CONTENTS

1 EXPERIENCE INDIA 7
   India Today 8
   What's New. 10
   What's Where 12
   India Planner. 14
   India Top Attractions 16
   Top Experiences 18
   Quintessential India 20
   FAQ. 22
   India with Kids. 24
   India Lodging Primer 25
   Great Itineraries 26

2 PORTRAIT OF INDIA 43
   Modern Indian Society 46
   History You Can See 50
   Religions of India 54
   Holidays and Festivals of India. . . .58
   Hindu Gods and Goddesses. 60
   Indian Cuisine 64
   Textiles and Shopping 70
   Indian Dance, Music, and
   Performing Arts 74

3 DELHI 77
   Welcome to Delhi. 78
   Eating Well in Delhi 80
   (Offbeat) Shopping in Delhi. 82
   Delhi's Holy Sites 84
   Exploring Delhi 90
   Old Delhi and Nearby 93
   Central Delhi. 101
   South Delhi. 110
   Where to Eat. 118
   Where to Stay. 127
   Nightlife and the Arts 131
   Shopping 136

4 SIDE TRIPS FROM DELHI 149

Fodor's Features

Getting Around India 31
The Taj Mahal. 166
Varanasi 198
Ajanta and Ellora Caves. 383

   Side Trips from Delhi 150
   Eating Well on Delhi Side Trips . . 152
   Planning. 155
   Agra and Environs. 159
   Khajuraho. 181
   Varanasi. 195

5 RAJASTHAN 213
   Welcome to Rajasthan 214
   Eating Well in Rajasthan. 216
   Camels: Ships of the Desert 218
   Rajasthan's Holy Sites 220
   Shopping in Rajasthan 222
   Planning. 225
   Jaipur and Environs. 232
   Udaipur and Environs. 261
   Jodhpur. 281
   Jaisalmer and Environs 291

6 MUMBAI 301
   Welcome to Mumbai 302

Eating Well in Mumbai 304

The Bazaars and Markets
of Mumbai 306

Mumbai's Holy Sites 308

Exploring Mumbai 320

Where to Eat 340

Best Bets for Mumbai Dining 342

Where to Stay 358

Best Bets for Mumbai Lodging . . . 359

Nightlife and the Arts 362

Shopping 369

Aurangabad, and the Ajanta
and Ellora Caves 378

7 GOA 395

Welcome to Goa 396

Eating Well in Goa 398

Goa Beaches 400

Planning 403

North Goa 408

Panaji 426

South Goa 436

8 KERALA 445

Welcome to Kerala 446

Eating Well in Kerala 448

Planning 451

Kochi 456

Central Kerala 469

Southern Kerala 477

Northern Kerala 482

UNDERSTANDING INDIA 487

TRAVEL SMART INDIA 491

INDEX 525

ABOUT OUR WRITERS 536

MAPS

Old Delhi 96

Central Delhi 104-105

South Delhi 111

Where to Eat and Stay
in Delhi 120–121

Agra 162

Fatehpur Sikri 178

Khajuraho 184

Varanasi 196

Jaipur 234–235

Udaipur 264

Jodhpur 284

Jaisalmer 295

Colaba, Fort, and
Marine Drive 322–323

Malabar Hill and Environs 331

CST and Environs 336

Where to Eat and Stay
in Mumbai 344–345

Excursions from Mumbai 380

Old Goa 435

Kochi 459

ABOUT
THIS GUIDE

Fodor's Ratings

Everything in this guide is worth doing—we don't cover what isn't—but exceptional sights, hotels, and restaurants are recognized with additional accolades. **Fodor's Choice** ★ indicates our top recommendations; ★ highlights places we deem highly recommended; and **Best Bets** call attention to notable hotels and restaurants in various categories. Care to nominate a new place? Visit Fodors.com/contact-us.

Trip Costs

We list prices wherever possible to help you budget well. Hotel and restaurant price categories from $ to $$$$ are noted alongside each recommendation. For hotels, we include the lowest cost of a standard double room in high season. For restaurants, we cite the average price of a main course at dinner or, if dinner isn't served, at lunch. For attractions, we always list adult admission fees; discounts are usually available for children, students, and senior citizens.

Hotels

Our local writers vet every hotel to recommend the best overnights in each price category, from budget to expensive. Unless otherwise specified, you can expect private bath, phone, and TV in your room. For expanded hotel reviews, facilities, and deals visit Fodors.com.

Ratings	Hotels & Restaurants
★ Fodor's Choice	
★ Highly recommended	🏨 Hotel
☕ Family-friendly	⤵ Number of rooms
	🍴 Meal plans
Listings	✕ Restaurant
✉ Address	⟝ Reservations
✉ Branch address	👔 Dress code
☎ Telephone	▭ No credit cards
🖷 Fax	$ Price
⊕ Website	
✉ E-mail	**Other**
🎫 Admission fee	⇨ See also
⊙ Open/closed times	☞ Take note
Ⓜ Subway	⛳ Golf facilities
⊹ Directions or Map coordinates	

Restaurants

Unless we state otherwise, restaurants are open for lunch and dinner daily. We mention dress code only when there's a specific requirement and reservations only when they're essential or not accepted. To make restaurant reservations, visit Fodors.com.

Credit Cards

The hotels and restaurants in this guide typically accept credit cards. If not, we'll say so.

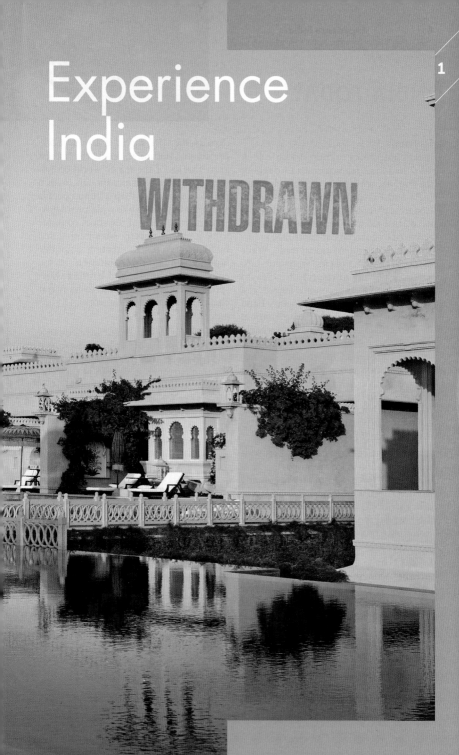

Experience
India

INDIA TODAY

Economy

India's independence from British rule in 1947 had huge repercussions throughout the country, which was then divided into India and Pakistan. The Indian National Congress party took control of India, and its socialist economy that ensued was characterized by government-controlled industry and limited international trade. While many beneficial policies were put into action, especially in respect of increased food production, the economy lagged, and in 1991 the International Monetary Fund bailed out the nearly bankrupt nation. Realizing the need for a new approach, the country opened its doors to economic reforms and began to embrace capitalism; significant economic changes were enacted, such as relaxed rules on foreign investment in trade, tax reforms, and inflation-curbing measures. Since then, the economy has been growing at an average pace of about 7% per annum.

Although agriculture is still the predominant occupation in India, employing 52% of the work force, the country's economy has diversified a great deal since independence in 1947: manufacturing, tourism, the hospitality industry, and the service sector have become major sources of economic growth.

In 2012 India had the second fastest-growing economy in the world, following burgeoning domestic demand for consumer goods and durables, as well as global demand for information technology and India's skilled, English-speaking software force.

For the most part, the Indian economy managed to dodge the economic slowdown that sent world economies into a downward spiral starting in 2008. Thanks to a relatively low dependence on exports, the GDP stayed at around 6.5% per annum, putting it among the highest growth rates of the major world economies. On the downside, though, with a population of more than a billion people and counting, issues like widespread poverty and inequality of resources continue to be a major concern. Maintaining and building new roads, creating equitable housing, countering sanitation issues, empowering women, and battling widespread corruption continue to be major challenges for the government.

Politics

In 2009 the United Progressive Alliance (UPA), a coalition of left-leaning national and regional parties was reelected, and Dr. Manmohan Singh, a veteran of the Congress party and a former finance minister, was chosen for the second time to lead the country as prime minister.

For much of the UPA's first term, the pressures of coalition politics influenced the central government's domestic and foreign policy—for instance, the Communist parties that were a part of the UPA until 2008 blocked the Indo-US bilateral accord on civilian nuclear cooperation, legislation that seeks to place India's civil nuclear facilities under international safeguards.

In the UPA's second term, the Congress party—the largest constituent party—has had a stronger presence in parliament.

Bilateral ties between India and Pakistan are a major focus of India's foreign policy, but peace talks between the two countries have been suspended since the terrorist attacks in Mumbai in November 2008, carried out by suspected Islamic terrorists from Pakistan.

Technology and Science

In recent years India has made large advances in information technology and software services, and thanks to a large, English-speaking workforce, the country has also emerged as a major hub for the outsourcing industry in general. Indeed, the country's software companies alone earn up to 90% of their revenue by providing technical support to companies from Europe and the United States. Although the global economic slowdown marginally affected the galloping growth of the software sector, the industry continues to drive India's economic growth.

Despite some failures, such as the loss of India's first unmanned moon orbiter in August 2009, India is pursuing significant milestones in space technology. The government announced that the Indian Space Research Organization aims to orbit Mars by 2014 and launch a manned mission to the moon by 2015.

Religion

India is a secular country, as laid down by the Indian Constitution, but the vast majority of the population is religiously observant. Eighty percent are practicing Hindus, and the remaining 20% is made up of various religions, including Islam, Christianity, Sikhism, Jainism, and Buddhism. In Mumbai there is a small but vibrant community of Parsis, as the Zoroastrians who settled in India several centuries ago are called. India also has as many as five native Jewish communities, who immigrated thousands of years ago and have their own unique customs. Religious festivals of many persuasions, such as Diwali (the Hindu Festival of Lights), the Muslim festival of Eid-ul-Fitr (which takes place at the end of Ramadan), and Christmas, are all celebrated with fervor.

The Arts

India has a rich cultural heritage dating back several thousand years. Classical music and dance have always been an important part of the social fabric, and each state has its own distinct folk styles as well, such as the Punjabi folk dance form of bhangra. The most popular of the modern-day performing arts, however, are the high-budget, song-and-dance extravaganzas that come out of Bollywood, as the Hindi film industry is popularly known. It is not unusual for India to produce nearly 3,000 movies a year, of which around a third would be feature films. In addition to Hindi films, many states also have thriving regional cinema industries. For instance, Chennai is home to the Tamil film industry, and Tamil superstar Rajnikanth is widely considered the highest-paid actor in the country.

India has had a rich legacy of literature, both in English and in regional languages. Since the early 1900s, when Bengali author Rabindranath Tagore won the Nobel Prize for Literature for the English translation of his collection of Bengali poems, *Gitanjali*, Indian writing has evolved and acquired a distinct voice of its own. British-Indian author Salman Rushdie's *Midnight's Children* (1981), which dealt with the coming of age of the country following independence, also marked the coming of age of contemporary Indian writing in English. His narrative style, which combines historical fiction with magic realism, has had a major influence on postcolonial Indian literature. Authors like Vikram Seth, Arundhati Roy, Amitav Ghosh, Jhumpa Lahiri, and Kiran Desai have powerfully conveyed the idea of a dynamic, ever-changing nation through their writing.

WHAT'S NEW

Slumdogs Live On

As most people probably know by now, back in 2008 a British film with a modest budget of US$15 million and a cast of virtually unknown Indian actors broke box-office records worldwide and catapulted Mumbai to international fame. *Slumdog Millionaire* director Danny Boyle's rags-to-riches story of a young man from a Mumbai slum who wins the Indian version of *Who Wants To Be A Millionaire* became the ticket to Hollywood for the film's young lead actors, Dev Patel and Freida Pinto.

Pinto, once a struggling model from Mumbai, has since graced international magazine covers and can be seen in Woody Allen's 2010 film *You Will Meet A Tall Dark Stranger* and in *Trishna,* Michael Winterbottom's 2012 take on the British classic *Tess of the D'Urbervilles.* Patel was recently seen in M. Night Shyamalan's *The Last Airbender,* though the box office was not impressed with the film, and in *The Best Exotic Marigold Hotel* alongside a roster of seasoned stars.

Perhaps the item most piquing the interest of fans, however, was the fact that after *Slumdog,* Pinto broke off her engagement to her former beau in Mumbai and has since been romantically linked to Patel.

The Commonwealth Games

In October 2010, Delhi played host to approximately 6,000 athletes from 71 countries who descended on the national capital for the Commonwealth Games. The event was a sort of coming-of-age for India, as the country had never before hosted an international sporting event of this magnitude. An estimated US$1.94 billion was spent on revamping Delhi's existing stadiums and constructing new ones and on accommodations for the athletes. A similar amount was spent on building and improving roads to facilitate transportation, including revamping Delhi's public transport system, and building a new airport terminal.

The overall expenditure on the Games far outstripped the initial estimate, and corruption charges marred the run-up to the event, but fears that the Games would be mismanaged were largely unfounded, and the 11-day event went off without too many hitches. Soon after the Games concluded, the government announced a high-level probe into the corruption charges, and Suresh Kalmadi, the president of the Indian Olympic Association, was forced to step down.

The Symbol of the Rupee

In 2010, the Indian government sent out a message about the growing strength of the Indian rupee against global currencies like the dollar and the euro by unveiling a new symbol for the rupee. With the symbol, a unique blend of the Roman "R" and the Devanagri (or Hindi) script "Ra," the Indian rupee joins the US dollar, the euro, the British pound, and the Japanese yen in having a distinct identity.

As part of the process, in 2009 the Indian government announced a public competition to create the symbol, and more than 3,000 people sent in their suggestions. D. Udaya Kumar, a professor at the elite Indian Institute of Technology, sent in the winning entry; he explained that his symbol "is a perfect blend of Indian and Roman letters" and that the design was inspired by the Indian tricolors "with two lines at the top and white space between." Although the new symbol will not be incorporated into currency notes, it will be added to major scripts and used in all official communication.

Delhi's Swanky New Airport

In 2010, India's busiest airport got a much-needed upgrade: the new Terminal 3 was unveiled at Delhi's Indira Gandhi International Airport. The swanky glass and steel terminal is larger than Madrid's T4 and Heathrow's T5 terminals and is expected to handle 34 million passengers per year—even more than Singapore's busy Changi airport. The T3 gives India's airports, infamous for their chaotic layouts and spartan facilities, a timely facelift. In addition to 168 check-in counters, and the ability to handle jumbo A-380 aircraft, the T3 also has sleep pods, a variety of restaurants and bars, and a large duty-free area.

Continued Globalization

International fast-food chain McDonald's was among the first global brands to set up base in India, way back in 1996. Over the ensuing years, they've tweaked their trademark products to better suit the Indian palate, and you won't find items like the McAloo Tikki (it has a potato cutlet in place of a meat patty), the Chicken Maharaja Mac (the Indian version of a Big Mac, with two grilled chicken patties, tomatoes, cheese, and spicy mayonnaise), or the Paneer Salsa Wrap anywhere else in the world.

A host of other international brands have since climbed on to the India bandwagon, including fast-food outlets like Domino's and Subway. Popular Spanish high-street fashion brands Vero, Moda, and Zara unveiled stores in Mumbai and Delhi in 2010, and denim manufacturer Diesel opened a store in Mumbai. And Starbucks' plan to bring its brand to India is finally set to materialize by the end of 2012; stay tuned for the whereabouts of your next latte.

Indian Art Booms

Indian art is becoming better known in the international art market, and the works of modern Indian masters have been fetching record prices at art auctions. In June 2010, for instance, veteran artist S.H. Raza's *Saurashtra,* a large acrylic on canvas work, was snapped up by a buyer for a staggering US$3.5 million at a Christie's auction in London. The sale set a new record for the amount paid for a work of modern Indian art at auction. Other artists, including M.F. Hussain—called the "Indian Picasso" by *Forbes* magazine—and others have found favor with international collectors, and the Indian art market is expected to continue gaining recognition and renown.

Recycling

Recycling isn't new to India, by any means. Indeed, recycling has been going for many decades, with ragpickers collecting paper, plastic, and metal waste that's then sold and resold up the chain of industry. Bottles and tins have always been reused until they break; newspapers are saved and resold, or used as insulation. The recycling of cow dung for fuel, building material, and many other uses has been going on for centuries. More recently India has become a center for recycling electronic waste. The country's own rapidly growing economy generates more than 50,000 tons of e-waste, and other countries have been sending their electronic waste to India as well—despite bans that prohibit the export of hazardous waste from rich countries to poor ones. In India most e-waste is dismantled and reprocessed by hand, without protective gear to guard against toxins such as lead and mercury that are known to be harmful. Something to think about.

WHAT'S WHERE

These numbers refer to chapter numbers.

3 Delhi. The capital of India is really two cities: the architecturally planned Central (New) Delhi (with South Delhi), the pride of British architect Edwin Lutyens, is characterized by broad tree-lined avenues. Old Delhi, by contrast, features labyrinthine alleys and narrow lanes, with the enormous Red Fort, stately Humayun's Tomb, and the Qutub Minar, the tallest stone tower in India.

4 Delhi Side Trips. Uttar Pradesh, the state neighboring Delhi, has several worthwhile attractions, most notably the Taj Mahal, in Agra. Just west of Agra is the former Mughal capital of Fatehpur Sikri, noted for its urban planning and architecture. In eastern Uttar Pradesh the holy city of Varanasi, on the Ganges, draws a constant stream of pilgrims to bathe in the river's holy water. The famous Hindu temples at Khajuraho are west of here in Madhya Pradesh.

5 Rajasthan. The "Land of Kings," once 18 princely kingdoms, is probably India's most-visited state. Historic palaces and forts are the prominent attractions here, along with the Pink City of Jaipur, the Jain temples in Ranakpur and Mount Abu, the

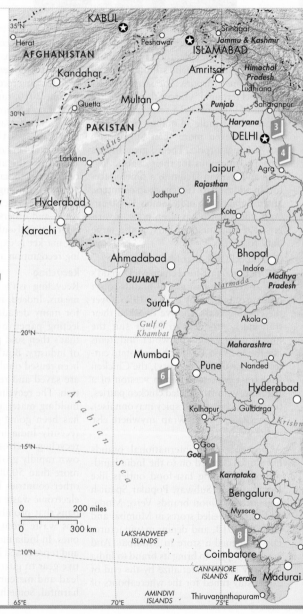

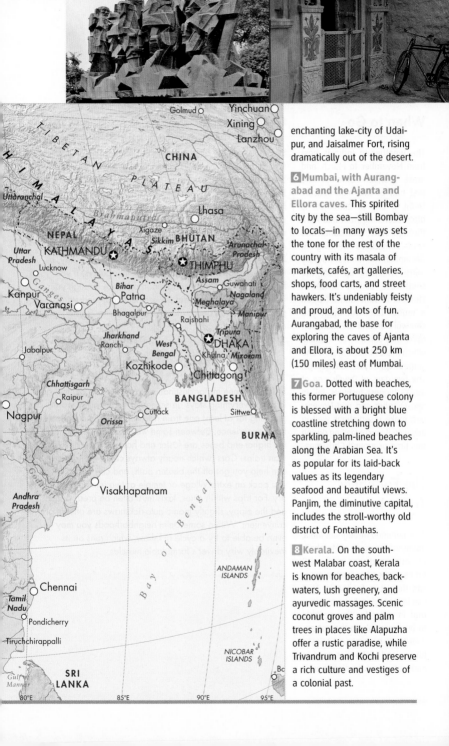

enchanting lake-city of Udaipur, and Jaisalmer Fort, rising dramatically out of the desert.

6 Mumbai, with Aurangabad and the Ajanta and Ellora caves. This spirited city by the sea—still Bombay to locals—in many ways sets the tone for the rest of the country with its masala of markets, cafés, art galleries, shops, food carts, and street hawkers. It's undeniably feisty and proud, and lots of fun. Aurangabad, the base for exploring the caves of Ajanta and Ellora, is about 250 km (150 miles) east of Mumbai.

7 Goa. Dotted with beaches, this former Portuguese colony is blessed with a bright blue coastline stretching down to sparkling, palm-lined beaches along the Arabian Sea. It's as popular for its laid-back values as its legendary seafood and beautiful views. Panjim, the diminutive capital, includes the stroll-worthy old district of Fontainhas.

8 Kerala. On the southwest Malabar coast, Kerala is known for beaches, backwaters, lush greenery, and ayurvedic massages. Scenic coconut groves and palm trees in places like Alapuzha offer a rustic paradise, while Trivandrum and Kochi preserve a rich culture and vestiges of a colonial past.

INDIA PLANNER

When to Go

The weather in India is best from November to March, and most tourists come in the first half of this high season. Delhi, a city of extremes, is often scorching from mid-April through June, and damp and cold—sometimes freezing—in December. The monsoon's daily rains, sweeping up from the southwest, usually arrive in Mumbai in June and hit Delhi a month later. Although you can work around the monsoon rains, they can lead to flooding, which makes traveling slow and sometimes even dangerous. The five days of Diwali, one of India's biggest festivals, fall in mid-October and mid-November; make reservations well in advance if you're visiting during this time or around Christmas.

The Foreigner Ticket Tax

As is common throughout India, admission to many of Mumbai's museums and sites is often 10 times higher for foreign tourists than it is for locals. That can be annoying, but remember that in order for these sights to be accessible to the not-so-well-to-do general public, institutions and authorities need to make up revenues elsewhere.

Getting Here

Delhi's huge new airport terminal is helping ease congestion at the busiest airport in the country. Flying into Mumbai is also an option, though long-needed improvements there are still a few years off. You'll need to take a taxi or have a driver pick you up from either airport: public transportation isn't a realistic option. Delhi's airport is about 30 minutes from the city center; it can take two hours to reach Mumbai's center from the airport. Allow lots of extra time for the transfer, especially if you arrive during the day, as roads are prone to bottlenecks and other delays. If you haven't arranged transportation in advance through your hotel, head to the prepaid government-approved stands past immigration and customs, and ignore touts offering other options.

Getting Around

Flying between major destinations can save lots of time, as long as everything stays on schedule. It's definitely worth planning for at least one train ride, though—it's a signature India experience. Between some well-traveled destinations, the higher-end buses are faster and have better schedules than trains. Cars (which nearly always come with drivers) can help you get off the beaten path, and can also help you pack an extra village or temple or two into your itinerary. For trips within cities, taxis must often be prearranged, and the zippy, slightly manic auto-rickshaws are often more convenient. Within some Delhi neighborhoods you may even be able to try a cycle rickshaw, which runs on its inevitably wiry driver's formidable muscles.

Dining

In a place as obsessed with food as India, unshowy neighborhood restaurants that cater to locals are often standouts. Luxury and business-class hotels often have so-called coffee shops; these are open 24 hours and always have a variety of cuisines, including a selection of Western dishes. Unless we mention otherwise, the restaurants we list are open daily for lunch and dinner. However, it's common for restaurants to close from roughly 3 to 6 pm, and they also stop serving by 11 pm or midnight. Only the most popular and heavily touristed restaurants, such as Delhi's Bukhara, require a reservation, although it's never a bad idea, and similarly it's only the highest-end restaurants that would have a dress code that requires a jacket or tie.

Packing Essentials

Go for loose, breathable, sturdy fabrics. Pants are better than shorts: they protect from the sun, and they won't make you stick out (shorts are inappropriate for most religious sites, in any case). Women should opt for pants or skirts or dresses that go below the knee. Pack light but sturdy walking shoes that are easy to take off (you'll need to do so to enter temples), strong sunscreen (the good stuff is costly and hard to find in India), toilet paper, moist towelettes, hand sanitizer, handkerchiefs (for drying off after washing your hands), insect repellent, and a flashlight.

Hiring a Guide

Guides can help you get more out of your sightseeing. Some are long-winded, so don't be afraid to gently turn the discussion to what interests you. And don't fall for the hard sell: you don't have to hire the first one you see—you can always go back and find that first one after you've had a chance to look around a bit. The guides at some sites, such as the Taj Mahal, are accredited by the local or national government, and in such places rates are fixed. Avoid going shopping with guides, because they will inevitably get a cut of the inflated prices you pay the stores.

Tours

Tours can be useful if you're not inclined to figure out the logistics of planes, trains, and hiring drivers. Make sure you shop around and know what you're paying for, though. Ask questions: How much can the tour be personalized? Will it be a group tour, or will it just be the people in your party? Finally, don't limit your research to just North American or European tour groups; many Indian tour companies put together well-regarded tours for foreign nationals, and their rates are often cheaper than their foreign competitors. *See the Travel Smart chapter for some specifics.*

Money

India's main unit of currency, the rupee, is worth roughly 1/55 of a US dollar. In 2010 the government adopted a new symbol for the rupee, but "Rs.," "Re.," and "INR" remain more common abbreviations. Because of governmental regulations, it's against the law to take rupees in or out of India, so you must obtain your rupees from an ATM after you land. When traveling, always carry some rupee bills, because charge cards are far from universally accepted. When paying for small items, keep in mind that many shopkeepers will have difficulty breaking large bills.

INDIA
TOP ATTRACTIONS

The Taj Mahal, Agra

(A) Despite the plethora of postcards and calendar images, nothing can prepare you for the architectural and awe-inspiring beauty of the Taj Mahal in Agra. An "elegy in marble" as some call it, the mausoleum immortalizes the love between Mughal king Shah Jahan and his wife, Mumtaz, for whom it was built.

Fatehpur Sikri, Agra

This former capital of the Mughal Empire was built by Emperor Akbar during the second half of the 16th century, though Akbar only lived here for about a decade. The red sandstone complex has elaborate palaces, beautiful courtyards, and a large mosque and is noted for its forward-thinking urban planning and blending of Indo-Islamic architecture.

Jama Masjid, Delhi

(B) India's largest mosque is built of deep red sandstone and still manages to retain an aura of calm and beauty, despite the crowds covering it and the timeworn streets surrounding it.

Humayun's Tomb, Delhi

(C) Ornate and yet calming, this complex of tombs in southern Delhi was a precursor to the Taj Mahal and is a stunning Mughal artifact in its own right.

Gateway of India, Mumbai

It might not be the most visually stunning monument you see in India, but the Gateway arch on Mumbai's waterfront is an undeniable focal point of the city: built to commemorate the visit of King George V and Queen Mary in 1911, it has seen the coming and going of important personages and ordinary folk and continues to be a site of vibrant city life.

Ajanta and Ellora, Mumbai Side Trip

(D) Dating back to 200 BC, the cave temples at Ajanta and Ellora are astounding for their intricate paintings and carvings. The Ajanta caves depict the life story of the Buddha, while the nearby Ellora caves feature Buddhist, Hindu, and Jain carvings. Both Ajanta and Ellora are UNESCO World Heritage sites.

Taj Lake Palace (Jag Niwas), Udaipur

(E) Rising out of Lake Pichola like a mirage, the Lake Palace is a real-life wonder. Now that it's a hotel, you'll need to get a room here to inspect the courts and fountains up close, but even if you admire it from afar, you'll still find it a memorable part of the scenery. Some of the best views are from the sprawling, equally stunning City Palace.

Fort, Jaisalmer

More than 5,000 people still live in this spectacular 12th-century citadel, which ascends strikingly out of Rajastan's Thar Desert. Inside is a network of temples, palaces, mansions, and tiny winding lanes.

Ghats (stairs), Varanasi

(F) Varanasi is one of the world's holiest cities, but it's the mighty Ganges that draws so many Hindus (roughly 1 million annually) and other visitors and pilgrims. Spend time along the waterfront *ghats* (stairs) where pilgrims pray, chant, and bathe, and you will get a sense of the city's spirituality and sanctity.

Churches of Old Goa

(G) The ultrabaroque 16th- and 17th-century churches of this Portuguese colony contain the final resting place of St. Francis Xavier, Goa's patron saint, and intricate chapels and carvings.

TOP EXPERIENCES

A Camel Ride in the Desert

What could be more spectacular than a windswept camel ride in Rajasthan's Thar Desert? The calm of the undulating dunes, the quiet of the landscape, perhaps the sun is just coming up over the horizon—it all contrasts so sharply with the commotion of urban India. The western desert town of Jaisalmer is a good place from which to venture out, but many other cities in Rajasthan, including Jaipur and Jodhpur, offer camel safaris. The town of Pushkar hosts a bustling and frenetic camel and livestock fair every November, which coincides with the peak travel season to northern India, and is another way to get up close to a camel.

Join in a Festival

There may be as many festivals in India as there are languages or gods (and that's a lot!), a concept that proves to what extent life in this huge country revolves around family, community, and devotion. Whether it's Diwali, the festival of lights, or the springtime holiday of Holi, where participants toss vibrantly colored powders and water balloons at one another, communities love to gather together and celebrate. During Ganesh Chaturthi in Mumbai, floatlike statues of the god are submerged into the water at Chowpatty Beach. Joining in on festivities that occur while you're in India is a great way to meet people and get a real feel for the country.

A Boat Ride along the Ganges

To sense the role the Ganges River plays in the lives of devout Hindus, take a dawn or dusk boat trip. Start from the sacred Dashashvamedha Ghat and head upstream or toward the southern end, near Assi Ghat. At sunrise, bathers flock to these 90 or so ghats, preparing for a purifying dip into the holy water. And at sunset, hundreds of *diyas* (clay lamps) are lit and floated across the river.

Splurge on a Few Nights at a Taj Hotel

For luxury that surpasses all standards, check into one of the Taj properties around the country, among the grandest in the land. A few of the brand's hotels, such as the landmark Taj Mahal Palace & Tower, Mumbai, or iconic Taj Lake Palace, Udaipur, are particularly splendid. If you're not quite up for the splurge for an overnight, stop for a cocktail or high tea.

Shopping Spree in Jaipur

Fashionistas and designers from across the country flock to the Pink City for semi-precious baubles and block-printed textiles. In Johari Bazaar, a central strip of pedestrian-friendly stalls, jewelers will string stones such as carnelian, turquoise, and pink quartz into necklaces on the spot. Even if you're not looking to buy, it's worth dropping by the Gem Palace, Jaipur's equivalent of Tiffany's, where you can ogle sparkling diamonds, emeralds, and rubies in stunning settings. And at cult-favorite textile shops like Anokhi and Cottons, choose from block-printed tunics and home accessories in bright hues and myriad patterns.

Mumbai Street Food off the Curb, or in a Restaurant

No other Indian city does savory street snacks quite like Mumbai, where stalls selling *pani puri* (canapés dipped into a chilled mint soup) and *pav bhaji* (a spicy mash of potatoes, onions, and tomatoes eaten with buttered bread) are around every corner. You can also try these local favorites at authentic restaurants like Elco or Swati Snacks if you want a cleaner environment.

Watch a Bollywood Movie

Indians easily rival—and probably surpass—Americans with their degree of movie-mania. The Indian film industry, better known as Bollywood (for the "B" in Bombay), churns out around 1,000 of these movies a year. They're hugely popular all across the country, with actors like Shah Rukh Khan and starlets such as Aishwarya Rai holding demigod status among the public. Plots tend to be simple but melodramatic, and there are usually plenty of musical interludes, so even though most films are in Hindi, it's pretty easy to get the gist of the story and be entertained by the song and dance. The people-watching is half the fun, too.

Pay Homage at a Temple or Mosque

With faith such an integral part of life, weekly or even daily visits to a place of worship are not uncommon for locals. Many places of worship are open to nonbelievers (some are not; specifics are noted in our reviews), and a visit to a temple, mosque, or church gives some insight into the devotion of so many. Sites like the Jama Masjid in Delhi or the Siddhivanayak Temple in Mumbai are among the more famous and can be quite busy, but smaller neighborhood places of worship are usually more tranquil. If you go, be respectful.

Experience the New India: Nightlife and Art Galleries

Tradition and ritual factor heavily in India's appeal to a first-time traveler, but the country is moving forward—fast—and there are plenty of modern cultural diversions. In urban centers, trendy bars and avant-garde art galleries are popping up almost overnight, attracting hip and stylish patrons. For a firsthand glimpse, visit the swanky bars and clubs that are becoming more and more prevalent in Delhi and Mumbai. An ambitious space with promising artwork, the two-story Devi Art Foundation, a privately owned space just outside Delhi, is essentially the country's first contemporary art museum. The smaller galleries that are proliferating in districts like Kala Ghoda in Mumbai are also good places to get a look at India's vibrant new art scene.

Ride the Rails

A relic of the British Raj, the train network that connects all of India is surprisingly efficient and extensive. Try to include a train journey in your itinerary if possible, as it is the best way to see the countryside and the smaller villages that are in many ways the heart of India today, even though the big cities may be the focus of travel. Be mindful, however, that the trip can entail rowdy neighbors and less than hygienic corridors. Lines like the Konkan Railway, running from Mumbai to Goa, are known for better service and cleaner quarters.

Eat Dessert

The spicier the meal, the sweeter the dessert: that seems to be the culinary rule of thumb in India. It's pretty much a given that India has a collective sweet tooth, but if the milky, syrupy desserts like *gulab jamun* (like a deep-fried donut, soaked in syrup) and *jalebi* (similar to gulab jamun, but the dough is a thin, pretzel shape, also deep-fried, and often soaked in syrup) prove too sweet for your palate, try the delicious Indian ice creams instead. Many feature tropical and seasonal fruits like the Alphonso mango, the *sitaphal* (custard apple), or the *chikoo* (a grainy, fleshy fruit that's caramel in color). Check out the Mumbai ice-cream parlor chain, Natural.

QUINTESSENTIAL INDIA

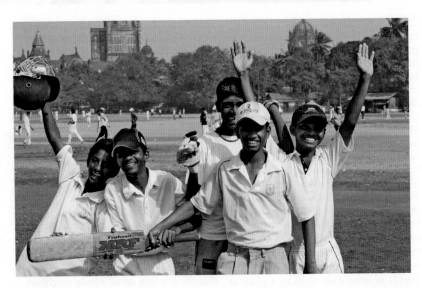

(Almost Always) Time for Tea

Drunk throughout the day, tea (called *chai*) is strong and formidably sweet: it's brewed with lots of milk and spices like ginger, cinnamon, and cardamom. Everyone in India makes time for tea—housewives take their tea breaks, office workers are served at their desk, and rickshaw drivers pull over for a roadside break—and so should you. And don't worry about standing on ceremony; it's not usually a drawn out affair: the tea, served in thick glasses, disappears as soon as it's cool enough to drink, and then it's time to get on with the day.

And Time for Tiffin

Indians want variety and big flavor in their food, and the tiniest towns as well as the biggest megapolises always have their share of tiny restaurants and stalls for buying *tiffin* (small meals or snacks) throughout the day. In the late afternoon, *chaat* (Indian street snacks) stalls set up

to sell offerings that are tangy, sour, sweet, crunchy, and delicious all at once. Along the road are *dhabas* (roadside eateries) that are so popular that even big-city restaurants attempt to imitate their culinary skills.

"Is That Your Final Price?"

The uninitiated can find bargaining an intimidating process, at least at first, but try it once or twice and you'll see how much fun it can be. Waiting for an offer, reacting with polite surprise, countering with a much lower offer, and repeating the process until someone either gives up or gives in—the mini-drama of bargaining is still the way most of India buys and sells. To bargain well, keep in mind that the best ammunition to have is knowing what something *ought* to cost, so it can be worth your time to visit some shops with fixed prices to get an idea. When you're ready to haggle, don't volunteer a price—you'll be too high. Wait for an offer, then

Should I book all my lodgings beforehand, or will I be able to do so once I'm there?

Although most cities along a traveler's route have ample accommodations, it's always a good idea to make reservations, especially for high-season travel (i.e., November to March). If you book with hotels that have a fair cancellation policy, you can often make alternate plans on arrival and cancel your original ones with a few days' notice.

Will all the food be very spicy and/or vegetarian? Will there be alcohol?

Most chefs and restaurants will happily adjust the spice level in dishes if told beforehand; you can also ask your waiter for nonspicy suggestions. Although a large percentage of the Indian population eats a strictly vegetarian diet, it's more common in the south, and most cities covered in *Essential India* have a variety of veg and nonveg restaurant options. Most vegetarian-only restaurants will have prominent signage to alert you. Alcohol is served at many hotels, restaurants, and bars, but note that some festivals and holidays are dry days.

Can I drink tap water?

Refrain from drinking all tap water. Stick with bottled water like Bisleri and Aquafina, and check the seal and date; empty water bottles are sometimes refilled with regular water and resold. You might also want to avoid fresh fruits and vegetables that you haven't washed or peeled yourself.

How should I deal with beggars and hawkers that approach me?

Unfortunately, while you might want to help, it's generally best to roll up car windows or walk away from beggars. Sometimes if you offer alms to one, several more quickly ambush you. With aggressive hawkers peddling their wares, walk away, say a firm "No," and avoid eye contact.

Is it safe to bring my valuables (i.e., jewelry) on my trip?

As with any travel, if you're afraid of losing it, we'd suggest you don't bring it—better safe than sorry. If you must bring valuables, keep them with you at all times, and this also applies to your passport and cash. Use basic street smarts by keeping your wallet in your front pocket and being alert.

What's the best way to bargain with vendors?

Compared to the West, bargaining is almost always expected in India, especially with street vendors and at smaller stalls. Once a price has been quoted, start your bargaining at about half of that. Don't be afraid to walk away either; it's not uncommon for a vendor to run down the street after a buyer—but don't waste your time, or the seller's time, if you have absolutely no intention of making a purchase.

Any last-minute advice?

The Fodor's forums are full of travel advice. For India, recommendations run the gamut from packing slip-on shoes because of how often you need to take them off when you visit temples to bringing ear plugs for many reasons, and especially in case your hotel is next to a mosque, street noise, or barking dogs. Ask your own questions, and read about the experiences of other travelers at www.fodors.com/community.

INDIA WITH KIDS

India might not be the typical family destination—there's no getting around the fact that it's dirty, and the unfamiliar can be a bit scary at times—but it's the kind of trip no child (or adult) will ever forget. Here are some ideas to help you plan.

Wildlife Safaris and Animal Rides

India abounds with national parks and reserves: the real-life setting and inspiration for Rudyard Kipling's *The Jungle Book*. An excursion to one of these parks, like Ranthambhore or Keoladeo, both in Rajasthan, can be a wonderful way for kids to learn about local flora and fauna. Also in Rajasthan, kids and grown-ups will almost undoubtedly get a thrill out of a camel safari in the desert. The Chokhi Dhani resort outside Jaipur has a nightly, carnival-like village fair on the resort grounds, complete with magic stalls and elephant rides that will captivate most kids—you can stay at the resort or just visit the village for an afternoon or evening (nighttime is livelier).

Kid-Friendly Museums and Sites

You could argue that all of India is a cultural museum for kids used to life in North America, but there are also specific sites and museums that appeal to the younger generation. The National Rail Museum in Delhi, for example, has old steam engines parked outside, and a toy train that kids can ride. For those interested in astronomy and observatories, the Jantar Mantar collections of outdoor solar instruments, including things like 90-foot-long sun dials, in Jaipur and Delhi can be fascinating (the one in Jaipur is the best preserved). A good guide is crucial if you want to understand how these huge stone-and-marble instruments can tell time, track the position of stars, and predict eclipses, all without a single computer—but even the small children will have fun climbing around these outdoor "sculptures." Parks and beaches are almost always good places to take children, and Kerala's beaches are legendary. In Mumbai you can escape the city congestion at the Hanging Gardens, a park in Malabar Hill overlooking the South Mumbai skyline and Arabian Sea, or head to Chowpatty or Juhu Beach—but don't go in the water.

Festivals

India's festivals are especially fun for younger audiences. From the kite-flying festival of Makar Sankranti to the throwing of colors and water balloons during Holi to the elaborate parade-and-float-driven Ganesh Chaturthi in Mumbai, participating in and viewing these festivals can be cultural immersion for kids without their even knowing it. They'll almost certainly come home with amazing stories to tell their friends.

Kids and Indian Food

Indian food might be different, but it doesn't have to be scary. If your kids are giving it a try for the first time, order less spicy versions and ask your waiter for suggestions that might appeal to picky eaters. In Mumbai, Cream Centre along Marine Drive is a classic crowd pleaser that caters to little clients, too. Dishes served here include the famed *chole bathure*, curried chickpeas (ask for the mild version) with a giant puffed bread—what child can resist a piece of bread larger than his or her own head? And for those times when you or your kids want some good old American comfort food, there are usually decent places to find the familiar: Italian restaurants serving pasta and pizza, for instance, are plentiful in tourist destinations.

INDIA LODGING PRIMER

Although Western travelers might expect to get more bang for their buck when it comes to lodgings in India, accommodations and facilities vary widely throughout the country. Luxury hotels may seem especially costly for this part of the world, but the facilities and service are nothing short of the royal treatment in most cases. At the same time, mid-tier hotels aren't always as consistent in service or facilities when compared with their Western counterparts, so adjusting your expectations before you arrive will make for a smoother stay. Prices peak sharply during the November to March high season—and even more so during the Christmas to New Year's week—so it's best to book in advance.

The following is an overview of the different types of lodging options you can expect to find in India. As anywhere else, to avoid any confusion on the ground, make sure to confirm your reservations and arrive as early as possible to check in, or let them know you'll be getting in late.

The lodgings we list in this book are ones we consider the best in their price range. Mid-range hotels will often have only a shower rather than a bathtub. Keep in mind that rates across the board have dipped a great deal from their highs earlier in the decade, so don't be afraid to bargain.

Luxury Hotels

The cream-of-the-crop luxury hotels in India often surpass their counterparts in the United States and Europe when it comes to service and general splendor—often in sumptuously converted palaces or *havelis* (mansions), or properties built using traditional architectural styles (like the intricate stonework and turreted balconies at several Rajasthan properties) and decorated with local artisanal crafts.

Although you might feel like you're shelling out quite a bit to stay at a Taj or an Oberoi, the price usually translates to the best location in town, a generous and delicious buffet breakfast, plush beds, marble baths, and wonderful service. Also look for heritage hotel chains like Neemrana, which has lovely properties. You'll see more and more familiar high-end names like Aman Resorts, the Four Seasons, and JW Marriott, but these tend to have a more contemporary look compared with the heritage properties.

Midrange Accommodations

While the mid-tier is where you might expect most properties to fall, India actually suffers from a dearth of mid-range lodgings, though the situation improves with each passing year. Recognizable chains like Marriott, Holiday Inn, Hilton, Sheraton, and Westin do have quite a few properties across the country, but the branding doesn't always guarantee a stay on par with a Holiday Inn in California or a Westin in Washington, DC. Their Indian counterparts might have rooms that look a bit worn, and service can be spottier than you'd expect.

Guesthouses and Budget Lodgings

Bed-and-breakfasts, better known as guesthouses in India, are plentiful across the country, especially in remote areas or smaller towns. They can vary widely in cleanliness, service, and even safety. Amenities will be limited, not all will have a restaurant or food available on the premises, and there's a good chance there will be shared bathrooms.

GREAT ITINERARIES

India is a huge country, and it would take months, or even years, to do a full-fledged tour of the country. We've narrowed this book down to what we consider the *essential* India, but even still, unless you have a *really* long vacation, you won't have time to see all the highlights. Keep in mind, too, that the best way to appreciate India is not to rush—in fact, the country tends to run in such a fashion that it's next to impossible to rush while you're here.

To further help you make the most of your time, India's Golden Triangle, spanning roughly 240 km (150 miles) on each of its three sides, links Mughal and Rajput sites in Delhi, Jaipur, and Agra. It's the most well-traveled tour in India, and for good reason: for many tourists, the sites here *are* India. What you see—the Taj Mahal, the impressive palace-fort and Islamic monuments in Old Delhi, and the timeless Pink City fairy tale that is Jaipur—are some of the most splendid edifices that India has to offer. Although you could visit most of these sights in a week, or even less, try not to make it a hurried affair if you can. Between the heat and the sometimes tricky dealings of getting around, traveling in India is often more exhausting than elsewhere, and an overpacked day rarely makes for a satisfying visit. We've outlined the basics of the Golden Triangle *below*, with some options and add-ons.

THE GOLDEN TRIANGLE, 11 DAYS

Delhi
3–4 days

Fly into Delhi to explore the old and new capitals. Hit the ground running with some light touring on the first day, perhaps doing some shopping or taking in

the lovely, pre-Mughal Lodi Gardens. Over the next two days, visit Old Delhi's major Mughal sites, including the Red Fort, Jama Masjid, and Chandni Chowk, now a hodgepodge market. Also highly worth a visit: the Mughal Humayun's tomb and the imperial buildings of the Raj-era. Pay a visit to the excellent collections at the National Museum as well, but make sure to also save time for just getting acquainted with Delhi weather, crowds, and food—the higher-end restaurants and shops in South Delhi are worth the trip. ⇨ *Delhi, Chapter 3.*

Option: If you prefer, head right out to Agra on your second day, leaving time to explore Delhi a little more afterward.

Jaipur
2–4 days

Set out early for Jaipur (it's about six hours by train or car; the flight is an hour, but factor in airport time). Alternatively, take an extra day and make an overnight stop at the Neemrama Fort Palace, built in the 15th century and now a luxury hotel about midway between Delhi and Jaipur. Once in Jaipur, head out to explore the city's unforgettable bazaars and monuments to see why it's called the Pink City. Set aside a half day to explore the Amber (Amer) Fort and Palace, just north of the city limits. ⇨ *Rajasthan, in Chapter 5.* Then head back to Delhi.

Side Trips: If you drive to Jaipur and have the time and desire, add in a few days for a side trip or two. About 160 km (100 miles) south of Jaipur is Ranthambhore National Park, the most likely place in India to see a tiger or other large cat outside of captivity. If you're inclined to explore more of Rajasthan, the "Land of Princes," head farther afield to either Udaipur, where the sprawling City Palace and Lake Palace

seem taken from a fairy-tale book, or the "Blue City" of Jodhpur, the site of the magnificent eight-gated Mehrangarh Fort, built in the 15th century.

Option: Skip Jaipur and go straight to Udaipur: there is more than enough in this magical city to keep you occupied for several days, and there are several spectacular side trips to places like the Jain Temple at Ranakpur.

The Taj Mahal (Agra) and Fatehpur Sikri
2–3 days

From Delhi, travel by road or take the train to Agra. If you're driving, make a stop during the two- to three-hour trip to visit the splendid royal remnants of the ancient Mughal capital Fatehpur Sikri (if you take the train to Agra, rent a car and driver and backtrack to Fatehpur Sikri). The fast train takes about three hours, but isn't at the most convenient times. Plan to stay overnight in Agra so you can fully appreciate the Taj Mahal and Agra's other sites, the impressive Agra Fort and the tomb of Etmad-ud-Daulah (the so-called "Baby Taj"). Then make your way back to Delhi. ⇨ *Chapter 4 Side Trips from Delhi.*

■ TIP ➔ **If this is your first time in India, it may seem like a good idea to rent a car and drive it yourself, but it isn't.** India's traffic is fierce and should only be tackled by seasoned drivers familiar with Indian roads and traffic conditions. Hire a car and driver, which costs only a little more than renting a car by itself.

Delhi is one of the most expensive places to stay in India. In the high season, Agra and Jaipur are a close second. These destinations are among the most popular tourist spots in India, so hotels book up quickly. If you have your heart set on a specific hotel, book early. Northern India

is also a popular circuit for guided tours. If you like the comfort of a knowledgeable guide and the structure of a set plan, consider a package tour. ⇨ *See the Travel Smart chapter in the back of this book for recommendations.*

Transportation: If getting there is half the fun in your mind, take a train. Although you give up some flexibility with a train, the countryside views are at least partial compensation, as is being able to avoid the loud, manic Indian driving style. If time is limited and you want to have as much freedom as possible with your route, then a car and driver is the better option.

ADD-ONS FROM DELHI: MUMBAI, GOA, AND KERALA

Mumbai
3–4 days

Fly to Mumbai from Delhi. To get your bearings in Mumbai, start with a visit to the city's most recognizable landmark, the Gateway of India (the nearby Taj Mahal

Palace and Tower hotel is a close second in fame). Then visit the Prince of Wales Museum, the Crawford Market, and other signature sights of Raj-era Bombay, ending your day with a visit to Chowpatty Beach, where food stalls and amusement rides line a stretch of sand that comes most alive on Saturday. Another thing that should not to be missed is some time for serious shopping in markets and for experiencing Mumbai's restaurants—two areas in which this often flashy city excels. On one morning, head to Elephanta Island, reached by boat from the Gateway of India; the Hindu and Buddhist cave sculptures there are masterful and mysterious. ⇨ *Mumbai, Chapter 6.*

Side Trip: Ajanta and Ellora Caves, 3 days

The Ajanta and Ellora Caves were built over a period of 700 years starting in the 2nd century BC. To get here, you first must go 400 km (250 miles) east of Mumbai to the city of Aurangabad. Plan on spending the good part of a day at each site (for a total of two days) to avoid getting sculpture fatigue. Aurangabad's impressive Daulatabad Fort, nearly a millennium old, is also worth a visit. ⇨ *Mumbai, Chapter 6.*

Transportation Tips: The number of trains making the seven-hour train ride from Mumbai to Aurangabad is limited, so it probably makes the most sense to fly there and back—it's a 45-minute trip each way. The Ajanta Caves can take up to three hours to reach from Aurangabad, and Ellora is about 30 minutes away. To use your time most efficiently, you will probably want to hire a car and driver to take you to the caves, rather than relying on tour buses.

Goa
4 days

If you're craving some beach time and a look at a totally different part of India, head south to the former Portuguese colony of Goa on the Arabian Sea. You can fly from Mumbai, or take the Konkan Railway, a gorgeous 12-hour trip that tracks the coastline and passes over nearly 150 major bridges on its complete route (book ahead for this popular train). In Goa you'll want to spend time eating seafood and sipping Kingfishers at a beach shack, but make sure to set aside time for a day trip to visit Old Goa's monumental 17-century cathedrals as well as the atmospheric Portuguese-influenced streets of Panjim. When you've had your fill of Goa's many charms, either fly or take the train back to Mumbai. ⇨ *Goa, Chapter 7.*

Kerala
4 days

Remote and serene, Kerala is on the southern coast of the Arabian Sea; you can get there by train or fly into Kochi, Trivandrum, or Calicut. Either way, you'll undoubtedly want to experience nature here. Rent a quaint houseboat for three days to just meander through the majestic backwaters that curve through green hills and the rice paddies of small villages—easily accessible via Kollam. A bit farther inland, the Western Ghats contain vast tea and spice plantations as well as beautiful wildlife. If you want to experience Kerala civilization, the old port city of Kochi is an enchanting mix of traditional South Indian culture and influences from the Portuguese, Jews, Syrian Christians, and Muslims who came this way in the past. ⇨ *Kerala, Chapter 8.*

ADD-ONS FROM DELHI: VARANASI AND KHAJURAHO

Varanasi, on the holy Ganges River, is the most sacred city for Hindus—and it may also be the oldest continuously populated city in the world. You can visit as a side trip from Delhi (leave time to also visit nearby Sarnath, a major Buddhist pilgrimage site) if you don't have enough time to do a thorough exploration of Uttar Pradesh, the state next to Delhi. The temples at Khajuraho are fascinating, but not easy to get to. If you plan to go, visit either on the way to or from Varanasi. Your best bet is to fly.

Varanasi
2–3 days

Fly from Delhi to Varanasi—traveling by train or car eats up a lot of time, and the roads in Uttar Pradesh are not the greatest. In Varanasi, spend your first day getting acquainted with the manic pace of the city's Old Town. Then make it an early night so that you can get up before dawn to take an early morning boat ride on the Ganges and witness morning ablutions along the river. After setting aside some time to wander and take in the Old Town's sights, sounds, and (yes) smells, take an auto-rickshaw south to the Bharat Kala Bhavan Museum, a college institution with some superb examples of local sculpture. ⇨ *Side Trips from Delhi, Chapter 4.*

Tips: The snarl of twisty alleys in Varanasi's Old Town can be incredibly hard to navigate, and while that's part of the thrill, it can be exhausting. Hire a guide from India Tourism for the first day to help you get your bearings, and avoid the touts until you're more confident here.

Varanasi is hectic, impressive, and probably unlike anywhere else you've ever been. But it's not that restful. Plan on heading somewhere a little less overwhelming after a visit here, or schedule in a little R & R at your hotel.

Side Trip: Sarnath, 1 day

After an early breakfast, head to Sarnath, just 11 km (7 miles) north of Varanasi, where the Buddha preached his first sermon. Take an auto-rickshaw or a taxi—you may want to hire the same driver to take you back at the end of the day. Sarnath's Deer Park contains a Buddhist temple, several 5th- and 6th-century monuments, and an outstanding archaeological museum. Have lunch at one of the nearby cafés, then return to Varanasi to see any last-minute sights and get ready for your return to Delhi.

Khajuraho
2 days

Fly to Khajuraho on your way to or from Varanasi and spend two days absorbing the exuberant, occasionally X-rated carvings that adorn the town's 10th- and 11th-century Hindu temples. ⇨ *Side Trips from Delhi, Chapter 4.*

BY HUMP AND BY TRUNK

In some regions, you may have the chance to take forms of transport that are a lot more unusual than a bus or car. Traveling on the back of an elephant, for instance, makes the steep approach to Amber Fort outside of Jaipur a breeze. As for camels, they're a common sight in Rajasthan, usually carrying cargo in the cities, but often transporting people out in the desert.

GETTING AROUND INDIA

India is huge country and getting around can be a challenge, so it pays (in time, money, and sanity) to be prepared. Knowing your travel options and the potential for delays will help you get the most out of your trip. With a little planning, getting there can be more than half the fun.

This is a country with a diverse geography and a still-developing infrastructure—which means there are plenty of potholes, lots of aggressive driving, and mysterious plane and train delays. It's important not to try to do too much, or there's a good chance you'll end up frustrated. "Expect the unexpected" are excellent words to live by when you're traveling in India.

If the places you'll be visiting are far apart and you're pressed for time, fly-ing is without question the best option. Trains can be almost as good as fly-ing, especially if you take an overnight train. A car and driver gives you the most freedom, and is often the most comfortable way to go, but not neces-sarily the fastest since Indian roads are often beset with intense traffic and lots of traffic jams. Buses are typically the worst option. When it comes to travel within a city, taxis and auto-rickshaws are best if you don't have a car and driver.

AIR TRAVEL

The domestic terminal of Chhatrapati Shivaji Airport in Mumbai

INTERCITY TRAVEL

Thanks to domestic carriers like Jet and Spice Jet, flying between cities in India is a practical and relatively affordable option that can save you a lot of time—especially if you have multiple destinations around Rajasthan.

ON TIME?

Flights usually run on or close to schedule, although the fog that descends on Delhi in December or January can bring the city and its airport to a standstill for hours. If you do plan on flying, keep in mind that Indian airports can often be a significant distance from your final destination, and that you'll need to factor in that transfer time.

DELHI'S AIRPORT

Delhi's huge T3 terminal, built in 2010 in part to accommodate tourists for the Commonwealth Games, handles all international flights as well as the domestic flights of Air India, Jet, and Kingfisher. Other domestic flights leave from Terminal 1; there is a shuttle bus between the terminals. In early 2011, the Delhi Airport Metro Express opened operations connecting T3 with the New Delhi Railway station. As of July 2012, service is suspended due to safety concerns but is expected to resume within a few months.

MUMBAI'S AIRPORT

Mumbai's airport is north of the city—as in Delhi, travel between the international and domestic terminals requires taking a shuttle. A major renovation, due for completion in 2014, will unite the domestic and international terminals. Currently, Mumbai's metro line does not reach the airport, though such a connection is likely in the future. Until then, it can take two hours or more to reach South Mumbai during rush hour.

⇨ *For more about transfers into either city from the airport, see the Getting Here and Around sections of the specific chapters. For airline contact info, see the Travel Smart chapter.*

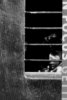

TRAIN TRAVEL

Taking the train

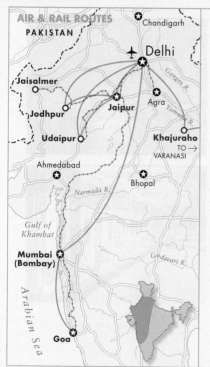

AIR & RAIL ROUTES

PAKISTAN

Chandigarh

Delhi

Ganges R.

Jaisalmer

Jaipur

Agra

Yamuna R.

Jodhpur

Udaipur

Khajuraho

TO →
VARANASI

Ahmedabad

Narmada R.

Bhopal

Gulf of
Khambat

Mumbai
(Bombay)

Godavari R.

Arabian Sea

Goa

TAKE THE TRAIN

A train ride in India remains one of the country's signature events; try to fit at least a short one into your India itinerary. Don't expect your trip to have much to do with the fabled luxury of an Orient Express, though, unless you've booked passage on the opulent Palace on Wheels *(see the next page)*.

PLAN AHEAD

To get the most out of any train ride, plan ahead; otherwise you might end up jammed into a hot compartment with far too many of your fellow passengers and their belongings, or—worse—stranded at a tiny station in the middle of nowhere because of a mix-up. Be aware, too, that train delays are far from uncommon, so pad your schedule, just in case.

Inside Mumbai's train station, Victoria Terminus, also called Chhatrapati Shivaji Terminus

ON THE TRAIN

In a country pretty well obsessed with hierarchies, it may not surprising that there are a full nine classes of train travel. Any class above sleeper is good.

Even first class on an Indian train might seem a bit down-at-the-heels to westerners, but in many ways that's part of the charm. First and foremost, after all, India's trains are a way to get from point A to B, and most of the passengers are Indians rather than tourists. In first class you're likely to find businessmen, politicians, and a smattering of families, perhaps with servants in tow. In the various second classes and the "chair cars" (with individual chairs as opposed to benches) are many more middle-class families. Chair classes, used for relatively short distances, also attract a range of middle-class travelers. The sleeper and unreserved classes have the broadest range and number of people, many of whom cram into narrow seats or just stand.

(top) Outside Victoria Terminus in Mumbai
(bottom) Delhi's Safdarjung train station

TRAIN CLASSES

Inside a second-class train compartment

CLASSES	ABBREVIATION	DESCRIPTION
1st a/c	1A	Your seat is in a lockable air-conditioned compartment with two or four benches that convert to sleeping berths at night. Not the best option for single women travelers, since your fellow travelers are likely to be male. Your compartment will have a small sink and light. Bedding is included.
2nd a/c	2A	Two or four berths that convert to two-tier, bunkbed-like sleepers, but with no lockable compartments. Bedding is included.
3rd a/c	3A	Similar to 2nd a/c, but with six berths in each seating bay (hence the "3," for three tiers). Good for families, but if you're not used to tight quarters, you might get claustrophobic.
3rd a/c economy	3E	This new train class is similar to 3rd a/c, but the berths are along the side of the train and have a little less space. Rare.
1st	FC	No a/c (the windows open instead), but otherwise similar to 1st a/c. Because this class is on its way out, the compartments are usually more dated than those in 1st a/c. Good for relatively short distances when it's not too hot.
A/C executive chair class	EC	Laid out like a standard train in the U.S.: rows of two or three seats on each side.
A/C chair class	CC	Similar in layout to executive chair class but less deluxe.
Sleeper	SL	Similar to 3rd a/c, but with no air-conditioning or reserved seats. Bring your own bedding. Unless you're traveling very light and are feeling adventurous, these cars are probably not for you.
2nd seating	2S	No reservations available. The cars have an open-air plan, with rows of padded or plain wood benches. This class gets crowded—avoid it for any trip longer than a couple of hours.

The toy train to Matheran

TOY TRAINS

The so-called "toy trains" of India, much beloved by tourists, were built to transport goods and overheated members of the Raj to the hill stations—towns up in the hills, to which

An aerial view of the Matheran toy train

members of the British empire would escape when the astonishing heat of summer got to be too much at the lower elevations. Although trucks and buses have made these narrow-gauge trains an anachronism, they remain a charming part of the transportation landscape. The final leg of the train trip to Matheran, a small hill station less than 60 miles east of Mumbai, is via the Matheran Hill Railway, which had its first run in 1907. To reach it, you'll first take a regular train from Mumbai Central (BCT) to Neral Junction (NRL), a 90-minute to two-hour trip. From there, a diesel toy train makes the two-hour trip on the railway three times daily, chugging into the forests and mists beneath Matheran on a two-foot-wide track with hundreds of curves. (*See the Mumbai chapter for more information.*)

Restaurant staff on the Palace on Wheels

LUXURY TRAINS

If you're looking for a luxe rail travel experience, there are several train lines in India that cater to just this desire. The Palace on Wheels travels to the Taj Mahal and other major sights in

Inside the Palace on Wheels

the Golden Triangle, while the Deccan Odyssey has stops in Mumbai, at the Ajanta and Ellora Caves, Goa, and several others destinations. Because these trains are all-inclusive, and because you travel from "port" to "port" while you sleep, it's sort of like being on a high-end cruise ship. Whether this is for you depends on how much the trains' opulent surroundings jibe with what you want from a trip. Among other issues, most meals are on the train and you may find yourself wishing that you could just find your own places to eat from time to time. In addition, luxury trains aren't immune from delays—and a hitch can trim off some time from sightseeing. Still, the comfort of such tours is hard to beat, and if money is no object, they're a tempting option. (*See the Rajasthan and Travel Smart chapters for more information.*)

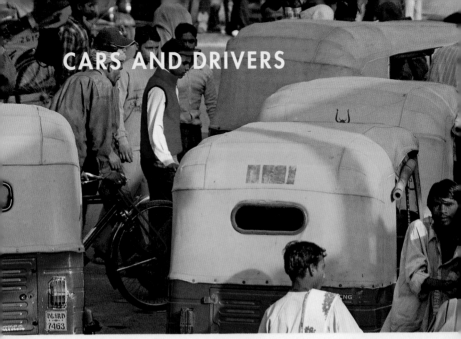

CARS AND DRIVERS

Auto-rickshaws in Delhi

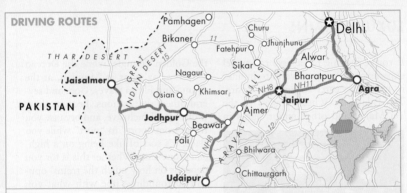

DRIVING ROUTES

Pamhagen
Churu
Delhi
Bikaner
11
Jhunjhunu
Fatehpur
THAR DESERT
Alwar
Sikar
Bharatpur
NH8
NH11
Nagaur
Khimsar
Jaisalmer
Jaipur
Agra
Osian
Ajmer
PAKISTAN
Jodhpur
Beawar
Pali
Bhilwara
12
Udaipur
Chittaurgarh

A CAR WITH A DRIVER

Even if there were a good supply of cars for rent in India, it wouldn't be a good idea to rent one and drive on your own. The traffic here often proceeds at a manic pace, it's not uncommon for drivers to disregard lanes markers (even the ones that separate different directions of travel), and sharing the road with trucks, scooters, auto-rickshaws, camels, bullocks, horses, and the occasional elephant is not something that anyone should try when they're also trying to have a vacation. Indeed, even being a passenger in a car can be disconcerting.

Instead, car rentals in India come with drivers, who are generally knowledgable and friendly and who can help make a day of sightseeing a true pleasure rather than the tiring slog it might otherwise be. In general, the drivers they choose will speak at least some English (make sure to ask)—in some cases, you may even want to ask your

Traffic in Mumbai

actual guide in addition to your driver, for any portion of your trip, you can arrange this at your destination or in advance through a tour operator (*see specific chapters for advice on this*). It's worth remembering that guides as well as drivers may sometimes have a financial interest in taking you to visit certain shops, restaurants, and other establishments.

WHAT KIND OF CAR?

The Ambassador, the classic Indian family car, is built like a tank to handle Indian road bumps and potholes; its design hasn't changed much since it was first built in 1958. Rent one if you can, at least for short trips—they are on their way out. Other more modern options, such as a Toyota Qualis or Innova or a Mahindra Scorpio, are roomier but lack the distinction of an "Amby."

driver (nicely, of course) to stop talking so much.

PRACTICALITIES

If your plans are likely to involve having a car and driver for more than half a day, it's a good idea to reserve ahead of time through a travel agent or tour company. The more information you have about your itinerary, the better a company can estimate the total fees. For long trips in most parts of the country air-conditioning is just about essential. In general, when you hire, a fee for the driver's meals and lodging is included in the price, as is gasoline. (Few drivers will drive at night and, given the perilous condition of the roads and the often-heavy truck traffic, you should steer clear of night travel by car.)

DRIVER VS. GUIDE

To a certain extent your driver might also act as a guide—he won't get out of the car at each stop and tell you interesting facts (although he might), but he can often suggest places to visit, or where to eat. If you want an

DHABAS: YOUR FRIEND ON THE ROAD

Dhabas are roadside truck stops that are especially prevalent in the Punjab regions of Pakistan and India, and if you're doing much driving in India, it's likely that you'll stop at one, if only to use the facilities and fill up on gas. If you're ready for a *tiffin* (snack), keep in mind that it's always best to eat at a dhaba that's doing lots of business. And since you're likely to be at least several hours from your hotel when you see one, it pays to be a little conservative about what you eat. If the place seems a little less than sanitary, there's nothing wrong with opting for some plain naan or a bag of wrapped potato chips and a soft drink rather than an order of tandoori chicken or saag paneer, tempting though the latter two may be. Dhabas have had such an influence on Indian cuisine that even upscale restaurants mimic their style and rich, rough-and-ready cuisine. These days you'll find dhabas popping up far from the dusty, busy highways that are their natural home.

TAXIS, AUTO-RICKSHAWS, AND BUSES

(left) A line of Ambassadors (right) A bus in front of the Hawa Mahal in Jaipur

TAXIS

For shorter trips within a city, taxis are available at airports, luxury hotels, and similar destinations, but they can't always be easily located if you're just out and about. One exception is in Mumbai: because auto-rickshaws are only allowed in the suburbs, taxis are much more common than they are in other cities. Taxis generally have meters, but that doesn't necessarily mean that the driver will use them: make sure to agree on a price if you can't reach agreement on using the meter.

AUTO-RICKSHAWS

Along with motor scooters, the iconic three-wheeled, yellow-and-black or yellow-and-green auto-rickshaws of India are the way a large proportion of the country gets from point A to B within cities and towns. Running on compressed gas or gasoline, their small engines can't handle steep hills or long distances, and their sides, open to the dust and fumes of the street, can be hard to take for too long. That said, their maneuverability in traffic means they're invaluable for short trips.

What you'll pay to zip along depends on your location, the time of day, and, often, your bargaining skills. In some places, auto-rickshaw drivers are fairly careful about using the meter, but it's much more common for them to quote a set fare instead. Make sure to work out a price before you get into a rickshaw—if you have the chance, ask a local to tell you how much a particular trip should cost. It's the rare ride that should cost more than 50 rupees, and most short trips are much less.

FINDING YOUR DESTINATION

Many drivers of auto-rickshaws, taxis, and hired cars know the city like the back of their hand, but it's also possible that your driver may have arrived in the big city just a few weeks before you showed up. To avoid problems, it's good to know the name of the neighborhood where you're headed, and preferably a nearby landmark, too, as well as the street address, which may not be used that often (phone numbers are also handy, since just about every driver will have a cell phone). You can probably assume that most drivers will know major hotels and tourist attractions, but for anything else, make sure that your address comes with a little context.

BUS TRAVEL

Buses are not the most comfortable option, but they do generally make good time, and their large number of departures is also handy.

TRAVEL TIMES

	DISTANCE	BY AIR	BY TRAIN
Delhi to Agra	203 km (126 mi)	1 hour	2.5 hours
Delhi to Jaipur	258 km (160 mi)	45 minutes	5 hours
Delhi to Mumbai	1,407 km (874 mi)	2 hours	16 to 22 hours
Delhi to Goa	1,912 km (1,188 mi)	2 hours	35 hours
Delhi to Varanasi	808 km (502 mi)	1.25 hours	9 to 13 hours
Delhi to Udaipur	663 km (412 mi)	1.25 hours	12 hours
Jaipur to Jaisalmer	614 km (382 mi)	no service	12 hours
Jaipur to Jodphur	332 km (206 mi)	1 hour	5.5 to 12 hours
Jodhpur to Jaisalmer	285 km (177 mi)	no service	5.5 to 7 hours
Mumbai to Jodphur	966 km (600 mi)	about 2 hours	17 to 20 hours
Mumbai to Goa	540 km (336 mi)	1 hour	7.52 to 12 hours
Mumbai to Aurangabad	388 km (241 mi)	45 minutes	6.5 to 7 hours
Delhi to Aurangabad	1,209 km (751 mi)	3.5 hours	about 30 hours
Varanasi to Goa	1,803 km (1,290 mi)	6 hours	39 hours
Jaipur to Udaipur	405 km (251 mi)	1 hour	8 to 10 hours

HONK HONK!

A colorful truck in Agra

Whether you're stuck in traffic in South Mumbai or barreling down the NH-8 highway to Jaipur, honking is always part of the ambient music accompanying a drive in India. But why? In India, it's standard practice to honk as you prepare to pass, to let people know what you're doing so that, hopefully, they'll cede more of the road to you (as you'll find out, lane designations are often completely disregarded). Other drivers honk to alert other drivers of their presence—and their impatience. Because a virile horn is such an important part of a car or truck, it's common for drivers to have after-market extra-loud versions installed.

Portrait of India

WORD OF MOUTH

"India is messy—crowded, dirty, and frenetic. But it is also vibrant, colorful, and so different from anywhere we have ever been. On the one hand, India is a modern society, but on the other, it seems as if things haven't changed much in hundreds of years . . . even wilder and more unexpected than we thought."

—Magster2005

Like the fragrance from the ubiquitous flower garlands, India is difficult to describe in exact terms. We can't completely prepare you for what you'll find, so instead, we will attempt to give a sense of the country through its different elements. From there, it's yours to experience.

From the desert of Rajasthan to the palm-fringed beaches of Goa, India is a study in contrasts. So how does the casual visitor get beyond the extremes of the sparkle of tourism's "Incredible India" and the squalor of the country's in-your-face poverty? A good place to start is with the subcontinent's lively **History,** marked by periods of unification and fragmentation, and sparked by associations with foreign traders and invaders—from the Portuguese and the English to Turkic and Mongol tribes. Indeed, the six decades or so of India as a modern nation is short compared to the region's past. An understanding of history will also help to decipher the morals and mores of **Modern Indian Society.**

Variety and contradiction are central themes in India. From the austerity of some types of vegetarianism to the excesses of spice-infused meats found in Indian **Cuisine,** and from the ascetic philosophies to extravagant rituals in its **Religions,** India is probably defined better by its deviations than by its norms. This makes for a densely populated portrait: from the panoply of **Hindu Gods and Goddesses** to the vibrant forms of **Indian Dance, Music, and the Performing Arts** and the packed calendar of **Holidays and Festivals**—every inch of India is alive with kaleidoscopic sight, sound, and color. Even in matters of economic consumption, contradiction is king, and **Shopping** options range from crafts and kitschy cultural artifacts to exquisite designer ware, all found at megamalls, high-end boutiques, traditional markets, and street-side stalls.

We've tried to distill India's head-spinning inconsistencies and rich traditions into the thematic pages that follow, starting points for an understanding of India, with an emphasis on the regions covered in this book. This background will help explain the nuances of even the most packaged of tours and—because the unexpected is inevitable in India—help you navigate situations that weren't part of your itinerary.

MODERN INDIAN SOCIETY

At once a stable society, comfortably couched in time-worn traditions, and a chaotic crucible of new ideas, modern India is distinguished by diversity and united by patriotism.

(top left) An information technology center outside of Delhi; (top right) A traditional Indian wedding; (bottom right) Dhobi ghat in Mumbai, where thousands of workers wash clothes by hand

There are countless issues that divide the country, including socioeconomic factors such as caste and access to basic needs and education; regional variations like the dozens of official languages and various different cuisines; religious differences that divide communities and often create distinct neighborhoods; and the deep gender inequality that transcends even the division between urban and rural populations. And yet there are many factors uniting the country. Even in terms of language, English and Hindi are common to most of urbanized India, at least at a basic level. And although major urban areas have been joined by roads (no matter the quality of these roads), the democratizing power of the Indian rail system is not to be underestimated. A shared history of colonialism, active media, a sprawling government bureaucracy, and an engaged political body help create a cohesive Indian society. And, of course, there is the fact that Indian people are, by and large, incredibly warm and welcoming.

ASTROLOGY

Modern India may be known for technology, but this doesn't negate the prevalence of superstitious tradition, and many Indians won't make decisions about business, love, or family without consulting the heavens or the cards. Marriages, if not made in heaven, should at least be consecrated on an auspicious date—on days deemed extra-auspicious for weddings, huge numbers of concurrent ceremonies occur.

URBAN VERSUS RURAL SOCIETY

Possibly the biggest difference in India is one that tourists rarely experience: the division between rural and urban life. India's cities are fueled by labor and resources from India's villages—the majority of the country's population still subsists on an agrarian lifestyle and economy—yet city and small-town life is worlds apart from the fields and dirt roads of the rest of India. While in the cities, access to electricity is frustrated by unannounced cuts and load-shedding, only about half of rural Indian households have any access to power at all. Education and potable water are also often elusive commodities outside of India's cities and towns. Idyllic glimpses of rural life are visible from the road or train—yellow-blossomed mustard fields in north India, coconut plantations along the coast, tractors loaded impossibly high with bales of cotton or other goods—but the realities of rural life are something a traveler will rarely get the chance to see. Interestingly, socioeconomic divisions of caste or occupation—though certainly still present—are less stark in rural areas than in urban ones.

RICH, MIDDLE CLASS, POOR

India's cities are microcosms and melting pots. A small, privileged elite drives (or is chauffeured) between the air-conditioned high-rises of south Mumbai, the gated colonies of south Delhi, the

exclusive resorts of Goa, and similar areas. The denizens of this privileged group frequent five-star restaurants, luxury boutiques, and private clubs. But this is just a tiny segment of society.

A large and rapidly growing middle class fuels urban economy, powering the country's information-technology hubs. More professionalized and better educated than their parents, members of the urban middle class also feed a mushrooming consumer-goods-and-services sector. Spending money is proof of success, and lavish weddings replete with yards of brocade, miles of fairy lights, tons of gold jewelry, and bushels of fresh-cut flowers are not uncommon. Coffee shops and fast-food outlets cater to and are staffed by members of middle-class society.

In stark contrast to the rich and the middle-class, India's populated areas are also home to millions of urban poor—from migrants who set up house in tarpaulin shelters while employed in construction and infrastructure projects to low-income families living in slum colonies characterized by open sewers. Many urban migrants live a double life—catering to the wealthy and middle class so they can send money to their families back in the village. Besides domestic help, low-income jobs include a wide range of workers—including porters, cycle-rickshaw drivers, salesmen of cheap goods, and more.

GENDER ROLES

Across all walks of life, women and men lead very different, often divergent, lives. While women work the fields and provide manual labor on construction sites right alongside men, these are roles born out of economic necessity. Middle-class and even elite women have less occasion to work outside of the home; although wealthier families may educate daughters as much as sons, the focus for women is squarely on marriage and raising children. Cutting across economic distinctions is a preference for boys—in some states female infanticide is still a serious problem, and it is illegal for doctors to disclose the sex of fetuses. Some villages have such a shortage of marriageable women that they have had to bring in brides from other regions of India—a practice that rubs against the older tradition of marrying within one's caste and culture.

MARRIAGE

Arranged marriages take place all across Indian society. Although the government prohibits child marriage, betrothals and weddings at a very young age still do take place in more remote areas. These days, however, the culture of dating also thrives in India's big cities. Couples can be seen everywhere in Delhi and Mumbai, flaunting their sexual freedom on the dance floors of clubs, sharing coffee and moony looks across a café table, or surreptitiously canoodling under a tree in a public park—often the most convenient meeting ground for poorer youngsters from more conservative families. Online dating is less of a casual affair than in the west, and dating sites are used predominately by middle-class families looking to set up marriages.

CASTE

Marriage classifieds (listings of eligible men and women, living in India or abroad, searchable by caste, religion, profession, and education, etc.) are only one of the many societal phenomena in which caste figures prominently. Caste in India can be as innocuous as a shared community history, signified by a particular last name, or as insidious as a derogatory slur. Although technically abolished, in practical terms caste identity still plays an important role in modern Indian society, particularly in politics. There is raging debate—akin to but far more polarizing than the American debate over affirmative action—over quotas for historically disadvantaged castes in government jobs or school admissions, for example, that plays out on the political stage both nationally and locally.

POLITICS

India's parliamentary democracy is rife with corruption and strange liaisons, and the average Indian is either actively cynical or openly engaged with politics—and sometimes both. A multiparty system means that there are significant blocs of special-interest parties besides the dominant Congress Party and BJP (Bharatiya Janata Party). Unfortunately, some of these parties mine religion to garner support, which can have the result of turning whole communities against each other.

RELIGION

Religion plays a large part in modern Indian society, and worship is an important component: people often pray regularly in temples, mosques, gurdwaras, and churches, but may also have family shrines at home, composed of icons, portraits, and statues. Ritual fasting is a regular occurrence in many religions, whether weekly for some very pious Hindus or yearly during Ramadan for devout Muslims. Religious conventions can often bleed into cultural ones, influencing diet, neighborhood, occupation, and clothing choice.

CLOTHING

Clothing in modern Indian society is a signifier of many things—gender, region, wealth, and profession—in addition to occasionally indicating religion. In general, men usually wear trousers or jeans with shirts or T-shirts. In south India and in rural areas, native forms of dress—long pieces of cloth called *lungis* or *dhotis*—are wrapped around the waist and legs, but loose-fitting pajama-type outfits are more common. These are topped with an undershirt, called a *banyan*, and perhaps a tunic or kurta. Headgear can also be an indicator of religion or region. Rajasthani men are known for their bright, coiled turbans (and grandiose mustaches), Sikh men sweep their long hair into streamlined turbans, and Muslim men usually wear skull caps when praying. Poorer or rural women of all religions tend to cover their heads with thin scarves, and urban Muslim women may keep their heads covered and wear body-covering robes as well. Traditional wear for women includes the more typically north Indian tunic or shirt, called a kurta or *kameez*. This is paired with loose pants, or *salwar*, gathered at the ankle. Skirts (*lehengas*) with blouses (*cholis*) are also popular, particularly as wedding wear. Saris, yards of cloth that can be tied many different ways around a petticoat and blouse, are worn all over India and come in many regionally and seasonally specific textiles and patterns. Urban women are quite comfortable in jeans and other Western wear, though exposing too much leg or cleavage in public is frowned upon (Mumbai and Goa are slightly more relaxed in this regard).

(top left) Lunch-wallahs transporting tiffin boxes; (bottom right) A traditional family in a small village in Rajasthan

HISTORY YOU CAN SEE

India's history is marked by periods of cultural and economic exchange and lively empire building. Among the obvious results are the ruins of ancient planned cities and the chaos of modern India's skyrocketing growth.

(top left) Rashtrapati Bhavan, in Delhi, where the president lives; (top right) A carving at Khajuraho; (bottom right) Stone chariot shrine at Hampi

Blessed with an abundance of natural resources, geographical diversity, and many access points along its coasts, India has historically been an attractive place for settlers and conquerors. Part of the reason for the subcontinent's continued diversity of culture and people is that residents have always been influenced by different forces at each of the area's different boundaries, which themselves have been rather fluid over the centuries. At various points, Indian empires have been some of the richest and most cultured in the world. Though its history is marked by cycles of destruction and construction, and despite a tendency to neglect all things old, India's past is very much alive in fabulous myths, recorded documents, and phenomenal physical artifacts and archaeological sites.

AGES OF ARCHITECTURE

Mughal architecture is a mélange of influences—vaulted spaces recalling Central Asian campaign tents, Persian domes topped with Hindu lotus finials, and Rajput-style pavilions with umbrella-like overhangs. The British adopted what they saw, adding Gothic and art deco touches. Examples of British construction include Victoria Terminus, the Gateway of India, and Rashtrapati Bhavan.

2

PREHISTORY

The subcontinent's oldest significant archaeological finds are from the planned cities of the Indus Valley Civilization, which peaked in western India, Pakistan, and points north in the period around 2600–1800 BC. Delhi's **National Museum** has a large collection of artifacts (pottery, toys, copper tools) from this era. Around 1500 BC, Indo-Europeans from Central Asia began to migrate to the region; their Indo-Aryan language was likely influenced by the subcontinent's indigenous Dravidian dialects to form Sanskrit. This gave rise to the Vedic Iron Age, characterized by the oral composition of Sanskrit texts—the underpinnings of Hinduism. Urban centers such as Kashi (modern-day **Varanasi**, the oldest continuously inhabited city in the world) emerged, and India began to be cut up into various monarchies and republics.

ANCIENT EMPIRES

Succeeding a handful of ancient kingdoms and forays by Macedonian conqueror Alexander the Great, the Hindu Maurya Empire (India's first) was founded in 321 BC. At its peak, under the Buddhist convert Emperor Ashoka, the kingdom encompassed most of the subcontinent. Ashoka built Buddhist shrines and temples at **Sarnath** (where the Buddha preached his first sermon) and at Sanchi. He also furthered the religion through edicts, often inscribed

on pillars. The **Ashokan pillar at Sarnath**, with four lions at the top, later provided the inspiration for modern India's state emblem.

Farther south lay the Dravidian kingdoms of the Cholas, Cheras, and Pandyas. These eventually gave way to other dynasties, while the decline of the Maurya Empire in the north led to smaller kingdoms with ever-shifting boundaries and incursions from the northwest. Most of the north was again united by the Gupta Empire during India's "Golden Age" from the 4th to 6th centuries. Under the tolerant administration of the Guptas, the arts and sciences flourished: the concept of zero, the heliocentric model, and the game of chess are all said to have been invented during this period. Meanwhile, the grandeur of the Vijayanagar Empire in the south, which was strong until the 17th century, is evident in the ruins at Hampi. The rest of India was ruled by other "Middle Kingdoms," like the Vakatakas in central India, who created the Buddhist cave paintings at Ajanta. By the 8th century, martial Rajput clans were a dominant ruling force in north India. Rajput factions built Gwalior's clifftop fort and **Khajuraho**'s erotically embellished temples; their descendents would go on to build forts and palaces in **Jaipur, Udaipur, Jaisalmer,** and other centers of power in **Rajasthan.**

MUSLIM RULERS

India's first Islamic states were several Turkic and Afghan territories, collectively called the Delhi Sultanate. The first, the Mamluk (Slave) Dynasty, was founded by Qutb-ud-din Aibak in the early 13th century. A slave-soldier whose leader had made incursions into north India, Aibak and his successors built Delhi's **Qutub Minar**. Next, the Turkic-Afghan Khilji rulers took over, expanding their territory west from the Ganges River and building Delhi's **Siri Fort**. Around the same time, the breakaway Bahmani Sultanate, which eventually fragmented into smaller kingdoms, carved out parts of the south's Vijayanagara Empire. In 1321, the Tughlaqs sultans came to power, ruling from Tughlaqabad (now in Delhi). Their rule was weakened in 1398, when Timur (Timurlane), a descendent of Genghis Khan, sacked the city. The Sayyid Dynasty ruled briefly, followed by the Afghan Lodhi sultans, some of whom are buried in the tombs in Delhi's **Lodhi Gardens**.

Relative stability came to north India with the first Mughal Emperor, Babur, who hailed from Central Asia and had Persian, Turkic, and Mongol ancestry. He established his rule in 1526, having defeated the Lodis and neighboring Rajputs. Babur's son was **Humayun**, whose **tomb** in Delhi is an example of the mixing of Islamic and Hindu cultures under the Mughals; it's considered a precursor to the Taj Mahal. Humayun's son, Akbar, reigned for half a century, starting in 1556. Based in **Agra** and nearby **Fatehpur Sikri**, Akbar expanded and consolidated Mughal power through marriage, conquest, and feudal ties. Greatly influenced by Sufi saints, Akbar was curious about and tolerant of other religions. The syncretic Mughal arts and architecture blossomed under his grandson, Shah Jahan, who built his city, **Shahjahanabad (Old Delhi)**, including the **Lal Qila (Red Fort)** and the **Jama Masjid**, as well as **Agra Fort** and, of course, the **Taj Mahal**.

COLONIALISM

Following the expansionist policies of the puritanical Emperor Aurangzeb (1658–1707), Mughal power was compromised by war, especially against the strong Maratha Empire, which had its center in Raigad, south of Mumbai.

Meanwhile, Queen Elizabeth I chartered the British East India Company, arguably the world's first corporation, in 1600. Competing with the Dutch, Portuguese, and French for mercantile control, the British East India Company opened trading posts and spread out, building India's **railroads**, from its **forts** in Madras, Calcutta, and Bombay (now Chennai, Kolkata, and Mumbai). The company steadily gained control over the subcontinent by pitting princely states against each other, leveraging economic power, installing governing and educational institutions, and through outright battle. In 1857, the company's Indian troops revolted. Variously called the Sepoy Mutiny or the First War of Independence, the rebellion's ripple effect gave the British government an excuse to clamp down. Raj architecture persists in **Delhi**, which succeeded Calcutta as the capital and is packed with imperial buildings, especially in the **India Gate** area. South Mumbai, too, is littered with Raj reminders; must-sees are the **Prince of Wales Museum** and **Crawford Market**.

INDEPENDENCE AND STATEHOOD

In 1947, after nearly a century of British Raj, India gained independence in the aftermath of World War II. Leading the push for independence through nonviolent resistance was Mohandas K. Gandhi, known as Mahatma (Great Soul). Gandhi and other leaders are honored at museums and memorials across the country, including Delhi's **National Gandhi Museum**, the **Gandhi Smriti** (where he was assassinated), and the **Nehru Memorial Museum**.

Independence came at a price, however. Before their soldiers sailed out from Mumbai's **Gateway of India**, the British partitioned the country, carving out West and East Pakistan (the latter now Bangladesh) as Muslim nations. The violence of Partition (the largest human migration in history, with a population exchange of millions), an early India-Pakistan war, and the problem of incorporating hundreds of princely states were huge challenges. The first prime minister, Jawaharlal Nehru, set about building a socialist nation—creating infrastructure, universities, and nationalized industries, and taking an active part in the fledgling Non-aligned Movement. In its first few decades, India also saw an agricultural revolution, war with China over disputed territory, and more conflicts with Pakistan. When Nehru's daughter, Indira Gandhi, became prime minister, she reacted to the threat of secessionist groups and economic problems by declaring a state of emergency in 1971. The backlash against her and her sons' leadership led to a more dynamic but less predictable coalition-driven Parliament and increased politicization of religion and caste. In the 1990s, economic reforms and the privatization of government-run corporations led to a booming economy and participation in global trade. Although its economy is still largely agrarian, India has become an offshore provider of skilled services with a large middle class, evident in the call centers and glittering malls that have sprouted around Delhi, Hyderabad, and elsewhere.

(top left) Humayun's tomb, Delhi; (bottom right) Photo of Jawaharlal Nehru, on the left, with Mahatma Gandhi, on the right

RELIGIONS OF INDIA

India may be a secular country constitutionally, but religion has a central and vital place in the daily lives of most of its citizens.

(top left) An illustration from the Ramayana; (top right) At a Hindu ceremony; (bottom right) Muslim woman praying at Jama Masjid

To just say that India is 80% Hindu oversimplifies the country's complex web of histories, identities, and institutions, many of which were codified in modern terms as "religions" only in the last few centuries. Leaving aside the fact that the population is more than 13% Muslim, with significant Christian, Sikh, and other minorities, even the majority Hindu community is extremely diverse. Regional identities often cut deeper than religion (thus Kashmiri Hindus eat meat while Hindus in Gujarat will not). On top of that, each of India's religions encompass age-old traditions that have survived modernity, new-age movements that focus on spirituality, and politically driven ideologies that justify themselves through mythology. But despite the fact that there are, occasionally, the kind of ugly conflicts that flare up in any pluralistic society, for the most part India is a place where you will find an amazing, often touching, degree of compassion—tolerance that extends to curiosity, and secularism that is expressed as humanity.

JUDAISM

The Jews have a long history in India, starting with the Cochin Jews arriving in Kerala around 500 BC. The Bene Israel came a few centuries later, followed by Middle Eastern and Central Asian Jews. More recently, the Bnei Menashe claimed to be a lost tribe of Israel and were recognized by Israeli rabbis. Some Ben Ephraim Jews, who were converted to Christianity in the 1800s, decided to re-embrace Judaism as recently as the 1980s.

2

HINDUISM

About 80% of India's population is Hindu. The world's third-largest religion, Hinduism is also often regarded as the oldest, with roots that stretch back 5,000 years. It may also be the most varied, as this millennia-old tradition is actually an amalgam of texts, schools, civilizations, and beliefs with a host of leaders and no single founder. Though Hindus generally believe in reincarnation, divinity itself may be multiple or monistic, and practice may involve dharma (moral duty), ascetic rigor (as in yoga), devotion through prayer, and many other forms of expression. Modern Hinduism draws from four major Vedic "texts"—Sanskrit ritual verses that were recorded orally beginning with the Iron Age Indus Valley civilization and later written down—as well as corollary philosophical and mystical discourses, treatises on the arts, and the epic poems the *Mahabharata* and the *Ramayana*.

Living Hinduism is just as multifaceted as its history. Visitors to India may witness or participate in many aspects of observance including ritual ceremonies, some with fire, ghee, milk, and offerings of flowers and sweets; temple worship, with offerings to deities represented by *murthis* (statues); or physical practices: ascetics who deny material comfort as an expression of devotion, yogis who push their bodies to the physical limit

in order to approach the divine, and ayurvedic doctors who prescribe herbal remedies and offer nutritional advice.

ISLAM

The country's largest minority, India's Muslim population is—including Pakistan's Muslims—second only to Indonesia's in numbers. As with Hinduism, Islam in India also encompasses many different schools and practices. Although India's earliest encounter with Islam was through Arab traders along the southwest coast, the religion's first real movement was through the north and west of the subcontinent in the 8th century, and it expanded from the 12th century onward under the Delhi Sultanate and then the Mughal Empire. Besides the strength of the Mughal seat of power around Delhi, Muslim communities grew around Islamic rulers around the country.

Like Muslims everywhere, Indian Muslims follow the Koran as the word of Allah revealed to Mohammad in the 7th century. Most Muslims in India belong to the majority Sunni sect, but there are significant portions of Shi'a Muslims as well, who believe in the importance of the Imams and of Mohammad's nephew, Ali. The spread of Islam in India also owes a great deal to mystical Sufi sects, whose founders created centers of learning, music, and charity.

CHRISTIANITY

India's third-largest religion (about 2% of the population), Christianity is most visible in south and southwest India and in the northeastern states. The earliest whispers of Christianity in India are accounts of the arrival of ("Doubting") Thomas the Apostle in Kerala in the 1st century and the establishment of Syrian Christian churches, which likely grew out of extant Indian Jewish communities and populations of Syrian immigrants. Later, European missionaries (like St. Francis Xavier, the Portuguese Jesuit) arrived to proselytize. Most Indian Christians follow Catholic or Orthodox practices, but some Protestant churches were also established.

As in other postcolonial countries, Indian Christianity has its own distinct flavors, from the colorful roadside shrines of Kerala to the excesses of Goan Carnival to the pronounced influence of gospel music in the northeast.

SIKHISM

Sikhism grew from the teachings of its founder, Guru Nanak Dev, in the early 1500s. Nanak, a Hindu, broke from that religion's rituals and began to preach a monotheistic faith based on meditation and charity. Nine more *gurus,* or teachers, followed in his footsteps, consolidating and spreading the religion over the next few centuries. Partially as a response to persecution under the later Mughals, Sikhism also acquired a martial flavor, and followers combined elements of both the soldier and the saint. The 11th guru and the spiritual authority for modern Sikhs is the *Guru Granth Sahib Ji,* a sacred text composed of the teachings of previous gurus and other Hindu and Muslim saints. With a majority of its population in the northwestern state of Punjab (the Golden Temple in Amritsar is the most important holy site), the Sikh community was directly affected by the violence of India's Partition, as well as suffering later injustices under the Indira Gandhi administration in 1984.

Often identifiable by their uncut hair (which the men tie up under turbans), practicing Sikhs also engage in the singing and chanting of passages of scripture (this can continue over days) and the serving of free daily meals at *gurdwaras* (temples).

BUDDHISM

Although Siddhartha Gautama attained enlightenment through meditation and became the Buddha, in 500 BC, in what is now the Indian state of Bihar, India has a surprisingly low percentage of the world's Buddhists. With its focus on moderation and individual duty over divisions of caste or divinity, Buddhism peaked in India with the conversion of the Maurya emperor Ashoka around 260 BC. The following centuries saw Buddhist rituals and institutions taking root outside of India, but within the country it was largely subsumed by other systems of faith. Today Buddhists in India include monks (mostly living along India's border with Tibet), low-caste Hindus who converted in large numbers over the last century to improve their social situation, and Tibetan refugees—including the Dalai Lama and his "government-in-exile" in Dharamshala. In spite of a relatively low number of adherents, Buddhism has had a profound impact on Indian society.

JAINISM

While Jainism appears in practice to be a more stringently ascetic, fiercely nonviolent cousin of Buddhism, the religion has most likely existed as a complement to and influence on Hinduism for thousands of years. Jains believe in reincarnation and do not believe in an all-powerful creator. However, Jains do follow 24 *tirthankaras* (teachers), the last of whom, Mahavir, was a contemporary of the Buddha. Jain temples house idols of these *tirthankaras*; these temples are also where you might see devout Jain monks or nuns who wear white and cover their mouths to avoid inadvertently swallowing and killing insects and microbes. Jain sects vary in degrees of asceticism (some even eschew clothing), but in general, Jains do not eat meat, garlic, or onions. Jain practices have been important to India's cultural identity, and while they represent just a small portion of the population, Jains are highly influential in political and economic spheres.

BAHÁ'Í FAITH

With the world's largest group of its followers living in India, and the landmark House of Worship (Lotus Temple) in Delhi, the syncretic Bahá'í Faith is a significant part of India's spiritual landscape. Founded in Persia in 1863, this faith seeks to unite the world's major religions and claims that Krishna, the Buddha, Abraham, Jesus, Mohammad, the Báb (a 19th-century holy man), and the religion's founder Bahá'u'llah were all divine messengers.

ZOROASTRIANISM

Though Zoroastrianism was once a major monotheistic world religion with Persian origins (founded by the prophet Zarathustra around 1200 BC), India now has the world's largest contingent of its followers, known as Parsis, a small but well-educated and influential group of Persians who settled in medieval western India. Though many have moved on, Mumbai has a sizeable group, including some prominent industrialists. Mumbai is also home to the Irani community—19th- and 20th-century immigrants who fled persecution in Iran.

(top left) Se (Cathedral), in Old Goa; (bottom right) Devotees inside Sis Ganj Gurdwara, a Sikh temple

HOLIDAYS AND FESTIVALS OF INDIA

With silk-garbed deities paraded through the streets, and special foods, dancing, and the ritual gifting of everything from saucepans to Swarovski, festivals and holidays bring together the most excessive and ascetic aspects of Indian culture.

(top left) At a Holi festival; (top right) An elaborate tableau for Durga Puja; (bottom right) Republic Day Parade

Holidays in India range from religious days of reflection to patriotic celebrations of nationalism, and festivals can mark time-honored trade fairs or harvest celebrations. Because this is a country of so many regions and religions—with different harvest seasons and different calendars based on the sun, the moon, or both—there are numerous new year's celebrations (sometimes overlapping), different commemorative days for religious or local founders, and any number of minor holidays. There's almost always something going on, and it's worth timing your visit to coincide with an event. Seeing the elaborate tableaux and dancing; witnessing the masses of people at temples, mosques, and churches; and joining the crowds eating at specially built food stalls adds an extra shine to any experience of India.

MAHA NAVRATI

Literally translated as "nine nights," this celebration, which takes place in October and November, marks the beginning of winter. It generally includes worshipping Shakti, the divine Hindu mother goddess. Bengalis honor Shakti in Durga Puja by creating thematic pandals or tableaux—three-dimensional representations that include a statue of Durga—which are then submerged in the river.

2

MAKAR SANKRANTI
This January 14 festival marks the end of winter and the beginning of the harvest season, depending on the region. In many places it's celebrated by flying brightly colored paper kites (often "fighting kites," on glass-encrusted string used to strike down other kites).

REPUBLIC DAY
January 26 marks the day that the Constitution came into being in 1950; celebrations include a parade in Delhi, with kitschy floats from every region.

HOLI
The Hindu and Sikh equivalent of Carnival, the northern spring festival of Holi is India's most colorful celebration. All social and religious groups get involved on the last and wildest day (in February or March) by throwing colored powder on each other.

INDEPENDENCE DAY
The celebration of India's independence on August 15 is a dignified affair, with flag-hoisting and speechifying.

EID-UL-FITR
The end of the fasting month of Ramadan consists of three days of feasting on special desserts, buying new clothes, visiting family, and distributing alms.

GANESH CHATHURTHI
Mumbai is the epicenter of this August/September celebration of the elephant-headed god, Ganesh, which involves

submerging Ganesh idols of all sizes and types in the sea.

DIWALI
Diwali is the Hindu New Year and the end of the harvest season. Often called the "festival of lights" because people line their homes with twinkling clay lamps, Diwali is celebrated over five days with firecrackers and gift-giving. On the third day people invite Lakshmi, the goddess of wealth, into their homes. The date varies each year, but is usually between September and November.

EID-UL-ADHA
Also called "Bakr-Id," Eid-ul-Adha marks the end of the Hajj (the Muslim pilgrimage to Mecca). It's celebrated by sacrificing a goat, echoing Abraham's willingness to sacrifice his son, and by distributing food to the poor. The date, based on the Islamic calendar, changes every year.

GURU NANAK JAYANTI
The most important Sikh holiday, also known as Gurpurab, marks the birth of Guru Nanak, the founder of the Sikh religion. It's celebrated with all-night chanting, singing hymns, and cooking meals for the poor. Based on the lunar calendar, it falls either in October or November.

CHRISTMAS
Christmas is celebrated across India with lights, tinsel, and midnight mass.

HINDU GODS AND GODDESSES

The vast pantheon of Hindu gods and goddesses originates in ancient Hindu mythology but plays an important role in modern life.

(top left) Durga Puja; (top right) Statue of Krishna; (bottom right) Statue of Vishnu

Most of the Hindu deities are represented in the two great Indian epics, the *Ramayana* and the *Mahabharata*, and in the ancient books of the Hindu religion known as the Vedas. The mythology surrounding the various gods and goddesses is steeped with lore of demons vanquished in the ongoing battle of good versus evil. The deities are richly portrayed, and each of their physical features is deeply symbolic. Many gods and goddesses are also characterized by their *vahana,* or vehicle, the traditional animal mount they ride.

A central concept is that of the Trimurti, which encapsulates the three basic cosmic actions: creation, maintenance, and destruction. These are, in turn, personified by Brahma the creator, Vishnu the maintainer or preserver, and Shiva the destroyer or transformer.

One of the key things to look for when you visit a Hindu temple is the intricate carvings and sculptures, which illustrate the gods and goddesses and provide interpretations of Hindu mythology.

PUJA

The tradition of daily *puja*, or prayer, is a central part of Hindu life. Paintings and sculptures of various deities are found in temples and home shrines, where lamps are lit and offerings of food are made to invoke the blessings of the gods. Specific gods or goddesses are often worshipped to deal with specific situations—anything from healing an ailment to doing well on a math test or having success in a business venture.

BRAHMA

The God of Creation, Brahma is the first god in the Hindu triumvirate, or Trimurti, and is associated with the daily coming and going of light and dark. He is said to have grown out of the navel of the sleeping Vishnu. Brahma is traditionally depicted with four heads (representing the four Vedas, the four holy books of the Hindu religion), sitting on a lotus. The legends tell that he once had a fifth head but it was lost after he lied to Vishnu and made Shiva angry. In his four arms he holds the Vedas, a *kamandalam* (water pot), a *suruva* (sacrificial spoon), and an *akshamala* (string of beads), which he uses to count time. Brahma has a swan as his *vahana*. Although Brahma is one of the three major gods in Hinduism, there are few temples dedicated to him, the most famous being the Brahma temple at Pushkar in Rajasthan.

VISHNU

Vishnu is the god of protection and maintenance, and the second entity in the Trimurti. He is commonly recognized by the blue color of his skin (the color of water) and with four arms that hold the *chakra* (a sharp spinning-discus-like weapon), a conch that produces the mantric Om representing the sound of creation, a lotus representing spiritual liberation, and a *gadha*, or mace. Vishnu is often shown reclining on the ocean, atop Adisesha (a serpent with

1,000 heads) and alongside his consort Lakshmi, the goddess of wealth. As the divine protector, he is believed to have assumed avatars and descended to Earth to rescue populations from evil rulers and forces, or to restore the balance between good and evil in the world. Thus far, he's come to Earth in nine different avatars, including one as Krishna, and Hindus believe that he will be reincarnated one last time, right before the end of this world. His wife Parvati represents his domestic and peaceful side. Mohini is the female form of Vishnu, and usually described as a supremely enchanting maiden.

KRISHNA

Krishna is an avatar, or incarnation, of Vishnu and is often depicted as a young boy or prince, usually with dark or black skin. He is said to be the embodiment of love and divine joy that destroys all pain and sin. He takes on many different personas, including prankster, lover, divine hero, and Supreme Being. Common representations show him lying back in a relaxed pose, playing the flute, though he is also represented as the divine herdsman, accompanied by cows or *gopis* (milkmaids). Some paintings show him with Radha, his *gopi* consort.

SHIVA

Shiva, the third of the Trimurti, is the god of destruction, and is generally worshipped in the form of the phallus (lingam) fixed on a pedestal. He is vested with the power to destroy the universe in order to re-create it—that is, he can destroy the imperfections that can transform the universe. His twin abilities to both create and destroy give an intimidating aura to his austere, meditative demeanor. He is usually portrayed residing high up in the Himalayas with an ash-smeared forehead, his body covered simply in animal skin, and a king cobra draped around his neck. He has a third eye, in the middle of his forehead, believed to be his source of knowledge and wisdom and also the source of his untamed energy, when it is unleashed. He is also often depicted as the Lord of Dance, a metaphor for his ability to masterfully maintain the balance in the universe.

LAKSHMI

The goddess of wealth and prosperity and the consort to Vishnu, Lakshmi is commonly depicted as a beautiful woman standing or sitting on a lotus. She has four arms representing the four ends of human life: *dharma* or righteousness, *kama* or desires, *artha* or wealth, and *moksha* or liberation from the cycle of birth and death. Her portrayal as the goddess of wealth is evident from the cascades of gold coins flowing from her hands. A representation of her can be found even now in nearly every household because of her power to bestow prosperity, and she is celebrated with much veneration during the festival of Diwali.

GANESH

Perhaps the most easily recognized of the Hindu gods, and certainly among the most endearing, Ganesh has an elephant head, large belly, and four arms, one of which holds a *laddu*, a ball-shaped popular Indian sweet. He is worshipped at the start of any new venture, and before exams, because he is considered to be the god who removes obstacles (*vignam*). He is variously depicted in seated, standing, and dancing postures, and is most often worshipped in people's homes for removing day-to-day challenges. His *vahana* is a tiny mouse, and he has several other names, including Ganapati, Gajanana, Vigneshwara, Pilliar, and Vinayagar.

MURUGAN

Also known as Subramanya or Kartikeya, Murugan is the second son of Shiva and Parvati. He is widely worshipped in southern India, especially in the state of Tamil Nadu. He is the God of War. Legend has it that he was so upset with his father, Lord Shiva, whom he believed showed preferential treatment to Ganesh, Shiva's other son, that Murugan left the Himalayas for a hill in the state of Tamil Nadu, in South India. It's there that the six most important shrines devoted to him are found; collectively they are known as Arupadai Veedu (literally "six battle camps"), and each is connected to one of the six stages of his life.

HANUMAN

The monkey god, Hanuman, is an ardent devotee of Lord Rama (one of the avatars of Vishnu) and he is among the key characters in the beloved Hindu epic, the *Ramayana*. The story goes that Lord Rama was banished from his father's kingdom for 14 years, during which time his wife Sita is abducted by the evil king Ravana and taken across the seas to Lanka. Hanuman, who belongs to the varanas, an apelike race of forest dwellers, joins Lord Rama in his mission to rescue Sita. Hanuman is revered and worshipped for his courage and valor in inspiring and leading Rama's army and for being steadfast in his devotion and loyalty to Rama. He is often depicted in temples with a mace in his right hand or kneeling before Lord Rama and Sita.

SARASWATI

As the goddess of knowledge, literature, music, and the arts, Saraswati is said to be the mother of the Vedas, the four holy books of Hinduism. She is also associated with intelligence, creativity, education, and enlightenment. Saraswati is usually pictured dressed in white, sometimes holding a palm-leaf scroll. Her *vahana* is a swan or a peacock. She is the consort of Brahma.

SHAKTI

Shakti is the divine Hindu mother goddess, a creative feminine force. The goddess Durga is the embodiment of her warrior side. Durga is often shown as the mother of Ganesha, Kartikeya, Lakshmi, and Saraswati. The female equivalent of the Trimurti concept is Tridevi (*devi* means goddess in Sanskrit), and can be represented as the conjoined forms of Lakshmi, Parvati, and Saraswati—essentially, the Shaktis of the Trimurti—Vishnu, Shiva, and Brahma, respectively.

KALI

Kali is the goddess of time and change, which come together as death. She has a dual nature of fierceness and motherliness. Although she represents death, she is also seen as a positive force because she is a destroyer of ego and therefore a granter of liberation and freedom of the soul. Kali is represented as the consort of Shiva, whose body she is often seen standing upon. Her *vahana* is a jackal.

(top left) A Ganesh idol at the Ganesh Chaturthi festival; (bottom right) An enormous Shiva statue

INDIAN CUISINE

Eating in India is an adventure, from the East-meets-West artistry of tandoori-style foie gras to the tangy jumble of flavors in a street snack.

(top left) An assortment of curries and rice dishes; (top right) A dosa with some aloo masala; (bottom right) A bowl of kheer with pistachios

This is a country united by its obsession with food, even as it is divided into infinite variations by region, religion, and economics. At the local level, friendships can be jeopardized over diverging loyalties to competing chai-sellers.

Still, visitors expecting a rigid, prohibitive food culture are often more surprised by the inclusive, evolving nature of Indian cuisines, which absorb and adapt ingredients and cooking techniques from all over the world. Despite many traditional taboos surrounding eating, there's a healthy amount of curiosity and sharing as well. In most cities you'll find diverse fare, from South India's famed breakfast dishes (*dosas, uttapams, idlis*) to North India's mouthwatering nonvegetarian dishes.

A growing respect for regional cuisines means that visitors are no longer subject to the sanitized menus of yore. Pay a little attention to the changing flavors around you and you'll never again think of Indian food as limited to kebab and curry.

STREET FOOD

In the busy by-lanes of India's urban centers as much as in its truck-stop towns, stalls and carts are a constant feature and the fuel of street life. For the faint of stomach, watching locals eat at these venues can be a vicarious pleasure—but in the big cities some vendors are sensitive to hygiene (look for signs indicating the use of bottled water), and some sit-down restaurants offer their own clean versions of street dishes.

UBIQUITOUS INDIAN DISHES

Daal, which in India refers to split pulses (lentils, beans, or split peas), is the country's most basic dish, generally boiled, spiced, and tempered with fried cinnamon, bay leaves, garlic, and onion. Variations in thickness and hue range from pale yellow (*moong daal*) to smoky black (*urad*).

Thanks to the inexorable force of Punjabi culture, **chicken tikka** is a widespread dish. Chicken pieces—usually boneless—are marinated in yogurt, lemon, ginger, garlic and spices, then skewered and baked in a clay oven (tandoor) or grilled over coals. Chicken tikkas are found in this simplest form or covered in various spiced gravies.

Though it consists of rice and sweetened, thickened milk, rice pudding is far too prosaic a translation of **kheer.** Ranging from Kashmir's fruit-flavored *phirnis* to coconut milk-based *payasams* in the south, kheer can also be made of broken wheat or vermicelli noodles. Often served in a shallow clay bowl, it can be garnished with nuts or topped with silver leaf.

Definitely a candidate for most ubiquitous dish, the "**Manchurian**" purports to be a Chinese specialty but is as Indian as *saag paneer*. Supposedly invented by Kolkata Chinese chef Nelson Wang in Mumbai in 1975, it consists of strips of battered and deep-fried poultry, doused

in a thickened soy-based sauce. Both chicken and veggie Manchurians are now found on every Indian Chinese menu in the country.

For many North Indians, South Indian food begins and ends with the **dosa.** Popular as a breakfast food, these crisp crepes are made of fermented ground-rice-and-lentil batter. They can be as big as small boats and are served with a thin lentil soup called *sambar*.

Only a small percentage of candies in any place are regional—the vast majority of Indian confectioners sell the brightly colored **Bengali sweets,** available in an astonishing variety of flavors and pretty, molded shapes. The catalyst for the invention of these candies—by one Nobin Chandra Das in 1860 Bengal—was the Portuguese introduction of intentionally curdling milk to make cheese; the candies too are based on curdled milk.

Whether it's called puchka, gol-guppa, **panipuri** or gup-chup, this delightful snack or "chaat" is found all over eastern, northern and western India. Street vendors crack open hollow puffed crisps, stuff them with bits of boiled vegetable (usually potato and chickpea), dunk them in tamarind sauce and lethally spiced mint-coriander water, and deliver them to salivating customers. Pop each panipuri into your mouth whole and wait for the fireworks.

EATING PHILOSOPHIES

Indian cuisines have evolved in anything but a vacuum. As part of a subcontinent, with landlocked borders along the silk route, India has always been at the crossroads of commerce between East and West, and its culinary traditions have benefited from centuries of cross-pollination.

When it comes to **eating meat**, scholars believe that even during Vedic times, meat was a regular fixture of the Indian diet. This included cattle, which are now considered strictly off-limits to most observant Hindus. In fact, nearly all items that are labeled "beef," "steak," or "burger" in India are actually buffalo meat. Only rarely is cow meat encountered in the country. Although the Hindu Vedas discuss meat-eating and animal sacrifice quite openly, these texts also mention the benefits of vegetarianism and allude to the later prohibition against killing cows.

The system of **ayurveda**, which focuses on six flavors (sweet, sour, salty, spicy, bitter, and astringent) and catalogs the benefits and ill effects of various spices, vegetables, fruits, and grains, is also rooted in these texts. Indians are hyperconscious of the consequences of this or that food and are quite fond of imparting advice on the subject—this is perhaps best exemplified in the obsessive attention paid to diet in Gandhi's autobiography.

It is commonly held by historians that the protected status of cattle arose first as an economically practical phenomenon and later became codified as religious practice. In general, **vegetarianism** is considered to have spread from North to South India, starting in the 4th century, propelled largely by the rise of Buddhism and Jainism. Contrary to popular belief, about a third of India's population is vegetarian. Add in vegetarians who eat eggs and the number is still less than half. Still, a third of a population this big is substantial, and the country's vegetarian options are arguably the most diverse, creative, and accessible in the world. Regions with high numbers of Jains (whose dietary restrictions surpass kosher laws in their complexity) have rich vegetarian traditions, making do even without onions, garlic, and other tubers.

INTERNATIONAL INFLUENCES

While everyday spices such as black pepper, cardamom, turmeric, and bay and curry leaf originated in India, many others that are just as commonly used were brought from the Mediterranean, Middle East, and Central Asia.

The Spice Traders. Fennel, coriander, cumin, fenugreek, saffron, and asafetida all came to India either over land, following Alexander the Great's route, or by sea, with Arab pepper merchants who plied the eastern coast. Syrian Christians also made their mark on South India, particularly enriching the nonvegetarian traditions of the Malabar region. Later, the Portuguese likely brought chillies and other New World plants to India. Also along eastern and western maritime trade routes, India absorbed tamarind from East Africa, cinnamon from Sri Lanka, and cloves from Southeast Asia.

The Mughal Empire. The Central Asian influence of the Mughals is the best-documented exchange in Indian culinary history. The early Mughal kings often left detailed descriptions of both native food and their own dietary habits. In his autobiography, Babur, the first Mughal king, pines for the grapes and melons of his Central Asian homeland and describes experimenting with planting these fruits in his new kingdom. Muslim rulers—both the Mughals in the north and the Nawabs of Lucknow and Bengal in the east and Hyderabad in the south—introduced elaborate courtly eating rituals to India, as well as the use of raisins, nuts, dried fruit, fragrant essences, and rich, ghee-soaked gravies. They brought their own technique of animal slaughter (halal) and introduced new ways to cook meat, including fine-ground mince dishes like *haleem*.

Colonizers. Indian cuisine adopted many imported plants introduced by the Portuguese, Dutch, and British traders and colonizers. Such integral ingredients as chillies, potatoes, tomatoes, maize, peanuts, and peanut oil are all New World additions; tea and soybeans are China's major contributions. Besides their role as traders, the British also brought their own culinary traditions to India. Anglo-Indian cuisine, which takes its cues from the chops, bakes, and puddings of Britain, has endured in the country-club culture of urban elites but has also influenced street snacks that are a twist on, for example, teatime sandwiches. The Portuguese introduced cottage cheese to east India, giving rise to the now omnipresent world of Bengali sweets.

Settler Groups. Smaller populations with their own distinct traditions (some of them nearly extinct in modern India) include various Jewish groups and Zoroastrians—both the Parsis who settled in Gujarat around the 10th century and the Iranis, who arrived later. Finally, the influence of India's Chinese population—descendants of settlers from the 19th century onward, and later Tibetan refugees—is formidable. Just as chicken tikka masala has become a national dish in Britain, dishes such as chilli chicken, "Manchurian," and chow mein are an undeniable part of India's culinary landscape.

(top left) A variety of spices, including coriander, cardamom pods, turmeric, cinnamon, bay leaves, black pepper, cloves, saffron, and red pepper; (bottom right) Tandoor prawns

THE INDIAN MEAL

Eating out in India could generally be divided into three categories: proper restaurants, holes-in-the-wall or open-air *dhabas* (the closest analogy would be café), and street food sold out of small stalls or carts. In someone's home or in a sit-down restaurant, a traditional, full meal follows certain general rules. Food is served in a *thali*—a stainless steel plate (silver on special occasions) with raised edges—and in small bowls. The thali contains condiments (a wedge of lime, salt, raw onions, pickles, or chutneys), possibly some fried items, and either rice or bread. The bowls contain servings of vegetable or meat dishes. There's a great deal of regional variation, but a sweet might be included with the savory food. In South India, a banana leaf might substitute for tableware, and in North India, street food or religious offerings are often served on plates made of stitched-together Banyan leaves. It's traditional to scoop up food with the tips of your fingers: curries are generally mixed with rice while torn-off bits of bread are used to pinch food between the fingers. Most places do offer Western cutlery as well.

Traditionally, a group of diners shares several dishes, and in *dhabas* you'd usually order a few things for the table. However, some upscale Indian restaurants have started experimenting with single-portion plating; their nouvelle-inspired dishes are well worth a taste.

COMMON SPICES

The word "masala," which loosely translates to "mixture of spices," has become a default adjective for all things Indian—and it's no wonder, given the infinite permutations of seasonings available to the Indian cook. Some of the most commonly used include cumin (*zeera*), turmeric (*haldi*), asafetida (*hing*), powdered and fresh coriander (*dhania*), cloves (*laung*), pepper (*kali-mirch*), dried or powdered red chillies (*lalmirch*), fennel seed (*saunf*), mustard seeds (*rai*), ginger (*adhrak*), garlic (*lasson*), cardamom (*elaichi*), cinnamon (*dalchini*), and bay (*tej patta*). A popular premixed powder called garam (hot) masala includes cumin, coriander, cinnamon, cardamom, and cloves.

COOKING METHODS

In general, special dishes tend toward lower heat and slower processes, while street food is generally quickly fried. But India's vast array of cooking processes includes sun-drying, parboiling, braising, steaming, dry-roasting, grilling, baking, and shallow and deep frying.

The use of the **tandoor,** a clay cylindrical oven, lit from the inside to bake flatbreads and meats, is widespread in North India. In this process, skewers of marinated meat are basted with ghee and suspended in the oven. The tandoor has been made famous by Punjabi restaurants, but it is used right across Central Asia and is an important component in both Mughal and Kashmiri cooking.

Frying is an essential part of street food, which includes a wide variety of fried snacks, from harder, storable munchies like plantain chips to savories and sweets that are meant to be eaten on the spot. The latter include *pakoras* (tempura-like vegetables dipped in gram flour batter), *samosas* (crispy pyramids stuffed with potatoes and peas), and much more. Several kinds of deep-fried wafers or hollow puffs also get incorporated into other snacks, like *paapdi chaat* or *golguppa.*

Most main dishes involve a combination of spices, either powdered or in a paste, fried and added to meat, vegetables, or lentils. **Slow-cooked** dishes are a special treat, and traditional methods include sealing the cooking pots with dough and burying them to cook their contents.

CONDIMENTS

Then there's the wonderful, colorful, and unending array of condiments that spice up every Indian meal. These might be freshly ground, spiced ingredients like mint, coconut, or peanuts. Or they might be sweet, vinegary, or acetic preservelike chutneys with slivers of mango or dates, or the syrupy, candied *murrabbas* made of fruit and vegetables like carrots or the medicinal Indian gooseberry (*amla*). Then there are *achhars,* spicy, oily pickles composed of everything from dried prawns to fiddlehead ferns, whose name describes their shape.

BREADS

Indian "bread" encompasses an assortment of flat or puffed, pale or golden, griddle-toasted, deep-fried or baked disks, triangles, and ellipses. Unleavened bread is generically called *roti,* and can be of varying thickness and made from refined, unrefined, and other types of flour. *Chapati* or *phulka* is a tortilla-like version made of wheat, cooked on a griddle, and finished on the flame. *Parathas,* rolled with oil to make layers, can be stuffed with all sorts of fillings and are almost a meal in themselves. Leavened breads, like *naan,* can be cooked in a tandoor, while the perfectly round *puri* and its giant cousin, the *bhatura,* are deep-fried so they puff up like crispy-soft balloons. Certain regions consume more rice than others, but every community will have its own recipes for rice and bread, and many meals involve eating both, usually one after the other.

(top left) A *thali* combination plate with a side of rice; (bottom right) Frying up some street food delicacies

TEXTILES AND SHOPPING

Vibrantly colored shawls, necklaces strung together on the spot, copper pitchers and serving bowls . . . these are a few of our favorite Indian things.

(top left) Dolls for sale at the flea market at Anjuna Beach in Goa; (top right) An embroidered pashmina; (bottom right) Painted pottery

With centuries-old crafts and textile traditions preserved from province to province, it's no wonder that shopping factors heavily in many travelers' itineraries when it comes to the Indian subcontinent. And these days, knowing where to shop is as important as knowing what to buy. In many cities you'll encounter bazaars and markets lined with street hawkers, where, unless it's a specific market for garments or jewelry, you'll mostly find trinkets like miniature Taj Mahal replicas and carved-wood coasters—and at all of these you can bargain down the prices.

As an alternative, government-run emporiums source good-quality handicrafts from various regions and sell them at fair but nonnegotiable prices. These emporiums (there's one in most cities) carry a great variety of goods, making them great for one-stop shopping or for getting an idea of what you should be paying at a market.

BARGAINING

Bargaining is customary at most markets and bazaars. Keeping a poker face while browsing will help so the seller won't see whether you're really attached to a particular item. Once you're ready to bargain, start below half the asking price: the salesperson will undoubtedly work you back up to half. If you don't intend to buy, it's best to just voice a firm *no* to any coaxing and move along.

2

PASHMINA SHAWLS

Pashmina refers to the cashmerelike wool from the goats that are indigenous to the Himalayas; these days, however, not all shawls labeled pashmina are made from this special wool. Many are silk-wool blends, or man-made viscose, making it important to really understand the fabric before buying. When possible, buy pashminas from government-run emporiums or reputable stores where you can ask questions about the fabric. Many shawls or wraps will also have some embroidery along the borders—look for neatly done threadwork, which gives a good clue about the shawl's quality.

SILVER AND STONE JEWELRY

From eye-catching stones to shimmering silver and gold, from traditional ethnic and tribal designs to chic contemporary pieces, jewelry shopping in India runs the gamut. Jaipur, India's gem-cutting capital, sees thousands of semiprecious stones passing through its gates to markets in Europe and North America. It does pay to carefully examine stones like amazonite, smoky topaz, and chalcedony, as glass beads are sometimes passed off as more precious baubles. If you find a wholesaler who will sell retail to individuals who walk in, these merchants are generally more legitimate because they're not looking to take advantage of retail customers. If you're shopping for silver pieces,

look on the back for a stamp that says 92.5% sterling silver to be assured it's the genuine article.

STONEWARE AND POTTERY

From coasters to jewelry boxes, stoneware, usually featuring floral inlay, is a popular souvenir. Merchants might try to convince you that the stone is marble, but it's more likely soapstone. Also look for terra-cotta and blue pottery, the making of which are traditions dating back thousands of years. Many blue pottery showrooms in Jaipur sell colorful, antique-style doorknobs, tiles, and platters.

COPPER AND BRASSWARE

Copper-bottom pots and pans might be all the rage at the moment, but copper kitchenware has been a long-standing tradition in India. Ask for *handi*-style pots (similar to a wok) and serving bowls. As for brassware, you'll find stunning Ganesh statues, incense-stick holders, and other household items. Many of these can be quite hefty, so be sure to keep your airline's suitcase weight limits in mind. With locations in many big cities, the popular Fabindia brand and the slightly more upscale Good Earth carry quality household products ranging from pottery and brass to linens and beauty products.

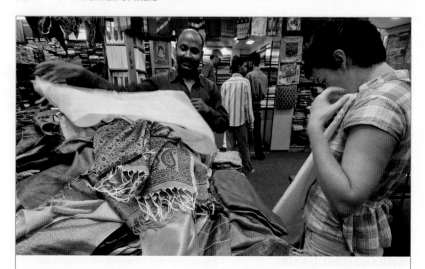

TEXTILES

Whether you're shopping for yourself or for convenient presents to take home, Indian textiles are a good way to go: perhaps block-printed tunics in bold hues, embroidered pillow covers, or quilted bedspreads. Established stores like Fabindia, Anokhi, and Cottons, which have locations in many cities, specialize in these types of textiles, as well as hand-woven table linens, rugs, and more, but you'll also find similar goods at markets all over the country. Look for a type of coarse cotton called *khadi* (popularized by Gandhi himself during the independence movement); it's highly durable but softens with each wash. Although textile traditions do vary from state to state, the most dramatic regional differences are visible in the sari, India's most iconic garment. Even if you don't want to purchase a sari, it's interesting to see how the borders or coloring change from one region to another.

SPICES

From cardamom to cloves, aromatic spices seem to fill the air wherever you are in India. Head to a local spice market to stock up on turmeric or cumin seeds at a fraction of the price of grocery stores back home—most merchants will even grind the spices for you on the spot. Be sure to bring back some garam masala, as well, a basic blend of ground spices used in many Indian dishes. The ingredients can vary slightly but usually include cloves, peppercorns, cumin, cardamom, star anise, and coriander seeds. A *masala dabba* is a traditional, round spice holder that has two lids and fits several smaller tins of spices inside, along with one or more spice spoons. These are good souvenirs, too, with or without spices included.

SOAPS AND BEAUTY PRODUCTS

With its history of ayurveda, or holistic medicine, that dates back thousands of years, India has always espoused the use of natural beauty products. Look for specialty brands like Forest Essentials, Kama Ayurveda, or even Himalaya Herbals (found at local pharmacies and chemists shops). Popular ingredients and herbs include rose, sandalwood, neem (the leaves and bark from a tropical evergreen-like tree), and *khus-khus* (an Indian grass used as an exfoliant).

MINIATURE PAINTINGS

Scenes of courtship, palace living, and the pursuit of the arts are often portrayed in the miniature watercolor and oil paintings available throughout the country. You'll undoubtedly find framed miniatures like these in New Delhi and Mumbai, but the art of miniature painting originated in Udaipur, making it worthwhile to look for these paintings in Rajasthan.

BOOKS AND CDS

Whether you're in search of a copy of the Bhagavad Gita or just the latest mystery novel, English-language bookstores are ubiquitous in India's big cities. Many have generous selections of Indian fiction, so it's easy to pick up works by authors like Vikram Seth, William Dalrymple, Rohinton Mistry, and others for a fraction of the price you'd pay Stateside. For Bollywood CDs or Indian instrumentals, you might not need to look farther than the bookstores as well, since many of them have extensive audio-visual sections.

ANTIQUES AND CARPETS

From rosewood furniture to ornate carpets, some people come to India specifically to search for top-notch furnishings at deep discounts. Since stores and dealers vary so greatly, though, it's best to employ a degree of caution when making big-ticket purchases. Getting an unbiased expert to come with you, or getting recommendations from a concierge, can help.

SHOES AND LEATHER GOODS

In general, you'll find more variety than you can choose from when it comes to sandals and shoes. From the classic Kohlapuri *chappal*, a thonglike flat sandal with a toe strap, to more modern wedge-heel and peep-toe sandals and shoes, Indians just love their footwear! Compared to street stalls, shoe chains like Metro and Catwalk in Mumbai or Delhi stock products of better quality and durability at reasonable rates. For other leather goods, such as wallets and purses, start by exploring the government-run emporiums or consider department stores like Shoppers Stop, which has more than a dozen locations across the country.

CONTEMPORARY CLOTHING

Although India's textile traditions continue to be preserved in provinces across the country, its modern fashion industry continues to go from strength to strength. Designers are moving forward to bring an Indian eye and aesthetic to modern-day silhouettes and garments. Several of them, including Manish Arora, Ashish N Soni, and Sabyasachi Mukherjee, have shown at international fashion weeks in Milan and New York. Whether at shopping complexes like Santushti in New Delhi or the Courtyard in Mumbai, you can find chic boutiques stocking chiffon and organza dresses, A-line skirts with delicate touches of embroidery, and accessories adorned with Indian fabrics or trimmings. Increasingly, many of these designers are also drawing on endangered traditional techniques and more eco-friendly weaving methods and incorporating them into their modern aesthetic.

(top left) Colorful fabrics; (bottom right) A miniature painting

INDIAN DANCE, MUSIC, AND PERFORMING ARTS

The appreciation of beauty, combined with a love of celebration and worship, is evident throughout India, especially in the realm of the performing arts.

(top left) Young girls practicing a traditional dance; (top right) A music performance at Mumbai's National Centre for the Performing Arts; (bottom right) An Indian music and dance performance

Centuries of different cultural influences and religious traditions make for a rich array of delights when it comes to the performing and visual arts. Ancient styles and themes continue to flourish alongside growing contemporary movements, and there are also varieties of performing arts that bring together features from throughout the ages.

Whether you choose to attend a formal dance or music performance, go to a Bollywood film, happen upon a street musician, or find yourself in the midst of a religious celebration, experiencing the vibrant forms of Indian culture will bring you closer to understanding the Indian way of life.

Mumbai's National Centre for the Performing Arts is a particularly good place to see live performances, although there are all sorts of formal and informal venues throughout the country.

RAMLILA

If you're in North India during the Navratri festival (see Holidays), try to see part of a Ramlila (literally, "Ram's play"). Actors—traditionally men and boys—wearing gaudy costumes and fake mustaches, dramatize the story of Ram, Prince of Ayodhya, who must fight the demon Ravana to rescue his kidnapped wife Sita. Some performances are makeshift, but others are hundred-year-old institutions. It's quite a spectacle.

MUSIC

Music is fundamental to Indian life, and it's almost impossible to walk from one end of a street to another without hearing an old Hindi film song crackling from a radio or the thumping bass of a gangster rap Bhangra mash-up from a passing car. Beyond this, however, there is a rich tradition of classical Indian music. Classical music is divided into Hindustani (predominately from North and Central India and heavily influenced by Persian traditions), and Carnatic (the melodic, formal tradition of the south). There is also a lively tradition of folk music, ranging from classical deviations to lusty rural songs about everything from the monsoons to migrant life. Nonclassical music can be boisterous—like Punjabi Bhangra—or steeped in refined sentimentality—like Bengali Rabindrasangeet (based on Rabindranath Tagore's lyrical works). Contemporary music ranges from Bollywood film music to Hindi (and other language) pop, rap, and hip-hop. In bars and clubs in the cities, it's not uncommon to find hard-rocking heavy-metal bands or classically trained fusion artists.

DANCE

Hand in hand with music is classical dance, of which there are a number of schools. Performances are enhanced by unusual and colorful costumes. Among dance performances to look for are the silk-clad and jewel-ornamented dancers

of the Bharatnatyam, Kuchipudi, and Mohiniyattam styles, which were once performed in temples; the exacting beat-driven Kathak, which evolved in royal courts; the grotesque and gorgeous makeup and wide skirts of Kathakali from Kerala; and gracefully delicate Manipuri from the northeast.

FILM

With such strong traditions of music and movement in Indian culture, it's not surprising that song and dance come together in Indian cinema. From the early days of sugar-sweet love songs and jaunty, jazzy numbers, Hindi films have absorbed and transformed many influences over the years, and these days the cinema produces endless pop and R&B-flavored film music. Independent cinema, once influenced by the New Wave movement of the 1950s and 1960s, continues to exist in the shadow of Bollywood but has also seen recent growth in experimental efforts and documentaries.

THEATER

Theater is also an important art form, and you might see troupes who perform special street plays on religious occasions or public service plays on issues like child labor or female infanticide. Folktales told through puppetry and the Western-style staging of Indian and other playwrights' works are also on the agenda.

DID YOU KNOW?

The words *Chandni Chowk* mean moonlit square or silver crossroads. This is one of the oldest and busiest markets in Old Delhi.

Delhi

WORD OF MOUTH

"If you want to combine boutiquey stores, interesting places to eat . . . ancient ruins and a lovely lake view, go to Haus Khaz (sic) Village. If you want to see ancient narrow winding streets, go to Old Delhi. You can see a lot in just a few days, so don't think it won't be worth it, even for a quickie trip."

—CaliNurse

WELCOME TO DELHI

TOP REASONS TO GO

★ **The Mughal Capital:** Delhi has a wealth of Mughal architecture— including Lal Qila (The Red Fort), Humanyun's Tomb, and Jama Masjid—that's survived for 450 years.

★ **Remnants of the Raj:** The British may have left in 1947, but colonial architecture still dominates Central Delhi, popularly known as Lutyens' Delhi: beautiful villas and large avenues lined with trees make this one of the most peaceful areas in the city.

★ **Shopping Nirvana:** From Western designer duds to beautiful silk Indian saris, there's an incredible selection of ready-to-wear and custom-made clothing in Delhi's variety of malls, shopping centers, and street markets.

★ **Taste of India:** Delhi is known as the unofficial food capital of India. From the best Mughlai cuisine (tandoori chicken done right) to tantalizing street food and international fare, you'll find kebabs and more around every corner.

1 **Old Delhi.** Anchored by Lal Qila (the Red Fort) and Jama Masjid, India's largest mosque, the walled Old City (originally called Shahjahanabad) provides the best glimpse into the city's treasured Mughal past, with a chaotic mix of colors and scents that stir the senses. Narrow, winding lanes branch off the main avenue, Chandni Chowk, crowded with wholesale markets, ancient shops, hidden monuments, and crumbling *havelis* (mansions).

2 **Central Delhi.** With the India Gate memorial at its heart, the capital built in interlocking circles by the British is now home to government buildings, parks, upscale markets, and the low-lying bungalows of the country's most powerful citizens.

3 **South Delhi.** The suburbs to the south of Central Delhi include semigated residential colonies, markets, and commercial districts. Here, too, are some of the oldest monuments in the capital, lovely parks, and charming locales such as Hauz Khas Village. It also has many of Delhi's can't-miss sites, including Humayun's Tomb and the Qutub Minar.

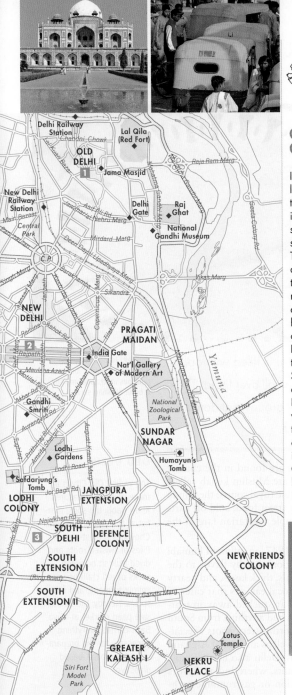

GETTING ORIENTED

3

India's wildly colorful, loud capital radiates from the broad avenues of its British-built center, its sprawl circumscribed by several concentric roads. The suburbs to the south are the most relevant for the first-time visitor. And just north of Central Delhi, the compact, dense Old City has its own internal warren of neighborhoods. Lodhi Road is a good demarcation between Central and South Delhi. Delhi is part of the 12,965-square-mile National Capital Region, which packs in more than 22 million people as well as satellite cities (like outsourcing hub Gurgaon) dotted with luxury high-rises and malls, in neighboring states.

EATING WELL IN DELHI

As a city of migrants, Delhi is filled with opportunities to sample food from all over India. There are, however, several key groups that dominate the city's food culture.

(top left) Mango kulfi; (top right) Aloo paratha (bread with potatoes in it); (bottom right) A bowl of nihari stew

Delhi's oldest food traditions are found in the chaotic lanes of the Old City. There are Muslim kebab sellers who claim to have cooked for the royal courts; the Hindu merchant class's lip-smacking street food, sold off carts and corner shops; and the simple vegetarian fare of the Old City's Jains.

Since India's independence in 1947, an influx of Punjabi migrants has brought that region's earthy flavor to the city. Cooked greens, creamy dals, thick lassis, and hearty breads feature prominently. Local eateries that cater to specific migrant communities are tucked away in markets and colonies, and you can find anything from South Indian vegetarian diners to northeastern spots specializing in spicy pork dishes, as well as a range of Afghani, Korean, and Japanese eateries. Delhi also has a couple of "nouvelle" Indian restaurants, where Indian flavors meet Western-style presentation or gastronomic techniques with striking results.

OLD DELHI

The walled Old City is a maze of edible treasures. Khari Baoli, the spice market at the end of Chandni Chowk, is a must-visit. Piles of twisted roots and dried fruit sit between sacks of red chilli powder, yellow turmeric, and other spices. Nearby, the wholesale paan market at Naya Bans carries everything necessary for the preparation of the betel-based digestive.

3

DAAL MAKHANI
A Punjabi staple, **daal makhani** (also known as *kaali daal*, or *maa ki daal*) is a nearly ubiquitous lentil stew, served by humble villagers and in superluxe hotel restaurants. Black urad beans and red kidney beans are tempered with a fry-up of garlic, ginger, tomato, and spices and ideally slow-cooked overnight on a coal fire. The *daal* is often finished with generous amounts of butter or cream.

PARATHA
Served with spicy achhaar pickles and yogurt, and topped with a dollop of butter, a **paratha** is a meal in itself. Whole wheat flour dough is rolled with oil before being panfried to create a flaky flatbread. The dough can be stuffed with anything; some fillings include radish, cauliflower, and sweet milk solids. "Mughlai" parathas include egg and are thicker. In Old Delhi, Gali Paranthe Wali, a lane dedicated to this originally Punjabi bread, has hosted prime ministers—who now peer down at diners from black-and-white photos.

KULFI
As early as the 16th century, Mughal emperors enjoyed the frozen dessert called **kulfi**. The Indian version of ice cream, standard *kulfi* is a mixture of milk solids (*khoya*) or cream, sugar, and pistachios—which are frozen in a conical metal or clay container sealed with dough. *Kulfi* is eaten as is, or with

starch vermicelli noodles (*faloodeh*). Besides flavors like pistachio and rose, Old Delhi *kulfiwallas* make fruit-flavored *kulfis*, sometimes frozen inside hollowed-out fruit, like mangoes.

NAGORI HALWA
Not well known but quintessentially Delhi, the **nagori halwa** breakfast is found almost exclusively in the Old City. It's a combination of three elements: small crisp breads made of deep-fried wheat and semolina flour; a mushy potato curry packed with fiery and warming spices; and a bit of *halwa*—a sweet preparation of semolina roasted in ghee and mixed with water. It's best eaten mixed all together for a delicious hot, sweet, and spicy combination.

NIHARI
Delhiites love their kebabs, and there are many options to be found in Delhi, but one nonkebab dish that nonveg residents cherish is **nihari,** a buffalo (since beef is not eaten) or goat stew cooked overnight in a virtual swimming pool of ghee. More scorching than the city's summer sun, *nihari* is usually eaten in the morning, especially in the foggy winter months. Legend has it that when Shah Jahan settled Delhi his doctor deemed the Yamuna River's water unfit for consumption; this firecracker of a dish, however, was believed to kill the germs.

(OFFBEAT) SHOPPING IN DELHI

Melding slangy street culture, hipster cool, fashion's excesses, and expat enthusiasm is a new trend in Delhi shopping: call it consumer design kitsch.

(top left) Colorful soap from Chumbak; (top right) A painted tea kettle by Aarohi Singh; (bottom right) Elephant dung paper products

With the state-run shops near Connaught Place, India's capital is still the central stop for crafts from all over the country; and its many Fabindia outlets are the go-to for casual native garb in natural-dyed fabrics and simplified cuts. But if you're looking for something a bit different, check out the new batch of fashion and design stores that market an Indian sense of humor with a hipster twist. You'll find chic boutiques and upstart brands that combine traditional handicraft traditions, preposterous color combinations, and sometimes a lewd sense of humor. The new purveyors of kitsch run the gamut from eco-conscious to hedonistic, excessive to elegant. What they share is a sense of raw creativity and a cosmopolitan design aesthetic that wouldn't be out of place anywhere in the world.

Happily Unmarried's Connaught Place store carries products like an ashtray shaped like a *sandaas*, or Indian-style squat toilet. Also fun are wine-bottle stoppers shaped like old-fashioned water pumps and CD stackers in cylindrical tiffin carriers. (✉ *Bombay Life Bldg., N35-A Connaught Pl., Outer Circle* ☎ *11/2331–3326* ⊕ *www.happilyunmarried. com;* other outposts in Select Citywalk mall, Khan Market)

Good Earth. Geared to the sophisticated shopper, Good Earth sells items like jewel-toned, pop-art cushion covers and other high-end home accessories. ✉ *9 Khan Market, Central Delhi* ☎ *11/2464–7175* ⊕ *www.goodearthindia.com* ✉ *Select Citywalk Mall, Saket, South Delhi* ☎ *11/2956–5600* ✉ *18 Santushti Shopping Complex, Chanakyapuri, Central Delhi* ☎ *11/2410–0108.*

Just Around the Corner. Find bright fashion and brands from around the country here. Look for Indian bobble-head dolls from Chumbak (⊕ *www.chumbak.in*), eco-Bollywood-stylings from Indigreen (⊕ *www.indigreen.co.in*), and elephant dung stationery from Haathi Chaap (⊕ *www.elephantpoopaper.com*). Upstairs is a retro kitsch-influenced fashion studio (☎ *11/4616–8007*). ✉ *36 Shahpur Jat, South Delhi* ☎ *96/5421–6252.*

Play Clan. The design collective (also in Mumbai and Goa) has collaborated with the likes of Paul Smith. Popular items are cushion covers and totes with maps of Indian locales, Mughal-ruler playing cards, T-shirts, and more (they even add custom kitsch to Converse shoes). ✉ *Select Citywalk Mall, Saket, South Delhi* ☎ *11/4053–4559* ⊕ *www.theplayclan.com* ✉ *17 Meher Chand Market, Lodhi Rd., Central Delhi* ☎ *11/2464–4393.*

Purple Jungle. This shop is a riot of color wrangled into kaleidoscopic order by two French expats. Packed into the ground floor are bags, cushions and home accessories—many using recycled products. Upstairs are pricier items like trays and hand-painted trunks. ✉ *16 Hauz Khas Village, South Delhi* ☎ *96509–43683, 11/2653–8182* ⊕ *www.purple-jungle.com.*

Also in Shahpur Jat, check out **Alter Ego** (✉ *87 B Shahpur Jat* ☎ *11/4175–1846*) and **The Wishing Chair** (✉ *86A Shahpur Jat* ☎ *11/4657–2121*), with whimsical products to spruce up your home.

Fish Fry. Bursting at the seams with fun fashion is iconic Indian designer Manish Arora's prête Fish Fry store. ✉ *3 Lodhi Colony Main Market, Lodhi Road, Central Delhi* ☎ *11/2463–8878* ⊕ *www.manisharora.ws* ✉ *G-10 Crescent at the Qutab, Lado Sarai, South Delhi* ☎ *11/2952–1582* ✉ *DLF Emporio Place, Nelson Mandela Marg, Vasant Kunj, South Delhi* ☎ *11/4606–0966.*

For more affordable Punjabi-hip clothes, try **1469** for Sikh-chic T-shirts (✉ *2 & 12 Janpath, Connaught Pl.* ☎ *11/2332–9461* ✉ *8 Defence Colony Market* ☎ *11/4155–6393* ⊕ *www.traditionalvalue.com*).

DELHI'S HOLY SITES

Brash, corrupt, political—the capital of India doesn't have a particularly spiritual reputation, yet Delhi, as the recurring seat of empires with vested religious and cultural interests, is a veritable melting pot of religiously significant sites.

(top left) At Hazrat Nizamuddin Dargah; (top right) The Akshardham Temple; (bottom right) The Bahá'í House of Worship (Lotus Temple)

Because the walled city of Old Delhi was divided into religious ghettos when it was first built by the Emperor Shah Jahan, it is home to a great variety of religious sites: the area is dotted with domes and spires of mosques, dozens of Hindu shrines to Shiva, the bustling Sisganj Gurdwara (an important Sikh site), and peaceful, marble-clad Jain temples.

Beyond Old Delhi, Sufi saints still draw thousands of visitors to their graves. Churches and cemeteries testify not only to the continued presence of South Indian Christians in Delhi, but also to the city as a place where scores of British lived and died. Among other things you can also find Buddhist monasteries and Bengali temples in this city.

HANUMAN MANDIR

In the thick of things near Connaught Place is **Hanuman Mandir**. Said to have mythic origins, the temple was constructed over the 16th and 17th centuries. Note the crescent-moon finial, typically associated with Islam. The surrounding area can be overwhelming, with beggars dressed as the monkey god worshipped here, women painting henna tattoos, and Delhi's best bangle market.

AKSHARDHAM TEMPLE
One of the newest additions to Delhi's spiritual scene is **Akshardham temple**: a theme park of polytheistic Hinduism. Despite criticism over its environmentally dubious location (a sprawling 90 acres on the Yamuna riverbank), this bulwark of pink sandstone and Italian marble—possibly the largest Hindu temple in the world—is undeniably dramatic. Set in landscaped gardens with a musical fountain, the temple incorporates traditional hand-carving and craftsmanship as well as a peacock-boat ride through dioramas of Indian history and mythology, and an IMAX film about the sect's founder.

HAZRAT NIZAMUDDIN DARGAH
In many ways the still-beating heart of spirituality in central Delhi is the mausoleum of saint Nizamuddin Auliya of the Sufi Chishti order. At **Hazrat Nizamuddin Dargah** Thursday evenings are enlivened by a troupe of Qawwals (who sing Sufi devotional music) and the distribution of food. You'll have to leave your shoes outside (tip a rose-petal seller to keep them safe).

JAMA MASJID
India's largest mosque, Masjid-i-Jahan-Numa ("world-showing mosque") as it is properly named, is a welcoming space with a well-loved, worn-in feel. Visitors are welcome any time except during prayers, and it is advisable to cover

your head as a sign of respect. Climb the minaret for an incredible view of the city and note the north gate's reliquary, which houses a beard hair and footprint of the Prophet Muhammad and an antique Koran.

SIS GANJ SAHIB GURDWARA
Right on Chandni Chowk itself is the Sikh **Sis Ganj Sahib Gurdwara**. It was on the site of this bustling *gurdwara* (temple) that the ninth Sikh leader, Guru Tegh Bahadur, was beheaded on order of the Mughal Emporer Aurangzeb in 1675. To learn more about Sikh martyrs, visit the gloriously kitsch Bhai Mati Das Bhai Sati Das Bhai Dyala Museum of Sikh history across the street. Delhi's grandest *gurdwara*, Bangla Sahib near Connaught Place, has gleaming golden domes that reflect in its large pond of holy water.

BAHÁ'I HOUSE OF WORSHIP
The Lotus Temple, as the **Bahá'i House of Worship** is also known, is probably Delhi's most iconic modern holy site and one of the most visited places in the world—designed by Canadian architect, Fariborz Sahba, it was built in 1986. The crowds can be thick on the approach to the building but it's surprisingly peaceful inside. Eminently egalitarian, the building has no point of focus for preaching and no obvious religious trappings.

Updated by
Sonal Shah

A city of many moods and identities, Delhi has evolved many personalities over its long, fraught history; it may not be the most beautiful city in India, but in many ways it is the grandest.

Here are the extremes that make India so compelling: the rich and the poor, the past and the present, the religious and the secular. Old Delhi's Mughul glory, Central Delhi's European grandeur, West Delhi's Punjabi opulence, and South Delhi's bars, boutiques, and massive houses—all come together with the poor, the pollution, and overpopulation.

Modern Delhi has its foundation on a city base that has been around for centuries. Various monuments lie scattered across the region revealing the numerous empires that have invaded Delhi and made it their home. Of these, the Mughals and British have left the deepest mark.

The city has grown exponentially over the years and continues to do so to accommodate the expanding population, currently estimated at more than 16 million, within a little less than 1,554 square km (600 square miles). It's part of the larger National Capital Region (NCR), which includes neighboring state suburbs like Ghaziabad, Faridabad, Noida, Greater Noida (all across the border in Uttar Pradesh), and Gurgaon (in Haryana). The latter is known in particular for its call centers and gleaming malls, which feed the consumer craze of India's rapidly expanding middle class.

In Delhi the different versions of modern India all coexist, and its contradictions quickly become abundantly clear to visitors. Newly minted junior executives ride in chauffeured, air-conditioned comfort as scores of children beg and hawk magazine in the streets.

PLANNING

MAKING THE MOST OF YOUR TIME
If you'll only be in Delhi a few days, note that the Red Fort and most museums are closed on Monday, and the Jama Masjid is closed to non-Muslims on Friday.

The best way to cover a lot of ground in Delhi is to hire a car, especially if you're on a limited schedule. Avoid tackling Old Delhi on your first day if you've never been to India before—its startling chaos can be overwhelming. Starting with New Delhi will also give you a better idea of the aesthetic and cultural dichotomy between the two areas. A drive through the graceful avenues of the British capital will ease you gently into the capital, but don't let it lull you into a state of pleasant, orderly inertia. The rest of the city requires that all your senses be in working order. Depending on your interests, visit South and Central Delhi's monuments (Humayun's and Safdarjang's tombs, the Qutub Minar, Lodhi Gardens, Hazrat Nizamuddin Dargah), some sites commemorating the leaders of India's independence movement (the Nehru Museum or Gandhi Smriti), a museum, or a temple or *gurdwara* (Sikh temple). When you're ready, plunge into Old Delhi—explore the Lal Qila (Red Fort) and the stunning Jama Masjid, then venture into Chandni Chowk. Make sure to eat at the famous Gali Paranthe Wali and the restaurant Karim's.

WHEN TO GO

HIGH SEASON: MID-NOVEMBER–MARCH

The most popular time to visit is during peak festive season, when cool temperatures (near-freezing at times) get people out of their homes, wrapped in shawls on the street, huddled around charcoal braziers at lawn parties, clutching hot kebab rolls in their hands. This is also peak cultural season; calendars are packed with music, dance, theater, and more. It does get cold though, and Delhi is especially foggy around New Year's, so try not to schedule any night-driving around then. Delhi's February sun has its own charming character, and seasonal trees turn the city into a riot of colors in the late winter.

LOW SEASON: MAY TO MID–AUGUST

The heat is intense from April until the monsoons arrive in July, after which rain and intense humidity add to the misery. Air-conditioning is a staple, and there's plenty to do indoors, from museums to malls, so don't let the outside stickiness deter you. Unfortunately, the rains shut the city down because of improper drainage, and the already intense traffic takes a turn for the worse, with people stuck on roads for hours on end.

SHOULDER SEASON: SEPTEMBER–OCTOBER AND MARCH–APRIL

Autumn and early spring bring mild, sunny days and the tourist crowds are thinner than in winter. Temperatures are comfortable, though a light sweater may come in handy in the evenings closer to the cold months.

GETTING HERE AND AROUND

AIR TRAVEL

All flights arrive and depart from Delhi's Indira Gandhi International Airport, along the southwestern edge of the city. It has separate domestic and international terminals that are quite a few miles apart but connected by a free hourly shuttle bus.

AIRPORT TRANSFERS   The airport is about a 45-minute drive from Delhi's center in light to moderate traffic (i.e., before 9 am or after 8 pm). Delhiites are proud of Terminal 3, the newest wing of the airport. It's being touted as the world's third-largest passenger terminal.

Major hotels provide airport transfers, otherwise taking a cab is your best bet. To avoid being overcharged, use the prepaid taxi service from a counter near the exit. Unfortunately, hucksters have set up similar services; ignore them. Your destination determines the fare, to which a small fee for each piece of luggage is added. Pay in advance at the counter, then take the receipt and exit. When you get outside, people might try to help you with your luggage; ignore them, and make sure they do not touch your things. Wheel your luggage down the ramp toward the black taxis with yellow tops, at which point the drivers will appear. If your receipt contains a taxi number, use that cab; if not, the drivers will decide among themselves who should take you. Tell the driver where you're going, and hold on to the receipt until you arrive. Tips are not expected unless they help with your luggage.

BUS TRAVEL

You're best off avoiding bus travel in Delhi: public buses are generally dirty, crowded, and unpleasant.

CAR TRAVEL

Hiring a car and driver is the best way to see the most of this sprawling city, especially for those with a limited amount of time. Most hotels can arrange a car, but they will also charge a premium for the service. Reputable travel agents do the same for less money (budget Rs. 1,000 or more per day for a basic car with air-conditioning and an English-speaking driver, for travel in Delhi only). Tip in advance if you want some extra-deferential, but exceedingly helpful service.

METRO TRAVEL

The city's metro service, which came into service in 2002, is air-conditioned, reliable, and state-of-the-art. With new stations and lines opening for service every few months, subway service is rapidly changing the face of the city. It's an inexpensive (starting at Rs. 8 per one-way trip) and convenient way to move between Connaught Place (Rajiv Chowk station), Lutyens' Delhi (Central Secretariat station), and Old Delhi (Chandni Chowk and Chawri Bazaar stations). For example, getting to Old Delhi from CP is three stops and takes about 15 minutes. There are currently five lines—red, yellow, blue, green, and violet. Maps are available at the official tourist office and often at your hotel concierge desk. The Rajiv Chowk station is massive; ask for directions as you go.

TAXI AND AUTO-RICKSHAW TRAVEL

Apart from a hired car, the best way to get around New Delhi is by black-and-yellow taxi or radio cab service. Most hotels and restaurants will gladly call you a cab, and major markets and tourist attractions usually have a taxi stand. Most drivers speak a little English. ■TIP→ **Tell the driver where you want to go and make sure he turns on the meter before you set off.** If he insists the meter is broken, get out of the car and find another cab. Most taxi drivers are honest, so it's not worth dealing with one who isn't.

The ubiquitous green-and-yellow auto-rickshaws are a good way to see the city from a different angle. But they aren't for the faint of heart, as the drivers zip through traffic at breakneck speed. Three-wheeled auto-rickshaws, known locally as "autos," are half the price of taxis and roughly half as comfortable—except in summer, when the open-air breeze keeps you cool while taxis trap the heat horrendously. The problem is that auto-rickshaw drivers refuse to use their meters (here they really often are broken, as the drivers deliberately break them), and if you look even remotely new to Delhi they will quote absurdly high fares. A trip around the corner costs Rs. 30, and a trip across the city should never cost more than Rs. 200. Government-run booths for prepaid auto-rickshaws can be found at Connaught Place, Basant Lok, Dilli Haat, and the Community Centre in Saket, among other places. Try to have exact change, as many drivers will claim to have none, and discussion is difficult, as most do not speak English.

In Old Delhi and other neighborhoods you can still hire a cycle-rickshaw. It's a great way to cruise Chandni Chowk, explore the maze of narrow lanes, and get from one sight to the next. A short one-way trip costs Rs. 30; work out a higher fare, up to Rs. 200, if you want to ride around for longer.

TRAIN TRAVEL

Delhi is the major hub for India's northern rail system, with five train stations. Most arrive at New Delhi Station, within walking distance of Connaught Place; Hazrat Nizamuddin, from which trains leave for Agra and points south; or Old Delhi Station. With luggage in tow and crowded streets, consider taking a taxi or auto-rickshaw to your hotel. Note that traveling by train in India is much different than in the US, in part due to the sheer number of travelers. Terminals are chaotic, and it can be unclear and confusing to determine when and from where your train is scheduled to leave. Trains are often also crowded and delayed. Your best bet, if you choose this means of travel, is to factor in plenty of extra time and a lot of patience. All stations have prepaid taxi and auto-rickshaw stands, though these can get quite busy.

EMERGENCIES

Most hotels have physicians on call. For emergencies, go to Indraprastha Apollo Hospital, Delhi's premier private hospital, southeast of town. From there you can call Meera Rescue if international evacuation is necessary; *do not* go to a government hospital. In a grave emergency, contact your embassy.

Although not equipped for trauma, the Max Medcentre—in conjunction with Harvard Medical International, one of India's major pharmaceutical companies—runs a first-rate clinic open daily from 8 am to 8 pm. Its hospital in Saket can treat complicated ailments and has many specialists. Many of the physicians are American-trained, and there's a 24-hour pharmacy on-site. The East–West Medical Centre is also a great resource for travelers, with ambulance service and regional evacuation, though it has no pharmacy.

Contacts East–West Medical Centre ⊠ *B-28, Greater Kailash I, South Delhi* ☎ *11/2469–9229, 11/2469–8865* ⊕ *www.eastwestrescue.com.*
Indraprastha Apollo Hospital ⊠ *Mathura Rd, Sarita Vihar, South Delhi* ☎ *11/2692–5801, 11/2692–5858* ⊕ *www.apollohospdelhi.com.*
Max Medcentre ⊠ *N-110 Panchsheel Park, South Delhi* ☎ *11/2649–9870* ⊕ *www.maxhealthcare.in.* **Meera Rescue** ⊠ *112 Jor Bagh, Central Delhi* ☎ *11/2469–3508, 11/2465–3170* ⊕ *www.meera-rescue.com.*

24-Hour Pharmacies Max Super Specialty Hospital ✉ *1 Press Enclave Rd., Saket, South Delhi* ☎ *11/2651–5050* ⊕ *www.maxhealthcare.in.*
New Delhi Medicos ✉ *12 Old RK Ashram Marg, Gate 5, Dr RML Hospital, near Connaught Place, Central Delhi* ☎ *11/2334–7151.*

INTERNET, MAIL, AND SHIPPING
Internet facilities can be found in most major markets, but are often holes-in-the-wall with a handful of grimy, outdated terminals. For laptop toters, Wi-Fi hotspots have sprung up.

One centrally located post office is on the roundabout just southwest of Connaught Place; another is the Eastern Court Post Office on Janpath. Hotels usually have mailing facilities, too. DHL outlets are available around the city, but you'll pay a premium—possibly as much as your own plane ticket—to ship anything heavy to the West (just sending documents will cost you at least $60). Use Speed Post at the main post office, which is a fraction of the price and usually reliable. Be prepared to wait (and wait some more).

Post Offices Main Post Office ✉ *Baba Kharak Singh Marg, at Ashoka Rd., Connaught Pl., Central Delhi* ⊕ *www.indiapost.gov.in.*

VISITOR INFORMATION
The Government of India Tourist Office south of Connaught Place is open weekdays 9 to 6 and Saturday 9 to 2, but it doesn't have anything a decent hotel can't offer. Its airport counters are open for major flight arrivals, and its train-station counters are open 24 hours.

Contacts Government of India Tourist Office ✉ *88 Janpath, Connaught Pl., Central Delhi* ☎ *11/2332–0005.*

EXPLORING DELHI

Most of sprawling Delhi is best navigated on wheels—hire a car, taxi, or auto-rickshaw to get around. In contrast, the narrow lanes of Old Delhi are a walker's delight, though you can hop on a cycle rickshaw if you get tired. Most people speak workable English, so don't assume there will be a language barrier.

The challenge Delhi presents is to find areas—beyond the Old City—in which walking is a viable mode of exploration. One of these areas is the central British-built commercial hub, Connaught Place. "CP" is a tourist magnet for its travel agent bucket shops, restaurants, and shops, as well as proximity to a number of mid-range and budget hotels. It's also the location of Delhi's main Metro station and a pleasant area to meander along colon-naded circles, or people-watch in the central park. There are plenty of shopping options nearby, including the street market, Janpath, where everything from brightly colored *kolhapuri* slippers to designer overstock to incense and natural soaps can be found. Keep in mind that even though it's commonly referred to as Connaught Place, the name was officially changed to Rajiv Chowk, which is what you'll see on metro stops and maps.

Around the hubs of Connaught Place and India Gate is the British-built city. This is the seat of the Indian government, with Rashtrapati Bhavan

The view down broad Rajpath Avenue from Rashtrapati Bhavan to India Gate is similar to the view up the Champs-Élysées in Paris, to the Arc de Triomphe.

(the Presidential Palace), the North and South Secretariats, Sansad Bhavan (Parliament House), and India Gate (a monument to British Indian Army soldiers killed in World War I and the Afghan wars) within a tight radius. Getting ice cream at India Gate's huge lawns or boating in the ornamental canals here are "very Delhi" things to do. Many museums are nearby, including the National Gallery of Modern Art and the National Museum.

Also here are the palatial residences of the affluent and lavish government bungalows. Khan Market, one of Asia's most expensive retail locations, is perfectly at home in this setting. It's also the place where Delhi's expats feel most at home, with its coffee shops and multiple ATMs. Down the road is Delhi's green lung, Lodhi Gardens, and several cultural centers, including mainstays India International Centre and India Habitat Centre (performances are pretty much on tap, especially in winter).

The mostly residential areas of South Delhi, West Delhi, North Delhi, and East Delhi (across the Yamuna) all have their own flavor, but visitors are most likely to venture into the neighborhoods, markets, and monuments of the first, roughly defined as south of Lodhi Road. In between semi-gated colonies are a good mix of urban villages, hectic alleyways, posh markets, and office complexes. Some of the city's oldest monuments can be found here, as well as some of its newest monuments to modernity: the massive malls squatting southward, en route to mega-suburb Gurgaon. The hippest of Delhi's hotspots though, is not a mall, but a gentrified urban village—Hauz Khas Village—with boutiques and independent restaurants nestled atop each other along narrow alleys, next to a 13th-century reservoir and several Sultanate ruins.

Some Delhi History

The ancient epic *Mahabharata* places the great town of Indraprastha on the banks of the Yamuna River, perhaps in what is now Delhi's Old Fort. Late in the first millennium AD, Delhi became an outpost of the Hindu Rajputs, warrior kings who ruled what's now Rajasthan. However, it was after 1191, when Mohammad Ghori of Central Asia invaded and conquered, that the city acquired its Islamic flavor. Other Afghan and Uzbek sultanates handed Delhi back and forth over the next 300 years, until the mighty Mughals settled in. Beginning with the invasion of Babur in 1526, the Mughals shifted their capital between Delhi and Agra until 1858, leaving stunning architecture at both sites, including the buildings at what's now known as Old Delhi.

The fall of the Mughal Empire coincided with the rise of the British East India Company, first in Madras and Calcutta and eventually throughout the country. When several of Delhi's Indian garrisons mutinied against their Company employers in 1857, the British suppressed them, moved into the Red Fort, and ousted the aging Mughal emperor. In 1911, with anti-British sentiment growing in Calcutta, they moved their capital from Calcutta to Delhi—the ultimate prize, a place where they could build a truly imperial city that would dwarf the older ones around it. Architect Sir Edwin Lutyens was hired to create New Delhi, a majestic sandstone government complex surrounded by wide, leafy avenues and traffic circles, in contrast to Old Delhi's hectic lanes.

When India gained independence on August 15, 1947, with Jawaharlal Nehru the first prime minister, the subcontinent was partitioned into the secular republic of India and the Muslim nation of Pakistan, which was further divided into West Pakistan (now Pakistan) and East Pakistan (now Bangladesh). Trapped in potentially hostile new countries, thousands of Muslims left Delhi for Pakistan while millions of Hindu and Sikh refugees streamed in—changing Delhi's cultural overtone almost overnight from Persian to Punjabi.

Since Prime Minister Rajiv Gandhi (grandson of Nehru) and his successor, Narasimha Rao, began to liberalize India's planned economy in the late 1980s and early 1990s, Delhi has experienced tremendous change. Foreign companies have arrived and hired locals for white-collar jobs, residential enclaves, and shopping strips have sprouted in every crevice, and land prices have skyrocketed. Professionals seeking affordable living space now move to the suburbs and drive into town, aggravating the already substantial pollution problem. At the same time, North Indian villagers still come here in search of work and build shanties wherever they can, sometimes in the shadows of forgotten monuments. It is they—Rajasthani women in colorful saris digging holes with pickaxes, men climbing rickety scaffolds in sarong-like lungis—who build new homes for the affluent. Many Delhiites say, with a sigh, that their city is in a perpetual state of flux.

OLD DELHI AND NEARBY

Old Delhi (6 km [4 miles] north of Connaught Place), or Purani Dilli, is also called by its original name Shahjahanabad, for the emperor, Shah Jahan, who built it. Havelis that line the gullies are architecturally stunning but irreversibly crumbling. Old Delhi's monuments—the Jama Masjid and the Red Fort that anchors the Old City—are magnificent, and the main artery, Chandni Chowk, should not be missed. It's a convenient metro ride to the Old City from Connaught Place.

Old Delhi is crowded and hectic, and the roads and footways are poorly maintained. It's best to chalk up all the bustle to added charm and just immerse yourself in the experience. It's one of the most incredible places to shop and eat, with lots of specialty markets crowding the area on both sides of Chandni Chowk—literally the "silver crossroad" but also meaning moonlit market or square. Kinari Bazaar and Katra Neel are two others, and are a tight squeeze with their maze of alleys. Gorgeous, intricately embroidered fabrics and appliqué materials, spices, herbs, and Indian sweets can be found in all. Watch out for Khari Baoli, Asia's largest spice market, toward the western end of Chandni Chowk (after Fatehpuri Masjid). You'll smell it before you see it.

Jama Masjid is the principle mosque in Old Delhi, and was built by Shah Jahan as well. It's the largest mosque in India, a colossal structure beautifully constructed out of red sandstone. The courtyard of the mosque can be reached from the east, north, and south gates by three flights of steps, all of which have religious significance. The northern gate has 39 steps, the southern side has 33 steps, and the eastern gate, which was once the royal entrance that Shah Jahan and his entourage used, has 35 steps. Arched colonnades and minarets surround the mosque itself, which rests on a platform. Apparently, the courtyard can hold up to 25,000 devotees.

The Red Fort, or Lal Qila, is another Old Delhi institution, and was also built by Shah Jahan as the main residence of the royal family. It's an important top attraction, and combines Indo-Persian architecture to perfection.

If you find yourself daunted by the throngs of people or just need a break after a few hours, try a cycle-rickshaw tour: for about Rs. 100 you can be carted around in a cycle-rickshaw (which seats two slim people) for about an hour. The rickshaw-*wallahs* (drivers) in front of the Red Fort are serious bargainers, but they know the city well, and many can show you places you wouldn't discover on your own.

The variety of traditional Indian food that can be found in Old Delhi is heavenly. Try the *kulfi* (a flavored frozen milk dessert) at places like Lala Dulichand, which serves the treat inside fruit. The *aam* (mango) and *anjeer* (fig) versions are to die for. Karim's, a restaurant right around the Jama Masjid, is another stop. Make sure you have cash on hand, because many of the smaller shops and stalls don't have credit card machines.

Commerce is everywhere along Chandni Chowk; it's a great place to stroll but keep a firm hold on your purse or other valuable possessions.

TOP ATTRACTIONS

Chandni Chowk. This was Delhi's former imperial avenue, where the Mughal emperor Shah Jahan rode at the head of his lavish cavalcade. That scene is hard to picture today, as bullock carts, bicycles, shuttle buses (cars are technically banned), freight carts, cows, auto-rickshaws, horse-drawn *tangas* (two-wheeled carts), and pedestrians create a constant, breathtaking bazaar. It runs from the Red Fort into the walled city, functioning as a major, if congested, artery. As in the days of the Mughals, commerce is everywhere: astrologers set up their charts on the pavement; shoemakers squat and repair sandals; sidewalk photographers with old box cameras take pictures for a small fee; medicine booths conceal doctors attending to patients; and oversize teeth grin from the windows of dentists' offices. Peer through a portico, and you might see men getting shaved, silver being hammered into paper-thin edible sheets, or any other conceivable form of commerce. While the scenes may seem archaic, the shopping is exactly where it's supposed to be so make sure you carry cash (safely tucked about your person). The stores in tinsel-filled Kinari Bazaar and Dariba Kalan, with its jewelry and gemstones, will make you want to empty your wallet. Also, lining just about every alley are the famous *halwais*, or "sweets-maker." Everything from staples such as fried orange jalebis to even more exotic confections is sold. Vendors can be found Monday to Saturday from 9 am to 7 pm at Dariba Kalan. ✉ *East–west artery from Red Fort 1.5 km (1 mile) west to Fatehpuri Masjid* ⊙ *Most shops closed Sun.* Ⓜ *Chandni Chowk.*

CLOSE UP

A Good Walk in Old Delhi

Start in Old Delhi with a morning tour of the **Lal Qila** (Red Fort), Emperor Shah Jahan's sprawling 17th-century capital. Exit the Red Fort onto **Chandni Chowk**. Chaos reigns supreme here, so gather your wits and watch your feet lest they be flattened by a cart or cycle-rickshaw. You'll pass a short but fragrant row of flower-sellers. About four blocks down the street on the left, identifiable by its small gold dome, is the marble **Sis Ganj Sahib Gurdwara**, a Sikh shrine. After a look around, continue down Chandni Chowk and cross three more lanes (*galis*); then, at Kanwarji's sweet shop (opposite the Central Bank of India), turn left on **Gali Paranthe Wali**. Continue down the lane, following its jogs to the right, until the T at the Sant Lal Sanskriti sari shop. Turn left into Kinari Bazaar, a sparkling bridal-trimming market where Hindu families can buy every item required, and then some, for their wedding festivities.

At 2130 Kinari Bazaar (a bric-a-brac shop called Krishna & Co.), turn right into one of Chandni Chowk's most beautiful lanes, Naughara Gali, where a community of Jains lives in some colorful old havelis. At the end of this peaceful alley is the **Svetamber Jain Temple**. Even if the temple is closed (as it is between 12:30 and 6:30 every afternoon), Naughara Gali offers a respite from the bustle of the bazaar.

Return to Kinari Bazaar and turn right, continuing until Kinari Bazaar intersects with **Dariba Kalan**, or "Silver Street." If you're in the market for jewelry or curios, check out the shops to the left; if not, turn right and head down Dariba Kalan to its end. Turn right again and you'll find yourself on a broad street in the brass and copper

district. Take the next right, then an immediate left under a stone arch. Now head up Chah Rahat, a typical narrow lane with old wooden balconies and verandas.

When Chah Rahat opens into a courtyard, take the hairpin turn to the left and follow the arrow on the sign for "Singh Copper and Brass Palace." After about 30 feet, a second sign directs you down an alley on the right. Singh's emporium is filthy, but has an interesting collection of miscellany.

From Singh's, return to the courtyard on Chah Rahat and take the short, narrow lane to the left. You'll emerge to see the splendid **Jama Masjid**, preceded by a somewhat incongruous tool bazaar. To reach the mosque's entrance, head right, then follow the bazaar to the left.

At the end of this long tour, you'll probably be ready for a proper Muslim meal. Make for Karim's, on the colorful lane heading away from the mosque's entrance, or take a cycle-rickshaw to Chor Bizarre. Another option, a bit farther afield, is to take a taxi or rickshaw to **Raj Ghat** and the **National Gandhi Museum**.

TIMING

Allow a full day—but not a hot one. Avoid Friday, when the mosque is closed to non-Muslims; Sunday, when most shops in Old Delhi are closed; and Monday, when the Red Fort is closed. (If Sunday and Monday are the only options, go for Monday. The bazaars are crucial to Old Delhi's flavor.) Note, too, that the Svetamber Jain temple is closed for most of each afternoon, so if art and architecture make your heart sing, try to start very early *or* right after lunch.

Chandni Chowk .. **2**

Gali Paranthe
Wali **4**

Jama Masjid **6**

Lal Qila **1**

National Gandhi
Museum **8**

Raj Ghat **7**

Sis Ganj
Sahib
Gurdwara **3**

Svetamber
Jain Temple **5**

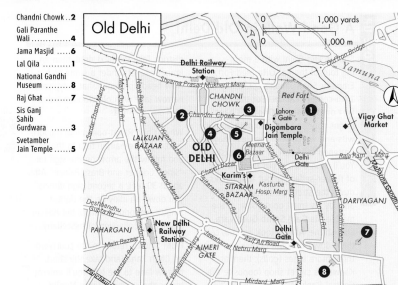

★ **Gali Paranthe Wali.** This narrow, festive lane is filled with shopkeepers selling fabric and saris, including the well-known Ram Chandra Krishan Chandra's, where young brides choose their red-and-gold finery. The lane is named for its other industry: the fabulous *paranthas* (fried flatbreads) that are sold here in no-frills open-air eateries. Stuffed or served with a variety of fixings, such as radishes, soft cheese, and seasonal vegetables, paranthas are delicious. The parantha makers moved into this lane in the 1870s, even though a couple of its original sari and jewelry shops still dot the lane. The three oldest and most famous of these parantha makers are Pundit Kanhaiyalal Durgaprasad (established in 1875), Pundit Dayanand Shivcharan (established in 1882), and Pundit Baburam Devidayal Paranthe Wali (from 1886). A few kitchens have seating, making them excellent places to refuel while looking upon photos of famous statesmen doing the same. ⊠ *South off Chandni Chowk, en route to Kinari Bazaar* Ⓜ *Chandni Chowk.*

Fodor's Choice **Jama Masjid.** An exquisite Islamic statement in red sandstone and mar-
★ ble, India's largest mosque was the last monument commissioned by Shah Jahan. Completed in 1656 after six years of work by 5,000 laborers, it's arguably one of the loveliest houses of worship in the world. Three sets of broad steps lead to two-story gateways and a magnificent courtyard with a square ablution tank in the center. The entire space

is enclosed by pillared corridors, with domed pavilions in each corner. Thousands gather to pray here, especially on Friday.

With its onion-shaped dome and tapering minarets, the mosque is characteristically Mughal, but Shah Jahan added an innovation: the stripes running smartly up and down the marble domes and minarets. The whole structure exudes peace and harmony—climb the south minaret to see the domes up close, complete with swarms of pigeons, and to see how finely the mosque contrasts with the commercial streets around it. (Women cannot enter the minaret without a man; if you're a woman traveling solo, enlist a man to help you, as the beauty of the architecture is best appreciated from above.) Look into the prayer hall (you can only enter after a ritual purification at the ablution tank) for the pulpit carved from a single slab of marble. In one corner is a room where Shah Jahan installed the marble footprints of the Prophet Mohammed. Each of the arched colonnades has black-marble inscriptions inlaid in white marble that relate the history of the building and extol the virtues of Shah Jahan's reign.

If you're feeling hungry, the restaurant Karim's *(⇨ see Where to Eat)* is in the shadow of the Jama Masjid. ⊠ *4.5 km (3 miles) north of Connaught Pl., across from Red Fort* ☎ *11/2326–8344* 🖾 *Free; Rs. 50 to climb minaret; camera or video camera fee Rs. 200* ☾ *Non-Muslims: winter, daily 8:30–12:15 and 1:45–half hr before sunset; summer, daily 7–12:15 and 1:45–half hr before sunset. Closed for prayer half hr each afternoon. Muslims: daily 5 am–8 pm* Ⓜ *Chawri Bazaar, Chandni Chowk.*

★ **Lal Qila** (*Red Fort*). Named for its red-sandstone walls, the Red Fort, near the Yamuna River in Old Delhi, is the greatest of Delhi's palace cities. Built by Shah Jahan in the 17th century, Lal Qila recalls the era of Mughal power and magnificence—imperial elephants swaying by with their *mahouts* (elephant drivers), a royal army of eunuchs, court ladies carried in palanquins, and other vestiges of Shah Jahan's pomp. At its peak, the fort housed about 3,000 people. After the Indian Mutiny of 1857, the British moved into the fort, built barracks, and ended the grand Mughal era; eventually the Yamuna River changed course, so the view from the eastern ramparts is now a busy road. Still, if you use your imagination, a visit to the Red Fort gives an excellent idea of what a fantastic city Shahjahanabad was.

The view of the main entrance, called **Lahore Gate,** flanked with towers facing Chandni Chowk, is unfortunately blocked by a barbican (gatehouse), which the paranoid Aurangzeb added for his personal security—to the dismay of Shah Jahan, his father. From his prison, where he was held captive by his power-hungry son, Shah Jahan wrote, "You have made a bride of the palace and thrown a veil over her face."

Once you pass through Lahore Gate, continue down the **Chhatta Chowk** (Vaulted Arcade), originally the shopping district for the royal harem and now a bazaar selling rather less regal goods. From the end of the arcade you'll see the **Naubat Khana** (Welcome Room), a red-sandstone gateway where music was played five times daily. Beyond this point, everyone but the emperor and princes had to proceed on foot. Upstairs, literally inside the gateway, is the Indian War Memorial Museum (Tuesday–Sunday 10–5; free), with arms and military regalia from several periods.

An expansive lawn leads to the great **Diwan-i-Am** (Hall of Public Audience)—you have now entered the Delhi of Shah Jahan. Raised on a platform and open on three sides, the hall is studded with some of the most emblematic arches in the Mughal world. In the center is Shah Jahan's royal throne, once surrounded by decorative panels that sparkled with inlaid gems. (Stolen by British soldiers after the Indian Mutiny, some of the panels were restored 50 years later by Lord Curzon.) Watched by throngs of people from the courtyard below, the emperor heard the pleas of his subjects; the rest of the hall was reserved for rajas and foreign envoys, all standing with "their eyes bent downward and their hands crossed." High above them, wrote the 17th-century French traveler François Bernier, under a pearl-fringed canopy resting on golden shafts, "glittered the dazzling figure of the Grand Mughal, a figure to strike terror, for a frown meant death."

Heading back north, you'll come next to the **Rang Mahal** (Painted Palace), once richly decorated with a mirrored ceiling that was dismantled to pay the bills when the treasury ran low. Home of the royal ladies, the Rang Mahal contains a cooling water channel—called the Canal of Paradise—that runs from the marble basin in the center of the floor to the rest of the palace and to several of the others. You can't enter this or any of the palaces ahead, so you must peer creatively from the side.

The emperor's private **Khas Mahal** has three sections: the sitting room, the "dream chamber" (for sleeping), and the prayer chamber, all with lavishly carved walls and painted ceilings still intact. The lovely marble screen is carved with the Scale of Justice—two swords and a scale that symbolize punishment and justice. From the attached octagonal tower the emperor Muthamman Burj would appear before his subjects each morning or watch elephant fights in the nearby fields.

The **Diwan-i-Khas** (Hall of Private Audience) was the most exclusive pavilion of all. Here Shah Jahan would sit on his Peacock Throne, made of solid gold and inlaid with hundreds of precious and semiprecious stones. (When Nadir Shah sacked Delhi in 1739, he hauled the famous throne back to Persia. It was destroyed a few years later after Nadir Shah's assassination.) A Persian couplet written in gold above a corner arch sums up Shah Jahan's sentiments about his city: "If there be a paradise on Earth—It is this! It is this! It is this!"

The **Royal Hammam** was a luxurious three-chamber Mughal bath with inlaid-marble floors. The fountain in the center supposedly had rose-scented water. Sometimes called a Turkish bath, the *hammam* is still used in many Muslim cultures. Peek through the windows for a look.

Next door to the hammam is the **Moti Masjid** (Pearl Mosque), designed by Aurangzeb for his personal use and that of his harem. The building is now closed, but the prayer hall is inlaid with *musalla* (prayer rugs) outlined in black marble. Though the mosque has the purity of white marble, some critics say its excessively ornate style reflects the decadence that set in late in Shah Jahan's reign.

Beyond the mosque is a typical Mughal *charbagh,* or four-section garden. Stroll through this quieter part of the fort to see some small pleasure palaces including the Zafar Mahal, decked out with carved

Outside the Jama Masjid

sandstone *jalis* (screens) and once surrounded by water. ✉ *Netaji Subhash Marg, eastern end of Chandni Chowk* 🎟 *Rs. 250; sound-and-light show, weather permitting, Rs. 60, purchase tickets 30 mins in advance* ☉ *Tues.–Sun. sunrise–sunset. Show times: Nov.–Jan., daily 7:30 pm–8:30 pm; Feb.–Apr., Sept. and Oct., daily 8:30 pm–9:30 pm; May–Aug., daily 9 pm–10 pm* Ⓜ *Chandni Chowk.*

Mumtaz Mahal. Behind the Diwan-i-Am, a row of palaces overlooks the now-distant river. To the extreme right is the Mumtaz Mahal, now the Red Fort Museum, with numerous paintings and relics from the Mughal period, some in better lighting than others. 🎟 *Free* ☉ *Tues.–Sun. 10–5.*

★ **Svetamber Jain Temple.** Properly called the Indraprastha Tirth Sumatinatha Jain Svetamber Temple, this splendid house of worship is painted head to toe with finely rendered murals and decorations covering the walls, arches, and ceilings. Reflecting the building's surroundings, some of the artwork shows Mughal influence. Look inside the silver doors of the shrine to Sumatinatha—the fifth of Jainism's 24 *Tirthankaras* (perfect souls)—to see some incredible original painting finished with gold leaf.

As interesting as the temple itself is the street it's located on. It's called Naughara Gali, which directly translates into Nine Houses Street (they date back to the late 18th century). Owned mainly by jewelers, this gated cul-de-sac somehow shuts out all the noise and chaos of the Old City. It's peaceful and charming and each of the houses is brightly painted in shades of pink and blue with floral motifs drawn intricately over the doorways. ✉ *Naughara Gali, Kinari Bazaar* ☏ *11/2327–0489* ☉ *Daily 5:30–12:30 and 6:30–8.*

The Raj Ghat memorial to Mahatma Gandhi

WORTH NOTING

National Gandhi Museum. Run by a private foundation, this museum across the Mahatma Gandhi Road from Raj Ghat houses a great many photographs, a display of spinning wheels with some information on Gandhi's *khadi* (homespun cotton) crusade, and some of the Mahatma's personal effects, including the blood-stained dhoti he was wearing at the time of his murder. The tiny art gallery has a poignant wooden sculpture, made by a South African, of Gandhi in a pose suggesting Jesus's Crucifixion. A film on Gandhi's life is shown on weekends at 4. ⊠ *Mahatma Gandhi Marg (Ring Rd.)* ⊕ *www.gandhimuseum.org* 🖃 *Free* ⊗ *Tues.–Sun. 9:30–5:30.*

Raj Ghat. After Mahatma Gandhi was shot and killed by a Hindu fanatic on January 30, 1948, his body was cremated on the banks of the Yamuna River; the site is now a national shrine called Raj Ghat, where tourists and pilgrims stream across the peaceful lawn to pay their respects to the saintlike "Father of the Nation." At the center of a large courtyard is a raised slab of black marble adorned with flowers and inscribed with Gandhi's final words, "Hai Ram!" (Oh, God!). An eternal flame burns at its head. The sandstone walls enclosing the shrine are inscribed with passages written by Gandhi, translated into several tongues including Tamil, Malayalam, Nepali, Urdu, Spanish, Arabic, and Chinese. Near Raj Ghat are the cremation sites of two other assassinated heads of state, Indira Gandhi and her son Rajiv (no relation to Mohandas). ⊠ *Mahatma Gandhi Marg (Ring Rd.)* 🖃 *Free* ⊗ *Daily sunrise–sunset.*

Sis Ganj Sahib Gurdwara. Old Delhi's most famous Sikh shrine is a restful place to see one of North India's emblematic faiths in practice. Built at various times between 1784 (when the Sikhs conquered Delhi) and the 20th century, it marks the site where the Mughal emperor Aurangzeb beheaded Guru Teg Bahadur in 1675, when the guru refused to convert to Islam. It's a gory story, but before his body could be quartered and displayed to the public as an example, it was stolen by disciples. He was cremated by his son, Guru Gobind Singh, the tenth and last great Sikh Guru. As in any *gurdwara* (Sikh temple), sections of the *Guru Granth Sahib* scripture are chanted continuously; depending on the season, you might also find decorations of tinsel, colored foil, and blinking lights. Leave your shoes at the opening about 30 feet to the right of the entrance, and cover your head before entering. Women: if you don't have a head covering, climb the stairs and ask the man on the left to lend you one (it's free). If you have any questions about Sikhism or the shrine after your visit, stop into the friendly information office to the left of the entrance to hear legends and symbols unfold. ⊠ *Chandni Chowk* ☉ *Daily 24 hrs* Ⓜ *Chandni Chowk.*

CENTRAL DELHI

Sometimes also called Lutyens' Delhi after the British urban planner and architect who was largely responsible for its design, Central Delhi houses the government center and the broad, imperial streets of power. Also sometimes referred to as "New Delhi" (as opposed to Shah Jahan's pre-British city), it begins around Connaught Place and extends about 6 km (4 miles) south. Most sights are south of Connaught Place.

TOP ATTRACTIONS

★ **Akshardham Temple Complex.** Rising over the traffic jams of National Highway 24 on the way to the eastern suburb of Noida lies a massive, 100-acre temple complex where religion and commerce meet. Completed in November 2005, the pink-stone religious emporium pays tribute to Bhagwan Swami Narayan (1781–1830), the founder of a worldwide spiritual movement that claims a million devotees. An architectural marvel built over five years and without using steel, the elaborate main temple and its soaring domes and 20,000 carved figures only appear ancient. This gleaming complex includes a giant movie theater and a 14-minute boat ride that is quite an experience. Whisking the visitor through 10,000 years of Indian culture, the ride could be mistaken for something straight out of Disney World—Indian style! Don't miss the Yagnapurush Kund and Musical Fountain, India's largest, which has an entertaining show echoing the Vedic sentiments of creation. Just viewing the exhibits takes at least two hours. Admission lines can be lengthy, so allow plenty of time. Security is airtight. ⚠ **All bags and purses, electronics (including mobile phones and cameras), and tobacco products are banned, so check them in or leave them at the hotel or in the car before you get in line.** But don't forget your wallet. While donations are voluntary, marketing is persistent. Exhibitions tend to shut an hour before the complex itself; the food court provides decent, cheap vegetarian meals and snacks for those who opt to spend the day.

✉ *Nizamuddin Bridge, East Delhi, Central Delhi, Delhi* ☎ *11/2201–6688* ⊕ *www.akshardham.com* ✉ *Free; exhibitions Rs. 170* ⊙ *Tues.–Sun.: 9:30–6:30* Ⓜ *Akshardham.*

Jantar Mantar. This odd grouping of what might seem like random sculptures is actually a huge sundial and open-air observatory. One of five such installations built by the Maharaja Sawai Jai Singh II of Jaipur in the early 18th century (the one in Jaipur is the best preserved), it's an interesting place to wander, though better understood with a good guide. The Samrat Jantar, the sundial, is the largest structure here, at 90 feet. The Hindu Chhatri, a small domed building, can tell when the monsoons are coming in and whether the weather will change. The Jai Prakash shows the sun's position at the time of the equinox. The Ram Yantra consists of two large buildings, both with open tops: they're used, together, to measure the altitude of stars. The Mishra Yantra consists of five instruments, which are used to measure the shortest and longest days of the year. ✉ *Sansad Marg, Connaught Pl., Central Delhi, Delhi* ☎ *11/2332–2474* ✉ *Rs. 100* ⊙ *Daily, sunrise to sunset* Ⓜ *Rajiv Chowk.*

★ **Lutyens' Delhi.** Rajpath—the broadest avenue in the city—leads to Delhi's British capital: Sir Edwin Lutyens' imperial city, built between 1914 and 1931 in a symbolically heavy-handed design after the British moved their capital from Calcutta to Delhi in 1911. (During construction, they hit marshy land prone to floods, so they reversed direction and put the bulk of their capital a few miles to the south.)

Starting from India Gate, at the lowest and eastern end of Rajpath, nearby land was allocated to numerous princely states, each of which built small palaces, such as the **Bikaner House** (now the Rajasthan tourism office) and **Jaipur House** (now the National Gallery of Modern Art). It might be said that this placement mirrored the British sentiments toward the princes, who lost much of their former power and status during the British Raj. Here, too, are the state Bhavans (houses), where you can taste the cuisine of each state.

Moving up the slowly inclining hill at the western end of the avenue, you also move up the British ladder of power, a concept inherent in the original design. First you come to the enormous **North and South Secretariats,** facing each other on Rajpath and reflecting the importance of the bureaucracy, a fixture of Indian society since the time of British rule. Identical in design, the two buildings have 1,000 rooms and miles of corridors.

Directly behind the North Secretariat is the Indian parliament house, **Sansad Bhavan,** a circular building in red and gray sandstone, encompassed by an open colonnade. Architecturally, the Indian design is meant to mirror the spinning wheel that was the symbol of Mahatma Gandhi, but the building's secondary placement, off the main avenue, may suggest the attitude of the British toward the Indian legislative assembly.

At the top of the hill is the former Viceroy's House, now called **Rashtrapati Bhavan,** where the President of India (not the prime minister) resides. It was built in the 20th century, but the building's daunting proportions seem to reflect an earlier, more lavish time of British supremacy. The Bhavan contains 340 rooms, and its grounds cover 330 acres. The shape of the central brass dome, the palace's main architectural feature,

The astronomical instruments at Delhi's Jantar Mantar are quite well preserved.

reflects that of a Buddhist *stupa* (shrine). The execution of Lutyens' design has a flaw: the entire palace was supposed to fill the vista as you approach the top of the hill, but the gradient is too steep, so only the dome dominates the horizon. And in a nicely ironic twist, a few years after the imperial city was completed, the British packed up and went home, and this lavish architectural complex became the grand capital of newly independent India.

Permission to enter Rashtrapati and Sansad Bhavan is almost impossible to obtain; unless you have contacts in high places, you'll have to satisfy yourself with a look at the poshest address in town from outside. ■ TIP → The extensive Rashtrapati gardens are open to the public in February and March (Tues.–Sun. 9:30–2:30; www.presidentofindia.nic.in). Heavy security is in place (no bags or cell phones, for instance), but a rare view of the impressive gardens is worth the hassle.

For an experience of imperial Delhi, stop for tea at the Imperial Hotel on Janpath; for a glimpse of Delhi's contemporary elite, browse at Khan Market. A stroll through Lodhi Gardens *(See South Delhi Top Attractions)* is a relaxing break and the India Habitat Centre or India International Centre are good bets if you have a taste for culture. ⊠ *Central Delhi, Delhi* Ⓜ *Central Secretariat.*

National Handicrafts and Handlooms Museum. Designed by the Indian architect Charles Correa, this charming museum near the Purana Qila houses thousands of artifacts and handicrafts. You're greeted outside by playful terra-cotta sculptures from Tamil Nadu. Inside, the annotations are sketchy, but the collection is fascinating. Items in the Folk and Tribal Art Gallery, including some charming toys, illustrate village life

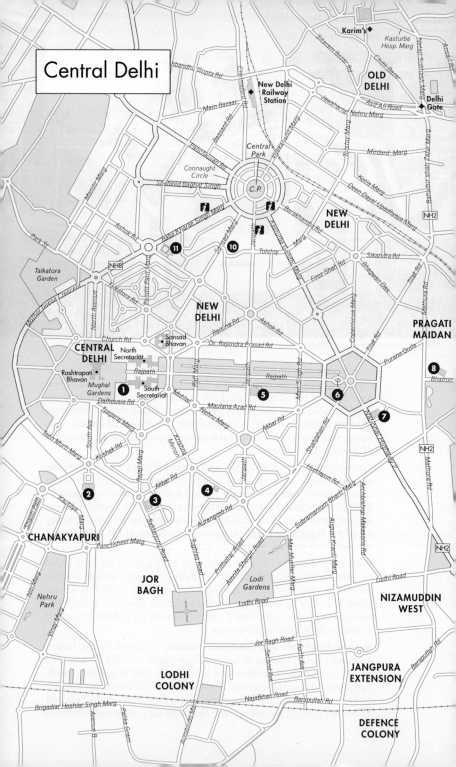

Akshardham Temple Complex **9**

Bangla Sahib Gurdwara **11**

Gandhi Smriti **4**

India Gate **6**

Indira Gandhi Memorial Museum **3**

Jantar Mantar **10**

Lutyens' Delhi **1**

National Gallery of Modern Art **7**

National Handicrafts and
Handlooms Museum **8**

National Museum **5**

Nehru Memorial Museum **2**

Vikas Marg

Geeta Colony Road

Dadri Road

Yamuna

National Highway 24 bypass

National
Zoological
Park

SUNDAR
NAGAR

NIZAMUDDIN
EAST

Hazrat
Nizamuddin
Railway
Station

0 _____ 1/2 mi

0 _____ 1/2 km

NH2

Mahatma Gandhi Marg

Barapulla Rd

KEY

i *Tourist information*

A view of the government buildings at Lutyens' Delhi

throughout India. In one courtyard you'll see a giant wooden temple car (cart), built to carry deities in festive processions; one of the adjacent buildings contains a lavishly decorated Gujarati haveli. The Courtly Crafts section suggests the luxurious lives of India's erstwhile royalty, and the entire upper floor is a spectacular showcase of saris and textiles. In the village complex out back, craftspeople demonstrate their skills and sell their creations in replicas of village homes. The museum shop is one of the best in Delhi, with high-quality art books and crafts. ⊠ *Bhairon Rd., off Mathura Rd., opposite Pragati Maidan, Central Delhi, Delhi* ☏ *11/2337–1641* ⊕ *nationalcraftsmuseum.nic.in* ▣ *Free* ⏱ *Tues.–Sun. 10–5* Ⓜ *Pragati Maidan.*

National Museum. The facade of this grand building imitates Lutyens' Presidential Palace: a sandstone dome is supported by classical columns of brown sandstone on a red-sandstone base. When you enter, you'll see a 13th-century idol—from the Konark Sun Temple in Bhubaneswar—of Surya, the sun god, standing beneath the dome. Such a statue is emblematic of the National Museum's strength—it showcases ancient, mainly Hindu, sculptures. An entire room is dedicated to artifacts from the Indus Valley Civilization, circa 2,700 BC; others display works from the Gandharan, Chandela, and Chola periods. Besides sculpture, also on exhibit are jewelry, painting, musical instruments, coins, carpets, and weapons, including Shah Jahan's sword. Be sure to pick up a brochure to help you navigate, and get the audio guide, included in ticket rates, which is also worth a listen. ⊠ *Janpath and Rajpath, India Gate, Central Delhi, Delhi* ☏ *11/2301–9272* ⊕ *www.nationalmuseumindia.gov.in* ▣ *Rs. 300; camera fee Rs. 300* ⏱ *Tues.–Sun. 10–5* Ⓜ *Central Secretariat.*

★ **Nehru Memorial Museum.** This colonial mansion, also known as Teen Murti Bhavan, was originally built for the commander of the British Indian Army. When the Viceroy's residence, Rashtrapati Bhavan (at the other end of South Avenue), became the home of India's president, India's first prime minister, Jawaharlal Nehru, took up residence here. Those interested in the Independence movement should not miss this landmark or the nearby Gandhi Smriti. Nehru's yellow mansion is fronted by a long, oval-shaped lawn; out back there's a tranquil flower garden. Inside, several rooms remain as Nehru left them, and extensive displays chronicle Nehru's life and the Independence movement. Move through the rooms in order: one by one, photographs, newspaper clippings, and personal letters tell the breathtaking story of the birth of the world's largest democracy. On your way out, stop and see the 14th-century hunting lodge next to the Nehru Planetarium. (The latter, good for children, has shows in English at 11:30 am and 3 pm.) ✉ *Teen Murti Marg, Central Delhi* ☎ *11/2301–7587* ⊕ *nehrumemorial.com* ☐ *Free; planetarium Rs. 50* ☉ *Tues.–Sun. 9–5:30* Ⓜ *Race Course.*

WORTH NOTING

Bangla Sahib Gurdwara. This massive *gurdwara* (Sikh temple) is always full of activity—no surprise, given Delhi's huge Sikh population, most of whom came here as refugees from Pakistan in 1947. If you can't make it to Amritsar to see the Golden Temple, come here to admire the distinctively ostentatious style of their temples. Sikh gurdwaras reflect both the symmetry of Mughal mosques and the chaos of Hindu temples. Bangla Sahib is built of white marble and topped with a shiny, gold onion dome.

The gurdwara stands on the site where Guru Hari Krishan, the eighth of 10 Sikh gurus who lived between 1469 and 1708, performed a small miracle. Before entering, remove your shoes and socks (check them at the counter on the left), get rid of cigarettes, and cover your head with a piece of cloth. As you walk up the stairs and enter the sanctum, you'll see people filling jugs of water from enclosed cisterns. Guru Hari Krishan used to distribute sanctified water to the sick, believing it had a miraculous healing effect on their mind, body, and soul, and people still treat the contents of these pools as holy water. Inside, devotees sit facing a small pavilion in the center that holds the *Granth Sahib* (Sikh scriptures). Hymns from the holy book are sung continuously from well before sunrise until approximately 9 pm, and you're welcome to sit and listen; if you fancy something cultural in the evening, come at about 9 to see the ceremony by which the book is stored away for the night. As you walk around inside, be careful to proceed in a clockwise direction, and exit on the right side in back. Out the door to the right a priest distributes *prasad*, a ritual that Sikhs share with Hindus and that resembles the Christian sacrament of communion: take a lump of this sugar, flour, and *ghee* (clarified butter) concoction with both hands, pop it into your mouth with your right hand, then rub the remaining ghee into your hands. ✉ *Bangla Sahib Lane, off Baba Kharak Singh Marg, near Connaught Pl., Central Delhi, Delhi* ☐ *Free* ☉ *Daily 4 am–9 pm* Ⓜ *Rajiv Chowk, Patel Chowk.*

Gandhi Smriti. Mohandas K. Gandhi, better known as the Mahatma (Great Soul), lived a life of voluntary poverty, but he did it in some attractive places. It was in this huge colonial bungalow, designed by a French architect for Indian industrialist G.D.R. Birla, that Gandhi was staying as a guest when he was assassinated in the back garden on his way to a prayer meeting. Gandhi's bedroom is just as he left it, with his "worldly remains" (only 11 items, including his glasses and a walking stick) mounted on the wall. Pictures and text tell the story of Gandhi's life and the Independence movement; there's also a collection of dioramas depicting events in Gandhi's life. In the theater, 10 different documentaries are available for viewing on request. Take off your shoes before entering the somber prayer ground in back; an eternal flame marks the very spot where Gandhi expired. This, not the National Gandhi Museum at Raj Ghat, is the government's official museum dedicated to the Mahatma. ⊠ *5 Tees January Marg, Central Delhi* ☎ *11/3095–7269* 🎟 *Free* ⊙ *Tues.–Sun., 10–5; museum closed 2nd Sat. in month* Ⓜ *Race Course.*

India Gate. Anchoring a traffic circle near the far end of Rajpath from the Indian government, this massive sandstone arch was designed by Lutyens in 1931, in memory of the 90,000 soldiers of the British Indian Army who fell in World War I and the Third Afghan War of the late 19th century. In the 1970s the government of India added a memorial to India's unknown soldier, the Amar Jawan Jyoti, beneath the arch. It has huge sentimental value to Indians. The Indira Gandhi Canal runs through the circle; if it's not dry, go boating! While traffic speeds neatly around the outer circle, vendors occupy the inner circle, and people amble and socialize on the lawns. Come in early evening and you'll find all sorts of activity, from men offering to make monkeys "dance" (for a fee) to impromptu cricket matches to youngsters splashing in the ornamental fountains. *The* thing to do is get an ice cream—Mother Dairy is one of the better brands. ⊠ *Rajpath, east end, Central Delhi, Delhi.*

Indira Gandhi Memorial Museum. On October 31, 1984, Prime Minister Indira Gandhi was shot outside her home by two of her Sikh bodyguards in retaliation for her violent suppression of a violent Sikh independence movement in Punjab, which included a military operation that entered Amritsar's Golden Temple. The murder sparked gruesome anti-Sikh riots in Delhi, and political turmoil ensued. The simple white bungalow in which Mrs. Gandhi lived from the 1960s to 1980s is now a small museum with endless photographs, quotations, and newspaper articles, plus a few rooms preserved as they were used. The photos get more interesting as you progress, and the museum ends with displays on Indira's son, Rajiv, himself prime minister from 1984 to 1991 before he, too, was assassinated. Displays include the sari, handbag, and shoes Mrs. Gandhi was wearing when she was killed, and the sneakers Rajiv was wearing during his even more grisly demise at the hands of a female suicide bomber who was retaliating for India's support of the Sri Lankan government during a civil war. Outside, the spot where Indira fell is marked and preserved. Popular with Indian tourists, the museum can get very crowded; allow extra time if you want

The gardens leading up to the Lotus Temple, also known as the Bahá'í House of Worship

to peruse things carefully. ⊠ *1 Safdarjung Rd., Central Delhi, Delhi* ☎ *11/2301–0094* 🎫 *Free* 🕑 *Tues.–Sun. 9:30–4:45* Ⓜ *Race Course.*

National Gallery of Modern Art. Facing India Gate, this neoclassical building was built by the British in the early 20th century as a palace for the Maharaja of Jaipur. With its small dome and large, open rooms, the structure makes a fine space for this art museum, established in 1954 to preserve Indian art forms (mainly painting) that developed after 1850. A large new wing was added in 2008 so that more of the extensive collection could be displayed. The displays are attractive by local standards but are unfortunately uneven and not always well explained. Highlights are the colorful paintings of Amrita Sher-Gil (the Frida Kahlo of India) and, upstairs, the myth-inspired works of Raja Ravi Varma and the Bengali Renaissance oils and watercolors of the Tagore family, Jamini Roy, and Nandalal Bose. There are a few representative works by contemporary masters such as M.F. Husain and Ganesh Pyne. Documentaries, shown daily at 11 and 3, explain Indian art. The old wing often hosts interesting temporary or traveling exhibitions. ⊠ *Jaipur House, India Gate, Central Delhi* ☎ *11/2338–4640* ⊕ *www.ngmaindia.gov.in* 🎫 *Rs. 150* 🕑 *Tues.–Sun. 10–5, Thurs. 10–8.*

SOUTH DELHI

South Delhi, the older suburbs and colonies of the new city, ironically has monuments even older than those in Old Delhi, such as the Qutub Minar, Kauz Khas, and numerous pre-Mughal tombs that lie abandoned in the midst of contemporary houses and apartments.

With a mix of government-built apartments, posh mansions and "farmhouses" of the elite, and refugee colonies from the 1950s, South Delhi also has the more recent addition of malls, particularly in Saket and Vasant Kunj. There is also plenty of soul and tradition. Getting some quiet meditation at the Lotus Temple is a must. The incredible urbanized villages of Hauz Khas and Shahpur Jat may turn up anything from vintage Bollywood posters to beautifully beaded slippers. Visit Nizamuddin East for a sufi music performance that will transport you to a spiritual plane.

The wealth of restaurants and bars that have opened here are packed on weekends.

TOP ATTRACTIONS

Bahá'i House of Worship (The Lotus Temple). The lotus flower is a symbol of purity and spirituality throughout India, and Delhi's Bahá'i Temple celebrates this in a unique architectural way. Designed by Fariborz Sahba, an Iranian-born Canadian architect, and completed in 1986, the building incorporates the number nine—the highest digit and, in the Bahá'i faith, a symbol of unity. The sleek structure has two layers: nine white marble-covered petals that point to heaven, and nine petals that conceal the portals. From a short distance it looks like a fantastic work of origami. The nine pools outside signify the green leaves of the lotus and cool the starkly elegant, usually silent marble interior. The interior conforms to that of all Bahá'i houses of worship: there are no religious icons, just copies of the Holy Scriptures and wooden pews. The road to the temple passes through a colorful temple bazaar connected to the nearby Kalkaji Mandir. ✉ *near Nehru Place, South Delhi, Delhi* ⊕ *www.bahaihouseofworship.in* 🖼 *Free* ☉ *Apr.–Sept., Tues.–Sun. 9–7; Oct.–Mar., Tues.–Sun. 9:30–5:30* Ⓜ *Kalkaji Mandir.*

Hauz Khas Village. The road south to the urban village of Hauz Khas is lined on both sides by ancient stone monuments, and the entire village is dotted with domed structures—the tombs of minor Muslim royalty from the 14th to the 16th centuries. At the end of the road is the tomb of Firoz Shah Tughlaq, who ruled Delhi in the 14th century. Hauz Khas means "Royal Tank," referring to the artificial lake visible from Firoz Shah's pillared tomb. The tank was actually built a century earlier by Allauddin Khilji as a water source for his nearby fort, then called Siri (the second city of Delhi). Back in the village, wander through the narrow lanes to experience a medley of old and new structures—expensive shops and art galleries in a medieval warren. ■ TIP→ **Find your way to the gardens near the ruin of a madrassa at the back of the village. The kindly old gentleman often playing cards can sometimes be coaxed into an impromptu Urdu lesson.** In the 1980s Hauz Khas was designated an upscale tourist destination, but of late it more accurately aspires to emulate Manhattan's West Village. After exploring, stop for a meal at

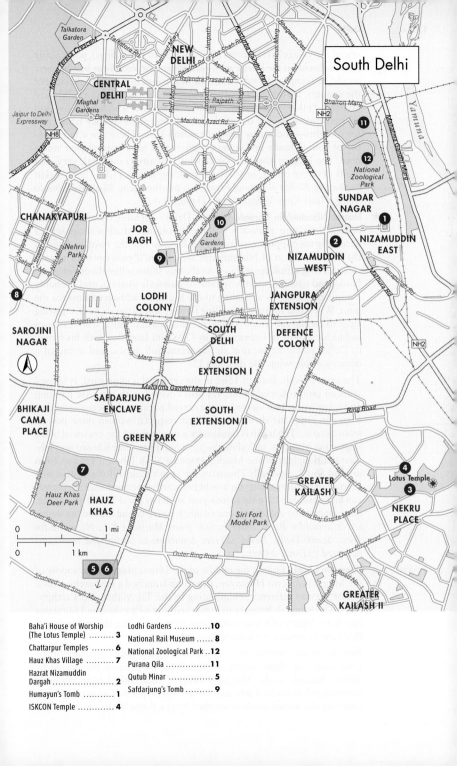

South Delhi

Baha'i House of Worship
(The Lotus Temple) 3
Chattarpur Temples 6
Hauz Khas Village 7
Hazrat Nizamuddin
Dargah 2
Humayun's Tomb 1
ISKCON Temple 4

Lodhi Gardens 10
National Rail Museum 8
National Zoological Park .. 12
Purana Qila 11
Qutub Minar 5
Safdarjung's Tomb 9

one of the village's restaurants *(⇨ See Where to Eat listings)*, particularly Park Balluchi (in the Deer Park), Naivedyam, or Yeti. Your best bet here would be Gunpowder which has the best South Indian food this side of the country. It also has a bird's-eye view of the lake and is a solid local favorite. "HKV" also has the popular TLR Café, which hosts live and DJ performances over the weekends—from reggae to rock bands and retro nights—and a new host of rooftop bars. There are a fair number of young, funky upcoming designers that have opened their stores here. The biggest store to look out for is White: a minimal, very cool multi-designer outlet, in the same building as the TLR. The Yodakin bookstore *(⇨ See shopping listings)* is another gem. ⊠ *off Aurobindo Marg, Hauz Khas Village, South Delhi, Delhi*.

★ **Hazrat Nizamuddin Dargah.** One of Delhi's greatest treats is hearing devout Sufis sing *qawwalis,* ecstatic devotional Muslim songs with a decidedly toe-tapping quality. To get here, follow the twisting lanes in the bazaar section of Nizamuddin West—you'll pass open-air restaurants serving simple meat-based meals, tiny shops selling Urdu-language books and cassettes (some by famous qawwali singers), and probably a number of beggars appealing to the Muslim tradition of alms for the poor. When you see vendors selling flowers and garlands, you're getting close to the *dargah* (tomb) of Hazrat Nizamuddin Aulia, who was born in Bukhara (now in Uzbekistan) in 1238 and later fled with his family to Delhi, where he became an important Sufi mystic and attracted a dedicated following. He died in 1325.

The saint's tomb, built in 1562 in the center of a courtyard, is topped with an onion-shaped dome. It's also covered with intricate painting and inlay work, best viewed on the carved parapet above the verandas. Men can enter the shrine to pay their respects; women must peer in from outside. The tomb is flanked by a mosque and the graves of other important Muslims, including the great Sufi poet Amir Khusro and Jahanara, a daughter of the Mughal emperor Shah Jahan. Evenings from around 5 to 7, especially Thursday, the saint's male followers often sing in front of the darga and you would best catch a performance. ⚠ Crowds can be dense, and it's easy to lose your wallet or purse before you notice. Keep money and valuables secured when you're in and around the darga. ⊠ *Nizamuddin Basti, enter bazaar from Mathura Rd., Nizamuddin West, South Delhi, Delhi* ☞ *Free, donations to shrine and musicians accepted* ☼ *Daily 24 hrs.*

Fodor's Choice **Humayun's Tomb.** Built in the middle of the 16th century by the widow of
★ the Mughal emperor Humayun, this tomb launched a new architectural era of Persian influence, culminating in the Taj Mahal and Fatehpur Sikri. The Mughals brought to India their love of gardens and fountains and left a legacy of harmonious structures, including this mausoleum, that fuse symmetry with decorative splendor.

Resting on an immense two-story platform, the tomb structure of red sandstone and white marble is surrounded by gardens intersected by water channels in the Mughals' beloved *charbagh* design: perfectly square gardens divided into four (*char*) square parts. The marble dome covering the actual tomb is another first: a dome within a dome (the

interior dome is set inside the soaring dome seen from outside), a style later used in the Taj Mahal. As you enter or leave the tomb area, stand a moment before the beveled gateway to enjoy the view of the monument framed in the arch.

Besides Humayun, several other important Mughals are buried here, along with Isa Khan Niyazi, a noble in the court of Sher Shah—who lies in the fetching octagonal shrine that precedes the tomb itself. The site's serenity belies the fact that many of the dead buried inside were murdered princes, victims of foul play. To see where Humayun actually died, combine this visit with a trip to the Purana Qila. ⊠ *Off Mathura Rd., Nizamuddin East, South Delhi, Delhi* 🖃 *Rs. 250* ⊙ *Daily sunrise–sunset.*

★ **Lodhi Gardens.** After Mughal warrior Timur ransacked Delhi at the end of the 14th century, he ordered the massacre of the entire population—acceptable retribution, he thought, for the murder of some of his soldiers. As if in unconscious response to this horrific act, the subsequent Lodhi and Sayyid dynasties built no city, only a few mosques and some mausoleums and tombs, the latter of which stand in what is now a delightful urban park. Winding walks cut through landscaped lawns with trees and small flowers, past schoolboys playing cricket, politicians taking some air, friends and lovers relaxing in the greenery, and parrots squawking. Lodi—The Garden Restaurant is a great place to get a meal post an evening walk. Made of wood and glass, it's as verdant as the garden itself. Near the southern entrance on Lodhi Road is the dignified mausoleum of Mohammed Shah, third ruler of the Sayyid dynasty, and some members of his family. This octagon, with a central chamber surrounded by verandas carved with arches, is a good example of the architecture of this period. Near the road is the open-air National Bonsai Park, with some nice specimens of the trees. The smaller, equally lovely octagonal tomb of Sikandar Lodhi, surrounded by a garden in the park's northwestern corner, has an unusual double dome. ⊠ *Lodhi Rd., southeast of Khan Market, South Delhi, Delhi* 🖃 *Free* ⊙ *Daily sunrise–sunset* Ⓜ *Jor Bagh.*

★ **Purana Qila** (*Old Fort*). India's sixth capital was the scene of a fierce power struggle between the Afghan Sher Shah and Humayun, son of the first Mughal emperor, Babur, in the 16th century. When Humayun started to build his own capital, Dinpanah, on these grounds in the 1530s, Sher Shah forced the emperor to flee for his life to Persia. Sher Shah destroyed what existed of Dinpanah to create his own capital, Shergarh. Fifteen years later, in 1555, Humayun returned and seized control, but he died the following year, leaving Sher Shah's city for others to destroy.

Unfortunately, once you enter the massive Bara Darwaza (Main Gate), only two buildings are intact. The **Qila-i-Kuhna Masjid**, Sher Shah's private mosque, is an excellent example of Indo-Afghan architecture in red sandstone with decorative marble touches—walk around to the "back" to see the beautiful front of the building. The nearby **Sher Mandal**, a two-story octagonal tower of red sandstone and white marble, became Humayun's library and ultimately his death trap: hearing the call to prayer, Humayun started down the steep steps, slipped, and fell to his death. On pleasant afternoons, every bush on these grounds hides a pair of young lovers in search of a little privacy. ✉ *Delhi Zoo, Off Mathura Rd., near Pragati Maidan, South Delhi, Delhi* 🎟 *Rs. 100* 🕙 *Daily sunrise–sunset* Ⓜ *Pragati Maidan.*

★ **Qutub Minar.** Named for the Muslim sultan Qutab-ud-din Aibak, this striking tower is 238 feet high, with 376 steps, and the tallest stone tower in India. Qutub-ud-din Aibak began construction in 1193; his son-in-law and successor, Iltutmish, added the top four stories. The result is a handsome sandstone example of Indo-Islamic architecture, with terra-cotta frills and balconies. At its foot lies the **Quwwat-ul-Islam Masjid,** the first mosque in India. The Muslims erected the mosque in the 12th century after they defeated the Hindu Chauhan dynasty—they built it on the site of a Hindu temple and used pillars and other materials from 27 demolished Hindu and Jain shrines. (Which explains why you see Hindu and Jain sculptures in the mosque.) The mosque is also famous for a 24-foot-high, 5th-century iron pillar, inscribed with six lines of Sanskrit. According to legend, if you stand with your back to the pillar and can reach around and touch your fingers, any wish you make will come true. (Unfortunately, it's now fenced off.) ✉ *Aurobindo Marg, near Mehrauli, South Delhi, Delhi* 🎟 *Rs. 250* 🕙 *Daily sunrise–sunset* Ⓜ *Qutub Minar.*

Safdarjung's Tomb. Delhi's last great garden tomb, built in 1754 for the prime minister of the emperor Mohammad Shah, is pleasantly located in the center of town. With its marble oversize dome and minarets, it can't compete with Humayun's resting place, but the finials and other details have a distinctly Mughul fineness, and the *charbagh* (four-section garden, which is a typical Mughal style) is a peaceful place to listen to the birds chirp. The site would be lovelier if water still ran through the four large channels in the gardens, but you have to imagine that part to complete the 18th-century scene. ✉ *Aurobindo Marg at Lodhi Rd., Jor Bagh, South Delhi, Delhi* 🎟 *Rs. 100* 🕙 *Daily sunrise–sunset* Ⓜ *Jor Bagh.*

WORTH NOTING

Chhattarpur Temples. If you're on your way south to Agra or Jaipur, drive a few miles beyond the Qutab Minar on Mehrauli Road and check out this massive Hindu temple complex. It's a mishmash of architectural styles, but the unifying factor—from the huge dome over the Shiva lingam to the 92-foot statue of the monkey god Hanuman—is the Punjabi Baroque architecture. It's quite a sight to take in: these huge temples looming on either side of the road. Enter through the sanctum with the devotees, stop at the idols to pay respects, and take some prasad on the way out. Many gods and goddesses are represented, but the inner sanctum is dedicated to Adhya Ma Katyan, a mother goddess. Hymns are sung all night during full moons. Make sure you're dressed respectfully or you'll stick out like a sore thumb. ✉ *Chhattarpur Rd, Chhattarpur, South Delhi, Delhi* 🎟 *Free* 🕙 *Daily sunrise–sunset* Ⓜ *Chhattarpur.*

ISKCON Temple. The International Society for Krishna Consciousness is better known as the Hare Krishna sect, and despite the 1960s association they are very much alive and kicking. In the 1990s ISKCON erected enormous, gleaming Krishna temples in several Indian cities, and these offer a unique glimpse into the remaining pockets of international

DID YOU KNOW?

The Qutub Minar minaret was inspired by the 213-feet tall Minaret of Jam in Afghanistan, but Qutub-ud-din Aibak, the Muslim sultan, had his built taller, at 238 feet.

Hinduism, with shaven-headed foreigners in saffron robes mingling with Indian colleagues, devotees, and tourists. Built impressively on a rock outcropping near a residential market, Delhi's temple is an amalgam of architectural styles: Mughal, Gupta, and the flashy Delhi style jokingly called Punjabi Baroque. The sanctum contains three idols—Balram Krishna, Radha-Krishna, and Laksman (along with Rama and Sita)—each representing a different incarnation of Lord Krishna. The art gallery behind the idols must be viewed in a clockwise direction, as this *parikrama* (revolution) is the only appropriate way to move around the gods. To learn more about Krishna, pop into the "Vedic Expo," where an upstairs collection of dioramas illustrate his life in the incarnation of Lord Chaitanya, and various sound-and-light shows (even a robotics display) enact the *Bhagavad Gita* scriptures and the ancient epic, the *Mahabharata,* from which the scriptures come. It's all a bit Southern California, but ISKCON's temples are by far the cleanest in India, and very welcoming to visitors. Finish with a meal at Govinda's, the on-site restaurant, where a delicious vegetarian buffet goes for Rs. 380. ⊠ *Sant Nagar Main Rd., East of Kailash, South Delhi, Delhi* ☎ *11/2623–5133, 11/2623–3400* ⚏ *Free* ☉ *Daily 4:30 am–12:45 pm and 4 pm–8:45 pm.*

☾ **National Rail Museum.** This large, mostly outdoor museum is a glimpse into the largest railroad system in the world. The 10-acre grounds are home to 75 authentic locomotives, bogies (railway cars), and even a working roundabout (a device that turns rail cars). Parked behind glass is the *Fairy Queen;* built in 1855, it's the oldest running steam engine in the world. It still takes nine trips a year to Sariska National Park and back for a weekend trip (contact the director of the museum if you're interested, but it's not worth the outrageous price). Inside the museum are displays that discuss the history of India's rail system. The museum is good not only for train buffs but also children, who love riding the tiny train that circles the grounds. ⊠ *Nyaya Marg, off Shanti Path, Chanakyapuri, South Delhi, Delhi* ☎ *11/2688–1816, 11/2688–0939* ⊕ *www.nrm.indianrailways.gov.in* ⚏ *Rs. 10* ☉ *Oct.–Mar., Tues.–Sun. 9:30–5; Apr.–Sept., Tues.–Sun. 9:30–7:30.*

☾ **National Zoological Park.** White tigers are the draw at Delhi's zoo, which was designed in the late 1950s by the German designer Carl Hagenbeck. There are many noteworthy animals roaming about, such as emus, gazelles, Indian rhinos, and a great many deer, not to mention some smart-looking waterbirds. Animals in cages, including the famous white tigers and Asiatic lions, are part of the national collection. The zoo is spacious and leafy, a virtual botanical garden for peaceful walks, and the central lake hosts numerous Central Asian migratory aquatic birds (pelicans, storks, and cranes) pausing on their way to Keoladeo National Park in Bharatpur, Rajasthan, for the winter. If you don't have time to make it to Bharatpur or a tiger reserve, this is a pretty good alternative. ⊠ *Mathura Rd., behind Sundar Nagar, South Delhi, Delhi* ☎ *11/2435–9825, 11/2435–8500* ⊕ *www.nzpnewdelhi.gov.in* ⚏ *Rs. 50* ☉ *Mid-Oct.–Mar., Sat.–Thurs. 9:30–4; Apr.–mid-Oct., Sat.–Thurs. 9–4:30.*

WHERE TO EAT

ABOUT THE RESTAURANTS

Restaurants are generally open daily 12:30 to 3 for lunch and 7:30 to 11 for dinner. Delhi's liquor laws have loosened in recent years and all restaurants serve alcohol unless we indicate otherwise. However, imported liquor is extremely expensive—inquire before you imbibe. Expect a 20% tax on your food and beverage bill.

Prices in the reviews are the average cost of a main course at dinner or, if dinner is not served, at lunch.

OLD DELHI

$$ NORTH INDIAN Fodor's Choice ★ 🍴 **Chor Bizarre.** Delhi's best-known Kashmiri restaurant is also one of its most beautiful, an art deco enclave with a tile floor, a spiral staircase leading nowhere, antique furniture and mirrors from various *chor* ("thieves'") bazaars. The bar is all dark wood and stained glass, and the salad bar is a 1927 Fiat roadster. Kashmiri food is milder than many Indian cuisines, exemplified by mutton *yakhni* (in a sauce of yogurt, cardamom, and aniseed) and mutton *mirchi korma* (in cardamom and clove gravy). Try a *tarami* platter to sample several dishes, and drink *kahwah,* fragrant Kashmiri tea. [$] *Average main: Rs. 425* ✉ *Hotel Broadway, 4/15A Asaf Ali Rd., just outside Old Delhi, near Delhi Gate, Old Delhi, Delhi* ☎ *11/4366–3600* ✣ *F1.*

$$ NORTH INDIAN 🍴 **Karim's.** This is an Old Delhi institution where mutton (which generally means goat in India) is king, especially in thick, rich gravies. Try *mutton Mughlai* or *badaam pasanda* ("almond delight," mutton in a slightly sweet gravy) for the full experience. Open from 7 am to midnight, it's off the street that runs out from the mosque's main entrance, Gate 1; about four shops down on the left, take the passageway into a small courtyard—you'll see large cauldrons of meaty concoctions, smoking kebabs on spits, and several indoor seating areas. The newer Karim's, **Dastar Khwan-e-Karim,** near Hazrat Nizamuddin Darga, is more restaurant-like. Alcohol is not served. [$] *Average main: Rs. 300* ✉ *Gali Kababian, near Jama Masjid, Old Delhi, Delhi* ☎ *11/2326–9880* 🌐 *www.karimhoteldelhi.com* 💳 *No credit cards* 🕓 *Closed daylight hours during Ramadan* [M] *Chawri Bazaar* [$] *Average main: Rs. 300* ✉ *168/2 Jha House Basti, Nizamuddin West, South Delhi, Delhi* ☎ *11/2435–8300* ✣ *E1.*

$ INDIAN Fodor's Choice ★ 🍴 **Lala Duli Chand Naresh Gupta.** A Delhi summer isn't complete without one of these famous *kulfis*—the frozen milk–based treats similar to ice cream. What makes this spot so unique is that you'll get your kulfi served in the fruit that it's flavored with: order apple, for instance, and you'll get an apple (it looks like a frozen candy apple) that splits open to reveal the delicious kulfi inside. They'll kulfi up just about any fruit, from mangoes to figs to kiwis. [$] *Average main: Rs. 100* ✉ *Bazaar Sita Ram, 934 Kucha Pati Ram, Old Delhi, Delhi* ☎ *11/2323–7085* [M] *Chawri Bazaar* ✣ *E1.*

CENTRAL DELHI

$$$ MODERN EUROPEAN Fodor's Choice ★ 🍴 **Basil & Thyme.** Celebrity chef Bhicoo Manekshaw, now in her 80s, still creates the daily specials and seasonal menus. There's no telling what she'll come up with, but you can bank on fresh flavors, such as carrot-and-orange soup, pita triangles with garlic butter, roast chicken stuffed with black mushrooms, or a "filo parcel" stuffed with vegetables and glazed with a coriander hollandaise. The room is a minimalist warm white, with stone floors and large windows overlooking the greenery of Santushti Shopping Complex. Alcohol is not served, but this lunch spot is a favorite of Delhi's upper crust and the embassy crowd. [$] *Average main: Rs. 500* ✉ *11 Santushti Shopping Complex, Chanakyapuri, Central Delhi, Delhi* ☎ *11/2467–4933* ✍ *Reservations essential* ⊗ *Closed Sun. No dinner* ✥ *D4.*

$$$$ VIETNAMESE ★ 🍴 **Blue Ginger.** Classy and expensive, with a tantalizing menu full of excellent choices, this is Delhi's only Vietnamese restaurant. Not sure whether to start with Taro prawns or the fresh summer rolls with chicken, shrimp and chives? We'd say order both; you won't be disappointed with the presentation or the flavor. It's equally hard to narrow down the main courses, but the stir-fried prawns with tamarind sauce is an excellent bet, as are lamb shanks in oyster sauce. The adjacent Blue Bar has one of the most innovative cocktail lists in town, so stop in before or after dinner. [$] *Average main: Rs. 1000* ✉ *Taj Palace Hotel, Sardar Patel Marg, Diplomatic Enclave, Chanakyapuri, Central Delhi, Delhi* ☎ *11/2611–0202* 🌐 *www.tajhotels.com* [M] *Dhaula Kuan* ✥ *B4.*

$$$$ NORTH INDIAN ★ 🍴 **Bukhara.** Served amid stone walls, rough-hewn dark-wood beams, copper urns, and blood-red rugs, Bukhara's menu hasn't changed in years, and its loyal clientele wouldn't have it any other way. The cuisine of the Northwest Frontier, now the Pakistan–Afghanistan border, is heavy on meats, marinated and grilled in a *tandoor* (clay oven). The *murgh malai kebab* (boneless chicken marinated with cream cheese, malt vinegar, and green coriander) is very good. Bukhara's famous *dal* (black lentils with tomatoes, ginger, and garlic) is now sold in grocery stores. Vegetarians choices are limited. Service can sometimes be perfunctory, especially for smaller groups. [$] *Average main: Rs. 1550* ✉ *ITC Maurya Hotel, Sardar Patel Marg, Diplomatic Enclave, Chanakyapuri, Central Delhi, Delhi* ☎ *11/2611–2233* 🌐 *www.itcwelcomgroup.in* ✥ *B4.*

$$$$ NORTH INDIAN Fodor's Choice ★ 🍴 **Dum Pukht.** Like the *nawabi* (princely) culture from which it's drawn, the food and style at this restaurant are subtle and refined. Chef Imtiaz Qureshi, descended from court cooks in Avadh (Lucknow), creates delicately spiced meals packed with flavor: *dum ki khumb* (button mushrooms in gravy, fennel, and dried ginger), *kakori kabab* (finely minced mutton, cloves, and cinnamon, drizzled with saffron), and the special *raan-e-dumpukht* (a leg of mutton marinated in dark rum and stuffed with onions, cheese, and mint). The formal room is white, blue, and hushed. [$] *Average main: Rs. 900* ✉ *ITC Maurya Hotel, Sardar Patel Marg, Diplomatic Enclave, Chanakyapuri, Central Delhi, Delhi* ☎ *11/2611–2233* 🌐 *www.itcwelcomgroup.in* ✍ *Reservations essential* ✥ *B4.*

$$$$ INDIAN ★ 🍴 **Fire.** Seasonal ingredients and unexpected flavor combinations update and transform Indian classics, making the Park Hotel's flagship eatery a real standout. Recent stunners included a savory banana stem

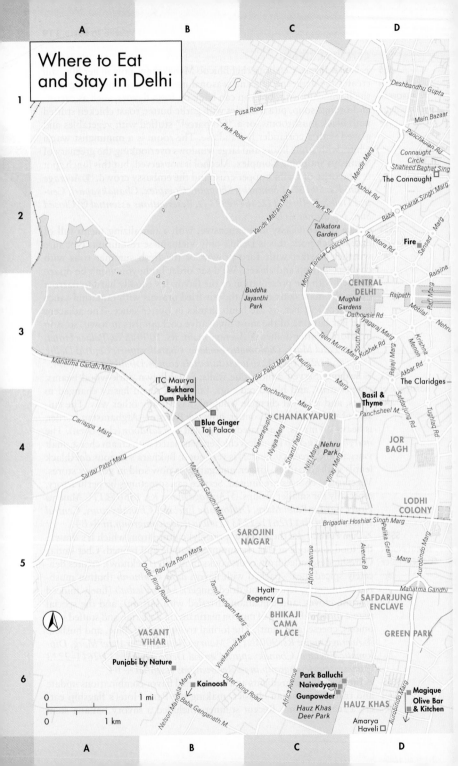

Where to Eat and Stay in Delhi

1

Deshbandhu Gupta

Pusa Road

Park Road

Main Bazaar

Panchkuian Rd.

Connaught Circle

Shaheed Baghat Sing

The Connaught

Mandir Marg

Ashok Rd

Baba Kharak Singh Marg

Sansad Marg

2

Vande Matram Marg

Park St

Talkatora Garden

Mother Teresa Crescent

Talkatora Rd

Fire

Raisina

Buddha Jayanthi Park

CENTRAL DELHI

Mughal Gardens

Rajpath

Rajpath Marg

Dalhousie Rd

Motilal

Nehru

Krishna Menon

3

Mahatma Gandhi Marg

Teen Murti Marg

South Ave

Jyagaraj Marg

Kushak Rd

Rajaji Marg

Akbar Rd

The Claridges

ITC Maurya
Bukhara
Dum Pukht

Sardar Patel Marg

Panchsheel Marg

Kautilya

Marg

Basil & Thyme

Safdarjung Rd

Tughlaq Rd

Cariappa Marg

Blue Ginger
Taj Palace

CHANAKYAPURI

Chandragupta Marg

Nyaya Marg

Shanti Path

Niti Marg

Panchsheel M.

JOR BAGH

4

Sardar Patel Marg

Mahatma Gandhi Marg

Vinay Marg

Nehru Park

LODHI COLONY

5

Outer Ring Road

Rao Tula Ram Marg

Tamil Sangam Marg

SAROJINI NAGAR

Brigadier Hoshiar Singh Marg

Africa Avenue

Avenue B

Palika Gram

Marg

Mahatma Gandhi

SAFDARJUNG ENCLAVE

Hyatt Regency

Aurobindo Marg

VASANT VIHAR

BHIKAJI CAMA PLACE

GREEN PARK

6

Punjabi by Nature

Nelson Mandela Marg

Baba Ganganath M.

Kainoosh

Vivekanand Marg

Outer Ring Road

Africa Avenue

Park Balluchi
Naivedyam
Gunpowder

Hauz Khas Deer Park

HAUZ KHAS

Aurobindo Marg

Magique

Olive Bar & Kitchen

Amarya Haveli

0 _____ 1 mi

0 _____ 1 km

A   B   C   D

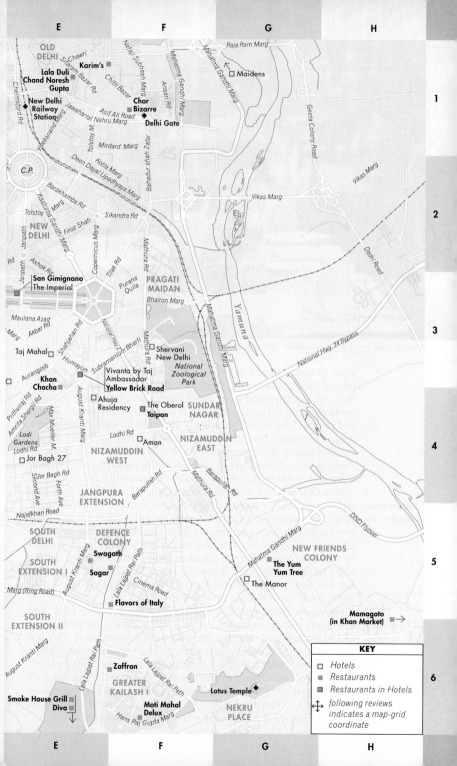

Magique restaurant has an atmospheric setting in the midst of the Garden of 5 Senses.

salad (it uses all parts of the fruit) and a surprisingly light, tomato-infused *dal* (stewed lentils). Regional classics with a twist, such as the fiery chicken chettinad from Tamil Nadu, are consistently delicious menu mainstays. Taster's menus offer a sample of the season's goods, and the carefully chosen wine list is presented by staff knowledgable enough to make informed recommendations, a rarity in Delhi. Service can be haughty. $ *Average main: Rs. 800* ⊠ *The Park New Delhi, 15 Parliament St., Connaught Pl., Central Delhi, Delhi* ☎ *11/2374–3000* ⊕ *www.theparkhotels.com* ⌂ *Reservations essential* ✛ *D2.*

$ ✕ **Khan Chacha.** Much expanded from its original hole-in-the-wall, with tables and standing room, you'll recognize this spot by the crowd of people clamoring for the kebabs hot off the grill. You won't notice the crowds though once you bite into your first chicken *tikka* or *paneer tikka roomali* roll (spiced chicken or soft cheese grilled and wrapped in a thin flatbread). Eat the succulent *seekh kebabs* (minced mutton rolls) before they get cold. $ *Average main: Rs. 120* ⊠ *50 Khan Market, Middle La., Central Delhi, Delhi* ☎ *98/1080–4114, 98/1115–2722* ▭ *No credit cards* Ⓜ *Khan Market* ✛ *E4.*

NORTH INDIAN
Fodor's Choice
★

$$ ✕ **Mamagoto.** "Mamagato" is Japanese for "play with your food" and this cheery restaurant, tucked behind a yellow door in the middle lane of Khan Market, is indeed a fun place for a low-key meal. This is a great spot to have a couple of cocktails and share several dishes. Choose items like the addictive crispy chilli potato from the "small plates" menu to pair with larger dishes like the "signature" Street Vendor's Panang Curry or crispy lamb with onions and peppers. $ *Average main: Rs. 300* ⊠ *53 Khan Market, first fl., Middle La., Central Delhi, Delhi* ☎ *11/4516–6060* ⊕ *www.mamagoto.in* Ⓜ *Khan Market* ✛ *H6.*

ASIAN

$$$$
ITALIAN
✕**San Gimignano.** Chef Ravi Saxena uses his Tuscan training to create playful, sensuous dishes in Delhi's most rarefied Italian restaurant. The three-course regional menu changes periodically, but you might find such fancies as a "flan" of spinach, black olives, and risotto with fresh basil-and-tomato sauce; tagliatelle with a fresh herb sauce of minced duck and Parmesan cheese; sliced grilled tenderloin with grilled polenta and marsala sauce; or grilled milk-fed baby lamb chop with grilled balsamic vegetables. The small wood-paneled rooms are inviting, and in winter you can dine on a terra-cotta patio in the fabulous garden. Service is excellent. $ *Average main: Rs. 950* ✉ *Imperial Hotel, Janpath, Connaught Pl., Central Delhi, Delhi* ☎ *11/2334–1234* ⊕ *www. theimperialhotel.com* ⌕ *Reservations essential* ✛ *E3.*

$$$$
CHINESE
✕**Taipan.** The formal Taipan is one of the finest Chinese restaurants in Delhi. The food is authentic, luscious, and artfully presented, and the view from the top of the Oberoi—over the Delhi Golf Course toward the high-rise buildings of Connaught Place—is grand. The menu highlights Cantonese and Szechuan cooking, including salt-and-pepper prawns, minced prawns with asparagus, Calcutta beckti fish in a *nonya* (spicy lemon) chilli sauce, and various duck dishes. The best-loved house specialty is dim sum, available in a daily fixed-price lunch—reserve in advance for this feast. $ *Average main: Rs. 900* ✉ *The Oberoi Hotel, Dr. Zakir Hussain Rd., next to Delhi Golf Club, Central Delhi, Delhi* ☎ *11/2436–3030* ✛ *F4.*

$$$
INTERNATIONAL
✕**Yellow Brick Road.** Delhi's insomniacs love this super-bright, tiny 24-hour coffee shop. The blinding-yellow striped wallpaper, vintage French-colonial posters, and distressed-yellow tables are a perfect cure for jet lag. The menu wears several hats, mainly North Indian and European, and everything is cheerfully presented. Vegetarian options are many, including tasty paneer dishes, ravioli *calabrese* (with spinach and basil), mushroom crepes, and sweet corn soup. The *chote miya biryani* (lamb in seasoned rice) is rich and filling. $ *Average main: Rs. 500* ✉ *Vivanta by Taj Ambassador Hotel, Subramani Bharti Marg, near Khan Market, Sujan Singh Park, Central Delhi, Delhi* ☎ *11/6637–3502* ⊕ *www.tajhotels.com* Ⓜ *Khan Market* ✛ *E4.*

SOUTH DELHI

$$$$
ITALIAN
✕**Diva.** Count on this popular, classy joint for delicious pizza and pasta—most of Delhi does—but if you're looking for something more substantial, mains like pan-seared lamb chops are also excellent, so make sure to ask about the daily specials. The excellent wine list is a draw here, too, as are top quality desserts like the apple pie with hazelnuts. $ *Average main: Rs. 800* ✉ *M-84 M Block Market, Greater Kailash 2, South Delhi, Delhi* ☎ *11/2921–5673* ⊕ *www.diva-italian. com* ⌕ *Reservations essential* ✛ *E6.*

$$$
ITALIAN
✕**Flavors of Italy.** Nestled in the heart of South Delhi, what started as a tiny ice-cream parlor has morphed into a large space with plenty of seating, both indoors and out. This is a staple for Delhi families, who come for basic, if overpriced, Italian dishes including fresh homemade pastas, a selection of thin-crust pizzas and calzones, bounteous salads, and main courses. Proprietor Tarsillo Nataloni is often on hand to make suggestions, and the beer is always super-chilled. $ *Average main:*

Rs. 550 ✉ 49–54C, Moolchand Flyover Complex, Ring Rd., Defence Colony, South Delhi, Delhi ☎ *11/2464–5644* Ⓜ *Lajpat Nagar* ✢ *F5.*

$$
SOUTH INDIAN

✕ **Gunpowder.** In the center of gallery-and-boutique-filled Hauz Khas village, this is a no-frills, no-fuss spot—though there is a gorgeous view of the reservoir. The restaurant is popular with Delhi denizens who appreciate the mouthwatering offerings on the menu. Coorg pork curry, Kerala mutton stew, *meen* (red fish) curry, and the parathas are top choices, but you can't really go wrong here. Call ahead for reservations, especially if you want to secure a spot on the outdoor balcony to catch sunset over the water. $ *Average main: Rs. 350* ✉ *22 Hauz Khas Village, 3rd fl., South Delhi, Delhi* ☎ *11/2653–5700* ⊕ *www.gunpowder.co.in* ✢ *C6.*

$$$$
MODERN INDIAN
Fodor'sChoice
★

✕ **Kainoosh.** Low-hanging lamps and delicate latticed screens set the refined mood at this upscale Indian restaurant where the extensive menu, with an "India through the ages" theme, covers the whole country. Quail with Rajasthani-influenced marinade is wonderfully succulent, the roti-wrapped leg of chicken with apricot chilli conserve is about as close to poetic as food can get. Their version of create-your-own *thali* (many dishes on one plate) is several steps above the usual: all the lamb options are excellent, as are the prawns, the okra, or anything with lentils. This is Indian food like you've never seen, or tasted, it. $ *Average main: Rs. 925* ✉ *DLF Promenade Mall, Nelson Mandela Marg, ground fl., Vasant Kunj, South Delhi, Delhi* ☎ *95/6071–5544* ⊕ *www.keya-kainoosh.com* ⌣ *Reservations essential* ✢ *B6.*

$$$$
ASIAN
Fodor'sChoice
★

✕ **Magique.** Tucked away in the verdant Garden of Five Senses amid fragrant frangipani trees and hedges strung with lanterns, Magique is one of Delhi's perennially popular restaurants. Wrought-iron candelabras cast a dreamy glow around the glass and wood interior, setting the scene for spectacular food and cocktails. Sip a golden martini—elderflower essence, vodka, and champagne—while you peruse the innovative menu. Starters include juicy crab and lychee wontons and watermelon and feta salad marinated in sake and sprinkled with pine nuts, while mains like char-grilled lamb chops, *khow suey* (a Burmese stew), and duck in tamarind sauce showcase the chef's range of influences. $ *Average main: Rs. 900* ✉ *The Garden Village, Gate 3, The Garden of 5 Senses, Said-ul-Ajaib, near Saket, South Delhi, Delhi* ☎ *11/2953–6767* ⊕ *www.magique.in* Ⓜ *Saket* ✢ *D6.*

$
NORTH INDIAN

✕ **Moti Mahal Delux.** This old-fashioned family restaurant serves North Indian comfort food. It's an update of an Old Delhi classic, Moti Mahal (now under seperate management). The meal of choice is butter chicken, otherwise known as chicken *makhni*, a tomato-based Punjabi classic that sticks to your ribs. The basic chicken curry is also good. There's no plain rice here; the so-called "plain *pulao*," zesty rice made with cumin, has a kick of its own. All meals are served with spicy little pickled onions. There are many other locations. $ *Average main: Rs. 260* ✉ *M-30 Greater Kailash I, South Delhi, Delhi* ☎ *11/2628–0480* ⊕ *www.motimahal.in* ☉ *Closed Tues.* ✢ *F6*

$
SOUTH INDIAN

✕ **Naivedyam.** This dark, soothing restaurant with gold-embossed paintings was designed by artisans from the Tamil Nadu town of Thanjavur. The food is Udupi, a vegetarian cuisine from a town near Mangalore.

All meals begin with a *rasam* (peppery soup) that must be the best in Delhi, and the rice dishes are a great introduction to South Indian home cooking. Try a *dosa*—a giant semolina or lentil-flour crepe filled with spicy potatoes—particularly the *maharaja sajjigemasala dosa,* which also includes vegetables. At night, look for the stained-glass entrance; by day, follow signs for the "South Indian Eating Panorama." Alcohol is not served. [$] *Average main: Rs. 120* ✉ *1 Hauz Khas Village, South Delhi, Delhi* ☎ *11/2696–0426* ✣ *C6.*

$$ MEDITERRANEAN 🍴 **Olive Bar & Kitchen.** Though sprawling in the shadow of the Qutub Minar, at Olive Bar & Kitchen you might believe you're in Santorini, or on the Italian Riviera. White on white is the color scheme, from the stucco walls to the pebbles in the courtyard to the cluster of white carnations on each table. The world cuisine has an emphasis on the Mediterranean, so you'll find options like a light-as-air goat-cheese soufflé, several pizza options, and pastas like the lasagna *verdure* or blue-cheese gnocchi, as well as Cajun spiced fish, Australian lamb chops, and Spanish style chicken *a la plancha.* [$] *Average main: Rs. 495* ✉ *Haveli 6–8, One Style Mile, Kalkadass Marg, near Qutub Minar, Mehrauli, South Delhi, Delhi* ☎ *11/2957–4444* 🌐 *www.olivebarandkitchen.com* ✣ *D6.*

$$ NORTH INDIAN 🍴 **Park Balluchi.** No, it's not Italian; it's Baluchistan, now in Pakistan. With glass on three sides to better enjoy the surrounding park, this kebab house serves amazing barbecue dishes: *nawabi kesri kabab* (chicken marinated in a saffron mixture, stuffed with chopped chicken, and grilled), *murg potli* (marinated chicken breast wrapped around minced mutton and flambéed), and *mewa paneer tukra* (soft cheese stuffed with nuts, currants, and mushrooms, marinated in cream and grilled). Kebabs are served all day; other dishes are not served between 3:30 and 6. Service can be extraordinarily slow and poorly informed. Reservations essential for dinner. [$] *Average main: Rs. 480* ✉ *Deer Park, Hauz Khas Village, South Delhi* ☎ *11/2685–9369* 🌐 *www.parkballuchi.com* ✣ *C6.*

$$$ NORTH INDIAN 🍴 **Punjabi by Nature.** It my no longer be the hip venue it once was, but its versions of hearty Punjabi classics like *murgh Punjabi masala* (the house chicken curry), *dal makhni* (black lentils with butter and cream), and *raan-e-Punjab* (a tender whole leg of lamb grilled just so) make up for it. In true Punjabi style, the over-the-top purple and gold interior remains, as does the most popular gimmick: *golgappas* (fried dough containers) filled with vodka instead of traditional spicy water. The noisy upstairs lounge is a fun place for a drink before a movie at nearby PVR Priya. [$] *Average main: Rs. 595* ✉ *11 Basant Lok, Vasant Vihar, South Delhi, Delhi* ☎ *11/5151–6666* 🌐 *www.punjabibynature.in* ✣ *B6.*

$ SOUTH INDIAN 🍴 **Sagar.** This no-frills, three-story vegetarian family joint bustles nonstop from 8 am to 11 pm. The dosa is king, and you can choose from 20 varieties, including some made with *rava* (semolina) rather than lentil flour. The vegetable *uttapam* (rice-flour pancake) is also good, and there's a North Indian menu with delicious *bhindi masala* (spicy okra). The wonderful *thalis,* or combination platters, are served from 11 to 3 and 7 to 11. [$] *Average main: Rs. 130* ✉ *18 Defence Colony Market, South Delhi, Delhi* ☎ *11/2433–3110* 🌐 *sagarratna.in* [M] *Lajpat Nagar* ✣ *E5.*

$$$$ MODERN EUROPEAN Fodor's Choice ★ 🍴 **Smoke House Grill.** The fashionable crowd clamors to get into this cousin of Mumbai's acclaimed Saltwater Grill, where the food is delicious and the drinks are desirable. Order anything with "smoke" in the name—from smoke-house chicken (two perfectly cooked smoked chicken breasts served with impeccably seasoned green beans and roasted potatoes) to smoked apple and rosemary pie. The smoked melon martini defies words, and the smoked apple mojito is even better. Unlike most see-and-be-seen places, service is unpretentious and friendly. The contemporary comic-book panels on blood-red walls and gleaming chrome staircase feels industrial—odd, but it works. Reservations are advised. [$] *Average main: Rs. 1300* ✉ *North Wing, VIPPS Center, LSC Masjid Moth, Greater Kailash II, South Delhi, Delhi* ☎ *11/4143–5530* 🌐 *www.smokehousegrill.in* ✣ *E6.*

$$ SOUTH INDIAN 🍴 **Swagath.** Delhi's original Mangalorean restaurant—specializing in seafood from the western coast between Goa and Kerala—is outstanding. Choose your sauce, then decide between fish, prawns, or crab. Anything served *sawantwadi* (in spicy mint-and-coriander sauce) is unforgettable, as is *gassi,* a mild coconut-flavored gravy, and the butter-pepper-garlic sauce. Another specialty is Chettinad food from Tamil Nadu, cooked in a very spicy black-pepper sauce (there's also decent Chinese and North Indian food). Mop up your food with *appam* or *neer dosa,* soft South Indian rice breads. The prim dining rooms are softly lit, and service is excellent. Doors are open all day. [$] *Average main: Rs. 475* ✉ *14 Defence Colony Market, South Delhi, Delhi* ☎ *11/2433–0930* 🌐 *www.swagath.in* [M] *Lajpat Nagar* ✣ *E5.*

$$$ ASIAN Fodor's Choice ★ 🍴 **The Yum Yum Tree.** Yum is the key word at this large but tastefully decorated Pan-Asian spot. The sushi attracts high praise, and selections from the extensive list of hot foods are also top-notch. For starters, try the crispy duck spring rolls with gooseberry sauce, barbecue pork buns (*bao*), or prawn and water-chestnut *har gao* (dumplings). Mains like sweet and crispy pork with pineapple, chilli roasted eggplant, and duck pancakes should be next. There are great desserts too, from the simple chocolate-dipped fresh figs to something more elaborate like cream-cheese-and-walnut-stuffed deep-fried wontons drizzled with strawberry coulis. [$] *Average main: Rs. 585* ✉ *Community Centre Market, 2nd fl., New Friends Colony, South Delhi, Delhi* ☎ *11/4260–2020* 🌐 *www.theyumyumtree.in* ✣ *G5.*

$$ NORTH INDIAN 🍴 **Zaffran.** Simple presentations of classic Punjabi and Mughlai fare such as *raan* (leg of mutton), tandoori naan, and *dal makhani* (lentils with tomatoes, ginger, garlic, and cream) draw top marks here thanks to fresh ingredients and a light hand with the oil and ghee (not the case at many North Indian joints). Zaffran also serves excellent spicy biryani (rice and meat, cooked together) and imports Parsi *kulfi* (ice cream) from a dairy in Mumbai. Despite it's popularity with families and the busy open kitchen, the minimalist blond-wood dining room is refreshingly calm, thanks largely to efficient, friendly, and knowledgeable staff. [$] *Average main: Rs. 485* ✉ *N-2 Kasbah restaurant complex, N-Block Market, Greater Kailash-I, South Delhi, Delhi* ☎ *11/4163–5000* 🌐 *www.kasbahrestaurants.com* ✣ *F6.*

WHERE TO STAY

ABOUT THE HOTELS

Unless we note otherwise, all the hotels we list have air-conditioning, bathrooms with tubs, currency exchange, and room service. Most have a doctor on call. In addition, all hotels have wireless or broadband Internet access and deluxe hotels have executive floors with special lounges and services for business travelers. You *must* reserve in advance for stays between October and February, as even the largest hotels fill up.

Prices in the reviews are the lowest cost of a standard double room in high season. For expanded hotel reviews, facilities, and current deals, visit Fodors.com.

OLD DELHI

$$ HOTEL **Maidens.** Opened in 1903, before New Delhi even existed, this is one of the city's oldest hotels, and with a Metro station adjacent, it's a speedy, air-conditioned ride from both Old Delhi and Connaught Place. **Pros:** coffee shop has a nice patio and an English feel, especially when British tour groups are in residence; renovations have brightened up the rooms. **Cons:** even with the metro, you are removed from the rest of the city; food and beverage options are limited. [$] *Rooms from: Rs. 5500* ✉ *7 Sham Nath Marg, Civil Lines* ☎ *11/2397–5464* 🌐 *www.maidenshotel.com* 🛏 *53 rooms, 3 suites* 🍴 *No meals* [M] *Civil Lines* ✥ *G1.*

CENTRAL DELHI

$$$$ HOTEL **The Claridges, Delhi.** In 1950, three years after Independence, an Indian family was talked into building a hotel with a British aesthetic, and the result was a winner: tasteful yet unpretentious, in a central yet quiet location. **Pros:** Sevilla, the Mediterranean eatery, gets high marks; excellent pool. **Cons:** rooms near the nightclub can be noisy. [$] *Rooms from: Rs. 15000* ✉ *12 Aurangzeb Rd., Central Delhi* ☎ *11/3955–5000* 🌐 *www.claridges.com* 🛏 *128 rooms, 12 suites* 🍴 *Breakfast* [M] *Race Course* ✥ *E4.*

$$$ HOTEL **The Connaught.** About 1 km (½ mile) from Connaught Place, this mid-size hotel is close to the center of things yet far enough away from the hubbub. **Pros:** rooms on the east side directly overlook a field-hockey stadium, which is more appealing than it sounds; attached RBS Travels agency provides round-the-clock service. **Cons:** small rooms; some travelers report extremely poor service here. [$] *Rooms from: Rs. 9000* ✉ *37 Shaheed Bhagat Singh Marg, near Shivaji Stadium, Connaught Pl., Central Delhi, Delhi* ☎ *11/2336–4225* 🌐 *www.theconnaughtnewdelhi.com* 🛏 *78 rooms, 9 suites* 🍴 *No meals* [M] *Rajiv Chowk* ✥ *D2.*

$$$$ HOTEL Fodor's Choice ★ **The Imperial.** Easily the most appealing hotel in Delhi, with a driveway lined by soaring king palms, the luxurious Imperial offers unparalleled service and location. **Pros:** top-notch restaurants and bar. **Cons:** extremely expensive; standard rooms on the small side. [$] *Rooms from: Rs. 10500* ✉ *Janpath, south of Tolstoy Marg, Connaught Pl., Central Delhi, Delhi* ☎ *11/2334–1234* 🌐 *www.theimperialindia.com* 🛏 *180 rooms, 43 suites* 🍴 *No meals* ✥ *E3.*

$$$ B&B/INN 🏨 **Shervani New Delhi.** In a central yet quiet location, The Shervani has good amenities—from electronic keys and wall safes to flat-screen televisions—in rooms that were renovated in 2006. **Pros:** staff is efficient, friendly, and willing to go out of its way for guests. **Cons:** in-house food options are limited; taxis at the neighborhood stand can be slow to arrive. [$] *Rooms from: Rs. 6000* ✉ *11 Sunder Nagar, Central Delhi, Delhi* ☎ *11/4250–1000* 🌐 *www.shervanihotels.com* 🛏 *19 rooms, 3 suites* 🍴 *Breakfast* ✥ *F3.*

$$$$ HOTEL 🏨 **Taj Mahal.** The Taj Mansingh, as it's locally known, is Delhi's premier social hotel, with nightly cocktail affairs, cultural events, and the occasional society weddings drawing the glitterati. **Pros:** centrally located in Lutyens' Delhi; popular with business travelers and celebrities, and the service is correspondingly slick; excellent dining options, including Varq and Wasabi by Marimoto. **Cons:** rooms on the small side. [$] *Rooms from: Rs. 23000* ✉ *1 Mansingh Rd., Central Delhi* ☎ *11/2302–6162* 🌐 *www.tajhotels.com* 🛏 *267 rooms, 27 suites* 🍴 *No meals* [M] *Khan Market* ✥ *E3.*

SOUTH DELHI

$$ B&B/INN Fodor's Choice ★ 🏨 **Ahuja Residency.** This little-known guesthouse is a jewel, Delhi's only combination of style and affordability, where hospitality and attention to detail are second to none. **Pros:** immaculately clean; fresh-squeezed juice at breakfast; organic bath products. **Cons:** reservations difficult to get; bathrooms have showers only. [$] *Rooms from: Rs. 5000* ✉ *193 Golf Links, Central Delhi, Delhi* ☎ *11/2462–2255* 🌐 *www.ahujaresidency.com* 🛏 *12 rooms* 🍴 *Breakfast* [M] *Khan Market* ✥ *F4.*

$$$$ HOTEL 🏨 **Aman.** An exclusive hotel at an exclusive address, the Delhi Aman is over-the-top luxury all the way, starting with the private pool nestled on the balcony of each of the rooms. **Pros:** luxurious to the hilt; next door to Khan Market and close to Lodhi Garden; excellent restaurants; great spa. **Cons:** staff can be hard to find when you need them; the price. [$] *Rooms from: Rs. 34365* ✉ *Lodhi Rd., Central Delhi, Delhi* ☎ *11/4363–3333* 🌐 *www.amanresorts.com* 🛏 *31 rooms, 36 suites* 🍴 *No meals* ✥ *F4.*

$$$ B&B/INN Fodor's Choice ★ 🏨 **Amarya Haveli.** Run by two charming Frenchmen, Amarya Haveli, in the quiet and cozy residential Hauz Khas enclave, is comfortably kitschy with themed rooms and friendly staff. **Pros:** chic, well-designed space; great en suite bathrooms. **Cons:** room service can be slow. [$] *Rooms from: Rs. 6900* ✉ *P-5, Hauz Khas Enclave, near Safdarjung Developmental Area, South Delhi, Delhi* ☎ *11/4175–9268, 11/4175–9267* 🌐 *www.amaryagroup.com/amarya-haveli* 🛏 *6 rooms* 🍴 *Breakfast* ✥ *D6.*

$$$ HOTEL 🏨 **Hyatt Regency.** For its size and range of amenities, the Hyatt has a surprisingly homey feel. **Pros:** the shopping arcade is easily the best in Delhi, with dozens of shops selling jewelry, handicrafts, Kashmiri carpets and more; the pool may take top honors, too. **Cons:** service can be impersonal; pricier than the competition. [$] *Rooms from: Rs. 8000* ✉ *Ring Rd., Bhikaji Cama Pl., South Delhi, Delhi* ☎ *11/2679–1234* 🌐 *www.delhi.hyatt.com* 🛏 *501 rooms, 6 suites* 🍴 *Breakfast* ✥ *C5.*

$$$$ HOTEL 🏨 **ITC Maurya.** A favorite with executives and dignitaries, the Maurya works hard to style itself as the swankest hotel in Delhi, and the whole place has the buzz of importance. **Pros:** knockout restaurants draw

The Imperial

Ahuja Residency

The Oberoi

as many locals as travelers, especially the famous Bukhara and Dum Pukht; pool and gym are best-in-class; business services get top marks. **Cons:** far from most major sites; chattering tour groups can dominate the atmosphere. $ *Rooms from: Rs. 19500* ✉ *Sardar Patel Marg, Diplomatic Enclave, Chanakyapuri, South Delhi, Delhi* ☎ *11/2611–2233* 🌐 *www.itchotels.in* 🛏 *411 rooms, 29 suites* 🍴 *Breakfast* ✥ *B4.*

$$ B&B/INN 🏨 **Jor Bagh 27.** Peace, proximity, and price are the benefits at this whitewashed guesthouse—popular with visiting UN and World Bank staffers—opposite Lodhi Garden. **Pros:** five minutes from Khan Market; serene neighborhood. **Cons:** some rooms are shabby—look at what's available before you settle in; breakfast is the only meal served here; generator cannot run all air-conditioners for very long, so this isn't your best bet in summer. $ *Rooms from: Rs. 4500* ✉ *27 Jor Bagh, South Delhi, Delhi* ☎ *11/2469–8647* 🌐 *www.jorbagh27.com* 🛏 *18 rooms* 🍴 *No meals* [M] *Jor Bagh* ✥ *E4.*

$$$$ HOTEL 🏨 **The Manor.** In one of Delhi's wealthiest residential neighborhoods, this is Delhi's premier boutique hotel with a stylish ultramodern interior, a nouvelle-Indian restaurant, and stunning, ultraprivate grounds. **Pros:** romantic, candlelighted restaurant. **Cons:** slightly off the beaten path and extremely difficult for drivers to locate; far from most sites and restaurants. $ *Rooms from: Rs. 10500* ✉ *77 Friends Colony West, South Delhi* ☎ *11/4323–5151* 🌐 *www.themanordelhi.com* 🛏 *15 rooms* 🍴 *Breakfast* ✥ *G5.*

$$$$ HOTEL Fodor's Choice ★ 🏨 **The Oberoi.** A beloved favorite of those who visit Delhi often, the city's first modern luxury hotel, built in 1965, is distinguished by its calm—even when it's packed, the sleek, black-marble lobby is peaceful. **Pros:** restaurants are among Delhi's finest; top-flight spa. **Cons:** extremely expensive. $ *Rooms from: Rs. 21500* ✉ *Dr. Zakir Hussain Rd., next to Delhi Golf Club, South Delhi, Delhi* ☎ *11/2436–3030* 🌐 *www.oberoihotels.com* 🛏 *252 rooms, 31 suites* 🍴 *No meals* ✥ *F4.*

$$$$ HOTEL 🏨 **Taj Palace.** Facilities are top-notch in this giant, boomerang-shaped hotel with first-rate business services and good leisure amenities. **Pros:** business services are best-in-class; has one of India's finest European restaurants. **Cons:** far from some tourist sites; in high season you'll battle package-tour crowds. $ *Rooms from: Rs. 23000* ✉ *Sardar Patel Marg, Diplomatic Enclave, Chanakyapuri, South Delhi, Delhi* ☎ *11/2611–0202* 🌐 *www.tajhotels.com* 🛏 *362 rooms, 40 suites* 🍴 *Breakfast* [M] *Dhaula Kuan* ✥ *B4.*

$$$$ HOTEL 🏨 **Vivanta by Taj Ambassador Hotel.** In an exclusive 1930s neighborhood dripping with late-Raj charm, this quiet Taj Group hotel's service is heart-warmingly friendly, and it costs a bit less than its glamorous siblings. **Pros:** excellent value for money; next door to Khan Market and close to Lodhi Garden. **Cons:** not as up-to-date as other, similarly priced properties. $ *Rooms from: Rs. 15500* ✉ *Subramania Bharti Marg, near Khan Market, Sujan Sing Park, South Delhi, Delhi* ☎ *11/2463–2600* 🌐 *www.tajhotels.com* 🛏 *76 rooms, 12 suites* 🍴 *No meals* [M] *Khan Market* ✥ *E3.*

NIGHTLIFE AND THE ARTS

THE ARTS

Delhi is India's cultural hub, if only because performers from all over the country come to the capital at least once a year to cultivate their national audience. Painting, music, dance, theater, and, of course, film are all well represented. The India Habitat Centre, a large, modern cultural center, has the best combination of all of the above; on any given evening, it hosts several good programs. The only problem is that hype is nonexistent, so you must be persistent to find out what's happening—pick up the biweekly *Time Out.* Failing that, the daily newspapers, especially the *Indian Express* and the *Hindustan Times,* are also good sources. The staff at your hotel may be able to help, too.

ART GALLERIES

Delhi's art scene is extremely dynamic. Contemporary Indian painting—which often blends traditional Indian motifs with Western techniques—is blossoming, but if you're looking to buy, bargains are hard to come by. Private galleries have mushroomed and art prices have skyrocketed. Most galleries are quite small, so if you want a broad view of what's happening, hire a car or taxi for an afternoon of gallery-hopping. Authenticating any major purchases is advisable. Pick up the latest *Time Out Delhi* for exhibit details and profiles of featured artists. Many galleries are closed on Sunday. Hauz Khas Village has a cluster of galleries.

Art Heritage. Part of a cultural institute with several galleries and performing spaces, Art Heritage has some of the finest exhibits in town. ⊠ *Triveni Kala, Sangam, 205 Tansen Marg, Mandi House, near Connaught Place, Central Delhi, Delhi* ☎ *11/2371–9470* ⊕ *www.artheritagegallery.com* Ⓜ *Mandi House.*

Delhi Art Gallery. A substantial collection of paintings by old masters and contemporary artists can be seen here; it often hosts comprehensive historical art exhibitions. ⊠ *11 Hauz Khas Village, South Delhi, Delhi* ☎ *11/2656–8166* ⊕ *www.delhiartgallery.com.*

★ **Devi Art Foundation.** Established by the Poddar family in 2008, the Devi Art Foundation, with it's sprawling exhibition area, is out of the way for the typical visitor—and the walk from the Metro station is unpleasant—but it's worth a visit for art enthusiasts. Shows on various themes are usually curated out of the permanent collection, which consists of long-time collector Lekha Poddar's folk art and historically significant acquisitions, as well as her son Anupam's trove of more cutting-edge contemporary works (he's a high-end hotelier). ⊠ *Sirpur House, Plot 39, Sector 44, Gurgaon, South Delhi, Delhi* ☎ *0124/488–8177* ⊕ *www.deviartfoundation.org* 🎫 *free* ☉ *Tues.–Sun. 11–7* Ⓜ *HUDA City Centre.*

Dhoomimal Gallery. It's a bit chaotic, with a focus on older contemporary artists, but this gallery is centrally located and large. ⊠ *G-42 and A-8 Connaught Pl., Central Delhi, Delhi* ☎ *11/4151–6056* ⊕ *www.dhoomimalgallery.com* Ⓜ *Rajiv Chowk.*

Gallery Espace. A small but remarkable space featuring both new and canonical artists, sometimes mixed together in interesting theme shows. ⊠ *16 Community Centre, New Friends Colony, South Delhi, Delhi* 🕾 *11/2362–6267* ⊕ *www.galleryespace.com.*

Habitat World. The various exhibition spaces here showcase painting, sculpture, Indian craft, and creativity of every kind. The main Visual Arts Gallery is just inside Gate 2. ⊠ *India Habitat Centre, Lodhi Rd., South Delhi, Delhi* 🕾 *11/2468–2222* ⊕ *www.indiahabitat.org.*

Lalit Kala Akademi. This government-run gallery is a large 1950s building showing several exhibits at once, usually of varying quality. ⊠ *Rabindra Bhavan, near Connaught Pl., Central Delhi, Delhi* 🕾 *11/2338–7243* ⊕ *lalitkala.gov.in* Ⓜ *Mandi House.*

Navratana. Navratana is a tiny but spirited hoard of old paintings, photographs, and movie posters, with a few contemporary works thrown in. ⊠ *2A Hauz Khas Village, South Delhi* 🕾 *11/45600–5300* ⊕ *www. navratana.com.*

Nature Morte. This is one of the most cutting-edge art and photography galleries in town. ⊠ *A-1 Neeti Bagh, opposite Kamla Nehru College, Neeti Bagh, South Delhi, Delhi* 🕾 *11/4174–0215* ⊕ *www.naturemorte.com.*

The Stainless. One of the more unusual galleries in Delhi, this space welcomes designers, architects, artists, and sculptors to display their work, and there is a permanent collection of stainless-steel installations. ⊠ *Mira Suites Complex, 1&2, Old Ishwar Nagar, Mathura Rd., Okhla Crossing, South Delhi, Delhi* 🕾 *11/4260–3167* ⊕ *www. thestainless.com.*

Vadehra Art Gallery. Respected for its permanent collection of 20th-century masters, this is also one of Delhi's best galleries for contemporary, established artists. There are several locations. ⊠ *D-40 Defence Colony, South Delhi, Delhi* 🕾 *11/2461–5368* ⊕ *www.vadehraart.com* Ⓜ *Lajpat Nagar.*

FILM

India's Mumbai-based film industry, known as Bollywood, produces more films annually than any other country in the world. Most Bollywood films are in Hindi, but anyone can understand them—most are romantic musicals, with dollops of family drama and occasionally a violent villain. Delhi cinemas show all the latest Hindi movies plus a few current Hollywood films, the latter tending toward action and young romantic comedy. To find out what's playing, check listings in the magazine section of any daily newspaper. If your movie of choice is a hot new release, consider buying tickets a day in advance; your hotel can help, and tickets can often be bought online.

PVR Plaza ⊠ *H Block, Connaught Pl., Central Delhi, Delhi* ⊕ *www.pvrcinemas.com* Ⓜ *Rajiv Chowk.*

PVR Saket ⊠ *Community Centre, Saket, South Delhi, Delhi* ⊕ *www.pvrcinemas.com* Ⓜ *Malviya Nagar.*

Art films from all over the world are shown at various cultural institutes; the monthly magazine *Time Out* has listings.

NAVJOT ALTAF
Touch – 2008
Duco paint on fiber glass
83.5 x 55 x 64 in. / 212.1 x 162 c...

Inside the Delhi Art Gallery

MUSIC AND DANCE

Great musicians and dancers are always passing through Delhi. Incredibly, most performances are free, but tickets ("passes") are sometimes required for high-demand performers.

India Habitat Centre. Several events take place here every evening. ✉ *Lodhi Rd., Lodhi Institutional Area, South Delhi, Delhi* ☎ *11/2468–2222* ⊕ *www.indiahabitat.org.*

India International Centre. This is an established performance space near the Habitat Centre. ✉ *40 Max Mueller Marg., Lodhi Estate, South Delhi, Delhi* ☎ *11/2461–9431.*

Kamani Auditorium. This is a long-standing venue for Indian classical music and dance. ✉ *1 Copernicus Marg, Mandi House, Central Delhi, Delhi* ☎ *11/4350–3351* ⊕ *www.kamaniauditorium.org* Ⓜ *Mandi House.*

Triveni Kala Sangam. In addition to the art galleries, regular dance performances and classes take place here. ✉ *205 Tansen Marg, near Connaught Pl., Central Delhi, Delhi* ☎ *11/2371–8833* Ⓜ *Mandi House.*

THEATER

India has an ancient dramatic tradition, and *nautanki* plays, which combine drama, comedy, and song, are still held in many villages. Delhi has an active theater scene in both English and Hindi, with many shows locally written, produced, and performed. Most run only for one weekend and don't travel afterward, so they can seem a bit unpolished even when they're fundamentally good.

India Habitat Centre. A regular venue for local theater troupes. ⊠ *Lodhi Rd., Lodhi Institutional Area, South Delhi, Delhi* ☎ *11/2468–2222* ⊕ *www.indiahabitat.org.*

LTG Auditorium. This is a veteran theater with performances by local and student groups. ⊠ *Copernicus Marg, Mandi House, near Connaught Pl., Central Delhi, Delhi* ☎ *11/2338–9713* Ⓜ *Mandi House.*

Shri Ram Centre. A constant stream of plays are staged here, some for one day only. ⊠ *4 Safdar Hashmi Marg, near Connaught Pl., Central Delhi, Delhi* ☎ *11/2371–4307* ⊕ *www.shriramcentre.org* Ⓜ *Mandi House.*

NIGHTLIFE

Delhi's nightlife is in a constant state of flux and among the growing set of young people who can afford it, the scene is intense. Various forms of the watering hole are now on offer, with the lounge bar emerging as the most successful formula. Though it doesn't rival the cosmopolitan feel of Mumbai, it seems as if a new lounge opens in Delhi every week. That said, the city's somewhat stodgy reputation is still partly deserved: All the major hotels have bars, but most are better suited for a collective nap with a few tired foreigners than a night of Indian camaraderie; they still shut by midnight and many nightclubs close not much later, though there are a few all-night venues. Hotel bars come in two stripes: aiming for a British Raj look and an older, quieter clientele, or raucous, late-night dance clubs. Drinks prices come close to those in London and New York. Those in search of late-night dancing and drinking sometimes head for the suburbs or five-star hotels that can stay open later.

The disco scene has undergone a transformation in recent years. Select places attract top international DJs and charge cover prices to match. Slowly electronic dance music is overtaking drunk renditions of classic rock and Bollywood favorites at most places. Overly casual attire (shorts, T-shirts, sandals on men) is typically frowned on, and closing times tend to vary with the mood of the city government that month.

CENTRAL DELHI
BARS AND PUBS
Baci. Baci is a charming Italian-style bistro that serenades with soft jazz. The sophisticated cocktail list has some delicious creamy drinks. Make sure you order the tiramisu with whatever you're drinking, especially the Irish coffee. ⊠ *23 Sunder Nagar Market, Central Delhi* ☎ *11/4150–7445.*

Blues. A vaguely Chicagoesque rock bar with occasional live music nights. ⊠ *N-18 Connaught Pl., Outer Circle, Central Delhi, Delhi* ☎ *11/4152–3486* Ⓜ *Rajiv Chowk.*

Q'BA. A cavernous space, a pleasant terrace with wonderful views, and well-mixed drinks that all add up to a pleasant nightspot. ⊠ *E-42/43 Connaught Pl., Inner Circle, Central Delhi, Delhi* ☎ *11/4151–2888* ⊕ *www.qba.co.in* Ⓜ *Rajiv Chowk.*

★ **Rick's.** A magnet for Delhi's beautiful people, with as many voices yelling into their cell phones as talking to each other. The booze selection is hard to beat, and the snacks are Southeast Asian. Go before 9 pm if you want a seat. ⊠ *Taj Mahal Hotel, 1 Mansingh Rd., Central Delhi* ☏ *11/2302–6162* Ⓜ *Khan Market.*

HOTEL BARS AND LOUNGES

1911. The large bar here is a classic watering hole decked out the way it looked during the Independence movement in the 1940s. The drink menu is massive, and lounge music keeps the vibe contemporary. ⊠ *Imperial Hotel, Janpath, Connaught Pl., Central Delhi, Delhi* ☏ *11/2334–1234* ⊕ *www.theimperialindia.com.*

Agni. Named for the Vedic fire god, the swanky Agni, in the lobby of the Park Hotel, attracts Delhi's party crowd, playing electronic interspersed with pop, hip-hop, and Bollywood hits. The door staff can be selective. ⊠ *The Park Hotel, 15 Parliament St., near Connaught Pl., Central Delhi, Delhi* ☏ *11/2374–3000* ⊕ *www.theparkhotels.com.*

Aqua. As the name suggests, Aqua is a giant outdoor space focused on a large swimming pool surrounded with lovely cabanas. It's well-heeled, especially when compared to its crazy next-door neighbor, Agni. ⊠ *The Park Hotel, 15 Parliament St., Connaught Pl., Central Delhi, Delhi* ☏ *11/2374-3000* ⊕ *www.theparkhotels.com.*

SOUTH DELHI

BARS AND PUBS

Hard Rock Café. This isn't especially India, but it does sometimes book some interesting bands (call for the weekly performance schedule). If you're homesick for the States, a plate of nachos, washed down with a margarita or two, will at least help you to the point where you don't know where on earth you are. ⊠ *M-110 DLF Place Mall, first fl., District Centre, Saket, South Delhi, Delhi* ☏ *11/4715–8888* Ⓜ *Malviya Nagar.*

Keya. Chic, chic, chic, and the cocktails are innovative and delicious: street-food-inspired concoctions include the betel-leaf martini and the sour mango mojito. It's one of the new classics in town and has a loyal following. ⊠ *DLF Promenade Mall, Nelson Mandela Marg., Vasant Kunj, South Delhi, Delhi* ☏ *95607–15533* ⊕ *www.keya-kainoosh.com.*

Magique. A Delhi favorite: it's hard to resist the alfresco charms, or the lure of the extremely evolved drinks list. Sit outside in the dewy breeze of a mist fan, on the large swing, with an Irish espresso martini, and you'll see what we mean. ⊠ *The Garden Village, Garden of 5 Senses, Said-ul-Ajaib, South Delhi, Delhi* ☏ *11/2953–6767.*

Smoke House Grill. The bar here is still a hot place for a drink—the wine selection is good, but innovative cocktails like the Smoke House Elixir are the real draw, and the place is buzzing on weekends. ⊠ *North Wing, VIPPS Center, LSC Masjid Moth, Greater Kailash II, South Delhi, Delhi* ☏ *11/4143–5530* ⊕ *smokehousegrill.in.*

Stone. This laid-back lounge with plenty of low-slung couches is where Expats head for quiet drinks and conversation over wood-fired pizza. ⊠ *Moets Restaurant Complex, 50 Defence Colony Market, Defence Colony, South Delhi, Delhi* ☏ *11/6569–7689* ⊕ *www.moets.com* Ⓜ *Lajpat Nagar.*

The Smoke House Grill is popular for dinner or just for drinks at the bar.

HOTEL BARS AND LOUNGES

Golf Bar. At the dark and publike Golf Bar, you're sure to hear cheesy pop and rock hits from the '80s onward (think wedding reception). Some nights it's just elderly gentlemen sipping whiskey-sodas, while other nights you may stumble on a party in full-swing. ⊠ *ITC Maurya Hotel, Sardar Patel Marg, Diplomatic Enclave, Chanakyapuri, South Delhi, Delhi* ☎ *11/2611–2233* ⊕ *www.itchotels.in.*

F Bar & Lounge. The lights pulse in this large, otherwise dark space till about 4 am on weekends. A hot spot for several years, F Bar is not far from Shiro in the Samrat Hotel, making disco-hopping a possibility. ⊠ *Ashoka Hotel, 50B Chanakyapuri, Diplomatic Enclave, South Delhi, Delhi* ☎ *11/2611–1066.*

Polo Lounge. While very much a hotel bar, this place can be very lively. The wood-paneled room has a curved bar, a leather sofa, a library with newspapers, an oddball collection of books, and sports channels playing on TV. ⊠ *Hyatt Regency, Ring Rd., Bhikaji Cama Pl., South Delhi, Delhi* ☎ *11/2679–1234.*

SHOPPING

Delhi is a shopping center for goods from all over India, making it the best place to stock up on gifts and souvenirs. Bargaining is often appropriate—and almost mandatory. A good rule of thumb: When the price is written down, it's probably fixed; when you have to inquire about the price, it's negotiable.

In shops where foreign customers are uncommon, the staff is likely to follow your every move with great interest. If this bothers you, simply state your objective or emphasize that you're just looking; they'll cooperate if you indicate nicely that you don't need to be followed around.

Old Delhi is an endlessly interesting place to shop, admittedly more for the experience than for what you'll take away. The sidewalks of Chandni Chowk are lined with clocks, baby clothes, tacky toys, blankets, and much more; the shops on Dariba Kalan are filled with silver and gold jewelry. Stalls behind the Jama Masjid sell metalware and utensils, and one street specializes in stationery, especially Indian wedding invitations. Kinari Bazaar glistens with Hindu wedding paraphernalia. Khari Baoli, west of Chandni Chowk toward Lahori Gate, is renowned for its wholesale nuts, spices, and Indian pickles and chutneys.

India has one of the world's foremost Oriental-rug industries, and there are carpet vendors all over Delhi. Unfortunately, carpet sellers are a notoriously dishonest crowd. In addition to being obnoxiously pushy, they are likely to sell you inauthentic merchandise at colossally inflated prices and then deny it later. There are some exceptions to this rule, but they tend to sell out of their homes rather than upscale showrooms—so call before you go.

Clothes shopping is one of Delhi's great pleasures. *Khadi,* the hand-spun, hand-woven cotton that Gandhi turned into a nationalist symbol during the Independence movement, has made a roaring comeback and is now worn by many Delhi women during the long, hot summer. You can experience khadi in a salwar-kameez—the classic North Indian ensemble of long tunic and loose pants, also popular in a variation called the kurta-churidar—and in Western-style tops and skirts. Some Indian fabrics can fade or bleed easily, so it's always a good idea to wash clothes first before wearing.

If you find yourself shopping for a sari, savor the experience of learning about this amazing handicraft. Silks and attractive cotton saris are sometimes sold at Dilli Haat market, depending on which vendors have set up shop that week. Silks are sold en masse at upscale stores in South Extension, Greater Kailash I, and Connaught Place, but the highest thumbs-up go to Kalpana and Padakkam.

For crafts and curios, Delhi's fixed-price government emporiums near Connaught Place offer good values to travelers with limited time. They're also conveniently open seven days a week. The best market for fine curios and antiques is in the exclusive leafy neighborhood of Sundar Nagar. In addition to the shops listed here, a few shops on the southern (right-hand) side of the market have collections of old optical instruments.

Jewelry is another popular item on visitors' shopping lists. India consumes more gold annually than any other country in the world, mainly because gold is an essential part of a bride's trousseau. With Delhi's upper middle class spending ever more money, and now chasing such Western fancies as diamonds and platinum, jewelry is big business here. The flashiest jewelry stores are clustered in South Extension, Greater Kailash I, and Connaught Place, offset by a handful of older shops in Sundar Nagar. Indian gold is 22-karat, and some Westerners tend to find its bright-yellow tone a bit too flashy. For a gold Indian piece in a subtler antique style, stroll through the market in Sundar Nagar. Hit the glitzier stores for the princess look. Indian jewelers as a group have been accused of adulterating their gold, but alas, you as a consumer will have no way to determine the content of each piece. Old Delhi is packed with jewelry and curio shops, though you have to search harder for fine designs. Stroll Dariba Kalan for the best selection of silver and gold.

As the center of India's English-language publishing industry, and, arguably, India's intellectual capital, Delhi has something of a literary scene. For those with hard currency, Indian books are great bargains, including lower-price local editions of titles published abroad. If you'll be in Delhi for a while, hunt down the elusive but excellent *Old Delhi: 10 Easy Walks,* by Gaynor Barton and Laurraine Malone (New Delhi: Rupa, 1997)—these painstakingly detailed routes are fascinating and manageable. The top hotels have small bookshops, but Khan Market has several of the capital's best.

South Delhi is best for discriminating music lovers.

Most shops are open six days a week, as each neighborhood's market area closes one day a week, usually Sunday, Monday, or Tuesday. Most shops in Old Delhi are closed on Sunday.

OLD DELHI

CLOTHING

Ram Chandra Krishan Chandra. In Old Delhi the venerable Ram Chandra Krishan Chandra has several rooms full of traditional silks. ⊠ *1976-1978 Chandni Chowk, near Gali Parathe Wali, Old Delhi, Delhi* ☎ *11/2327–7869* Ⓜ *Chandni Chowk.*

CRAFTS AND CURIOS

Shivam Zari Palace. In Old Delhi, Shivam Zari Palace and its neighbors sell inexpensive Hindu wedding paraphernalia such as turbans, fabric-covered boxes, *torans* (auspicious door hangings), tiny brass gods, and shiny bric-a-brac. ⊠ *2178 Kinari Bazaar, Old Delhi, Delhi* ☎ *11/2327–7617* Ⓜ *Chandni Chowk.*

Singh Copper & Brass Palace. Several dusty floors here are filled with brass, copper, and wood artifacts. ⊠ *1167 Chah Rahat Gali, near Jama Masjid, Old Delhi, Delhi* ☎ *11/2327–7486* Ⓜ *Chandni Chowk.*

JEWELRY

Multan Enamel Mart. Along with other stores in the area, Multan Enamel Mart sells old and new silver jewelry and curios by weight. ⊠ *No. 246–247 Dariba Kalan, Old Delhi, Delhi* ☎ *11/2326–4012* Ⓜ *Chandni Chowk.*

CENTRAL DELHI

BAZAARS AND MARKETS

Connaught Place. Open every day but Sunday from about 10 to 7:30, this is the former commercial district of the British Raj. Pillared arcades and a wheel-shaped layout make it a pleasant place to stroll, especially the inner circle, though you have to get used to the intermittent entreaties of hawkers and beggars. Shops run the gamut from scruffy to upscale. Beneath the green park at the center of Connaught Place is **Palika Bazaar,** a cheap underground market with all the charm of a Times Square subway station. Avoid it: it's a favorite haunt of pick-pockets, and many shopkeepers are dishonest. ⊠ *Central Delhi, Delhi.*

Khan Market. This is one of the capital's most pleasant and popular markets—though it's not cheap—with dozens of fine shops selling books, CDs, cameras and film processing, drugs, ayurvedic cosmetics, clothing, home decorations, imported magazines, and imported foods. The shops are open roughly 10 to 7 every day but Sunday; some of the cafés and restaurants stay open for dinner. The crowd is thick with Delhi intelligentsia and expats. ⊠ *Central Delhi, Delhi* Ⓜ *Khan Market.*

Santushti Shopping Complex. Open every day but Sunday from 10 to 6 or 7, this Chanakyapuri shopping opportunity is a collection of posh and arty boutiques scattered around a small, quiet garden across from the Ashok Hotel in the Diplomatic Enclave. Prices match those in the West, but this is a relaxing place to stroll and browse. Clothing is the main draw, followed by home furnishings, jewelry, leather, and ayurvedic beauty products. The restaurant Basil & Thyme serves excellent contemporary Euro-American food. ⊠ *Central Delhi, Delhi* Ⓜ *Race Course.*

BOOKS

Bahri Sons. This place is stuffed to the ceiling with dusty nonfiction, particularly academic history, politics, and Indian heritage. ⊠ *Subramaniam Bharti Marg, Opposite main gate, Khan Market, Central Delhi, Delhi* ☎ *11/2469–4610* ⊕ *www.booksatbahri.com* Ⓜ *Khan Market.*

The Bookshop. Strong on literary fiction, including hot new titles from abroad. ⊠ *13/7 Jor Bagh, Main Market, Central Delhi, Delhi* ☎ *11/2469–7102* Ⓜ *Jor Bagh.*

CMYK. Come here for art and design books, and perhaps one of the occasional movie screenings (call or drop in for the schedule). ⊠ *15–16 Meher Chand Market, Lodhi Rd., Central Delhi, Delhi* ☎ *11/2464–1881.*

Faqir Chand. This bookstore carries a fair number of coffee-table books. ⊠ *15A Khan Market, Central Delhi, Delhi* ☎ *11/2461–8810* Ⓜ *Khan Market.*

Full Circle. Spirituality, self-help, and coffee-table books are the specialty here. ⊠ *23 Khan Market, Central Delhi, Delhi* ☎ *11/2465–5641* ⊕ *fullcirclebooks.in* Ⓜ *Khan Market.*

NEED A BREAK? **Café Turtle.** Two flights up, in the Full Circle bookshop, Café Turtle serves light bistro food, exotic fruit juices, and excellent Western desserts in a smart contemporary setting, with music from the record shop below. The terrace is very pleasant in winter. ⊠ *23 Khan Market, Central Delhi, Delhi* ☎ *11/2465–5641* ⊕ *www.cafeturtle.com* Ⓜ *Khan Market.*

CLOTHING

SARIS **Banaras House.** This store sells the rich brocaded silks of Varanasi. ⊠ *N-13 Connaught Pl., Central Delhi, Delhi* ☎ *11/2331–4751* Ⓜ *Rajiv Chowk.*

Kalpana. Like an upscale version of Dilli Haat, Kalpana has exquisite traditional saris from all over India plus gorgeous Kashmiri shawls. ⊠ *F-5 Connaught Pl., Central Delhi, Delhi* ☎ *11/4152–3738* Ⓜ *Rajiv Chowk.*

Padakkam. An incredible collection of one-of-a-kind saris—mostly South Indian silks, but also interesting cottons—and Kashmiri shawls. ⊠ *17 Santushti Shopping Complex, Chanakyapuri, Central Delhi, Delhi* ☎ *11/2467–1417* Ⓜ *Race Course.*

MEN'S FABRIC AND TAILORS

D. Vaish & Sons. The oldest and finest men's tailors are in Connaught Place. D. Vaish & Sons has a huge selection of fabric and can tailor both men's and women's Western suits, not to mention Indian outfits, for about US$80 plus fabric. ⊠ *17 Regal Bldg., Connaught Pl., Central Delhi, Delhi* ☎ *11/4150–0850* ⊕ *www.dvaish.com* Ⓜ *Rajiv Chowk.*

Mohanlal & Sons. This tailors shop whips up men's Western and Indian suits at very low prices. ⊠ *B-21 Connaught Pl., Central Delhi, Delhi* ☎ *11/4151–3891* ⊕ *www.mohanlalsons.com* Ⓜ *Rajiv Chowk.*

Vedi Tailors. This company has a good reputation. ⊠ *M-60 Connaught Pl., Central Delhi, Delhi* ☎ *11/2341–6901* ⊕ *www.veditailors.com* Ⓜ *Rajiv Chowk.*

WOMEN'S FABRIC AND SALWAR-KAMEEZ SETS

Fabindia. A Delhi institution, this emporium is stuffed with block-printed kurtas, salwars, churidars, dupattas, Western tops, and skirts in subtle colors for trendy Delhiites, their mothers, expats, and tourists. Quality can vary. Avoid Saturday, when the place is a madhouse and it's difficult to get your hands on the stock. There are also branches in Khan Market, the Delhi airport, Green Park, a mall in Vasant Kunj and elsewhere. ⊠ *B-28 Connaught Place, Central Delhi, Delhi* ☎ *11/4151–3371* ⊕ *www. fabindia.com* ☉ *Closed Sun.* Ⓜ *Rajiv Chowk* ⊠ *N-14 N Block Market, Greater Kailash, South Delhi, Delhi* ☎ *11/2646–5497* ⊕ *fabindia.com.*

Kanika. Beautiful, if somewhat pricey, salwar-kameez sets in contemporary cuts of traditional fabrics are sold here. ⊠ *M-53 Connaught Pl., Central Delhi, Delhi* ☎ *11/2341–4731* Ⓜ *Rajiv Chowk.*

Khanna Creations. This is a good place for handsome salwar-kameez, some hand-embroidered, and raw fabric sets in great colors and patterns at good prices. Their in-house tailor can create a salwar-kameez in as little as four hours for Rs. 300. ⊠ *D-6 Connaught Pl., Central Delhi, Delhi* ☎ *11/4151–7907* Ⓜ *Rajiv Chowk.*

Tulsi. The supple garments and home furnishings here are made of handwoven silk, linen, and cotton. ⊠ *19 Santushti Shopping Complex, Chanakyapuri, Central Delhi, Delhi* ☎ *11/2687–0339* ⊕ *www. neerukumar.com* Ⓜ *Race Course.*

CRAFTS AND CURIOS

Bharany's. Specializing in jewelry, this store also sells rare old shawls and wall hangings from all over India. ⊠ *14 Sundar Nagar Market, Central Delhi, Delhi* ☎ *11/2435–8528* ⊕ *www.bharanys.com.*

Central Cottage Industries Emporium. Purchase crafts from all over the country here; they will ship items abroad too. ⊠ *Jawahar Vyapar Bhavan, Janpath, opposite Imperial Hotel, near Connaught Pl., Central Delhi, Delhi* ☎ *11/2332–3825* ⊕ *www.cottageemporium.in* Ⓜ *Rajiv Chowk.*

Curio Palace. There's an overwhelming array of silver and brass curios here, with much of the brass oxidized for an antique look. ⊠ *17 Sundar Nagar Market, Central Delhi, Delhi* ☎ *11/2435–0560.*

Shopping at Dilli Haat

Friends Oriental Arts. Among the bizarre, kitschy miscellany at Friends Oriental Arts are Kashmiri lacquerware, antique glassware, and old optical instruments. ⊠ *15 Sundar Nagar Market, Central Delhi, Delhi* ☎ *11/2435–8841.*

Ladakh Art Gallery. Distinctive silver items and small, tasteful Hindu icons are offered by this gallery. ⊠ *10 Sundar Nagar Market, Central Delhi, Delhi* ☎ *11/2435–5424* ⊕ *www.snsvo4.seekandsource.com/ladakh.*

Natesan's. This exclusive store has elaborate Hindu sculptures in bronze and teak. ⊠ *13 Sundar Nagar Market, Central Delhi, Delhi* ☎ *11/2435–9320.*

★ **state emporiums.** The many state emporiums, strung out over three blocks, can keep you busy for hours: the Kashmir store specializes in carpets, Karnataka in sandalwood, Tripura in bamboo, and so on. ⊠ *Baba Kharak Singh Marg, near Connaught Pl., Central Delhi, Delhi* Ⓜ *Rajiv Chowk.*

HOME FURNISHINGS
Anokhi. This store is loved for its block-print cotton home furnishings and gifts, including tablecloths, bedcovers, makeup bags, bathrobes, and cloth-bound journals. ⊠ *32 Khan Market, Central Delhi, Delhi* ☎ *11/2460–3423* ⊕ *www.anokhi.com* Ⓜ *Khan Market* ⊠ *Santushti Shopping Complex, Chanakyapuri, Central Delhi, Delhi* ☎ *11/2688–3076* ⊕ *www.anokhi.com* ☽ *Closed Sun.* Ⓜ *Race Course.*

Good Earth. All sorts of housewares are available here, including linens, pottery, and brass. There's a store in the Santushti Shopping Complex

Dressing the Part

Many traveling women (and a few traveling men) are inspired to buy an Indian outfit to wear for the duration of their trip. Here's a primer:

The traditional North Indian women's ensemble of a long tunic over loose pants is known as a salwar-kameez. Today it is equally common in a variation called the kurta-churidar. The word *kameez* is a general term meaning "shirt," whereas *kurta* specifies a traditional Indian tunic worn by both women and men. The pants worn beneath women's kurtas take two forms: the *salwar*, which is very loose, with only a slight gather at the ankle, and the *churidar*, which is loose in the thigh but tight along the calf, bunched up near the ankle like leggings. Presently the churidar is in greater vogue than the salwar, and true fashionistas now wear very short (above the knee) kurtas over thigh-tight churidars, a look with a Western element: it favors skinny women. Most women opt for knee- or calf-length kurtas.

The outfit is usually finished with a matching *dupatta* or *chunni*, a long scarf draped over the chest with the ends dangling in back, traditionally 6 feet long and 3 feet wide. These days you're free to drape the dupatta however you like; slinging it back from the neck, or even forward from the neck (Western-style), gives the outfit a modern twist. Just beware of dupattas made of stiff or starchy fabric—no matter how beautiful they look, you will probably find them unwieldy. A dupatta is particularly useful in places like Old Delhi and Nizamuddin, where you can pull it over your head as a kerchief if you feel too conspicuous.

You won't have to invest much in any of these items; at Fabindia or Dilli Haat you can buy a smart trio of kurta, churidar or salwar, and dupatta for US$25–US$50. Another option at Dilli Haat and some fabric stores is to buy uncut "suit fabric," a smartly matched set of three pieces of fabric meant to be sewn into the full regalia. If you buy suit fabric, simply take it all to a tailor (ask any market merchant to suggest one; most are holes-in-the-wall), allow him to measure you, tell him what kind of neckline you fancy and whether you want a churidar or salwar, and come back for your custom-made "suit." This can take a few days, but the tailoring costs about US$10 and these ensembles are very attractive.

Men's kurtas are traditionally paired with a churidar or with loose, straight-legged "pyjamas." Most urban Indian men wear Western shirts and trousers, but Delhi's politicians keep the white cotton kurta-pyjama and the more formal *dhoti* (a loose, bunchy men's skirt) alive and kicking. Formal silk kurta-churidars are trotted out only for weddings.

Many Western women who buy salwar-kameez choose muted colors, perhaps on the premise that light skin tones need light fabric tones. Unfortunately, muted colors often make Westerners look washed-out and even more "foreign." Be bold! Women of all complexions are flattered by the jewel tones of many Indian clothes.

and one in Saket as well. ⊠ *Khan Market, 9 ABC, Central Delhi, Delhi* ☎ *11/2464–7175* ⊕ *www.goodearth.in* Ⓜ *Khan Market.*

Neemrana Shop. This upscale shop has some beautiful India-inspired women's clothing, men's kurtas, and household gifts at Western prices. ⊠ *23B Khan Market, Central Delhi, Delhi* ☎ *11/2462–0262* Ⓜ *Khan Market.*

JEWELRY
Cottage Gallery. In business for more than 30 years, Cottage Gallery has necklaces, bracelets, and earrings, including some antiques. ⊠ *Claridges Hotel, 12 Aurangzeb Rd., Central Delhi, Delhi* ☎ *11/3955–5000* Ⓜ *Race Course.*

Ivory Mart. There's a huge selection of lovely necklaces in updated traditional styles. Reproductions of antique *kundan* jewelry, in which several gems are set in a gold-outlined design, are a specialty. ⊠ *F-22 Connaught Pl., Central Delhi, Delhi* ☎ *11/2331–0197* ⊕ *www.ivorymartjewellers. com* Ⓜ *Rajiv Chowk.*

Lotus Eaters. The interesting chunky silver, and a few gold pieces, are all very expensive. ⊠ *Santushti Shopping Complex, Central Delhi, Delhi* ☎ *11/2688–2264* Ⓜ *Race Course.*

Mehrasons. This place is a bit of a factory—service is surly, but the selection is immense. ⊠ *68 Janpath, near Connaught Pl., Central Delhi, Delhi* ☎ *11/4567–0700* ⊕ *www.mehrasonsjewellers.com* Ⓜ *Rajiv Chowk.*

Meyer Jewellers. Beautiful silver and gold jewelry, especially necklaces, is in tasteful traditional styles, including gemstone wedding sets. ⊠ *4 Sundar Nagar Market, Central Delhi, Delhi* ☎ *11/2435–8664.*

Roopchand. Some eye-popping regal pieces in antique styles are among the offerings here. ⊠ *C-13 Connaught Pl., Central Delhi, Delhi* ☎ *11/2341–1709* Ⓜ *Rajiv Chowk.*

MUSIC
Mercury. It looks ordinary, but Mercury is strong on Indian classical music and *ghazals* (Urdu-language love songs). ⊠ *20 Khan Market, Central Delhi, Delhi* ☎ *11/2469–0134* ⊕ *www.atmercury.in* Ⓜ *Khan Market.*

Music Street. The shelves here are mostly stocked with Hindi-film pop and DVDs. ⊠ *B-29 Connaught Pl., Central Delhi, Delhi* ☎ *11/2332–1171* Ⓜ *Rajiv Chowk.*

TEA AND COFFEE
Asia Tea House. Next door to Mittal, Asia Tea House (previously known as Regalia) sells fine teas and tea paraphernalia. ⊠ *12 Sundar Nagar Market, Central Delhi, Delhi* ☎ *11/2435–0115.*

Fodor's Choice ★ **Mittal Tea House.** Stuffed to the ceiling with Indian teas, herbs, and spices, this tea house has a charming owner, Vikram Mittal, who will tell you everything you ever wanted to know about tea. ⊠ *12 Sundar Nagar Market, Central Delhi, Delhi* ☎ *11/2435–8588* ⊕ *www.tea-india.com* ⊠ *8A Lodhi Colony Market, South Delhi, Delhi* ☎ *11/2461–5709* ⊕ *www.tea-india.com.*

SOUTH DELHI
BAZAARS AND MARKETS

Dilli Haat. This government-run food and crafts bazaar invites artisans from all over the country to sell their wares directly. More than 60 do so at any given time; the vendors rotate every two weeks according to changing themes such as handicrafts, textiles, or Rajasthani goods. Constants include Kashmiri shawls, Lucknavi *chikan* (white embroidery on pastel cotton), woodwork, pottery, cotton dhurries and simple children's toys from around the country. At the back of the bazaar 25 stalls serve regional food from around the country, a rare opportunity to sample Goan fish curry, Bengali fish in mustard sauce, and Kerala chicken stew outside their states of origin. Best of all, doors are open daily from 10 to 9 (10 to 10 in summer). Admission is Rs. 20. ⊠ *Aurobindo Marg, South Delhi, Delhi* ☎ *11/2611–9055* Ⓜ *INA Market.*

Hauz Khas Village. In the narrow medieval alleys of South Delhi's Hauz Khas Village, boutiques and shops in converted old homes sell crafts, curios, jewelry, artisanal furniture, and clothing (mostly glitzy Indian wear). Newer design stores include places like White and Shrivan Narresh. The back alley also has fun vintage stores where you can find movie posters from Hollywood and Bollywood films. Most stores are open every day but Sunday from 10:30 to 6 or 7. ⊠ *South Delhi, Delhi.*

INA Market. Across the street from Dilli Haat, this colorful market is open every day but Monday. This is one of Delhi's most exciting food bazaars, with shops full of imported packaged foods giving way to a covered fruit-and-vegetable market complete with coolies (porters) ready to carry your choices in a basket while you shop. Dry-goods merchants sell spices, nuts, and Indian salty snacks, and meat is prepared and sold on a muddy lane in back. This is the place to find the best incense. ⊠ *Aurobindo Marg, South Delhi, Delhi* Ⓜ *INA Metro Station.*

Lajpat Nagar Market. Middle-class locals stock their households at this lively market. Several Western brand names have outlets here, but Lajpat is best known for cheap kitchenware, curtains, Indian clothing, raw fabric, and shoes. A good place to take in the chaos and sample some street food, it's open every day but Monday from about 10:30 to 8. ⊠ *South Delhi, Delhi* Ⓜ *Lajpat Nagar.*

Sarojini Nagar Market. Popular with locals for its endless array of cheap clothing, from Indian nightgowns and flashy kurtas to rejected Western export apparel—note how much is charged for brand-name T-shirts and sweats compared with what you pay back home. The fruit and vegetable bazaar is great fun, especially at night. The market is open every day but Monday from about 10:30 to 8. ⊠ *South Delhi, Delhi.*

BOOKS

Fact and Fiction. In South Delhi, this store caters to the diplomatic community with books on international affairs, history, science, and language study. ⊠ *39 Basant Lok, Vasant Vihar, South Delhi, Delhi* ☎ *11/2614–6843.*

Classic Chaats

No trip to India is complete without some Indian snack food. The most popular street foods are *papri chaat* (fried wafers piled high with potatoes, chickpeas, yogurt, and chilli powder), *chole bhatura* (also known as chana bhatura—spicy chickpeas with fried, airy *puri* bread), and *golgappas* (fried dough in a hollow golf-ball shape, which you fill with a spicy mixture of potatoes, chickpeas, tamarind, and coriander sauce), *pakoras* (battered and fried vegetables, cheese, or chicken), and the Mumbai delicacy known as *bhel puri* (spicy rice with bits of onion). The best places to nosh on these snacks, other than in the bylanes of Old Delhi, are in neighborhood markets. Here are a few recommendations in Central and South Delhi.

The Bengali Sweet House (27–37 Bengali Market, near Connaught Pl., Central Delhi; metro: Mandi House) is a classic spot for evening golgappa outings.

At Bikanervala (Rajiv Ghandi Handicraft Bhavan, Baba Kharag Singh Marg, 1st fl., near Connaught Pl., Central Delhi) you can sample Gujarati snacks: khandvi is a delicious panfried snack made from a seasoned batter of chickpea flour and buttermilk, then cut into rolls and sprinkled with coconut and coriander; dhokla is a savory, fluffy, steamed cake made with chickpea flour, mustard seeds, and an inch of sugar and topped with coriander leaves.

Nathu's (2 Sundar Nagar Market, Central Delhi; www.nathusweets.com) is the perfect place to kick back after shopping for high-end souvenirs, with its robust Indian sweets and pleasant seating area. The nearby Sweets Corner supplies the fried stuff outdoors.

Under a charming tin ceiling at the Evergreen Sweet House (S-30 Green Park Market, South Delhi; metro: Green Park), a large crowd stuffs itself with chole bhatura and vegetarian thalis (combination platters).

Prince Paan Box (M-Block Market, eastern corner, Greater Kailash-1, South Delhi) is where you will find one of Delhi's most popular paanwallahs, attracting a crowd at all hours. They're also known, of course, for their paan, betel-nut leaves wrapped around various ingredients. There's no seating here.

Yodakin. Opened by the independent Yoda Press to provide an alternative to the big international conglomerates, Yodakin stocks an interesting mix of cutting edge books, music, and movies. It's a fun place to browse. ⊠ *2 Hauz Khas Village, South Delhi, Delhi* ☎ *11/4178–7201* ⊕ *www.yodakin.com.*

CARPETS

Carpet Cellar. This store has a vast selection; there's also a shop in Santushti. ⊠ *1 Anand Lok, Khel Gaon Marg, Siri Fort Rd., South Delhi, Delhi* ☎ *11/4164–1777.*

Janson's Carpets. Jasim Jan, of Janson's Carpets, delivers exactly what he describes—carpets old and new, silk and wool, Persian and tribal—and at fair (not cheap) prices. ⊠ *A-14 Nizamuddin East, South Delhi, Delhi* ☎ *11/2435–5615, 98111–29095 cell phone.*

Novel Exports. The family that runs Novel Exports comes from Kashmir, and they have stunning Kashmiri carpets, shawls, jewelry, and lacquered papier-mâché items. ⊠ *D-23 Jangpura Extension, South Delhi, Delhi* ☎ *11/2431–2226.*

CLOTHING

SARIS **L'Affaire.** Flamboyant party wear at prices to match. ⊠ *M-59 M Block Market, Greater Kailash I, South Delhi, Delhi* ☎ *11/2923–9974* ⊕ *www.laffaire.net.*

Nalli. This is a Chennai-based chain specializing in gold-trimmed silks from the Tamil town of Kanchipuram. The South Extension location is larger than the Connaught Place one. ⊠ *F-44 South Extension I, South Delhi, Delhi* ☎ *11/2462–9926* ⊕ *www.nalli.com* ⊠ *P-7/90 Connaught Pl., Central Delhi, Delhi* ☎ *11/2374–7154* Ⓜ *Rajiv Chowk.*

WOMEN'S **Cottons.** You guessed it—this store sells a variety of ethnic and Western-
FABRIC AND style cotton casuals. It's closed on Tuesday. ⊠ *11 N Block Market,*
SALWAR- *Greater Kailash, South Delhi, Delhi* ☎ *11/4163–5108.*
KAMEEZ SETS
Daman Choli. Bright, tastefully decorated cotton salwar-kameez are sold here, and they have a convenient while-you-wait alteration service. ⊠ *V-1 Green Park, South Delhi, Delhi* ☎ *11/2656–2265* Ⓜ *Green Park.*

Dilli Haat. This outdoor market usually has the capital's largest selection of cheap, distinctive cotton kurtas and raw salwar-kameez fabric. Designs vary widely, from Rajasthani mirror work to gossamer Maheshwari cotton to *ikat* weaves from Orissa—and stalls change for various themed exhibitions. ⊠ *Aurobindo Marg, South Delhi, Delhi* ☎ *11/2611–9055* Ⓜ *INA.*

Kilol. Some of the most stunning salwar-kameez fabric sets in India are available here, with color-drenched crêpe dupattas topping off soft, block-printed cottons. They're stacked on shelves upstairs. ⊠ *N-6 N Block Market, Greater Kailash I, South Delhi, Delhi* ☎ *11/2924–3388* ⊕ *www.kilol.com.*

NEED A
BREAK?
Market Café. In Khan Market, this café serves light Western salads, pastas, and desserts and refreshing cold drinks in an airy contemporary setting. ⊠ *8 Khan Market, Central Delhi, Delhi* ⊕ *www.marketcafe.in* ⊙ *Daily 10 am–10:30 pm* Ⓜ *Khan Market.*

CRAFTS AND CURIOS

Cottage of Arts & Jewels. This subterranean treasure trove is a musty jumble of old prints, photos, maps, curios, and junk. ⊠ *50 Hauz Khas Village, South Delhi, Delhi* ☎ *11/2696–7418.*

India Arts Palace. This is an absolute hurricane of Indian ephemera, with dangling colored lanterns, Hindu icons, cute animal curios, drawer pulls, and so forth. ⊠ *33 Sundar Nagar Market, South Delhi, Delhi* ☎ *11/2435–7501* ⊕ *www.indiaartspalace.net.*

La Boutique. This shop pleases the eye with painted wooden items from Rajasthan, plus Hindu and Buddhist icons and other curiosities. ⊠ *20 Sundar Nagar Market, South Delhi, Delhi* ☎ *11/2435–0066* ⊕ *www.laboutiqueindia.com.*

HOME FURNISHINGS

Fabindia. This is a good place for cheap, attractive cotton tablecloths, placemats, bedcovers, curtains, and rugs. ⊠ *N-5, 7 N Block Market, Greater Kailash, South Delhi, Delhi* ☎ *11/4669–3733* ⊕ *www.fabindia.com.*

JEWELRY

Aakaar. It's hard to find, but its arty silver baubles are hard to resist. Enter from Khel Gaon Marg and park near the electricity plant behind Siri Fort. ⊠ *5-L Shahpur Jat, South Delhi, Delhi* ☎ *11/2649–7632.*

Bharany's. Traditional gold earrings and beaded necklaces in muted colors and styles are the specialty of this shop. ⊠ *14 Sundar Nagar Market, South Delhi, Delhi* ☎ *11/2435–8528* ⊕ *www.bharanys.com.*

Ethnic Silver. Supremely elegant pieces, especially earrings, will tempt buyers here. The store is open daily until 9 pm. ⊠ *9A Hauz Khas Village, South Delhi, Delhi* ☎ *11/2696–9637.*

Hazoorilal. The jewelry here has relatively modern designs. ⊠ *M-44 M Block Market, Greater Kailash I, South Delhi, Delhi* ☎ *11/4173–4567* ⊕ *www.hazoorilal.com.*

MUSIC

Music World. Delhi's largest music store is where uniformed youngsters help you find your heart's desire in any category, Indian or international. ⊠ *Ansal Plaza, Khel Gaon Marg, near South Extension II, South Delhi, Delhi* ☎ *11/2625–0411* ⊕ *www.musicworld.in.*

3

Side Trips from Delhi

AGRA AND THE TAJ MAHAL, FATEPHUR
SIKRI, KHAJURAHO, AND VARANASI

WORD OF MOUTH

"Varanasi: probably the most fascinating city on the planet,
teeming with chaos, culture, and spirituality."

—crosscheck

"I wouldn't want to be without the experience of the Taj Mahal."

—Amy

SIDE TRIPS FROM DELHI

TOP REASONS TO GO

★ **Fatehpur Sikri:**
Easily visited in conjunction with the Taj Mahal, this UNESCO World Heritage Site, the former Mughal capital, is astounding for its prescient urban planning and architecture.

★ **Khajuraho:**
The temples of Khajuraho, built between the 9th and 10th centuries, are famous for their exquisite sculptures, especially the erotic ones; it is also a UNESCO World Heritage Site.

★ **The Taj Mahal:**
One of the most iconic sites in the world, the Taj is even more enchanting in real life; the minute detail is awe-inspiring.

★ **Varanasi:** One of the holiest cities in the world, Varanasi is unlike anywhere else you'll go; it can be quite a culture shock, but it's a truly awesome, unforgettable experience. Nearby Sarnath is the site of the Buddha's first teachings.

1 Agra and Fatehpur Sikri. Full of squalor and magnificence alike, this is the architectural heart of North-Central India, with over-the-top creations left by the Mughuls, including the Taj Mahal and the abandoned fortress-city of Fatehpur Sikri.

2 Khajuraho. In contrast to Agra's chaos, Khajuraho projects extreme calm amid equally impressive temples built by the Chandelas.

GETTING ORIENTED

The places covered here may be the most awe-inspiring region of this tremendous country, and if you plan to visit India only once in your lifetime, this is the place to go, tourist traps and all. With a sprawling population, North-Central India is composed of the states of Uttar Pradesh (Northern Province in English) and Madhya Pradesh ("Middle" Province, as Madhya means Middle). It's fairly easy to move from one place to another as the area is well connected, mainly by plenty of trains.

NEPAL

Basti Gorakhpur Motihari
Gopalganj
Azamgarh Muzaffarpur Darbhanga Purnia
Jaunpur Chhapra Samastipur
Ghazipur Patna Baruni
Sarnath Dumraon Jamalpur
BIHAR Bhagalpur
Varanasi Jamui
Sasaram Nawada
Gaya
Bodhgaya

JHARKHAND

0 — 100 mi
0 — 100 km

CHHATTISGARH

3 **Varanasi and Sarnath.** These two cities are cornerstones of Hinduism. Varanasi is a maze of nameless lanes and corridors, making it well suited to getting blissfully lost amid its constant din. The Ganges flows through this sacred city, which is one reason why thousands of *sadhus* (holy men) flock to it all year round.

EATING WELL ON DELHI SIDE TRIPS

The day-to-day fare of people across Uttar Pradesh's distinct regions tends to be utilitarian and vegetarian. However, there is a strong tradition of street food as well.

(top left) Paan ingredients in a betel leaf; (top right) Barbecued kakori kebabs of spicy minced lamb; (bottom right) Dumpukht biryani in a clay pot

The Awadh region, with Lucknow as its traditional center, has a vibrant culinary history that arose from the royal courts of the Muslim Nawabs who ruled the area. Considered to be very refined, Awadhi cuisine is reminiscent of the Mughal traditions of Delhi, Agra, and Kashmir and the Nawabi cuisine of Hyderabad, but it is distinct from these. Awadhi *bawarchis* and *rakabdars* (cooks and specialty cooks) are most-often credited with inventing the "dumpukht" style of sealing ingredients like rice, spices, and meat in an earthen pot and slow cooking them.

Agra's better hotels offer a taste of nonvegetarian Awadhi food, but Varanasi is mostly limited to simple vegetarian restaurants and international backpacker-friendly cafés. The city's importance as a Hindu holy site has led to the popularization of bland, "sattvik" food, made by using vegetarian ingredients deemed conducive to meditation.

DIGESTIVE AID

Chewed as a digestive all over India, **paan** is a slightly intoxicating slug of areca nut and other ingredients wrapped in a betel leaf. It often includes varieties of tobacco, which can be left out on request. *Paan* can also include chutneys, spices, and sweets. Every *paanwallah* (paan vendor) has his own way of doing things. Beginners should ask for a sweet or "mitha" *paan*, "no tambacu."

PETHA

Resembling blocks or cylinders of marble cut from the Taj Mahal itself, **petha** is Agra's most famous sweet. Usually white and slightly translucent, this somewhat gelatinous confection is made, improbably, from boiled and sweetened winter melon. There's also a yellow version called *angoori petha*. The sweet varies in consistency from soft and syrup-filled to crunchy and nearly crystalline. *Petha* is sold by weight in cardboard boxes at the train station and all over Agra, and comes in many flavors like rosewater, *paan* (betel), and coconut.

LITTI CHOKHA

A laborer's staple, the dish called **litti chokha** is especially common in eastern Uttar Pradesh and in the neighboring state of Bihar. Similar to Rajasthan's *batti* (and sometimes referred to by that name), the *litti* is a tough ball of baked dough made of *sattu*, a roasted gram-based flour particular to the region. Around Varanasi and farther afield, you may see stalls serving *litti* with *chokha*—a vegetable accompaniment of eggplant, potato, or tomato.

MALLAIYO

One of the more fussy foods you may find in Varanasi is a yellow dairy dessert called **mallaiyo**. Like the version of the dish found in Delhi (where it's called *daulat ki chaat*), *mallaiyo* is an airy, saffron-scented concoction that

magically melts away on your tongue. Traditionally, this is a winter morning sweet: to prepare it, milk has to be thickened and allowed to foam, then set overnight. The foam is then skimmed off and sold as *mallaiyo*.

KAKORI KEBABS

Tender, melting morsels of meat called **kakori kebabs** are a common menu item in Uttar Pradesh. You can try these kebabs at the better restaurants in Agra, especially those that serve Awadhi food. Minced twice and tenderized with *papain* (from raw papaya), this delicately spiced dish is typically eaten with a large, very thin and soft *roomali roti* (handkerchief bread). Various theories as to the origin of the kebab include its provenance as a dish for a toothless Nawab and as a dish cooked to impress a British officer.

DUMPUKHT BIRYANI

An elaborate dish that originated in the royal Awadhi court, **dumpukht biryani** consists of rice and meat suffused with aromatic spices. The spices are tied up in a muslin cloth, so as not to disintegrate in the dish. Half-cooked lamb (or other meat) and rice are layered in a clay pot, which is then sealed with dough and slow-cooked over low heat. Although you won't find good *dumpukht biryani* in Varanasi, it's well worth sampling at one of Agra's better restaurants or in Delhi.

Updated by
Malia Politzer

Anchored by Agra (home of the Taj Mahal), Khajuraho, and Varanasi, this section of the Hindi heartland is one of the most culturally and spiritually rich areas in India.

Agra was a seat of the Mughals' power, and their legacy remains (partially intact) for us to marvel at. Dominated by Muslim influences in culture, art, architecture, and cuisine, the city is a testament to the beauty and grandeur of Mughal aesthetics, most notably in the form of the Taj Mahal and Fatehpur Sikri.

Some 440 km (273 miles) southeast of Agra, in the northern part of Madhya Pradesh, the sleepy village of Khajuraho predates the Mughals. Khajuraho was founded at the end of the classical age of Hindu civilization, and is home to stunning Hindu and Jain temples that are famous for their erotic, often explicit sculpture. Excavations here have also uncovered a long-forgotten complex of Buddhist temples.

According to legend, Varanasi was founded by the Hindu god Shiva, and it's said to be one of the oldest populated cities in the world—about 3,000 years old. In many ways, the city (still sometimes called by its Raj-era name, Benares), in southwestern Uttar Pradesh, is the antithesis of Khajuraho. Quite the opposite of the small, sparsely populated village, Varanasi teems with pilgrims, hospice patients, ascetics, priests, Hindu pundits, and international citizens of many religions. Its famous *ghats* (wide stone stairways leading down to the Ganges) are both key religious sites and secular promenades. Writer Mark Twain explained its charm perfectly. He called it "older than history, older than tradition, older even than legend and looks twice as old as all of them put together." Hindus believe that a person who dies here will gain salvation and freedom from the cycle of birth and rebirth. Sarnath, on the outskirts of Varanasi, is where the Buddha is said to have preached his first sermon after his enlightenment. The ruins and temples here draw Buddhist pilgrims from all over the world.

PLANNING

WHEN TO GO

HIGH SEASON: MID-OCTOBER TO MARCH

The weather at this time is fresh and nice, but hotels tend to charge premium rates. December and January are the best times to visit, but it can get quite cold so remember to pack some warm clothes. Conversely, it could be the worst time to visit the Taj Mahal, because you're simply trading the sun for sky-high prices and unbelievable amounts of foot traffic. The weather from early February to mid-March is wonderfully temperate.

LOW SEASON: APRIL TO AUGUST

If you decide to go to Agra from April to early July, even Indians might look at you as if you're crazy. There's no denying that this region is at its hottest then, making sightseeing in Agra and Khajuraho, which involves hours in the sun, borderline unbearable, especially while looking at the red sandstone monuments, which radiate heat. Temperatures will be well above 100 degrees Fahrenheit, with monsoon showers picking up toward the end of July and continuing through August. Temperatures during this period will be in the 80s, rain is intermittent, and hotel rates go down, so this is a good time to get a deal.

SHOULDER SEASON: SEPTEMBER TO MID-OCTOBER

During this period the weather just begins to cool, and while you might still be unlucky enough to catch a shower or two, is a great time to visit. Some hotels still give discounts for off-peak season.

GETTING HERE AND AROUND

The recently opened Yamuna Expressway has reduced driving time from Delhi to Agra to 2½ hours, making driving a convenient but somewhat pricey option. Taking the train—just a 3-hour commute—is a good alternative.

AIR TRAVEL

As of late 2012, all flights to Agra have been suspended. The airports in Khajuraho and Varanasi are all connected by air from Delhi, with flights by Air India and Jet. SpiceJet also flies between Delhi and Varanasi.

AIRPORT TRANSFERS Khajuraho Airport is 5 km (3 miles) from town; the taxi ride costs about Rs. 200.

Bhabatpur, the nearest airport to Varanasi, is 22 km (14 miles), or a 45-minute drive, from most hotels. A taxi costs about Rs. 350 or Rs. 500 (air-conditioned) to the Cantonment area, or from Rs. 400 to Rs. 600 into the city proper.

AUTO-RICKSHAW AND TAXI TRAVEL

Auto-rickshaws and taxis are a cheap, convenient option for getting around in all the big cities, and can also be hired for an entire day of sightseeing. Be prepared to bargain, though.

Fares for an auto-rickshaw ride, especially one in Agra, depend on several factors, including how wealthy you look, how far you want to go, how many times you want to stop, the time of day, and whether it's raining. You can generally expect to pay about Rs. 600 for a half day,

Rs. 800 for a full day. If you're not comfortable with the price you're given, look for another auto-rickshaw, and if you don't want to haggle, take a metered taxi or book a car.

Auto-rickshaws are a fast way to scoot through crowded city streets, but the fumes from other automobiles can be horrendous at busy times. When traffic is heavy, take an air-conditioned taxi with the windows closed, especially if you're coming from one of the hotels far from the ghats. Ask your hotel or the tourist office for the going rate, and agree on a fare in advance.

BUS TRAVEL

Traveling to these cities via bus is the cheapest option, but it's only for the truly adventurous, because local schedules are difficult to come by and service is spotty. If you're taking off from Delhi, the bus stations are large and can be chaotic and hard to deal with. You can book a seat on a private, air-conditioned bus for travel between the cities through any local travel agent.

Within cities, local bus lines are the only form of public transportation. In general, they are too crowded and difficult to use for the average foreign visitor.

CAR TRAVEL

Hire a car and driver only through your hotel or tour operator; UP Tours, the government of Uttar Pradesh's tour arm *(⇨ Tours)*; the Madhya Pradesh State Tourism Development Corporation *(⇨ Visitor Information)*; or a recommended local travel agent.

For trips to Agra from Delhi, contact Dhanoa Tours and Travels. Rates start around Rs. 7,500 and go up to Rs. 10,000 for a day trip, depending on the size of the vehicle and whether there's air-conditioning. The price includes tax and a driver. Expect to pay about Rs. 1,000 extra for a worthwhile detour to Fatehpur Sikri.

Prices in Agra are generally Rs. 6–Rs. 8 per kilometer. A non-air-conditioned car for four hours or 40 km (25 miles) should cost about Rs. 600–Rs. 700—the minimum charge. For overnight excursions, add a halt charge of Rs. 400. The standard charge for a trip to Fatehpur Sikri is Rs. 1,200, but prices are always negotiable. You can hire a taxi at the train station under a fixed-rate system. If you'd prefer not to be taken to the driver's choice of stores, restaurants, or hotels (where he gets a commission), say so firmly up front.

In Khajuraho, a hired car can be convenient if you want to wander outside town or can't walk the 3 km (2 miles) to the most distant temples. A non-air-conditioned car should cost about Rs. 500 for two hours or 30 km (18 miles). You can hire a taxi for about Rs. 6 per km.

Contacts Dhanoa Tours and Travels ✉ *Hara Marg, near Malcha Marg Market, Chanakyapuri, Central Delhi, Delhi* ☎ *11/2688–6051.* **Touraids Travel Service.** One of the largest travel agencies in Northern India, Touraids Travel provides hotel bookings, train and bus tickets, and travel advice. ✉ *46 Gopichand Shivhare Rd., Agra Cantonment, Agra, Uttar Pradesh* ☎ *562/222–5029, 562/222–5074* ✍ *touraids@sancharnet.in.*

CYCLE-RICKSHAW TRAVEL

You can get the latest rate estimates for cycle-rickshaws from the local India Tourism office. Cycle-rickshaws should cost no more than Rs. 70 per hour in Agra or Khajuraho. They're a particularly pleasant way to get around Khajuraho, especially to the outlying temples. Distances are long in Varanasi, so a cycle-rickshaw is better for a leisurely roll through the Old City (it frees you from fighting the crowds) than for cross-town transportation. A trip from the Cantonment to the ghats should cost about Rs. 100. If you hire a cycle-rickshaw for the day, agree on the price in advance and expect to pay about Rs. 250.

TRAIN TRAVEL

Train service is superb, as the region is connected by several local and express trains originating in Delhi and other major cities, and taking the train to Agra is a good option. Otherwise, if your time is limited, you're probably better off flying. *For more info about train travel, see the Travel Smart chapter.*

TOURS

Outbound Travels in Delhi can arrange flights and coordinate flights with train or car travel to help you make the most of limited travel time. UP Tours (Uttar Pradesh's tour agency) has a vast offering of tours, including Buddhist circuit tours and a daily guided bus tour of Fatehpur Sikri, Agra Fort, and the Taj Mahal for Rs. 1,700 per person (this covers transportation, guide, and admission fees, including the Rs. 750 admission to the Taj); a half-day tour of Fatehpur Sikri alone is Rs. 550. For a personal guide, ask your hotel or contact the nearest India Tourism office.

Contacts **Outbound Travels**. This company provides customized itineraries, books train and plane tickets, and hotel bookings for trips across India. ✉ *216A/11 Gautam Nagar, 3rd fl., South Delhi, Delhi* ☎ *11/4164–0565* ⊕ *www.outboundtravels.com*. **UP Tours** ✉ *64 Taj Rd., Agra, Uttar Pradesh* ☎ *562/222–6431* ⊕ *www.up-tourism.com* ✉ *Cantonment Railway Station, Varanasi, Uttar Pradesh* ☎ *542/250–6670.*

VISITOR INFORMATION

If you are planning your trip from New Delhi, the India Ministry of Tourism's office on Janpath is worth a visit.

You can pick up maps and information about approved guides at the India Ministry of Tourism offices in Agra, Khajuraho, and Varanasi's Cantonment, and at an information desk at Varanasi's airport. The Madhya Pradesh State Tourism Development Corporation, one of India's better state tourist offices, has friendly staff and information on Khajuraho.

The Uttar Pradesh State Tourism Development Corporation arranges tours and cars in Agra. The New Delhi office (centrally located near the Imperial Hotel) has maps, brochures, and information on approved guides. The best information at Varanasi's Uttar Pradesh State Tourism office is in Hindi, but the staff can still help you, and there's a satellite desk at the train station.

Tourist Offices India Ministry of Tourism ⊠ *88 Janpath, Central Delhi, Delhi* ☎ *11/2332–0005 to 0008* ⊕ *www.incredibleindia.org.* ⊠ *Opposite Western Group of temples, Khajuraho, Madhya Pradesh* ☎ *768/6242–0347* **Madhya Pradesh State Tourism Corporation** ⊠ *Chandella Cultural Center, Rajnagar Rd., Khajuraho, Madhya Pradesh* ☎ *768/627–4051* ⊠ *At airport and bus station, Khajuraho, Madhya Pradesh* ⊕ *www.mptourism.com.* **Uttar Pradesh Tourist Office** ⊠ *Chandralok Bldg., 36 Janpath, Central Delhi, Delhi* ☎ *11/2332–2251* ⊕ *www.up-tourism.com* ⊠ *64 Taj Rd., Agra, Uttar Pradesh* ☎ *562/222–6431* ⊠ *Hotel Mrigdava Campus, Sarnath, Uttar Pradesh* ☎ *542/259–5965.*

ABOUT THE RESTAURANTS

Restaurants on this route generally serve kebabs and other grilled meats, *birianis* (rice casseroles), and the rich almond-and-saffron-scented concoctions of Mughlai cuisine. Most hotels offer a menu of Indian (with choices from various regions), Continental, Chinese (sort of), and sometimes Thai or Japanese dishes; Khajuraho has several Italian restaurants. Small places in villages along the way have simple local vegetarian dishes that are often delicious and cheap. Also keep an eye out for South Indian joints, where a delicious spiced-potato-filled *dosa* (crisp rice crepe) will fill you up for a 20 rupees or less and is tremendously satisfying. Most restaurants are open from 7 to 10 for breakfast, noon to 3 for lunch, and 7:30 to 11 for dinner; hotels often have a 24-hour or all-day coffee shop.

Prices in the reviews are the average cost of a main course at dinner or, if dinner is not served, at lunch.

ABOUT THE HOTELS

India's main hotel groups are represented in this region, providing increased amenities and efficiency at increasing prices. More and more good, air-conditioned hotels cater to India's upper-middle class and businesspeople, but such places are often quite generic. Outside the old British cantonment areas, where most top hotels are clustered, and often closer to the center of town, you'll find clean, well-run guest houses and small Heritage Hotels. Unless otherwise noted, all hotels listed have air-conditioning and private baths.

Prices in the reviews are the lowest cost of a standard double room in high season. For expanded hotel reviews, facilities, and current deals, visit Fodors.com.

PLANNING YOUR TIME

It's a good idea to take the express train to Agra to avoid Delhi traffic. To see the Taj and related sights without being completely rushed, plan on spending at least one night in Agra.

Most people visit Khajuraho in conjunction with Varanasi: the best idea is to fly here either on your way to or from Varanasi. Plan to spend two days exploring the Chandela temples.

Varanasi requires at least two days, including half a day for Sarnath. Again, the best option is to fly from Delhi, perhaps stopping in Khajuraho.

EXPLORING AGRA, VARANASI, AND KHAJURAHO

Agra and Varanasi are at opposite ends of Uttar Pradesh. Both lie on the Gangetic plain, also known as the Northern Plain, which stretches across most of Northern India. The countryside in both areas is similar: a dry landscape planted with sugarcane, mustard, and wheat in winter. In Khajuraho, 418 km (260 miles) southeast of Agra—sort of midway, but south, between Agra and Varanasi—you'll get a good sense of the natural environment, because it's an uncongested area. The monsoon hits harder to the east, around Varanasi, so the terrain there is a little more lush.

AGRA AND ENVIRONS

The fastest way to drive to Agra from Delhi is via the Yamuna Expressway, or you can take the other, more historic route, which follows the Grand Trunk Road—a royal route established by India's Mughal emperors in the 16th and 17th centuries, when their capital alternated between Delhi, Agra, and Lahore (now in Pakistan). If you get an early start, you can see Agra's sights in one very tiring day: start at Akbar's Tomb, 10 km (6 miles) north of Agra, then move on to Etmad-ud-Daulah's Tomb, the Taj Mahal, and Agra Fort.

A short drive farther, toward Jaipur, is Akbar's deserted dream city at Fatehpur Sikri. Many visitors find this atmospheric place as rewarding as the Taj Mahal.

AGRA

200 km (124 miles) southeast of Delhi.

It's safe to say that Agra, a sprawling city of nearly 1.5 million inhabitants, would not be on many tourists' maps if it weren't for one thing: the Taj Mahal. Yes, it is crowded and congested, but imagine walking down an avenue of stores selling tiny replicas of the Taj Mahal, with guides and hawkers vying for your attention . . . and then passing through a massive doorway and seeing the Taj Mahal in all its splendor. It's a magical moment. As you find out more, you'll discover that other amazing sights are also worth the trek. You can drive to the old fortress city of the Mughals, Fatehpur Sikri, as well as Agra's fort.

In this Mughal stronghold every successive emperor added something new to prove his cultural sensibilities and his power. Under the Mughal emperor Akbar (1542–1605) and his successors Jahangir (1605–27) and Shah Jahan (1628–58), Agra flourished. However, after the reign of Shah Jahan's son Aurangzeb (1658–1707) and the gradual disintegration of

NORTH CENTRAL'S FESTIVALS

Agra's Taj Mahotsav (10 days in February) is a festival celebrating the arts, crafts, and culture of North India. The Khajuraho Festival of Dance (a week between late February and March) is geared primarily to visitors. It's a spectacular event that attracts classically trained dancers from all parts of the country, who perform against a magnificently floodlighted backdrop of the temples.

In Varanasi there's a major religious festival practically every week, but their dates shift every year (check ⊕ www.incredibleindia.org for upcoming dates). Varanasi's great bathing days, when thousands stream down the ghats into the Ganges, include Makar Sankranti (January), the full moon of the Hindu month Kartik (October or November), and Ganga Dussehra (May or June). Durga Puja (September or October) ends with the city's large Bengali community marching to the river at sunset to immerse large mud-daubed images of the goddess Durga. The Bharat Milap festival, held in October or November, occurs the day after the major Hindu festival of Dussehra. It marks Lord Rama's return from exile (from the epic *Ramayana*). It's held in Nati Imli in Varanasi.

Buddhists from Tibet and all over Asia celebrate their festivals in Sarnath. The Buddha Jayanti is celebrated on a full moon day in April or May. It celebrates the Buddha's birth anniversary as well as his day of enlightenment.

the empire, the city passed from one invader to another before the British took charge early in the 19th century. The British, particularly Governor General Lord Curzon (in office 1898–1905), did much to halt and repair the damage inflicted on Agra's forts and palaces by raiders and vandals.

Much of Agra today may be crowded and dirty, and some of the Mughal buildings are irrevocably scarred. But the government has taken steps to protect the city's most important site from pollution, closing the streets around the Taj Mahal to gas-fueled vehicles (visitors are ferried from a remote parking lot by battery-powered buses) and relocating small factories and fire-burning shops away from the area. Still, Agra's monuments remain strewn like pearls in ashes, evoking that glorious period in Indian history when Agra was the center of the Mughal empire.

■ TIP→ Opening hours change constantly; inquire in advance at your hotel or the Uttar Pradesh State Tourist Office.

GETTING AROUND

It's a good idea to spend a night in Agra and start tackling the sights early in the morning, if only because you'll get a couple of hours in before the hot sun begins to bear down. It's true that the Taj at sunrise is glorious, but if you happen to sleep in, don't worry. Hotels and tour guides tend to make a big deal about the best times of day to see the Taj Mahal, but this legendary mausoleum is spectacular whenever you choose to visit, so you shouldn't feel despondent if you arrive at noon as opposed to sunrise or sunset. (A midday visit, however, *would* be the worst time to forget your sunglasses.) Another thing to remember is that the Taj Mahal is extremely crowded at all hours of the day, so don't assume that an early start will necessarily save you from the relentless foot traffic.

A GOOD TOUR

Assuming you see the Taj Mahal first (and that's certainly not mandatory), it's easy to take leisurely drives to the rest of the sights and be ready to unwind by early evening. Drive 5 km (3 miles) north of the Taj Mahal—about a 20-minute drive on a congested road—to **Etmad-ud-Daulah's Tomb** and then 8 km (5 miles) northwest—about a half-hour drive, with traffic—to **Akbar's Tomb.** (Also known as Sikandra for the town it's in, this monument is often overlooked, but it's an impressive sight that's well worth a stop.) From here it's a 12-km (7-mile), or 45-minute, drive northeast to **Agra Fort,** where it's easy to spend an hour or more. If you have the time and energy, drive southwest for an hour (37 km [23 miles]), to **Fatehpur Sikri.**

4

If you're day-tripping from Delhi with a car and driver, it's a must to leave by 5 am to avoid terrible traffic. You can see Akbar's Tomb and Etmad-ud-Daulah's Tomb on the way to the Taj Mahal, at which you'll easily arrive before noon. Spend the afternoon visiting the Agra Fort or Fatehpur Sikri, then hit a good restaurant before heading back to Delhi.

TIMING

Any time between September through March is a good time to visit. Winters here are cool and sometimes quite cold in December and January, so make sure you have some layers packed if you visit at that time.

If you try to pack all of Agra's sights into a day that starts in Delhi, you'll have a long, tiring day; starting fresh in the morning from Agra will make for a full, but fairly easy day. Consider staying a second night at your hotel and dividing your excursions between two days to eliminate that constant hectic feeling that Agra's crowds, congested traffic, and sights often impart.

ESSENTIALS

Government-approved tourist guides can be found through the local tourist offices.

Contacts Uttar Pradesh Tourist Office. This is a good resource for local transportation queries, and they have a list of government-approved drivers and tour guides at market rates so you will not be cheated. Their recommendations for restaurants and hotels, however, are less reliable. ⊠ *64 Taj Rd., Agra, Uttar Pradesh* ☎ *562/222–6431* ⊕ *www.up-tourism.com* ⊘ *Closed Sun.*

EXPLORING

★ **Agra Fort.** The architecture of this fort—one of the area's 7 World Heritage Sites (and India's 30), along with the Taj Mahal and Fatehpur Sikri—reflects the collective creative brilliance of Akbar, his son Jahangir, and grandson Shah Jahan. The structure was built by Akbar on the site of an earlier fort. A succession of Mughal emperors lived here, including Humayun, Akbar, Jehangir, Shah Jahan, and Aurangzeb. It was from here that the country was governed, and the fort contained the largest state treasury and mint. As with similar Mughal facilities in Delhi and Lahore, the word "fort" is misleading: the complex is

Agra Fort **4**
Akbar's Tomb **3**
Etmad-ud-Daulah's
Tomb **2**
Taj Mahal **1**

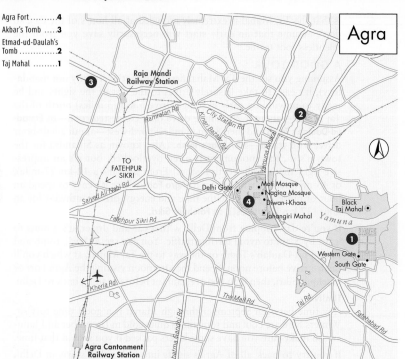

really a fortified palace, containing royal apartments, mosques, assembly halls, and a dungeon—the entire cityscape of an imperial capital. A massive wall 2½ km (1½ miles) long and 69 feet high surrounds the fort's roughly triangular shape. With the Yamuna River running at its base, the fort was also protected by a moat and another wall, presenting a daunting barrier to anyone hoping to access the treasures within.

This was originally a brick fort, and Ibrahim Lodi held it for nine years until he was defeated and killed in the battle of Panipat in 1526. The Mughals captured the fort post Panipat along with masses of treasure which included one of the most famous gems in the world, the Koh-i-Noor diamond. The emperor Babur stayed in the fort in the palace of Ibrahim, while Humayun was crowned here in 1530. Emperor Akbar decided to make it his capital when he arrived in Agra in 1558. He rebuilt it with red sandstone from the Barauli area in Rajasthan, and the whole process took eight years.

It was during the reign of Akbar's grandson, Shah Jahan, that the fortress took on its current "marbeled" state. It's quite sad that Shah Jahan was imprisoned by his own son Aurangzeb toward the end of his life. A legends says that Shah Jahan died in the Muassamman Burj, a tower with a marble balcony with an excellent view of the Taj Mahal, the monuments he created.

The fort's entrance is accessible through the Amar Singh Gate (also called the Lahore Gate, for the city in modern-day Pakistan that it faces). It was named for Amar Singh Rathore, a legendary general who served the Mughals. North of this entrance sits the fort's largest private residence, the **Jahangiri Mahal,** built by Jahangir as a harem, mainly for his Rajput wives. (Akbar's own palace, closer to the entrance, is in ruins.) Measuring 250 feet by 300 feet, the Jahangiri Mahal juxtaposes *jarokhas* (balconies) and other elements of Hindu architecture with pointed arches and other Central Asian influences imported by the Mughals. The palace's central court is lined with two-story facades bearing remnants of the rich, gilded decoration that once covered much of the structure.

After Jahangir's death in 1628, Shah Jahan assumed the throne and started his own buildings inside the fort, often tearing down those built by his father and grandfather in the process and adding marble decorations (it is said that he was partial to the material). The **Anguri Bagh** (Grape Arbor) shows the outlines of a geometric garden built around delicate water channels and chutes. The 1637 **Khas Mahal** (Private Palace) is an early masterpiece of Shah Jahan's craftsmen. The central pavilion, made of white marble, follows the classic Mughal pattern: three arches on each side, five in front, and two turrets rising out of the roof. Of the two flanking pavilions where Shah Jahan's two daughters resided, one is of white marble and was supposedly decorated with gold leaf; the other is made of red stone. The arched roofs of all three pavilions are stone interpretations of the bamboo architecture of Bengal. In one part of the Khas Maha a staircase leads down to the palace's "air-conditioned" quarters—cool underground rooms that were used in summer. It's famous for its paintings on marble.

The octagonal tower of the **Mussaman Burj** has fine inlay work and a splendid view down the river to the Taj Mahal. This is where Shah Jahan is said to have spent the last seven years of his life, imprisoned by his son Aurangzeb but still able to look out on his greatest monument, the Taj Mahal. It is said that Shah Jahan built the tower for his wife Mumtaz Mahal (he also built the Taj Mahal for her). On the northeastern end of the Khas Mahal courtyard stands the **Sheesh Mahal** (Palace of Mirrors), built in 1637 as a bath for the private palace and dressing room for the harem. Each of the two chambers contained a bathing tank fed by marble channels.

The emperor received foreign ambassadors and other dignitaries in the **Diwan-i-Khas** (Hall of Private Audience), built by Shah Jahan in 1636–37. Outside, the marble throne terrace holds a pair of black and white thrones. The black throne, carved from a single block of marble, overlooks the Yamuna and, according to the inscription, was used by Shah Jahan; the white throne is made of several marble blocks and was his father's seat of power. Both thrones face the **Machhi Bhavan,** an enclosure of fountains and shallow pools, and a number of imperial offices.

To the empire's citizens and to the European emissaries who came to see these powerful monarchs, the most impressive part of the fort was the **Diwan-i-Am** (Hall of Public Audience), set within a large quadrangle. This huge, low structure rests on a 4-foot platform, its nine cusped

Agra's massive fort

Mughal arches held up by rows of slender supporting pillars. Here the emperor sat and dispensed justice to his subjects, sitting on the legendary Peacock Throne.

Northeast of the Diwan-i-Khas is the **Nagina Masjid,** a private mosque raised by Shah Jahan for the women of his harem. Made of white marble and walled in on three sides, it has typical cusped arches, a marble courtyard, and three graceful domes. While in the Nagina Masjid, royal ladies could buy beautiful items from tradesmen who set up a temporary bazaar for them in front of its balcony. Nearby is the lovely **Moti Masjid,** a perfectly proportioned pearl mosque (*moti* means pearl) built in white marble by Shah Jahan. ⊠ *Yamuna Kinara Rd., Agra, Uttar Pradesh* ☞ *Rs. 300 (Rs. 250 with a ticket to Taj Mahal)* ⊘ *Daily sunrise–sunset.*

Akbar's Tomb. Akbar's resting place, in what's now the small town of Sikandra, was begun by the emperor himself in 1602 and completed after his death by Jahangir. Topped with white marble and flanked by graceful minarets, this mausoleum of rough red sandstone sits in a typical Mughal garden called a *charbagh*—four quadrants separated by waterways. The garden, however, is not well tended, and Jat raiders (who invaded Agra after the fall of the Mughul empire) destroyed much of the gold work that once adorned the tomb, though the British partially restored it. In a domed chamber three stories high, the crypt is inscribed with the 99 names of Allah, plus the phrases *Allah-o-Akbar* (God is great) at the head and *Jalla Jalalahu* (Great is His glory) at the foot. It's a charming spot to visit; you'll spot many langurs (long-tailed monkeys) and deer in the gardens. Akbar had originally meant this to be the official resting place for the Mughals, but it didn't turn out that way:

only two of his daughters are buried here. ■TIP→ You can actually see the tomb's enormous gateway, topped with bright tilework, from the train from Delhi—look out the left window 10 or 15 minutes before the train is due to reach Agra. ⊠ *Sikandra, 10 km (6 miles) north of Agra on Grand Trunk Rd. to Delhi, Agra, Uttar Pradesh* 🖃 *Rs. 110* ⏱ *Daily 6–5:30.*

★ **Etmad-ud-Daulah's Tomb.** The empress Nur Jahan (Jahangir's favorite wife) built this small, gorgeous tomb for her father, Mirza Ghayab Beg (pronounced Baig), a Persian nobleman who became Jahangir's chief minister. Beg was also the grandfather of Mumtaz Mahal, the wife of the emperor Shah Jahan. The monument, one of Agra's loveliest, was supposedly built by workers from Persia. The tomb incorporates a great deal of brown and yellow Persian marble and marks the first use of Persian-style marble inlay in India—both features that would later characterize the style of Shah Jahan. Particularly in its use of intricate marble inlay, this building was a precursor of, and very likely an inspiration for, the Taj Mahal (for this reason it has earned the somewhat goofy nickname of the "Baby Taj"). The roof is arched in the style of Bengali terra-cotta temples, and the minarets are octagonal, much broader than the slender cylinders of the Taj Mahal—in its fine proportions this mausoleum almost equals that masterpiece. Inside, where the elegant decoration continues, the central chamber holds the tombs of Etmad-ud-Daulah and his wife; other relations are buried in adjacent rooms. Most travelers to Agra never see this place, but its beauty and tranquility are extraordinary, and its well-maintained gardens make it a wonderful place to pause and reflect. ⊠ *5 km (3 miles) north of Taj Mahal on left bank of Yamuna River, Agra, Uttar Pradesh* 🖃 *Rs. 110* ⏱ *Daily sunrise–sunset.*

Fodor'sChoice ★ **Taj Mahal.** *See the highlighted feature in this chapter.*

WHERE TO EAT

$$$$ ✕ **Bellevue.** You can have breakfast, lunch, and dinner here at this airy
INTERNATIONAL indoor restaurant, which looks out on the Oberoi's gardens, and has a
★ distant view of the Taj. Bellevue is stylishly decorated, with chic brown-and-white tile floors, plush turquoise booths and dusky wooden tables and chairs. Indian food is the specialty—try their *murgh tikka masala*, a chicken dish with a tomato-based gravy. The huge menu includes *chaats* (Indian snacks) as well as pasta and European dishes. 💲 *Average main: Rs. 1200* ⊠ *Oberoi Amarvilas, Taj East Gate Rd., Agra, Uttar Pradesh* ☎ *562/223–1515.*

$$ ✕ **Dasaprakash.** The light and spicy South Indian vegetarian dishes
SOUTH INDIAN served at this town favorite are a nice change from Agra's usual rich
★ Mughlai fare. The Formica tables and fake Tiffany-style lamps evoke an American pizza joint. The food is excellent and service is fast. The *thali* (a sampler combination plate) may include crisp *appam* (fried bread made from rice flour) and *rasam* (thin, spicy lentil soup), as well as fluffy *idlis* (steamed rice cakes) and *dosas* (rice crepes). Also available are an unusual selection of fresh juices and a great dessert menu with ice creams and floats. 💲 *Average main: Rs. 360* ⊠ *1 Meher Cinema Complex, Gwalior Rd., Agra, Uttar Pradesh* ☎ *562/246–3535* ⊕ *www. dasaprakash.in.*

Continued on page 173

THE TAJ MAHAL

Described as an "elegy in marble," the Taj Mahal is an epic monument to Emperor Shah Jahan's beloved wife. Seeing the magnificent structure in person reveals the minute details of its decoration and its construction, and the incredible symmetry of the elements.

The Taj Mahal is one of the most recognizable, most reproduced images in the world, and the tale of love and loss that sparked its creation is almost as incredible as the monument's beauty. It was built by the fifth Mughal emperor, Shah Jahan, in memory of his third but favorite wife, who was called his Mumtaz Mahal (the Jewel of the Palace). As the legend goes, she asked him to build her a monument so beautiful that the world would never forget their love. She died after giving birth to their thirteenth child, and six months after her death a huge procession brought Mumtaz Mahal's body to Agra, where Shah Jahan began the process of honoring her request with the Taj Mahal. Construction of the monument began in about 1632, and it took 20,000 laborers a period of about 17 years to complete the vast, bejeweled, white marble tomb on the banks of the Yamuna River. The building's perfect proportions, scale, and exquisite detail make it a vision unlike anything else. It was made a UNESCO World Heritage site in 1983.

Up close the intricately crafted and colorful detail of the building is apparent, but from far away, the magnificent structure appears all white—though depending on the sun and the time of day it takes on different hutes. At sunrise it takes on a pinkish hue; at sunset it's a lemon yellow, then orange. Once the sun goes down, the marble is pure white against a black sky.

(top) An artist's rendition of Mumtaz Mahal
(right) The reflecting pool leading up to the Taj Mahal is a typical element of Islamic gardens and courtyards

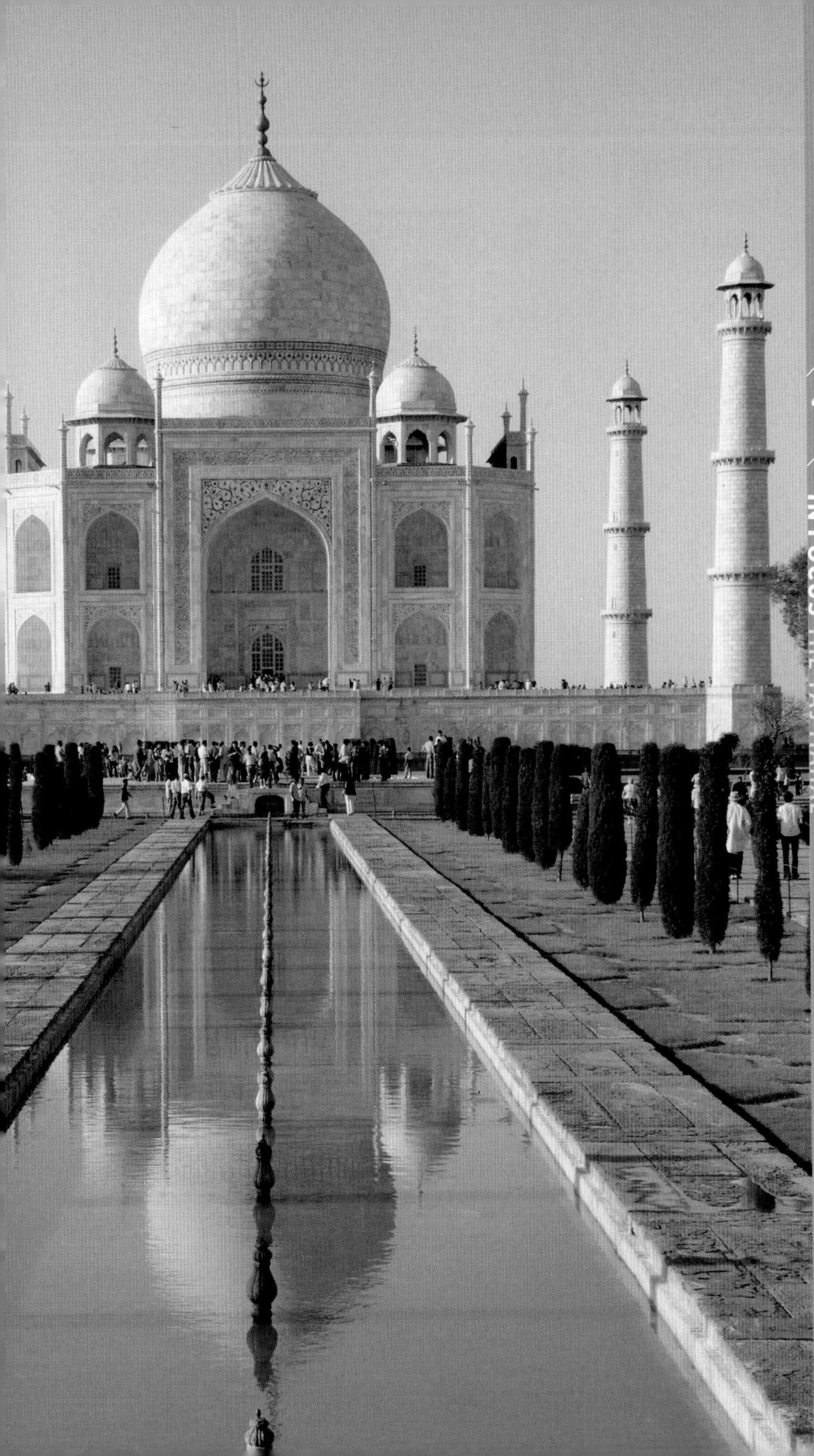

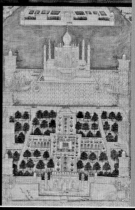

ENTRANCE

You enter the grounds through a huge sandstone gateway boldly emblazoned with an inlaid Koranic inscription.

THE GARDENS

The Taj Mahal stands at the end of a large garden that is divided into four sections by pools of water. Midway between the entrance and

(top left) Emperor Shah Jahan standing on a globe (top middle) Entrance to the Taj Mahal (top right) Interior of the mosque (bottom left) The Taj Mahal in early morning (bottom middle) An artist's drawing of the Taj Mahal (far right top) The lotus pool (far right bottom) Map of the Taj

the Taj is a large pool, called the Lotus pool because of it's lotus-shaped water spouts. The water reflects the Taj, and standing in front of the lotus pool makes for a popular photo op.

The garden in front of the Taj is said to symbolize Paradise, because Islamic texts of the period describe Paradise as a garden of abundance with four rivers separating it into four quadrants.

THE TOMB

The 190-square-foot central marble building, the mausoleum or pavilion, is the focus of the structure, and it stands on two bases: sandstone on the

bottom level, and marble on the top (measuring 313 square feet) that has been worked into a chessboard design.

The mausoleum's central archway is deeply recessed, as are the smaller pairs of companion archways along the sides and the beveled corners of the 190-square-foot structure.

Behind the main pavilion, the Yamuna River winds along its broad, sandy bed.

THE DOME

The Taj Mahal's most extraordinary feature is its onion-shaped dome, crowned by a brass finial mounted in a scalloped ornament: an inverted Hindu motif of the lotus. The

dome uses the Central Asian technique of placing a central inner dome, in this case 81 feet high, inside an outer shell to attain the extraordinary exterior height of 200 feet; between the two is an area nearly the size of the interior hall itself.

MINARETS
There are four slender, marble minarets—one at each corner of the Taj platform. They blend so well into the general composition that it's hard to believe each one is over 130 feet tall. The minarets were built at a slight tilt away from the tomb so that, in case of an earthquake, they'd fall away from the building.

MOSQUES
On opposite sides of the Taj Mahal are two majestic sandstone buildings: on the left is a mosque; the one on the right is believed to have been built as a mirror image, for symmetry, but may also have been used as a guesthouse.

MUSEUM
The small Taj Mahal Museum stands near the mosque to the left of the Taj. It contains Mughul memorabilia and provides some historical background to the Taj, as well as paintings of the famous

couple, manuscripts, letters, and a display of precious stones used in the construction of the Taj.

INSIDE THE MAUSOLEUM

The Taj Mahal is a glorious example of the refined aesthetics of the Mughals. In addition to the magnificent architecture of the buildings and the layout of the gardens, the mausoleum itself, likened to a jeweled box, showcases a range of artforms. One of the recurring motifs throughout the Taj are the many flower forms: flowers were believed to symbolize paradise on earth.

Carved marble screen

CARVED MARBLE SCREENS
Directly under the marble dome lie what look like the coffins of Mumtaz Mahal and Shah Jahan (photo at left), surrounded by a screen chiseled from a single block of marble, with latticework as intricate as lace. In fact, however, both are buried in a crypt below, in deference to the Islamic tradition that no one should walk upon their graves.

Crypt

CRYPT
Visitors are no longer allowed to go downstairs to the main crypt area (photo at right) where the bodies of Mumtaz Mahal and Shah Jahan are buried because of the vandalism that has occurred over the years.

INLAY WORK
Pietra dura, a type of mosaic work, is believed to have originated in Italy and later imported to Asia. It makes use of colorful, cut stones set in marble to create images. The intricate designs in the Taj use semi-precious stones including agate, carnelian, coral, jasper, lapis lazuli, malachite, tiger's eye, and turquoise, set in different shades of marble, sandstone, and slate. Look closely at the tiny flowers and detailed stonework on each petal and leaf in the Taj. The work is so fine that not even a magnifying glass reveals the tiny breaks between stones, yet a single one-inch flower on the queen's tomb has 60 pieces.

Inlay work

CARVED RELIEF WORK
Panels of carved flowers, foliage, and vases decorate the lower parts of the walls inside the mausoleum.

Carved relief work

CALLIGRAPHY
Inlaid calligraphy of black marble ornaments the undecorated surfaces of the mausoleum. The banner-like inscriptions on the arches are passages from the Koran.

Calligraphy

VISITING TIPS

The Taj Mahal, seen from the bank of the Yamuna River

Hours: The Taj is open Saturday to Thursday, from sunrise to sunset. It's closed on Fridays. The Taj Mahal museum is open Saturday to Thursday 8 am to 5 pm.

Admission: Rs. 750; museum Rs. 5

Best time to visit: Many people say that sunrise or sunset is the best time to see the Taj Mahal, for the glorious colors. Though the Taj Mahal is glorious any time of day, midday is probably the worst time to visit because of the bright sun reflecting off the white marble (bring your sunglasses). By all means, go early to beat the heat, but don't count on having the place to yourself, as there are almost always crowds at the Taj Mahal.

Night Viewing: The Taj is open for viewing 5 nights per month, on the full moon and two nights before and after, except Fridays and during Ramadan. Limited numbers of tickets are sold one day in advance (your hotel might be able to arrange tickets for you), for a half hour visit between 8:30 pm and 12:30 am. Admission price is the same as during regular hours. It's a romantic way to see the Taj but definitely not a substitute for a day-time visit. ✉ *Taj Ganj, Taj Rd. 282001* ⊕ www.tajmahal. gov.in/

To buy night-view tickets: Archaeological Survey of India. ✉ Agra Circle, 22 The Mall, Agra (10 am to 6 pm). ☎ *562/222–7261* or *562/222–7262*

DID YOU KNOW?

The two mosques on either side of the Taj Mahal provide stability. The Taj is built on a "floating" marble platform that doesn't have a foundation; the two mosques weigh down the platform. This was done because a massive earthquake had destroyed a major part of Agra in 1505, and the builders of the Taj were worried that another earthquake might destroy the magnificent building.

$$$$
NORTH INDIAN
★

✕**Esphahan.** Through the Amarvilas' illuminated Mughal courtyard and grand marble lobby, this intimate den celebrates local craftsmanship, with square pillars of red sandstone and white marble and carved wooden screens. Through the glass wall of the kitchen you can watch the chefs at work. The menu emphasizes the frequently elaborate and rich Lucknowi cuisine. Specialties include *Esphahani raan* (leg of lamb, marinated for 24 hours, roasted for 6 to 8 more, deboned, then cooked crisp in the tandoor). The tiger prawns marinated in citrus yogurt are good too. Live instrumental music, including sitar performances, adds to the mood throughout the week. Ⓢ *Average main: Rs. 1300* ✉ *Oberoi Amarvilas, Taj East Gate Rd., Agra, Uttar Pradesh* ☎ *562/223–1515.*

$$$$
INDIAN

✕**Jhankar.** Occupying an elegant, airy space open to the lobby of the Taj View Hotel, Jhankar has a menu of excellent Indian dishes that include the house specialty, *aloo dum chutneywale* (potatoes with dried fruits and herbs simmered in a mint and coriander sauce). Also terrific is the Agra delicacy *magazi murgh korma* (chicken in yogurt, cashews, and poppy seeds, garnished with rose petals and melon seeds). Flavors are subtle and distinct; many herbs and vegetables come from the kitchen garden. Ⓢ *Average main: Rs. 1200* ✉ *Taj-View Hotel, Fatehabad Rd., Taj Ganj, Agra, Uttar Pradesh* ☎ *562/223–2400 to 18.*

$$$$
INDIAN
★

✕**Mughal Room.** A ceiling of faux twinkling stars floats over an interior of rich reds, with brass trays hanging on walls and tables set with silver goblets. The panoramic view from a wall of windows takes in both the Taj Mahal and the Fort, while after dark live *ghazals* (Urdu love songs) set the mood for Mughlai cuisine. Behind a display window, a chef can be seen making such delicious dishes as *bajari tikka* (chicken cubes marinated in cream and yogurt, coated with spices, topped with cashews) and *kabuli naan* (bread stuffed with dried fruits and cheese, sprinkled with cumin seeds). Ⓢ *Average main: Rs. 900* ✉ *Clarks Shiraz, 54 Taj Rd., top fl., Agra, Uttar Pradesh* ☎ *562/222–6121 to 27.*

$$$$
INDIAN
★

✕**Peshawri.** Rustic wood tabletops resting on tree-trunk bases, plush, bright-orange seat cushions, and hammered copper plates and goblets create a dark, romantic mood, complemented by the simple, delicious barbecue cuisine of the North West Frontier, in what's now Pakistan. All kinds of meats are freshly prepared over open flames and served with rich, aromatic sauces. The ultra-rich *dal bukhara* (a combination of whole black lentils, tomatoes, ginger, and garlic along with plentiful ghee and cream) is slow-roasted for hours and makes a perfect choice for any vegetarians in the group. Reservations are recommended: it gets packed. Ⓢ *Average main: Rs. 800* ✉ *ITC Mughal Hotel, Taj Ganj, Agra, Uttar Pradesh* ☎ *562/402–1700.*

$$
INTERNATIONAL

✕**Pinch of Spice.** One of Agra's choice destinations for Mughal food, this sleek, modern restaurant is decorated in rich shades of purple, beige, and orange, and lighted by glittering glass chandeliers. The five-page menu includes Chinese and European dishes, but their North Indian cuisine is what makes the restaurant so popular with the locals. Try their signature butter chicken and *dal bukhara* (slow-cooked black lentils) and wash it down with a "paan shot," a creamy liquid breath freshener served after every meal. Massively popular, this restaurant is usually crowded, so it's best to make a reservation for dinner. Ⓢ *Average main:*

Rs. 400 ⊠ 23/453 Wazirpura Rd., Sanjay Pl., opposite Sanjay Cinema, Agra ☎ 562/400–9004 ⊕ www.pinchofspice.in.

$$
NORTH INDIAN
✕ **Sai Khandelaa.** A grand facade and entrance welcomes you into this simple but elegant restaurant, with a long history of serving delicious North Indian and Mughal cuisine. With its white walls adorned with paintings of Indian princesses, white linen tablecloths, and royal blue chairs, the restaurant feels traditionally Indian, and the equally traditional menu includes both vegetarian and meat-based dishes. $ *Average main: Rs. 400 ⊠ Sadar Bazar, Taj Rd., opposite Hotel ITC Mughal, Agra ☎ 562/222–7003 ⊕ www.saikhandelaa.com.*

$
ECLECTIC
✕ **Taste of Maya Restaurant.** One of the loveliest rooftop restaurants in Agra, this is a relaxing place to enjoy a coffee, or glass of wine in the evening by candlelight. Shaded from the sun by an enormous pipal tree, half-a-dozen tables covered with Rajasthani-dyed cloths are set up on a blue Moroccan tile floor, amidst a garden of potted plants. The menu is eclectic, with mostly Chinese and Indian fare. It's also a great place for breakfast—one of the few restaurants outside of five-star hotels that serves fresh seasonal fruit juice and organic bread. Recommended for breakfast and dinner. $ *Average main: Rs. 200 ⊠ 18/184 Purani Mandi Circle, Fatehabad Rd., Taj Ganj, Agra ☎ 97191–07691 ⊕ www.mayainmagic.com* ▭ No credit cards.

WHERE TO STAY
For expanded hotel reviews, visit Fodors.com.

$$$$
RESORT
★
▦ **ITC Mughal.** This huge complex has an overwhelming range of activities night and day—there's even a mock village, complete with cyclerickshaws and fake wedding ceremonies in which couples can dress up like an Indian bride and groom. **Pros:** you'll never be bored; the spa is incredible. **Cons:** so huge you may need a map. $ *Rooms from: Rs. 11500 ⊠ Fatehabad Rd., Taj Ganj, Agra, Uttar Pradesh ☎ 562/402–1700 ⊕ www.itcwelcomgroup.in* ⤴ *233 rooms, 7 suites* ❘⊙❘ *Breakfast.*

$$$
RESORT
☾
▦ **Jaypee Hotel Palace.** The largest hotel-resort in all of Agra, the Jaypee sits on nearly 25 acres of lawns and gardens and, in addition to the usual type of resort amenities, has an in-house bowling alley and theater, with an arcade and playroom to keep children happy. **Pros:** lots of in-house amenities; a good place to bring children. **Cons:** easy to get lost on the grounds; not for those seeking cozy lodgings. $ *Rooms from: Rs. 7500 ⊠ Fatehabad Rd., Agra ☎ 562/233–0800 ⊕ www.jaypeehotels.com* ⤴ *350 rooms* ❘⊙❘ *No meals.*

$
B&B/INN
▦ **N. Homestay.** It would be difficult to find a more warm and inviting hostess than Naghma Haider, who runs this homestay—and even offers cooking classes—in the spacious, three-story home she shares with her delightful, easygoing family. **Pros:** a great cultural experience; the family is a fount of local knowledge. **Cons:** you are in someone's house, so you won't necessarily have privacy outside of your room. $ *Rooms from: Rs. 1499 ⊠ 15 Ajanta Colony, Vibhav Nagar, Agra ⊕ www.nhomestay.com* ⤴ *6 rooms* ▭ No credit cards ❘⊙❘ *Breakfast.*

$$$$
RESORT
Fodor'sChoice
★
▦ **Oberoi Amarvilas.** One of India's best resorts emulates the opulent lifestyle of the Mughal emperors—complete with your own butler—and has a breathtaking view of the Taj Mahal. **Pros:** gorgeous views; flawless service; free rides to the Taj Mahal and guide services. **Cons:** extremely

expensive. $ *Rooms from: Rs. 41000* ✉ *Taj East Gate Rd., Agra, Uttar Pradesh* ☎ *562/223–1515, 800/562–3764* ⊕ *www.oberoihotels.com* ⇆ *106 rooms, 7 suites* ⊙| *No meals.*

$
HOTEL

⬚ **Ray of Maya.** Less than a 10-minute walk from the western gate of the Taj Mahal, this clean, cozy, and elegant place is ideal for couples and singles on a budget who don't want to rough it. **Pros:** cozy, intimate, and economical; top of the Taj visible from rooms 6 and 8. **Cons:** while the inside is lovely, the exterior isn't much to look at; lots of stairs; toiletries not provided. $ *Rooms from: Rs. 3000* ✉ *Purani Mandi, Fatehabad Rd., Agra* ☎ *562/405–2665* ⊕ *www.mayainmagic. com* ⇆ *7 rooms* ⊙| *No meals.*

$$$
RESORT
⟳

⬚ **Taj Gateway.** Luxury without outrageous prices and rooms with a good, though distant, view of the Taj Mahal make this a popular choice. **Pros:** upscale amenities for a decent price; great activities and entertainment for kids (and adults). **Cons:** the hotel's popularity, and its small lobby, can make it seem extremely crowded. $ *Rooms from: Rs. 9500* ✉ *Fatehabad Rd., Taj Ganj, Agra, Uttar Pradesh* ☎ *562/660–2000* ⊕ *www.tajhotels.com* ⇆ *95 rooms, 5 suites* ⊙| *Breakfast.*

$$$
HOTEL
⟳
★

⬚ **Trident Agra.** Built around a large garden courtyard with fountains, water spilling over rocks, a soothing expanse of green lawn, and a pool, this place is a real oasis in Agra. **Pros:** a thoughtful feature—rare in India—is two handicap-accessible rooms; kids' club. **Cons:** rooms are close to the lobby. $ *Rooms from: Rs. 9000* ✉ *Fatehabad Rd., Agra, Uttar Pradesh* ☎ *562/223–5000, 800/11–2122* ⊕ *www.hilton. com* ⇆ *136 rooms, 2 suites* ⊙| *Breakfast.*

$$$$
RESORT
⟳

⬚ **Wyndham Grand Agra.** A night here feels a bit like staying in a Mughal palace, with sweeping beige and white marble arches, manicured gardens, gurgling fountains, and elaborate rooms. **Pros:** five restaurants offer plenty of dining options. **Cons:** rooms are far from the lobby. $ *Rooms from: Rs. 10500* ✉ *7th Mile Stone, Fatehabad Rd., Agra* ☎ *562/223–7000* ⊕ *www.wyndhamgrandagra.com* ⇆ *160* ⊙| *Breakfast.*

SHOPPING

Tourist shops are generally open daily from 10 to 7:30. Many Agra shops sell hand-knotted dhurries and other rugs, jewelry made from precious and semiprecious stones, brass statues, and marble inlays that continue the form and motifs seen in the city's great monuments. Resist drivers and touts who want to take you to places offering special "bargains"; they receive big commissions from shopkeepers, which you pay in the inflated price of the merchandise. Beware, too, of soapstone masquerading as marble: this softer, cheaper stone is a convincing substitute, but you can test it by scraping the item with your fingernail—Indian marble won't scrape. Finally, for what it's worth, local lore has it that miniature replicas of the Taj Mahal bring bad luck.

Agra Marble Emporium. This large, three-room marble shop sells side tables, knickknacks, and souvenirs, and you can often see workers carving marble in the front of the shop. All marble can be shipped internationally. ✉ *A Block No. 4, Taj Nagri Phase-2, Fatehabad Rd., Agra* ☎ *562/327–9345, 562/223–2321* ⊕ *www.agramarbleemporium.com.*

Cottage Industries Exposition. This chain of privately owned stores (not to be confused with the government-run Central Cottage Industries) carries high-quality rugs (mostly Kashmiri), silks, gemstones, and, like everyplace else in Agra, marble inlay. Prices are extremely high—bargain fiercely. ⊠ *39 Fatehabad Rd., Agra, Uttar Pradesh* ☎ *562/222–6813.*

Cottage Industry. Good kashmiri stoles, dhurries, and other carpets are available here. ⊠ *18 Munro Rd., Agra, Uttar Pradesh* ☎ *562/222–6019.*

> ### THE MARBLE MECCA
>
> It's believed that the Taj Mahal's marble may have come from the mines of Makrana, a small Rajasthani village 400 km (250 miles) to the west that's renowned for its marble supply. The artisans creating marble inlay in Agra today are likely using Makrana marble, and they're believed to be descendants of those who mined the marble or did the inlay work on the Taj.

Ganeshi Lall and Son. This reliable, family-owned jeweler, established in 1845, specializes in older pieces and also creates new ones; the M.G. Road location, adjacent to the owner's home and open only by appointment, is a museumlike gallery of very fine old textiles, paintings, wood carvings, and some jewelry. Past clients have included major museums and Jacqueline Kennedy Onassis. ⊠ *ITC Mughal, Fatehabad Rd., Agra, Uttar Pradesh* ☎ *562/233–0181* ⊠ *13 M.G. Rd., Agra, Uttar Pradesh* ☎ *562/246–4567.*

Kohinoor. This company has been designing jewelry using cut and uncut emeralds and other precious stones since 1862; a special connoisseur's room is open by appointment. Don't miss the little museum of fantastic 3-D *zardoji* (embroidered paintings). Some paintings, known as Shams, have been encrusted with gems by the master of the technique, Shamsuddin (some are for sale). ⊠ *41 M.G. Rd., Agra, Uttar Pradesh* ☎ *562/236–4156, 562/236–8855.*

Oswal Exports. Excellent examples of inlaid white, pink, green, and black marble are produced here; you can watch as the artisans do their work and learn the technique. ⊠ *30-B Munro Rd., Agra, Uttar Pradesh* ☎ *562/222–5710, 562/222–5712.*

Subhash Emporium. This was the first store to revive Agra marble work in the 1960s. Ask to see some of the incredible pieces in the private gallery to give you a better perspective on quality. ⊠ *18/1 Gwalior Rd., Agra, Uttar Pradesh* ☎ *562/222–5828 to 30.*

FATEHPUR SIKRI

Fodor'sChoice ★ *37 km (23 miles) southwest of Agra.*

The capital of the Mughal Empire for only 14 years (from 1571 to 1585), the majestic red sandstone buildings of the now uninhabited fortified city of Fatehpur Sikri are remarkably well preserved, and showcase elegant architecture and an inspired sense of planning.

In a sense, Fatehpur Sikri was built on faith: in 1569, so the story goes, the Mughal emperor Akbar was driven to despair because he didn't have a male heir. He made a pilgrimage to visit the mystic Salim Chisti, who blessed him. The blessing evidently worked, as Akbar had a son within the next year, naming him Salim (the future emperor Jahangit) in honor of the saint. Two years later, Akbar began building a new capital in Chisti's village of Sikri, later renaming it Fatehpur Sikri (City of Victory) after a great triumph in Gujarat. Standing on a rocky ridge overlooking the village, Fatehpur Sikri originally had a circumference of about 11 km (7 miles). Massive walls and seven gates enclosed three sides, and a lake (now dried up) protected the fourth. When the British came to Fatehpur Sikri in 1583 to meet Akbar, they were amazed to see a city that exceeded contemporary London in both population and grandeur—with more rubies, diamonds, and silks than they could count.

What remains is a beautiful cluster of royal dwellings on the top of the ridge, landscaped with lawns and flowering borders. The structures elegantly blend architectural styles from Persia as well as Akbar's various Indian holdings, a reflection of the synthesizing impulse that characterized the third and greatest of the Mughal emperors. Also notable is how Akbar synthesized Muslim and Hindu beliefs here. The magnificently carved Brahma pillar is testament to his stand on communal harmony. Akbar ruled here for only 14 years before moving his capital—perhaps in pursuit of water, but more likely for political reasons—to Lahore and then eventually back to Agra. Because it was abandoned and never resettled, the city was not modified by later rulers, and thus is the best reflection of Akbar's aesthetic and design philosophies. Fatehpur Sikri now stands as an intriguing ghost town, reflecting a high point in India's cultural history.

GETTING HERE AND AROUND
To reach Fatehpur Sikri from Agra, hire a car and driver or join a tour. The drive takes about an hour. There are ticket offices at the Jodh Bai Palace entrance, Diwan-i-Am.

TIMING
Fatehpur Sikri is best visited early in the morning. Set out from Agra by about 6:30 am to avoid traffic. You'll be done well before 11 am, which is when the heat begins to really kick in. Plan to spend at least two or three hours wandering the grounds. Wear good walking shoes; there's a lot of ground to be covered here.

EXPLORING
Buland Darwaza (Great Gate). The usual starting point for exploring Fatehpur Sikri is the Buland Darwaza (Great Gate) of the **Jama Masjid**, near the parking lot, but the cluster of hawkers and guides nearby can be unrelenting. If you arrive by car, you can avoid this minor annoyance by asking to be dropped at the subsidiary entrance at the northeastern end of the city, where the following tour begins. Coming from Agra, bear right just after passing through **Agra Gate**, the main one in Akbar's day. The tour ends at the Great Gate, so have your driver meet you there.

Approaching the Fatehpur Sikri complex, you'll walk through the **Naubat Khana,** a gate that was manned by drummers and musicians during imperial processions. Just ahead on the right is the **Mint,** a workshop that may have minted coins.

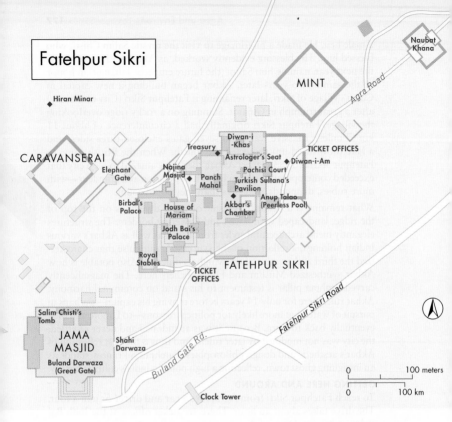

Fatehpur Sikri

Naubat Khana

Hiran Minar

MINT

Agra Road

CARAVANSERAI

Elephant Gate

Najina Masjid

Treasury

Diwan-i-Khas

Astrologer's Seat

TICKET OFFICES

Diwan-i-Am

Pachisi Court

Panch Mahal

Turkish Sultana's Pavilion

Birbal's Palace

House of Mariam

Akbar's Chamber

Anup Talao (Peerless Pool)

Jodh Bai's Palace

Royal Stables

TICKET OFFICES

FATEHPUR SIKRI

Fatehpur Sikri Road

Salim Chisti's Tomb

JAMA MASJID

Shahi Darwaza

Buland Gate Rd.

Buland Darwaza (Great Gate)

Clock Tower

0   100 meters

0   100 km

A few steps from the museum is the **Diwan-i-Am** (Hall of Public Audience), a large courtyard 112 meters long and 55 meters wide (366 feet by 181 feet) with colonnades on three sides. Ahead is the balcony where the emperor sat on his throne to meet subjects or observe celebrations and other spectacles. Through chiseled marble screens, the women of the court would watch as Akbar, the empire's chief justice, handed down his decisions: it's said that those condemned to die were impaled, hanged, or trampled under the feet of an elephant. What looks like a square two-story building with domed cupolas at each corner is the **Diwan-i-Khas** (Hall of Private Audience). Inside it's actually one tall room where Akbar sat on an elaborate elevated platform and, it's thought, conducted meetings with his ministers. Supported by a stone column topped with a giant lotus flower intricately carved in stone, it's connected by causeways to four balconies with window seats on which the ministers sat. The throne's position is thought to have symbolized the center of the world or, alternatively, the one god sought by several major religions; it also may have had a practical side, shielding the emperor from would-be assassins.

Across from the hall is the **Treasury**, also known as **Ankh Michali** (Hide and Seek), said to be named for Akbar's reported playful habit of playing the game with his harem inside the broad rooms and narrow passageways. The deep recesses in the walls, though, suggest that it may have been used as a treasury. Adjacent is the **Astrologer's Seat,** a platform where Akbar's royal astrologer sat. Pass through the court-yard paved with a board on which Akbar played *pachisi* (an early form of parcheesi that used slave girls as pieces), into the pavilion centered by the **Anup Talao** (Peerless Pool), a square pool with a central plat-form, connected by four bridges. Below the basement of the pavilion is an excavated underground palace whose entrances cleverly concealed it until archaeologists, led by reports from Akbar's day, discovered it. The emperor would come to these rooms, constructed at the center of a water-filled tank, to escape the summer heat. Unearthed within them was the 12-foot-high stone bowl (now displayed on the pavilion) used to store water transported from the Ganges—the only water Akbar would drink. At the edge of the pool is the **Turkish Sultana's Pavilion,** a charm-ing structure covered with elaborate Persian carvings in floral and zigzag patterns. It is said to have been the home of the emperor's Turkish wife, but was more likely a place to relax by the pool and have a quiet conver-sation. Separated from the sultana's pavilion as well as from the official buildings of the palace by the Anup Talao are Akbar's private chambers.

The Imperial Harem, where the women of Akbar's household resided, consists of several buildings connected by covered passages and screened from view of the more public areas. The **Panch Mahal** is a breeze-catching structure with five arcaded stories (*panch* in Hindi), each smaller than the one below. Its 176 columns are carved with tiny flowers or other motifs (no two of the first floor's 56 columns have the same design). As Fatehpur Sikri's tallest building, it affords grand views of the city and the surrounding landscape from its upper stories. When the women prayed, they did so behind the screened arches of the **Najina Masjid** (Small or Jewel Mosque), behind the Panch Mahal across a small garden. The largest residence in the complex is the Gujarati-influenced **Jodh Bai Palace,** more properly called Principal Haram Sara, because behind its eunuch-guarded entrance lived a number of the emperor's wives rather than just that of his Hindu wife Jodh Bai. The **Hawa Mahal** (Palace of the Winds) is a cool vantage point from which women could peek out at the court unseen from beautifully carved stone screens.

The **House of Mariam** (on a diagonal between Jodh Bai's Palace and the Panch Mahal) is the home of either Akbar's Christian wife or, more likely, his mother. Look for the faded paintings of horses and elephants on the exterior walls. Some of the brackets supporting the eaves are carved with scenes from mythology. **Birbal's Palace,** which sits a few yards northwest of Jodh Bai's Palace and the Hawa Mahal, was named for the emperor's playfully irreverent Hindu prime minister. Because it's unlikely that he would have lived inside the harem, the ASI ascribes it to Akbar's two senior wives. The palace's ornamentation makes use of both Hindu and Islamic motifs.

The big open colonnade behind the harem is known as the **Royal Sta-bles** because the stalls were once thought to have housed elephants and horses; however, it is more likely that it was the quarters of the serving women, and that the open stalls were enclosed by curtains tied to the stone rings once thought to have tethered the animals. At the

One of the red sandstone buildings at Fatehpur Sikri

edge of the city complex, by Sikri Lake, you should be able to see the **Hiran Minar** tower, decorated with six-pointed stars and hexagons, from which elephant tusks protrude (the originals have been replaced with stone tusks). If it's open, there are 53 steps that take you to the top of the tower, from where you have a bird's-eye view of Fatehpur Sikri.

Follow the path down to the east gate of the **Jama Masjid** (Imperial Mosque); built around 1571 and designed to hold 10,000 worshippers, it's still in active use. Note the deliberate incorporation of Hindu elements in the design, especially the pillar decorations. The **Shahi Darwza** (Emperor's Gate) is on the eastern side of the mosque; only the Emperor and his courtiers were allowed to pass through this gate. The sandstone gateway is fully carved in geometrical design, and has two arches, one on top of the other; a lotus-bud motif runs through the smaller arch.

In the courtyard of the Jama Masjid (opposite the Buland Darwaza) lies **Salim Chisti's tomb**, surrounded by walls of marble lace, each with a different design. Begun upon the saint's death in 1571 and finished nine years later, the tomb was originally faced with red sandstone, but was refinished in marble by Jahangir, the heir Akbar's wife bore after the saint's blessing. From here you can cross the courtyard and exit through the imposing Buland Darwaza. Tombs of those people lucky enough to be buried by the revered saint are in this area. And here is the **Buland Darwaza** (Great Gate), at the southwestern end of the city. The beautiful inscription etched on it translates to "The world is but a bridge, pass over but build no houses on it." With its beveled walls and inset archways, the southern gate rises 134 feet over a base of steps that raise it another 34 feet, dwarfing everything else in sight. Akbar built it after conquering Gujarat, and it set the style for later gateways, which the Mughals built habitually as symbols of their power.

The various upper stories of Fatehpur Sikri are now closed to visitors because of the proliferation of graffiti. ✉ *Rs. 260* ⏱ *Daily sunrise–sunset.*

> **NEED A BOY?**
>
> Many people believed that Salim Chisti, the famous Muslim saint, could perform miracles. Women of all faiths still come to his tomb to cover it with cloth and tie a string on the marble latticework in hopes of giving birth to a son.

NEED A BREAK?

Gulistan Tourist Complex. The simple Indian restaurant at the Gulistan Tourist Complex, just down the road from Fatehpur Sikri on the way to Agra, is a convenient and welcoming lunch stop. ☎ 561/3288–2490.

KHAJURAHO

395 km (245 miles) southeast of Agra and 379 km (235 miles) south-west of Varanasi.

The UNESCO World Heritage Site temples of Khajuraho are known for their carved erotic images, but they are also examples of advanced architecural styles. The soaring *shikharas* (spires) of the temples are meant to resemble the peaks of the Himalayas, the abode of Lord Shiva. The spire of each temple rises higher than the one before it, as in a range of mountains that seems to draw near the heavens. Designed to inspire the viewer toward the highest human potential, these were also the builders' attempts to reach upward, out of the material world, to *moksha*, the final release from the cycle of rebirth. It's definitely worth a visit here, though getting to Khajuraho is not easy.

This small rural village in the state of Madhya Pradesh was once the religious capital of the Chandelas, one of the most powerful Rajput dynasties of Central India, from the 10th to 12th century. They built 85 temples here, 25 of which remain to give a glimpse of a time when Hindu art and devotion reached its apex. When the dynasty eventually succumbed to invaders, Khajuraho's temples lapsed into obscurity until their rediscovery by the British explorer Captain T.S. Burt in 1838.

During the Chandelas' rule, the temples' royal patrons were rich, the land was fertile, and those at the top lived the good life, trooping off to hunts, feasts, and theater, music, and dance performances. This abundance was the perfect climate for creativity, and temple-building emerged as the major form of expression. There were no strict boundaries between the sacred and the profane, no dictates on acceptable deities: Shiva, Vishnu, Brahma, and the Jain saints were all lavishly honored here. Among other things, Khajuraho represents an incredible testament of the strength of human devotion and faith.

Excavations have also uncovered a complex of Buddhist temples. Despite the interest in heaven, the real focus was Earth, particularly the facts of human life. Here, immortalized in stone, virile men and voluptuous women cavort and copulate in the most intimate, erotic, and sometimes bewildering postures. Khajuraho represents the best of Hindu temple sculpture: sinuous, twisting forms, human and divine, pulsing with life, tension, and conflict. But its Buddhist side is more serene.

A number of sculptural motifs run through the temples. Certain gods, for instance, have directional positions: elephant-headed Ganesh faces north; Yama, the god of death, and his mount, a male buffalo, face south. Other sculptures include the *apsaras* (heavenly maidens), found mainly inside, and the Atlas-like *kichakas,* who support the ceilings on their shoulders. Many sculptures reflect everyday activities, such as a dance class, and there are sultry *nayikas* (mortal women) and plenty of *mithunas* (amorous couples). The scorpion appears as an intriguing theme, running up and down the thighs of many female sculptures as a kind of erotic thermometer.

Of the extant temples, all but two were made from sandstone mined from the banks of the River Ken, 30 km (19 miles) away. The stone blocks were carved separately, then assembled as interlocking pieces. Though each temple is different, all observe precise architectural principles of shape, form, and orientation and contain certain essential elements: a high raised platform, an *ardh mandapam* (entrance porch), a *mandapam* (portico), an *antrala* (vestibule), and a *garbha griha* (inner sanctum). Some of the larger temples also have a walkway around the inner sanctum, a *maha-mandapam* (hall), and subsidiary shrines at each corner of the platform, making a complete *panchayatana* (five-shrine complex).

No one knows why erotic sculptures are so important here, though many explanations have been suggested. The female form is often used as an auspicious marker on Hindu gateways and doors, in the form of temple sculptures as well as domestic wall paintings. In the late classical and early medieval periods, this symbol expanded into full-blown erotic art in many places, including the roughly contemporary sun temple at Modhera, in Gujarat, and the slightly later one at Konark, in Orissa. A common folk explanation is that the erotic sculptures protect the temples from lightning; and art historians have pointed out that many of the erotic panels are placed at junctures where some protection or strengthening agent might be structurally necessary. Others say the sculptures reflect the influence of a Tantric cult that believed in rever-sals of ordinary morality as a religious practice. Still others argue that sex has been used as a metaphor: the carnal and bestial sex generally shown near the bases of the temples represents uncontrolled and baser human appetites. They're metaphors of leaving bodily desires behind, to follow a spiritual path. Conversely, the couples deeply engrossed in each other, oblivious to all else, represent a divine bliss, the closest humans can approach to God.

GETTING HERE AND AROUND

Khajuraho Airport, 5 km (3 miles) from the city, is connected via Jet and GoAir to Delhi, Varanasi, and Mumbai. If you're going by train, one good option is to take the UP Sampark Kranti Express, which comes in from Delhi H. Nizamuddin Station to Khajuraho three times a week (Tuesday, Friday, and Sunday). Khajuraho is about a five-hour drive from Varanasi, 6½ hours from Agra, and more than 9 hours from Delhi.

Khajuraho is so small that bicycles, cycle-rickshaws, and/or walking are the best available options for getting around, rather than taxis or auto-rickshaws. For Rs. 50–Rs. 70 you can **rent a bicycle** for the day from one of the many places across from the bus stand, behind the museum, and from some hotels. It's a great way to get around this relatively traffic-free town and to explore the small streets of Khajuraho village, the old residential area near the Eastern Group of temples that teems with shops, animals, and children. Entrepreneurial boys will gladly guide you around for Rs. 50.

TIMING

Dance Festival. In late February or early March, Khajuraho holds an annual, week-long dance festival, set in part against the backdrop of the temples. This superb event attracts some of the country's best performers. Contact the tourist office for more information. ✉ *Khajuraho, Madhya Pradesh*.

Kandariya. From August through mid-April, for Rs. 300 you can see folk dances from all over India performed nightly at 7:30 and 8:30 pm at Kandariya, a theater attached to the shop **Shilpgram**. ✉ *Bamitha Rd., near Jhankar Hotel, Khajuraho, Madhya Pradesh*.

ESSENTIALS

Madhya Pradesh Tourism ☎ 755/255–3006 ⊕ www.mptourism.com.

> ## EVENING ENTERTAINMENT
>
> **The sound-and-light show** at Khajuraho is a popular 50-minute extravaganza, which runs in Hindi and English every evening (except during the summer monsoon season) at the Western Group, traces the story of the Chandela kings and the temples from the 10th century to the present. Showtime varies based on sunset, so confirm it with your hotel or the tourist office. Buy tickets at the tourism office. ✉ *Khajuraho, Madhya Pradesh* ⊕ *www.mptourism.com* 🎟 *Rs. 300* ⊗ *English-language show: 6:30–7:25*.

4

WESTERN GROUP OF TEMPLES

Most of the Western Group of temples, the richest and largest group, are inside a formal enclosure whose entrance is on Main Road, opposite the State Bank of India. Although the rest of the town's temples are always accessible and free, these are open daily from sunrise to sunset and have an admission charge of Rs. 250.

The first three temples, though considered part of the Western Group, are at a slight distance from the enclosure.

Chausath Yogini Temple. The oldest temple at Khajuraho is set on a granite outcrop southwest of the Shivsagar Tank, a small artificial lake. It may have been built as early as AD 820. It's dedicated to Kali (a form of the Goddess Durga, Slayer of Demons), and its name refers to the 64 *chausath* (female ascetics) who serve this fierce goddess in the Hindu pantheon. A little more than half that number have survived. Unlike its counterparts, which are made of pale, warm-hued sandstone, this temple is made of granite. ✉ *Khajuraho, Madhya Pradesh*.

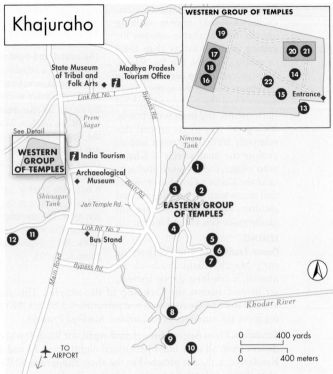

Temples ▼

Adinath **5**

Bijamandala **9**

Brahma **3**

Chaturbhuj **10**

Chausath
Yogini **11**

Chitragupta **19**

Devi
Jagdamba **17**

Duladeo **8**

Ghantai **4**

Javari **2**

Kandariya
Mahadev **16**

Lakshmana **15**

Lalguan
Mahadeva **12**

Mahadeva **18**

Matangesvara ..**13**

Nandi **21**

Parsvanath **6**

Parvati **22**

Shantinath **7**

Vamana **1**

Varaha **14**

Vishvanath **20**

Lalguan Mahadeva. Lying in ruins, with the original portico missing, this Shiva temple is 600 meters west of Chausath Yogini. It is historically significant because it was built of both granite and sandstone, marking the transition from Chausath Yogini to the later temples. ⊠ *Khajuraho, Madhya Pradesh.*

Matangesvara Temple. Just outside the boundary of the Western Group stands this temple, which has its own gate to the left of the entrance. It's the only one still in use here; worship takes place in the morning and afternoon. The lack of ornamentation, the square construction, and the simple floor plan date this temple to the early 10th century. It has large bay windows, a projecting portico, and a ceiling of overlapping concentric circles. An enormous lingam (a phallic symbol associated with Shiva), nearly 8½ feet tall, is enshrined in the sanctum. ⊠ *Khajuraho, Madhya Pradesh.*

Archaeological Museum. Across the street from Matangesvara Temple, this museum displays exquisite carvings and sculptures that archaeologists have recovered from the temple sites. The three galleries attempt to put the works into context according to the deities they represent. ⊠ *Main Rd., Khajuraho, Madhya Pradesh* ☎ *768/627–2320* ⌚ *Rs. 5* ☉ *Mon.–Sat. 10–5.*

Varaha Temple. Just inside the main entrance gate, to your left, next to a small Lakshmi temple, is this beautiful temple dedicated to Vishnu's Varaha avatar (his incarnation as a boar). It was built circa 900–925. Vishnu assumed this form in order to rescue the earth after a demon had hidden it in the slush at the bottom of the sea. In the inner sanctum, all of creation is depicted on the massive and beautifully polished sides of a stone boar, which in turn stands on the serpent Shesha. The ceiling is carved with a lotus relief, which represents the flowering of the crown chakra, the spiritual center. ⊠ *Khajuraho, Madhya Pradesh*.

★ **Lakshmana Temple.** Across from the Varaha Temple is this temple dedicated to Vishnu. It is the only

> **DON'T MISS THE DETAILS**
>
> The number of carvings can seem overwhelming, but keep an eye out for work into which the carvers injected their own views of life, often with a sense of humor. In the Western Group there is an elephant turning his head and laughing at the couple having sex beside him. In another carving a man has covered his face in embarrassment, but he's still peeping through his fingers at what's going on nearby. It's well worth hiring a guide, for the Western Group at least, who can point out the more quirky aspects.

complete temple remaining. Along with Kandariya Mahadeva and Vishvanath, this edifice represents the peak of achievement in North Indian temple architecture. All three temples were built in the early to mid-10th century, face east, and follow an elaborate plan resembling a double cross, with three tiers of exterior sculpture on high platforms. The ceiling of the portico is carved with shell and floral motifs. The support beam over the entrance to the main shrine shows Lakshmi, goddess of wealth and consort of Vishnu, with Brahma, Lord of Creation, on her left and Shiva, Lord of Destruction, on her right. Around the exterior base are some of Khajuraho's most famous sculptures, with gods and goddesses on the protruding corners, erotic couples or groups in the recesses, and apsaras and *sura-sundaris* (apsaras performing everyday activities) in between. Along the sides of the tall platform beneath the temple, carvings depict social life, including battle scenes, festivals, and more X-rated pursuits. According to the inscription on the Lakshmana Temple, it was built by King Yasovarman. The whole temple was built to house an image of Vishnu given to him by his Pratihara overlord, Devapala. This image (it can still be seen here) was originally brought over from Tibet. ⊠ *Khajuraho, Madhya Pradesh*.

Fodor's Choice **Kandariya Mahadev.** This temple, which lies west of the Lakshmana, is
★ the tallest and most evolved temple in Khajuraho in terms of the blending of architecture and sculpture, and one of the finest in India. Probably built around 1025–50 by King Vidyahara (the greatest of the Chandela kings), it follows the five-shrine design. Its central spire, which towers 102 feet above the platform, is actually made up of 84 subsidiary towers built up in increments. The feeling of ascent is repeated inside, where each succeeding portico rises a step above the previous one, and the inner sanctum is higher still; dedicated to Shiva (Mahadev is another name for Shiva), this inner sanctum houses a marble lingam

with a 4-foot circumference. Even the figures on this temple are taller and slimmer than those elsewhere. The rich interior carving includes two beautiful *toranas* (arched doorways). Outside, three bands of sculpture around the sanctum and transept bring to life a whole galaxy of Hindu gods and goddesses, mithunas, celestial handmaidens, and lions. ⊠ *Khajuraho, Madhya Pradesh.*

Devi Jagdamba Temple. This temple was originally dedicated to Vishnu, as indicated by a prominent sculpture over the sanctum's doorway. It now honors Parvati, Shiva's consort, but because her image is black—a color associated with Kali—it's also known as the Kali Temple. From the inside, its three-shrine design makes the temple appear to be shaped like a cross. The third band of sculpture has a series of erotic mithunas, considered some of the finest sculpture of this type in all of Khajuraho. The ceilings are similar to those in the Kandariya Mahadev, and the three-headed, eight-armed statue of Shiva is one of the best cult images in Khajuraho. ⊠ *Khajuraho, Madhya Pradesh.*

Mahadeva Temple. Sharing the platform with the Kandariya Mahadev and the Devi Jagdamba, this small temple is now mostly a ruin. Now dedicated to Shiva, it may originally have been a subsidiary temple to the Kandariya, probably dedicated to Shiva's consort. In the portico stands a remarkable statue of a man caressing a mythical horned lion. ⊠ *Khajuraho, Madhya Pradesh.*

Chitragupta Temple. This temple that's just north of the Devi Jagdamba also resembles it in construction. In honor of the presiding deity, the sun god Surya, the temple faces east, and its cell contains a 5-foot-tall image of Surya complete with the chariot and seven horses that carry him across the sky. Surya also appears above the doorway. In the central niche south of the sanctum is an image of Vishnu with 11 heads; his own face is in the center, and the other heads represent his 10 main incarnations. Sculptural scenes of animal combat, royal processions, masons at work, and joyous dances depict the lavish country life of the Chandelas. It also has an ancient three-story stepped tank (water reservoir). ⊠ *Khajuraho, Madhya Pradesh.*

Vishvanath Temple. Two staircases lead up to this temple, the northern one flanked by a pair of lions and the southern by a pair of elephants. The Vishvanath probably preceded the Kandariya, but here only two of the original corner shrines remain. On the outer wall of the corridor surrounding the cells is an impressive image of Brahma, the three-headed Lord of Creation, and his consort, Saraswati. On every wall the female form predominates, portraying some women's 10th-century occupations: writing a letter, holding a baby, applying makeup, or playing music. The nymphs of paradise are voluptuous and provocative, the erotic scenes robust. An inscription states that the temple was built by Chandela King Dhanga in 1002. The temple sits on a terrace to the east of the Chitragupta and Devi Jagdamba temples. ⊠ *Khajuraho, Madhya Pradesh.*

Nandi Temple. This simple temple, which faces Vishvanath, houses a monolithic statue of Shiva's mount, the massive and richly harnessed bull Nandi. ⊠ *Khajuraho, Madhya Pradesh.*

Carvings on the Kandariya Mahadev

Parvati Temple. The small and heavily rebuilt temple, near Vishvanath, was originally dedicated to Vishnu. The present icon is that of the goddess Ganga (a representation of the river Ganges) standing on her mount, the crocodile. ⊠ *Khajuraho, Madhya Pradesh.*

<table>
<tr><td>NEED A
BREAK?</td><td>Blue Sky. Exit the gate, and across the street from Vishvanath and Nandi temples is Blue Sky, a favorite café that's on the main road. Don't miss the view from the 2nd floor and rooftop terraces. ⊠ Main Rd., near Western Group of Temples, Khajuraho, Madhya Pradesh ☎ 7686/274-120.</td></tr>
</table>

★ **State Museum of Tribal and Folk Arts.** There's an excellent collection here, consisting of more than 500 artifacts of terra-cotta, metal, and wood crafts, paintings, jewelry, and masks from all over Madhya Pradesh and the Bastar region (known for tribal crafts) in the neighboring state of Chhattisgarh. ⊠ *Chandela Cultural Complex, Rajnagar Rd., Khajuraho, Madhya Pradesh* ☎ *768/627–4051* ⊠ *Rs. 50* ☉ *Tues.–Sun. noon–8.*

EASTERN GROUP OF TEMPLES

Scattered around the edges of the old village of Khajuraho, the Eastern Group of temples includes three Brahma and four Jain temples. Their proximity attests to the religious tolerance of the times in general and the Chandela rulers in particular.

Vamana Temple. Northernmost is the late-11th-century Vamana Temple, dedicated to Vishnu's dwarf incarnation (though the image in the sanctum looks more like a tall, sly child). The sanctum walls show unusual theological openness, depicting most of the major gods and goddesses;

Vishnu appears in many of his forms, including the Buddha, his ninth incarnation. Outside, two tiers of sculpture are concerned mainly with the nymphs of paradise, who strike charming poses under their private awnings. The pretty view from this temple includes barley fields. ⊠ *Khajuraho, Madhya Pradesh.*

Javari Temple. Small and well-proportioned, this temple is just south of the Vamana and roughly contemporary with it. It has a simplified three-shrine design: the two main exterior bands of sculpture bear hosts of heavenly maidens. It's also dedicated to Lord Vishnu. ⊠ *Khajuraho, Madhya Pradesh.*

Brahma Temple. This granite-and-sandstone temple, one of the earliest here (circa 900), is probably misnamed. Brahma, a titular member of the triad of Hinduism's great gods, along with Shiva and Vishnu, rarely gets a temple to himself. (The only other famous Brahma Temple is at Pushkar, in Rajasthan.) It differs in design from most of the other temples here, particularly in the combination of materials and the shape of its spire. Nearby is Ninora Tal, one of the largest tanks in Khajuraho. ⊠ *Khajuraho, Madhya Pradesh.*

Ghantai Temple. All that's left of the temple here are its pillars, festooned with carvings of pearls and bells. Adorning the entrance are an eight-armed Jain goddess, Chakreshvari, riding the mythical bird Garuda and a relief illustrating the 16 dreams of the mother of Mahavira, the founder and greatest figure in Jainism and a counterpart to the Buddha. The temple sits south of the Vamana, Javari, and Brahma temples, toward the Jain complex. ⊠ *Khajuraho, Madhya Pradesh.*

Adinath Temple. The late-11th-century Adinath Temple, a minor shrine, is set in a small walled compound southeast of the Ghantai temple. Its porch and the statue of the Tirthankara (literally, Ford-Maker, a figure who leads others to liberation) Adinatha are modern additions. Built at the beginning of the Chandelas' decline, this temple is relatively small, but the spire and base are richly carved. ⊠ *Khajuraho, Madhya Pradesh.*

Parsvanath Temple. This temple was built in the mid-10th century during the reign of King Dhangadeva. It is the largest and finest in the Eastern Group's Jain complex and holds some of the best sculpture in Khajuraho, including images of Vishnu. In contrast to the intricate calculations behind the layout of the Western Group, the plan for this temple is a simple rectangle, with a separate spire in the rear. Statues of flying angels and sloe-eyed beauties occupied with children, cosmetics, and flowers adorn the outer walls. The stone conveys even the texture of the women's thin garments. ⊠ *Khajuraho, Madhya Pradesh.*

Shantinath Temple. Although it has been remodeled extensively, this early-11th-century temple does contain some old Jain sculpture. ⊠ *Khajuraho, Madhya Pradesh.*

SOUTHERN GROUP OF TEMPLES

The Southern Group, the smallest, includes two impressive temples from the 12th century. They are the Chaturbhuja Temple (which has a massive, carved image of Vishnu) and the Duladeo Temple, one of the last temples of the Chandela era.

Duladeo Temple. Though built in the customary five-shrine style, this 12th-century temple looks flatter and more massive than most Khajuraho shrines. About 900 yards south of the Eastern Group's Ghantai, it stands near the Khudar rivulet. Probably the last temple built in Khajuraho, the Duladeo lacks the usual ambulatory passage and crowning lotus-shaped finials. Here, too, in this temple dedicated to Shiva, eroticism works its way in, though the amorous figures are discreetly placed. ✉ *Khajuraho, Madhya Pradesh.*

Bijamandala Temple. As part of continuing explorations since 1999, the largest temple yet—4 meters longer than the Kandariya Mahadeva—has been partially unearthed. On the Bikamandala you can see multiple tiers of beautifully carved moldings and a Shiva lingam placed on a marble pedestal. Images of Vishnu and Brahma have been found as well, and it also houses a lovely image of Saraswati. Archaeologists surmise that the temple, begun in the late 10th or early 11th century and between the Duladeo and the Chaturbhuj, may never have been completed, judging by the remains and unfinished statues found on the site. ✉ *Khajuraho, Madhya Pradesh.*

Chaturbhuj Temple. This small 12th-century temple, nearly 3 km (2 miles) south of Duladeo, is often ignored given its distance from the main complex. It has an attractive colonnade entrance and a feeling of verticality thanks to its single spire. Inside, its impressive four-armed image of Vishnu in a sunken sanctum may be the single most striking piece of sculpture in Khajuraho. The exterior sculpture here is not nearly as impressive as other examples in the area, but the temple is definitely the best place in Khajuraho to watch the sun set. In the north corner there is a rare image of the goddess Narsimhi, who has a lion's face and a human body. ✉ *Khajuraho, Madhya Pradesh.*

WHERE TO EAT

$ ITALIAN

🍴 **Bella Italia.** A simple, no-frills rooftop restaurant, with plastic tables and chairs, adorned only by a few potted plants, the main draw for Bella Italia is the food. This restaurant specializes in fresh homemade pastas, including lasagna, fettucini, and ravioli. Thin-crust pizzas are decent, and the crepes—both savory and sweet—are delicious. Try the Nutella crepe topped off with ice cream for a special treat. [$] *Average main: Rs. 250* ✉ *Jain Temple Rd., Khajuraho, Madhya Pradesh* ☎ *98934–54795.*

$ INTERNATIONAL

🍴 **Blue Sky Restaurant.** Across from the Vishvanath and Nandi temples, Blue Sky is open for all meals. It has a great view of the entire Western Group from its second-floor and rooftop terraces. The view's the thing, but the food's not bad. You can just stop by for a *lassi* (a yogurt-based drink) or tea, breakfast on omelets, porridge (oatmeal), and Indian

DID YOU KNOW?

The Lakshmana Temple is one of the oldest temples at Khajuraho, and the only complete temple left standing. It's covered in sculptures depicting all aspects of life, including erotic pursuits.

items; at lunch and dinner there are soups and salads, plus Indian, Chinese, Italian, and Japanese choices. ■ **TIP→ At dinner you can watch the sound-and-light show from your table.** [$] *Average main: Rs. 200* ✉ *Main Rd., near Western Group of Temples, Khajuraho, Madhya Pradesh* ☎ *7686/274–120* 💳 *No credit cards.*

$ KOREAN 🍴 **Korean Cafe.** On the second floor of the Shanti Hotel, overlooking the lake, this small restaurant offers a refreshing break from Indian and continental cuisine. Don't be fooled by its no-frills, white interior and plain wooden furniture—it serves shockingly authentic and tasty Korean cuisine, including two types of *kimchi* (fermented vegetables with spices) made fresh daily, *Gim-bop* (rice, meat, egg, and vegetables rolled in edible seaweed), steamed chicken, and "Korean thali," with omelet, sticky rice, and kimchi. Owner, Nikki Shivhare, who speaks fluent Korean, takes great pride in the authenticity, and imports all ingredients (including rice) from Korea. [$] *Average main: Rs. 250* ✉ *Shanti Hotel, opposite Shiv Sagar Lake, near Western Group of Temples, Khajuraho, Madhya Pradesh* ☎ *7686/274–560* 💳 *No credit cards.*

$$ ITALIAN 🍴 **Mediterraneo.** Eat on the rooftop or in a small dining room at this Italian restaurant near the Western Group. Like most of the restaurants in Khajuraho that aren't connected to a hotel, there are no frills here. The pizzas, one of the many pasta dishes (the carbonara has actual bacon), or standbys like eggplant Parmigiana or lamb cacciatore may just do the trick when you're tired of the Indian-continental-Chinese menu popular in tourist areas throughout India. At breakfast, you can order crepes and omelets. [$] *Average main: Rs. 300* ✉ *Jain Temple Rd., opposite Surya Hotel, Khajuraho, Madhya Pradesh* ☎ *768/627–2246* 💳 *No credit cards.*

$ INTERNATIONAL 🍴 **Raja Café.** This charming, two-story outdoor restaurant has a distinctly European aesthetic, with a Spanish-style courtyard—where marble-top tables are shaded by an enormous Neem tree—and a fantastic terrace with a stunning view of the Western Temples. The food is a mix of Indian and continental fare, and highlights include freshly baked pastries and wood-fire pizzas. [$] *Average main: Rs. 250* ✉ *Opposite Western Temples complex, Khajuraho, Madhya Pradesh* ☎ *94251–41307 cell phone.*

$ INTERNATIONAL 🍴 **Shambala Chill Out Restaurant, The Green View.** This colorful and hippyish Indian restaurant has a great view of the temples. Don't expect anything too posh on the menu, but everything is cooked well and the staff (an Indian-Swedish husband-wife duo) are friendly and can tweak dishes to your specifications. Cuisines encompass Indian, Chinese, and European, with plenty of vegetarian choices. [$] *Average main: Rs. 250* ✉ *In front of the Western Group of Temples, Khajuraho, Madhya Pradesh* ☎ *99932–13301 cell phone* 💳 *No credit cards.*

WHERE TO STAY

For expanded hotel reviews, visit Fodors.com.

$$$ HOTEL ★ 🏨 **Chandela.** Though without the usual sparkle of a Taj Hotel, this is a fine property (close to the temples) with lots of amenities and an unusual (for India) attention to safety issues. **Pros:** warm, friendly service; all rooms have smoke detectors and sprinklers. **Cons:** restaurant is small, occupying a windowless area behind the lobby. [$] *Rooms from: Rs. 6000* ✉ *Airport Rd., Chhatarpur District, Khajuraho, Madhya Pradesh* ☎ *768/627–2355, 768/627–2364* 🌐 *www.tajhotels.com* 🛏 *89 rooms, 5 suites* 🍴 *Breakfast.*

$$$ HOTEL 🏨 **Hotel Clarks Khajuraho.** A 10-minute drive from the main group of temples, this is a clean and tastefully decorated hotel, and though it rather lacks personality, it does have an excellent range of sport and leisure options on-site. **Pros:** good value-for-money; plenty to do. **Cons:** somewhat nondescript. [$] *Rooms from: Rs. 6000* ✉ *Between airport and temples, off main road, Khajuraho, Madhya Pradesh* ☎ *7686/274–038, 7686/274–056, 7686/274–421* 🌐 *khajuraho.hotelclarks.com* 🛏 *100 rooms, 4 suites* 🍴 *Breakfast.*

$ HOTEL 👍 🏨 **Hotel Tourist Village.** Affordable and charming, this hotel, run by the Madhya Pradesh Government, is built in the style of a "traditional village," and although it's a 10-minute walk from the bustle and noise of the main road, it feels much more remote. **Pros:** quiet, relaxing ambience; economical. **Cons:** white tube lights in the rooms detract from the village charm. [$] *Rooms from: Rs. 1490* ✉ *Near Vidhyadhar Colony, Khajuraho, Madhya Pradesh* ☎ *7686/274–062* 🌐 *www.mptourism.com* 🛏 *11 rooms* 🍴 *Breakfast.*

$ HOTEL 🏨 **Jhankar.** The lobby feels a bit like that of a college dorm, with plaid furniture and an Internet room in plain sight, but government-run Jhankar does have comfortable accommodations for a reasonable price. **Pros:** small and easy to navigate. **Cons:** some walls are moldy and riddled with chipping paint; staff isn't very friendly. [$] *Rooms from: Rs. 2000* ✉ *Airport Rd., Khajuraho, Madhya Pradesh* ☎ *768/627–4063, 768/627–4194* 🛏 *19 rooms* 🍴 *No meals.*

$$$ RESORT 🏨 **Ken River Lodge.** Near Panna National Park, about a half hour from Khajuraho, this lodge is perfect for nature lovers, with basic mud huts and cottages with hot water and private baths, but no phones, TVs, or air-conditioning. **Pros:** very secluded, with no tourist traps in sight. **Cons:** far from town, making transportation expensive; monkeys regularly (and loudly) run across the roofs. [$] *Rooms from: Rs. 7000* ✉ *Near Madla Village, Panna District, Khajuraho, Madhya Pradesh* ☎ *7686/275–235 at the lodge, 98100–24711 cell phone, 98102–53436 cell phone for reservations* 🌐 *www.kenriverlodge.com* 🛏 *10 cottages, 10 huts* 🕒 *Closed May–Sept.* 🍴 *All meals.*

$$$$ HOTEL 🏨 **Lalit Temple View Khajuraho.** The closest hotel to the temples, the Lalit has a great view of the World Heritage Site, which you can enjoy while lounging in the manicured garden, sipping cocktails next to the pool. **Pros:** a five-minute walk from the main temples; food available 24 hours; kids' playground on-site. **Cons:** very expensive. [$] *Rooms from: Rs. 15000* ✉ *Opposite Circuit House, Khajuraho, Madhya Pradesh* 🌐 *www.thelalit.com* 🛏 *43 rooms, 4 suites* 🍴 *Breakfast.*

4

$$$ HOTEL 🏨 **Radisson Hotel Khajuraho.** There's no shortage of amenities at this hotel—wellness center, recreation center, business center—and the Western Temples are just a kilometer away. **Pros:** impeccably kept; feels fresh; pay an extra Rs. 40 per night and the Radisson contributes money to a well-known charity that develops programs for poor children across the country. **Cons:** feels like a big-city hotel, with no intimate charms. [$] *Rooms from: Rs. 6500* ✉ *Bypass Rd., Khajuraho, Madhya Pradesh* ☎ *768/627–2777* 🌐 *www.radisson.com/khajurahoin* 🛏 *86 rooms, 4 suites* 🍴 *Breakfast.*

$$ HOTEL ★ 🏨 **Ramada Khajuraho.** The friendly owner's enthusiasm for giving his hotel the grandest look in town makes for great value, and some rooms have temple views. **Pros:** a lot of bang for your buck compared with others in town; discounts are possible. **Cons:** despite its grandeur, the character is predictable, and you might wonder why you need such luxury in a sleepy Indian village. [$] *Rooms from: Rs. 4500* ✉ *Airport Rd., Khajuraho, Madhya Pradesh* ☎ *768/627–2302* 🌐 *www.ramadakhajuraho.com* 🛏 *79 rooms, 6 suites* 🍴 *Breakfast.*

$$ HOTEL 🏨 **Usha Bundela.** With friendly staff, large rooms, and great prices, this nice hotel hits the spot for travelers on a budget without sacrificing on location and style. **Pros:** puppet shows are held on the lawn in the evenings; yoga and meditation classes can be arranged. **Cons:** pool looks very worn and has a green tinge. [$] *Rooms from: Rs. 4000* ✉ *Temple Rd., Khajuraho, Madhya Pradesh* ☎ *768/627–2386* 🌐 *www.ushalexushotels.com* 🛏 *65 rooms, 1 suite* 🍴 *Breakfast.*

SHOPPING

Numerous shops around the Western Group of temples sell curios, including humorous knockoffs of Khajuraho's erotic sculptures, as well as tribal metalwork.

Kandaryia Shilpgram. This large crafts shop is owned by the Agra marble-inlay maker Oswal. It's associated with a government project that hosts craftspeople from all over India for residences during peak travel season; you can watch the artisans at work as you shop. ✉ *Bamitha Rd., near Jhankar Hotel, Khajuraho, Madhya Pradesh* ☎ *768/627–2243* 🕒 *Mar.–Sept.*

Tijori. This two-story shop has fine, beautifully displayed crafts, such as new and antique silver and gold jewelry, diamonds from a local mine, silver boxes and vases, enameled silver elephants, sandalwood carvings, small and very large brass statues, Varanasi and Kashmiri carpets, papier-mâché, and silk and paper paintings. ✉ *Ramada Khajuraho, Airport Rd., Khajuraho, Madhya Pradesh* ☎ *768/627–2302.*

SIDE TRIPS

If you have time, take an extra day to explore and picnic in the beautiful countryside around Khajuraho.

Gharial Sanctuary. Drive or bike to the Gharial Sanctuary on the Ken River, 28 km (17 miles) away; the park was set up to protect the slender-snouted crocodile and has some lovely waterfalls. Madhya Pradesh

Tourism office will have information about renting a jeep, and can provide directions. ⊠ *Khajuraho, Madhya Pradesh.*

Khajuraho Village. Backed by the distant mountains, Khajuraho Village—the old residential part of town near the Eastern Group of temples—is a typical Indian village. Contact the Ministry of Tourism office in Khajuraho for directions, or to request a guide. ⊠ *Khajuraho, Madhya Pradesh.*

Panna National Park. October through June, hire a jeep and driver to take you to Panna National Park to see wildlife that includes antelope, deer, and a lot of monkeys; if you're lucky (and arrive very early in the morning or in late afternoon and hire a guide at the park or come with Ken River Lodge), you'll see one of the 35 elusive tigers in the Panna Tiger Reserve. Sign on for the elephant safari for Rs. 400. The best viewing season is January through March. (Sightings are said to be better at Bandhavgarh Park, but that's a five-hour, 237-km [147-mile] drive from Khajuraho). Entry is Rs. 500 per person, plus Rs. 150 for a jeep safari. ⊠ *31 km (19 miles) SE of Khajuraho, Khajuraho, Madhya Pradesh* ⊕ *www.pannanationalpark.net.*

VARANASI

406 km (252 miles) east of Khajuraho; 765 km (474 miles) southeast of Delhi.

A visit to Varanasi, formerly known as Benaras or Benares, or as Kashi (meaning "resplendent with light"), is an experience unlike any other. This is the epitome of a holy city, inundated with religious pilgrims and sacred cows, yet it is also a city firmly grounded in the commerce and reality of day-to-day existence. A visit here is thrilling but exhausting, and never boring.

Along the left bank of the Ganges, a river believed by Hindus to hold the power of salvation in every drop, Varanasi is one of the most sacred places in the world, considered by many to be the spiritual heart of India. Every year the city welcomes millions of pilgrims for whom the water—physically fouled by the pollution of humans both living and dead—remains spiritually pristine enough to cleanse the soul.

About 90 *ghats*, or steps, line this 6-km (4-mile) stretch of the Ganges, wedding the holy river to the chaotic city above it—a maze of streets and alleys crammed with derelict palaces, homes, and about 2,000 temples and shrines (most of these holy sites are closed to people not of the temple religion), where you'll see funeral processions, cows and goats munching on whatever they can find, and, especially near the Golden Temple (Kashi Vishvanath) and centrally located Dashashvamedh Ghat, assertive hawkers and phony guides.

The most essential thing to do in Varanasi is to take a boat ride along the Ganges, preferably at dawn or sunset, to see the ghats and the rituals being performed—it's also a peaceful respite from the chaos of the city.

Sarnath, just a few kilometers north of Varanasi, is a peaceful park and the historic center of the Buddhist world, where the Buddha preached

Varanasi

TO AZAMGAR
TO BABATPUR AIRPORT
Raja Bazar Rd.
Sanskrit Univ. Rd.
Varanasi City Station
Varanasi Junction Station
UP Tourist Office
JAITPURA
ADAMPURA
Station Rd.
St. Kabir Rd.
KOTWALI
Rabindranath Tagore Rd.
Malaviya Bridge
TO ALLAHABAD
Vidyapeeth (Limba) Rd.
Nai Sarak Rd.
CHOWK
Thatheri Bazaar
Panchganga Ghat
Raja Sir Motichand Rd.
GODAULIA
Scindia Ghat
Manikarnika Ghat
Luxa Rd.
Rathyatra Mahmurganj Rd.
Bhadaini Road
Man Mandira Ghat
Prayaga Ghat
Darabhanga Ghat
Ganga (Ganges) River
Caowki Ghat
Harish Chandra Ghat
Hanuman Ghat
Shivala Ghat
Chet Singh Ghat
Jain Ghat
Anandamayi Ghat
Tulsi Ghat
Assi Ghat
BHELUPURA
Durgakund Rd.
Sankat Mochan Rd.
Asi
Ravidas Ghat
University Rd.
NAGWA
RAMNAGAR
Ramnagar Rd.
Pontoon Bridge
BANARAS HINDU UNIVERSITY
National Highway 7

0   1 mi
0   1 km

Bharat Kala Bhavan Museum **6**

Dashashvamedh Ghat **2**

Durga Temple **4**

Kashi Vishvanath Temple ... **1**

Ramnagar Fort and Palace **7**

Sankat Mochan Temple **5**

Shitala Temple **3**

his first sermon, revealing the Eightfold Path that became the central tenets of Buddhism. It is an easy, and peaceful, place to visit.

GETTING ORIENTED

Varanasi is on the west bank of the Ganges, which is intersected by two smaller rivers: the Varana, to the north, which winds by the Cantonment area (often abbreviated as Cantt) and joins the Ganges near Raj Ghat, and the Asi, a small stream in the south. The ghats stretch along the river from Raj Ghat in the north to Assi Ghat in the south; beyond Asi is the university, across the river from Ramnagar Fort and Palace. The city itself spreads out behind the ghats, where there are smaller hotels and restaurants; the larger chain hotels are in the Cantonment area, about 20 minutes from the river by auto-rickshaw.

Traditionally, Varanasi is divided into three sections named after important temples to Shiva. Omkareshvara is the namesake temple in the northern section, which is probably the oldest area but is now impoverished and seldom visited by pilgrims. The central section is named after Kashi Vishwanath, the famous "Golden Temple." Vishwanath itself means "Lord of the Universe," one of Shiva's names, and there are many Vishwanath temples. The southern area, the Kedar Khand, is named for Kedareshvara, a temple easily spotted from the river thanks to the vertical red and white stripes painted on its walls, a custom of the South Indian worshippers who are among the temple's devotees.

GETTING AROUND

Varanasi is a chaotic place, and although you can certainly find your own way around, you might want to hire a guide for your first day to help you get oriented: it will cost you about Rs. 700 for a half day, and about Rs. 1,100 for an eight-hour full day. You can book a guide through your hotel, or through the Indian Tourism Office. A guide will also know which temples and mosques are open only to their own sects; he may be able to help get you in.

Out on your own, walking is your best bet within the old city, and if your feet get tired, or you get lost, take an auto- or cycle-rickshaw.

Varanasi's airport is about 23 km (14 miles) from the Cantonment area, or 30 km (19 miles) from the riverfront area.

ESSENTIALS

India Ministry of Tourism. You can also find official tourist counters at the airport and train station. ⊠ *15B The Mall* ☎ *542/250–1784* ⊕ *www.incredibleindia.org.*

EXPLORING

★ **Bharat Kala Bhavan Museum.** No one interested in Indian art should miss this museum on the campus of Banaras Hindu University. The permanent collection includes brocade textiles, excellent Hindu and Buddhist sculptures, and miniature paintings from the courts of the Mughals and the Hindu princes of the Punjab hills. One sculpture with particular power is a 4th-century Gupta-dynasty frieze depicting Krishna (an incarnation of Vishnu) holding up Mt. Govardhan to protect his pastoral comrades from the rain. Have your car or rickshaw wait for you, as transportation can be hard to find on the university's sprawling campus. It's a good idea to go with a guide, since the upkeep of the

Continued on page 204

VARANASI

Also known as Kashi (City of Light) or Kashika (Shining One), Varanasi is one of the holiest cities on earth: there are more than 700 temples and counless shrines here—though none of these are more holy than the Ganges River itself.

Each drop of Ganges water is believed to hold the power of salvation: immersing oneself in it is said to cleanse one not just of sins in this life, but of all the sins of past lives, too. As a result, millions of pilgrims come to this city every year to take part in ritual cleansing. Dying here and being cremated is believed to give instant enlightenment and freedom from the cycle of rebirth.

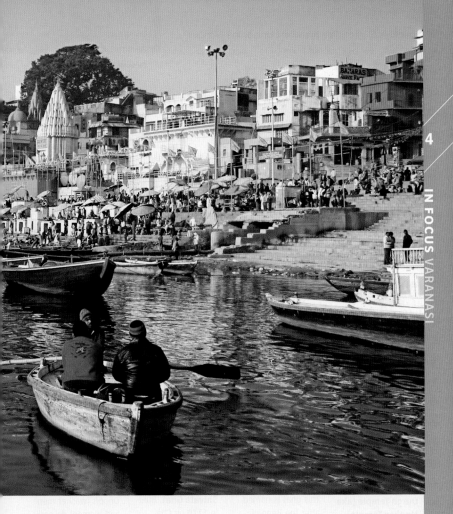

While the water here might be spiritually pure, the Ganges is also one of the dirtiest bodies of water in the world, and drinking it or bathing in it carries the risk of infection. To get the full experience of the river (without actually going in), take a boat ride, preferably as the sun comes up in the morning. From this vantage point you'll see not only the various *ghats* (stairs down to the river) but also the daily rituals and prayers that are a part of this incredible city: everything from elderly men sitting cross-legged in prayer or meditation, to young men exercising, people washing clothes, and various and sundry people and animals bathing.

Above, Dashashvamedh ghat on the banks of the Ganges River, in Varanasi.

ALONG THE GANGES

Roughly 82 ghats line the west bank of the Ganges, stretching out over about 6 km (4 mi); each has a different historical or ritual significance.

Chet Singh Ghat

Dashashvamedh Ghat

Chausath Yogini Temple

Dashashvamedh Ghat

Prayaga Ghat

Darabhanga Ghat

Caowki Ghat

Lali Ghat

Harish Chandra Ghat

Hanuman Ghat

Shivala Ghat

Chet Singh Ghat

Jain Ghat

Durga Temple (Monkey Temple)

Anandamayi Ghat

Tulsi Ghat

Assi Ghat

Bhadani Rd.

Pandit Manmohan Malviya Rd.

> **Dashashvamedh** is one of the busiest ghats along the Ganges. This is a good place to hire a boat (*see full listing*).

Assi Ghat. This southernmost ghat marks the place where the Assi River and the Ganges meet.

On the eastern side of the river is the **Ramnagar Fort and Palace** (*see full listing*).

Durga Temple (aka Monkey Temple). Inland and a short walk from Assi Ghat, the monkey temple is recognizable by its mulitiered spire (*see full listing*).

Tulsi Ghat. This ghat was named for Tulsi Das, the great 16th-

century Hindu poet who wrote the epic Ramcharitmnanas while he was in Varanasi; the poet's house and temple are close by as well. Legend has it that the manuscript fell into the water and did not sink, but floated instead, and was saved. Cultural activities often take place at this ghat.

Anandamayi Ghat. This ghat is named after the Bengali (female) saint Anandamayi Ma who died in 1982. The ashram that she founded here attracts thousands of devotees.

Jain (Bachraj) Ghat. Previously part of the adjoining ghat, the

Jains made this their own in the early 20th century. The Jain temple here is quite impressive.

Chet Singh Ghat. The reddish color of the fort at Chet Singh ghat stands out, although you won't see many bathers here because it's said that the currents here are dangerous. The ghat is historically notable as being the spot where the maharaja of Varanasi was defeated by the British in the mid 1800s.

Shivala Ghat. Built in 1770 by Chet Singh, the maharaja of Varanasi, the ghat has a large mansion and temple.

Hanuman Ghat. Legend has it that this ghat was built by Lord Ram (the original name was Ra-

mesvaram ghat), and that the ghat is dedicated to his favorite disciple: Hanuman. Because Hanuman is a symbol of strength, you can often see local wrestlers and body builders here.

Harish Chandra Ghat. This cremation ghat has been modernized and has an electric crematorium. It's also known as Adi Manikarnika, which means "original creation ground."

Lali (Dhobi) Ghat. *Dhobis* (washer men and women) do early morning laundry here, beating the clothes against the stones in the river.

Caowki Ghat. A huge ficus tree at the top of the steps makes this ghat recognizable. Under

Man Mandira Ghat

Nepali Ghat

Manikarnika Ghat

Vishvanath Temple

Scindia Ghat

Aurangzeb's Mosque

Panchganga Ghat

KEY

🔲	Ghats
	Mosques
⛰	Temples
⛵	Boats

Ganga River

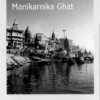
Manikarnika Ghat

the tree many stone figures of snakes are arranged.

Darabhanga Ghat. You can recognize this ghat by the Greek-style pillars.

Chausath Yogini Temple. A steep set of stairs leads from the Chausath Yogini ghat to the temple of the same name. Originally devoted to a Tantric cult that is also associated with an important ruined temple at Khajuraho, it's now dedicated to Kali (the goddess most popular with Bengalis), known here simply as "Ma"—Mother. The worshippers are mainly white-sari-clad widows from Varanasi's Bengali quarter; in the early morning you'll see them coming for the *darshan* (vision) of Kali after bathing in the Ganges.

Prayaga Ghat. This ghat marks the location where the Ganges, the Yamuna, and the invisible Sarasvati rivers all come together. The temple is not often used, however, except by boatmen, who store their boats here.

Man Mandira Ghat. Maharajah Jai Singh, of Jaipur, built his palace here, along with one of his 5 observatories (the most famous is the Jantar Mantar in Jaipur).

Vishvanath (Golden) Temple. With its gold-plated spire, this temple is easy to spot on the skyline. It's the most sacred shrine in Varanasi *(see full listing).*

Nepali Ghat. One of the more prominent ghats, Nepali has a golden lion outside a pagoda-like temple, built by the royal family of Nepal. Many Nepalese live in the area.

Manikarnika Ghat. Varanasi's main burning ghat is a focal point for most trips along the river, and the traditional funeral pyres burn 24 hours a day. Boats keep a distance, out of respect, but you can still see the fires. At the top of Manikarnika's steps is a small, deep pool, or *kund,* said to have been dug by Vishnu at the dawn of creation and thus to be the first *tirtha*— literally, "ford," and figuratively a place of sacred bathing. Shiva is said to have lost a jeweled ear-ring *(manikarnika)* as he trembled in awe before this place, one of the holiest sites in Varanasi.

Scindia Ghat. This ghat is notable for its ornate temple, which was so heavy that it collapsed into the river and is now partially submerged.

Aurangzeb's Mosque. The Alamgir Mosque, known as Aurangzeb's Mosque, was built by the Mughul emperor Aurangzeb over the remains of the Hindu temple that had previously stood here. When Aurangzeb conquered Banaras, he had ordered destruction of all temples. The mosque's dramatic vantage point overlooking the Ganges gives it a prominent place in the skyline. The mosque is closed to non-Muslims.

Panchganga Ghat. Below Aurangzeb's Mosque, this is an important bathing point. It's the mythical meeting place of the 5 sacred rivers and images of the river goddesses are displayed here.

Ramnagar Fort

PRACTICAL MATTERS (FAQ)

Where can I hire a boat? The most popular place to hire a boat is at Dashashvamedh Ghat—essentially in the middle of Varanasi, and convenient if you're staying near the water. You can also hire one at Assi Ghat, the southernmost end of the ghats. It's a good idea to arrange your boat trip the afternoon before, then get up and meet your boatman early the next morning so that you can be out on the water as the sun comes up.

How much will it cost? Rates are negotiable, but it should cost about Rs. 125–150 for about a two- to three-hour trip.

Where do I want to go? The most popular routes are any that take you past the Manikarnika cremation ghat, the main burning ghat. In general, though, the people and their rituals are more sightworthy than the ghats themselves.

When should I go? The best time to be on the river is as the sun comes up in the morning, when people and pilgrims are getting ready to start the day.

Saris draped on the stairs to dry

At morning prayer

Crowds bathing in the sacred Ganges

A *sadhu* (holy man)

Morning traffic on the Ganges

विजा
VIJAYA

A painting on a temple wall

Climbing the steep
ghat stairs

A *puja* offering to the Gods

Darabhanga Ghat

The Ganga Arti ceremony

GANGA ARTI

Take a boat ride on the Ganges at sunrise, but come back to the water's edge in the evening, as the sun goes down for *Ganga Arti* (*arti* means prayer), at Dashashvamedh Ghat. The steps fill with people singing Vedic hymns, lighting lamps, and praying along with the priests. It can get very crowded, so you might even want to hire another boat so that you can witness the whole scene from the water, without dealing with the crush on the ghat.

museum is a bit haphazard and you might need someone who knows his way around and can turn the lights on. ⊠ *Banaras Hindu University, Lanka, Varanasi, Uttar Pradesh* ☎ *542/230–7621* ⊕ *www.bhu.ac.in* 🎟 *Rs. 40* ☼ *Mon.–Sat. 11–4:30.*

Fodor'sChoice
★
Dashashvamedh Ghat. At roughly the midway point of Varanasi's ghats, this is a convenient and popular spot, always busy with hawkers and pilgrims, and a good place to hire a boat. It's one of the holiest ghats, the site of ancient sacrificial rite: the name literally means "ten-horse sacrifice." **Ganga Arti** is an *arti* (prayer ceremony) performed at Dashashvamedh Ghat every night at sunset. The steps fill with people singing Vedic hymns, lighting lamps, and praying along with the priests; if you're out on a boat at this time, you can take in the whole scene without having to deal with the crush on the ghat. ⊠ *East of Godaulia Crossing, Chowk, Varanasi, Uttar Pradesh.*

Durga Temple. This 18th-century shrine, dedicated to the goddess Durga, Shiva's consort, stands beside a large, square pool of water due west about a kilometer from Assi Ghat. The multilevel spire (five lower ones, and one on top) symbolizes the belief that the five elements of the world (earth, air, water, fire, and ether) merge with the Supreme. The shrine is also called the Monkey Temple because there are monkeys everywhere, and they'll steal anything (keep all food and water safely out of sight). The temple is closed to non-Hindus, but the courtyard is accessible to all. ⊠ *Durgakund Rd.* ☼ *Daily sunrise–noon and 2–sunset.*

▮ NEED A BREAK?

Vaatika Café. The Vaatika Café, an easygoing, inexpensive second-floor outdoor eatery with tables looking out on Assi Ghat, serves excellent thin-crust pizza made in an Italian oven with real mozzarella, as well as home-made pasta dishes, bona fide espresso, and fresh homemade apple pie. ⊠ *B-1/178 Assi Ghat, Varanasi, Uttar Pradesh* ☎ *98380–94111, 94513–97331* ⊕ *www.pizzeriavaatika.in.*

Kashi Vishvanath Temple. Known as the Golden Temple because of the gold plate on its spire—a gift from the Sikh maharaja Ranjit Singh of Punjab in 1835—this is the most sacred shrine in Varanasi. It's dedicated to Shiva, whose pillar of light is said to have appeared on this spot. Foreigners are only admitted through Gate 2, and are required to bring passports and register prior to entering. Various forms of the *arti* prayer ceremony are performed outside at 3:30 am, noon, and 7:30 and 11 pm. It's located in the Old City above the Ganges, between Dashashvamedh and Manikarnika ghat: to get here, walk from Dashashvamedh Road down the relatively broad, shop-lined lane (Vishvanath Gali, the main sari bazaar) to Vishvanath Temple. The lane turns sharply right at a large image of the elephant-head god Ganesh, then passes the brightly painted wooden entrance to the 1725 **Annapurna temple** (Annapurna was Vishvanath's consort), on the right. On the left, look for the silver doorway usually manned by a police officer—this is the entrance to the Kashi Vishvanath Temple. The present temple was built by Rani Ahalyabai of Indore in 1776, near the site of the original shrine, which had been destroyed by the emperor Aurangzeb. Nearby is the **Gyanvapi Mosque,** built by Mughal emperor Aurangzeb after he destroyed the

CLOSE UP

The Economics of Burning

Public cremation is the norm for Hindus throughout India, but the spiritual implications of being cremated in Varanasi make dying here an especially celebratory occasion. The idea is that because the Ganges is so holy, a spiritual cleansing in this water means easier achievement of *moksha, the* release from the cycle of rebirth. In Varanasi bodies are wrapped in silk or linen—traditionally white for men, red or orange for women—and carried through the streets on bamboo stretchers to the smoking pyres of the burning ghat. Then, after a brief immersion in the Ganges and a short wait, the body is placed on the pyre for the ritual that precedes the cremation. Funeral parties dressed in white, the color of mourning, surround the deceased. Photographing funeral ghats is strictly forbidden, but you are allowed to watch.

So dying in Varanasi will get you closer to achieving purification and *moksha*—but even here, there are still obstacles to achieving the ultimate release from the cycle of rebirth, and money is the most common problem. A proper wood cremation ceremony, even in one's hometown, involves basic expenses that much of India's poor majority simply cannot afford. The most expensive aspect is the wood itself, costing about Rs. 150 for 40 kg. With a minimum requirement of about 300 kg, the price of wood cremation starts at Rs. 1,125. Other supplies include ghee (clarified butter), sandalwood powder, and cloth to prepare the body—and there's a tax to be paid, too. The total price for the ritual usually comes to a minimum of Rs. 2,000. Add to that the cost of traveling to Varanasi, and the prospect of honoring the dead at the bank of the Ganges becomes financially daunting—many of the poorest people in India make only Rs. 2,000 a month or less.

To help with cost, traditional funeral pyres share space at the burning ghat with Varanasi's one electric cremation center. Burning a body here costs just Rs. 500, a fraction of the cost of wood cremation, though still expensive by Indian standards. A lack of money, in fact, is probably the best explanation for a body drifting by during a boat ride on the Ganges. It's unlawful to offer dead bodies to the river now, except in the case of a pregnant woman, a child younger than 5, someone with smallpox, someone who has been bitten by a cobra, or a holy man—Hindus believe that gods live inside these bodies, so they can't be burned. But in the absence of money for a cremation, poor relatives often have no other choice but to break the law if they want to honor the dead in the holiest of waters.

4

temple that stood here: the building's foundation and rear still show parts of the original temple. As a result of Hindu revivalist attempts to reconsecrate the site of the former temple, the area is usually staffed with police and fenced with barbed wire. It's normally very sedate, however, and is an important starting point for Hindu pilgrims. ⊠ *Vishvanath Gali, Varanasi, Uttar Pradesh* ⊘ *Daily 4 am–11 pm.*

Ramnagar Fort and Palace. Across the Ganges from the river ghats is the 17th-century, red sandstone palace of the Maharaja of Varanasi, who still lives here (if the flag is up, he's in residence) and performs ceremonial and charitable functions. Inside, there are some interesting collections—stop at the Durbar Hall and the Royal Museum—but the place is sadly run-down and the objects are not well maintained. It's sort of fascinating, though, to see the state of decay: a case full of beautiful black musical instruments, for example, is so completely white with dust and the case so covered with grime that it's almost impossible to see anything, and the royal costumes are ratty. Still, there are palanquins and howdahs in ivory, goldplate, or silver (completely tarnished); old carriages and cars; furniture; portraits of maharajas; and arms from Africa, Burma, and Japan. The palace was built to resist the floods of the monsoon, which play havoc with the city side of the river. (It should cost about Rs. 1200 to take a taxi here and have him wait for an hour or two; negotiate beforehand.) Note that the fort is closed to visitors during monsoon season if the weather is bad. ✉ *End of Pontoon Bridge, off Ramnagar Rd., Varanasi, Uttar Pradesh* ☎ *542/233–9322* 🎟 *Rs. 12* ⏲ *Daily 10–5.*

Sankat Mochan Temple. One of Varanasi's most beloved temples—as well as one of its oldest—Sankat Mochan (Deliverer from Troubles) was built in the late 16th century. Though the city has encroached all around it, the building still stands in a good-size, tree-shaded enclosure, like temples elsewhere in India. (Most temples in Varanasi are squeezed between other buildings.) Although most of the city's major shrines are dedicated to Shiva or various aspects of the mother goddess, Sankat Mochan belongs to Hanuman, the monkey god, revered for his dedicated service to Rama, an incarnation of Vishnu whose story is told in the *Ramayana.* The best time to see Sankat Mochan is early evening, when dozens of locals stop for a brief visit at the end of the workday, and on Tuesday and Saturday—days sacred to Hanuman—when worshippers come in large numbers to pay their respects. The temple is closed to non-Hindus. ✉ *Durgakund Rd., Varanasi, Uttar Pradesh* ⏲ *Daily 5 am–11 pm.*

Shitala Temple. This unassuming but very popular white temple near Dashashvamedh Ghat is dedicated to Shitala, the smallpox goddess. Despite the eradication of smallpox, Shitala is still an important folk goddess in North India. The temple is closed to non-Hindus. ✉ *Shitala Ghat, Varanasi, Uttar Pradesh* ⏲ *Daily 5 am–11 pm.*

WHERE TO EAT

$$ ECLECTIC 🍴 **Amrapali.** At this big wood-paneled restaurant lit by crystal domes and overlooking a garden full of palm trees, the lunch and dinner buffets—including several soups, steamed vegetables, and a great dessert section—are excellent. Or you can choose from four separate menus, including kebabs, tandoori dishes, and thalis (served with superbly soft, warm naan), plus Chinese and continental dishes. [$] *Average main: Rs. 400* ✉ *Clarks Varanasi Hotel, The Mall, Cantt, Varanasi, Uttar Pradesh* ☎ *542/250–1011.*

$ CAFÉ 🍴 **Bread of Life Bakery.** Close to the Assi Ghat, this is an impressive haven for homesick Western palates and a great place for breakfast after a morning boat ride—the pancakes are real and so is the maple syrup, which is rare in India. Stop in anytime to write postcards over coffee and chocolate-chip cookies, apple strudel, an éclair, or some Black Forest cake. Simple lunches and dinners include omelets, quiches, sandwiches, soups and stews, pastas, and some Chinese dishes. All profits of the café and the art gallery upstairs go to charities, or are used for the employees' education. $ *Average main: Rs. 200* ⊠ *B-3/322 Shivala, Varanasi, Uttar Pradesh* ☎ *542/227–5012* ⊟ *No credit cards.*

$$
ECLECTIC

✕**Canton Royale.** Behind the colonial facade of the Surya Hotel, the Canton Royal is a simple but elegant restaurant, with vaulted ceilings, statues, and framed pictures of Benaris royalty. The menu is eclectic, spanning European, Mediterranean, Mexican, and Chinese, but the Indian is the best—and this is one of the few restaurants in Varanasi that serves nonvegetarian food. The tandoori chicken and mutton curry are both delicious, and the *aloo dum Banarasi* (potatoes stuffed with paneer in a spicy tomato gravy), a dish native to Varanasi, is recommended. You can dine inside or in the lovely gardens. $ *Average main: Rs. 450* ⊠ *Surya Hotel, S-20/51A-5 The Mall, Varanasi* ☎ *542/250–8465, 542/250–8466* ⊕ *hotelsuryavns.com.*

$
MIDDLE EASTERN

✕**Haifa.** Connected to Hotel Haifa, this restaurant's specialty is Middle Eastern food. It's basically a long room with nondescript tables and lots of tourists flowing in and out—and no wonder, because it's incredibly cheap and the only place in town to sample freshly made Middle Eastern treats. An entire Middle Eastern "thali" consisting of hummus, *baba ghanoush* (eggplant mashed with spices and olive oil), *labneh* (strained yogurt), falafel, and potato costs only Rs. 70. In case you're sticking to Indian, there's plenty of that, too, along with Chinese and continental, also at rock-bottom prices. $ *Average main: Rs. 150* ⊠ *B-1/107 Assi Ghat, Varanasi, Varanasi, Uttar Pradesh* ☎ *542/231–2960.*

$$
ASIAN FUSION

✕**I:ba Café.** A chic, eclectic interior—cane "tikki roofs" concealing the tops of beams, cozy floor couches, dangling bells, dry corn husks—sets a stylish scene that's only rivaled by the food. A Japanese and Indian husband-wife team run the operation, serving varied cuisines, including Indian, pizzas, pastas, Thai and Korean, but the Japanese is the best: delicious vegetable tempura, tasty chicken *gyoza* (dumplings), teriyaki chicken, sticky rice bowls, and a variety of *raman* (noodle) dishes. The nonvegetarian items on the menu are limited to chicken and mutton; no beef or fish is served here. $ *Average main: Rs. 400* ⊠ *B3/335B, Krimkund, Shivala, Varanasi.*

$
INDIAN

✕**Kerala Cafe.** As the name implies, South Indian food is on the short menu at this no-frills, popular little diner that's lined with narrow, dingy booths and filled with mostly Indian pilgrims. The specialty is dosas—specifically masala dosas—and they're terrific, full of juicy chunks of potatoes, onion, and peas. In addition to choices like plain, tomato, or coconut *uttapams* (Indian-style pancakes), *idlis* (steamed bread made of rice flour), and *vadas* (deep-fried savory "doughnuts"), they do a great lemon rice with peanuts and a sprinkling of coriander leaves, and beautiful puffy *pooris* (fried bread) as big as your head. It's open for breakfast. $ *Average main: Rs. 200* ⊠ *Bhelupura Crossing, Varanasi, Uttar Pradesh* ⊟ *No credit cards.*

$ INTERNATIONAL 🍴 **Lotus Lounge.** There's a wonderful view from this simple outdoor terrace restaurant, which is right along the Ganges. The setting itself is simple—a mix of tables and chairs on white Moroccan tiles, and tables with floor seating; the only real adornment is a large mural of the Buddha. The food is as pleasing as the view, with an eclectic menu of dishes including chicken schnitzel, vegetable moussaka, Thai coconut curry, and mushroom *makhani* (with butter). The mushroom and spinach Indian pakoda with fig dip and the eggplant slices with spicy yogurt sauce are both delicious. [$] *Average main: Rs. 280* ✉ *D14/27 Mansrowar Ghat, Varanasi* ☎ *9838/567–717* 💳 *No credit cards.*

WHERE TO STAY

There are two options in Varanasi: you can stay near the water, where most of the lodgings are smaller and right in the midst of the action; or you can stay in the Cantonment area, about a 20-minute rickshaw ride away, where the more established, larger hotels are located. The latter area has less character, but it's definitely quieter and less chaotic.

For expanded hotel reviews, visit Fodors.com.

WATERFRONT

$$ B&B/INN ★ 🏨 **Hotel Ganges View.** Still the residence of a well-to-do family, this guest house has small, beautiful rooms with quirky charm—one has a jungle painting and stone shrine (with goddess) that you sleep under—and a great veranda overlooking the river and Assi Ghat. **Pros:** the veranda is the best place in town to watch the endless stream of pilgrims and tourists. **Cons:** it's pretty noisy, particularly in rooms without a/c; narrow stairs to the front door make access difficult. [$] *Rooms from: Rs. 5500* ✉ *Assi Ghat, Varanasi, Uttar Pradesh* ☎ *542/231–3218, 542/329–0289* 🌐 *www.hotelgangesview.com* 🛏 *15 rooms* 💳 *No credit cards* 🍽 *No meals.*

$$$ HOTEL 🏨 **Jukaso Ganges.** Accessed by boat from the nearby Dasaswamedh Ghat, this stunning sandstone heritage hotel on the Ganges is perfect for a romantic getaway or a personal retreat. **Pros:** excellent river views, including from the yoga meditation room. **Cons:** boat access impossible during monsoon, and it's quite a trek overland; monsoon floods the lobby. [$] *Rooms from: Rs. 10000* ✉ *CK 1/14 Patni Tola Chowk, Varanasi* ☎ *542/240–6667* 🌐 *jukaso.co.in* 🛏 *15 rooms* 🍽 *No meals.*

$$ HOTEL 🏨 **Palace on Ganges.** In this century-old building on Assi Ghat, rooms are styled after Indian states—Gujarat (brightly colored drapes studded with mirrorwork), Rajasthan (elaborately carved doors and furnishings), Assam (lots of bamboo)—while delivering modern comforts. **Pros:** magnificent view from the rooftop; library well-stocked with cultural and history books. **Cons:** you'll have to climb a flight of stairs just to get to the front door. [$] *Rooms from: Rs. 5500* ✉ *B-1/158 Assi Ghat, Varanasi, Varanasi, Uttar Pradesh* ☎ *542/231–4304 to 05* 🌐 *www.palaceonganges.com* 🛏 *42 rooms* 🍽 *No meals.*

$ HOTEL ★ 🏨 **Pradeep.** A shining example of inexpensive lodging in an expensive tourist town, summed up by the words that accompany the huge portrait of Mahatma Gandhi in the lobby: "A customer is not an interruption on our work—he is the purpose of it." **Pros:** exceptionally warm and sincere service. **Cons:** some rooms don't have windows; rooms near the road are noisy; usually quite crowded. [$] *Rooms from: Rs. 2800* ✉ *Jagatganj, Varanasi, Uttar Pradesh* ☎ *542/220–4963, 542/220–4594, 542/220–7231* 🌐 *www.hotelpradeep.com* 🛏 *45 rooms* 🍴 *No meals.*

$$$$ B&B/INN 🏨 **Suryauday Haveli.** Built in the style of a traditional "Nepali courtyard" by the royal family of Nepal, this boutique property sits directly on the banks of the Shivala Ghat. **Pros:** luxurious rooms; relaxing aura; exellent service. **Cons:** windows in all the rooms are a bit small. [$] *Rooms from: Rs. 16000* ✉ *B-4/25 Shivala Ghat, Nepali Kothi, Varanasi* ☎ *542/654–0390, 542/227–6820, 80/4130–6352 for reservations* 🌐 *www.suryaudayhaveli.com* 🛏 *13 rooms, 1 suite* 🍴 *Breakfast.*

CANTONMENT

$$$ HOTEL 🏨 **Clarks Varanasi.** The best thing about staying here may be the restaurant, Amrapali (⇨ *See Where to Eat listings*), but it's also a good choice if you prefer a quiet location amid upscale properties. **Pros:** a 24-hour coffee shop and well-stocked shopping arcade. **Cons:** a bit far from the unique hustle and bustle of Varanasi. [$] *Rooms from: Rs. 7500* ✉ *The Mall, Cantt, Varanasi, Uttar Pradesh* ☎ *542/250–1011 to 20* 🌐 *www.clarkshotel.com* 🛏 *102 rooms, 3 suites* 🍴 *Breakfast.*

$$ HOTEL 🏨 **Hotel Cresent Villa.** With its contemporary Western interior design, this hotel doesn't have much local character, but it's clean, affordable, and within walking distance of the Ganges and the ghats. **Pros:** close to the river; free Internet. **Cons:** lacking in personality; some areas could use a bit of maintenance. [$] *Rooms from: Rs. 4500* ✉ *126-A Lane No. 6, Ravindrapuri Colony, Varanasi* ☎ *542/227–6191* 🌐 *cresentvilla.com* 🛏 *11 rooms* 🍴 *Breakfast.*

$$ HOTEL 🏨 **Hotel India.** A less expensive option in the Cantonment area, this hotel has a choice of five restaurants. **Pros:** affordable, with plenty of dining options. **Cons:** halls are dark, with worn green carpet that makes things look a bit shabby overall. [$] *Rooms from: Rs. 5000* ✉ *59 Patel Nagar, Cantt, Varanasi, Uttar Pradesh* ☎ *542/250–7593 to 97* 🌐 *www.theindiahotel.com* 🛏 *64 rooms, 2 suites* 🍴 *Breakfast.*

$$$$ HOTEL ★ 🏨 **Taj Gateway Hotel Ganges.** Although its spacious lobby bustles with large tour groups, the rooms at this Taj property are cozy and quiet, particularly if you get an upper-story room facing the adjacent Nadesar Palace *(See below)*. **Pros:** lots of space to take peaceful walks without fear of being run over in this crowded city; quite posh. **Cons:** a tour-group magnet. [$] *Rooms from: Rs. 10500* ✉ *Nadesar Palace Grounds, Varanasi, Uttar Pradesh* ☎ *542/666–0001 to 19* 🌐 *www.tajhotels.com* 🛏 *120 rooms, 10 suites* 🍴 *Breakfast.*

$$$$ RESORT Fodor's Choice ★ 🏨 **Taj Nadesar Palace Hotel.** This restored heritage palace provides the most luxurious accommodations in Varanasi, as it did in its heyday, when guests of the Maharaja of Benarisi included Queen Elizabeth, Lord Mountbatten, Jahawalar Nehru, and the King of Persia. **Pros:** extraordinarily luxurious; you will feel like royalty here. **Cons:** extremely expensive. [$] *Rooms from: Rs. 29650* ✉ *Off Raja Bazar Rd., Varanasi* ☎ *542/666–0002, 542/250–3016* 🌐 *www.tajhotels.com* 🛏 *10 suites* 🍴 *Breakfast.*

4

SHOPPING

The city's shops are open generally from 10 to 8; the larger shops close on Sunday, but the street sellers and smaller shops are open daily. One of India's chief weaving centers, Varanasi is famous for its silk-brocade saris, which start at around Rs. 2,000. Some saris are still woven with real gold and silver threads, though in most noncustom work the real thing has been replaced by artificial fibers. (You can see the fabric being woven by entire families in Muslim neighborhoods like Qazi Sadullahpura.)

★ **Banaras Art Center.** Regional and other Indian art, folk art, and crafts—bronzes, terra-cottas, marble sculptures, wood carvings, paintings—are displayed here in many rooms of an old home. ⊠ *B–2/114 Bhadhaini, Shri Krishna Kunj, near Bread of Life Bakery, Varanasi, Uttar Pradesh* ☎ *542/231–3615, 542/231–1715.*

Cottage Industries Exposition. Come here for excellent Varanasi weaves in silk and cotton, a vast rug room, plus brasswares and Kashmiri embroidered shawls. Everything is expensive. ⊠ *Mint House, Nadesar, across from the Taj, Varanasi, Uttar Pradesh* ☎ *542/250–0814.*

Dharam Kumar Jain & Sons. Operating out of their home near Thatheri Bazaar, this company has an extraordinary private collection of old brocade saris, pashmina shawls, and other textiles. ⊠ *K 37/12 Sona Kuan, Varanasi, Uttar Pradesh* ☎ *542/233–3354.*

Mehta International. In the Cantonment area around the corner from the Radisson, this is a large showroom with a wide selection of fine saris, scarves, bed covers, fabric, and some elaborately worked tapestries. ⊠ *S 20/51 Varuna Bridge, Varanasi, Uttar Pradesh* ☎ *542/250–7364.*

Thatheri Bazaar. Among the brass vendors, on a small lane 50 meters north of the Chowk, some shops sell silks and woolens to a local crowd. ⊠ *Varanasi, Uttar Pradesh.*

Vishvanath Gali. Most hotels sell silk-brocade saris in their shops, but the main bazaars for saris are in Vishvanath Gali—the lane leading from Dashashvamedh Road to the Kashi Vishvanath Temple, where the customers are mainly pilgrims and tourists. Try to go early—it gets quite crowded in the afternoon! ⊠ *Varanasi, Uttar Pradesh.*

NIGHTLIFE AND THE ARTS

Nagari Natak Mandal. Infrequent concerts of some of Varanasi's—and India's—best musicians are hosted here. There are also numerous music festivals. Ask your hotel to check the local Hindi newspaper, *Aj,* for events while you're in town, or check the English-language papers yourself. ⊠ *Kabir Chowra, Varanasi, Uttar Pradesh.*

SARNATH

11 km (7 miles) north of Varanasi.

Sarnath is where Gautama Buddha first taught the Buddhist Dharma. In 528 BC Siddhartha Gautama came to Sarnath about five weeks after having attained enlightenment at Bodhgaya, and here he preached his first sermon (now called Dharma Chakra Pravartan, or Set in Motion the Wheel of Law) in what is today Sarnath's Deer Park.

Legend has it that the Buddha was incarnated as King of the Deer in the deer park—the name "Sarnath" comes from Saranganath, which means "Lord of the Deer." In the Deer Park you can buy some carrots for a few rupees and feed the current denizens.

When the Buddha arrived at Sarnath, he revealed his Eightfold Path leading to the end of sorrow and the attainment of enlightenment. Three hundred years later, in the 3rd century BC, the Mauryan emperor Ashoka arrived in the area; he was a convert to Buddhism and had made it the state religion. In Sarnath he had several stupas (large, mound-shape reliquary shrines) built, along with a pillar with a lion capital that was adopted by independent India as its national emblem—it's called the Ashoka pillar. The wheel motif under the lions' feet represents the *dharma chakra*, the wheel (*chakra*) of Buddhist teaching (*dharma*), which began in Sarnath. The chakra is replicated at the center of the Indian national flag.

Sarnath reached its zenith by the 4th century AD, under the Gupta dynasty, and was occupied into the 9th century, when Buddhist influence in India began to wane. By the 12th century Sarnath had more or less fallen to Muslim invaders and begun a long decay. In 1836 Sir Alexander Cunningham started extensive excavations here, uncovering first a stone slab with an inscription of the Buddhist creed, then numerous other relics. It was then that the Western world realized that the Buddha had been an actual person, not a mythical figure. Most of the sites are in a well-manicured park behind a gate (admission is Rs. 100).

GETTING HERE AND AROUND
Sarnath is an easy taxi or auto-rickshaw ride from Varanasi; be prepared to bargain. India Tourism also arranges a three-hour trip (giving you two hours to explore) from Cantonment area hotels or its office for Rs. 500.

Chaukhandi Stupa. The first monument you come to in Sarnath, on the left-hand side of Ashoka Marg on the way to the park, is this shrine that is believed to have originally been a terraced temple during the Gupta period (the 4th to 6th century). Govardhan, the son of Raja Todarmal (who later became a governor under Akbar's rule), built an octagonal tower to commemorate the visit of Emperor Humayun, the father of Emperor Akbar. The event is recorded in Arabic in a stone tablet above the doorway on the north side.

Dhamekh Stupa. Dappled with geometric and floral ornamentation, the stone-and-brick Dhamekh Stupa is the largest surviving monument in Sarnath at 143 feet in height and 748 feet in diameter at the base. Built around 500 AD, Dhamekh is thought to mark the place where the Buddha delivered his sermon, though excavations have unearthed the remains of an even earlier stupa of Mauryan bricks of the Gupta period (200 BC). An Ashoka pillar with an edict engraved on it stands near the stupa.

Mulagandha Kuti Vihari Temple. Built in 1931, the temple joins the old foundations of seven monasteries. The walls bear frescoes by a Japanese artist, Kosetsu Nosu, depicting scenes from the Buddha's life, and relics of Sakyamuni Buddha are enshrined here. On the anniversary of the temple's foundation—the first full moon in November—monks and devotees from all parts of Asia assemble here. The temple is behind a separate gate just outside the park.

★ **Sarnath Archaeological Museum.** At the entrance to this excellent museum is Ashoka's Lion Capital, moved here from its original location in the park. The museum represents the oldest site in the history of India's Archaeologial Survey. Other beautiful sculpture is here as well, including lots of Buddhas; still more of Sarnath's masterpieces are in the National Museum, Delhi, and the Indian Museum, Kolkata. ⊠ *Ashoka Marg at Dharmapal Marg* ☏ *542/259–5095* ⊕ *asi.nic.in* ⌷ *Monument Rs. 100; museum Rs. 5* ⊙ *Sat.–Thurs. 9–5.*

Rajasthan

WORD OF MOUTH

"Udaipur City Palace is a must. More like a museum than a fort."
—crosscheck

"Best fort in Rajasthan is the one in Jodhpur. The maharaja has installed an elevator so guests can go to the top, then take a leisurely stroll downward."

—indianapearl

WELCOME TO RAJASTHAN

TOP REASONS TO GO

★ **Appreciate Jaipur's Pink architecture:** Dusty-pink Jaipur is the gateway to Rajasthan's beautiful palaces, forts, culture, and food.

★ **Marvel at the diversity of Rajasthan's landscapes:** You can travel from the golden sand dunes in Jaisalmer to Udaipur's lovely Lake Pichola, which is set against the Aravali mountains.

★ **Admire the Massive Mehrangarh Fort:** Standing dramatically on a hill, this massive fort is one of Jodhpur's most imposing treasures.

★ **Make a palace your home:** Spend a night in one of the many opulent palaces and forts that have been converted into heritage hotels around Rajasthan.

★ **Go on a shopping spree:** Hopefully, there's room in your suitcase for the jewelry, clothes, fabric, carpets, leather-bound journals, silver, and everything else that has caught your eye—or buy an extra bag to hold your goodies.

1 Jaipur and Environs. The modern and ancient worlds collide in Rajasthan's bustling capital. Highlighted by the Hawa Mahal and the City Palace, this town is both an architectural delight and a shopping hot spot for carpets, textiles, and jewelry. Excursions from Jaipur include the Shekhawati region, known as India's open-air art gallery because of the frescoes on the walls of the old *havelis*, or ancient homes of merchants.

2 Udaipur and Environs. With the Lake Palace floating in the middle of Lake Pichola, the White City is charming and serene. If you're feeling adventurous, you can hike up to Monsoon Palace for stunning bird's-eye views. From here there are spectacular day trips like the Jain temples at Ranakpur and Mount Abu, and the medieval citadel of Chittaurgarh.

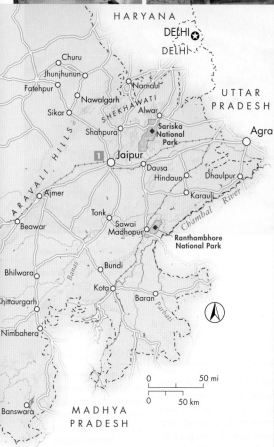

GETTING ORIENTED

The largest state in India, Rajasthan is in the northwestern part of the country, sharing a border with Pakistan. The Aravali mountain range runs north–south almost the entire length of the state. The hot, dry northwest region is dominated by the Thar Desert; the milder south is known for its lakes and greenery. Jaipur, the state capital, is an hour's flight from New Delhi—options for traveling around Rajasthan include air, train, and road.

5

3 Jodhpur. The blue houses in the Old City here contrast with the desert landscape and the imposing Mehrangarh fort. The congested Old City is fun to explore, and the fort is a short auto-rickshaw ride away.

4 Jaisalmer and Environs. The Golden City is synonymous with its majestic fort, and a visit here just isn't complete without a jeep or camel safari, or a visit to the Sam Sand Dunes.

EATING WELL IN RAJASTHAN

A major part of Rajasthan is also known as Marwar (literally "the land of dead" because not much grows there), and traditional cuisine revolves around the robust plants of the desert and the scarcity of water.

(top left) Creamy safed maas; (top right) A Rajasthani thali (plate); (bottom right) Ghevar, a popular sweet

The lack of fresh green vegetables led to the use of gram (chickpea) flour and the development of dry, long-lasting foods, and because water was scarce, many dishes were cooked in ghee (clarified butter) or milk, making them quite rich. Food tends to be heavily spiced, too, perhaps for preservation. The area was predominantly Hindu and Jain—both vegetarian religions—but besides the restrictive but rich meat-free cuisine, the ruling Rajputs were avid hunters and contributed a variety of game dishes, many heavily influenced by the Mughals.

Tourist areas in Rajasthan—besides the better hotels—are a bit thin on authentic eating out options, especially for nonvegetarian fare, but *thali* meals (with a variety of different dishes) are usually available at casual eateries and offer a taste of Marwari home cooking. You'll also find a dazzling range of snacks and sweets.

COOKING SCHOOL

There are several places in Udaipur where travelers can pick up the basics of Rajasthani cooking: **Meenakshi's** (☎ 91/98290–59319); **Spice Box** (☎ 91/29424–24713 ⊕ www.spicebox.co.in); **Hotel Krishna Niwas** (☎ 91/29424–20163 ⊕ www.cookingclassesinudaipur.com); and **Shashi Cooking Classes** (☎ 91/99293–03511 ⊕ www.shashicookingclasses.blogspot.com).

LAAL MAAS

A dish fit for Rajasthani royalty, **laal maas** (literally "red meat") is the state's best-known nonvegetarian entrée. This spicy dish is usually made with goat, marinated in ginger, garlic, and yogurt, then cooked in ghee with red chilli powder. It's sometimes confused with a similar dish called *jungli maas* (wild meat), which is more of a confit, and probably originated on hunting trips where only basic, nonperishable ingredients were available.

SAFED MAAS

The yin to *laal maas*'s yang, **safed maas** or "white" meat is another goat or lamb main dish—creamy white and wonderfully fragrant. The parboiled meat is massaged with yogurt before being sautéed in a fry-up of ghee, onion, ginger, garlic, cardamom, cloves, cinnamon, white peppercorn, and red pepper seeds. The meat is then finished with a paste of poppy seeds, cashew, dried coconut, almond, milk solids (*khoya*), and a hint of saffron or rosewater.

DAAL BATTI CHURMA

A true desert dish, **daal batti churma** is a staple of Rajasthani cuisine. The rustic *baati* is a ball of unleavened bread made of wheat, semolina, and ghee. Traditionally, these are cooked on coals to form a firm, slightly squashed sphere, which may be stuffed with peas and other fillings. *Baati* is eaten

with a hot mixed-lentil dal. *Churma* is a sweet accompaniment of ground-up whole-wheat *baati* or other bread mixed with ghee and melted *jaggery* (unrefined sugar).

GATTE KI SABZI

One of Rajasthan's vegetable substitutes, *gatte* are sausage-shape gram-flour dumplings that are spiced and then boiled. *Gatte* can be eaten in a variety of ways, but the most typical dish is **gatte ki sabzi,** in which the dumplings are fried before they're mixed into a curry of yogurt, with a little more gram flour for thickening, and some mild spices. If you like this, try curry dishes made from pappadams or *mangodi* (sundried ground-lentil dumplings).

GHEVAR

One of the most eye-catching of Indian sweets, **ghevar,** which look like halved bagels with the cratered surface of an English muffin—can be seen stacked up on confectionary shelves, especially around the Teej festival in late summer. Crispy, with a slightly soft interior, the *ghevar* is made from batter that gets its riddled texture from the bubbling heat of the ghee in which it is deep-fried. The crisp golden disc is then soaked in sugar syrup flavored with the fresh-tasting screwpine flower essence (*kewra*) and sometimes topped with silver leaf, spice, and nuts.

CAMELS: SHIPS OF THE DESERT

Taking a camel ride in the Thar desert is one of the most unforgettable experiences of a trip to India. If you can, start off before sunrise, so that you can watch the sun come up over the sand dunes.

(top left) A colorfully outfitted camel; (top right) Sunset in the Thar Desert; (bottom right) Camel safari

Camels are an indispensable part of the local landscape and economy in Rajasthan, and you'll see them wherever you go in the state. Apart from pulling loads (and that includes tourists on safaris), camels are also highly valued for their milk, meat, hair, leather, and even their droppings (used for fertilizer and dried for cooking fuel).

Camel owners usually dress their animals with flair: red, green, and gold saddle covers and tasseled bridles are signs of the well-dressed camel. They're also rather gentle creatures—contrary to popular belief—and you'll no doubt form a bond with yours.

⇨ *For camel-safari tour contacts, see listings throughout the chapter, and in the Tours section of the Planning information.*

DESERT SUPERFOOD

Camel milk is rich in nutrients, and is a common food source for desert people worldwide. In India's desert regions the milk is consumed regularly, and a few enterprising people—Sara's Dairy, for instance—even create camel-milk ice cream. Fans claim that it's easier to digest than cow's milk, but some travelers have reported tummy aches after consuming camel-milk products.

WHERE TO GO ON SAFARI?

It's easy to book a camel safari once you're in Rajasthan: Jaisalmer is the most popular place to take a safari, but other destinations like Pushkar and Jodhpur are good, too. You can choose to go for anything from several hours to several days, or even several weeks. On a day trip, your guide will probably take you through a local village, maybe stopping for something to eat.

SIMPLE OR LUXURY

Overnight safaris range from simple and inexpensive—a one-night trip to a local campsite—to luxury glamping ("glamorous" plus "camping") excursions. A lower-end, one-night safari will cost from around Rs.1,500, which includes a camel, a guide, a cot under the stars, and a basic dinner of dal and rice. Higher-end tours cost at least twice as much, and include more comfortable tented accommodations, multicourse meals, and even a jeep service to carry supplies and luggage between campsites. Water is not always included, so check to see if you need to pack your own.

WHAT TO BRING?

It's important to come prepared, be it a daytrip or a longer safari. The desert sun is very strong, so wear sunglasses, a brimmed hat, and high-power sunscreen (ideally one that doubles as an insect/mosquito repellent) even if you don't generally get sunburned. Long-sleeved

shirts and full-length trousers are also a must—both for sun protection and to stop your legs from chafing. Wear solid shoes or boots with socks to avoid bites from small insects that live in the sand. Pack a scarf to protect your face in case of a sandstorm.

WHEN?

Overnight camel safaris typically run from late August to mid-April; in May, June, and July temperatures in the Thar Desert peak above 120 degrees, which is dangerously hot for anyone from outside the desert to make such a venture. Only male camels are used during the winter mating season, as adding females into the mix can cause the animals to bolt or even attempt mating, regardless of whether there's a rider on their back.

LEARNING TO RIDE

Although learning to ride a camel is easier than learning to ride a horse, it still takes a bit of getting used to. On short trips you might be tied to your guide's camel; on a longer trip, you will be taught to "drive" the camel yourself. Camel bridles are attached to pegs in the camel's nose, and camels are steered with reins. Camels have remarkably sensitive flanks, so you won't need to kick the way you would with a stubborn horse—a little practice and a few nudges with your legs is usually enough to get your steed to pick up the pace.

RAJASTHAN'S HOLY SITES

Although Rajasthan is best known for its forts, palaces, and desert expanses, this huge state is also home to some of India's most awe-inspiring sacred sites.

(top left) One of Pushkar's many temples; (top right) The main gate of the Karni Mata Temple; (bottom right) Inside one of the Jain temples at Ranakpur

The Jain temples in the southern part of Rajasthan are popular destinations; visitors marvel at the white-marble architecture and intricately carved designs that embellish the temples walls and pillars. The best-known Jain holy sites in the state include the temples at Ranakpur near Udaipur and at Dilwara in Mount Abu. There are also a number of significant Hindu temples in Rajasthan. Pushkar has one of the world's few temples dedicated to Bramha, the god of creation in the Hindu trinity. The Eklingji temple complex near Udaipur was built by royalty and is dedicated to Shiva (the destroyer). Not everyone, however, feels the need to actually visit the Karni Mata temple at Deshnoke (popularly known as the Rat Temple among tourists) near Bikaner: it's known as an abode for thousands of rats, which are considered sacred. A popular Muslim pilgrimage site is just outside Pushkar, in Ajmer: Dargah Sharif is the shrine of Sufi saint Khwaja Moinuddin Chisti, and is among the most important pilgrimage sites for South Asian Muslims.

SWASTIKAS

Visitors to Rajasthan are often shocked to see images of the swastika—a symbol associated with Nazism in the West—on walls, doorways, and temples. The swastika is sacred to Hindus, Buddhists, and Jains, who place it prominently in all of their temples and holy books. Sadly, Hitler misappropriated the holy symbol, turning it on its side and making it into his party's logo.

DARGAH SHARIF

In Ajmer's Old Town the white-marble Dargah Sharif is one of the finest examples of Mughal architecture in the state. This is the shrine of Khwaja Moinuddin Chisti, a Sufi saint of Persian descent who is best known for his service to the impoverished. Chisti's shrine is sacred to Muslims, but visited by people of all faiths. Every year, pilgrims from across the subcontinent flock to Dargah Sharif to commemorate the Chisti's Urs, the anniversary of the saint's death.

DILWARA TEMPLES

The five temples of Dilwara in Mount Abu attract Jain pilgrims from across the country and people of all faiths with an interest in art and architecture. Each temple is devoted to a different *tirthankar* (enlightened being who is repeatedly reborn to impart the knowledge he has gained) from the Jain faith. The pillars, arches, and domes represent some of the finest marble artisanship in the country.

RANAKPUR TEMPLE

Between Udaipur and Jodhpur, this magnificent Jain temple venerates the *tirthankar* Rishabha. The four sides symbolize the four directions, each with a similar facade, and the interior features an almost mazelike series of 1,444-plus intricately carved marble pillars. There's also a small, much older temple, dedicated to the sun.

EKLINGJI TEMPLE COMPLEX

A pleasant drive from Udaipur through the Aravali mountains, Eklingji village is famous for its 108-strong temple complex, the highlight of which is the 15th-century Shiva Temple (some parts date back to the 8th century). There's a unique four-sided, four-faced black-marble image of Shiva here, miniature replicas of which will be eagerly offered to you in the village bazaar. Every Monday evening the Maharaja of Udaipur visits the temple privately.

PUSHKAR BRAMHA TEMPLE

It seems like there's a temple every few feet in Pushkar—many restrict access to foreigners and non-Hindus, but the most famous temple, the red-spired 14th-century Brahma Temple, allows people of all backgrounds. The town's lake is also a holy spot unto itself, and many of Pushkar's priestly residents earn a living performing *pujas* (ceremonies) at the shore.

KARNI MATA

Near the Pakistan border the town of Deshnoke is home to the Karni Mata temple, dedicated to a 14th-century female sage who was believed to be an incarnation of the goddess Durga. The temple is best known, however, for its large population of rats, which some people estimate at being around 20,000. The rodents are considered sacred, and are fed by the temple's caretakers.

5

SHOPPING IN RAJASTHAN

When it comes to shopping, Rajasthan has something for everyone. From elegant silk saris to kitschy wooden camels, even the most frugal visitor is likely to leave the state with some goodies tucked in their luggage.

(top left) Indian bangles at a market in Jodhpur; (top right) Handmade leather shoes; (bottom right) Bandhani fabric

Rajasthan is well known as a destination with all sorts of craftspeople, and each region has its own distinct specialties. Jaipur is at the hub of the state's tourism industry and has handicrafts from across the state; if you want something with a local flair here, pick up a piece of blue pottery or a pair of emerald earrings. Jodhpur is a good place to shop for glass bangles as well as mirrored and sequined bedspreads—or wood furniture if you are willing to pay for shipping. Udaipur is known for miniature paintings and marble work. In Jaisalmer the key word is camel leather—patchwork bed covers, shoes, purses, and even book covers are made from the desert animal's hide. Yellow sandstone statues and knickknacks are also popular in Jaisalmer. The best deals can be found in local markets—large emporia and shops in "craft villages" tend to mark their items up to recover the huge com-

BUYER BEWARE

Every year, unsuspecting tourists fall prey to shady self-professed "gem dealers," who befriend foreign visitors and try to get them to transport gems back to their home countries. The victims are then asked to leave a deposit for the jewels, which are inevitably nothing more than tin and glass. Most tourists don't realize they've been scammed until they're thousands of miles away.

JEWELRY

Rajasthan has been known for its fine selection of jewelry for centuries, and you're sure to find something special, no matter what your budget. The state is a major exporter of precious and semiprecious gems, and good deals on precious jewelry abound—just make sure you buy from a reputable source. Popular purchases include glass bangles, silver anklets, rings, pendants, and *meenakari* (enamel) rings and bracelets. More traditional are the *kundan* pieces: elaborate gold and gem jewelry with designs dating from the Mughal era.

LEATHERWORK

Handcrafted leatherwork is popular in Rajasthan, and you can find purses, journals, and traditional slippers, or *jootis*, at bargain prices. Shopkeepers always claim that their products are made from camel hide, but sometimes cowhide is passed off as camel leather to avoid offending Hindus. Watch out for overly pungent leathergoods (sniff before you purchase), and if you do end up with something smelly, seal the item in a plastic bag along with some fabric-softener/dryer-sheets and baking soda.

PAINTINGS

Rajasthan is famous for paintings in the *phad, pichwai,* and miniature styles. The *phad* is a red, green, and yellow scroll depicting the life of a local hero; the dark and richly hued *pichwais,* hung

in temples, are cloth paintings depicting Lord Krishna in different moods. Miniature paintings are created using squirrel-hair brushes on paper, silk, marble, or bone, and usually depict wildlife and courtly scenes, or illustrations of religious stories and mythological themes.

POTTERY

Pottery is a huge industry in Rajasthan, and the blue pottery here is quite famous. Most people believe that blue pottery originated in Rajasthan, but it's actually of Turko-Persian origin and only emerged in India in the 18th century. The craft nearly went extinct, but was revived in the 1960s and 1970s. The name blue pottery is misleading—although blue is the traditional hue for this kind of work, it's available in an array of colors.

TEXTILES

Rajasthan has a rich textile tradition. *Bandhani* (tie-dye) has its origins in this part of the country, but don't expect to find the psychedelic designs popular in 1960s America—Rajasthan's tie-dyes are often only one or two colors embellished with tiny white circles. Handmade block-printing is also popular, and is made by using wooden stamps (mostly with patterns of paisley, elephants or camels) to transfer natural dyes onto fabric. Detailed embroidery and appliqué, often featuring mirror work, are also popular.

Updated by Abhishek Madhukar

Steeped in tales of chivalry and romance, and famous for its striking desert landscape, massive forts, and fabulous palaces, Rajasthan represents, for many, the quintessential India. With the legendary cities of Jaipur, Jodhpur, Udaipur, and Jaisalmer, built by the mighty Rajput warriors, and the indigenous tribal and artisan communities, Rajasthan is a unique combination of royal and tribal India.

The variety of Rajasthan's landscape is unparalleled: the region is packed with awe-inspiring forts, sparkling palaces, tranquil lakes and gardens, and exquisite temples and shrines. The crafts and folk art produced here are world-renowned. Once called Rajputana ("Abode of Princes"), this vast land consisted of more than 22 princely states before most of them were consolidated into modern Rajasthan in 1949. Each of the 22 states was ruled by a Rajput, an upper-caste Hindu warrior-prince, and the Rajputs were divided into three main clans: the Suryavanshis, descended from the sun; the Chandravanshis, descended from the moon; and the Agnikuls, who had been purified by ritual fire. When they were not fighting among themselves for power, wealth, and women, the Rajputs built the hundreds of forts, palaces, gardens, and temples that make this region so enchanting.

The Rajputs' contribution to cultural life in Rajasthan lives on to this day, and with the amalgam of so many states, each with its rituals and ways of life, Rajasthan is extremely culturally diverse. Communities vary in everything from the colors of their sandstone buildings to the languages they speak—a local saying has it that you hear a new language (dialect) every 4 km (2½ miles). Travelers will notice the brilliant colors of the local women's *lehangas* (long skirts with separate veils), designed to stand out against the starkness of the desert. Women also wear elaborate jewelry, and Rajasthani men are famous for their turbans—called *saafas*—which vary in style from region to region and caste to caste; the style of wearing high turbans with a tail is preferred by Rajputs, for instance, while *pagris* (compact turbans, often orange) are worn by businessmen. Even facial hair is unique in these parts: Rajputs, in particular, sport long, Salvador Dalí–like handlebar moustaches.

Although Rajasthan has many social problems, most notably widespread rural poverty, low literacy rates, and child marriages, its cities and people remain lively. Cultural festivals, crafts fairs, and religious gatherings take place throughout the year. With its bright colors and rich folk traditions, and the sheer variety of experiences it has to offer the traveler, Rajasthan easily earns its place as one of India's most popular tourist destinations.

PLANNING

WHEN TO GO

HIGH SEASON: OCTOBER TO FEBRUARY

The high season for Rajasthan officially begins in October, though the large Spanish tour groups begin arriving in August and September. The peak is November through mid-February when the weather is at its best, the days are perfect for sightseeing and evenings are pleasant—and can even be chilly in the desert areas. Temperatures rarely rise above the mid-80s, but the sun is still strong, so cover up if you're susceptible to sunburn. Many hotel rates are close to double those charged in low season, and monuments are crowded with group tours. This is also when the Ranthambhore National Park is open and the winter migratory birds come to Bharatpur (Keoladeo Ghana) Bird Sanctuary.

LOW SEASON: MAY TO JULY

These summer months can be unbearably hot, with temperatures, particularly in desert cities like Jaisalmer and Jodhpur, at times soaring close to 120 degrees. It's almost impossible to endure a full day of sightseeing. As a result most hotels are vacant and offer great deals—often less than half their usual rates—and the monuments are either deserted or sparsely dotted with a few random tourists.

SHOULDER SEASON: AUGUST TO SEPTEMBER AND MARCH TO APRIL

As long as you don't mind the monsoon, this is not a bad time to visit. The weather is neither at its best or its worst, and crowds can easily be avoided. However, hotel deals are not as highly discounted as in the low season, and the wildlife parks are closed because they sometimes flood.

GETTING HERE AND AROUND

Rajasthan is India's largest state, and if you try to cram too much into one trip you may find yourself spending more time on the road than at your destinations. It can be helpful to use a travel agent for advice on getting around—they're seemingly everywhere you look in the touristy parts of Rajasthan's major cities, and they can help you reserve train and bus tickets for a nominal fee, and most are happy to offer destination advice, though not always unbiased as far as hotels or accommodations are concerned.

AIR TRAVEL

There are domestic airports in Jaipur, Jodhpur, and Udaipur (there's also an airport in Jaisalmer, but civilian flights no longer operate for security reasons, though there is talk of opening it up again, possibly in 2013). Indian Airlines flies between the three and connects Rajasthan with Delhi and Mumbai. The Udaipur–Jodhpur sector sometimes sells out during peak season, as there's no rail connection between the two cities, so reserve in advance. Popular domestic airline carriers to and around Rajasthan include Jet Airways, Air India, IndiGo and SpiceJet. All of these airlines have websites, so searching for tickets is easier than ever.

AIRPORTS AND TRANSFERS Jaipur's Sanganer Airport is about 13 km (8 miles) south of town; a taxi into town costs about Rs. 250 if you call for a radio taxi, or Rs. 550 by private taxi. Jodhpur's airport is 5 km (3 miles) from the city center; a taxi into town costs about Rs. 450. Udaipur's Dabok Airport is 25 km (16 miles) from the city center; the ride costs about Rs. 750.

BUS TRAVEL

If convenience and a cheap price are more important to you than a super-comfortable journey, travel by bus—but keep in mind that the quality of buses in India varies widely. The state-run Volvo buses are a good option for intercity travel. Some "tourist" buses end up picking up hitchhikers, so by the time you reach your destination people are sitting in the aisles and sometimes even on the roof. If you don't mind an adventure, or if you have no other choice, by all means take a bus. Otherwise, take a train or rent a car and driver. The easiest way to get a bus ticket in advance is not from the bus stations, but from many of the private vendors in tourist areas. Your hotel reception or concierge might be able to help (for a fee).

CAR AND DRIVER TRAVEL

It's not cheap, but having a car and driver to yourself is highly efficient if you're short on time, as distances between points of interest are usually long, and direct trains can sometimes be hard to come by. You can hire a car and driver through your hotel or a recognized travel agent—hiring through your hotel is usually more expensive because the hotel will tack on a finder's fee. A car and driver should cost about Rs. 13 to Rs. 15 per km (½ mile), not including tolls. An extra Rs. 200 to Rs. 300 per day is usually tacked on for overnight trips. If you organize a car directly through the driver, it will be cheaper, but check the vehicle and driver out properly the day before you start.

Expect to spend about Rs. 5,000 for a thorough tour of the region from Delhi to Jaipur in a small air-conditioned car with room for three passengers, or about Rs. 6,500 in an air-conditioned larger vehicle that can carry five passengers. Know that because the driver has to return to his point of origin, you pay the round-trip fare even if you're going one-way.

ROAD CONDITIONS Aside from major national highways crossing through Rajasthan, the state highways are not in very good shape, and the going is slow: The Delhi–Jaipur Highway (NH–8) is well paved, but once you're off the highway the roads are full of potholes, and it takes a long time to travel even short distances. When calculating driving time, plan to cover 40 kph–50 kph (25 mph–31 mph) at best. That said, driving is an excellent way to see the Indian countryside and glimpse village life.

Jaipur is a five- to six-hour drive from Delhi on National Highway (NH) 8. This is a congested industrial road with a high accident rate, so prepare for a trying experience.

Road surfaces are rough in and out of Jodhpur, and the going is slow. Don't expect to average more than 40 km (25 miles) per hour. Udaipur is on National Highway 8, one of the better roads, which links Mumbai and Delhi. Again, expect your road speed to top out at 40 kph (25 mph).

A car with driver will cost around Rs. 12 to Rs. 15 per kilometer, or less if you opt out of air-conditioning. Get in touch with your hotel's travel desk or an independent travel agent for car-rental options—the latter is more likely to give you a reasonable rate.

RAJASTHAN IS BIG

Rajasthan is big—very big—with long stretches between the most popular destinations. If you have limited time, stay in one place and explore the surrounding area rather than rushing through all the highlights. If you have to choose one city to focus on, Udaipur is probably your best bet—it's the most enchanting and tourist-friendly of Rajasthan's four major tourist cities—but if you only have a couple of days, you may be better off sticking to Jaipur, which is closest to Delhi and Agra.

5

TAXIS AND AUTO-RICKSHAW TRAVEL

Taxis are unmetered in Jaipur, Jodhpur, and Udaipur, so ask your hotel for the going rate and negotiate with the driver before you set off; hire one through your hotel or the RTDC's Tourist Information Center (⇨ *See Visitor Information, below, for contacts*). Depending on the distance to be covered, a taxi for half a day will cost about Rs. 800, and for a full day about Rs. 1,600. A full day usually equates to 8 hours and 80 kilometers (50 miles) within the city limits; a set sightseeing city tour may cost less.

Auto-rickshaws in Jaipur are metered, but the meters are hardly ever used. Insist on setting the price in advance and negotiate. The rate should be no more than Rs. 8 per km (½ mile), with a minimum total of Rs. 15. Auto-rickshaws in Jodhpur and Udaipur are unmetered, so agree on a price before departing. You can also hire an auto-rickshaw by the hour, for about Rs. 100 per hour. Note that all of these rates go up by 25% to 50% after 11 pm.

TRAIN TRAVEL

In Rajasthan if you want to travel overnight, it's safer and more comfortable to take the train than a bus or car. Trains offer classes of service for all budgets (seats and sleepers, air-conditioning and non-air-conditioning, reserved and unreserved). Trains do get crowded, though, during peak season, and you may want to investigate special "tourist quotas" that set aside seats for foreign travelers. Check with a travel agent rather than deal with the crowds and administrative chaos at the train station, and book as far ahead as possible.

Because of Jaisalmer's proximity to the Pakistan border there are no commercial flights, although there has been talk of flights recommencing in 2013. Until that happens a train is the best method of getting there.

The Shatabdi Express, an air-conditioned chair-car train (the local term for a train carriage with only seats, no sleeping arrangements), travels every morning from New Delhi, departing at 6 am to arrive at Jaipur by 10:30 am. The DEE Double Decker leaves Delhi S Rohilla station at 5:35 pm and reaches Jaipur at 10:05 pm. The BDTS Garib Rath leaves Delhi Cantt station at 9:35 am and arrives at 2:10 pm. Daily trains connect Udaipur with Jaipur, Ajmer, Chittaurgarh, and Delhi. Trains also run out from Delhi to Jaisalmer and Jodhpur as well as Jodhpur to Jaisalmer, but they're significantly slower than the road routes. *Contact the Indian Railways Catering and Tourism Corporation Ltd for more information, and see the In Focus: Transportation feature in the Experience chapter, and the By Train section of the Travel Smart chapter for more information about train travel in India.*

The famed Palace on Wheels is a luxury train that runs across the state, connecting major sights. It's quite expensive, and not everyone feels that the accommodation standards merit the train's high prices. Note that if the train is running behind schedule, you might miss some sites.

Train Information **Indian Railway Catering and Tourism Corporation Ltd** ☎ 11/3934–0000 ⊕ www.irctc.co.in **Palace on Wheels** ☎ 11/2338–1884 *in Delhi, 888/463–4299 US and Canada, 800/845–6201 in Europe* ⊕ www.palaceonwheels.com.

EMERGENCIES

If you need a doctor or a 24-hour pharmacy, ask at your hotel: they'll know the closest place and can send someone to get medicine, or find a doctor. There are emergency help lines and ambulance numbers for all major cities—108 is the emergency number for ambulance service in Rajasthan.

INTERNET

Internet cafés with high-speed connections can be found in all of Rajasthan's major tourist destinations, though the service can fluctuate. Wi-Fi is harder to come by, except at top-end hotels.

MONEY MATTERS

ATMS ATMs are widely available in Rajasthan. In major cities it's also possible to get a credit-card advance from a bank. Almost all ATMs take foreign credit cards.

CURRENCY Nearly all hotels exchange foreign currency for their guests. You'll get
EXCHANGE better rates at banks, but the hassle of waiting in line may outweigh the money-saving. There are also Thomas Cook and Western Union kiosks in all four major cities, usually open daily from 10 am to 6 pm.

TOURS

Royal Desert Safari in Jaisalmer organizes treks, camel safaris, and nights in the desert around Bikaner, Jodhpur, and Jaisalmer, as well as visits to traditional villages, craftspeople's homes, little-known fairs, and ashrams. Karwan Tours in Jaipur can also help with general travel arrangements, including a hired car with driver to any location in Rajasthan. Le Passage to India functions both as an agent and as an operator, and offers custom tours as well as reliable cars and drivers in all major Rajasthan towns. Parul Tours and Travels is a tour operator. Rajasthan Tourism Development Corporation also organizes city tours and excursions. It's usually easiest to book tours through your hotel or a travel agent, although a few operators allow direct booking. If you are

Festivals in Rajasthan

The dates of most of Rajasthan's festivals are determined using the Hindu calendar, so timing varies from year to year.

Pushkar's Camel Fair is in October or November, the Jaisalmer Desert Festival in January or February, Jaipur's Gangaur Festival and Udaipur's Mewar Festival are in March or April, and Mount Abu's Summer Festival is in June. Jodhpur's RIFF (Rajasthan International Folk Festival) is usually in late October or November.

The Jaipur Literature Festival in January attracts authors from around the world; speakers at the 2012 festival included Nobel laureate J.M. Coetzee, Oprah Winfrey, William Dalrymple, Tom Stoppard, Kiran Nagarkar, Steven Pinker, and Richard Dawkins. The Dalai Lama will be a keynote speaker in 2013.

booking through an agent, shop around—sometimes agents will try to undercut the competition by offering small discounts on their offerings: there are usually several agents next to each other on the same street, so you can go from one to another.

Tour Contacts Karwan Tours ✉ *Bissau Palace Hotel, outside Chandpol gate, near Saroj Cinema, Jaipur* ☎ *141/230–8103.* **Le Passage to India** ✉ *101 Ganpati Plaza, M.I. Rd., Jaipur* ☎ *141/511–5415, 982/905–1387* ⊕ *www.lpti.com* ✉ *14/21 Lake Palace Rd., first fl., Udaipur* ☎ *0294/510–0422, 0294/510–0432* ✉ *Shop 04, Geeta Ashram Rd., Hanuman Circle, Jaisalmer* ☎ *299/225–0355, 299/225–0354* ✉ *Airport Rd., Ratananda circle, opposite R.S.E.B. sub station, Jodhpur* ☎ *291/251–0859.* **Parul Tours and Travels** ✉ *32 Lal Ghat, opposite Kankarwa Haveli, Udaipur* ☎ *0294/242–1697* ⊕ *www.rajasthantravelbycab.com.* **Royal Desert Safaris** ✉ *Nachna Haveli, Gandhi Chowk, Jaisalmer* ☎ *2992/252–538* 🖷 *2992/251–402* ⊕ *www.campsandsafaries.com.*

VISITOR INFORMATION

Many hotels provide regional information and travel services. In Jaipur, Jodhpur, Udaipur, and Jaisalmer the Tourist Information Centers of the Rajasthan Tourism Development Corporation (RTDC) provide information, travel assistance, and guides. *Jaipur Vision* and the *Jaipur City Guide*, available in most hotels, are periodicals with visitor information and up-to-date phone numbers.

Tourist Offices Rajasthan Tourism Development Corporation ✉ *Swagatam Complex, Station Rd., Jaipur* ☎ *141/255–4970, 141/237–5466, 141/237–5835* ⊕ *www.rajasthantourism.gov.in.*

ABOUT THE RESTAURANTS

Rajasthan's culinary traditions are heavily influenced by its desert setting and in some parts of the state, sweets open the meal. Food tends to be highly spiced, perhaps for preservation. Instead of the rice and vegetables that are popular in regions with more rainfall, Rajasthani cuisine includes a lot of lentils and corn. Both posh, pricey restaurants and local dives are bound to serve regional food, so try some local delicacies.

Prices in the reviews are the average cost of a main course at dinner or, if dinner is not served, at lunch.

ABOUT THE HOTELS

The most opulent hotels in India—and perhaps in the world—are in Rajasthan. You can literally live like a king in one of several converted palaces, surrounded by glittering mirrored walls, tiger skins, and stained-glass windows. Rajasthan is also famous for Heritage Hotels, a group of castles, forts, and havelis that have been converted to elegant accommodations.

Prices in the reviews are the lowest cost of a standard double room in high season. For expanded hotel reviews, facilities, and current deals, visit Fodors.com.

PLANNING YOUR TIME

The ideal way to see Rajasthan is first to fly to Jaipur, Jodhpur, or Udaipur and then tackle nearby towns by train, bus, or private car. Ideally you should start at Jaipur, make your way around by car, and end up in Udaipur, from where you can fly to Mumbai or Delhi. Overnight train journeys between major cities in air-conditioned sleeper coaches are a cheap way to travel without wasting too much time or money on hotel stays. For instance, you could start in Jaipur and work your way to Udaipur, then to Jodhpur, Jaisalmer, and back to Delhi.

There are plenty of sights and day trips to be taken from each of these major destinations. Don't miss the Jain temples in Ranakpur and the Kumbalgarh fort, both of which are fantastic day-trip options from Udaipur. One day and a night in Jodhpur is plenty, but make sure you give yourself at least two nights in Jaisalmer—spend one night in town and the second night on an overnight desert safari on camelback. *For more about planning a Rajasthan itinerary, see the Great Itineraries in the Experience chapter.*

If you only have a few days to visit Rajasthan, we suggest picking one city to visit, and try to make a few day trips from there, rather than cram in several of the larger cities. While Jaipur is the most popular destination in Rajasthan for its proximity to Delhi and Agra, Udaipur is a fairy-tale sort of place, with its beautiful lakeside palaces and havelis, and the many nearby attractions.

EXPLORING RAJASTHAN

You could easily spend months in Rajasthan. The state's southwestern corner centers on Udaipur, a hilly town of palaces and artificial lakes, with the nearby hill station of Mount Abu, while central Rajasthan is anchored by Jodhpur, home to a glorious fort and the eye-catching blue houses of the Brahmin caste. Jaipur, the state capital, is in the east, toward Delhi. Western Rajasthan, largely given over to the Thar Desert, can best be explored via camel or jeep from the golden city of Jaisalmer. In the northeast, between Jaipur and Delhi, the Shekhawati region is home to lovely painted havelis, the mansions of prosperous merchants. The southern and eastern regions also have a number of good wildlife parks.

CLOSE UP

The Brave Rajputs

For centuries, many Hindu Rajputs valiantly resisted invasion, including attempts by the Muslim Mughals. Their codes of battle emphasized honor and pride, and they went to war prepared to die. When defeat on the battlefield was imminent, the Rajput women would perform the rite of *jauhar,* throwing themselves onto a flaming pyre en masse rather than live with the indignity of capture. With the exception of the princes of Mewar, major Rajput states such as Jaipur, Bikaner, Bundi, and Kota eventually stopped fighting and built strong ties with the Mughals. The Mughal emperor Akbar was particularly skilled at forging alliances with the Rajputs; he offered them high posts in his court, and sealed the deal with matrimonial ties (he married two Rajput princesses). Those kingdoms who sided with Akbar quickly rose in importance and prosperity.

Raja Man Singh I of Jaipur was the first to marry his aunt to Akbar. As the emperor's brother-in-law and trusted commander-in-chief, Man Singh led Mughal armies to many victories, and both rulers benefited immensely. A traditional saying: *"Jeet Akbar ki, loot Man Singh ki"* translates as "The victory belongs to Akbar, the loot to Man Singh". In addition to securing wealth, these marriages opened the Rajput households to the Mughals' distinctive culture. The same people who initially sacrificed their lives to resist the Mughals quickly adapted themselves to Mughal domination and started borrowing heavily from Mughal aesthetics. Skilled craftsmen from the Mughal courts were enticed to Rajasthan to start craft schools, fomenting what would become a golden age of Indian

art and architecture. The Mughals' influence in Rajasthan is still visible in everything from food to architecture, from intricate miniature paintings to musical styles, and from clothing to the tradition of *purdah* (covering the head and face with a veil).

The beginning of the 18th century marked the decline of the Mughal period, and with it came the decline of the Rajputs. The incoming British took advantage of the prevailing chaos. Not only did they introduce significant administrative, legal, and educational changes in Rajasthan, they also exposed the Rajputs to new levels of excess. The British introduced polo and other equestrian sports, the latest rifles and guns, *shikar* (hunting) camps, Belgian glass, French chiffons, Victorian furniture, European architecture, and—eventually—fancy limousines. The influence extended to Rajput children: sons were sent to English universities, and daughters to finishing schools in Switzerland.

While the rest of India launched its struggle for independence, many Rajput princes ended up defending the Raj. Unwilling to give up their luxury and power, they did their best to suppress rebellion outside their own kingdoms by sending soldiers to help the British forces. When India became independent, the Rajput princes and kings merged their kingdoms into one state as part of the new nation, but they were allowed to keep the titles to their palaces, forts, lands, jewels, and other possessions. The Indian government has since taken over much of the royal properties. Stripped of feudal power, many maharajas became hotel owners, while others have turned their properties over to leading hotel chains.

Dancers at Jaisalmer's Desert Festival

JAIPUR AND ENVIRONS

Jaipur, the state capital, is worth a few days' visit: it's a delightful mixture of modernity and folk tradition. Don't be surprised to see camels pulling carts on the main streets, mingling ill-temperedly with vehicular traffic. With its towering forts and impressive city palace, Jaipur is a good indicator of what to expect as you progress to interior Rajasthan. It's also a good base from which to visit other towns and parks in the region. The craft villages of Sanganer and Bagru, just outside Jaipur, are populated almost entirely by artisans, and you're free to stop in and watch them make fine paper and block-print textiles by hand—don't expect great bargains though. The Hindu pilgrimage town of Pushkar is known for its annual camel festival, held in October or November. For an unusual experience, take a long day trip to Bundi, as famous for its intricate stepwells and charming little lanes as it is for being one of Rudyard Kipling's former residences. To escape civilization altogether, go bird-watching at Bharatpur's Keoladeo National Park or on a tiger safari at Ranthambhore (which may or may not result in spotting a tiger), though you'll need to check the latest government restrictions on "tiger tourism."

JAIPUR

261 km (162 miles) southwest of Delhi; 343 km (213 miles) east of Jodhpur; 405 km (252 miles) northeast of Udaipur.

There is a Rajasthani proverb that asks, *"Je na dekhyo Jaipario, To kal men akar kya kario?"* ("What have I accomplished in my life, if I have not seen Jaipur?").

Flanked on three sides by the rugged Aravali Hills, and celebrated for the striking, if somewhat run-down, pink buildings in the old part of the city, Jaipur is the capital of Rajasthan, and a good starting point for a trip through the region. It's a spirited place: a jumble of colorful native clothes—*ghagharas* (skirts),

complex turbans, and sturdy *jutis* (pointed shoes)—sidewalk shops overflowing with pottery and dyed or sequined fabric, and streets packed with camel carts, cycle-rickshaws, and wandering cows. The salmon-color Old City is where you'll spend most of your time: most of the sights you'll want to see are here, and it's full of appealing bazaars with colorful textiles and trinkets—look for *lac* (resin) bangles, steel utensils, and copper ornaments—and *mehendi* (henna) artists. Mirza Ismail (or M.I. Road as it's popularly known) is the main drag. It's a bit touristy and hectic in the Old City, so be prepared to deal with a lot of touts and bargain hard if you want to purchase something at one of the bazaars.

Jaipur was named after Maharaja Sawai Jai Singh II, an avid scientist, architect, and astronomer who founded the city in 1727 when he moved down from Amber, the ancient rockbound stronghold of his ancestors. It's known for being one of the first planned cities in the world, and it's said to epitomize the dreams of the ruler and the creative ideas of his talented designer and builder, Vidhydar. The city they planned is rectangular in shape, and divided into nine blocks based on the principles of the ancient architectural treatise *Shilp Shastra*. Every aspect of Jaipur—streets, sidewalks, building height, and number and division of blocks—was based on geometric harmony, environmental and climatic considerations, and the intended use of each zone. Part of the city is still enclosed in 20-foot-high fortified walls, which have eight gates.

GETTING HERE AND AROUND

Although you can fly to Jaipur, most people get here either by train or road. The train station and the city's main bus stand are less than half a mile apart, so if you don't have much luggage and need to transfer from a bus to train, or vice versa, you can easily walk from one to another.

To get around in the city, auto-rickshaws are your best bet; cycle-rickshaws are equally good for short distances—just be sure to negotiate a fare before you climb aboard. Note that parts of the walled Pink City

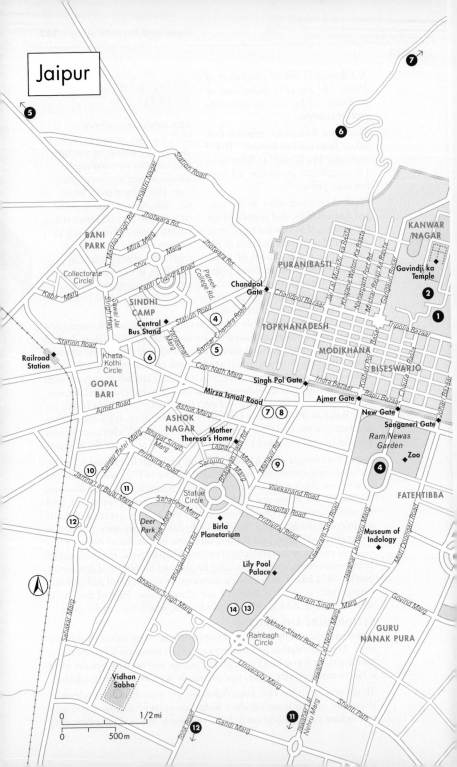

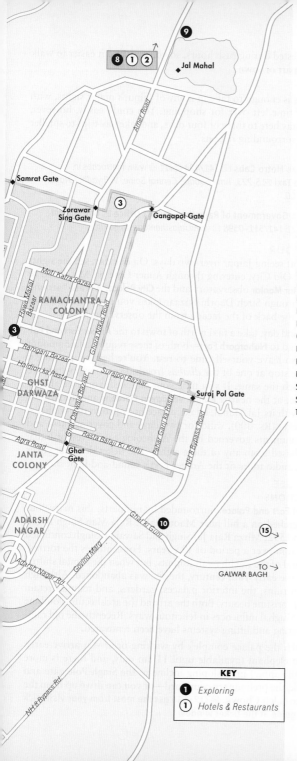

Exploring ▼

Albert Hall Museum **4**
Amber Fort and Palace **8**
Apno Gaon **5**
Chokhi Dhani **12**
City Palace **2**
Hawa Mahal **3**
Jaigarh Fort **7**
Jantar Mantar **1**
Jawahar Kala Kendra **11**
Kanak Vrindavan Gardens **9**
Nahargarh Fort **6**
Sisodia Rani ka Bagh **10**

Hotels & Restaurants ▼

Alsisar Haveli **4**
Café Kooba **11**
Copper Chimney **6**
Hotel Arya Niwas **5**
Hotel Diggi Palace **9**
Natraj **7**
Neemrana Fort Palace **2**
Niros **8**
Oberoi Rajvilas **15**
Pratap Bhawan Home Stay **10**
Raj Mahal Palace **12**
Rambagh Palace, Jaipur **14**
Samode Haveli **3**
Suvarna Mahal **13**
Tree of Life **1**

Jal Mahal

⑨

⑧①②

→

Samrat Gate

**Zorawar
Sing Gate**

③

Gangapol Gate

Amer Road

❸

Mott Katra Bazaar

**RAMACHANTRA
COLONY**

Hawa Mahal Bazaar

❸

Ramganj Bazaar

Haldion ka Rasta

Ghora Nikas Road

Surajpol Bazaar

**GHST
DARWAZA**

Ghat Darwaza Bazaar

Rasta Balaji Ki Kothi

Pahar Ganj ka Rasta

Suraj Pol Gate

Agra Road

**JANTA
COLONY**

**Ghat
Gate**

**ADARSH
NAGAR**

Adarsh Nagar Rd.

⑩

Ghat ki Guni

Govind Marg

⑮

TO →
GALWAR BAGH

NH 8 Bypass Rd.

NH 8 Bypass Road

KEY

❶ *Exploring*

① *Hotels & Restaurants*

get very congested during rush hours, so you may find it easier to walk through this part of town.

TIMING

Two full days is enough to take in many of Jaipur's major sights, with a little bit of time left over for shopping. You could easily, however, extend your stay here to three or four days, and take day trips to smaller towns in the surrounding regions.

ESSENTIALS

Taxi Companies Metro Cabs ☎ 141/424–4411 ⊕ www.metrocabs.in. Pinkcity Radio Taxi ✉ S-223, Time Square, Central Spine, Vidhyadhar Nagar ☎ 141/515–5100.

Tourist Offices Government of Rajasthan Tourist Office ✉ Government Hostel, M.I. Rd. ☎ 141/511–0598 ⊕ www.rajasthantourism.gov.in.

A GOOD TOUR

You're best off seeing Jaipur over two days. On one day, see the sights in the walled Old City, entering through Ajmer Gate off M.I. Road to reach the **Jantar Mantar** observatory and the **City Palace**. A walk "around the block" through Sireh Deorhi Bazaar takes you to the **Hawa Mahal** (you can see the back of the facade from the observatory).

On your second day, take a taxi north of town to the **Amber Fort and Palace** and then go to **Nahargarh Fort**—both of these require a fair amount of walking, so leave yourself time to rest. You're best off packing a lunch, or else stop at one of the *dhabas* (roadside eateries), which are all pretty much the same. If you time your day well, you'll be able to see the sun set at the nearby **Kanak Vrindavan Gardens** and admire the Man Sagar with its Jal Mahal, a lake palace not open to the public. A combined ticket (Rs. 300), valid for two days and covering these and all other monuments governed by the Archeological Survey of India, can be purchased from any of these sights. The ticket does not cover camera fees, audio tours or the Amber Fort's sound-and-light show.

WHAT TO SEE

TOP ATTRACTIONS

☼ ★ **Amber (Amer) Fort and Palace.** Surrounded by ramparts, this marvelous fortress is perched on a hill near Maota Lake. Raja Man Singh began building it in 1592; Mirza Raja Jai Singh and Sawai Jai Singh continued the construction over a period of 125 years. For centuries the fortress was the capital of the Kachhawah Rajputs, but when the capital shifted to Jaipur in the early 18th century, the site was abandoned. Although the fort is in ruins, the interior palaces, gardens, and temples retain much of their pristine beauty. Both the art and the architecture combine Rajput and Mughal influences in felicitous ways. Recently the old rainwater harvesting and lifting systems have been renovated.

You approach the palace complex by walking or, if you arrive early, by riding an elephant (available until 11 am only, and there is more demand than supply) up a sloping incline to the **Singh Pole** gate and **Jaleb Chowk,** the preliminary courtyard—or you can drive up from the rear end into Jaleb Chowk. ■TIP→ To get the most from your visit, pick up an audio guide at the ticket window.

JAIPUR'S HERITAGE BROUGHT TO LIFE

Virasat Experiences, run by enterprising local youths, organizes meticulously designed walking tours that bring alive diverse elements of the city's living heritage that underpin the main monuments. The off-beat tours—a leisurely two- to three-hour walk, including a break for tea and food sampling—begin (morning and evening) at the heart of the old walled "Pink" city, and explore hidden, derelict, abandoned homes, temples, monuments, and buildings. The knowledgeable guides point out living crafts, culture, and traditional cuisines (including sweet making) with a historical perspective, and walks can be customized to specific interests. The fee includes all admission fees, temple donations, food sampling and tea; tip of Rs. 100 per person, to a maximum Rs. 500 for a group, is customary. Virisat Experiences also organize tours in Jodhpur and Udaipur. Book at least one day ahead. ⊠ Om Niwas Hotel, E-23 Kaushalya Marg, Bani Park, Jaipur ☎ 141/5109090, 94140–66260 ⊕ www.virasatexperiences.com ⊠ Rs. 1500.

Two flights of stairs lead up from Jaleb Chowk; to start, skip the one leading to the Shiladevi Temple and take the one leading directly to the palace. In the next courtyard, the pillared **Diwan-i-Am** (Hall of Public Audience) contains alabaster panels with fine inlay work—the kind of craftsmanship for which Jaipur is famous. Typical of the Mughal period, the rooms are small and intimate, whereas the palace's successive courtyards and narrow passages are characteristically Rajput.

One of the elaborately carved and painted gates is known as **Ganesh Pol,** after the elephant god Ganesh. From a latticed corridor above it, the queen—always in purdah, or hiding—would await the king's return from battle and sprinkle scented water and flowers down upon him. Each room shows some vestige of its former glory, especially the **Sheesh Mahal** (Palace of Mirrors), with glittering mirror work on the ceiling. Narrow flights of stairs lead up to the lavish royal apartments, and beyond the corridors and galleries there'll find the small, elegant **Char Bagh** garden. Take in the views of the valley, the palace courtyards, the formal gardens abutting the octagonal pool next to the lake, and the vast **Jaigarh Fort,** the ancient fortress on the crest of the hill above you. Also on the upper floor is **Jas Mandir,** a hall with filigreed marble *jalis* (screens) and delicate mirror and stuccowork.

On your way out, peek into the 16th-century **Shiladevi Temple** to the goddess Kali, with its silver doors and marble carvings. Raja Man Singh installed the image of the goddess after bringing it here from lower Bengal (now Bangladesh). Exit the palace by the gate near the temple, and just a few minutes down the road is the 16th-century **Jagat Shiromani** temple. Dedicated to Krishna, this exquisitely carved marble-and-sandstone temple was built by Raja Man Singh I in memory of his son. ⊠ *Delhi Rd., 11 km (7 miles) north of Jaipur, Amber* ☎ *141/253–0844, 141/253–1042* ⊠ *Rs. 200; sound-and-light show Rs. 250* ⊙ *Daily 8:30–5:30 (last admission 4:45); sound-and-light shows (summer only) 7:30 or 8 pm.*

City Palace. This complex of pavilions, courtyards, and chambers was begun by Jai Singh II in 1727, and wings were added by later maharajas. If you're standing in the outer courtyard, the marble and sandstone building directly in front of you is the **Mubarak Mahal** (Guest Pavilion), built by Maharaja Madho Singh in the late 19th century. Now a museum, it's an ideal place to admire at close range some of the royals' finest brocades, silks, and hand-blocked garments and robes, many made in nearby Sanganer and some dating from as far back as the 17th century. The collection also includes musical instruments. The **armory** in the northwest corner of the courtyard has one of India's best collections of arms and weapons, including an 11-pound sword belonging to Akbar's Rajput general. Some of the paints used on the beautiful, 18th-century ceiling are believed to have been made from crushed semiprecious stones.

> ### FOR YOUR SWEET TOOTH
>
> Jaipur is especially known for its desserts: look for *ghevar* (lentil-batter funnel cake), *pheeni* (strawlike sweets made of refined flour), *jalebis* (fried, twisty orange sweets), *malpua* (deep-fried syrupy pancakes), and *churmas* (tasty wheat-flour dumplings in a sweet gravy).

In the inner courtyard, through the gateway guarded by two stone elephants, is the art gallery, housed in the cavernous **Diwan-i-Am** (Hall of Public Audience). Built in the late 18th century, the building has a magnificent, vintage-1930s painted ceiling, rows of gray marble columns inside the courtyard, the second-largest chandelier in India, and two silver pots so large that they are mentioned in the *Guiness Book of World Records*. The art includes scores of miniatures from the Mughal and various Rajput schools, rare manuscripts, and 17th-century carpets from the Amber Palace. From the inner courtyard, enter the Zenana (ladies') courtyard on the left to see the seven-story **Chandra Mahal** (Moon Palace). Built by Jai Singh II, this attractive cream-colored building was the official residence of the last maharaja, "Bubbles" (born 1931)—Lieutenant Colonel Sawai Bhawani Singh—who passed away in 2011; his family still lives on the upper floors. The ground floor has sumptuous chandeliers, murals, and a painting of an old maharaja. A "Royal Grandeur" tour is available, taking you close, but not quite into, the royal family's quarters and their guest rooms. ⚠ Watch out for touts claiming that you need a guide to tour the palace—you don't. ✉ *Center of the Old City, enter the complex at the Virendra Pole gate, Pink City* ✉ *Palace Rs. 300; camera free; video-camera Rs. 200* ☾ *Daily 8:30–5:30 (last tickets sold before 5).*

★ **Hawa Mahal.** Jaipur's photogenic Palace of Winds was built by Maharaja Sawai Pratap Singh in 1799 so that the women of the court could discreetly take some air and watch the activity on the street below. Every story has semi-octagonal overhanging windows, and each has a perforated screen. This curious five-story structure, named after the westerly winds that blow cool breezes through the windows, is just one room wide, so the wind easily passes through the building and cools the interior (servants also threw water on the lattice, so any breeze would

CLOSE UP

Jaipur's Village Complexes

Rajasthan is a largely rural state, and the local villages still maintain unique lifestyles, with traditional entertainments and ways of life. It's a fascinating other world from what Westerners are used to. Travelers with little time and limited personal contact with the locals, though, aren't generally going to get invited to an authentic village to see how people really live—and language barriers can be an issue if you do. A popular alternative is to visit what is known as "village complexes," essentially artificial replicas of the real thing that feature souvenir stands, cultural entertainment programs, and regional cuisine. Popular with Indian and overseas tourists alike, these villages feel a bit like theme parks, but the cuisine and traditional entertainment is authentic, so they're quite worthwhile. Two good ones to visit when you're in Jaipur are Chokhi Dhani and Apno Gaon (see Jaipur, What to See). Apno Gaon is closer to town and on a smaller scale than Chokhi Dhani, a large, over-the-top complex. Both include a feast of local delicacies and entertainment in the admission price, but there might be an extra charge for things like camel and elephant rides—and, of course, there will be shopping opportunities.

be cooled by the water, and would lower the temperature). The building facade has a delicate honeycomb design with close to 1,000 windows, and is fashioned from pink sandstone. ✉ *Sireh Deorhi Bazaar, Pink City* ☎ *141/261–8862* ✉ *Rs. 50 (free Mon.)* ☉ *Sat.–Thurs. 9–4:30.*

NEED A BREAK?

Laxmi Misthan Bhandar. Known affectionately as LMB, Laxmi Misthan Bhandar is a sweet shop famous all over Rajasthan for its fresh and sumptuous sweets, including *ghevar* (lentil-batter funnel cake), *mave ki kachori* (a milk-base pastry), and savory snacks like *raj kachori* and samosa, though the sugar-laden delicacies may be a bit too sweet for the average foreign visitor. LMB also has a restaurant adjoining the sweet shop, which serves a large selection of rather oily Indian specialties. The *shahi* (royal) thali has an impressive 15 items. ✉ *Johari Bazaar, Ajmer Rd., Behind Hawa Mahal, Pink City* ☎ *141/256–5844.*

★ **Jantar Mantar.** Jai Singh II was well aware of European developments in the field of astronomy, and wanted to create one of the world's finest observatories. He supervised the design and construction of five remarkable facilities in northern India, of which this is the largest and best preserved. Built in 1726 out of masonry, marble, and brass, it's equipped with solar instruments called *yantras*, which look like large, abstract sculptures, and are remarkably precise in measuring celestial data. Such accuracy was desired for creating astrological predictions. If you don't have a guide with you, try to recruit one to explain how these devices work, as they're fascinating and, for nonscientists, somewhat complicated. Avoid the observatory at noon, as it can be very hot. ✉ *Tripoliya Bazaar, near entrance to City Palace, Pink City* ✉ *Observatory Rs. 200; camera free* ☉ *Daily 9–4:30.*

Nahargarh Fort. The scenic hilltop location of Naharharh Fort provides breathtaking views of Jaipur and its natural defenses. Initially built by Sawai Jai Singh in 1734, it was enlarged to its sprawling, present-day glory in 1885 by Sawai Madho Singh, who commandeered it as a lookout point. Cannons placed behind the walls recall the days when artillery was positioned against potential attackers below. The Rajasthan tourist board runs a terrace snack bar at the fort, but if you want a full meal, you're probably better off packing a picnic. The palace of nine queens—with nine separate apartments for the wives of Maharaja Ram Singh—within the fort is also worth a short visit. The massive channels that carried rainwater from Nahargarh to Jaigarh Fort, a few miles away, where it was stored in large tanks as part of a rainwater harvesting system, can still be seen from the approach road. ⊠ *10 km (6 miles) north of Jaipur off Amber Rd.* ⬚ *Rs. 50; camera fee Rs. 30; video-camera fee Rs. 70* ⊙ *Fort daily sunrise–sunset; palace daily 10–5:30.*

> ## WHAT'S WITH THE PINK?
>
> The buildings of Jaipur were originally yellow colored, which you can still see on the backs of the buildings—the capital was painted pink (really more of a salmon color), however, when Prince Albert, consort of Queen Victoria, visited India in the middle of the 19th century. The idea stuck, and by law buildings in the Old City must still be painted pink. As a result Jaipur is commonly referred to as the Pink City.

WORTH NOTING

Albert Hall Museum. The oldest museum in Jaipur is worth a visit just for its architecture—the sandstone-and-marble Indo-Saracenic-style building dates from the late 19th century. The collection, which unfortunately is neither well maintained nor well organized, includes folk arts, miniature paintings, traditional costumes, unexpected exhibits of yoga postures, and visual explanations of Indian culture and traditions. Filming and photography are allowed at no extra cost. ⊠ *In Ram Niwas Gardens, Adarsh Nagar* ⬚ *Rs. 150; audio tour Rs. 110; camera free* ⊙ *Daily 9–5.*

Apno Gaon. Camel rides, playground swings, traditional music, and puppet shows are part of the experience at this cultural village *(see also Jaipur's Village Complexes)*, but the emphasis is on the food, which is so good that even locals come here to feast. For an all-in price (Rs. 250), you'll get a large platter of vegetarian food in a Rajasthani thali cooked with farm-fresh, organic vegetables, *gatte ki sabji* (chunks of chick-pea-based sausage cooked curry style)—a favourite with locals—*bhajra* (millet) delicacies, and milk-based desserts. Be prepared to sit on the ground and eat with your hands. It's more fun to come here at night. ⊠ *14 Sikar Rd., Loha Mandi Rd.* ☎ *98878–64030, 94133–43477* ▭ *No credit cards* ⊙ *Daily 11–11.*

Chokhi Dhani. About a 45-minute drive from Jaipur, this large replica cultural village *(see also Jaipur's Village Complexes)* includes a huge buffet meal in the admission price, consisting of pretty much every regional vegetarian dish you can imagine as well as a huge selection of sugary desserts. Come hungry and expect to sit on benches or on the floor in a lantern-lit hut to eat. Performance tents and clearings around the compound host traditional dances, including the dramatic fire dance, folk singing, *katputli* (puppet shows), and juggling. Entertainment is also included in the admission fee, and tipping is discouraged. If you're here at sunset, you'll see the traditional village *aarti* (prayer ceremony). Camel and elephant rides are available, and there are plenty of vendors selling every type of Rajasthani tchotchke under the sun. There's a hotel on-site, although not in authentic village style—it's much more luxurious—and its restaurant and bar, serving regular Indian fare, offer an alternative to the buffet. ⊠ *Tonk Rd., 19 km (12 miles) south of Jaipur via town of Vatika* ☎ *141/516–5000, 141/516–5015* ⊕ *www. chokhidhani.com* ☞ *Rs. 400, including dinner and cultural show.*

Jaigarh Fort. Originally the royal treasury, this fort has large water tanks for storing rainwater that's been channeled down the hill from imposing Nahargarh. There are fantastic views of Jaipur from the watchtower. A large monkey population now provides endless entertainment and a certain amount of annoyance in the center of the fort, where visitors marvel at the Jaivana Cannon, the largest wheeled cannon in the world, measuring over 20 feet long and weighing in at around 50 tons. Guides are available at the entrance—an English-speaking one will charge about Rs. 100. It's possible to drive from Jaigarh to Amber, but be sure to get a driver who knows the way through the narrow lanes. ⊠ *About 7 km (4 miles) from Jaipur, off Amber Rd.* ☞ *Fort Rs. 75; camera fee Rs. 50; video-camera fee Rs. 200; vehicle Rs. 50* ☉ *Daily 9–5.*

Jawahar Kala Kendra. Jaipur's center for arts and crafts was founded by the state government with a specific vision: to create a space for understanding and experiencing culture and folk traditions amid the chaos of urban life. The center also hosts occasional theatrical and musical performances. You can drop by to meet some of the locals who exhibit and perform here, or just to collect information on cultural events. ⊠ *Jawaharlal Nehru Marg, opposite Jhalana Institutional Area, Moti Dhungri* ⊕ *jawaharkalakendra.rajasthan.gov.in* ☉ *Daily 10–6; concerts some evenings; offices weekdays only.*

Kanak Vrindavan Gardens. This picturesque set of gardens and temples is just below the majestic Amber and Nahargarh forts. From here you can get a good look at the Jal Mahal Palace in Man Sagar Lake. The gardens also make a great picnic spot, especially if you like to people-watch. If you're lucky you might even catch a glimpse of Bollywood's brightest filming a Hindi movie. ⊠ *Amber Rd., Man Sagar* ☞ *Rs. 25* ☉ *Daily 8–5.*

Sisodia Rani ka Bagh. On the road to Bharatpur stands one of many palaces built for the *ranis*, or queens, of Sawai Jai Singh II. Built in 1779, the palace, though in a state of disrepair, still looks lovely against the backdrop of hills. The palace is furnished with murals illustrating hunting scenes and the romantic legend of Krishna and Radha, while the terraced garden is dotted with fountains and frequented by prancing peacocks and monkeys. ⊠ *8 km (5 miles) east of Jaipur on road to Bharatpur* ☞ *Rs. 25* ☉ *Daily 8–6.*

The Jantar Mantor Observatory in Jaipur

OFF THE
BEATEN
PATH

Galwar Bagh. Known by locals and rickshaw-wallahs simply as Monkey Temple, Galwar Bagh is a popular pilgrimage site and temple complex on the outskirts of town. The temple itself is called **Gulta Ji Mandir;** it's a 30-minute walk from the ceremonial gate called Gulta Pol, located at the far eastern edge of the city. If you visit on a hot day, make sure to bring plenty of water, though avoid carrying unsealed food, as this can attract monkeys, who generally have no qualms about mugging unsuspecting humans for their lunch. The walk leads you over a small mountain pass and past a few small temples and shrines. Jaipuri Hindus believe that at the site of the Gulta Ji Mandir a local saint named Gala Rishi—nicknamed Gulta Ji—brought forth a spring of holy water from the Ganges that filled a water reservoir 18 feet deep. The waters here are believed to be spiritually connected to the Ganges—if you bathe here, you are said to get the same benefits as a pilgrimage to the Ganges, but as with the Ganges, spiritual cleanliness does not equal physical cleanliness, and we don't recommend going in. The temple, which venerates Lord Brahma, Creator of the Universe, is in violation of a curse by Brahma's wife Savitri; she confined his temples to Pushkar. ⊠ *Outside Suraj Gulta Pol, near Agra Rd.* ⌷ *Free; camera fee Rs. 50* ⊙ *6–10:30 and 4–6:30.*

WHERE TO EAT

$$ ✕ **Café Kooba.** Once a casual hangout for Jaipur's well-heeled underfor-
EUROPEAN ties, this is also a popular spot for tourists in the know and expatriate students from North America and Europe. The menu focuses mostly on continental food, including some East-meets-West fusions of pastas with Indian curry sauce (best avoided). Wood-fired pizzas are Kooba's specialty and are among the best in town. Weather permitting head

CLOSE UP

Palace on Wheels

If you have limited time, one of the most exciting and convenient ways to see Rajasthan is aboard the *Palace on Wheels*. This train, which runs September through April, takes you on one of the most luxurious rail journeys in the world, through a region well known for its historic architecture, varied wildlife, and heady culture. The eight-day-journey begins in Delhi, from where you travel to Jaipur, the capital of Rajasthan, with its "pink" city, forts, palaces, and ornately outfitted elephants. From there you travel across the desert to Jaisalmer, whose fort is a vision in sandstone, and to Jodhpur with its magnificent and well-preserved Mehrangarh Fort. Then you continue on to Ranthambhore, where you might spot tigers in the wild, and Chittaurgarh—at the heart of chivalrous Mewar state. At Udaipur, the city of lakes, you have a chance to lunch at the famous Lake Palace hotel (the James Bond movie *Octopussy* was filmed here). The last leg of the journey takes you to Bharatpur, which bird-watchers, especially, will enjoy. You'll also go to Fatehpur Sikri, chosen capital of the Mughal emperor Akbar, and finally Agra, where the stunning, ethereal Taj Mahal is the crowning experience of the breathtaking week.

The destinations, however, are only half the fun. The train's 14 splendid coaches are replicas of those once owned by the viceroy of colonial India and the rulers of the princely states of Rajputana, Gujarat, and Hyderabad, and the plush accommodations allow you to sink blissfully into an unforgettable experience of India's sophisticated royal past while watching rural scenery through elegant, wood-frame picture windows. Bedchambers have private baths, while the train's shared facilities include two dining cars and a lounge coach with a bar and library. Service is warm and attentive, and each coach has a captain and an attendant. Your ticket on board this opulent train—it's about US$520 per person per night for standard double occupancy (there are hefty surcharges over the Christmas–New Year period)—covers taxes, all meals, including those taken off the train, entrance fees to every monument and national park, and cultural entertainment. Beverages (alcoholic and nonalcoholic), camera fees, Wi-Fi and some other items are not included. The *Palace on Wheels*' well-planned route allows you to take in a lot in a week, though it's more antiseptic than the typical India experience and some travelers don't appreciate being herded around in a group. *For contact information, see the Planning section.*

5

to the rooftop terrace. To lure the local young crowd Kooba has pool tables, Play Station, and other games, and Sheesha smoking corners (anticipating the end of a temporary local ban). Beer and wine are served. [$] *Average main: Rs. 400* ✉ *F 40, Jamna Lal Bajaj Marg, 1st fl., above Shopper's Paradise, C-Scheme* ☎ *141/511–6343.*

$$$ INDIAN 🍴 **The Copper Chimney.** Taking its name from the copper chimney at its center, this restaurant, with beautiful etched glass windows, has a regular clientele of business people, local elite, and international tourists. Although the menu has continental and Chinese selections, the Copper Chimney is best known for its heavy, North Indian dishes. The *palak*

paneer (peas with cheese) and the sweet-and-sour lassis are exceptional. This is also a good place to try the traditional *lal mas* (mutton in gravy), Rajasthani-style *kadai* chicken (cooked in a heavy wok, and spicy), or *Tandoor* (clay oven) meat dishes. $ *Average main: Rs. 600* ✉ *M.I. Rd., near G.P.O., Panch Batti* ☎ *141/237–2275.*

$

NORTH INDIAN

✕ **Nataraj.** This all-vegetarian restaurant, popular with locals, is a terrific place for Indian tea and dessert, although it's a little rough around the edges, and one of the few places open for breakfast—if you're in the mood for stuffed *paranthas* (whole-wheat flatbread) or *idlis* (South Indian steamed rice cakes). The house specialty is *bundi ki laddu* (sugary, deep-fried chickpea-flour balls), and the *rasgulla* (cheese balls in a sugary syrup) and *ras malai* (sweet cheese dumplings smothered in cream) melt in your mouth. The silver thali has a good assortment of vegetables and breads—one of the best on M.I. Road. $ *Average main: Rs. 150* ✉ *M.I. Rd., Panch Batti* ☎ *141/237–5804, 141/510–2804.*

$$$

INTERNATIONAL

✕ **Niros.** This Jaipur institution might be the most popular restaurant among the city's upper middle class. Amid mirrors and marble floors, it serves good Indian and Chinese food, as well as continental dishes. Specialties include *reshmi* kebab (skewered boned chicken), *paneer tikka* (soft Indian cheese with skewered tomatoes, onions, and green peppers), and mutton *tikka masala* (simmered in a spicy tomato-and-butter sauce). Service is relatively prompt. They serve beer and wine, or try a cold coffee topped with ice cream. During peak tourist season reservations are advisable. There are seats outside if you have to wait for a table. $ *Average main: Rs. 600* ✉ *M.I. Rd., Panch Batti* ☎ *141/237–4493, 141/221–8520* ⊕ *www.nirosindia.com.*

$$$$

INDIAN

Fodor's Choice

★

✕ **Suvarna Mahal.** Once the maharaja's throne room, this grand hall has a soaring, frescoed ceiling, tapestry-covered walls, gold-plated silverware, and a staff eager to elaborate on the history and decoration as well as the menu. Service is impeccable. The specialties are cuisines from the royal kitchens of Hyderabad, Punjab, Awadh, and, of course, Rajasthan; try *murgh tikka zaffrani* (chicken marinated in yogurt and saffron and cooked in a tandoor) and *dahi ka mass* (lamb cooked in a yogurt-base curry). A good vegetarian choice is *papad ki sabzi* (vegetables cooked in gravy). For dessert *Ras Malai* is soft, creamy and juicy. $ *Average main: Rs. 4000* ✉ *Rambagh Palace, Bhawani Singh Rd., Rambagh* ☎ *141/221–1919* ⚄ *Reservations essential* 🏛 *Jacket and tie* ⊘ *No lunch.*

WHERE TO STAY

For expanded hotel reviews, visit Fodors.com.

$$$

HOTEL

Fodor's Choice

★

🏨 **Alsisar Haveli.** This gorgeous and opulent haveli—one of the most popular family-run heritage hotels in the city—is close to the Old City, tucked away in a narrow alley that keeps out urban noise, and has numerous courtyards and alcoves in which to chill out. **Pros:** good value; jeep and camel safaris can be arranged. **Cons:** some rooms are dark and lighting is a bit depressing; a few bathrooms are cramped; staff can be slow to respond. $ *Rooms from: Rs. 6000* ✉ *Sansar Chandra Rd., Chandpol* ☎ *141/236–4685, 141/510–7167, 141/510–7157* ⊕ *www.alsisarhaveli.com* ⇘ *45 rooms* ⦿ *No meals.*

Important residents hanging out in front of the wall to Jaipur's Old City

$ 🏨 **Hotel Arya Niwas.** Trusted, reliable, comfortable, and probably the
HOTEL   most efficient family-run hotel in Jaipur, the Arya Niwas has that ideal
combination of convenience to the heart of the city and cushioning
from its noise and chaos. **Pros:** centrally located; value for money;
efficient. **Cons:** serves only vegetarian food and no alcohol. $ *Rooms
from: Rs. 2200* ✉ *Sansar Chandra Rd., behind Amber Tower, off M.I.
Rd., Jaipur* ☎ *141/407–3450, 141/407–3400* ⊕ *www.aryaniwas.com*
🛏 *87* ⦿ *Breakfast.*

$$ 🏨 **Hotel Diggi Palace.** In Jaipur's leafy C-Scheme neighborhood, this is
HOTEL   the venue for the famous Jaipur Literature Festival every January; the
rest of the year it's quite peaceful, and a charming but not too distant
alternative to staying in the rowdy Old City. **Pros:** great value; quiet
most of the year. **Cons:** even the high-end rooms lack the opulence it
could offer. $ *Rooms from: Rs. 5000* ✉ *Shivaji Marg, Sawai Man Singh
Rd., C-Scheme* ☎ *141/237–3091* ⊕ *www.hoteldiggipalace.com* 🛏 *31
rooms, 39 suites* ⦿ *Breakfast.*

$$$ 🏨 **Neemrana Fort Palace.** This 15th-century fort, now a heritage hotel,
RESORT   is one of the finest retreats in India, perched on a plateau in the Aravali
Fodor'sChoice   Hills with stunning views. **Pros:** even some bathrooms have lovely views;
★   morning and afternoon tea with cookies is included; stunning sunsets.
Cons: fixed meal times; original building full of stairs and steep ramps;
can get crowded on weekends. $ *Rooms from: Rs. 6000* ✉ *Neemrana
village, 150 km (94 miles) north of Jaipur, off NH–8* ☎ *1494/299900,
11/2435–6145, 11/4666–1666* ⊕ *www.neemranahotels.com* 🛏 *25
rooms, 34 suites* ⦿ *Breakfast.*

$$$$ RESORT Fodor's Choice ★ **Oberoi Rajvilas.** This fabulous retreat, 20 minutes outside Jaipur, is a destination unto itself, whether you want to splash out on a private villa with its own pool, enjoy a spacious standard room, or revel in a romantic luxury tent on the grounds. **Pros:** large spa and beautiful pool; impeccable service; lavish breakfasts; staff may well remember your name. **Cons:** expensive; outside Jaipur and traffic jams hamper getting in and out for sightseeing. [$] *Rooms from: Rs. 41000* ✉ *Goner Rd., Babaji-ka-Mod, 18 km (11 miles) from Jaipur* ☎ *141/268–0101* 🌐 *www.oberoihotels.com* 🛏 *71 rooms, 3 villas, 13 tents* 🍴 *No meals.*

$ B&B/INN **Pratap Bhawan Home Stay.** Perfect for foodies, wildlife enthusiasts, and those who like to engage with locals, this cozy home stay, in an upscale residential area, is run by an energetic young couple—one a naturalist who runs wildlife tours, the other a food enthusiast who offers cooking classes. **Pros:** warm, personal service from knowledgeable owners; good home cooking; good value. **Cons:** simple, basic facilities; locomotive horns from nearby railroad can disturb light sleepers. [$] *Rooms from: Rs. 3500* ✉ *A-4 Pratap Bhawan, Jamnalal Bajaj Marg, C-Scheme, Jaipur* ☎ *98298–74354 cell phone, 98290–74354 cell phone* 🌐 *www.pratapbhawan.com* 🛏 *3* 🍴 *Breakfast.*

$$ HOTEL **Raj Mahal Palace Hotel.** If you want a central location and don't mind sacrificing quality for the sake of staying in a real palace run by the local royal family, this is just the place. **Pros:** moderately priced considering room size and character; nice neighborhood. **Cons:** rooms vary a lot—inspect several before choosing; noise from nearby train station can disturb at night; service is slow and staff not very proactive. [$] *Rooms from: Rs. 5500* ✉ *Sardar Patel Marg, C-Scheme, Civil Lines* ☎ *141/414–3000* 📠 *141/222–1787* 🌐 *www.rajmahalpalacejaipur.com* 🛏 *29 rooms, 6 suites* 🍴 *Some meals.*

$$$$ HOTEL Fodor's Choice ★ **Rambagh Palace, Jaipur.** Simply the best address in town, this wistfully romantic palace was once home to the maharaja of Jaipur and his legendary and beautiful wife, and preserves much of its history while providing up-to-the-minute comforts. **Pros:** lovely original indoor pool and newer outdoor pool; efficient, helpful service. **Cons:** not walking distance to the tourist sites; Wi-Fi not free; rooms above restaurant can be noisy. [$] *Rooms from: Rs. 26500* ✉ *Bhawani Singh Rd., Rambagh* ☎ *141/221–1919* 🌐 *www.tajhotels.com* 🛏 *79 rooms, 33 suites* 🍴 *Some meals.*

$$$$ HOTEL Fodor's Choice ★ **Samode Haveli.** Hidden amid the lanes of the Pink City, this stately heritage hotel preserves its Rajasthani character and harbors a few surprises, including elegant gardens and a beautiful open-air pool with pool-side bar. **Pros:** charmingly decorated main dining room; huge rooms; grounds have swings for kids. **Cons:** fancier rooms are very expensive; vehicle access problematic during rush hours. [$] *Rooms from: Rs. 13000* ✉ *Near Ganga Pole, Pink City* ☎ *141/263–2407, 141/263–2370, 141/263–1942* 🌐 *www.samode.com* 🛏 *39 rooms* 🍴 *Breakfast.*

$$$$ RESORT **Tree of Life.** This haven from the chaos of Jaipur, nestled in the Aravali hills yet within an hour's drive of the city sights, offers secluded villa accommodations, spa treatments, and a chance to interact with the community. **Pros:** professional, personal service by owner and staff; stylish and modern. **Cons:** far from Jaipur; not best suited to one-night

stays. $\boxed{\text{\$}}$ *Rooms from: Rs. 20000 ⊠ Delhi–Jaipur Hwy., Kukas, Kacher-awala, Jaipur* ☎ *96020–91000 cell phone* ⊕ *www.treeofliferesorts.com* ⇆ *14 rooms* ⦿ *All meals.*

NIGHTLIFE AND THE ARTS

If you want a night on the town, your best bet is one of the hotel bars, which are usually open from about 11 am to 3 pm and 7 pm to 11:30 pm. Many hotels stage cultural programs for their guests, such as the dance performances with dinner at the Panghat banquet hall, at the Rambagh Palace.

The Fire Ball (TFB). Hotel nightclubs such as this open around dinner-time but shut by midnight. A local crowd will come here to dance on Saturday (the only night there's a disco); otherwise it's just a pub. ⊠ *Ramada Hotel, Govind Marg, Raja Park* ☎ *141/406–666* ⊕ *www. ramadajaipur.com.*

Rajmandir movie theater. This historic Art Deco movie theater is the place to experience Bollywood films. Widely visited by Indian and foreign tourists (the films are in Hindi without subtitles, but you get the gist of the action even if you don't understand the language), Rajmandir is still constantly flooded with locals, who sing, cheer, and whistle throughout each film. Shows are usually at 12:30, 3, 6:15, and 9:30, but times may vary by 15 to 30 minutes, according to the length of the film. Tickets for popular new releases sell out quickly on weekends, but you can buy in advance—your hotel reception or concierge should do this for you for a small fee. ⊠ *16 Bhagwandas Rd., next to McDonald's, near Panch Batti* ☎ *141/237–9372, 141/237–4694.*

Ravindra Rang Manch. In the heart of the city, surrounded by gardens, this theater and cultural organization hosts occasional dinner-and-dance programs. It also plays host to famous classical musicians and theater groups performing Indian classics and epics at the open-air amphithe-ater, especially during and around Indian festivals like Holi and Diwali. Most are free or with nominal charge; some are by invitation. ⊠ *Ram Niwas Gardens* ☎ *141/261–9061.*

SHOPPING

Rajasthan's craftspeople have been famous for centuries for their jewel settings, stonework, blue pottery, enamel, lacquer, filigree work, *bhan-dani* (tie-dye), and block-printed silk and muslin. You'll find all this and more in Jaipur, but watch out: Your drivers and/or guides are likely to insist that they know the best shops and bargains in the city (they get a commission on whatever you purchase). If you have a specific shop in mind, be firm. Don't rely on the phrase "government-approved"; it's meaningless. The following shops are reliable, but you're bound to find others in your explorations. Note that many shops are closed on Sunday.

ARTS AND
CRAFTS

Artchill. This is Jaipur's leading gallery of contemporary art. There's a larger branch with an exhibit area of more than 5,000 square feet, in Amber Fort, with a wide-ranging collection of oil paintings, watercol-ors, and graphics by eminent artists such as Jatin Das, Arpana Caur, and Paritosh Sen. ⊠ *Lakshmi complex, M.I. Rd., Panch Batti* ☎ *141/403–4964, 98290–11964 cell phone, 141/253–0025* ⊕ *www.artchill.com.*

The Anokhi museum in Jaipur, affiliated with the popular shop, is a great place to learn about Indian textiles.

Khadi Ghar. A good place to pick up practical gifts, this national cooperative sells natural herbal soaps and shampoos, oils, incense, Khadi (hand spun/woven) textiles and clothing, leather goods, and handicrafts. ⊠ *320 M.I. Rd., Jaipur* ☎ *141/237–3745* ⊘ *Closed Sun.*

Khazana Walon ka Rasta. For specialty shops, wander through this lane in the old Pink City (accessible through Chandpol gate), and watch stone-cutters create artworks in marble. Bargaining is recommended. ⊠ *Chandpol.*

P.M. Allah Buksh and Son. Established in 1880 and still selling the finest hand-engraved, enameled, and embossed brassware—including oversize old trays and historic armor—this is a great place to look for antique metalwork. ⊠ *M.I. Rd., Panch Batti* ☎ *141/401–2786.*

Rajasthali. If you have limited time and lots of gifts to buy or don't relish bargaining, head to this enormous, government-run emporium in the center of Jaipur. It's always flooded with crafts and textiles, though you might have to sift through a bewildering variety before you find what you want. ⚠ Be aware that touts and rickshaw drivers may try to take you to fake Rajasthali showrooms, which are privately run by the same name and charge exhorbitant prices. ⊠ *M.I. Rd., opposite Ajmeri Gate* ☎ *141/237–2974* ⊕ *www.rajasthali.gov.in.*

Tilak Gitai. A special treat for lovers of miniature paintings is a trip to the home of award-winning artist Tilak Gitai, who creates exquisite miniatures in classic Mughal, Rajput, Pahari, and other styles. Using antique paper, Gitai applies colors made from semiprecious stones, then real gold and silver leaf, in designs so fine he'll give you a magnifying glass to admire them. This is not a quick visit, but it's a great way to spend a few hours with a friendly Rajasthani family and learn about Indian art. Prices start at a few hundred rupees and soar to a few hundred thousand. ⊠ *E-5 Gokhle Marg, C-Scheme* ☎ *141/237–2101* ⊕ *www. splendidindianart.com.*

NEED A BREAK? **Lassiwallah.** Across the street from Niros restaurant is the well known Lassiwallah—on the periphery of a long chain of imposters, the real thing can only be found under the sign "Kishan Lal Govind Narayan Agarwal." You may have to wait behind a line of locals waiting to get their daily glass of lassi. Served in disposable red-clay cups (which means they haven't been washed with unclean water), the lassis come with a dash of hard cream on top, and are only available in medium and large sizes. As with any street food, there's no absolute guarantee that they haven't been diluted with water, but the popularity of the place (they sometime sell out by 3) should reassure you. ⊠ *M.I. Rd., across from Niros, Panch Batti* ☎ *141/2378682.*

BEAUTY **Forest Essentials.** India's answer to L'Occitane is cheaper and has a wide range of ayurvedic as well as naturally made and herbal products, including fragrances, oils, creams, soaps, and skin and beauty products. ⊠ *341 M.I. Rd., Jaipur* ☎ *141/402–9284* ⊕ *www.forestessentialsindia.com.*

JEWELRY **Chameli Valon ka Rasta.** If you're willing to bargain, head for this lane within the walls of the old city to negotiate for silver and semiprecious jeweled ornaments, trinkets, and small toys. ⊠ *off M.I. Rd.*

Amrapali Jewels. A favorite among trendy and wealthy Indians for its whimsical silver and ornamental trinkets, as well as semiprecious stone artifacts. ⊠ *M.I. Rd., Panch Batti* ☎ *141/237–7940, 141/236–2768* ⊕ *www.amrapalijewels.com.*

Bhuramal-Rajmal Surana Showroom. For precious jewels, including gold ornaments, seek out this showroom, known worldwide for its *kundan* (a glasslike white stone) and *mina* (enamel) work. It has some reasonably priced silver jewelry featuring traditional patterns on contemporary styles. ⊠ *368 J.L.N. Marg, Moti Dhungri* ☎ *141/257–0429, 141/257–0430* ⊕ *www.suranas.com.*

★ **Gem Palace.** Shop here for Jaipur's best gems and jewelry, and a small collection of museum-quality curios, and you'll join the ranks of a royal clientele that includes Prince Charles and many members of Rajasthan's royal families. Even the princess of Jaipur, Maharani Gayatri Devi, might be found here bargaining for a good deal. Prices range from US$2 to US$2 million. ⊠ *M.I. Rd., Panch Batti* ☎ *141/237–4175.*

POTTERY **Jaipur Blue Pottery Art Center.** A broad selection of Rajasthan's fetching blue pottery is available here, including a large selection of tiles, bathroom fittings, cups, plates, and decorative items. Clay pots are made on the premises. ⊠ *Amber Rd., near Jain Mandir* ☎ *141/263–0116.*

Neerja International. The blue pottery here is particularly funky—the designer, owner Lela Bordia, has been at the forefront of the movement to keep the craft alive for more than three decades, and has exhibited all over the world. Her wares are made in nearby villages, helping to create jobs in rural areas. ⊠ *Anand Bhawan, Jacob Rd., Civil Lines* ☎ *141/411–2609* ⊕ *www.neerjainternational.com.*

5

Shekhawati, Rajasthan's Open-Air Art Gallery

Known as Rajasthan's open-air art gallery because of the frescoes painted on the walls of ornate havelis in the region, Shekhawati—about 160 km (100 miles) from Jaipur or 200 km (124 miles) from Delhi—makes an intriguing day trip. Influenced by the Persian, Jaipur, and Mughal schools of painting, Shekhawati's frescoes, many of which date back to the early 19th century, illustrate subjects ranging from mythological stories and local legends to hunting safaris and scenes of everyday life. You'll even find illustrated experiences with the British and cars or planes. The introduction of photography in 1840 gave Shekhawati's painters still more to work with.

The painters were called *chiteras* and belonged to the caste of *kumhars* (potters). Initially, they colored their masterpieces with vegetable pigments; after mixing these with lime water and treating the wall with three layers of a very fine clay, the chiteras painstakingly drew their designs on a last layer of filtered lime dust. Time was short, as the design had to be completed before the plaster dried, but the technique ensured that the images wouldn't fade.

The havelis themselves are quite spectacular, with courtyards, exquisitely latticed windows, intricate mirror work, vaulted ceilings, immense balconies, and ornate gateways and facades. They date from the British Raj, during which traditional overland trading routes to Central Asia, Europe, and China were slowly superseded by rail and sea routes. Only a handful of the havelis have survived—some have been restored by their owners, and a few have been converted into hotels. In **Sikar,** formerly the wealthiest trading center, look for the Biyani, Murarka, and Somani havelis. **Lachhmangarh** features the grand Char Chowk Haveli, particularly evocative of the prosperous Marwari lifestyle. In the village of **Churi Ajitgarh,** unusually erotic frescoes are painted behind doors and on bedroom ceilings in the Shiv Narain Nemani, Kothi Shiv Datt, and Rai Jagan Lal Tibrewal havelis. The frescoed temples of **Jhunjhunu** make for interesting comparisons: visit Laxmi Nath, Mertani Baori, Ajeet Sagar, and Qamrudin Shah Ki Dargah Fatehpur. Warrior-statesman Thakur Nawal Singh founded **Nawalgarh** in 1737, and the town has some of the best frescoes in Shekhawati, in the Aath, Anandilal Poddar, Jodhraj Patodia, and Chokhani havelis, as well as at the Roop Niwas Kothi hotel.

Logistics: Hire a guide from Delhi or Jaipur, making sure they know the Shekhawati area; get an early start to make the most of your time, and be prepared to spend a lot of time driving from site to site, since the havelis are quite spread out. *The havelis listed above are the ones to prioritize.*

A painted *haveli* in Shekhawati

TEXTILES

Fodor's Choice ★

Anokhi. This is a leading shop for designer and ethnic wear, mostly in cotton, with hand block prints and paisley patterns. The selection includes saris and other clothing—both Indian and casual Western—and it has the prettiest *lehengas* (skirts) in the state. You can also get beautiful bedspreads, quilts, and cloth bags here. ⊠ *C-11, KK Square, Prithviraj Rd., 2nd fl., C-Scheme* ☎ *141/400–7244, 141/400–7245* ⊕ *www.anokhi.com.*

Anokhi Museum. To learn more about the hand block printing and textiles with natural pigments and dyes that you might want to shop for, check out this museum on your way in our out of Amber Fort (there is a small shop, too). ⊠ *Chanwar Palkiwalon ki Haveli, Kheri Gate, Amber Fort* ☎ *141/253–0226, 141/400–7245* ⊕ *www.anokhi.com/museum/visit.html* ☉ *Closed Mon.*

★ **Cottons.** Managed and staffed by women, Cottons carries simple, attractive clothes for men and women, as well as small bags, quilts, and other decorative household items. ⊠ *Hari Bhawan, 4 Achrol House, Jacob Rd., Civil Lines* ⊕ *www.cottonsjaipur.com.*

Soma. Catering to the ultra-elegant crowd, Soma is filled with vibrant colors. Here you'll find chutneys, clothing for women and children, and decorative fabrics, including fabulous, hand-painted white cloth lamp shades. ⊠ *A5, Jamnalal Bajaj Marg, 2nd fl., C-Scheme* ☎ *141/237–3346* ⊕ *www.somashop.com.*

OFF THE BEATEN PATH

Sanganer (16 km [10 miles] south of Jaipur on Tonk Rd., near the airport) and Bagru (35 km [22 miles] southwest of Sanganer on Ajmer Road) are crafts towns that you can visit to see Rajasthani artisans in action. In Sanganer nearly every family is involved in the production of block- and screen-printed textiles, blue pottery, or handmade paper.

Salim's Paper. Whatever handmade paper you've seen back home may well have come from Salim's, a factory where you can see each step of the process. Some of the thick, beautiful papers are made with crushed flower petals; it's fun to see them thrown into the mixture of cotton and resin. ⊠ *Gramodyog Rd.* ☎ *141/273–0222, 141/273–0444* ⊕ *www.salimspaper.com.*

Bagru is famous for its hand-printed cloth industry, and the simple, popular designs made here feature earthen colors of green, brown, black, and blue.

■TIP➔ Come out here to see artisans in action, but don't expect to get better deals than in town just because you are buying from the source—the products here are marked up to cover the huge commissions they dole out to taxi drivers.

TIGER, TIGER

There are three national parks in the Delhi/Jaipur area. Ranthambhore (161 km [100 miles] south of Jaipur) is your best bet if tigers are your priority, but you'll still only have a 30% to 40% chance of seeing one; also check the latest government restrictions on "tiger tourism." Keoladeo National Park in Bharatpur (150 km [93 miles] east of Jaipur, 55 km [34 miles] west of Agra) is mainly a destination for bird-watchers, though there are also some interesting flora and fauna. There is also Sariska, which is the closest park to Jaipur (110 km [68 miles]) but there are no tigers and it's not well run.

RANTHAMBHORE NATIONAL PARK

161 km (100 miles) south of Jaipur.

Fodor's Choice ★ **Ranthambhore National Park.** If you want to see a tiger in the wild, Ranthambhore is the best park in Rajastan to visit, although new government regulations state that visitors must keep minimum distance of 20 meters from all wildlife (50 meters if you're in a vehicle) and that vehicles may only remain at a sighting point for up to 15 minutes. The park encompasses 1,334 square km (515 square miles) of rugged terrain (though only a very limited section about 20% is open to visitors), and is home to a vast ecosystem of flora and fauna. Ranthambhore is noted for its tiger and leopard populations, although you still have only a 30% to 40% chance of seeing a large cat on any given expedition. The best time to see tigers is right before the monsoon, in summer, when the tigers emerge to drink at small water holes—when it's dry and the water table is low, the tigers are forced out of hiding to quench their thirst. What you will definitely see are numerous peacocks, *sambar* (large Asian deer), *chital* (spotted axis deer), *chinkara* (gazelles), wild pigs, jackals, crocodiles, and often sloth bears.

Sighting a wild tiger in Ranthambhore is an exciting experience. First, of course, you will hear the jungle sounds that warn of a tiger's presence. Monkeys and peacocks scream loudly and the deer in the area become agitated and nervous. Ranthambore became a tiger reserve in 1973 under the Project Tiger program, which was launched in an effort to save India's dwindling population of Bengal Tigers. Despite conservation efforts, though, the tiger population in Ranthambhore is small: recent estimates put the park's tiger population at around 40, although the number varies from source to source. Sighting a leopard is much more difficult, as these cats live on high, inaccessible slopes and are extremely shy.

The park is run by the Indian government, and the rules are inflexible: you can only enter the park in an official government jeep, and the jeeps keep strict hours, daily from 6:30 am to 9:30 am and 3:30 pm to 6:30 pm (the timings may vary by 30 minutes during summer and winter months when the park opens later in the morning). Book a jeep in advance, or save yourself the hassle and book through your hotel (it's worth the service charge). You can also explore the surrounding region: the 10th-century **Ranthambhore Fort,** perched on a nearby hill, is one of Rajasthan's more spectacular military strongholds. Dastkar, a craft-and-textile shop on the Ranthambhore Road, is run by a non-government organization.

The government-run **Jhoomar Baori** (12 rooms, Rs. 3,300–Rs. 6,000) offers the chance to spend a night near the animals, but little else. It can be booked through Rajasthan Tourism Development Corporation (RTDC) offices across the state. A better option is to stay at one of the hotels along Ranthambhore Road and take a morning safari. The neighboring town of Sawai Madhopur has numerous hotels, but most are basic. ☎ *7462/220–808 Sawai Madhopur Tourist Information Center* 🌐 *www.rajasthantourism.gov.in* 🎟 *Rs. 391 per person; up to 6 people per jeep* 🕓 *Oct.–June.*

5

WHERE TO STAY

For expanded hotel reviews, visit Fodors.com.

$$$$ RESORT Fodor's Choice ★ 🏨 **Oberoi Vanyavilas.** On the edge of the Ranthambhore Tiger Reserve, this is ideal for those who want to "camp" in sheer luxury—one of the best resorts not just in the area but in all of India. **Pros:** natural surroundings and camping-like experience that doesn't skimp on luxury; hospitable staff. **Cons:** expensive. [$] *Rooms from: Rs. 35000* ✉ *Ranthambhore Rd., Sawai Madhopur* ☎ *7462/223–999* 🌐 *www.oberoihotels.com* 🛏 *25 tents* 🍴 *No meals.*

$$$ RESORT 🏨 **Ranthambhore Regency.** This is the most comfortable mid-price place on the Ranthambhore Road, with a helpful owner—a mine of local information—committed to making your Ranthambhore experience pleasant. **Pros:** friendly staff; clean rooms. **Cons:** meals are buffet-only. [$] *Rooms from: Rs. 7000* ✉ *Ranthambhore Rd., Sawai Madhopur* ☎ *7462/223–456, 7462/221–176* 🌐 *www.ranthambhor.com* 🛏 *22 rooms, 40 cottages, 1 suite* 🍴 *All meals.*

$$$$ RESORT 🏨 **Vivanta by Taj – Sawai Madhopur.** This Art Deco lodge, the only heritage hotel in Ranthambore, is convenient for the national park as well as being something of a destination in its own right. **Pros:** near the train station; just a 20-minute drive to the park. **Cons:** rooms are not particularly elegant or fancy. [$] *Rooms from: Rs. 36000* ✉ *Ranthambhore Rd., Sawai Madhopur* ☎ *7462/220–541, 7462/223–500* 🌐 *www.vivantabytaj.com* 🛏 *24 rooms, 12 suites* 🍴 *No meals.*

Two tigers in the bushes at Ranthambhore

BHARATPUR

150 km (93 miles) east of Jaipur; 55 km (34 miles) west of Agra; 18 km (11 miles) west of Fatehpur Sikri.

Deeg. Built in the 1730s, Deeg was the first capital of the Jat state and is known for its graceful palaces and gardens, complete with swings and ancient fountains. Indian families find this a charming location for a picnic. Check with your hotel about the condition of the fountains—sometimes they are not working and the lake is dirty. The Jal Mahal (water palace) has fountains that are run to musical accompaniment during August and September when the local fair is held. ⊠ *34 km (21 miles) north of Bharatpur.*

Keoladeo National Park. Founded by the Jat ruler Suraj Mal in 1733, the city of Bharatpur is famous for the Keoladeo National Park (also known as the Ghana Bird Sanctuary), once the duck-hunting forest of the local maharajas. This UNESCO World Heritage site is home to many mammals and reptiles—blue bulls (antelope), spotted deer, otters, and Indian rock pythons—but birds, especially waterbirds, are the main attraction. It's an ornithologist's dream—29 square km (10 square miles) of forests and wetlands with 400 species, more than 130 of which are resident year-round, such as the Saras crane, gray heron, snake bird (Indian darter), and spoonbill. In winter, birds arrive from the Himalayas, Siberia, and even Europe.

The best way to see the park is on foot or by boat (Rs. 150 per person, per hour, depending on boat type, though these are usually unavailable due to lack of rains; check at entrance), but there are plenty of other options. The park's main artery is a blacktop road that runs from the entrance gate to the center. Surrounded by marshlands but screened by bushes, this road is the most convenient viewpoint for bird-watching and is also traveled by cycle-rickshaws (Rs. 75 per hour, but drivers usually expect more, plus a tip of at least Rs. 50), bicycle (Rs. 25 and 40 per trip), and the park's electric bus (Rs. 50 per person). The rickshaw drivers, trained by the forest department, are pretty good at finding and pointing out birds. You can also rent a bicycle and head into more remote areas; just remember that most roads are unpaved. The excellent guides at the gate (Rs. 100 per hour; Rs. 150 for groups of five or more) are familiar with the birds' haunts and can help you spot and identify them.

Try to bring a bird guidebook: former royal-family member Salim Ali's *The Birds of India* is a good choice. The best time to see the birds is early morning or late evening, November through February; by the end of February, many birds start heading home. Stick around at sunset, when the water takes on a mirrorlike stillness and the air is filled with the calls of day birds settling down and night birds stirring.

A simple government-run restaurant at the Ashok RTDC offers decent Indian food, sandwiches, and drinks, but service is slow. ✉ *5 km (3 miles) south of city center* ☎ *5644/222–777* 📷 *Rs. 400, video-camera fee Rs. 400* ⊙ *Daily 6 am–6:30 pm.*

Lohagarh Fort. In Bharatpur's Old City, this fort is also known figuratively as the Iron Fort, though it's built of mud. The structure might seem fragile, but it was tested by a British siege in 1805: armed with 65 pieces of field artillery, 1,800 European soldiers and 6,000 Indian sepoys did manage to win the battle, but they failed to break down the invincible fort. 📷 *Fort free; museum Rs. 50* ⊙ *Daily 10–5.*

WHERE TO STAY

For expanded hotel reviews, visit Fodors.com.

$$$ 🏨 **Laxmi Vilas Palace Hotel.** Rural and old-fashioned, this cozy heritage
HOTEL hotel is the best place to stay in Bharatpur and is still home to descen-
★ dants of the former maharaja's brother. **Pros:** excellent value; impressive architecture. **Cons:** lacks the luxury of fancier hotels in its category; slow service. 💲 *Rooms from: Rs. 6500* ✉ *Old Agra Rd., Kakaji Ki Kothi* ☎ *5644/231–199, 5644/223–523* ⊕ *www.laxmivilas.com* 🛏 *16 rooms, 12 suites* 🍽 *No meals.*

PUSHKAR

★ *146 km (90 miles) southwest of Jaipur.*

With more than 500 temples, Pushkar is one of Hinduism's holiest sites and an interesting place to visit even when the famous camel fair (in October or November) isn't being held. In its narrow car-free main bazaar, sadhus, tribals, hippies, and five-legged cattle (such birth deformities are considered lucky) vie for space with shops selling everything from religious paraphernalia to water bongs. Although goods from all over Rajasthan find their way to the bazaar, because Pushkar is such a holy city, no alcohol or meat can be sold here—some restaurants get around the alcohol restriction by serving beer in coffee mugs to their regular customers, but by no means should you count on being able to get anything alcoholic—something to think about if you were planning to spend New Year's here.

Pushkar's religious significance derives from the Vedic text, *Padma Purana,* which describes how the town was created. Lord Brahma, Creator of the Universe, was looking for a place to perform the *yajna*—a holy ritual that involves placing offerings into a sacrificial fire for Agni, the fire god—that would signify the beginning of the human age. He dropped a lotus from his hand and Pushkar was where it struck the ground.

GETTING HERE AND AROUND
Pushkar, best reached by road, is quite small, and everything worth seeing is in walking distance.

ESSENTIALS
Tourist Offices **Rajasthan Tourism Tourist Information Centre** ✉ *Hotel Sarovar, Pushkar Lake, Pushkar* ☎ *0145/277–2040.*

EXPLORING
Bathing ghats *(flights of steps).* Many of the marble ghats on Pushkar Lake—a must-visit—were constructed for pilgrims by royal families who wanted to ensure power and prosperity in their kingdoms throughout Rajasthan by appeasing the gods. When you pass an entrance to a ghat, be prepared for a priest to solicit you by simply offering you a flower—he'll want you to receive a blessing, known as the "Pushkar Passport". He'll lead you to the water's edge, say a prayer, and will ask you to recite a blessing in Sanskrit (you'll repeat after him). Then he'll paste a *tilak* (rice and colored powder dot) on your forehead and tie a *raki* (a string bracelet, denoting a blessing) to your wrist. After the ceremony, you're expected to give a donation: don't give more than Rs. 100 (or you can negotiate the sum as soon as he approaches you).

The ghats get extra busy during auspicious pilgrimage times, especially during the Kartik Purnima, the full moon during the Hindu month of Kartik, around October or November (also the time of the Pushkar Camel Fair): there may be tens of thousands of people here to get blessings from local Brahmins. The peaceful parts of the ghats can be accessed from the eastern shore of the lake, close to Sunset Café. ✉ *Pushkar.*

Brahma Temple. In the center of town, this is Pushkar's most important temple in spite of its unimpressive architecture and the modern feel created by reconstruction. Although many say it's the sole temple dedicated to Brahma in the world, in reality there are a few others. Pilgrims visiting the temple climb a long stairway into the walled area to take the blessings of the god—in the form of small sweets. There are varying versions of legend concerning the temple, but most have to do with Brahma's wife Savitri, who refused to attend the ceremony. Impatient, Brahma married the goddess Gayatri (some say she was a milkmaid), and when Savitri found out, she put a curse on Brahma, declaring that the earth would forget him completely. She then relented, but said that Brahma could only be worshipped in Pushkar. ⊠ *Pushkar* ⊙ *Closed 11 am–3 pm.*

⟳ **Camel Fair.** If you really want an experience, go to Pushkar during its famous annual Camel Fair. Every October or November—depending on the lunar calendar—people flock here to see the finest camels parade around the fairground in colorful costumes. People come to buy, sell, and trade camels, and to race one camel against another. A good male camel goes for about US$250. In addition to the camel activities, there are cultural programs during the day and music and dance performances in the evenings. The town is packed during festival time, so make sure you reserve a room at least several weeks—if not longer—ahead of time. Several tented camps with modern conveniences also mushroom during the fair. Contact the Rajasthan Tourism Development Corporation (RTDC) in Jaipur for more details. ⊠ *Pushkar* ⊕ *www. pushkar-camel-fair.com (temporary, just prior to event).*

Dargah Sharif. The shrine of the Sufi saint Khwaja Moinuddin Chisti is in the heart of Ajmer, a city about 11 km (7 miles) southeast of Pushkar. The shrine is very significant for South Asian Muslims, and is visited by Muslims and non-Muslims alike, especially during Urs, the anniversary of the saint's death, which takes place during six days in the Islamic month of Rajab (around September or October). Be prepared to deal with crowds and aggressive beggars on the street leading to the dargah, whenever you visit. Ajmer itself isn't much of a destination, so most people pass through on their way to Pushkar, then backtrack for a half-day visit to the shrine. While you're here, the 19th-century **Nasiyan Temple** is worth a visit as well: the detailed display depicting the Jain story of the world's creation inside the temple is mesmerizing. It's near Agra Gate, or just ask people how to find the Jain temple. ⊠ *Ajmer.*

Savitri Temple. Make an early start to check out the Savitri Temple on a hill overlooking Pushkar Lake. The climb up the long flight of stairs leading up the hill takes between a half-hour and an hour, and the view at sunrise is worth it. △ Be careful of menacing monkeys, which tend to grab anything edible; don't venture out to the temple if it is getting dark—it may be badly lit and dangerous. ⊠ *Pushkar.*

WHERE TO EAT

$ ✕ **Café Enigma.** This four-story family-run restaurant is a good choice
ECLECTIC for continental cuisine (think veggie burgers and Israeli salads) as well as Indian classics with spice levels suited to the Western palate. It's also a good place for breakfast—they usually stock a few pastries from the nearby bakery, and their *paranthas* (potato-stuffed flatbreads) are fresh and not too oily. They also serve "real" filter coffee. Sit up on the rooftop terrace for views of Pushkar and the surrounding desert. $ *Average main: Rs. 150* ⊠ *Near Old Rangji Temple, Choti Basti, Pushkar* ☎ *99834–41449* ▭ *No credit cards.*

$ ✕ **Moon Dance Garden Restaurant.** Just off the main road on the way to the
ECLECTIC bus stand, this small, quaint garden café serves a huge selection of continental dishes, including homemade pasta, baked macaroni and cheese, and fabulous tandoor-fired pizzas. They also have a small "German

Looking out over Pushkar Lake

Bakery" selling desserts and pastries, perfect for a light breakfast. On rainy days you can sit in the covered semi-indoor area, which features the low cushion seating that's common throughout Rajasthan. $ *Average main: Rs. 250* ✉ *Naya Rangi Mandir (Vishnu temple), Choti Basti, Pushkar* ☎ *94146–66966 cell phone* ▭ *No credit cards.*

$$$ ✕ **Prince's Restaurant.** This lakeside restaurant inside the Hotel Pushkar
INDIAN Palace is popular with large tour groups and has buffet service for all three meals, plus a few snack and à la carte options; it's generally Indian buffet food with some continental and Chinese dishes. The food is good, but the main reason to come here is for the restaurant's terrace garden, which looks out over Pushkar's sacred lake; there are sometimes music and dance performances staged here at dinnertime, which add to the atmosphere. There's also indoor seating for hot days. $ *Average main: Rs. 600* ✉ *Hotel Pushkar, Choti Basti, off Pushkar Bazaar (the main street), Pushkar* ☎ *145/277–3001, 145/277–2401* ⊕ *www.hotelpushkarpalace.com.*

$$ ✕ **Sunset Café.** If you like to people-watch, this small terrace restaurant
INTERNATIONAL is the place to be. Come in the early evening, when scores of tourists and locals gather in front of the restaurant on Pushkar Lake's eastern shore to watch the sun set. Expect to see an eclectic mash-up of dreadlocked backpackers, ornately adorned gypsies who have come from the desert to sing and dance, and plenty of local priests eager to perform *pujas* (Hindu ceremonies). The continental cuisine isn't bad either though many tourists prefer either Indian or Italian; the Veg Sizzlers are popular here. $ *Average main: Rs. 350* ✉ *Parikrama Marg, next to Pushkar Palace, Choti Basti, Pushkar* ☎ *145/277–2382, 145/277–2725* ▭ *No credit cards.*

WHERE TO STAY

For expanded hotel reviews, visit Fodors.com.

$$$ HOTEL 🏨 **Pushkar Palace.** In the best location in town, this small palace sits above its own *ghat* (private stairs leading down to the lake) and has fabulous, panoramic views of Pushkar. **Pros:** lakeside location; good food; great views. **Cons:** as elsewhere, room rates skyrocket during the Pushkar festival and all meals must be included at this time; no pool. [$] *Rooms from: Rs. 7000* ✉ *Choti Basti, off Pushkar Bazaar (the main street), Pushkar* ☎ *145/277–3001, 145/277–2401* 🌐 *www.hotelpushkarpalace.com* 🛏 *48 rooms, 5 suites* 🍴 *All meals.*

$$$ RESORT 🏨 **Pushkar Resorts.** The spirit of the maharajas blends well with the comforts of resort living here, and guests can relax poolside under the shade of a palm tree far from Pushkar's chaotic main bazaar, a 15-minute jeep ride away. **Pros:** rooms with a view; nice pool. **Cons:** need a car to get into town. [$] *Rooms from: Rs. 6000* ✉ *Motisar Rd., Village Ganhera, outside Pushkar, Pushkar* ☎ *145/277–2944, 145/277–2945* 🌐 *www.hotelspushkar.net* 🛏 *40 rooms* 🍴 *All meals.*

5

UDAIPUR AND ENVIRONS

Romantic Udaipur, the major city here, warrants several days or more since the Aravali Hills and the Mewar region that surround the city have several fascinating day-trip destinations. The Mewar region is known for its rich military history—while much of what is now known as Rajasthan was taken over by the fierce Mughal emperor Akbar, Mewar maintained its autonomy—and the region's forts, including the impressive medieval citadel of Chittaurgarh and the remarkable fort at Kumbalgarh, not far from Ranakpur, are intriguing remains of this military might. Expect to also see marble palaces, elaborate gardens, serene temples, lush forests, and sparkling lakes. There are several famous temples and religious sites in the area, too, that are well worth visiting, including the spectacular Jain Temples in Ranakpur and Mount Abu and the Shiva temple complex at Eklingji; an overnight trip is recommended for a visit to Mount Abu.

UDAIPUR

Fodor's Choice ★ *405 km (251 miles) southwest of Jaipur; 335 km (207 miles) southeast of Jodhpur.*

Romantic old-world charm, soothing lakes, and fairy-tale palaces are what draw so many visitors to the Mewari city of Udaipur, known as the City of Lakes—many call this the Venice of the East. The city of Udaipur was founded in 1567, when, having grown weary of repeated attacks on the old Mewar capital of Chittaur—Chittaur is the historic name of the area, and Chittaurgarh literally means "the fort of Chittaur"—Maharana Udai Singh asked a holy sage to suggest a safe place for his new capital. The man assured Udai Singh that the new base would never be conquered if it was established on the banks of Lake Pichola, and thus was born Singh's namesake, Udaipur.

Evening falls at the Pushkar camel fair

Despite being one of Rajasthan's largest cities, with a population of more than half a million people, modern Udaipur still feels like a small town. Added perks are the weather, which is balmy year-round except for the summertime heat between April and July, and the fact that the locals are extremely friendly.

Five main gates lead into Udaipur's Old City: they are Hathi Pol (Elephant Gate) to the north; Kishan Pol to the south; Delhi Pol to the northeast; Chand Pol (Moon Gate) to the west; and Suraj Pol (Sun Gate) to the east.

Anchoring Udaipur's Old City are the famed City Palace and Lake Palace—the latter in the middle of Lake Pichola, and now a hotel run by Taj Hotels Resorts and Palaces. The Old City itself is built on tiny hillocks and raised areas, its lanes full of twists and turns, with plenty of charming little niches to be discovered. The major landmarks in the new section are Chetak Circle, Sukhadia Circle, and Sahelion Ki Bari gardens.

GETTING HERE AND AROUND

Most of Udaipur's top attractions are on the east shore of the lake, in the Old City, and if you stay near the Jagdish Temple or the City Palace, in the heart of the Old City, you'll be able to reach most of the sites on foot. If you follow the main road downhill from the Jagdish Temple, you'll wind up at the Ghanta Ghar (clock tower)—the road continues north all the way to the city center in the newer, and far less enchanting, part of Udaipur. There are a number of hotels and restaurants on the west shore of the lake, too. The easiest way to get from one side to the other is to cross the small bridge at Chand Pol, on the narrow northern edge of the lake. Auto-rickshaws are also widely available—don't pay more than Rs. 100 for an auto-rickshaw ride anywhere within the main city.

TIMING
Udaipur is lovely, and while you can get through most of the sights if you stay here for only two days, three or four will give you time to explore the Old City's many winding lanes or go on a day trip—there are several intriguing ones: from Udaipur you can explore the ornately carved Jain temples of Ranakpur and Mount Abu, or see the magnificent forts at Chittaurgarh and Kumbalgarh.

ESSENTIALS
Taxi Companies Travels to India ✉ *1–2 Aakar Complex, University Rd., Keshav Nagar* ☎ *294/241–5881* ⊕ *www.travelstoindia.com.*

Tourist Offices Government of Rajasthan Tourist Office ✉ *Fateh Memorial, Suraj Pol* ☎ *294/241–1535* ⊕ *www.rajasthantourism.gov.in.*

A GOOD TOUR
Head straight to the Old City and start with a visit to the **City Palace, Jagdish Temple,** and the clock tower area, where you can then have some lunch and explore the winding and hilly streets teeming with shops selling clothing, silver jewelry, and leather-bound journals made with handmade paper. In the afternoon, take a boat ride on **Lake Pichola,** stopping to explore the Jag Mandir Island Palace. Then wind down your day with an evening sound and light show back at the City Palace. Finish your day with dinner at the legendary Taj Lake Palace hotel (make reservations). Alternatively, take your boat ride in the evening, when the sun begins to set.

TIMING You can cram these activities into one very full day, but you should really spend at least two days in this glorious city, especially if you want to also fit in a trip to the arts-and-crafts village of Shilpgram, see some of Udaipur's art galleries, or check out the views from the **Sajjan Garh** (aka the Monsoon Palace) or the **Neemach Mata** temple.

WHAT TO SEE
TOP ATTRACTIONS
★ **City Palace.** The sprawling maharana's palace—the largest in Rajasthan—stands on a ridge overlooking the lake. Begun by Udai Singh and extended by subsequent maharanas, the sand-color City Palace rises five stories tall, with a series of balconies. Cupolas crown its octagonal towers, which are connected by a maze of narrow passageways. The City Palace is part of a complex of palaces—two have been converted to hotels and one houses the current titular maharana, Arvind Singh of Mewar. Part of the palace houses a museum; its entrance is near the Jagdish Mandir; the entrance to the City Palace Hotel is at the bottom of the hill, to the south. The rooms inside the City Palace Museum contain decorative art: beautiful paintings, colorful enamel, inlay glasswork, and antique furniture. It's useful to have the explanatory site publication, available in the bookshop, or get an audio guide at the admission point. The hour-long sound-and-light show held at the palace's Manek Chowk chronicles the history of the House of Mewar. The English-language version starts at 7 pm (7:30 pm in April), but check ahead, as timings can change without notice. ✉ *City Palace Complex* ☎ *0294/252–8016* 🎟 *Rs. 100, or Rs. 275 with audio guide; camera fee Rs. 200* ⊙ *Daily 9:30–5:15 (last admission 4:30).*

Bagore ki
Haveli 3

Bharatiya Lok
Kala Mandal 6

City Palace 1

Jagdish
Temple 2

Lake Pichola 4

Neemach
Mata 8

Sahelion
Ki Bari 7

Sajjan Garh 5

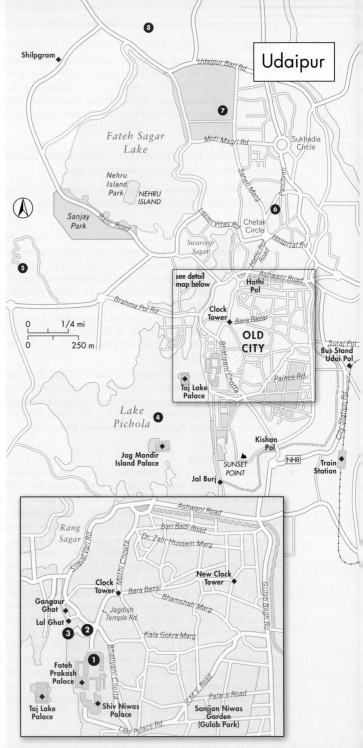

★ **Jagdish Temple.** This 17-century Hindu temple, the oldest in the city, was commissioned by Maharana Jagat Singh and is a major landmark in Udaipur's Old City. It's usually abuzz with devotees and tourists, especially during the morning and evening *aarti* (prayer ceremony), when vendors set up makeshift flower stalls along the temple walls and sell offerings of marigolds. The temple is dedicated to Jagdish (an incarnation of Vishnu), and songs sung in his praise are often played through loudspeakers high on the temple's edifice. You're welcome to step inside, although the engravings on the temple's exterior walls are more interesting to look at. ⊠ *Jagdish Mandir, just north of City Palace* ☉ *Daily, sunrise–sunset.*

FodorsChoice **Lake Pichola.** You can't leave Udai-
★ pur without seeing the stunningly romantic **Lake Palace** (Jag Niwas),
which seems to float serenely on the waters of Lake Pichola. A vast, white-marble fantasy, the palace has been featured in many Indian and foreign films, including the James Bond film *Octopussy*. Unfortunately, the palace's apartments, courts, fountains, and gardens are off-limits unless you're a guest at the Taj Lake Palace Hotel (⇨ *Where to Stay, below*). The equally isolated, three-story **Jag Mandir Island Palace** occupies Jag Mandir Island at the southern end of the lake, and is open to visitors from 10 to 6 (take a boat over). This palace has an elegant restaurant, the Darikhana (it serves Indian and continental cuisine, and is only open for dinner), as well as a more casual all-day café. Built and embellished over a 50-year period beginning in the 17th century, Jag Mandir is made of yellow sandstone, lined with marble, and crowned by a dome. The interior is decorated with arabesques of colored stones. Shah Jahan, son of the Mughal emperor Jahangir, took refuge in Jag Mandir after leading an unsuccessful revolt against his father. Legend has it that Shah Jahan's inspiration for the Taj Mahal came from this marble masterpiece. One-hour motorboat cruises (Rs. 300, or Rs. 500 for the sunset cruise), including a stop at Jag Mandir, leave from the jetty on the hour (daily 10–5). Check for the exact spot at ticket counter; book a day ahead during the busy season.

Gallery. Overlooking Lake Pichola from a gallery adjoining the magnificent
NEED A Durbar Hall in Fateh Prakash Palace, Gallery serves high tea between 3 pm
BREAK? and 7 pm. There's a full tea (cakes and scones with jam and cream, tea or coffee) as well as sandwiches. If you're visiting the crystal gallery above the restaurant, your Rs. 500 ticket also includes a soft drink, plain tea, or

---

THE LAKES SPILL OVER IN UDAIPUR

After a drought in 2000, Pichola Lake dried up: boys played cricket and cows grazed in the lake bed. The Taj Lake Palace hotel was a sad sight, sitting in what looked more like a puddle than a lake, and elephants and jeeps ferried guests from the "lakeshore." During the 2005 monsoon the skies finally opened and the lakes filled up in days; locals and the tourism industry heaved great sighs of relief. By 2008 the lake had dried up again, and it remained relatively parched until the 2010 monsoon, when heavy rains again filled the lake. Since then the monsoons have been good and the lake remains quite full.

5

coffee at the Surya Darshan Bar. (The crystal gallery houses the palace's early-19th-century collection of Birmingham crystal, with everything from wine decanters to beds.) ⊠ *Fateh Prakash Palace, City Palace Complex* ☎ *294/252–8016 to 19.*

Neemach Mata. This hilltop temple in the new part of town is dedicated to the goddess of the mountain, and the climb to its summit (no vehicles are allowed) is rewarded by a beautiful view of the whole city and its lake. It's a steep, 20-minute climb on a paved, zigzag path, but you can pause often on the way up to take in the view (and catch your breath). Wear comfortable shoes. ⊠ *North of Fateh Sagar Lake.*

Sajjan Garh. High in the Aravali Hills just outside Udaipur, this fort–palace glows golden orange in the night sky, thanks to the lights that illuminate it. Once the maharana's Monsoon Palace, it's now rather dilapidated, and serves as a radio station for the Indian Army. The panoramic view is spectacular from the fort's lofty tower, and locals claim you can see distant Chittaurgarh on a clear day. The winding road to the top of Sajjan Garh, surrounded by green forests, is best covered by car (you can take an auto-rickshaw, but the ride will be long and bumpy). On foot, it's a 45-minute uphill walk. A fee is required for vehicles at the gate leading up the hill. ☎ *Rs 160; camera free; vehicle fee Rs. 130* ☉ *Daily 8–6.*

OFF THE BEATEN PATH

Shilpgram. This rural arts-and-crafts village 3 km (2 miles) west of Udaipur contains a complex with 26 re-creations of furnished village huts (authentic right down to their toilets) from various states across India, including Rajasthan, Gujarat, Maharashtra, and Odisha, with tribal relics on display. The town comes alive in December with the **Shilpgram Utsav,** when artists and craftspeople from around the country arrive to sell and display their works. Puppet shows, dances, folk music, and handicrafts sales take place year-round, however. You can tour parts of the compound on a slow camel ride. There is a basic *dhaba* (eatery) inside the compound serving Indian food and tea. ⊠ *Rani Rd., near Fateh Sagar Lake* ☎ *294/243–1304* ⊕ *www.shilpgram.org* ☎ *Rs. 50; camera fee (still and video) Rs. 50* ☉ *Daily 11–7.*

WORTH NOTING

☉ **Bagore ki Haveli.** It's fun to explore the many rooms and terraces of this elegant 18th-century haveli on Gangaur Ghat. It was built by a prime minister of Mewar. One-hour folk-dance performances are organized every evening at 7 (time may change, so check on arrival)—get there at least 30 minutes early for good seats. ⊠ *Gangaur Ghat* ☎ *294/242–2567* ☎ *Rs. 30; dance performance Rs. 100; camera fee Rs. 100; video-camera fee Rs. 100* ☉ *Daily 10–5:30; dance performance at 7 pm.*

☉ **Bharatiya Lok Kala Mandal.** This folk-art museum displays a collection of puppets, dolls, masks, folk dresses, ornaments, musical instruments, and paintings. The museum is known for its short afternoon (noon–1) and evening (6–7) puppet shows—this is the reason to come here, because the museum itself is not well maintained. ⊠ *About 500 yds. north of Chetak Circle, Panch Batti, near Mohta Park* ☎ *0294/252–9296* ☎ *Museum Rs. 40, evening program Rs. 50 (prices subject to change)* ☉ *Daily 9–7.*

Udaipur's City Palace

Sahelion Ki Bari. Udaipur's famous Garden of the Maidens was founded in the 18th century by Maharana Sangam Singh for the 48 young ladies-in-waiting who were sent to the royal house as dowry. Back then, men were forbidden entrance when the queens and their ladies-in-waiting came to relax (though the king and his buddies still found their way in). The garden is planted with exotic flowers and themed fountains that have carved pavilions and monolithic marble elephants. The fountains don't have pumps: designed to take advantage of gravity, they run on water pressure from the lakes. If the fountains are not working, ask one of the attendants to turn them on. The pavilion opposite the entrance houses a small **children's science center.** For some touristy fun, you can dress up in traditional Rajasthani garb and have your picture snapped by a local photographer. ✉ *Saheli Marg, north of the city, near Bharatiya Lok Kala Mandal* 🎫 *Rs. 5 (subject to change); camera free* ⏰ *Daily 8–8.*

WHERE TO EAT

$$$ ECLECTIC 🍴 **1559 AD.** Named after the year when Udaipur was founded, 1559 occupies an elegant colonial bungalow, with the option of dining alfresco in the large garden. The interior is romantically lighted, and the food ranges from Rajasthani game birds (farmed, not hunted), prepared in traditional Indian and European styles, to salmon, rack of lamb, and baby back ribs. Indian meat dishes like *laal maas* (hot mutton curry) or *keema matar* (minced meat with peas) are among the favorites. There's a café with an authentic espresso machine and a bar with a decent selection of wines. [$] *Average main: Rs. 700* ✉ *P.P. Singhal Marg, near Fateh Sagar, Udaipur* ☎ *294/243–3559* 🌐 *www.1559ad.com.*

$$$ INDIAN 🍴 **Ambrai.** On the shore of Lake Pichola opposite Lal Ghat, this pleasant and popular outdoor restaurant with a bar has a hidden approach via narrow lanes, the restaurant has stunning views of the City Palace complex and the Lake Palace. It serves good Indian fare: standards include *paneer do piaza* (soft white cheese in an onion gravy) and mutton *rajputana* (spicy, Mewari-style) along with decent continental and Chinese dishes. There's a pleasant bar, and the restaurant is open for all three meals. If you're here at dinner, insure the staff places a mosquito repellant coil under your table. [$] *Average main: Rs. 500* ✉ *Opposite Lal Ghat* ☎ *294/243–1085* 🌐 *amethaveliudaipur.com.*

$ CAFÉ 🍴 **Café Namaste.** This little roadside bakery and café sells fresh pastries and cakes, as well as delicious, real espresso—a rarity outside of India's major cities. They can even make entire cakes to order on pretty short notice. If you come for breakfast, try the soft cinnamon rolls, apple crumble or date and walnut pie. The café is on a busy thoroughfare (and there are drains outside), but you can take your coffee and pastry upstairs to Natural City View, the rooftop restaurant owned by the same people (the latter is good for Indian and continental meals). [$] *Average main: Rs. 100* ✉ *339 Ashoka Haveli, Gangaur Ghat Marg, Udaipar* ☎ *294/242–2303, 294/241–9427.*

$$$ NORTH INDIAN ★ 🍴 **Jagat Niwas Palace Terrace Restaurant.** In a converted haveli at the end of one of Lal Ghat's labyrinthine lanes, this restaurant has retained the mansion's lovely design and has spectacular views of the Lake Palace, especially at night, when the vistas capture the incredibly romantic essence of the city. To see the brilliantly illuminated palace seemingly float on the water from a cushioned alcove is a signature Udaipur experience. There is a decent range of continental and Indian food—*Fish à la Jagat* is a highlight during fishing season; otherwise try the *Lal Maas* (red meat curry). There's nightly live music during peak season. [$] *Average main: Rs. 600* ✉ *23–25 Lal Ghat* ☎ *294/242–2860, 294/242–0133* 📠 *294/241–8512.*

$ VEGETARIAN 🍴 **Maxim's.** On a rooftop, with views of the Jagdish Temple, this renowned backpacker establishment borrows its name from the famous Parisian restaurant. This Maxim's is strictly vegetarian, with a huge selection of Indian dishes—from Chinese food to baked beans on toast. The owner takes pride in using only the freshest ingredients, and vegetables are cleaned using purified water. Adventurous eaters might try the Rajasthani Pizza, a greasy concoction of cheese, veggies, and tomato sauce, sandwiched between two chapattis and deep fried. The lassis here are some of the best in town. Beer and sheesha are also available. [$] *Average main: Rs. 180* ✉ *Near Jagdish Temple, Jagdish Chowk* ☎ *94–1423–9762* 💳 *No credit cards.*

$$ EUROPEAN 🍴 **Palki Khana.** Inside the City Palace complex, this casual café is a perfect post-museum stop—sit outside if you like to people-watch. The menu emphasizes standard continental café fare, such as salads, sandwiches, pizza, and pasta; try the yummy "mochachillo" (espresso shake) for a caffeine kick. Beer and an extensive variety of international and Indian wines are also available. If you have tickets for the sound-and-light show, you can watch it over dinner (Rs. 400; reservations required) on the patio; if you want dinner but don't have show tickets, you'll have

to wait until the café reopens at 9 pm. $ *Average main: Rs. 300* ⊠ *Shiv Niwas Palace, City Palace Complex* ☎ *294/252–8016, 294/252–8017* ⊕ *www.hrhhotels.com.*

$$
INDIAN

✕ **Rainbow Restaurant.** Popular with younger tourists and backpackers, this family-run restaurant is a great place for real Espresso coffee (Lavazza capsules) and superior juices—the menu has an incredibly long list of fresh fruit juices and funky "mocktails." The restaurant is open for breakfast, lunch, and dinner and Tandoori food is the favorite—try the *chicken palak* (chicken cooked curry style in spinach sauce), served with high-quality basmati rice. It's also a good spot from which to gaze over Lake Pichola and the Lake Palace as the sun goes down. $ *Average main: Rs. 300* ⊠ *27–28 Lal Ghat, Lake Pichola, Udaipur* ☎ *294/9460631484* ⊙ *Closed 10 pm–7:30 am.*

$$
ITALIAN

✕ **Savage Garden.** This Mediterranean-style, three-story restaurant is tucked away in the heart of Udaipur's Old City, and there is seating inside and out. Service may not be great, but the food makes up for it—even the menu, just a page long, is a refreshing change from the sheaves of standard Indian, Chinese, and continental options elsewhere. Owned by a German expat, the restaurant specializes in homemade pastas, some with an Indian twist, and all dishes are prepared with filtered water. Beer and wine are available, as is free Internet, and a selection of unusual locally made cutlery is also sold here. $ *Average main: Rs. 300* ⊠ *22, inside Chandpol* ☎ *294/242–5440* ▭ *No credit cards.*

$$$
INTERNATIONAL

✕ **Sunset Terrace.** Overlooking Lake Pichola, this café benefits from a constant breeze, and sitting on the terrace feels as if you've joined the aristocracy and have unlimited leisure. The menu includes Indian, European, and Chinese dishes, with a fixed-price menu as well as à la carte options. Favorite options here include the *paneer lababdar* (cottage cheese in an onion and tomato gravy) and the *safed maas,* a local lamb dish cooked in cream sauce. Live instrumental music adds to the romance in the evenings. What the place scores in location and atmosphere it loses in food and service. $ *Average main: Rs. 700* ⊠ *Fateh Prakash Palace, City Palace Complex* ☎ *294/252–8016 to 19* ⌂ *Reservations essential.*

$$$
INTERNATIONAL

✕ **Upre.** The name of the Lake Pichola Hotel's restaurant means "upstairs" in the local dialect, and that's exactly what it is—a rooftop spot beside the pool, with spectacular views of the City Palace Complex and lake, especially charming when they are lighted up after dark. Run by the same family that runs 1559 AD, this is a favorite among locals and tourists, who come for the good-quality food at reasonable prices. The menu features Italian, Mexican, and Chinese dishes alongside the Indian food—mutton *dhungar* (smoked) is a specialty. The restaurant also has a well-stocked bar. $ *Average main: Rs. 500* ⊠ *Lake Pichola Hotel, outside Chand Pol, Lake Pichola, Udaipur* ☎ *294/243–1197* ⊕ *www.1559ad.com.*

WHERE TO STAY

For expanded hotel reviews, visit Fodors.com.

$$$$
RESORT

⊡ **Fateh Garh.** Environmentally friendly, community minded, luxurious, and with an interesting back-story, this is one of Udaipur's newest boutique hotels, perched atop a hill adjacent to the Monsoon Palace. **Pros:**

friendly, polite service; great food. **Cons:** far from the Old City; policy of employing locals can affect efficiency. [$] *Rooms from: Rs. 14000* ✉ *Sisarma 6 km (4 miles) from Udaipur* ☎ *294/241–3845* 🌐 *www.fatehgarh.in* 🛏 *45 rooms, 3 suites* 🍴 *Some meals.*

$ HOTEL 🏨 **Jagat Niwas Palace Hotel.** Overlooking Lake Pichola, this converted 17th-century haveli is one of the best medium-budget places to stay in Udaipur and with all the recent improvements, you'd be hard pressed to find better value (or better views). **Pros:** unsurpassed views of the lake and Aravali hills; best value in town; short walk from shopping and restaurants. **Cons:** narrow approach; no pool or elevator. [$] *Rooms from: Rs. 3600* ✉ *23–25 Lal Ghat* ☎ *294/242–2860, 294/242–0133* 🌐 *www.jagatniwaspalace.com* 🛏 *25 rooms, 4 suites* 🍴 *No meals.*

$ HOTEL 🏨 **Lake Pichola Hotel.** For the price, this hotel has some great features, including a rooftop pool and restaurant, rooms with private terraces, suites with Jacuzzi or steam room, and a lakeside location. **Pros:** city and lake views; good service. **Cons:** difficult approach through narrow, crowded lanes. [$] *Rooms from: Rs. 3500* ✉ *Outside Chandpol, on western side of Lake Pichola* ☎ *294/243–1197* 🌐 *www.lakepicholahotel.com* 🛏 *28 rooms, 4 suites* 🍴 *No meals.*

5

$$$$ HOTEL Fodor's Choice ★ 🏨 **Oberoi Udaivilas.** On Lake Pichola, with sublime views of the Lake Palace, City Palace Complex, and ghats, this is one of India's most luxurious (and expensive) hotels—a contemporary palace in its own right. **Pros:** luxurious spa; great service and surroundings; expansive garden and sanctuary. **Cons:** extremely expensive; rather remote from the old city (but a boat provides a shortcut); service can become intrusive. [$] *Rooms from: Rs. 40000* ✉ *Haridasji ki Magri* ☎ *94/243–3300, 800/562–3764 reservations from US and Canada* 🌐 *www.oberoihotels.com* 🛏 *87 rooms, 5 suites* 🍴 *No meals.*

$$$$ HOTEL Fodor's Choice ★ 🏨 **Taj Lake Palace.** This exclusive 250-year-old white-marble palace—location for the James Bond film *Octopussy*—floats like a vision in the middle of Lake Pichola, and you arrive, of course, by boat. **Pros:** exemplary service to match unique palatial setting; boat service to shore available all hours. **Cons:** astoundingly expensive, and taxes can push up food and beverage costs by 25%. [$] *Rooms from: Rs. 36000* ✉ *Lake Pichola* ☎ *294/242–8800* 🌐 *www.tajhotels.com* 🛏 *66 rooms, 17 suites* 🍴 *Some meals.*

$$$ HOTEL 🏨 **Trident Hilton.** A relatively affordable option among Udaipur's luxury hotels, the Trident is removed from the downtown bustle, amid acres of beautiful gardens on Lake Pichola. **Pros:** heated pool is pleasant day or night; peaceful; attentive service always comes with a smile. **Cons:** uninspiring rooms are on the small side; location is not central. [$] *Rooms from: Rs. 8000* ✉ *Haridasji Ki Magri, Mulla Tulai* ☎ *294/243–2200* 🌐 *www.tridenthotels.com* 🛏 *139 rooms, 4 suites* 🍴 *No meals.*

$$ HOTEL 🏨 **Udai Kothi.** Who can pass up regal accommodations at cut-rate prices, particularly when its rooftop is one of the liveliest places in town? **Pros:** great value for the money; beautiful rooftop pool. **Cons:** only the suites have lake views; a long walk from the main sites. [$] *Rooms from: Rs. 5000* ✉ *Hannuman Ghat, outside Chandpol* ☎ *294/243–2810 to 12* 🌐 *www.udaikothi.com* 🛏 *39 rooms, 7 suites* 🍴 *No meals.*

SHOPPING

Udaipur's main shopping area is around the Jagdish Temple. You'll discover interesting nooks and crannies around here, but watch out for touts. There are plenty of stores to explore and items to buy, including leather-bound journals, wooden toys, silver, Udaipuri and Gujarati embroidery, and miniature paintings in the Mughal and Rajput styles, though most of these paintings are machine-made prints, a fact reflected in the wide disparity in prices between originals and others. If you want to buy original art, ask the proprietor to show you his best pieces—and plan to bargain.

ART **B.G. Sharma Art Gallery.** Udaipur has many galleries that exhibit original work by burgeoning artists, which attracts serious art buyers. The B.G. Sharma Art Gallery has nearly five decades of work by B.G. Sharma, one of the preeminent miniature painters in India, who recently passed away. Unlike most artists of miniature paintings, Sharma produced original ideas rather than copying traditional pictures, and made a huge contribution to advancing the Mughal, Kishangarh, and Kangra painting styles. Now that his sons run the business it has become commercialized and lost its charm, but some of Sharma's legacy remains. Check the authenticity of anything you want to buy. ⊠ *3 Saheli Marg* ☎ *294/241–9201* ⊕ *www.bgsharmaart.com* ⊘ *Closed Sun.*

Gallery Pristine. Specializing in both contemporary and folk art, this gallery has many small pieces by Shail Choyal, a guru of contemporary Indian painting. Other highlights include the stylized work of Shahid Parvez, a well-known local artist. ⊠ *60 Bhatiyani Chohatta, Palace Rd.* ☎ *294/242–3916.*

Ganesh Art Emporium. This is a trendy little shop focusing on a gifted young artist, Madhu Kant Mundra, whose oeuvre includes more than 125 funky representations of Lord Ganesh. Don't miss the artistic refrigerator magnets, sculptures, and antique photographs. ⊠ *152 Jagdish Rd.* ☎ *294/242–2864.*

Kamal Sharma Art Gallery. You can often see the artist at work here. Kamal Sharma paints mainly birds and animals on paper, marble, silk, and canvas, in contemporary and traditional styles. All the works are for sale. ⊠ *15-A New Colony, Kalaji-Goraji* ☎ *294/242–3451* ⊕ *www.kamalsharma.net.*

HANDICRAFTS **Rajasthali.** If your time is limited, head straight to the area around the Jagdish Temple, where you'll find an array of shops stocking an almost overwhelming variety of leather-bound journals, deity statues, and knickknacks; if bargaining isn't your thing, though, head to an emporium instead. The government-run Rajasthali emporium sells high-quality Rajasthani arts and handicrafts, and is a good place to pick up a wool-stuffed washable quilt with a Rajasthani motif. The showroom at Jagdish temple is a bit run down and looks dusty with limited items but the prices here are fixed. ⊠ *Jagdish Chowk, near Jagdish Temple* ☎ *294/241–5346.*

Sadhna. One of the oldest NGOs in India, working for the advancement of the village poor, Sadhna works with rural women in the Udaipur district and trains them to produce traditional appliqué work on cushion covers, bedspreads, silk stoles, bags, kurtas, light quilts, and jackets. Sadhna has gained popularity over the years, and the women also tour around the country to exhibitions in major cities during festivals. There's another branch near the Jagdish Temple in the Old City. ⊠ *Seva Mandir Rd., Old Fathepura* ☎ *294/245–4655* ⊕ *www.sadhna. org* ⊘ *Closed Sun.*

University of Arts. While you're in the Jagdish Temple area, make sure you check out the collection of more than 500 handmade wooden puppets in varying shapes and sizes at this small shop. Ask the proprietor, Rajesh Gurjarjour, an excellent puppeteer, for a private demonstration. Embroidered jackets, handcrafted soft toys, and knick-knacks are also for sale. ⊠ *166 Jagdish Marg, off City Palace Rd.* ☎ *294/242–2591.*

JEWELRY **Ganta Ghar.** From Jagdish Temple, stroll down to the Ganta Ghar (clock tower) and the area around it, a base for silver jewelry. Browse freely, but take care not to purchase items that are merely coated with silver-tone paint. Most of the silver shops here are run-of-the mill and offer little variation in style and price.

Gehrilal Goverdhan Singh Choudhary. More unusual jewelry is on offer here, with a good selection of antique jewelry as well as contemporary designs with stonework. Goverdhan Singh has been collecting jewelry from tribal sources and gypsies for a decade. Choudhary has been in the business more than two decades, and has exhibited several times abroad. ⊠ *72 Jagdish Marg* ☎ *294/241–0806.*

NEED A
BREAK?

Lala Mishtan Bhandar. Next door to Gehrilal Goverdhan Singh Choudhary, near the Clock Tower, is a sweet stall, Lala Mishtan Bhandar, where you can satisfy your sweet tooth and refuel with the best *gulab jamun* (fried milk balls in syrup) and *imarti* (pretzel-shaped pastries dipped in sugary syrup) in town. It's open late till 10 pm. ⊠ *Jagdish Chowk, Near Ghantaghar.*

EKLINGJI AND NAGDA

22 km (14 miles) north of Udaipur.

★ **Shiva Temple Complex.** A pleasant and scenic drive from Udaipur through the Aravali Hills, Eklingji is a small village famous for its 15th-century Shiva Temple Complex (some parts date back to the 8th century). There's a unique four-sided, four-faced black-marble image of Shiva within an enclosing silver grille, miniature replicas of which will be eagerly offered to you in the village bazaar. Morning and evening, devotees sing and chant hymns in praise of Shiva. Every Monday evening the Maharana of Udaipur visits the temple privately. Aside from religious festival times, this is a peaceful spot and a good place to experience a living Hindu temple. The temple is closed at certain times of the day; ask at your hotel about best times to visit. Cameras, shoes, and socks are not allowed inside; lockers are available. ⊠ *Eklingji, Rajasthan.*

The private pools of the Oberoi Udaivilas hotel

RANAKPUR

★ *96 km (60 miles) northwest of Udaipur.*

Jain Temple. A comfortable two- to three-hour drive from Udaipur, the 15th-century Jain Temple at Ranakpur is one of the most stunning examples of Jain temple architecture in the country, dedicated to Adi-nath, the first Jain *Tirthankar* (a holy person who has attained enlightenment and takes rebirth to pass on the knowledge to others); this is also a less-crowded, more convenient, and perhaps equally impressive, alternative to the temples at Mount Abu. Legend has it that the temple, which is dedicated to Lord Rishabadeva, was built after it appeared in a dream to a minister of the Mewar king. One of the five holiest places for India's Jains, the three-story temple is surrounded by a three-story wall and contains 27 halls supported by 1,444 elaborately carved pillars—no two carvings are alike. Below the temple are underground chambers where statues of Jain saints were hidden to protect them from the Mughals. The view of the white-marble complex rising up from the fertile plain is awe-inspiring—the relief work on the columns is some of the best in all of India. As you enter, look to the left for the pillar where the minister and the architect provided themselves with front-row seats for worship. Another pillar is intentionally warped, to separate human works from divine ones—the builders believed only gods could be perfect, so they intentionally added imperfections to some of the columns to avoid causing insult. Outside are two smaller Jain temples and a shrine adorned with erotic sculptures and dedicated to the sun god. There are a few priests around who speak a little English and will act as a guide; in return, you should make a small donation. Leather items—shoes, belts, wallets, and more—are not allowed inside the temple (neither are menstruating women) and there are strict instructions about dress code. ■TIP→ Although there are a couple of hotels in the vicinity, Ranakpur is best visited as a day trip from Udaipur, maybe stopping at Kumbalgarh Fort en route. ✉ *Temple free; camera fee Rs. 50; video-camera fee Rs. 150* ⊗ *Non-Jains, daily 11:30–5.*

KUMBHALGARH

84 km (52 miles) north of Udaipur.

★ **Kumbhalgarh.** Isolated and serene, this formidable **fort** was a refuge for Mewari rulers in times of strife. Although there's less to see here than at Chittaurgarh, the grandeur is stunning and the countryside that separates it from Udaipur makes for a beautiful, and not too bumpy, drive. It's also close enough to Ranakpur to visit both in one day.

Built by Maharana Kumbha in the 15th century, the fort ramparts run 4 km (2½ miles) and the outer wall encloses an area of 83 square km (32 square miles). At one time its ramparts nearly encircled an entire township, self-contained to withstand a long siege. The fort fell only once, to the army of Akbar—whose forces had contaminated the water supply. The fort was also the birthplace of Maharana Pratap. The **Badal Mahal** (Cloud Palace), at the top, has an awesome view of the surrounding countryside. There's a small café at the fort that serves light snacks and tea. ⊠ *Kumbalgarh, Rajasthan* ✉ *Rs. 100* ⊗ *Daily 9–5.*

Kumbalgarh Sanctuary. Surrounding the fort, the modern-day Kumbalgarh Sanctuary is home to wolves, leopards, jackals, nilgai deer, sambar deer, and various species of birds, and makes for great treks. Inquire at the Government Tourist Office in Udaipur if you're interested in going on a two-hour morning jeep safari here. It's a pretty part of the country, though the wildlife is nothing too out of the ordinary. ⊠ *Kumbalgarh, Rajasthan.*

MOUNT ABU

185 km (115 miles) west of Udaipur.

GETTING HERE AND AROUND
The road to Mount Abu is winding and rough in some areas, so make sure to leave early in the morning if you're making a day trip from Udaipur. Ideally, you should plan for an overnight stay.

EXPLORING
High in the Aravali Hills, Mount Abu is Rajasthan's only hill station, and it attracts hordes of tourists from the neighboring state of Gujarat, who come to enjoy the town's cool climate and pretty lakes. As a result, you'll find a large number of restaurants here serving the famously sweet Gujarati thalis. It's also a great place to stop if you like taking long walks or are simply looking to escape the heat during the unforgiving pre-monsoon months (April and May), although you may want to give it a miss if you're short on time.

5

Mount Abu is a major pilgrimage center for Jains, who come here for the famous **Dilwara Temples,** a group of five awe-inspiring carved temples that were built of marble between the 11th and 13th centuries. Each is dedicated to a different Thirthankar (enlightened ascetic). The 13th-century Luna Vasahi and the 11th-century Vimal Vasahi temples are of special note. The highlight of the Luna Vasahi is its ceilings, covered with interconnected marble carvings; the Vinak Vasahi, with its intricately carved white-marble columns and dome, is equally splendid.

Nakki Lake, resting between green hills, is believed to have been carved out by the gods' fingernails.

At **Sunset Point** you can take in a romantic Mount Abu sunset, but don't expect peace and quiet—this is the major sunset spot in town, and you'll likely be joined by plenty of other tourists, especially on weekends and Indian holidays.

Mount Abu's ashram-cult hotspot, **Brahma Kumaris Spiritual University,** attracts thousands of followers from all over the world—members of the sect don white robes or saris and study spiritual knowledge or Raja yoga meditation—you'll undoubtedly see them around town.

Guru Shikhar. Past Peace Park, on Guru Shikhar Road, is Guru Shikhar, the highest point between South India's Nilgiri Hills and the Himalayas, in the north. From here you can enjoy excellent views of the countryside. ⚠ Don't venture this way after dark—the winding forest roads make for hazardous driving. ⊠ *about 12 km (8 miles) out of Mount Abu.*

Peace Park. The Brahma Kumaris, a spiritual and educational institution that's spread across the globe, designed the Peace Park which lies about 16 km (10 miles) outside of town, on the edge of a nature reserve; it has a series of beautiful gardens and is good for a break from the bustle of the city, if you have a car to get you there. ⊕ *www.brahmakumaris. com/campus/peacepark* ☉ *Daily sunrise–sunset.*

WHERE TO STAY

For expanded hotel reviews, visit Fodors.com.

$$
HOTEL
🛏 **Palace Hotel (Bikaner House).** Besides once being the summer residence of the Maharaja of Bikaner, this was for decades also the center of Mount Abu's aristocratic social life and it's still an elegant and hospitable getaway. **Pros:** service is excellent; free Internet; lovely grounds. **Cons:** no pool; conferences may impact on the experience. $ *Rooms from: Rs. 4500* ⊠ *Delwara Rd.* ☎ *2974/235–121, 2974/238–673* ⊕ *www. palacehotelbikanerhouse.com* ⇆ *17 rooms, 16 suites* ❑ *No meals.*

CHITTAURGARH

112 km (69 miles) northeast of Udaipur.

Chittaurgarh. If any one of Rajasthan's many forts were to be singled out for its glorious history and chivalric lore, it would be Chittaurgarh. It's also gargantuan in size, and there's plenty to explore on a day trip from Udaipur.

This was the capital of the Mewar princely state from the 8th to the 16th centuries, before Maharana Udai Singh moved the capital to

Udaipur, and the sprawling hilltop fort occupies roughly 700 acres on a hill about 300 feet high. It was besieged and sacked three times: after the first two conquests, the Rajputs recovered it, but the third attack clinched it for the Mughals for several decades.

The first attack took place in 1303, when the Sultan of Delhi Allauddin Khilji became so enamored of Rani Padmini that he set out to attack the fort and win her in battle. Some 34,000 warriors lost their lives in this struggle, but the Sultan did not get Padmini: she and all the women in the fort committed *jauhar*—mass self-immolation—in anticipation of widowhood and assaults by invading armies. Frustrated, Khilji entered the city in a rage, looting and destroying much of what he saw. Chittaurgarh was also the home of the saint-poet Mirabai, a 16th-century Rajput princess and devotee of Lord Krishna who gave up her royal life to sing *bhajans* (hymns) in his praise.

The massive fort encompasses the palaces of the 15th-century ruler **Rana Kumbha,** where Udaipur's founder Udai Singh was born, as well as the palace of **Rani Padmini.** Legend has it that Khilji fell in love with Padmini by gazing at her reflection in the pond in front of her palace. Also worth visiting in the fort are the victory towers—the ornate **Vijay Stambh** and **Kirti Stambh**—and a huge variety of temples, including **Kunbha Shyam, Kalika Mata,** and the **Meera temple** associated with the devotional poetess Mirabai. The **Fateh Prakash Mahal** displays some fine sculptures. Plan to spend at least half a day in Chittaurgarh. Note that the sites are spread out and it can get quite sunny, so you may want to drive between some points. You can find a guide by the Rampole entrance to the fort or near the Rana Kumbha. ⊠ *Rajasthan* ☉ *Daily 10–5.*

BUNDI

★ *210 km (130 miles) south of Jaipur; 279 km (173 miles) from Udaipur.*

GETTING HERE AND AROUND

Although Bundi can easily be reached by train from Jaipur (via Kota), it's even more convenient to rent a taxi with a driver and get there by road (it's about a four-hour drive). Bundi can be done as a day trip, but it's more relaxing if you spend the night. The town is small enough to be navigated on foot, and most of the attractions are within a mile of each other. If you get tired of walking, auto-rickshaws are easy to find.

WHAT TO SEE

The magical little town of Bundi, with its winding lanes and unusual step wells, appears to have been plucked straight from a fairy tale. It's a perfect getaway from the commotion of Jaipur.

The area now known as Bundi was populated by tribal people until the 13th century, when it was taken over by a clan of Rajputs, and after that was ruled by various dynasties until the town was incorporated into the Republic of India after India's independence from the British. Rudyard Kipling is Bundi's most famous former resident, and it is popularly believed that it was during his stay in the little town that he decided to write *Kim*.

Most popular is the 14th-century **Taragarh** (Star Fort), tucked into a hillside above the town (but still within about 1½ km [1 mile] of the center). The rundown fort was originally constructed to defend the principality of Bundi from invasion, although these days its biggest draw is its great views of the town and the surrounding countryside. Sunset is the best time to visit, but don't forget a flashlight for the way down. **Bundi Palace** is another must-see, both for its impressive architecture and the amazingly well-preserved murals depicting the life of Lord Krishna that grace its interior walls. The palace also has its own *chitrashala* (art gallery), where beautiful old paintings are displayed. Bundi is also well-known for its dozens of *baoris* (step wells), which were used by local women to gather water in large vessels in the days before indoor plumbing and hand pumps. The most interesting of these is the steep **Raniji ki Baori** (Queen's Well), which is covered with carvings and stone latticework. The interiors of the nearby identical twin step wells, **Nagar Sagar Kund,** feature banister-free flights of stairs that crisscross down into the well bellow—though you're not allowed to descend yourself.

WHERE TO STAY
For expanded hotel reviews, visit Fodors.com.

$ ⌂ **Hotel Braj Bhushanjee.** Family-owned and -operated, this hotel in a
HOTEL 200-year-old haveli preserves many of its original features, including carved stonework, and art lovers will appreciate the striking Bundi School of Painting murals and other artwork. **Pros:** excellent location; warm staff. **Cons:** only vegetarian food served; no alcohol. $ *Rooms from: Rs. 3500* ⌂ *Below palace, opp. Ayurvedic Hospital, Bundi, Rajasthan* ☎ *0747/244–2322, 0747/244–2509* ⊕ *www.kiplingsbundi.com* ⌂ *24 rooms* ⦿ *Breakfast.*

$ ⌂ **Hotel Bundi Haveli.** This boutique heritage hotel, furnished with
HOTEL antiques, is in the heart of the town, with great views of the palace and fort. **Pros:** charming character; clean. **Cons:** staff is not always professional; restaurant is expensive. $ *Rooms from: Rs. 1500* ⌂ *107 Balchand Parra, Near Naval Sagar Lake, Bundi, Rajasthan* ☎ *0747/244–6716* ⊕ *www.hotelbundihaveli.com* ⌂ *10 rooms, 2 suites* ⦿ *No meals.*

JODHPUR

343 km (215 miles) west of Jaipur; 266 km (165 miles) northwest of Udaipur.

Jodhpur, Rajasthan's second-largest city, is known as the Blue City because of the azure-painted houses of the Old City, which are especially impressive when viewed from the ramparts of Mehrangarh Fort. The city, at the base of a sandstone ridge, was the capital of the Marwar kingdom for five centuries, and it's encircled by a 9-km (6-mile) wall, which keeps out the desert sands. It was named after its 15th-century founder, Rao Jodha, chief of the Rathore clan of Marwar. The clan traces its lineage to Lord Rama, hero of the ancient Hindu epic *The Ramayana.*

One of the murals depicting the life of Lord Krishna, at Bundi Palace

There isn't that much to do in Jodhpur, aside from a few sites including the incredible Mehrangarh Fort, and many people use the city as a jumping-off point for Jaisalmer, or as a place to overnight on the way to Jaipur or Udaipur.

Getting around Jodhpur is relatively easy. Take an auto-rickshaw up the hillside and walk through the massive, impeccably maintained Mehrangarh Fort, saunter through the Umaid Bhawan Palace Museum, and wander through the chaotic and colorful markets full of fruit, textile, and handicraft stalls near the city's clock tower. If you have time, Jodhpur is an especially good place from which to take a camel safari into the desert.

GETTING HERE AND AROUND

The older part of the city that extends between the clock tower and the base of the Meherangarh Fort consists of narrow lanes, and it's faster and easier to walk in this part of town than it is to go by car or auto-rickshaw. For attractions farther afield, auto-rickshaws can easily be hailed on the street.

TIMING

You could squeeze in all the main attractions in one full day, though this won't leave you much time to shop or really get a feel for the city, so try to spend two days here.

ESSENTIALS

Tourist Offices Government of Rajasthan Tourist Office
✉ RTDC Hotel Ghoomer Campus, High Court Rd. ☎ 291/254–5083
🌐 www.rajasthantourism.gov.in.

A GOOD TOUR

Spend your morning at the majestic **Meherangarh Fort** (which has a good audio tour). If you're adventurous, you could even go for a zip on the fort's Flying Fox zip-line course. Then head into town for a quick lunch, and, if it's not too hot for a stroll, take a short taxi drive 9 km (6 miles) north of Jodhpur to the **Mandore Gardens**, where you can walk off your lunch. If you have extra time, visit **Mahamandir**. End your day at the **Umaid Bhawan Palace Museum**—walk through the museum before it closes at 5, then linger for a drink and dinner and enjoy the fabulous sunset views.

TIMING With this plan you can tour Jodhpur in a day, covering the essentials. If you have more time, spend your second day visiting sites like the Jaswant Thada crematorium and doing a bit of shopping.

WHAT TO SEE

Jaswant Thada. The royal marble crematorium was built in 1899 for Maharaja Jaswant Singh II. Capping the enormous white structure are marble canopies under which individual members of the royal family are buried. You may see people bowing before the image of the king, who is considered to have joined the ranks of the deities. ⊠ *500 yds. northeast of Mehrangarh Fort* 🎫 *Rs. 30; cameras Rs. 25; video-cameras Rs. 100* ☉ *Daily 9–5.*

Mahamandir. Built in 1812 just outside Jodhpur, this old, walled monastery complex (*mahamandir* means "great temple") still contains a few hundred houses and a school. The monastery belongs to the Nath community, warrior-priests who worked closely with the royal family to arrange support in times of war. Mahamandir is best known for the 84 beautifully carved pillars that surround it. Prayers are offered morning and evening in the main temple. Check locally for best times to visit. ⊠ *4 km (2½ miles) northeast of Jodhpur.*

Mandore Gardens. Within the old Marwar capital at Mandore, these gardens house the exquisitely sculpted red-sandstone *davals* (memorials) to former rulers. The Hall of Heroes depicts 16 colorfully painted heroes and deities carved from a single piece of stone. The small **museum** on the grounds has sculptures from the 5th to the 9th centuries as well as ivory and lacquer work. It's definitely worth a visit here for the davals, but the gardens are not well maintained, and are no longer the picnic-spot destination they used to be. ⊠ *Mandore, 8 km (5 miles) north of Jodhpur.* 🎫 *Gardens free; Museum Rs. 50* ☉ *Gardens: daily sunrise–sunset; Museum: Sat.–Thurs. 10–4.*

NEED A BREAK?

Shri Misrilal Hotel. In the highly competitive world of lassi wallahs, only the strong survive and this one has survived since 1927, making it the oldest in Jodhpur. Standing in the shadow of Jodhpur's famous clock tower, and misleadingly called a hotel, it's a longtime favorite among locals and foreigners. Look past the simple interior and neon lighting, and choose a flavor—make sure to specify whether you want salty or sweet, and note that the lassis here are consumed with a spoon. ⊠ *Ghanta Ghar (Clock Tower), Sadar Market* ☎ *291/254–0049.*

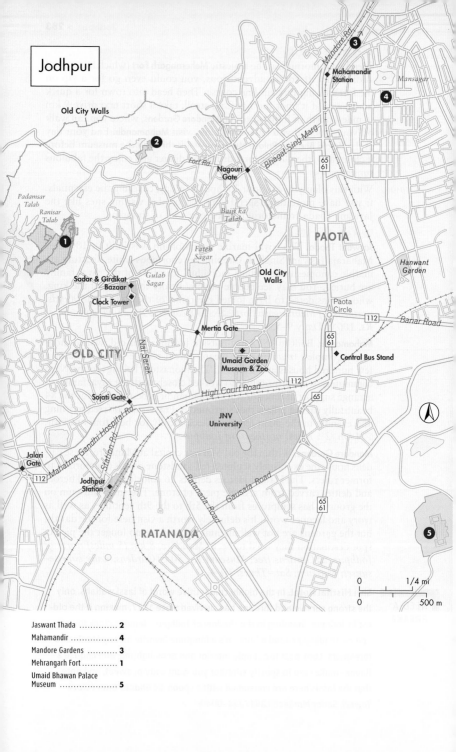

Jodhpur

Old City Walls

② Nagouri Gate

Fort Rd.

Bhagat Singh Marg

65 61

Mandore Rd.

③

④ Mahamandir Station

Mansagar

PAOTA

Padamsar Talab

Ranisar Talab

①

Baiji ka Talab

Fateh Sagar

Gulab Sagar

Old City Walls

Hanwant Garden

Paota Circle

112

Banar Road

Sadar & Girdikat Bazaar

Clock Tower

OLD CITY

Nai Sarak

Mertia Gate

Umaid Garden Museum & Zoo

65 61

112

Central Bus Stand

Sojati Gate

High Court Road

112

65

JNV University

Jalari Gate

112

Mahatma Gandhi Hospital Rd.

Station Rd.

Jodhpur Station

RATANADA

Ratanada Road

Gausala Road

65 61

⑤

0   1/4 mi
0   500 m

Jaswant Thada **2**
Mahamandir **4**
Mandore Gardens **3**
Mehrangarh Fort **1**
Umaid Bhawan Palace
Museum **5**

Mehrangarh Fort. This enormous hilltop fort was built by Rao Jodha in 1459, when he shifted his capital from Mandore to Jodhpur. Looking straight down a perpendicular cliff, the famously impregnable fort is an imposing landmark, especially at night, when it's bathed in yellow light. Approach the fort by climbing a steep walkway, passing under no fewer than eight huge gates—if you're not up for the hike, you can take an auto-rickshaw instead for about Rs. 100 or 150 from Clock Tower, or take the elevator (Rs. 20) up two levels from the ticket office. The first gate, the Victory Gate, was built by Maharaja Ajit Singh to commemorate his military success against the Mughals at the beginning of the 18th century; the other seven commemorate victories over other Rajput states. The last gate, as in many Rajput forts, displays the haunting handprints of women who immolated themselves after their husbands were defeated in battle.

> ## JODHPUR'S SWEETNESS
>
> Jodhpur's famed tradition of hospitality, known as *mithi manuhar*, frequently takes the form of offers of food. Such items, especially *mithai* (sweets), are not to be missed. When you're offered a *mave ki kachori* (milk-based pastry), *besan ki barfi* (a fudgelike sweet made of chickpea flour), *mirchi bada* (fried, breaded green peppers), or *kofta* (deep-fried balls of potatoes or vegetables), don't resist: the offer will be repeated until you take some.

Inside the rugged fort, delicate latticed windows and pierced sandstone screens are the surprising motifs. The palaces—**Moti Mahal** (Pearl Palace), **Phool Mahal** (Flower Palace), **Sheesh Mahal** (Glass Palace)—and the other apartments are exquisitely decorated; their ceilings, walls, and floors are covered with murals, mirror work, and gilt. The palace museum has exquisite rooms filled with lavish royal elephant carriages (*howdahs*), palanquins, thrones, paintings, and even a giant tent. It also has an interesting weapons gallery. From the ramparts there are excellent views of the city; the blue houses at sunset look magical. If you're up for it, you can strap on a harness and take a zip-line tour around the fort with **Flying Fox** (⇨ *see contact info in Sports and the Outdoors*); it's not for the weak of heart. The fort is possibly the best-maintained historic property in all Rajasthan, and offers an audio tour with headphones (included in the admission price for foreigners) with recorded commentary in six languages, including English. ✉ *Fort Rd.* ☎ *291/254–8790, 291/254–9790* ⊕ *www.mehrangarh.org* ✑ *Rs. 300 (including audio tour and lift); camera fee 100; video-camera fee Rs. 200* ☉ *Daily 9–5:30 (8:30–5 in summer).*

Umaid Bhawan Palace Museum. Built between 1929 and 1942 at the behest of Maharaja Umaid Singh during a long famine, this public-works project employed 3,000 workers. Now part museum, part royal residence, and part heritage hotel, its art-deco design makes it unique in the state. Amazingly, no cement was used in construction; the palace is made of interlocking blocks of sandstone, something to admire when you stand under the imposing 183-foot-high central dome. The museum's collection includes royal finery, local arts and crafts, miniature paintings, stuffed big cats, and a large number of clocks. You may catch a glimpse of the titular Maharaja of Jodhpur, who still lives in one large wing of the palace, but in any case you won't miss the magnificent peacocks that strut around the palace's marble *chattris* (canopies) and lush lawns. Photography is allowed on the lawns but not in the museum. ⊠ *Umaid Bhawan Palace, Airport Rd.* ☏ *291/251–0101* ☏ *Rs. 50 (free to hotel guests); camera fee 30 Rs.* ☉ *Daily 9–5.*

WHERE TO EAT

$$$

NORTH INDIAN

✕ **Chokelao Terrace.** Sip a chilled beer and enjoy spectacular views of Jodhpur city at this romantically lit restaurant high up within Mehrangarh Fort. Notable more for its ambience than the food, this touristy outdoor eatery is as good an option as any within the Old City, and it's especially fitting after an evening tour of the fort. Try the traditional Rajasthani food (veg and non-veg thalis), as well as standard tandoori favorites like *paneer tikka.* $ *Average main: Rs. 700* ⊠ *Mehrangarh Fort* ☏ *291/255–5389* ▭ *No credit cards* ☉ *No lunch.*

$$$

NORTH INDIAN

✕ **Indique.** After a long day of sightseeing, stop at this good but basic rooftop hangout at the Hotel Haveli in the Old City. Go for a sundown drink or dinner and take in stunning views of the nearby lake, the fort, the clock tower, and the Umaid Bhawan Palace. The mostly Indian menu includes a couple of continental dishes at reasonable prices and a decent list of drinks on the bar menu. Note that the steps leading four stories up to the restaurant are quite steep. $ *Average main: Rs. 500* ⊠ *Hotel Haveli, Gulab Sagar* ☏ *291/329–3328, 291/263–8344* ▭ *No credit cards* ☉ *No lunch.*

$

INDIAN

✕ **Janta Sweet Home.** Jodhpur's most famous sweet shop, bustling Janta Sweets is a hot favorite with locals and a good place to sample regional delicacies. Test your chilli tolerance level with the spicy *mirchi bada*, a huge pepper that's been breaded and deep-fried. For something sweeter, try the local specialty: mawa kachori (a pastry filled with nut-based sweetmeats). Indianized vegetarian versions of American-style fast food—think pizzas and burgers—are also available with plenty of local beverage options like lassi. $ *Average main: Rs. 150* ⊠ *3 Nayi Sarak* ☏ *291/263–6666, 291/262–5559* ⊕ *www.jantasweethome.com* ▭ *No credit cards.*

$$

VEGETARIAN

★

✕ **Jhankar.** Although this little garden restaurant is one of the newest in Jodhpur, it has quickly established itself as a popular spot for travelers to relax and meet new people over a cup of rich *masala chai.* Owned by a Jain, the restaurant is strictly vegetarian and alcohol-free, but even meat eaters will marvel at the Indian house specialties, such as the *Navratan Korma* (a rich curry of vegetables, fruits, and nuts). Jhankar is at its best after dark, when tiny twinkling lights strung through the trees lend a whimsical air to the setting. $ *Average main: Rs. 300* ⊠ *Fort Rd., Makarana Mohalla* ☏ *291/261–2590.*

$$$$

INTERNATIONAL

✕ **Marwar.** One of the better attempts at upscale cuisine in Jodhpur, the restaurant is a part of Taj group's Hari Mahal hotel. The neo-Mughal-style restaurant serves continental and Indian food, with a few Rajasthani specialties, and there is a buffet as well as à la carte options. Try Jodhpuri *gatta* curry (steamed chickpea flour dumplings in yogurt-base gravy); the spicy Jodhpuri *maas* (lamb) curry is also typical of this region. Pasta dishes are a nice break from the usual Indian fare: the penne *arrabiata* is particularly good. On most nights live Indian classical music is performed. $ *Average main: Rs. 1000* ✉ *Vivanta by Taj – Hari Mahal Hotel, 5 Residency Rd.* ☎ *291/243–9700* ⊕ *www.vivantabytaj. com* ✍ *Reservations essential.*

$$$
NORTH INDIAN
✕ **On the Rocks.** This jungle-theme restaurant is aptly named, not because it has a well-stocked bar, but because the ground inside the mostly outdoor restaurant is gravel. A popular place with locals as well as tour groups, it can get lively over peak season and weekends, when the crowds come in to swing to the music in the cave-like bar called Rocktails. On the same road as Ajit Bhawan hotel and close to numerous shopping boutiques, it's an ideal rest stop for a quick drink or lunch. The food here is rich and hearty, and the tandoori specialties are famous with the local upwardly mobile crowd. $ *Average main: Rs. 600* ✉ *Circuit House Rd., next to Ajit Bhawan Hotel* ☎ *291/510–2701.*

$$$$
INTERNATIONAL
✕ **Risala.** If you're looking to feel like royalty and splurge on a wining and dining experience, head to this elegant, formal dining room adorned with portraits from the royal collection—or opt for the balcony overlooking luscious gardens. The contemporary European and unique Indian dishes are a welcome change from the usual Indian and Rajasthani fare, and if you like seafood, you're in luck—try the prawn curry in a tomato cream sauce. Service is impeccable. The drinks menu is extensive, and includes internationally sourced wines. Non-hotel guests may have trouble securing a reservation during the busy season. $ *Average main: Rs. 3000* ✉ *Umaid Bhawan Palace, Airport Rd.* ☎ *291/251–0101* ✍ *Reservations essential.*

$$$
ECLECTIC
✕ **Sir Pratap.** This multi-cuisine restaurant in the Gateway Hotel is a good place for the health conscious—they have plenty of low-calorie options. The feel of the place is not as romantic as some of the restaurants in the Old City, but if you have children, you'll want to bring them here for the sprawling grassy lawns flanking the restaurant. It's worth coming out on weekends, when they open the pool up to non-guests and serve a buffet dinner. $ *Average main: Rs. 650* ✉ *Banar Rd.* ☎ *291/226–3430* ⊕ *www.thegatewayhotels.com.*

WHERE TO STAY

For expanded hotel reviews, visit Fodors.com.

$$$$
RESORT
Fodor'sChoice
★
▦ **Ajit Bhawan.** This small, enchanting palace and village complex has several intriguing perks, like a garage full of royal vintage cars available for rent. **Pros:** warm and inviting; cozy bar; free Wi-Fi; paths and lanes connecting rooms create a spacious outdoor feel; large rooms. **Cons:** far from the Old City; tented rooms can be noisy; service can be slow during peak times. $ *Rooms from: Rs. 13000* ✉ *Circuit House Rd.* ☎ *291/251–3333, 291/251–1410* ⊕ *www.ajitbhawan.com* ⤳ *106 rooms, 20 Suites, 10 tents* ❚⊙❙ *Breakfast.*

$
HOTEL
▦ **Devi Bhawan.** One of the more moderately priced hotels in Jodhpur, Devi Bhawan is run by a friendly young couple, Prithviraj and Rambha Singh. **Pros:** on a quiet street away from the city; good service, clean rooms, excellent value; free Wi-Fi. **Cons:** not as many facilities as other places. $ *Rooms from: Rs. 2800* ✉ *1 Ratanada Circle, Defence Lab. Rd.* ☎ *291/251–1067* 🖷 *291/251–2215* ⊕ *www.devibhawan.com* ⤳ *21 rooms* ❚⊙❙ *No meals.*

$
B&B/INN

Hotel Haveli. An affordable option for those interested in staying in the heart of the Old City, this hotel also has a rooftop restaurant with excellent views of the city. **Pros:** entrance on quiet street in the otherwise bustling Old City; impressive facade. **Cons:** no pool; multistory building with no elevator; can feel cramped. $ *Rooms from: Rs. 1000* ✉ *Makrana Mohalla, behind clock tower, opposite Toorji Ka Jhalra (a step well)* ☎ *291/261–4615, 291/264–7003* ⊕ *www.hotelhaveli.net* ⟿ *24 rooms* ❏ *No meals.*

$
HOTEL

Karni Bhavan. Outstanding hospitality is the hallmark of this homey hotel, but you'll enjoy the interestingly themed rooms and the dinners with entertainment too. **Pros:** large airy rooms; fabulous hospitality. **Cons:** away from action in the Old City; no gym or spa; ordinary pool. $ *Rooms from: Rs. 3300* ✉ *Palace Rd., Ratnada* ☎ *291/251–2101, 291/251–2102* ⊕ *www.karnihotels.com* ⟿ *25 rooms, 5 suites* ❏ *No meals.*

$$
HOTEL

Pal Haveli. This 300-year-old haveli (family home) is in the heart of the chaotic labyrinth of central Jodhpur, with views of the Mehrangarh Fort above, and scores high on location and heritage. **Pros:** centrally located; fairly priced. **Cons:** no pool; congested traffic can make getting in and out difficult. $ *Rooms from: Rs. 5000* ✉ *Gulab Sagar, near clock tower, Jodhpur* ☎ *291/329–3328, 93504–08034 cell phone* ⊕ *www.palhaveli.com* ⟿ *21* ❏ *No meals.*

$$$$
HOTEL
Fodor'sChoice
★

Umaid Bhawan Palace. You can live like (and with) royalty at this magnificent palace—one of Rajasthan's grandest hotels—which has featured in many movies and hosted at least one international celebrity wedding. **Pros:** a haven away from the city; impeccable service; the massive lawn is great for walks. **Cons:** very expensive; not walking distance to the city center; some rooms lack privacy. $ *Rooms from: Rs. 32500* ✉ *Off S.H.61, north of Jodhpur Airbase* ☎ *291/251–0101* ⊕ *www.tajhotels.com* ⟿ *22 rooms, 42 suites* ❏ *No meals.*

NIGHTLIFE AND THE ARTS

If you're looking for nightlife, you'll find Jodhpur rather sedate; your best bet is one of the hotel bars, which are usually open from 11 am to 2:30 pm and 6 pm to 11 pm, though some bars, like the Trophy Bar at the Umaid Bhawan Palace, are only open to hotel guests.

Geoffrey's. This fully equipped bar is reminiscent of an English pub. It's popular among the upwardly mobile Jodhpuri crowd as well as with hotel guests. ✉ *Park Plaza Hotel, Airport Rd., Ratanada* ☎ *291/510–5000* ⊕ *www.sarovarhotels.com.*

Mehrangarh Fort. Festivals and exhibits are hosted here throughout the year; inquire at the Tourist Information Center *(see Planning section)* or your hotel to see if anything is going on while you're here. ✉ *Fort Rd.* ☎ *291/254–5083 (Tourist Information Center).*

OUTDOOR ACTIVITIES

Many hotels offer excursions to outlying villages, and most can arrange camel and jeep safaris on request.

Blue House Guest House. If your hotel doesn't arrange excursions, try Manish Jain at the Blue House Guest House; he organizes reasonably priced trips. ✉ *Sumer Bhawan, Moti Chowk* ☎ *291/262–1396* ⊕ *www.guesthousejodhpur.com.*

Inside Jodhpur's Mehrangarh Fort

☾ **Flying Fox.** This expat-owned outfitter runs zip-line tours of Mehrangarh
★ Fort, an extraordinary way to get dramatic views of the city. If you
book three days in advance you get a discount. Lower age limit is 10
years. ⊠ *Mehrangarh Fort* ☎ *98109–99390 cell phone, 291/211–1989*
⊕ *www.flyingfox.asia.*

SHOPPING

Sadar Bazaar. Jodhpur's vibrant bazaars are among the city's key sights,
particularly Sadar Bazaar and the Girdikot Bazaar, near the clock tower.
Wandering among the tiny shops dotting these crowded, narrow lanes
in the heart of town, you'll get a real feel for the life and color of
Marwari jewelry, underwear, steel utensils, kitchenware, leather shoes,
trinkets, wedding clothes—you can find just about everything here
(including locksmiths and indigenous dentists sitting side by side on
the street), many of the local spice merchants here deal in saffron and
other spices from all over India. Beware of tourist markups and young
men guiding you to their "uncle's store." There are also plenty of stores
to shop in if you don't like haggling in bazaars—most notably the
government-run emporium.

M.V. Spices. A wide selection of spices is available here, clearly marked
and packed in plastic for travelers with a passion for cooking Indian
food. There's also an outlet on Nayi Sadak, which is easier to find than
the main shop, and a stand at the entrance to Mehrangarh Fort. ⊠ *Shop
209B, Sadar Market, near clock tower* ⊕ *www.mvspices.com.*

For boutique shopping, visit Rani Bagh, a cluster of high-end retail
shops just outside the Ajit Bhawan hotel that sells antiques, silver jewelry, and clothing.

Amarpali. Come here for gorgeous traditional and contemporary silver and gold jewelry. ✉ *Shop no. 4, Rani Bagh, Ajit Bhawan, Circuit House Rd.* ☎ *291/325–0544* ⊕ *www.amrapalijewels.com* ☉ *Daily 11–8.*

Anokhi. The local outlet of the popular brand Anokhi sells good-value Western clothes with an Indian flair, including cotton and hand block prints. ✉ *Shop No. 5, Rani Bagh, Ajit Bhawan, Circuit House Rd.* ☎ *291/251–7178, 291/251–7179* ⊕ *www.anokhi.com* ☉ *Closed Wed. May–July.*

Gems & Jewels Palace. This good local jewelry store specializes in tradional bridal jewellery styled according to Rajasthani royal tradition. ✉ *Rani Bagh, Ajit Bhawan, Circuit House Rd.* ☎ *291/251–6666.*

Tulsi. Worth a stop for classic and contemporary textiles and home furnishings. ✉ *Circuit House Rd., next to Ajit Bhawan hotel, Rani Bagh* ☎ *291/510–2583* ⊕ *www.neerukumar.com.*

Elsewhere in Jodhpur are shops like the following.

Bhandari Exports. Wood items are designed according to customer requirements, while maintaining the roots of the artisans' creative process. Antiques are also sold. ✉ *Old Police Line, Raika Bagh* ☎ *291/251–0621.*

Lalji Handicrafts Emporium. Woodwork, antiques, leatherwork, and brass furniture feature in the collection here, which also includes unique painted boxes and *jharokhas* (carved doorways or windows) made of dark wood with brass decoration. This place is a joy if you love antiques. ✉ *Opposite Umaid Bhawan Palace* ☎ *291/251–7377* ⊕ *www. laljihandicrafts.com.*

National Handloom Corporation. For textiles, including cotton dress fabric, and other handicrafts—hidden among the rows of discounted toasters and kitschy house decorations—check out this four-story emporium. ✉ *Nayi Sadak* ☎ *291/506–1103, 291/503–1198.*

OFF THE BEATEN PATH

Guda Vishnoi. This is one of several immaculately kept villages of the Vishnoi community, a Hindu caste that takes its name from the 29 edicts its members agree to follow. In 1520, during a 20-year drought, the saint Jamboji came to the Vishnoi to ease their troubles by finding new water sources for them, and creating natural springs. Jamboji made a pact with the Vishnoi that if they accepted his commandments, they would never experience a water shortage again. The next year, the drought ended. The Vishnoi, who have faithfully kept to the teachings of Jamboji for almost 500 years, are one of Jodhpur's most distinct scheduled castes. Part of their pact was to respect the land and treat animals like their family—very protective of their environment, they look harshly on anyone who appears to hurt their sacred deer and antelope populations. Notable around here are the rare migratory birds, such as the godavan and sara cranes, that pass through the area. The Vishnoi are extremely outgoing and hospitable—they will invite you into their home for a cup of chai or *amala*, a mixture of opium and water traditionally reserved for special occasions and lazy days. Remember to bring your camera—you might just see a barasingha or blackbuck at dusk. Note that the area is difficult to navigate, as there are no real landmarks, so ask at your hotel or reputable travel agent for transportation arrangements and make sure you come with a tour guide. ✉ *25 km (16 miles) south of Jodhpur.*

JAISALMER AND ENVIRONS

The stark, compelling beauty of the Thar Desert draws travelers to far-western Rajasthan—for good reason. Jaisalmer, a medieval city resplendent with golden buildings and a towering citadel, is an intriguing city in its own right, and is an excellent base for camel safaris into the desert and for day trips to the photogenic Sam Sand Dunes and Desert National Park.

JAISALMER

Fodor'sChoice ★ *663 km (412 miles) northwest of Udaipur; 285 km (177 miles) northwest of Jodhpur; 570 km (354 miles) west of Jaipur.*

Jaisalmer seems like a mirage: its array of sandstone buildings are surrounded by the stark desert and illuminated in a gold hue by the sun. The medieval city is defined by its carved spires and palaces and the massive sandcastle-like fort that towers over the imposing wall that encircles the town. Jaisalmer is a remote and unusual city; it's out of the way, but it's worth it if you want to see a different side of India, and definitely if you want to take a camel safari.

Founded in 1156 by Rawal Jaisal, Jaisalmer is on the western edge of Rajasthan's Thar Desert, about 160 km (100 miles) east of the India–Pakistan border. The city started as a trade center: from the 12th through the 18th centuries, rulers here amassed their wealth from taxes levied on caravans passing through from Africa, Persia, Arabia, and Central Asia. Smugglers were also known to frequent Jaisalmer to work the profitable opium trade. The rise of Mumbai (known then as Bombay) as a major trading port in the 19th century, however, began to eclipse Jaisalmer.

Today Jaisalmer draws travelers attracted by the city's fairy-tale architecture and the mystery and harsh, remote charm of the desert. At night the golden fort is bathed in light, which illuminates its seemingly impregnable walls (most of the buildings inside are made out of yellow sandstone).

Jaisalmer is also known for its ornate 19th-century havelis—city mansions with facades so intricately carved that the stonework looks like lace. It's also worth wandering through the mazelike alleys and bazaars, although the shopkeepers here can be annoyingly pushy, perhaps because they see fewer tourists than elsewhere in Rajasthan.

Camel safaris are a good way to see the desert. These are great fun, but choose your outfitter carefully—don't skimp and choose a cheap one. Take a light scarf to protect your face in case of a sandstorm, wear sunglasses, and use sun protection lotion.

In terms of lodgings, you can stay inside the fort area, but most of the hotels and guesthouses are outside its golden walls; if you do choose to stay in the fort, make sure to choose accommodations that use sustainable plumbing methods, because an increase in tourism over the past few decades has led to an increase in water drainage and this, in turn, has caused structural damage to the fort's foundation.

5

GETTING HERE AND AROUND

Jaisalmer is not easy to reach. There is a small military airport, but at this writing there are no commercial flights, although there is talk of having a civil airport functional by the end of 2013. From Jodhpur, Jaisalmer is about six hours by car or train; from Jaipur the train ride is about 12 hours; from Delhi it's a grueling 17–18 hours by train. There are no direct trains to Jaisalmer from Udaipur.

With clean lanes, little traffic, and few crowds, Jaisalmer's fort and the surrounding areas are easily covered on foot (heat permitting), although you can also take an auto-rickshaw from the base of the fort to other parts of town. Rickshaws are not metered, so be sure to bargain and fix a price before setting off.

TIMING

Spend at least two nights in Jaisalmer. If you plan to go on a camel safari, set aside at least one extra night for this.

ESSENTIALS

Taxi Companies Hanuman Travels ✉ *Hanuman Circle* ☎ *2992/250–340.* **Swagat Travels** ✉ *Hanuman Circle* ☎ *2992/252–557, 2992/252–057.*

Tourist Offices Tourist Reception Centre ✉ *Near Gadsisar Lake Circle* ☎ *2992/252–406* ⊕ *www.rajasthantourism.gov.in.*

A GOOD TOUR

In Jaisalmer it's next to impossible to follow a straight path—the city is a maze of streets and passageways—so trust your instincts and don't be afraid to ask the locals for directions. You can't get too lost, because Jaisalmer is fairly small. The major landmark is the **Golden Fort,** which is every bit as labyrinthine as the rest of the city; allow several hours to explore the attractions within. After visiting there, walk north to the **Salim Singh-ki Haveli, Patwon-ki Haveli,** and **Nathmal-ki Haveli.** Finally, you can hail an auto-rickshaw—or hop a camel, if you've arranged this with a local travel agent the day before—and head southeast toward **Gadsisar Lake** and the nearby Folklore Museum. You can end your day with a puppet show at the Desert Culture Centre.

TIMING You can do this tour in a day. If you spend a second day in town, visit the royal cenotaphs at **Bada Bagh** and then head out of the city to **Sam Sand Dunes** for a sunset camel ride back.

WHAT TO SEE

TOP ATTRACTIONS

Bada Bagh. Outside of Jaisalmer proper and on the shore of an artificial lake, this site is home to a collection of cenotaphs of Jaisalmer's Rajput rulers. The gardens are especially notable, with so much lush greenery (when there's no drought) that they resemble a beautiful oasis. There are royal cenotaphs in the gardens as well, with canopies under which members of the royal family are buried. Notice the beautifully carved ceilings and equestrian statues of the former rulers. The city's vegetables and fruits were once grown here in the extensive gardens. ✉ *6 km (4 miles) northwest of Jaisalmer* 🖼 *Rs. 100; camera fee Rs. 50; video camera fee Rs. 150* ☉ *Daily 9–6.*

Desert Culture Centre. Near Gadsisar Lake, this center is run by the same person who runs the Folklore Museum, and admission to this interesting anthropological museum is included in the Folklore Museum entry fee (the two museums may end up in the same building in the future, so check before you visit). The culture centre has a collection of artifacts about music, culture, and life in the desert. They host daily puppet shows at 6:30, with another at 7:30 pm during peak season. ⊠ *Gadsisar Circle* ☎ *2992/253–723* 🖃 *Rs. 50 (free with admission to Folklore Museum); puppet show Rs. 50* ☉ *Daily 10–5.*

Fodor's Choice
★ **Golden Fort (Sonar Qila).** Jaisalmer's dazzling 12th-century fort, often likened to an oversized sandcastle, is unquestionably the most charming aspect of an already very charming city. Some 250 feet above the town, the fort has been inhabited for centuries; it's protected by a 30-foot-high wall and has 99 bastions, and several great *pols* (gateways) jut outward from the battlements. Built of sandstone and extremely brittle, the fort is rumored to be an architectural time bomb, destined to collapse in the face of a particularly aggressive sandstorm. So lovely is this structure that the poet Rabindranath Tagore (1861–1941) was inspired to write a poem *Sonar Kila* after seeing it; this, in turn, inspired another creative Bengali—Satyajit Ray made a famous film by the same name.

Inside the web of tiny lanes are Jain and Hindu temples, palaces, and charming havelis. The seven-story **Juna Mahal** (Old Palace), built around 1500, towers over the other buildings and is now home to the **Jaisalmer Fort Palace Museum and Heritage Centre.** A visit to the museum is worth the time: enter via the **Satiyon ka Pagthiya** (Steps of the Satis), where the royal ladies committed *sati*, self-immolation, when their husbands were slain. 🖃 *Free. Museum Rs. 300, includes audio tour; camera fee Rs. 100; video camera fee Rs. 200. Jain temples Rs. 30, camera fee Rs. 70; video camera fee Rs. 130* ☉ *Fort always accessible. Museum daily 9–5. Jain temples daily 8 am–noon.*

Jain temples. Make sure to visit the eight Jain temples within the fort. They were built from the 12th to 16th centuries, and house thousands of carved deities and dancing figures in mythological settings. There are a few rules to observe: photographing some sculptures is not allowed; you'll have to leave any leather items at the gate—Jains worship life in all forms, so leather is sacrilegious; and menstruating women are asked not to enter the temple. ⊠ *Inside Fort* 🖃 *Rs. 120, including camera fee* ☉ *Daily 8–noon.*

Gyan Bhandar. Within the fort, the Jain temple complex library contains more than 1,000 old manuscripts—some from the 12th century, written on palm leaf, with painted wooden covers—and a collection of Jain, pre-Mughal, and Rajput paintings.

Patwon-ki Haveli. Outside the fort, about 1½ km (1 mile) from the Gopa Chowk entrance, are the Patwon-ki Havelis—literally "five mansions"— a string of connected grand homes built by the Patwa brothers in the 1800s. The Patwas were highly influential Jain merchants back when Jaisalmer was an independent principality. The Patwa brothers forbade the repetition of any motifs or designs between their mansions,

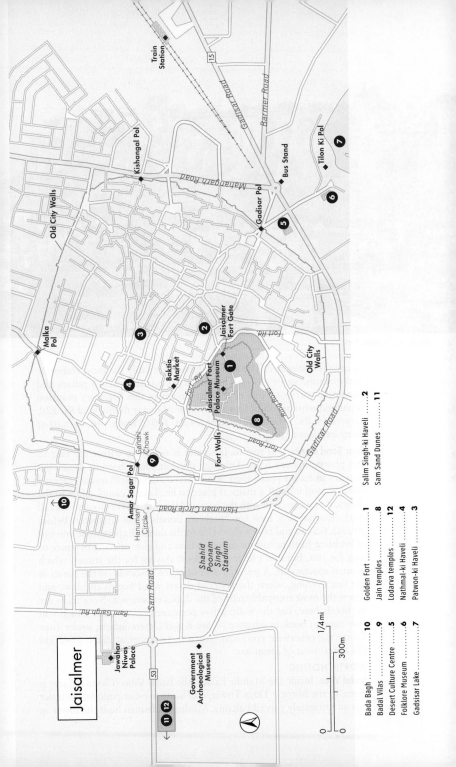

Jaisalmer

Train Station

Gadisar Road

Barmer Road

15

Old City Walls

Kishangal Pol

Mahangarh Road

Bus Stand

Tilon Ki Pol **7**

Gadisar Pol

6

5

Malka Pol

Jaisalmer Fort Gate

2

Fort Rd.

3

Bakhta Market

Fort Rd.

1

Jaisalmer Fort Palace Museum

Old City Walls

4

Fort Road

Fort Walls

8

Gandhi Chowk

9

Fort Road

Gadisar Road

Amar Sagar Pol

Hanuman Circle Road

10

Hanuman Circle

Sam Road

Shahid Poonam Singh Stadium

Ram Garh Rd

53

Jawahar Niwas Palace

Government Archaeological Museum

11 12

1/4 mi

0   300m

0

Bada Bagh **10**
Badal Vilas **9**
Desert Culture Centre **5**
Folklore Museum **6**
Gadsisar Lake **7**

Golden Fort **1**
Jain temples **8**
Lodarva temples **12**
Nathmal-ki Haveli **4**
Patwon-ki Haveli **3**

Salim Singh-ki Haveli **2**
Sam Sand Dunes **11**

Jaisalmer's "Golden Fort"

so each is distinctive. The first of these is arguably the most elaborate and magnificent of all—in addition to exquisitely carved pillars and expansive corridors, one of the apartments in this five-story mansion is painted with beautiful murals. ✉ *Near Mahavir Bhawan* 🎟 *Rs. 120; camera fee Rs. 100; video camera fee Rs. 100* ⏱ *Daily 9–6:30 (part of complex closed Sun.).*

★ **Sam Sand Dunes.** No trip to Jaisalmer is complete without a visit to this photographer's feast. Although the dunes have become somewhat touristy in recent years, their wind-carved ripples still create fantastic mirages, and it's still a magical place to be. Take a camel safari to the dunes, if you can cope with the heat and the time it takes to get here (all day). Alternatively, look for "parked" camels a few kilometers before you reach Sam, and take a short ride to the dunes. Expect some amount of heckling from persistent camel owners and girls offering to dance or sing for you, but don't let it put you off staying for the sunset, which is often spectacular. A peculiar sort of peace descends on the dunes in the late evening, when the icy cold desert wind begins to blow, and this is the most enjoyable part of the dunes experience. Note there are no hotels here, but there are a few permanent camps, for which you may need to book in advance (➪ *See Royal Desert Safaris, under Tour Contacts*); otherwise you must return to Jaisalmer at night. ✉ *42 km (26 miles) west of Jaisalmer.*

WORTH NOTING

Badal Vilas. Inside the Mandir Palace, the Badal Vilas (Cloud Palace) is home to the historic **Tazia Tower**, a delicate five-tier pagoda; each tier has an intricately carved balcony. Muslim craftsmen built the tower in the shape of a *tazia*—a replica of a bier carried in procession during Mohurram, a Muslim period of mourning. ✉ *Mandir Palace, Gandhi Chowk* 🎫 *Rs. 50* ⊙ *Daily 8–6.*

Gadsisar Lake (*Gadi Sagar Tank*). Built in the 12th century, this freshwater lake surrounded by numerous golden-hue shrines is frequented by a spectacular and diverse avian community. Plan for a camel ride, a picnic, and perhaps a short paddleboat excursion, and bring some bread to feed the catfish. ✉ *About 1 km (½ mile) southeast of Jaisalmer's fort* 🎫 *Free* ⊙ *Daily 10–5.*

Folklore Museum. Near the shrines and behind the main bus stand is the small Folklore Museum, built in the style of a traditional home.

Lodarva Temples. The founder of Jaisalmer, Rawal Jaisal, lived here before shifting his capital to Jaisalmer proper. The ruins of the former city are interesting: the Jain temple complex is known for its *nag devta* (snake god), a live snake that appears on auspicious days and nights. The snake is worshiped because, as legend goes, it has been protecting this temple for thousands of years. The temples are famous for their graceful architecture and detailed carving. ✉ *16 km (10 miles) northwest of Jaisalmer* 🎫 *Rs. 120 including camera* ⊙ *Daily 9–6.*

Nathmal-ki Haveli. Near the Patwon-ki Havelis, this 19th-century haveli was carved by two brothers, each working independently on his own half; the design is remarkably harmonious, though you can spot small differences. You can stop to admire the facade, but the family still lives inside. 🎫 *Free.*

Salim Singh-ki Haveli. The interior of this still occupied haveli, which was built in about 1815, is in sad disrepair, but the mansion's exterior is still lovely—it has an overhanging gallery on its top floor. Note the haveli's ventilation systems: the projecting windows and stone screens keep the buildings cool even in the searing summer months. 🎫 *Rs. 50; camera free; video camera fee Rs. 50* ⊙ *Daily 9–6.*

WHERE TO EAT

There aren't that many good restaurants in Jaisalmer, but these are our favorites. Otherwise, the better hotels are your best bet for a savory meal.

$ ✕ **8 July Restaurant.** Run by an eccentric Indo-Australian and his wife
CAFÉ Rama Bhatia, this restaurant serves simple snacks, pizzas, vegetable dishes, waffles, and wonderful coffee milk shakes throughout the day—the ice cream and freshly baked bread are made on the premises, from scratch. Indian dishes on the menu include egg curry and *pav bhaji* (vegetable curry with bread), a popular street-food snack served throughout Maharashtra and Mumbai. Homesick Brits and Australians should note that Marmite and Vegemite can be purchased here. The restaurant is just inside the fort, up a staircase, and has beautiful views of Jaisalmer's Old Palace. 💲 *Average main: Rs. 100* ✉ *Fort* ☎ *2992/252–814* ▭ *No credit cards.*

$ ✕ **Jaisal Italy.** At the base of the fort, this little Italian restaurant has a
ITALIAN lovely vibe, and the food is decent, too. The interior is simple yet far from rustic, and the open rooftop area is perfect for people-watching. The menu focuses on vegetarian Italian pasta dishes and pizza, as well

as good espresso and tiramisu. They also serve Spanish-style tortillas, quite a rarity in India. *Average main: Rs. 250* *by First Gate of fort* *2992/253–504* *No credit cards.*

$ NORTH INDIAN **K.B. Cafe.** Rajasthani vegetarian food is the specialty at this small family-owned rooftop restaurant, but don't expect the palate-burning dishes that Rajasthan is known for—the spice levels here are significantly toned down to suit the westerners. If you haven't yet tried the quintessentially Rajasthani dish *dal bati churma* (lentils, rolls, and sweetened wheat and butter paste, sort of the Rajasthani equivalent of bread and butter), this is the place to do so. For a taste of something local, try the Marwari Thali, an assortment of regional vegetarian dishes served with rice and chapatis. The café has Wi-Fi connectivity. *Average main: Rs. 150* *K.B. Lodge Hotel, Opposite Patwon ki Haveli* *2992/253–833* *No credit cards.*

$$ ECLECTIC **Saffron Restaurant.** The majority of the restaurants in Jaisalmer are vegetarian, prompting travelers in search of meat-based dishes to flock to this quiet rooftop restaurant at the Nachana Haveli hotel complex. The menu includes a variety of Indian food, as well as Chinese and Italian options, but the emphasis is on traditional Rajasthani dishes and tandoor (Indian clay oven roasts). Continental specialties include roast chicken with potatoes, as well as a selection of gratins and sizzling platters. There's also a large selection of all-day breakfast dishes. The restaurant sells beer, wines and other alcohol at very affordable prices. *Average main: Rs. 400* *Nachna Haveli Hotel, Goverdhan Chowk* *2992/252–110, 2992/255–565* *www.nachanahaveli.com.*

$$$ NORTH INDIAN **Trio.** Serving rich North Indian and Rajasthani food, as well as some Chinese and continental dishes, this rooftop restaurant is an old favorite with travelers. Try the *tandoori thali*, a combo platter of various chicken and vegetable items baked in a tandoor oven. Regulars like the *murg makhni* (butter chicken) and *baiga bhaji* (eggplant curry). The tented rooftop has a kitschy though charming look, with good views of the fort from the smaller open terrace area. Trio can get packed with prebooked tour groups, so check whether you need a reservation for dinner during the peak season. *Average main: Rs. 500* *Gandhi Chowk, near Amar Sagar Gate, Mandir Palace* *2992/252–733.*

WHERE TO STAY

For expanded hotel reviews, visit Fodors.com.

$$$ HOTEL **Fort Rajwada.** It might not be particularly convenient, but the architecture and interior design here are particularly interesting and the suites are nothing short of extravagant. **Pros:** beautiful architecture and interiors. **Cons:** outside town; unfriendly staff; can get busy with large tour groups. *Rooms from: Rs. 7500* *No. 1 Hotel Complex, Jodhpur-Barmer Link Rd.* *2992/253–233, 2992/254–608* *www.fortrajwada.com* *98 rooms, 5 suites* *Breakfast.*

$$$ HOTEL **The Gateway Hotel Rawalkot.** This cozy hotel on the edge of town, with a great view of the fort, has exceptionally warm staff and a deal more character than Jaisalmer's other modern hotels. **Pros:** quiet; friendly and helpful staff. **Cons:** a bit inconveniently located away from the main sights in Jaisalmer; availability of hot water is sometimes an

issue. $ *Rooms from: Rs. 9000* ✉ *Jodhpur Rd.* ☎ *2992/251–874, 2992/252–638* 🌐 *www.thegatewayhotels.com* 🛏 *31 rooms, 11 tents in season* 🍴 *No meals.*

$$$ HOTEL 🏨 **Gorbandh Palace.** This expansive retreat is a good option if you're looking for a break from the city center. **Pros:** spacious property; nice pool. **Cons:** slightly institutional looking rooms; corridors could do with better lighting. $ *Rooms from: Rs. 8000* ✉ *1 Tourist Complex, Sam Rd.* ☎ *2992/253–801 to 7* 🌐 *www.eternalmewar.in or www.hrhindia.com* 🛏 *80 rooms, 3 suites* 🍴 *Some meals.*

$$$ HOTEL 🏨 **Jawahar Niwas Palace.** Still owned by the Maharaja of Jaisalmer, this elegant palace, with spectacular views of the fort, has a kind of faded charm that some find appealing, while its large rooms and old-style furniture hint at past glories. **Pros:** elegant, old-fashioned setting; spacious lawns. **Cons:** bathrooms are in need of a refurb; lacks efficient service. $ *Rooms from: Rs. 6000* ✉ *1 Bada Bagh Rd.* ☎ *2992/252–208, 2992/252–288* 📠 *2992/250–540* 🌐 *www.jawaharniwaspalace.co.in* 🛏 *22 rooms* 🍴 *No meals.*

$$$ HOTEL 🏨 **Killa Bhawan.** The location of this ancient hotel, built into the walls of the fort, could not be better, the views are great, and its eco-friendly approach has merit. **Pros:** fabulous views from the terrace; room rate includes breakfast. **Cons:** approach past drains can be off-putting; plumbing problematic; some rooms have shared bathrooms; no bar, but alcohol available on request. $ *Rooms from: Rs. 6500* ✉ *Fort, 445 Kotri Para* ☎ *02992/251–204* 🌐 *www.killabhawan.com* 🛏 *5 rooms, 3 suites* 🍴 *Breakfast.*

$ HOTEL 🏨 **Nachana Haveli.** A 10-minute walk from the Golden Fort, this 18th-century haveli exudes old-world charm and is owned and run by descendants of the Maharaja Kesri Singh, who ruled over Jaisalmer during the 1700s. **Pros:** central; reasonably priced; free Wi-Fi. **Cons:** no pool; basic amenities; some windowless rooms. $ *Rooms from: Rs. 3500* ✉ *Gandhi Chowk* ☎ *2992/252–110, 2992/255–565* 🌐 *www.nachanahaveli.com* 🛏 *12 rooms, 2 suites* 🍴 *No meals.*

CAMEL SAFARIS

Safari prices vary dramatically depending on the itinerary and the level of tourist crush. You can book an excursion yourself, or have your hotel do it—but make sure you check exactly what you're going to get for the price asked. Camel safaris are slow; if you're pressed for time, try combining them with jeep travel. One option is to contact the Rajasthan Tourism Development Corporation's Tourist Reception Center (☎ *2992/252–406*) for reservations.

Royal Desert Safaris. The oldest and most-established agent in town offers trips to nearby villages and overnight sojourns in the desert. ✉ *Nachna Haveli, Gandhi Chowk* ☎ *2992/252–538, 2992/251–402* 🌐 *www.campsandsafaries.com.*

For more about camel safaris, see the "Camels: Ships of the Desert" boxed feature.

5

SHOPPING

Jaisalmer is famous for its mirror work, embroidery, and woolen shawls. Local artisans also make attractive, good-quality wooden boxes, silver jewelry, and curios. The main shopping areas are **Sadar Bazaar, Sonaron Ka Bas, Manak Chowk,** and **Pansari Bazaar,** all within the walled city, near the fort and temple areas. Sonaron Ka Bas, in particular, has exquisite silver jewelry. Avoid solicitors dispensing advice, take time to browse carefully, and bargain hard.

Khadi Graamudyog. This shop has *khadi* (hand-spun cotton) shawls, Nehru jackets, scarves, and rugs. There is also a branch outlet at Hanuman Chowk. ⊠ *Dhibba Para, near fort, in the walled city.*

Mumbai

WORD OF MOUTH

"Bombay . . . is definitely worth a visit, because it has a "buzz" (rather like NYC) and also a colonial feel since the British had a major base here."

—bombayteddy

WELCOME TO MUMBAI

TOP REASONS TO GO

★ **All of India in one city:** Mumbai is both modern and old-fashioned, rich and poor, beautiful and ugly—all of India concentrated in one metropolis.

★ **One big feast:** From down-home seafood joints to upscale temples of gastronomy, many of Mumbai's restaurants are the best in India.

★ **Experience India's bazaars:** The buzz of a typical Indian bazaar is fascinating, and Mumbai is packed with them; time to get shopping.

★ **Check out Chowpatty:** No visit to Mumbai would be complete without a nighttime stroll along this carnivalesque stretch of beach.

★ **The Ancient Caves of Ajanta and Ellora:** Take a side trip to see the awe-inspiring carvings and paintings, basing yourself in Aurangabad.

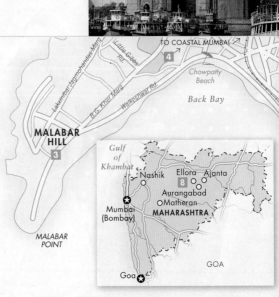

1 **Colaba.** The tip of Mumbai's peninsula is one of the oldest parts of the city, home to the majestic Taj Mahal Palace Hotel, the Gateway of India, and the Colaba Causeway, which is the city's main commercial drag.

2 **Fort and Marine Drive.** From the winding lanes of quaint Kala Ghoda (a tiny enclave within the Fort District) to the long promenade of Marine Drive, this neighborhood provides a good wander, and the best seafood in town.

3 **Malabar Hill and Environs.** Mumbai's richest neighborhood also houses some of the city's most important holy sites.

4 **Central Mumbai.** A bit of a no-man's-land when it comes to sightseeing, the densely populated center of the city does offer up a number of choice dining and lodging options.

5 **CST and Environs.** In the shadow of Mumbai's massive Victorian train station, this is where you'll find the city's best street food and the biggest, busiest bazaars.

6 **Elephanta Island.** Just a short ferry ride from South Mumbai lie the ancient caves of Elephanta: a historic getaway from the ultramodern city.

7 **Juhu, Bandra, and the Western Suburbs.** The neighborhoods along the northwestern side of the

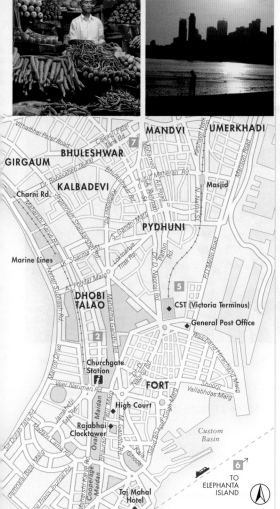

GETTING ORIENTED

Mumbai is not only India's largest city, it's also one of the largest cities in the world, both in size and population. Nearly 20 million are crammed into an area of a little more than 4,000 square km (1,600 square miles)— that's about 5,000 people per square km (11,000 people per square mile). On a peninsula jutting out of the western coast of India and facing the Arabian Sea, in the state of Maharashtra, Mumbai is roughly equidistant from the three other main Indian cities of New Delhi, Kolkata, and Chennai.

6

peninsula and on the suburban train line are growing fast. Juhu, probably the northernmost suburb tourists are likely to visit, offers a number of nice hotels, and Juhu Beach—great for a sunset walk. Bandra is home to Bollywood's studios, and where most of India's

biggest celebrities live. Other suburbs have restaurants that make a visit worthwhile.

8 Aurangabad and the Caves. Aurangabad, about 400 km (250 miles) east of Mumbai, is a base for exploring the astounding cave temples of Ellora and Ajanta.

EATING WELL IN MUMBAI

Mumbai has a robust tradition of eating out for cheap—you can dine out on a dime at working-class diners or stretch your dollar at bars and cafés—but it's also a modern metropolis with an exciting, extensive, and relatively affordable cosmopolitan dining scene.

(top left) A plate of bhel puri; (top right) Potato snacks on display in the Zaveri bazaar; (bottom right) A bowl of lamb dhansak

With its origins as a fishing village, Mumbai is blessed with a strong coastal culinary tradition. And because it's also a historic port of commerce, Mumbai also has absorbed influences from foreign traders and settlers (among them, Portuguese, Iranians, and Brits) and Indian communities that came here for trade. Maharashtrian food, marked by the use of peanuts, coconut, and chilies, dominates home cooking and the city's street-food options. Also significant are the culinary traditions of the Gujarati Hindu and Jains, and the Parsi populations of the city—the former two for their elaborate vegetarian contributions and the latter for its Persian- and British-influenced dishes. Regionally themed thalis are a popular way to sample an assortment of dishes from distinct cuisines.

DABBAWALAS

Dabbawalas, or tiffin carriers, are a symbol of Mumbai's industriousness. An institution since the late 1800s, they ensure that hundreds of thousands of professionals get fresh, home-cooked meals delivered daily to their offices. Wives and mothers fill containers, which are picked up and delivered by foot, bicycle, and train via a supply chain organized by an efficient system of coded marks.

BHEL PURI

Probably the most common street food you'll see in Mumbai is **bhel puri**; the crunchy, piquant, puffed-rice snack is sold on literally every street corner. Best savored during a stroll on Chowpatty Beach, *bhelwallas* blend the puffed rice with onion, tomato, coriander, and a sprinkling of powdered spices like cumin, rock salt, and chilli; a chutney made of tamarind, dates, and jaggery (a kind of brown sugar); and a chutney made of coriander, mint, green chillies, and peanuts. The addictive combination is tossed with fine shreds of fried gram flour and, sometimes, raw mango, then served on stitched-leaf plates.

PAV BHAJI

Pav, the local word for leavened bread, comes from the Portuguese *pão*; "bhaji" is a curried vegetable dish. The combination, **pav bhaji**, is served late into the night on Mumbai's streets, but also in fast-food places and even hotel restaurants. A spicy mash of potato that's been fried and simmered into an orange paste is sopped up with soft white-bread rolls that have been lightly toasted with butter on a griddle. Slivers of raw onion, a squeeze of lemon, and a coriander garnish add a sharp kick.

DHANSAK

The flagship dish of the Parsi community, **dhansak** is a labor-intensive production that constitutes the big weekend

meal. This stew always includes lentils and is usually made with lamb and vegetables like radishes and gourds. Dhansak lends itself to adaptation, though, and can be made with fish, chicken, or paneer. It's a filling dish that can be eaten with bread or rice.

BATATA VADA

Mumbai's answer to french fries, **Batata vada** are mashed-potato patties coated with batter and deep-fried into a crisp-and-soft salty snack that's irresistible when fresh. Both the potatoes (*batata*) and the gram-flour batter are spiced, and the fritters are served with green chilli chutney. Every Mumbai barfly has his favorite go-to spot for a postdrinking *vada pav*: a *batata vada* sandwiched in greasy, fried-bread bun. Yum.

MODAK

An unusual dish found in Mumbai and parts of south India is **modak**, a type of sweet dumpling. In Maharashtra, modak are usually prepared for the late-summer Ganesh Chaturthi holiday, as they're thought to be the favorite treat of the elephant-headed god celebrated on this day. Filled with coconut and unrefined sugar, these rice-flour dumplings can be steamed and eaten with ghee. Another version less particular to this region uses different flour and deep-fries the dumplings.

THE BAZAARS AND MARKETS OF MUMBAI

Mumbai is not a city for sightseeing in the traditional sense—it's more a destination that you need to experience through your five senses, and there's no better way to do this than by going shopping in one of the city's teeming bazaars.

(top left) Produce at Crawford market; (top right) A relics shop in Chor Bazaar; (bottom right) Flower garlands for sale

No one comes to Mumbai to shop at luxury boutiques—indeed, the locals don't, either, because high import taxes make it cheaper to buy name brands like Gucci abroad—they come to experience the racing pulse and frenzied pace of the markets. From handcarts tottering down crowded lanes, overloaded with antiques in Chor Bazaar, to succulent street food on the bylanes of Bhendi Bazaar, to the overwhelming madness of the wholesale trade at Crawford Market, to the glittering gold of Zaveri Bazaar, Mumbai knows how to shop. If you consider yourself a bargainer, this is the place to test your skills—Mumbai merchants are some of the trickiest in the world, so be prepared to cut whatever price you're quoted in half, and then in half again.

THE ART OF THE BARGAIN

Unlike other parts of the world, where bargaining can sometimes take on a mean-spirited tone, in India the back-and-forth is part of the joy of shopping. Here bargaining is a game both you and the merchant are in on, so have fun with it: he's going to go high, so you should go extremely low, then walk away when he won't come down. He'll call you back, with a smile on his face.

ANTIQUES, CHOR BAZAAR

Tourists—and locals—spend hours in crowded Chor Bazaar for the chance to dig out a hidden gem, lost for ages beneath mountains of ancient antiques. Although the market's best finds are probably long gone, there is still the chance you might get lucky with vintage furniture or prints from decades gone by, but only if you bargain, and bargain hard. Chor is the Hindi word for thief, and if you're not firm—or don't have a local to help you with your purchasing—you're likely to get taken for a ride. ■TIP→ Do a round of the bazaar, taking notes on the items you like and which stall they're in; then, if you have a local friend, send him or her around the next day to buy the items for you, at a fraction of the quoted price.

ANYTHING AND EVERYTHING (IN BULK), CRAWFORD MARKET

For an all-encompassing Mumbai market experience, look no farther than Crawford Market, where you can find everything from household goods to wholesale vegetables to live poultry to knickknacks—it's definitely worth checking out, even if you're not planning to buy any of the above. To see Crawford in all its glory, go on a weekday, when the market, housed in a 140-year-old British Raj–era building, is packed with housewives (or, more likely, their maids) bargaining over the price of Alfonso mangoes, tableware sets, and

ziplock bags. ■TIP→ Steer clear of the area that sells pets; the dogs, cats, and birds in this section of the market are not treated very well, and the scene can be quite depressing.

CLOTH, MANGALDAS MARKET

More than 1,000 shops cram the far side of Crawford Market, in an area called Mangaldas, where the best fabrics in town are available at rock-bottom prices (sold by the bolt). If you're looking to get Indian clothing made, this is the place to pick up the fabric you need. If you sew a little yourself, Mangaldas is a must-visit.

STREET FOOD AND JEWELRY, ZAVERI AND BHENDI BAZAARS

This pair of bazaars pretty much blend into one another, north of Crawford Market, and if you're looking for gold or, better yet, the best street food in Mumbai, this is the place to go. Shady is the name of the game here—from the money-laundering operations that most of the jeweler's in Zaveri engage in to the questionable hygiene of most of the street-food stalls on Khao Galli and Muhammad Ali Road; but if you want a great deal on jewelry, or have the stomach and the desire to taste the best of what Mumbai's carnivorous side has to offer, this is it.

MUMBAI'S HOLY SITES

Although it's not generally known for its religious heritage, Mumbai has a holy legacy going back hundreds of years, with sites dedicated to most of the world's major religions scattered throughout the city.

(top left) The Knesseth Eliyahoo synagogue; (top right) At the Haji Ali shrine; (bottom right) Mount Mary church, in Bandra

Not surprisingly, Hindu sites dominate any religious-oriented tour of Mumbai—from Siddhivinayak, central Mumbai's grand temple to Lord Ganesha, to Malabar Hill's peaceful, isolated Banganga water tank—but the city is also home to one of the world's most unique mosques (Haji Ali Shrine, whose location in the Arabian Sea means it's only accessible during low tide) and colorful synagogues (the sky-blue Knesseth Eliyahoo synagogue in Kala Ghoda). So if you need a break between booming bazaars and bumping bars—though, to be fair, some of these sites are likely to be just as busy as the hottest clubs in town—wander over to one of Mumbai's many temples, churches, mosques, or synagogues. *(Contact information is given here, unless there are full listings in the body of the chapter.)*

PAYING RESPECTS

How to be suitably respectful in a place of worship can be a little confusing—whether to take off your footwear, cover your head, or remove your hat. Keep the following in mind: If you see a pile of shoes outside a temple, remove yours as well; if you see a collection box in front of an idol, drop in a coin or two; and if you're still not sure what to do, ask a local.

HAJI ALI SHRINE

One of the most unusual mosques in the world lies in the middle of the Arabian Sea, just off one of Mumbai's busiest intersections. At high tide it looks like an isolated island in the middle of a bay. But during low tide the narrow 1 km (½-mile) pathway to the 500-year-old tomb is revealed. It's especially busy on Thursday and Friday, when upward of 40,000 pilgrims visit the site.

BANGANGA WATER TANK

According to the Hindu epic the *Ramayana*, the god Rama stopped at this spot while searching for his wife Sita, and asked his brother Lakshmana for some water. Lakshmana shot an arrow into the ground and water gushed out, creating what would become Banganga. The first water tank is said to have been built here in the 11th century, and a more formal version was constructed in the 1700s. The current tank, built in the early 20th century, is a serene spot.

SIDDHIVINAYAK TEMPLE

Pilgrims travel from far and wide—often on foot—to visit the Siddhivinayak Temple, dedicated to Ganesh, the elephant-headed god. The shrine is renowned throughout the Hindu world for its purported wish-granting properties, and attracts worshippers of every stripe—from Bollywood beauties to industrial titans to slum dwellers. Tuesday is Ganesh's day, and the road to

the temple is especially busy. ✉ *Prabhadevi, Central Mumbai* ☏ *22/2422–3206* ⊕ *www.siddhivinayak.org.*

KNESSETH ELIYAHOO SYNAGOGUE

This pale, light blue synagogue stands out among the gray and brown British Raj buildings of winding Kala Ghoda. It's worth a visit more for its exteriors than its interiors—the sparsely attended services are a reminder of Mumbai's dwindling Jewish population.

JAIN TEMPLE

Officially known as Babu Amichand Panalal Adishwarji Jain Temple, but usually just referred to as the Jain temple, this small but very opulent (thanks to its diamond merchant benefactors) temple sits atop Malabar Hill, full of ornate sculptures and elegant frescoes, and topped with an arched dome extravagantly emblazoned with the 12 signs of the zodiac. The Jain temple is a testament to the wealth and status of a people who make up but a fraction of one percent of the Indian population.

CATHOLIC BANDRA

Tucked between Bandra proper and Bandra Reclamation is the Catholic village of Bandra—a small slice of Goa here in the big city. With tiny, winding lanes, small bungalows, a few churches, and a simple, village atmosphere, it's an interesting place to wander if you're in the suburbs.

Updated by
Neil Munshi

Delhi may be the capital city, but it's Mumbai that encapsulates all the dynamic, chaotic parts that make up modern India. This is where you'll find everything from succulent street food to haute cuisine, bargain-basement bazaars to the finest haute couture, humbling poverty to staggering wealth, sacred temples to hedonist nightclubs. Mumbai *is* India—vibrant, hectic, frustrating, enervating, and exhilarating, warts and all.

Mumbai is a city of extremes, where slum-dwelling strivers making dollars a day serve Bollywood stars and industrial billionaires. It's a 24-hour city stocked with some of the best late-night street food in the world, as well as fine-dining restaurants of renowned chefs. It's a cosmopolitan city of people from all over India that's nonetheless home to strident parochialism. It's a city of dreams for millions of Indians that, at the same time, affords so few any measure of comfort. And it's a beautiful city of silver towers when viewed by twilight from the new Bandra-Worli Sea Link bridge over the Arabian Sea that connects the Western suburbs to the city, but which quickly descends into a maze of winding—often dirty—streets and alleys when viewed up close.

Sensory overload is the name of the game on the island formerly known as Bombay (and yes, many locals still call it by its previous moniker). The first thing that hits you when you arrive at the airport is the smell—spicy, fishy, and, to be honest, often not altogether pleasant. Next comes a crazed cab ride through the seemingly lawless streets (should your driver run a red light or, just as likely, drive on the wrong side of the road, remain calm). Then a traffic jam in the midst of a veritable symphony of honking, in which barefoot children, often holding infants, and tragically disfigured men and women knock at your window, begging for change. Persevere through, though; embrace and try to understand the natural hazards of the Third World, and you'll find yourself in the middle of a vibrant, often beautiful city.

PLANNING

WHEN TO GO

HIGH SEASON: DECEMBER TO MARCH

Every year, Mumbaikars wait for the one-month period between mid-January and mid-February when the weather turns breezy and clear—a welcome respite from the sweltering heat (or pouring rain) that otherwise swamps the city. If you hit that sweet spot, you're gold—and you'll have also just missed NRI season, when the Non-Resident Indian relatives of locals visit from abroad during Christmas vacation (and prices explode). Because most tourists arrive in Mumbai in winter, it's important to make hotel and transportation arrangements ahead of time.

LOW SEASON: APRIL TO MID-SEPTEMBER

Mumbai's first summer starts at the tail end of March and lasts until the monsoon hits, usually in mid-May; the rainy season lasts until mid-September, when another hot season comes around. None of these times are particularly pleasant—it is ungodly hot, then raining buckets, and then ungodly hot again. But those willing to test their mettle will find two joyous surprises: low lodging prices, and a monsoon that is not nearly as bad as you'd imagined (though hardly a walk in the park).

SHOULDER SEASON: MID-SEPTEMBER TO NOVEMBER

The Hindu festival season, when there seems to be (and often is) a religious holiday every other day, begins in August, but really starts rolling in September, attracting both domestic and international tourists. It will be hot, but the Ganpati festival—which sees the city transport massive idols of the elephant-headed god, Ganesh, to the sea—and other such festivities may just make it worth the sweat.

GETTING HERE AND AROUND

AIR TRAVEL

Mumbai's international airport, Chhatrapati Shivaji International Airport, previously called Sahar International Airport—note that it may be helpful to give your taxi driver that name (Sa-hair) when you're on your way to the airport, instead of trying to pronounce the new one, to avoid confusion—is 30 km (19 miles) north of the city center in Sahar. The domestic airport is at Santa Cruz, 4 km (2½ miles) away from the international airport. Arrive at the airport at least 75 minutes before takeoff for domestic flights, two to three hours before international flights (some airlines require three hours). ■TIP→ **Mumbai airports are packed to their gills these days, and there are long queues for scanning luggage and checking in.** However, in recent years a huge effort has been put into renovating both airports (international and domestic), and things are finally looking up. The recently renovated domestic airport is now one of India's finest airports, and is of international standard. Both airports have 24-hour business centers available to holders of major credit cards.

Most international flights arrive in the middle of the night. Be prepared: Airports in Mumbai, like those in Delhi, Kolkata, or Chennai, may be among the poorest run, compared to those in other countries. Because airports typically run at or beyond capacity, many flights arrive at the same time, and luggage belts and trolleys are few. Your luggage may arrive after an interminable wait. ■TIP➔ Make sure you secure a free baggage trolley first and send the touts (and assorted individuals posing as porters, luggage loaders, personal trolley pushers, hotel/taxi providers, or customs clearance aids) packing. Station yourself close enough to the right belt; check any stacks of luggage lined up against the wall in case your suitcases have come earlier.

If you have a lot of luggage, you can get a porter as soon as you disembark—right at the door of the airplane—they work for the airport and are identifiable by their uniforms. If you hire one, get his name, and he will meet you after you go through immigration, at the baggage belt. Do not negotiate rates beforehand—if he tries to do so, hire someone else. Pay him between Rs. 100 and Rs. 300 depending on how helpful he's been.

Immediately after you exit the customs hall there is a row of tourist counters for hotels, taxi hire, car hire, tourist information, and cell-phone-cards, and currency exchange booths. If someone is meeting you at the airport, understand that he or she will have no idea when you will emerge from the airport, given the wait at immigration or at the baggage concourse, so don't panic.

AIRPORTS AND TRANSFERS
The trip from Chhatrapati Shivaji International Airport downtown to south Mumbai should take about 45 minutes if you arrive before 7:30 am or after 11 pm (many international flights arrive around midnight). At other times, traffic near the city center can increase your trip by as much as 90 minutes. Most hotels provide airport transfers starting at Rs. 900 and going up to Rs. 2,500; some offer complimentary transfers if you're staying in a suite or on an exclusive floor or if the hotel is close to the airport.

To avoid hassles with taxis over prices, we strongly recommend heading to the prepaid-taxi counter outside the baggage-and-customs area to hire a regular cab, either air-conditioned or non-air-conditioned. Your rate is determined by your destination and amount of luggage, and is payable up front; Rs. 450 by day and Rs. 500 at night should get you to the center of town from the international airport, and from the domestic airport Rs. 50 less (tips aren't necessary). If you want an air-conditioned taxi and do not spot one, call Group Mobile Cool Cab Service or Gold Cabs, but remember, you'll have to wait even longer. Air-conditioned taxi fares are 25% higher than non-air-conditioned cabs. A trip to Colaba, for example, from the international airport will set you back Rs. 450 by day and Rs. 500 at night, and from the domestic airport Rs. 50 less. A word to the squeamish: Most of the standard black-and-yellow cabs operating in Mumbai were built well over 20 years ago and seem to be held together by little more than duct tape and the driver's ingenuity. If you end up with an old Prestige (modeled on a Fiat), expect to see dirty, smelly upholstery (the drivers also sleep in the cars), a jerry-rigged trunk, and, quite possibly, a hole or two in the rusted metal floor. If you're on a budget, it's the way to go; but if you can afford it, spring for an overpriced Avis car, which includes a driver.

SOME MUMBAI HISTORY

Mumbai initially consisted of seven marshy islands—Colaba, Old Woman's Island, Bombay, Mazgaon, Worli, Mahim, and Parel—that belonged to the Muslim kings of the Gujarat sultanate. The Muslims passed the parcel to the Portuguese (who occupied much of western India in the 16th and 17th centuries), who in turn passed it in 1661 to England's King Charles II as part of a dowry in his marriage to the Portuguese Princess Catherine de Braganza. The British established a fort and trading post that grew quickly in size and strength.

Soon enough, land reclamation joined the seven small islands into one, grafting a prototype for today's multifarious metropolis—today the islands, except for Old Woman's Island, are neighborhoods within Mumbai.

The pride of the British in Bombay, and in their power over western India, is memorialized in the city's most celebrated landmark—the Gateway of India, built to welcome King George V to India in 1911. Ironically, it's now near a statue of the young 17th-century Marathi leader, Shivaji.

■ TIP➡ Even though metered taxis are available outside the domestic airport, and a police officer notes the taxi's license plates before dispatching you on your way, we advise against taking one. The cabbies waiting at the domestic airport are often cheats with meters that run double-time.

A metered (not prepaid) taxi from the domestic airport to the downtown/south Mumbai area should cost about Rs. 300, and from the international airport about Rs. 350 (more expensive at night). In any case, do not take a taxi that's outside the queue, or accept the offer of a taxi that's parked somewhere that requires you to walk out of the main airport area.

Finally, keep in mind that the route over Mumbai's brand-new Bandra-Worli Sea Link will cost you an extra Rs. 75, exclusive of what you've prepaid. The bridge, which cuts travel from the leafy Bandra to not-quite-midway-point Worli from 40 minutes to 7, offers stunning views of the ever-growing Mumbai skyline, and is definitely worth the extra money to save time.

Airport Information Chhatrapati Shivaji International Airport ⊕ *www.csia. in.* **Gold Cabs** ☎ *22/3244–3333, 22/3244–9999* ⊕ *www.mumbaigoldcabs.com/ index.asp.* **Group Mobile Cool Cab Service** ☎ *22/2490–5151, 22/2490–5152.*

BUS TRAVEL
For inner-city travel, Mumbai has a good bus system, but navigating long routes and big crowds make it highly inadvisable.

CAR TRAVEL
Fairly good roads connect Mumbai to most major cities and tourist areas. Hiring a car and driver gives you a chance to watch the often-beautiful surroundings whiz by. Note that the driving can also be loud, hair-raising, and is definitely less than time-efficient for long distances.

Some distances from Mumbai: Aurangabad 388 km (241 miles); Panaji (Goa) 597 km (371 miles); Delhi 1,408 km (875 miles); Kochi (Kerala) 1,384 km (860 miles).

CARS AND DRIVERS In certain areas, such as bazaars, you really have to walk for the full experience. Aside from these, having a car at your disposal is the most convenient way to travel around Mumbai, as you can zip (or crawl, depending on the time of day) around town without the repeated hassle of hailing taxis and haggling over fares. To arrange a hired car, inquire at your hotel's travel desk or contact a travel agency (you'll probably pay much more if you book through your hotel). You'll get lower rates from private agents like Adarsh, Euro Cars, or Travel House: Rs. 1,600 to Rs. 1,800 for a full day (8 hours, or 80 km [50 miles]) in a car (Uno or Indica; small cars) with air-conditioning, and Rs. 1,500 or more for an air-conditioned sedan car like a Maruti Esteem. Rates go up for Toyotas, Mercedes, and other luxury cars.

GANESH CHATURTHI

For two weeks every year, usually between August and September, Mumbai explodes with impromptu parades to celebrate Lord Ganesha, the elephant-headed god. During the Ganesh Chaturthi festival, idols of the god are worshipped throughout the city and then taken to the sea to be immersed—and no beach is quite as popular as Chowpatty. If you happen to be in Mumbai during this time, you'll witness thousands of people walking, dancing, and singing down the street toward Chowpatty, where elaborately adorned idols as small as six inches and as large as three stories are dunked into the water.

Contacts Adarsh Rent a Car ✉ *Asmita Mogra Co-op. Soc., Bldg. No. 3, Shop No. 3, Jijamata Marg, Andheri East* ☎ *22/2837–7294, 22/3096–9675.* **Euro Cars** ✉ *105 Madhava, Bandra Kurla Complex, Bandra East* ☎ *22/2659–2929, 22/4074–4074* ⊕ *www.eurocars-india.com.* **Travel House** ✉ *Crescent Business Park, 301/302, Andheri Kurla Rd., 3rd fl. Near Saki Naka Telephone Exchange, Andheri East* ☎ *22/4077–4071, 22/4077–4072* ⊕ *www.travelhouseindia.com.*

TAXI AND AUTO-RICKSHAW TRAVEL

Mumbai's sights are spread out, so getting around by taxi is a sensible—and cheap—option. You can flag down yellow-top black taxis anywhere in the city. Insist that the driver turn on the meter, a rusty contraption on the hood of the car, before setting off—in fact, if you turn the meter yourself, the driver is less likely to scam you. Because the meters haven't been adjusted for quite some time, it takes some arithmetic to compute the latest (higher) fares, based on the meter reading. Drivers must show you their revised tariff cards, but they sometimes "misplace" them, or whip out a chart for air-conditioned cabs, or show you fares chargeable after midnight. At this writing the legal fare was around 17 times the total amount shown on the meter, based on roughly Rs. 17 for the first kilometer and about Rs. 10 for each additional kilometer.

Silver-and-blue air-conditioned taxis can also be flagged—the rates are about 25% higher, usually Rs. 22 for the first kilometer and Rs. 14 for each subsequent, but the cabs are new and comfortable.

In the last few years on-call air-conditioned taxi services have been springing up—and the drivers are usually reliable. Meru and MegaCab are the best services, but even they can miss your scheduled pick-up time, so book the car for at least a half-hour earlier than you actually have to leave if you're headed to the airport. Still, they're generally worth it for the sheer comfort.

You can hire an air-conditioned taxi for a full day (8 hours or 80 km [50 miles], whichever comes first) for Rs. 1,000, and a half day (4 hours) for Rs. 550. Ask your hotel what the going rates are in case they've gone up. ■TIP➜ Hiring a car and driver is much cheaper than hiring a taxi for extended periods, and you can negotiate your price. Also, because there is no contract, you're not locked in, and if you don't like a particular driver, you can hire a different one the next day.

Auto-rickshaws are permitted only in Mumbai's suburbs, beyond Bandra, where you can flag them down on the street. As with regular taxis, insist on paying by the meter and ask to see the tariff card.

Both Mega Cabs and Meru Cabs have an automated phone system, but if you stay on the line you'll eventually speak to an agent, and they'll send a confirmation by text message.

Contacts **Mega Cabs** ☎ 22/4242–4242 ⊕ www.megacabs.com. **Meru Cabs** ☎ 22/4422–4422 ⊕ www.merucabs.com.

TRAIN TRAVEL

Mumbai has two main train stations for travel outside of Mumbai (they also both act as stations for the local railroad). Chhatrapati Shivaji Terminus, more commonly called Victoria Terminus, is the hub of India's Central Railway line. Mumbai Central Station is the hub of India's Western Railway line. Make sure to go to the right train station.

To avoid the pandemonium at the stations, have a travel agent book your ticket; this costs a bit more but saves time and stress. Or book online: Indian Railways has a decent website (⊕ *www.indianrailways. com*) or, better yet, go to ⊕ *www.yatra.com*—India's version of Expedia—where you can now book Indian Railway tickets in a much more user-friendly format. For information on confirming a ticket or on arrivals and departures ask a local to make the phone call.

If you decide to book in person, head for the tourist counter established specially for foreign travelers. Eliciting information about trains on the telephone is usually impossible—local stations have no phone number, the national lines are usually busy, and the interactive voice-response numbers are in Hindi.

Train Information **Chhatrapati Shivaji Terminus** *(CST, Victoria Terminus, or VT).* ⊠ *D. Naoroji Rd.* **Mumbai Central Station** ⊠ *Adjacent to Tardeo, Central Mumbai.*

EMERGENCIES

Pharmacies (chemists) in Mumbai are usually open daily until about 9 pm, and most hotels have house physicians and dentists on call. The chemists at Nanavati Hospital and Royal Chemists are both open 24 hours. Your consulate can also give you the name of a reputable doctor or dentist. Otherwise, try the emergency room at Breach Candy

Playing cricket in one of Mumbai's public parks

Hospital and Research Center or Jaslok Hospital. Mumbai emergency services can't respond to an emergency as quickly as these services do in parts of the world with better roads and more manageable traffic.

Medical Care Breach Candy Hospital and Research Center ✉ *60 Bhulabhai Desai Rd., Breach Candy* ☏ *22/2367–1888, 22/2367–2888.* **Jaslok Hospital** ✉ *Dr. G. Deshmukh Marg, near Haji Ali, Peddar Rd.* ☏ *22/6657–3333.* **Lilavati Hospital** ✉ *Bandra Reclamation* ☏ *22/2642–1000.*

24-Hour Pharmacies Bombay 24 Hour Chemist ✉ *New Marine Lines, near Bombay Hospital, Marine Drive* ☏ *22/2200–4051, 22/2200–5070.* **Nanavati Hospital 24 Hour Chemist** ✉ *SV Rd., Juhu* ☏ *22/2618–7038.*

VISITOR INFORMATION

Don't count on hotels to stock general tourist information. The Government of India Tourist Office, near the Churchgate train station, has useful material; it's open weekdays 8:30–6, Saturday and holidays 8:30–2. There's information on trains, and the office oversees knowledgeable, multilingual tour guides, available directly from the office or through the MTDC (Maharashtra Tourism Development Corporation), or just about any travel agency. Rates are approximately Rs. 500 per half-day for groups of one to four, Rs. 700 for a full eight-hour day (your guide will have lunch when you do, and you should pay for his lunch). Additional fees of Rs. 350 apply for trips beyond 100 km (62 miles), and for those involving overnight stays the rates could be still higher. Multilingual guides charge Rs. 300 extra, in addition to the regular fee.

The MTDC is open daily 9–6. Both MTDC and the Government of India Tourist Office have 24-hour counters at the airports. The MTDC also has counters at Chhatrapati Shivaji Terminus (Victoria Terminus) and the Gateway of India (it's a booth where the boats to Elephanta Island dock). MTDC phone numbers are not that useful, as they are always busy—visit in person or check the website.

Tourist Offices Government of India Tourist Office ⊠ *123 Maharishi Karve Rd., Churchgate* ☏ *22/2207–4333, 22/2207–4334, 22/2203–3144, 22/2203–3145 recorded tourist background on Goa, Mumbai, Ahmedabad, and Aurangabad* ⊕ *www.incredibleindia.org.* **Maharashtra Tourism Development Corporation (MTDC)** ⊠ *Madame Cama Rd., opposite L.I.C. Building, Nariman Point* ☏ *22/2284–5678* ⊕ *www.maharashtratourism.gov.in.*

PLANNING YOUR TIME

Spending two days in Mumbai is like sprinting a marathon. Even though the city may lack monuments and historic sites, this is a place you have to experience to understand (and enjoy). Try cramming all of Mumbai into two days and you're likely to end up hating it, but give it a little longer and the abstract cacophony will start to make more sense and, ultimately, grow on you. Otherwise, the only impression you're likely to get is: hot, crowded, smelly, filthy. Give it a bit of time, and you'll begin to appreciate the madness, as opposed to being overwhelmed by it. So, we suggest spending a week in Maharashtra, with 4–5 days in Mumbai and a weekend trip to the Ellora and Ajanta caves, 370 km (229 miles) northeast of the city—you can take a round-trip overnight train for about Rs. 1,200 to Aurangabad, the best place to base yourself for trips to the caves; but for the time-crunched, one-way, one-hour flights cost around Rs. 3,000. If you have an extra day or two, head up to Matheran (110 km [66 miles] away) or one of the other quaint hill stations nearby, where Maharashtra's landscape fuses stark, semiarid mountains, and rock formations with lush, green countryside.

In Mumbai it's important to catch the flavor of the colonial city: This means walking around the Gateway of India, the Prince of Wales Museum, and Victoria Terminus. To take in a bazaar, head to Crawford Market or stroll down Colaba Causeway to do some bargain hunting. Lunching at a seafood restaurant in Fort and snacking at Chowpatty Beach off Marine Drive are both great experiences, as is people-watching with a beer at Leopold Café in Colaba. A trip to the western suburbs—Bandra and Juhu, among others—will give you a good perspective on how the city has grown, and where it's going next. A day trip to the ancient Elephanta Caves will show you where it came from.

DISCOVER DHARAVI

Slum tours. In recent years so-called "slum tours" of one of Asia's largest slums, Dharavi, have become something of a cottage industry in Mumbai, especially after the popularity of the movie *Slumdog Millionaire*, which was set here. While the idea may seem akin to "poverty voyeurism," many of the companies who conduct the tours do so on a not-for-profit basis, and have explicit no-camera-allowed policies.

THE GREAT BOMBAY NAME CHANGE

In the mid-1990s, a far-right government decided to change Bombay's name to Mumbai, a name often used in local languages, and which comes from Mumba Devi, the patron Hindu goddess of the island's original residents, the Koli fishermen. Many residents still call their city Bombay, however. The renaming of the city was simply the grandest example of an epidemic that has swept the former Bombay in the last 20 or so years—Crawford Market became Mahatma Jyotiba Phule Market, Victoria Terminus became Chhatrapati Shivaji Terminus, Marine Drive became Netaji Subhash Chandra Bose Marg. And those are just the big ones; indeed, nearly every road and lane in Mumbai has more than one name. Not only that, but each intersection often has its own name, too, and each individual corner might also have its own moniker (they're often named by local government officials or rich locals for members of their families).

The fact is, though, that as a tourist—and even as a local—you don't need to know any of the new names: No one calls Marine Drive anything but Marine Drive, and no one calls the Causeway anything but the Causeway. Although you will get the odd "CST" for Victoria Terminus, no one uses the new full name, so don't worry about pronouncing it: VT will do just fine.

On such a tour you'll normally meet up with a guide at Churchgate or Mahim Station, and take the train with a group of no more than six other tourists to Dharavi, which is near the Mahim neighborhood. Here you'll see the variety of cottage industries—from jewelry making to recycling to leather working to blacksmithing—that make up an estimated US$600 million dollar annual economy. You'll see poverty, but Dharavi is not the kind of place you saw in those early scenes in *Slumdog*: it's a vibrant, functioning community, with its own post office, schools, temples, mosques, churches, and police force. It is, on balance, an incredibly safe place (and you'll be with a local guide) full of people striving for a better life in Mumbai, willing to live in cramped confines and not knowing where their next meal will come from—or even if there will be a next meal. One of the most popular tour operators, Reality Tours and Travel, explicitly takes no tips, and makes no profit: they use the fees (Rs. 400 per person) to fund a community center and a kindergarten in the area. ✉ *Mumbai* ☎ *98208–22253* ⊕ *www.realitytoursandtravel.com.*

In South Bombay—"Town" to the locals—colonial mansions, remnants of the British Raj, share space with towering high-rises, and long, rectangular parks, known as *maidans*. To the east, in the labyrinthine streets of Kala Ghoda, the sky-blue Knesseth Eliyahoo synagogue looms. South, the majestic Taj Mahal Palace Hotel holds court with the massive Gateway of India. On the western coast, the Queen's Necklace—as the lights along Marine Drive are affectionately known—stretches out past the carnival food and games of Chowpatty Beach to tony Malabar Hill, where the Hanging Gardens provide some of the city's best nonskyscraper views. Farther north, the Haji Ali shrine, a popular pilgrimage spot for Muslims the world over, sits in the middle of the Arabian Sea like an ancient island tomb. Beyond that, the brand-new Bandra-Worli Sea Link connects the south to leafy Bandra, the king of the western suburbs, where Bollywood stays and plays. In between, and beyond, lie the very things that make Mumbai so confounding, and alluring, and so quintessentially Indian.

EXPLORING MUMBAI

There's plenty to see in Mumbai, but it's not generally in the form of stationary monuments like those in London, Paris, or Delhi. The art of experiencing Mumbai lies in eating, shopping, and wandering through the strikingly different neighborhoods and the various markets. Think of Mumbai as a 50-km (30-mile) -long open-air bazaar.

Colaba, headed by Gateway of India, is the tourist district and main drag for visitors, and from the Gateway of India to Colaba Market, along the main road, is a walkable stretch of hotels, pubs, restaurants, and interesting shops. Churchgate and Nariman Point are the business and hotel centers, and major bank and airline headquarters are clustered in skyscrapers on Nariman Point.

The district referred to as Fort—which includes Mumbai's hub, Flora Fountain—is filled with narrow, bustling streets lined with small shops and office buildings, as well as colleges and other educational facilities. Another upscale residential neighborhood, Malabar Hill, north of Churchgate on Marine Drive, is leafy and breezy, with fine, old stone mansions housing wealthy industrialists and government ministers.

Shopping and people-watching are most colorfully combined in Mumbai's chaotic bazaar areas, such as Chor Bazaar, Zaveri (jewelry) Bazaar, and Crawford Market (aka Mahatma Jyotiba Phule Market). Many of the city's newest and trendiest shops and restaurants are now out in the suburbs—where more and more people have been moving due to soaring real-estate prices and a lack of space—but South Mumbai still retains some of the very best.

Some travelers opt to stay in the suburbs, either in Bandra, at the end of the new Bandra-Worli Sea Link, or in Juhu, a popular coastal suburb between Mumbai and the airports (about 20 km [12 miles] north of the city center). Juhu's beaches aren't clean enough for swimming, and the place can be scruffy, but staying out here is a good way to observe everyday Indian life beyond the shadow of Mumbai's skyline. Sunday nights bring families down to the beach for an old-fashioned carnival, complete with small, hand-powered Ferris wheels, and lantern-lit snack stalls hawking sugarcane.

COLABA

Mumbai's hot spot—full of bars, restaurants, and a long stretch of street stalls selling everything from clothing to black-market DVDs to brassware and handicrafts set in front of name-brand stores from Nike, Puma, Lacoste, and many others—Colaba is a bit of a one-stop shop for

The Gateway of India, with the Taj Mahal Palace hotel in the background

all of Mumbai. Beginning at Regal Circle, which is named for the 1930s art deco Regal Cinema, Colaba stretches southward, through winding lanes and bustling streets. You can stop by the Taj Mahal Palace Hotel for high tea and gaze out at the Gateway of India, standing sentinel over the sea, then wander up through cramped lanes filled with shops to the Colaba Causeway, South Mumbai's main drag. On the Causeway, you can haggle for knockoffs and bootlegs—start at one-third the asking price, at a maximum—or shop in the "official" stores if you're not in the bargaining mood, then stop in at Leopold Café or Café Mondegar for a beer, a snack, and some people-watching before heading deeper down into Colaba, where more stores, bargains, bars, and food await. Colaba is an easy place to end up spending an entire day just wandering, eating, drinking, and shopping with nothing particular in mind, so plan on spending some time here.

WHAT TO SEE

Elephanta Caves. A quick 30-minute ferry ride from bustling South Mumbai, the Elephanta Caves are an ideal half-day trip for anyone who wants a relatively quick glimpse of India's ancient history. Once you arrive at the island, you climb a steep hill, on rough-hewn steps, past trinket sellers and beggars, to get to Shiva Cave; greenery abounds. The temple, carved out of the basalt hillside, is 130 square feet. Inside, each wall has elaborate, 16-foot-tall rock carvings of Lord Shiva, the destroyer, in his many forms, depicting famous events from the Hindu epics. The main sculptures are on the south wall, at the back.

The central recess has the most outstanding sculpture, the unusual Mahesamurti, the Great Lord Shiva—an 18-foot triple image. Its three

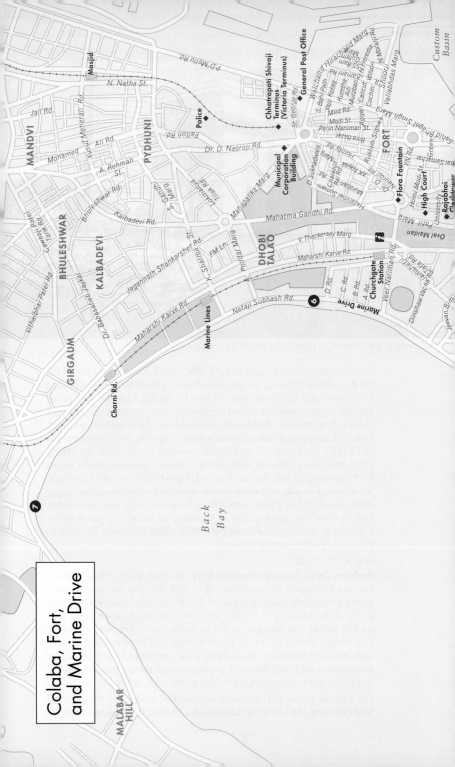

Colaba, Fort,
and Marine Drive

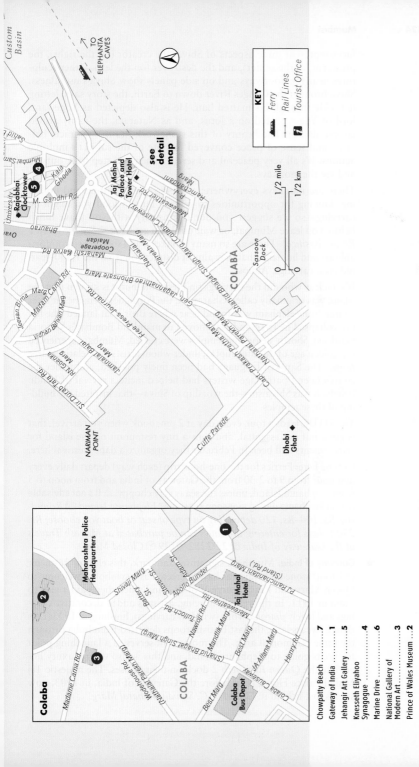

Colaba

Maharashtra Police Headquarters

Shivaji Marg
Apollo Bunder
Adam St.
Steren St.
Battery St.
Tulloch Rd.
Nawroji Rd.
Mandlik Marg
P J Ramchandani Marg
Taj Mahal Hotel
Shahid Bhagat Singh Marg
Meherwather Rd.
Madame Cama Rd.
Wodehouse Rd. (Nathalal Patch Marg)
Colaba Causeway (Shahid Bhagat Singh Marg)
Best Marg
Best Marg
Best Marg
Henry Rd.
JA Allana Marg
Colaba Bus Depot
(Stand Rd.)
COLABA

Custom Basin
TO ELEPHANTA CAVES

University
Rajabhai Clocktower
M. Gandhi Rd.
Kala Ghoda
Bhaurao
Oval
Maharshi Karve Rd.
Cooperage Maidan
Cross Maidan
Barrack Marg
Natraj
Taj Mahal Palace and Tower Hotel
see detail map
P. J. Ramchandani Marg
Meherwather Rd.
Jeevan Bima Marg
Madam Cama Marg
Vidhan Bhavan Marg
Free Press Journal Rd.
Gen. Jagannathrao Bhonsale Marg
Capt. Prakash Pethe Marg
Nathalal Parekh Marg
Shahid Bhagat Singh Marg
Jamnalal Bajaj Marg
RN Goenka Marg
Sir Durab Tata Rd.
NARIMAN POINT
Cuffe Parade
COLABA
Sassoon Dock
Dhobi Ghat
Mumbai Samachar Marg
Sand

KEY
Ferry
Rail Lines
Tourist Office

0   1/2 mile
0   1/2 km

Chowpatty Beach 7
Gateway of India 1
Jehangir Art Gallery 5
Knesseth Eliyahoo Synagogue 4
Marine Drive 6
National Gallery of Modern Art 3
Prince of Wales Museum ... 2

faces represent three aspects of Shiva: the creator (on the right), the preserver (in the center), and the destroyer (on the left). Other sculptures near the doorways and on side panels show Shiva's usefulness. Shiva brought the Ganges River down to Earth, the story says, letting it trickle through his matted hair. He is also depicted as Yogisvara, lord of Yogis, seated on a lotus, and as Nataraja, the many-armed cosmic dancer. The beauty of this stonework lies in the grace, balance, and sense of peace conveyed in spite of the subject's multiple actions. It's all very peaceful and serene. Then you step back outside and see the monkeys.

There are monkeys everywhere: climbing trees, hooting and hollering, looking for opportunities to get any human food you might be carrying—so we suggest you don't bring any with you (have lunch before you leave Mumbai, or wait until you get back ⇨ *See the Need a Break: Basilico*). There are so many monkeys, and they are so comfortable around humans, that they almost distract you from the 1,500-year-old rock carvings. Almost.

It's unclear who did the carvings on Elephanta but it is known that the island was originally called Gharapuri; the Portuguese renamed it after a large stone elephant was found near where their boat landed (the figure collapsed in 1814 and was moved to mainland Bombay's Victoria Gardens). Shortly before the temples were created, Mumbai experienced the golden age of the late Guptas, under whom artists had relatively free range. The Sanskrit language had been finely polished, and under the court's liberal patronage writers had helped incite a revival of Hindu beliefs. It was Shivaism—the worship of Shiva—that inspired the building of these temples.

The MTDC leads a tour, every day at 2 pm (book when you arrive), that is good but not essential, and runs a tiny restaurant on the island for refreshments and beer. In February they organize a dance festival here.

Getting here: Ferries for the one-hour trip (each way) depart daily every half hour from 9 to 2:30 from the Gateway of India and from noon to 5 from Elephanta Island, unless the sea is very choppy. ⚠ It's not advisable to visit Elephanta during monsoon season. ✉ *Elephanta Island* 🚢 *Roundtrip Rs. 100–Rs. 120 depending on type of seat or boat you choose; Rs. 250 tickets for entering the caves can be purchased at Mahesh Travels at the Gateway of India* ☎ *22/2282–0139* ⊘ *Closed Mon.*

★   **Gateway of India.** Mumbai's signature landmark, this elegant 26-meter (85-foot) stone archway was hastily erected as a symbol of welcome to Queen Mary and King George V of England when they paid a visit to India in 1911. In the years following, artisans added decorative carvings and lovely *jharoka*-work (window carvings), finishing in 1923. Less than 25 years later, the last British troops departed from India through the same ceremonial arch. The monument serves as a launching point for boats going to Elephanta Island, and this is also where luxury liners like the *Queen Elizabeth 2* dock on their cruises. The majestic Taj Mahal Palace Hotel, built before the Gateway of India, in 1903, now stands just behind it. ✉ *End of C. Shivaji Maharaj Marg.*

Kalash Parbat Hindu Hotel. For decades Bombayites have come to seedy Kalash Parbat Hindu Hotel, which isn't actually a hotel, to indulge their craving for Indian-style vegetarian junk food, such as *chana bhatura* (giant *puris,* or puffed bread, served with spicy chickpea curry), *samosas* (stuffed vegetable turnovers), *sev puri* (deep-fried crackers layered with potato and chutney), *ragda pattice* (spicy potato cakes), *pani puri* (fried lentil-and-potato-stuffed puffs), and other intricate snack food and *kulfi* (Indian-style ice cream). The place is a bit down-at-the-heels, but the food preparation is clean, and the piping hot, tasty food makes a visit well worth it. Go slow, though: the uninitiated may find the oily food difficult to digest. ⊠ *Sheela Mahal, 1st Pasta Lane, off Colaba Causeway* ☎ *22/2287–4823, 22/2284–1972* ⊙ *Daily 11–11.*

FORT AND MARINE DRIVE

Long, rectangular parks—known as *maidans*—split Marine Drive starting at the Fort neighborhood, each one filled from end to end with countless overlapping cricket games. At one end there might be a gentle match between players in full white regalia, while the next comparable stretch of land is filled with 10 side-by-side matches, barefoot players whipping the ball and hurling their bodies through the air, laughing and talking trash. To the west, past Flora Fountain and the surrounding street-side secondhand booksellers, you'll find Churchgate Station and the Queen's Necklace (as Marine Drive's curved line of street lights is called), where some of the city's best hotels sit. To the east, past the 130-year-old Gothic High Court building and Mumbai University's 260-foot Rajabhai Clocktower, in the labyrinthine streets of Kala Ghoda (a small area within the Fort neighborhood), the city's best seafood restaurants await, along with a completely incongruous, beautiful baby-blue synagogue. In Fort, the side streets are filled with vendors selling secondhand books and bootleg software and DVDs, all at rock-bottom prices. Fort is a great place to see the kind of grandeur the British had in mind when they dreamed up "Bombay," and Marine Drive offers a wonderful walk along the Arabian Sea.

WHAT TO SEE

Fodor's Choice ★ **Chowpatty Beach.** It's not much of a beach in the resort sense, but Chowpatty and the rest of long, elegantly curved Marine Drive are the essence of the mammoth, cheeky, beautiful seaside beast that is Mumbai. Chowpatty is a taste of the bazaar and *mela* (festival) rolled into one. By day—weekday, that is—it's a quiet, uncluttered stretch of sand, but by night it transforms into a carnival of food and hawkers and touts and amusements of every kind, all lit up like Christmas Eve. In a rapidly changing city, it retains some of the simple pleasures in which Mumbaikars indulged before the economy skyrocketed—and it remains an equalizer of sorts, with parents of every class and caste bringing their families here for an evening of fun. For the casual traveler, it offers a window into the many colors—and smells and tastes and sounds—of Mumbai.

Crowds of people at Chowpatty Beach

A hundred species of salesmen throng the beach in the evening, and especially on Sunday, selling everything from glow-in-the-dark yo-yos and animal-shaped balloons to rat poison. Men stand by with bathroom scales, offering complacent strollers a chance to check their heft. Hand-operated Ferris wheels and carousels are packed with children. A few stalls nearby distribute Mumbai's famously satisfying fast food—crunchy *bhel puris* (puffed-rice snacks), *ragda pattices* (spicy potato cakes), and *paav bhaji* (fried vegetable mash eaten with bread). From the beach, walk southeast down Marine Drive toward Nariman Point and you'll bump into flotillas of evening strollers, cooing couples wandering past the waves in a daze, and dogs and kids being walked by their respective nannies. ⊠ *Chowpatty*.

NEED A BREAK?

Cream Centre. Cream Centre, an old and very popular vegetarian eatery, is the best address in the city for delicious *chana bhatura*: the piping-hot, football-size puris made from white flour and yeast are served with a spicy chickpea concoction and raw onions and lemons. Just as good are the stuffed parathas, felafel, *lassis* (yogurt-based drinks), and hummus. ⊠ *Fulchand Niwas, 25B Chowpatty Seaface, opposite Chowpatty Beach, Marine Drive* ☎ *22/2367–9222, 22/2367–9333* ⊙ *Daily noon–midnight.*

Jehangir Art Gallery. Mumbai's chief contemporary-art gallery hosts changing exhibits of well-known Indian artists. Some of the work is lovely, and all of it is interesting for its cultural perspective. There's usually plenty of art outside as well—when it's not monsoon season the plaza in front of the building is full of artists selling their work. ⊠ *M.G. Rd., Kala Ghoda, Fort* ☎ *22/2284–3989* 🖭 *Free* ⊙ *Daily 11–7.*

Knesseth Eliyahoo Synagogue. The old Baghdadi synagogue at the southern edge of Fort is the attractive and ornate, sky-blue Knesseth Eliyahoo Synagogue, across from Jehangir Art Gallery and behind Rhythm House. Built in 1884, it has lovely stained-glass windows and intricately constructed second-floor balconies. You can visit daily between 10 and 6:30, and are welcome for Sabbath prayers on Friday evenings. ⊠ *V.B. Gandhi Rd., Kala Ghoda, Fort* ☎ *22/2283–1502.*

NEED A BREAK?

Café Samovar. Next to a bit of courtyard greenery in the Jehangir Art Gallery, Café Samovar is a popular, laid-back place for a fresh lime soda or a mutton samosa. Their meat-stuffed *parathas* (griddle-fried whole-wheat pancakes) and chicken rolls are also tasty. ⊠ *M.G. Rd., Kala Ghoda, Fort* ☎ *22/2284–8000* ⊙ *Mon.–Sat. 10–7.*

Marine Drive. This 3-km (2-mile) -long boulevard by the Arabian Sea offers, along its lengthy promenade, one of the best walks in Mumbai. After you've had your fill of the busy city, head out for a wander—if you're in the mood, you can stroll all the way from Nariman Point up to Malabar Hill. On the way, stop by **Dome**, on top of the InterContinental Hotel in Churchgate for a sunset drink, or grab a snack at Chowpatty Beach, which is famous for Mumbai street food. If you're here at night, scope out the famed Queen's Necklace, as the streetlights along C-shaped Marine Drive are affectionately known.

NEED A BREAK?

Status. This is a convenient spot along the seaside stroll to sample long, crispy dosas bathed in butter, in all their crackling perfection. Weight-watchers can opt for an oil-free version. Equally good are the *idlis* and *rava* (semolina) dosas. Alternatively, you can try the various *pulaus* (rice dishes) and quick lunches on the menu. ⊠ *Regent's Chamber, Jamnalal Bajaj Rd., Nariman Point* ☎ *22/2287–2281.*

★ **National Gallery of Modern Art.** A great place to see the works of legendary Indian artists M.F. Hussein and F.N. Souza, this imposing, classical-looking circular building has interiors that bring to mind a shrunk-down version of New York's Guggenheim Museum. Built in 1911 by Gateway of India architect George Wittet, it was once the Sir Cowasji Jehangir Public Hall, and the venue for the concerts of violinist Yehudi Menuhin and the rallies of Mahatma Gandhi—the hall still has the acoustics to match. Modern Indian art is displayed in an uncrowded, easy manner on four floors. It's not as spectacular as the Prince of Wales Museum across the street, but it's quiet, and worth a visit, especially if you're an art lover. On the top floor is Atul Dodiya's interesting interpretation of Bill and Chelsea Clinton's visit to India, hung alongside a portrait of Vladmir Putin on his visit. ⊠ *M.G. Rd., near Regal Cinema, Fort* ☎ *22/2288–1969, 22/2288–1790* ⊕ *www.ngmaindia.gov.in* ⊠ *Rs. 150* ⊙ *Tues.–Sun. 11–6.*

Prince of Wales Museum. Topped with Moorish domes, Mumbai's finest Victorian building and principal museum houses 30,000 artifacts, divided between art, archaeology, and natural history. While the building is stunning, the artifacts, most of which are extremely interesting,

DID YOU KNOW?

The 3-km (2-mile) -long, C-shape Marine Drive is one of Mumbai's quintessential features. It's also known as the Queen's Necklace because at night the street lights look like a string of pearls.

Mumbai's Jewish Heritage

Jews were once a prominent stream in Mumbai's population. It's believed there were three strains of Indian Jews—Maharashtrian (Bene Israel) Jews, Cochini Jews, and Baghdadi Jews. The Bene Israel Jews, considered by some to be the Lost Tribe of Israel, supposedly arrived (shipwrecked) in India in the early centuries of the Common Era (some say as far back as 500 BC) and settled along the Konkan coast south of Mumbai. The Cochini Jews, who were spice traders, arrived in approximately AD 1000 and settled in Kerala, in the town of Cochin (Kochi) on the Malabar Coast. Jewish immigration began in earnest in India, however, in the 1800s, and by the 1900s there may have been up to 50,000 Jews in India. These days there are about 5,000 left—most migrated to Israel in the 1950s. Baghdadi Jews, from Iraq and Syria, settled mainly in Mumbai and Kolkata; there's still a small but active population of Iraqi Jews in Mumbai.

Left behind by historic Jewish communities in Mumbai is an assortment of synagogues (see What to See listings).

are unfortunately shown in a slightly dusty environment, with not great lighting. The picture gallery contains scores of Mughal and Rajput miniature paintings, works by European and contemporary Indian artists, and copies of magnificent cave-temple paintings from Ajanta. ■TIP➜ The museum was renamed the Chhatrapati Shivaji Maharaj Vastu Sangrahalaya, but don't ask for directions to this—no one uses that name. ⊠ M.G. Rd., near Regal Cinema, Fort ☎ 22/2284–4519, 22/2284–4484 ⊕ www.themuseummumbai.com ✄ Rs. 300 ◷ Tues.–Sun. 10:15–5:45.

MALABAR HILL AND ENVIRONS

This tony area is at the far end of Marine Drive, where some of the richest and most powerful people in Mumbai live. It's also probably the best place to see the sheer amount of money this city is made of—take, for instance, Antilia, the "quaint" house industrialist Mukesh Ambani recently completed on Altamount Road. Its US$2 billion price tag, 560-foot height (27 floors), and 400,000 square feet of living space make it the most expensive, and largest, residential home on the planet. (That the 600-person-staffed behemoth is a mere 10 km (6 miles) from Dharavi, one of the largest slums in Asia, where 1 million people share less than 2½ square km (1 square mile) of land, highlights the extent of India's massive income gap.) Along the switchback roads of Malabar Hill you'll also find the ancient Babulnath Temple (a Shiva temple), the austere Jain Temple, the spring-fed Banganga water tank, and the verdant Hanging Gardens.

A GOOD TOUR

■TIP➜ Do this tour by taxi; it's totally acceptable to have your taxi driver wait for you—he may ask for extra money for "waiting time," and Rs. 20 or so should do the trick.

Malabar Hill and Environs

KEY

＋ Rail Lines

Babulnath Temple **3**
Banganga Water Tank **6**
Haji Ali Shrine **1**
Jain Temple **5**
Kamala Nehru Park **2**
Mani Bhavan **4**

TO MATUNGA

MAZAGAON

Dockyard Rd.

Dockyard Rd.

Sandhurst Rd.

UMERKHADI

Mafet Rd.

Manson Rd.

Dr. Maishari Rd.

Wadi Bunder Rd.

Keshavji Naik Rd.

Masjid

Jail Rd. (East)

Mahatma Jyotiba Phule Market
(Crawford Market)

N. Natha St.

P.D'
Mello Rd

Police

Palton Rd

Jail Rd.

MANDVI

PYDHUNI

Ramchandra
Bhatt Marg

Ibrahim
Rahimtulla Rd.

Mohamed Ali Rd.

Yusuf Meherali Rd.

A. Rahman St.

S. Marg

Lokmanya Tilak Rd.

Sir Jamshedji Jijibhoy Rd.

Mirza Galib
Marg

KHARA
TALAO

Maulana Azad Rd.

S.V. Patel Rd.

Chowkalkar Rd.

Bhuleshwar Rd.

Kalbadevi Rd.

Mohd Shahid
Maru Marg

Maulana Azad Rd.

Dinshaw
Dimtumkar
Rd.

BHULESHWAR

KALBADEVI

Maulana Ramchandra
Shaukatali Rd.

CENTRAL
MUMBAI

Jehangir Boman Behram Marg

KAMATIPURA

R-S Nimbar Rd.

KHETWADI

GIRGAUM

Maulana Marg

Jagannath Shankarsheth St.

Dr. Babasaheb Jaykar

Dr. Anandrao Nair Rd.

Maulana Azad Rd.

Vithalbhai Patel Rd.

Dr. Maharshi Karve Rd.

K. Sharma Rd.

Marine Lines

Pattho

Rapurao Marg

Dr. Daadasaheb Bhadkamkar Marg

Charni Rd.

TARDEO

Grant
Rd.

Jaofer
N. Naik Marg

V. N. Naik Marg

Jaofer Dadaji Rd.

Sitaram Patkar

Chowpatty
Beach

Ramtazar Rd.

Gopalrao Deshmukh Rd.

CUMBALLA
HILL

Bhulabhai Desai Rd.

August Kranti Marg

Kamala
Nehru Park

②

③

①

④

Little Gibbs
Rd.

Walkeshwar Rd.

⑤

Laxmibai Jagmohandas Marg

B.G. Kher Marg

MALABAR
HILL

⑥

Arabian Sea

0 ──── 1 mi

0 ──── 1 km

After checking the tides to time your visit just right, take a taxi to the **Haji Ali Shrine** and have your taxi wait for you while you walk out on the jetty. Then drive to **Kamala Nehru Park,** take some air, enjoy the views, and walk to the **Jain Temple.** From here you can either walk or take a taxi along Walkeshwar Road to the **Banganga water tank** area. Finally, have your taxi take you to **Babulnath Temple** and Gandhi's former home, **Mani Bhavan.**

TIMING This tour takes about three to four hours, depending on traffic.

TOP ATTRACTIONS

Babulnath Temple. To get the flavor of a large, traditional Indian temple that's nevertheless jammed in the heart of a busy city, a visit to the Babulnath Temple is a must. And climbing the few hundred steps to reach the temple, perched on a hillside, will also reward you with a panorama of South Mumbai. The first Babulnath Temple was apparently built by Raja Bhimdev in the 13th century and named after the *babul* trees (a type of acacia native to India) that forested this area. The architecture of this imposing shrine, one of Mumbai's most important, isn't especially remarkable, but it's interesting to watch the melée of worshippers coming, going, and milling about. Outside are rows of flower sellers hawking a temple-visitation kit—coconut plus flowers plus rock sugar—and a cluster of vendors concocting sweets in *karhais* (large woks) in the open air. Temple authorities are sometimes prickly about allowing foreigners into the innermost areas, but it's worth a try; more often than not they don't object. For Rs. 2 you can avoid the climb and take the elevator. ⊠ *Babulnath Rd.*

★ **Banganga Water Tank.** This serene, under-visited temple complex is considered one of the city's holiest sites. It's also the oldest surviving structure in Mumbai. The small, somewhat dilapidated temples are built around a holy pool of water and surrounded by the ever-encroaching houses of Mumbai's newer residents. Cows and people mingle freely here, as do bathers who come to sample the "healing powers" of the water, and life around here harks back to earlier, more traditional times. A special musical festival takes place on its banks in winter. ⊠ *Walkeshwar Rd., take the lane just beyond Ghanshyamdas Sitaram Poddar Chowk* ⊡ *Free.*

★ **Mani Bhavan.** This charming, old-fashioned three-story Gujarati house, painted brown and cream and in a quiet, tree-shaded Parsi neighborhood on Malabar Hill, was the home of Mahatma Gandhi from 1917 to 1934. Now overseen and lovingly maintained by the Gandhi Institute,

THE DHOBI GHATS

Dhobi ghats are where washermen (dhobis) pound clothes clean day and night in enormous open-air laundries. Mumbai actually has several, but the Cuffe Parade ghat is the most conveniently located for tourists. If you're feeling more adventurous, a visit to Mumbai's main dhobi ghat, near Mahalakshmi Station, a kilometer (half mile) beyond the racecourse, may make for better photo ops; here about 200 washermen are at work in an area covering 7 acres—it's best viewed from the railroad bridge leading into Mahalakshmi Railway Station.

it houses a library and an interesting and attractively presented small museum on Gandhi's life and work. Gandhi's simple belongings are displayed in his room, including his original copies of the Bible, the Koran, and the Bhagavad Gita (a famous discourse within the ancient Indian epic, the *Mahabharata*); other displays include spectacular colorful miniature dioramas of his life, photographs, and some important and moving letters from the fight for Indian independence. Don't miss the humble and polite letter to Adolf Hitler asking him to not go to war. ⊠ *19 Laburnam Rd., near Nana Chowk, Gamdevi* ☎ *22/2380–5864* ⟟ *Rs. 10* ☽ *Daily 10–5:30.*

WORTH NOTING

Haji Ali Shrine. Set far out on a thin, rocky jetty in the Arabian Sea, this striking, dilapidated white shrine was built in honor of the Muslim saint Haji Ali, who drowned here some 500 years ago on a pilgrimage to Mecca. When a coffin containing his mortal remains floated to rest on a rocky bed in the sea, devotees constructed the tomb and mosque to mark the spot. The shrine is reached by a long walkway just above the water. ■ TIP➔ At high tide the walkway is submerged, making the shrine unreachable. But walking there when the sea has completely receded is not too romantic, because the exposed rocks smell of garbage; choose a time in between. The walkway is lined with destitute families and beggars ravaged by leprosy, some writhing, chanting, and (calling on the Muslim tradition of giving alms) beseeching you as you make your way down—a deeply discomfiting experience, but one that is unfortunately quintessentially Mumbai. Inside, the shrine is full of colored-mirror mosaics and crowded with worshippers praying over the casket, which is inevitably covered with wilted flower garlands. Men and women must enter through separate doorways. On many evenings a busker plays *quawalis* (a style of Muslim music) after the sunset prayers. There's no admission charge, but you may consider giving between Rs. 20 and Rs. 50 to the mosque charity box. The shrine closes at 10 pm. ⊠ *Off Lala Lajpatrai Marg, near Mahalaxmi Race Course, Central Mumbai.*

Jain Temple. What may be the most impressive temple in Mumbai belongs to the prosperous, strictly vegetarian Jains, the largely Gujarati followers of Lord Mahavira. The colorful interior of their main Mumbai temple is filled with marble, but at the same time it's understated and peaceful—check out the intricate work on the walls and ceilings. Jain worship here is rather different from the general chaos at Hindu temples; it's more introspective and humble in aspect, which reflects the Jain faith. At around 8 am daily, freshly bathed Jain devotees in swaths of unstitched off-white cloth walk here barefoot from their nearby—often quite ritzy—homes to pay homage to the splendid idol of Adinath, an important Jain prophet. (Jains show respect by arriving clean and without shoes—originally Jains used to wear only a silk cloth, the highest quality and hence most respectful material, but plenty now also wear cotton, and many others simply make do with ordinary clothes.) ⊠ *B.G. Kher Marg, Teen Batti, near Walkeshwar.*

Kamala Nehru Park. Children love playing on the "Old Woman Who Lived in a Shoe" structure here, at this small park on the eastern side of

Inside Mumbai's Hanging Gardens

the top of Malabar Hill. It's primarily a children's playground—and an old-school one at that, so if your kids are used to the finer things, this park may seem impossibly quaint—but also has gorgeous views of the city below that are worth checking out if you happen to be in the area. From the special viewpoint clearing you can see all of Marine Drive and the Mumbai skyline, from Chowpatty Beach to Colaba Point—try to come up after dark to see why Marine Drive, sparkling with lights, is known as the Queen's Necklace. Just across the road another park, the **Hanging Gardens** (also known as the Pherozeshah Mehta Gardens), also has pleasant views and a topiary garden. A few minutes north of here, heading down the hill, are the **Towers of Silence**, where Mumbai's Parsis—followers of the Zoroastrian faith—dispose of their dead. Pallbearers carry the corpse to the top of one of the towering cylindrical bastions, where it is left to be devoured by vultures and crows (a roughly two-hour process) and decomposed by the elements. None of this is visible to would-be onlookers, even relatives, and high walls prevent any furtive peeping. ⊠ *B.G. Kher Marg* ⊙ *Daily 6 am–9 pm.*

CENTRAL MUMBAI

Unlike most other cities, the center of Mumbai has few historical sites, though it does include Mahalaxmi, home of the city's race track. Densely populated, it also encompasses areas like Tardeo, Parel, and Worli, but with its cluster of gray tower blocks is, quite frankly, not the sort of place many tourists are going to want to visit. However, it is home to some of the best restaurants in the city, and that alone may warrant a trip.

WHAT TO SEE

Magen Hassidim Synagogue. This is probably Mumbai's most active synagogue, but being in Byculla, it's not really much of a tourist destination and, as a Hasidic synagogue, may not be as open to visitors as some of the reform places of worship. This Bene Israel shrine is in the Muslim area of Madanpura. Although the communities of Baghdadi and Cochini Jews have dwindled to just a few thousand, the Bene Israel community continues to modestly prosper. The congregation and caretakers at this well-attended shrine (with about 750 members) can lend insight into the future of this community: Magen Hassidim is the face of India's modern Jews, the ones who generally don't plan to migrate to Israel and who are now part of the nation's mainstream. ⊠ *Maulana Azad Rd., near Fancy Market and Jula Maidan, Madanpura, Central Mumbai* ☎ *22/2301–2685.*

CST AND ENVIRONS

Colaba may have the Causeway, but the commercial hub of Mumbai is centered on the bustling bazaars near Chhatrapati Shivaji Terminus. Although CST—also often referred to by its colonial acronym, VT, which stands for Victoria Terminus—is a sight in and of itself; nearby you'll find three of Mumbai's most important bazaars and the city's best Muslim food. It's the perfect place to see a true slice of "Bombay" as it was before the high-rises, fancy hotels, and fine-dining restaurants moved in.

WHAT TO SEE

Chor Bazaar (*Thieves' Bazaar*). This narrow thoroughfare, smack in the heart of classic Muslim Mumbai, is lined with dozens of stores crammed with antiques and general bric-a-brac: clocks, old phonographs, brassware, glassware, and statues; some of it quite cheap. Over the years the value and breadth of much of this stock has dwindled, but there's still a chance that you'll find an unusual, memorable piece. Haggle. In the same lane a number of shops are engaged in the profitable business of constructing new furniture that looks old; many will openly tell you as much. Some shops do stock genuine antique furniture from old Parsi homes. Around the corner, stolen cell phones and car stereos are being hawked. The Thieves' Bazaar got its name because it's always been the kind of place that sold goods that fell off the back of the truck—or back of the camel—and even today you can't be too sure of the provenance of your purchases. Getting to the Chor Bazaar will take you on a tour of an interesting and very staunchly Muslim neighborhood, where life has a completely different flavor from elsewhere in the city. One street away is an interesting mosque belonging to the Bohri Muslims—the architecture and the people are a mix of Yemeni, Egyptian, Indian, and African—just ask people to point you in the direction of Bohri Masjid (or Mosque). ⊠ *Mutton St., off Sardar Vallabhbhai Patel Rd., off Mohammed Ali Rd., Mandvi, CST and Environs* ☉ *Sat.–Thurs. 11–7.*

CST (Chhatrapati Shivaji Terminus), aka Victoria Terminus. Built by the British in 1888, this is one of Mumbai's—and probably the world's—busiest

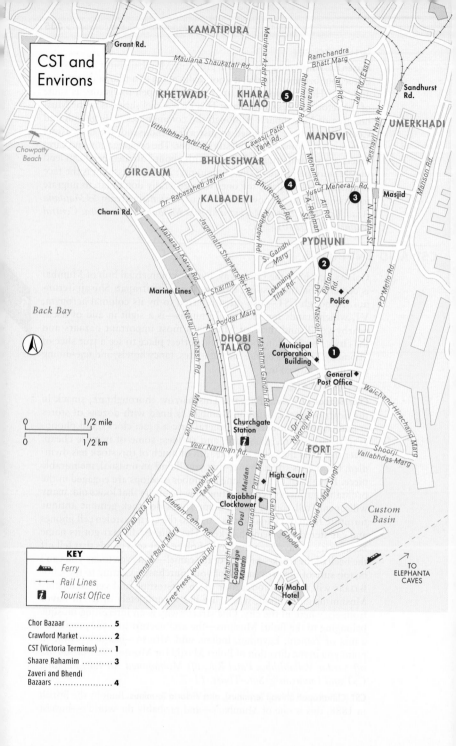

CST and Environs

KAMATIPURA

Grant Rd.

Maulana Shaukatali Rd.

Maulana Azad Rd.

Ramchandra Bhatt Marg

Sandhurst Rd.

KHETWADI

KHARA TALAO

5

Ibrahim Rahimtulla Rd.

Jail Rd.

Jail Rd. (East)

UMERKHADI

Vithalbhai Patel Rd.

Cawasji Patel Tank Rd.

MANDVI

Keshavji Naik Rd.

Manson Rd.

Chowpatty Beach

GIRGAUM

BHULESHWAR

Mohamed Ali Rd.

Yusuf Meherali Rd.

Masjid

Dr. Babasaheb Jaykar

Bhuleshwar Rd.

A. Rehman St.

4

3

N. Natha St.

Charni Rd.

KALBADEVI

Mahatshi Karve Rd.

Jagannath Shankarsher St.

Kalbadev Rd.

S. Gandhi Marg

PYDHUNI

P. D'Mello Rd.

Marine Lines

K. Sharma St.

Lokmanya Tilak Rd.

2

Patton Rd.

Dr. D. Naoroji Rd.

Police

Back Bay

Netaji Subhash Rd.

A. Poddar Marg

DHOBI TALAO

Municipal Corporation Building

Maharshi Tata Rd.

Mahatma Gandhi Rd.

1

General Post Office

Walchand Hirachand Marg

Marine Drive

Churchgate Station

Dr. D. Naoroji Rd.

FORT

Shoorji Vallabhdas Marg

Veer Nariman Rd.

High Court

Sir Durab Tata Rd.

Jamsheti Tata Rd.

Madam Cama Rd.

Maharshi Karve Rd.

Oval Maidan

Patil Marg

M. Gandhi Rd.

Bhaurao

Rajabhai Clocktower

Kala Ghoda

Sahid Bhagat Singh

Custom Basin

0   1/2 mile
0   1/2 km

Jamnalal Bajai Marg

Cooperage Maidan

Free Press Journal Rd.

Taj Mahal Hotel

TO ELEPHANTA CAVES

KEY

🛥 Ferry

✛ Rail Lines

ℹ Tourist Office

Chor Bazaar **5**

Crawford Market **2**

CST (Victoria Terminus) **1**

Shaare Rahamim **3**

Zaveri and Bhendi Bazaars **4**

A Good Walk of Mumbai's Markets

This walk is not for the timid: It will be harried, the traffic is usually crazy, and the streets are dirty, but this is Mumbai, and the experience can't be beat.

Start off at grand, Victorian **CST**, then head north, just past the station, to **Crawford Market** (renamed Mahatma Jyotiba Phule, which no one ever uses). This is one of Mumbai's biggest wholesale fruit, poultry, and vegetable markets—though you can also buy retail—and it teems with traders and local buyers. To get around, it's best to just ask a local to point you in the direction of what you're looking for (or a good landmark), because street names mean almost nothing in Mumbai, and the roads here are winding and confusing. ■TIP➔ You're about to enter the belly of the bazaar beast, so keep an eye on your wallet, and it's a good idea not to carry anything of great value with you. Head north and you'll end up on **Muhammad Ali Road**, the city's great Muslim ghetto, though its ragged appearance and, frankly, filthy streets make it not for the faint of heart. Muhammad Ali Road begins to blend with **Bhendi Bazaar**, which, in turn, blends into **Zaveri Bazaar**, and these two bazaars contain all of Mumbai's best goldsmiths, as well as the city's not-so-secret money-laundering industry. Grab lunch in the air-conditioned confines of **Shalimar Restaurant** (✉ Bhindi Bazar Corner, Masjid Bunder Sind Harsh Road ☎ *022/2345–6630*) in Bhendi (order the *rand biryani*, a spicy rice dish made with goat leg), then hang a left to **Chor Bazaar**, where you'll dodge wooden carts piled high with goods and wind through the labyrinth of alleys, picking through thousands of shops and stalls for dirt-cheap antiques, vintage Bollywood posters, and furniture. ■TIP➔ If you can, bring a local with you and, after making a round together, have them go back and do the bargaining and purchasing for you, with you out of sight—they'll get much better deals without a foreigner around. Next, head back toward Muhammad Ali Road and Bhendi Bazaar for some of the best Muslim street food Mumbai has to offer. If you're strong of stomach, go to Haji Tikha Wali (ask a local, he's well known) for *kheeri tikka*, marinated cow udders grilled right in front of you. Or, if it's late at night, to Walliji Paayawala, for cooked, spicy goat hooves with coarse Irani bread. During the day, you can get *chana bateta*, chickpeas cooked with spleen (yes, we know how terrible all of this sounds, but there's no honest way to prettify it and this is seriously tasty food if you can keep yourself from thinking about what you're eating); there's a whole row of stalls—just go for the one with the longest line. If you're adventurous, and relish food from regions far and wide, you won't be disappointed. And, on the honestly off chance you end up spending the night on the toilet, at least you'll do so knowing you tried the best there is.

Timing: This walk will take a full day, and, again, it's not for the faint of heart—or those unwilling to experience India on its own chaotic, messy terms. Note that Crawford Market is closed Sunday, and Muhammad Ali Road, Bhendi Bazaar, and Chor Bazaar are essentially closed—that is, completely empty of the Muslims who make up their majority—on Friday, the holy day.

6

train stations, overflowing at rush hour with enormous, surging, scurrying crowds who use the suburban lines that also originate here (Mumbai's suburban trains carry eight million people a day). Although it's been renamed Chhatrapati Shivaji Terminus, it's still commonly called Victoria Terminus or just VT, and it bears a hefty statue of Queen Victoria on its imposing dome, the haughty structure combining Indian and Victorian–Gothic architecture for an Eastern version of London's St. Pancras station. Why visit? To spend a few minutes admiring the enormous, incredible building, which is even more arresting lit up at night. If you're brave, walk around the corner to the modern suburban extension of the station around rush hour—9 am or 5:30 pm—and experience Mumbai's maddening crowds. Even better, take a ride on a local train; many say you have not experienced Mumbai unless you have ridden one. ⊠ *D. Naoroji Rd., CST.*

★ **Crawford Market.** Renamed Mahatma Jyotiba Phule market decades ago (before the relatively recent renaming Bombay and Victoria Terminus), but still known by its original name, this building was designed in the 1860s by John Lockwood Kipling (father of Rudyard, who was born in this very neighborhood). The market's stone flooring supposedly came from Caithness, Scotland. Check out the stone relief depicting workers on the outside of the building. Come here early in the morning for a colorful walk through Mumbai's fresh-produce emporium, and if it's late spring or early summer, treat yourself to a delicious Alphonso mango—the experience has had many people rhapsodize that they've never truly had a mango until they ate one of these. Everything from cookies and party streamers to white mice and cane baskets is sold in other sections of the market—the meat section can be a bit hair-raising. In the middle lane (Sheikh Memon Street) of Crawford Market, is the chaotic **Mangaldas Market**, a covered, wholesale cloth market with a tremendous variety of fabrics at hundreds of indoor stalls. Across the street from the market's main entrance on the west, spread across a trio of lanes, is a smaller but popular bazaar area called **Lohar Chawl**, where the selection ranges from plastic flowers to refrigerators. ⊠ *D. Naoroji Rd., at L. Tilak Rd., CST and Environs* ⊗ *Mon.–Sat. 11:30–8.*

NEED A BREAK?

Rajdhani. Rajdhani serves up hot Gujarati and Rajasthani *thalis* (combination platters; Rs. 299) in spartan, clean surroundings. It's just a tiny bit north of Crawford Market. Eat sparingly, because the restaurant uses a lot of ghee (clarified butter) in its dishes, which are also slightly (and authentically) sweet. ⊠ *Sheikh Memon St., Lohar Chawl, near Crawford Market, Mandvi* ☎ *22/2342–6919* ⊗ *Mon.–Sat., noon–4 and 7–10:30; Sun. noon–3:15.*

Shaare Rahamim (*Gate of Mercy*). North of Crawford Market via P. D'Mello Road, past Carnac Bunder and right next to the Masjid train station, is the hard-to-find Shaare Rahamim, built in 1796. The mildly dilapidated synagogue is still in use, and you're welcome to peek inside. ⊠ *254 Samuel St., Mandvi, CST and Environs.*

Zaveri and Bhendi Bazaars. A little beyond Fort in the neighborhood of Kalbadevi—a 10-minute walk northwest of Crawford Market—

Outside Victoria Terminus, Mumbai's main train station, also known as Chhatrapati Shivaji Terminus (CST)

Bombay's crowded, century-old jewelry markets have shops filled with fabulous gold and silver in every conceivable design. The two bazaars are so intermingled at this point that it's impossible to tell where one ends and the other starts. If you notice people walking past with plastic bags full of cash, try not to stare—this is also a major hub for (certainly illegal, widely known, wholly tolerated) money laundering, completely out in the open, with no security measures in place. ■ TIP→ One of the lanes leading off Zaveri Bazaar is called Khao Galli (literally "Eat Lane") and its endless food stalls feed most of the bazaar workers daily; it's here that you'll find some of Mumbai's best—and most unusual—non-veg street food. ⊠ Sheikh Memon St., Kalbadevi ⊗ Mon.–Sat. 11–7.

Mumbadevi Temple. At the Bhuleshwar (the name of a neighborhood) end of Zaveri Bazaar is the six-century-old Mumbadevi Temple, a noisy, busy structure that houses the mouthless but powerful patron goddess who is the city's namesake. *Aarti*, evening prayers, take place at 6:30 pm. ⊠ CST & Environs ☎ 22/2242–4974.

JUHU, BANDRA, AND THE WESTERN SUBURBS

The suburbs that make up the majority of Mumbai lie north of the island city, and spread out for miles on end, but visitors are likely only to visit the two main ones: Juhu and Bandra. Both house Mumbai's rich and famous, including most of its Bollywood stars (and studios). Being right in the middle of Mumbai, the main feature of **Juhu** is Juhu Beach, but it's not the kind of sandy oasis for swimming, or even sunbathing, even though it was recently cleaned up—you'll notice the locals, fully clothed, jumping around in the water, but theirs is a stronger constitution, so limit yourself to a sunset stroll. Instead, tourists are best advised to either find accommodations in Juhu or come to sample one or two of its many bars and clubs. **Bandra,** the hub of hip Mumbai, is full of boutiques, trendy restaurants, and expats, and though it's low on sightseeing it's high on eating and drinking spots. If Bollywood's your thing, ask your cabbie or rickshaw driver to take you past the towering homes of superstars Shahrukh Khan or Salman Khan,

or past historic Mehboob Studios. If it isn't, stop in for a drink at one of the many watering holes on Waterfield Road. Beyond Juhu and Bandra, other suburbs, such as Khar and Santa Cruz, are only worth a trip for the culinary offerings of certain restaurants.

WHERE TO EAT

ABOUT THE RESTAURANTS

Mumbai is India's melting pot, as well as its most cosmopolitan city, so it's no surprise that you can find nearly every regional Indian cuisine here, and some quality international food, too. You'll also find options ranging from casual to super chic.

Seafood from the Konkan coast—from Maharashtra south through Goa and all the way to Mangalore, in Karnataka—is a Mumbai specialty. The many seafood restaurants in Fort, from upscale Trishna to old-school Apoorva, have some of the best food in Mumbai. "Lunch home" is a typical Mumbai name for the slightly dingy seafood joints that bring in the crowds at lunchtime. North India is represented as well, with kebabs and tandoori. If you're looking for kebabs, head to restaurants specializing in Punjabi or Mughlai cuisine, or, if you have a fairly strong stomach, go to Khao Galli near Bhendi Bazaar (⇨ see CST and Environs); the late-night kebab snack option is Bade Miya behind the Taj Mahal Palace Hotel. Meat-heavy dishes from the Northwest Frontier (the area of undivided India that's partly in modern-day Pakistan) are also popular, and closely related to Mughlai food: check out Neel, at the Mahalaxmi race track in Central Mumbai, for upscale versions. On the other end of the spectrum are Gujarati vegetarian thalis—combination platters of various veggies and lentils, though the ones in Mumbai tend to be a bit oilier than those from elsewhere in India. Soam, at the top of Marine Drive, is a great upscale place for thalis, where they're less oily. You may also encounter some Jain food, which is also vegetarian but cooked without any root vegetables—and that includes onions and garlic. You'll find authentic South Indian vegetarian food—*dosas* (fried, crepelike pancakes), *idlis* (steamed rice cakes), *wadas* (also spelled *vadas*; savory fried, and often flavored, lentil-flour doughnuts), and simple, light *thalis* (combination platters)—all over the city.

There are many multicuisine restaurants around the city—usually fairly cheap, tacky joints that make good kebabs, decent Indo-Chinese food, and terrible continental food.

People eat late in India. Lunch is generally around 1-ish, and dinner is anytime between 8:30 pm and midnight—if you're meeting local friends, expect to eat around 9:30 or 10 pm. If you plan on eating at 7, reservations probably aren't necessary, and you can expect a fairly empty restaurant; if you want to eat at 6, call ahead: your restaurant may not even be open for dinner yet. Locals generally dress for dinner. They aren't formal, but they are usually well turned out. Shorts and the grunge look are only acceptable at cafés.

It's worth noting, too, that if you're staying in South Bombay, there's no need to head out to the suburbs to eat, but if you're staying outside the city center there are plenty of quality food options if you don't feel like going downtown to eat.

Prices in the reviews are the average cost of a main course at dinner or, if dinner is not served, at lunch.

6

CENTRAL MUMBAI

$$$$ NORTH INDIAN Fodor's Choice ★

🍴 **Neel.** Hand's down the best upscale Indian food in town, this restaurant in a beautifully designed building at the track makes the journey to the city center utterly worthwhile. Portions are big—as are the prices—and the food is heavy but sophisticated. Start with a *seekh kebab* (minced chicken or mutton with spices) or the mutton *shorba* (bone marrow soup), followed by *raan*, a North Indian–style leg of lamb with roasted apples, or *bindhi kali mirch* (spicy okra), and *dal makhani* (a buttery black lentil dish) with rice, or any of the dozen great breads—flaky *lachha paratha* is recommended. [$] *Average main: Rs. 1500* ✉ *Tote on Turf, Mahalaxmi Racecourse, Gate 5 or 7, Mahalaxmi, Central Mumbai, Mumbai* ☎ *22/6157–7777* ✣ *C1.*

$$ INDIAN Fodor's Choice ★

🍴 **Oh! Calcutta.** Rarely packed, even on Saturday night, because its in the infrequently visited centre, Oh! Calcutta serves the city's best Bengali food in a fine-dining environment of dark-wood set off by simple black-and-white archival photos from the British raj. The food is exquisite, and if it's all too unfamiliar, defer to the waiters—some of the best in the city—to choose something, based on your specifications. Start with Roshun Bhapa Maach, a steamed *bekti* (a freshwater fish) marinated with *kashundi* (Bengali-style mustard), green chilli paste, and garlic. For a main course, you can't go wrong with the *aam kashundi kakra* (breaded stir-fried crabmeat in an orange-mango mustard sauce). [$] *Average main: Rs. 700* ✉ *Rosewood Hotel, Tulsi Wadi La., near Tardeo A/C Market, Central Mumbai* ☎ *22/2496–3114* ✣ *F4.*

$$$ EUROPEAN

🍴 **The Tasting Room.** Popular with rich Mumbai housewives—who pack the place for lunch during the week—this Mediterranean restaurant serves gourmet food in a relaxed setting. On the top-floor veranda of Good Earth (a designer furniture store), the Tasting Room shares its hosts' penchant for subtle Indian minimalism in warm earth tones. Although the ladies who lunch tend to get a little loud midday, dinner

BEST BETS FOR MUMBAI DINING

With so many restaurants to choose from, how to decide? Fodor's writers and editors have chosen their favorites, by price, cuisine, and experience, in the lists below.

Fodor's Choice ★

Apoorva, p. 351
Britannia & Co., p. 352
Kebab Korner, p. 353
Neel, p. 341
Oh! Calcutta, p. 341
The Pantry, p. 353
Soam, p. 354
The Table, p. 350
Wasabi, p. 350

By Price

$

Apoorva, p. 351
Britannia & Co., p. 352
The Pantry, p. 353
Soam, p. 354
Zaffran, p. 355

$$

Oh! Calcutta, p. 341
Woodside, p. 351

$$$

Kebab Korner, p. 353
The Table, p. 350
Trishna, p. 354

$$$$

India Jones, p. 352
Neel, p. 341
Wasabi, p. 350

By Cuisine

INDIAN

Apoorva, p. 351
Britannia & Co., p. 352
Kebab Korner, p. 353
Koyla, p. 367
Neel, p. 341
Soam, p. 354
Status, p. 327
Zaffran, p. 355

SEAFOOD

Apoorva, p. 351
Gajalee, p. 356
Mahesh, p. 353
Oh! Calcutta, p. 341
Trishna, p. 354

ASIAN

Busaba, p. 343
India Jones, p. 352

ITALIAN

Suzette, p. 354
Vetro, p. 354

JAPANESE

Wasabi, p. 350

AMERICAN

The Pantry, p. 353
The Table, p. 350

By Experience

MOST ROMANTIC

Aurus, p. 355

HOT SPOT

Busaba, p. 343
The Pantry, p. 353
Woodside, p. 351

BEST HOTEL DINING

India Jones, p. 352
Vetro, p. 354
Wasabi, p. 350

BEST BRUNCH

Indigo, p. 346
The Pantry, p. 353

is quite the calm affair. The watermelon and feta salad is extremely popular, and makes a good starter, as do the port-poached beets. For mains, you can't go wrong with the lamb ragu with spaghetti. [$] *Average main: Rs. 1200* ✉ *Raghuvanshi Mansions, Raghuvanshi Mills, Senapati Bapat Marg, Lower Parel, Central Mumbai* ☎ *22/2495–1954, 22/6572–0342* ⊕ *F4.*

COLABA

$ INDIAN 🍴 **Bade Miya.** Not for the faint of heart when it comes to hygiene, Mumbai's most famous kebab stand sits behind the Taj Mahal Hotel like a promise it'll never change. Always packed, always greasy, and always tasty, it's perfect for a late-night snack, but not necessarily the place for an early dinner—the grime is less apparent after dark. Try the chicken *bhuna* (shredded chicken in a spicy red-brown gravy), the chicken *baida* roti (a sort of Indian quesadilla, with chicken and egg), or, for the more adventurous, the *bheja* fry (fried goat brains in a spicy gravy). There's also a strictly vegetarian tandoor. [$] *Average main: Rs. 200* ✉ *Tullock Rd., behind Taj Mahal Hotel, Colaba* ☎ *22/2284–8038, 22/2285–1649* 💳 *No credit cards* ⊕ *C4.*

$$ ASIAN ★ 🍴 **Busaba.** Pan-Asian is a dirty term in the hands of most restaurants, but this small, hip joint proves that it *is* possible to do it all, and do it well. The most popular dish, with good reason, is the Khao Suey, a Burmese coconut-based soup that you assemble yourself—you get a bowl of noodles, a bowl of broth, and small bowls of ingredients like chives, veggies, chicken, crushed peanuts, etc. The Korean *bibimbap* (a combination of vegetables, meat, and rice) and beef *bulgogi* are also great. Start with the beef tenderloin skewers, pepper prawns, or any of the *momos* (dumplings). [$] *Average main: Rs. 900* ✉ *2 Mandlik Rd., near Cotton World, behind Taj Mahal Hotel and Palace, Colaba* ☎ *22/2204–3769* ⊕ *C5.*

$ BRITISH 🍴 **Café Churchill.** Dingy—but not dirty—Churchill's specializes in British-style comfort food, perhaps a welcome break from all the Indian food you'll be eating. The red-and-white vinyl interior fits the food, and although the cheap chow may be starchy and simple, sometimes roast beef and gravy with steamed veggies and mashed potatoes really hits the spot. The desserts, though—oh my!—are some of the best Mumbai has to offer: at any given time you'll find five kinds of chocolate cake (brownie, truffle, you name it), and five kinds of cheesecake in the dessert case. You might be tempted to have dessert for dinner. [$] *Average main: Rs. 350* ✉ *103-B Colaba Causeway, opposite Cusrow Baug, Colaba* ☎ *22/2204–2604* 💳 *No credit cards* ⊕ *C5.*

$ CAFÉ 🍴 **Café Mondegar.** Just down the block from Regal Cinema, Monde's is similar in atmosphere and cuisine to its older brother Leopold's up the road. It's a great place to grab a beer—unlike Leo's, they don't have a full liquor license—and it's always packed. Opt out of the characterless air-conditioned room and instead post up at one of the cramped tables in the main space, where the jukebox plays at full blast and the walls are covered with cartoon murals of Mumbai life. Continental and Chinese cuisine are available, or you could stick to the greasy french fries and onion rings. [$] *Average main: Rs. 200* ✉ *Colaba Causeway, Colaba* ☎ *22/2202–0591, 22/2283–0586* ⊕ *C4.*

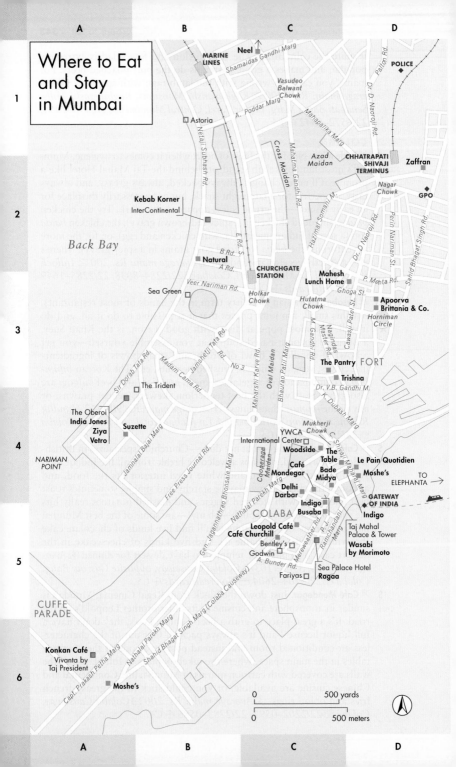

Where to Eat and Stay in Mumbai

A **B** **C** **D**

1

MARINE LINES
Neel
Shamaidas Gandhi Marg
Vasudeo Balwant Chowk
A. Poddar Marg
Mahatma Gandhi Rd.
Mahapalika Marg
Pallon Rd.
Dr. D. Naoroji Rd.
POLICE
Astoria
Netaji Subhash Rd.
Azad Maidan
CHHATRAPATI SHIVAJI TERMINUS
Nagar Chowk
Zaffran
GPO

2

Kebab Korner
InterContinental
E Rd. S
Harniman-Somani M.
Dr. D. Naoroji Rd.
Perin Nariman St.
Sahid Bhagat Singh Rd.

Back Bay

B Rd. S
A Rd.
Natural
CHURCHGATE STATION
Cross Maidan
Mahatma Gandhi Rd.
Nagindas Master Rd.
P. Mehta Rd.
Mahesh Lunch Home
Ghoga St.
Apoorva
Brittania & Co.
Cawasji Patel St.
Horniman Circle

Sea Green
Veer Nariman Rd.
Holkar Chowk
Hutatma Chowk

3

Sir Dorab Tata Rd.
Madam Cama Rd.
Jamshetji Tata Rd.
No. 3
Maharshi Karve Rd.
Oval Maidan
Bhaurao Patil Marg
M. Gandhi Rd.
The Pantry
FORT
Trishna
Dr. V.B. Gandhi M.
K. Dubash Marg

The Trident

The Oberoi
India Jones
Ziya
Vetro
Suzette
Jamnalal Bajaj Marg

4

NARIMAN POINT
Free Press Journal Rd.
Mukherji Chowk
C. Shivaji Maharaj Marg
YWCA
International Center
Woodside
Café Mondegar
The Table
Bade Midya
Le Pain Quotidien
Moshe's
TO ELEPHANTA →
GATEWAY OF INDIA
Cooperage Maidan
Nathalal Parekh Marg
Delhi Darbar
Indigo
Busaba
Indigo

5

Gen. Jagannathrao Bhonsale Marg
Leopold Café
Café Churchill
COLABA
Bentley's
Godwin
A. Bunder Rd.
P. J. Ramchandani
Taj Mahal Palace & Tower
Wasabi by Morimoto
Sea Palace Hotel
Fariyas
Ragaa
Merewether Rd.

CUFFE PARADE

6

Konkan Café
Vivanta by Taj President
Capt. Prakash Petha Marg
Nathalal Parekh Marg
Shahid Bhagat Singh Marg (Colaba Causeway)
Moshe's

0   500 yards
0   500 meters

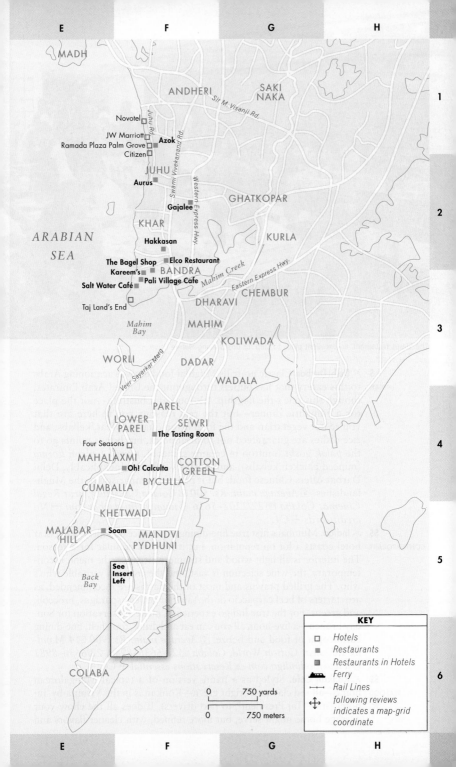

E F G H

MADH

ANDHERI SAKI NAKA

Sir M. Visanji Rd.

1

Novotel

JW Marriott
Azok

Ramada Plaza Palm Grove
Citizen

JUHU

Aurus

Gajalee

GHATKOPAR

2

KHAR

ARABIAN
SEA

KURLA

Hakkasan

The Bagel Shop Elco Restaurant

Kareem's BANDRA

Salt Water Café Pali Village Cafe

Taj Land's End

Mahim Creek

Eastern Express Hwy.

CHEMBUR

DHARAVI

Mahim
Bay

MAHIM

3

KOLIWADA

WORLI

DADAR

Veer Savarkar Marg

WADALA

PAREL

LOWER
PAREL

SEWRI

The Tasting Room

Four Seasons

4

MAHALAXMI

COTTON
GREEN

Oh! Calcutta

BYCULLA

CUMBALLA

KHETWADI

MALABAR
HILL

Soam

MANDVI
PYDHUNI

5

Back
Bay

See
Insert
Left

KEY
☐ Hotels
◼ Restaurants
◼ Restaurants in Hotels
⚓ Ferry
┼──┼ Rail Lines
✛ following reviews indicates a map-grid coordinate

COLABA

6

0   750 yards

0   750 meters

E F G H

The Status restaurant, an excellent place to stop for *dosas* along Marine Drive

$ 🍴 **Delhi Darbar.** Classic no-frills Mughlai food draws vacationing Arabs
INDIAN to this eatery that has outlets throughout the United Arab Emirates, though this one's the flagship. It's loud and bustling—not the place for a romantic dinner—but the real reasons you're here are that you're not vegetarian and the food is top quality. Meat, kebabs, and rice dishes are guaranteed not to disappoint, but bonus points go to the *palak gosht* (mutton in creamy spinach), *murgh badami korma* (minced chicken kebabs), and mutton Kashmiri. Inexplicably, Delhi Darbar offers Chinese food, but it pales in comparison to the Mughlai dishes. [$] *Average main: Rs. 500* ✉ *Colaba Causeway, near Regal Cinema, Colaba* ☎ *22/2202–5656* 🌐 *www.delhi-darbar.com* 💳 *No credit cards* ✥ *C4.*

$$ 🍴 **Indigo.** Mumbai's first true fine-dining experience outside of a five-star
CONTEMPORARY hotel coasts a lot on reputation, but it remains popular for a reason. The interior is all light wood and summery elegance, the menu is contemporary, the wine selection is vast, and the crowd a veritable who's who. The grilled prawns and most of the pastas are recommended, as are starters of beef carpaccio or the salad of grilled asparagus, broccoli, and greens. For the true Indigo experience, make a reservation for Sunday brunch—a five-hour, all you can eat and drink, top-shelf, fine-dining cornucopia of food and booze. [$] *Average main: Rs. 900* ✉ *4 Mandlik Rd., near Cotton World, Colaba* ☎ *22/6636–8980, 22/6636–8981* 🌐 *www.foodindigo.com* ✍ *Reservations essential* ✥ *C4.*

$$ 🍴 **Konkan Café.** Styled as a haute version of a typical Mangalorean
SEAFOOD home—all red clay and bright green—Konkan is in the Vivanta by Taj
★ hotel (still "Taj President" to taxi drivers). It does all the chow your average home might serve, but more refined, with cleaner flavors and

CLOSE UP

Mumbai's Greatest Seafood Hits

Clams, squid, prawns, lobsters, crabs, and fish, rubbed with a spicy red masala or spiked with a green masala or simmered in a thick fragrant coconut gravy: this is what you'll find emanating from kitchens along the Konkan coast of India, stretching from Mumbai to Mangalore to Goa. If you love seafood, help make your Mumbai trip memorable by sampling the best of Konkan seafood cuisine.

Here's a list of what to look for on menus:

Prawn *gassi*: small prawns simmered in a thick, tangy, spicy red coconut gravy

Prawn curry: thinner than a *gassi*, also red, with *kokum* (a sour berry)

Masala prawns: prawns marinated in garlic and spices and then panfried

Teesri masala: tiny clams cooked in a dry coconut masala

Bombay duck *bombil*: this Mumbai specialty has nothing to do with duck: Bombay duck is actually a type of fish—in this dish it's batter-fried with semolina, and is light and flaky; in all honesty, it's not for everybody

Surmai, pomfret, and *rawas*: these three famous, fleshy fish of the region are either marinated and fried, baked in a tandoor, or cooked into a curry

Masala crab: crab cooked in thick, almost dry, green or red masala

Neer dosa: a light crumpled soft-rice dosa meant especially for eating with seafood

Kori roti: a dry, crumbly rice roti

Appam: a Kerala-style steamed kind of dosa available in some Konkan joints

elegant presentation: food is served on copper thali plates lined with banana leaves. The prawn *gassi* (Mangalorean curry) is spicy and delicious, and the crab dishes will not disappoint, but breads tend to be rather dry. Still, it's probably the only coastal restaurant to offer a great, if expensive, bottle of wine. [$] *Average main: Rs. 1000* ✉ *Vivanta by Taj hotel, 90 Cuffe Parade, Colaba* ☎ *22/6665–0808* 🌐 *www.vivantabytaj.com* ✍ *Reservations essential* ✥ *A6*.

$$ BELGIAN ★ 🍴 **Le Pain Quotidien.** This Belgian bakery, a stone's throw from the Gateway of India, offers great breads, fresh ingredients, and a giant communal table—great pop-in when you're sweating it out in South Bombay. It has the best croissants and baguettes in the city, fresh, large salads (try the Caesar or Caprese), and its specialty: *tartines* (open-face sandwiches)—the roasted chicken and smoked mozzarella is recommended. There are hot dishes, too, and evening specials might include grilled salmon or seared lamb chops. It's a good option for those who need a break from Indian food and want to check email on the free Wi-Fi. [$] *Average main: Rs. 500* ✉ *Dhanraj Mahal, C.S.M. Rd., Apollo Bunder, Colaba, Mumbai* ☎ *22/6615–0202* 🌐 *www.lepainquotidien.in* ✥ *D4*.

$ CAFÉ ★ 🍴 **Leopold Café.** When it defiantly reopened just four days after the first shots of the November 2008 terrorist attacks were fired and 10 people were killed, the crowds were so big the police had to shut the place down all over again. The following day it was open again. Order a

Street-Food Favorites

Unlike most other Indian cities that start snoozing as early as 8 pm, Mumbai buzzes around the clock. Food carts appear every few yards serving *chaats* (Indian street snacks), and even the simplest food is transformed into something impressive. The choices are enormous—there are hot, spicy vegetable sandwiches, slices of green mango peppered with masala, sizzling kebabs, Chinese noodles with vegetables, fresh strawberry milk shakes, carrot juice, *kulfi* (cream-based Indian ice cream), fresh-sliced mango with creamed, spicy boiled chickpeas, fried fish, potato turnovers, masala peanuts, coconut water, green-chilli omelets in buns, and an almost endless array of exotic snacks associated with Mumbai, *such as those listed here.*

Much of this snack food is created right at the side of the road on open grills and stoves and then assembled in front of you. As you would imagine, the hygiene may be a little suspect. But don't let that deter you, or you may miss out on some carnival-like happenings and some excellent local food. If you sample any of these street-side treats, follow some rules. Try food served hot on the spot. If the plates don't look clean, ask that food be either served or packed in a disposable container (a fresh plastic bag, a cup created from leaves, a paper plate, or newspaper) or bring your own container. Carry your own spoon and paper or plastic cup, if you want. And don't worry—the vendors usually understand enough English to see the process through. Finally, those vendors who attract the biggest crowds and fame are likely to be safer than those who are ignored.

MUMBAI'S STREET-FOOD CLASSICS

Bhel puri: Puffed rice tossed with cubes of boiled potatoes, slices of tomatoes, peanuts, tamarind sauce, chopped onion, and *sev* (a savory, deep-fried treat made of chickpea flour).

Dahi puri: Tiny, flat, white-flour *puris* (deep-fried bread) layered with boiled potatoes, three types of chutney made from tamarind, dates, and cilantro, plus mung-bean sprouts and topped with curd and chopped cilantro leaves.

Sev puri: The same white-flour puris *as above,* or crackers, layered with boiled potatoes, three types of chutney made from tamarind, dates, and cilantro.

Pani puri: Deep-fried, globular puris, also known as *golgappas,* that have been cracked open and filled with date water, tamarind sauce, mung-bean sprouts, and potatoes.

Ragda pattice: Spiced and mashed potatoes shaped into cutlets and fried on a griddle. These are served with hot white-pea curry and a few sauces.

Dahi bada: Large flat dumplings of white lentils, which are deep-fried to make *badas,* and are then dipped in water to soak out the oil. The badas are broken into pieces and served spiced with a variety of masala powders, tamarind sauce, cilantro chutney, and yogurt.

Pav bhaji: Mashed potatoes that are fried on a hot griddle for an hour with peas, tomatoes, and butter—until it's become a juicy, spicy, potato mash. It's then served with sliced onions, lemons, and butter-fried buns called *pavs.*

Wada pav: A cutlet made of mashed potatoes, spice, cilantro, and ginger that's coated in chickpea flour and deep fried—which is then stuffed into a pav lined with hot garlic and red-chilli chutney.

Aanda pav: A spicy omelet made with chillies, onions, masala, and a bunch of spices, which is then fried and slapped into a pav.

Baida roti: Minced meat mixed with beaten egg is wrapped in white-flour dough that's been tossed by hand into thin sheets; the square, layered pancake is then fried on a hot griddle with oil.

Bheja fry: Spicy red masala and tomatoes fried with goat brains—it's really tasty!

Boti roll: Spicy pieces of grilled lamb kebab, chutney, and sliced onions rolled into a *roomali* roti (a thin, hand-tossed, and roasted white-flour pita).

Sheekh kababs: Minced, spiced lamb cooked on a skewer barbecue-style and served with chutney.

Chicken tikka: Marinated chicken pieces that have been roasted on an open-air barbecue and are served with chutney.

Mutton or chicken biryani: Long-grained basmati rice simmered with spice and mutton or chicken for many hours.

Masala dosa: A lentil- and rice-flour pancake fried on a griddle with plenty of ghee (clarified butter) and stuffed with a spicy potato mixture.

WHERE IS IT SERVED?
Bade Miya *(see full listing in Where to Eat),* next to Gokul Bar on Tullock Road, off Shahid Bhagat Singh Road (enter the lane next to Café Mondegar and take the next right) is an open-air

stall that has been supplying hungry Mumbaikars with kebabs and *baida* (white-flour) rotis for more than 50 years; they're open through the night until the early morning. Also check out the Elco food stalls and the Elco Restaurant *(see full listing in Where to Eat)* in Bandra.

Head to Kailash Parbat or Swati Snacks *(see the Need a Break boxes for full contact info)* to sample bhel puris and sev puris. Also visit Shiv Shankar Tiwari's Dahi Puri stall on B. Road (aka Karmveer Pandit Shobhnath Mishra Marg) off Marine Drive, next to the InterContinental hotel.

There's a fellow outside Churchgate Station—ask around for the omelet *pav* man, as his stand doesn't have a name—who makes the best *aanda pav* in town; he starts in the evening and is open into the wee hours of the morning.

bottle of ice-cold Kingfisher beer to wash down the hearty, typical bar food—chicken tikka, french fries, that kind of thing. Surprisingly, the Chinese food is actually the better bet: the beef with chilli peppers can't be beat, and the chicken fried rice and the chilli chicken are highly recommended. [$] *Average main: Rs. 400* ✉ *Colaba Causeway, Colaba* ☎ *22/2287–3362, 22/2202–0131* 🌐 *www.leopoldcafe.com* ✣ *C5.*

$$ CONTEMPORARY
🍴 **Moshe's.** The jewel of the Moshe's empire, this elegant, European-style restaurant is where chef Moshe Shek, a Mumbai Jew, puts his culinary skills on display. It offers some of the city's best international food—pastas in creamy sauces, eggplant *roulade,* crusty cheese garlic bread (baked on the premises), Israeli stuffed chicken, hearty soups, and the highly recommended char-grilled *rawas* (Indian salmon). Fresh bread and some of the city's best pastries are also available: try the cheesecake. **■ TIP→ Reserve an inside table—though the outdoor patio is lovely, it's sometimes engulfed in the stench of the fisherman's village across the road.** [$] *Average main: Rs. 800* ✉ *7 Minoo Manor, Cuffe Parade, off Wodehouse Rd., Colaba* ☎ *22/2216–1226* 🌐 *www.moshes.in* ✍ *Reservations essential* ✣ *A6.*

$$ NORTH INDIAN
🍴 **Ragaa.** On the ground floor of the Sea Palace Hotel, Ragaa serves surprisingly good Indian food and also has outdoor seating for dining to the sound of the ocean. The service is not great, and it can take a while to get your drinks and food, but when they arrive they are cheap and of good quality. Try the spinach *chaat* (fried breaded spinach with spicy tomato on top), the buttery *dal makhani* (a rich, dark lentil dish), and the kebab platter. After your meal, head up to the rooftop bar for an after-dinner cocktail. [$] *Average main: Rs. 600* ✉ *Sea Palace Hotel, Sea Front, Colaba, Mumbai* ☎ *22/6112–8080* ✣ *C5.*

$$$ MODERN AMERICAN Fodor's Choice ★
🍴 **The Table.** One of Mumbai's best restaurants, The Table was launched by a pair of Indian restaurateurs and a young American chef from San Francisco. The lofted upper floor is perfect for romantic dinners, while below the large, eponymous, communal table extends from the bar for a more lively and sociable setting. The small plates tend to be the best, with particularly high marks for the zucchini spaghetti (literally spaghetti made from the vegetable) in a light buttery sauce with almonds, the tuna tataki, the spicy lamb burgers, and the meatballs, smothered in sauce and topped with cheese and fried onions. The large plates don't disappoint either. [$] *Average main: Rs. 1400* ✉ *Kalash Peshi Building, Chhatrapati Shivaji Maharaj Marg, Apollo Bundar, Colaba, Mumbai* ☎ *22/2282–5000* ✣ *C4.*

$$$$ JAPANESE ★
🍴 **Wasabi by Morimoto.** Wildly expensive, Wasabi attracts a rich clientele who don't mind spending an extra few thousand rupees for fresh, delectable sushi in a town that almost entirely lacks any, even of the barely edible variety. On the second floor of the Taj Mahal Palace hotel and styled after an upscale but fairly authentic Japanese sushi joint, the restaurant offers great service, a nice view toward the Gateway of India, and—we cannot emphasize this enough—great sushi. If you've got the cash, try one of the tasting menus (6 to 12 courses), which will take you through the best dishes, from whitefish carpaccio to rock-shrimp tempura to salmon nigiri. [$] *Average main: Rs. 2000* ✉ *Taj Mahal Palace &*

At the sushi bar in Wasabi by Morimoto

Tower, Colaba ☎ 22/6665–3366 ⊕ *www.tajhotels.com* ⤓ *Reservations essential* ⊹ *C4.*

\$\$
BRITISH
✕ **Woodside.** The only real bar in town is modeled on an English pub, plays decent music (though sometimes too loud), has great bar food, and free Wi-Fi. It has some of the best-priced alcohol in town and is the only such place that's neither a trendy lounge playing club music or a dingy permit room. It's also a great place to stop in after a day's walking. Try the pizzas—pepperoni, four cheese, and pesto chicken are excellent, and the margherita's no slouch—the burgers, the chicken nuggets, or Franco's meatballs (a lamb and pork mix in a tangy tomato sauce). \$ *Average main: Rs. 600* ⊠ *Indian Mercantile Mansion, Wodehouse Rd., Regal Circle, Colaba, Mumbai* ☎ 22/2287–5752 ⊹ *C4.*

FORT AND MARINE DRIVE

\$
INDIAN
Fodor's Choice
★
✕ **Apoorva.** If you're searching for an authentic seafood lunch home— read: unpretentious, tasty, and cheap—this old-school Kala Ghoda mainstay is spot on: slightly dingy, full of locals, with a too-cold a/c section that smells faintly of moth balls. The king prawn *gussi*, a spicy red masala dish, is the best thing on the menu, though the tandoori pomfret (an Indian Ocean fish) is a close second. Whatever main dish you choose—especially any fish with a dry green Hyderabadi treatment— order a couple of *neer dosa* as accompaniment: think rotis, but much lighter and fluffier, and made of rice; most Konkan restaurants have them, but none do them better than Apoorva. \$ *Average main: Rs. 400* ⊠ *Vasta House (Noble Chambers), S. A. Brelvi Marg, near Horniman Circle, Fort* ☎ 22/2287–0335, 22/2288–1457 ⊹ *D3.*

The Great Irani Café

Mumbai has a special breed of teahouse that's on the way out. Called "Irani joints" in local parlance, these corner shops were begun by the first waves of Zoroastrians, called the Iranis, who migrated to India in the 10th century from Persia to escape religious persecution. (Those who were part of later waves are referred to as Parsis.) In following centuries thousands and thousands more Zoroastrians arrived in India. A community of about 50,000 remains in the country today, the majority in Mumbai.

Irani cafés probably arose out of the Iranis' need for a place to gather and exchange news. Simply furnished with solid wood chairs and cloaked in the appearance of yesteryear, they remain places where customers can tarry over endless cups of sweet tea for just a couple of rupees. Visiting these seedy, century-old cafés is a chance to glimpse a culture that has all but vanished. The clientele is usually very ordinary Mumbai *wallahs* (dwellers), more often than not

old-timers who have been having chai and buns for the last 40 years in the same spot. Equally eccentric is the menu, an odd selection of chai, "cutting chai" (a half-cup of tea), *bun-maska* (a bun with butter), and typical Parsi cutlets, patties, rolls, fruitcakes, and confectionery. Amid the ancient mirrors, upright chairs, marble tables, elaborate balconies, and portraits of the Prophet Zarathustra is sometimes a sign acquainting you with the dos and don'ts of the particular establishment. Beer is sometimes served. But credit cards? Goodness, no. Early or mid-morning is a good time to visit.

As McDonald's and coffee chains overtake Mumbai, though, traditional Irani cafés are dying out, almost overnight being converted to fast-food joints or else turning upscale and adding Chinese food or spaghetti to their menus. The few that are still left can be found in the Fort area *(See also Britannia & Co. in Where to Eat, under Fort and Marine Drive).*

$
INDIAN
Fodor'sChoice
★

✕**Britannia & Co.** Office workers come here for the world-famous chicken berry pulao—and Boman Kohnior, whose father founded the restaurant in 1923, still takes their orders. When he chants—and he will—"fresh lime soda sweet to beat the Mumbai heat!" you will order just that, but it's that pulao, with rice, chicken, gravy, and dried fruit, that will keep you coming back. Parsi food is only available in Mumbai, and this is one of the oldest Parsi restaurants that, thankfully, hasn't tried to go upscale. It's simple, fast, heavy, blissfully unhealthy food served in a dingy-looking shop with simple tables. $ *Average main: Rs. 400* ⊠ *Wakefield House, Strott Rd., opposite New Custom House, Ballard Estate, Fort* ☎ *22/2261–5264* ⊜ *Reservations essential* ⊟ *No credit cards* ☾ *No dinner* ✛ *D3.*

$$$$
MODERN ASIAN

✕**India Jones.** Though the name implies something quite different, this restaurant actually serves pan-Asian food, and attracts a mix of couples and families out for a special occasion. A bubbling pond with wooden statues greets customers to an interior decked out with traditional Asian accoutrements—mini yellow catamaran sails over the lights, giant Japanese orchids, and various Asian scripts on the walls. For starters, try the

Malaysian beef tenderloin satay, and follow with *Da long xai* (ginger-flavored, wok-fried lobster with water chestnuts and asparagus) or the *rung koo mun shao,* another Malaysian dish made with braised, skin-on chicken and mixed vegetables. $ *Average main: Rs. 1400* ✉ *Trident Hotel, Nariman Point* ☎ *22/6632–4343* ✦ *A4.*

$$$
INDIAN
Fodor's Choice
★

✕ **Kebab Korner.** If you're used to 100-rupee kebabs, this hotel restaurant will serve up a shock, but though they don't come cheap, the succulent kebabs are perfect for those who don't want to risk Delhi belly (yes, even in Mumbai it's called that) at a hygienically challenged late-night spot. Elegant and subdued, with excellent waitstaff, the restaurant's only drawback is the minimum 25-minute wait for your food—but good things take time, and the chicken *seekh* kebabs (ground chicken and spices), Chilean sea bass served in a green *hariyali* (spinach and mint) masala, and the chicken *pahadi* kebab (chunks of saffron-tinged chicken topped with egg whites) are worth the wait. $ *Average main: Rs. 1400* ✉ *InterContinental Hotel, 135 Marine Dr., Churchgate* ☎ *22/3987–9999* ⊕ *www.ichotelsgroup.com* ☾ *No lunch* ✦ *B2.*

$$
SEAFOOD

✕ **Mahesh Lunch Home.** Somewhere between Apoorva and Trishna—geographically as well as atmospherically—Mahesh is another legendary Fort seafood restaurant that attracts the office lunch crowd as well as packing them in during the evenings. The character has been stripped out of the place since they decided to go upscale, and the floor-to-ceiling marble might be a bit much, but the food remains reliably authentic. With that in mind, pass on the butter/pepper/garlic concoctions and stick to the traditional Konkan fare, like prawn *gussi* (a spicy red curry), *rawas* (a local fish), and fried kane (a bony Mangalorean fish). Decades into its existence, it's still *the* place for the freshest fish in town. $ *Average main: Rs. 700* ✉ *8-B Cawasji Patel St., Fort* ☎ *22/6695–5559, 22/6695–5554* ⊕ *www.maheshlunchhome. com* $ *Average main: Rs. 700* ✉ *Kings Apt., Juhu Tara Rd., Juhu* ☎ *22/5695–5554, 22/5695–5559* ✦ *D3.*

$
CAFÉ

✕ **Natural.** Serving the best ice cream in town, Natural—which has the taste of Indian *malai* (sweets so creamy they're almost like cheese)—seems to be everywhere. Established in 1984 in Juhu, Natural now has outlets throughout the country. Open until around midnight—depending on the shop—Natural shops attract students and families alike on most weekend nights. All of the ice cream is made with fresh fruit or nuts, and contains no preservatives; highly recommended are the tender coconut, roasted almond, or seasonal Indian fruit flavors like cinnamon-tinged *chikoo* (a caramel-flavored fruit also known as sapodilla), custard apple, or mango. $ *Average main: Rs. 200* ✉ *Jyoti Sadan, 137 Marine Dr., next to InterContinental Hotel, Churchgate* ☎ *22/2202–7426, 22/6610–8000* ⊕ *www.naturalicecreams.in* ▭ *No credit cards* ✦ *B2.*

$
MODERN
AMERICAN
Fodor's Choice
★

✕ **The Pantry.** Under the same ownership as Woodside, this new restaurant dispenses with the pubby atmosphere to focus on simple, rustic cuisine using local ingredients. The food is excellent and incredibly reasonably priced considering how refined it is, and although it'd be nice if it had a wine license—the white interiors, open kitchen, and general atmosphere fairly scream "Wine Bar!"—the excellent baked goods and mains more than make up for the lack of booze. Try the creamy potato pie, the grilled chicken or pulled pork sandwich, along with the grilled *rawas* and literally any of the breads or pastries, and get ready for the best salads in town. $ *Average main: Rs. 450* ⊠ *Yeshwant Chambers, Military Square La., Kala Ghoda, Fort, Mumbai* ☎ *98206–40695* ☾ *No dinner* ✦ *C3.*

$
INDIAN
Fodor's Choice
★

✕ **Soam.** Families, vegetarians, and foreigners who can't handle street food flock here for healthy Gujarati food. Granted, the use of ghee (clarified butter) is quite liberal, but not all dishes use it—like the various kinds of *chaat* (veggie and bread snacks). The spicy potato patties stuffed with peas and smothered in savory yellow *dal* are highly recommended, as is *palak moong dal* (yellow lentils sautéed with spinach), vitamin *bhel* (a light veggie salad), and spinach and cheese samosas. The modern take on classics doesn't deter the locals and it's likely to be packed, but you'll soon get a seat amid the pale yellow walls, wooden benches, and loud aunties. $ *Average main: Rs. 400* ⊠ *Sadguru Sadan, ground fl., across from Babulnath Mandir, Chowpatty, Marine Drive* ☎ *22/2369–8080* ✦ *E5.*

$
FRENCH
★

✕ **Suzette.** With two Frenchmen at the helm, this tiny crepe joint serves authentic and healthy organic buckwheat pancakes at fair prices. It gets packed with office jockeys on weekday lunchtimes, but they don't linger, so the longest wait time is 10 minutes. Try the Méditerranée, with grilled chicken, olive tapenade, mozzarella, and tomatoes, or the Italie, with arugula, tomato coulis, mozzarella, and oregano, or build your own crepe from their extensive list of ingredients. Salads are washed in bottled water and totally safe. Sweet crepes come with various combinations of Nutella, jam, fruit, and cream. There's another branch in Bandra. $ *Average main: Rs. 400* ⊠ *Atlanta Bldg., Nariman Point, Mumbai* ☎ *22/22880055* ⊕ *www.suzette.in* ✦ *A4.*

$$$
SEAFOOD
★

✕ **Trishna.** Four words: Butter; Pepper; Garlic; Crab. Even if that was all this legendary Kala Ghoda restaurant served, they'd be full year-round. The succulent crab is available in myriad treatments—with Indian and Western spices, green *hariyali* masala, black (spicier) Hyderabadi masala—and they maintain the quality that's made it a favorite with locals and tourists alike for more than 30 years. But there's more to the menu than crab—prawns, squid, pomfret (a classic Indian Ocean fish) are there too, and it's always fresh. The interiors have a tacky 1980s feel, but you're here for the food, not the interior design. $ *Average main: Rs. 1200* ⊠ *7 Rope Walk La., next to Commerce House, Kala Ghoda, Fort* ☎ *22/2270–3213, 22/2261–4991* ✦ *C3.*

$$$
ITALIAN

✕ **Vetro.** This Italian restaurant at the Oberoi hotel has become known as the best in town. Granted, Mumbai is not exactly known for its carbonara, so the bar isn't set too high, but Vetro could stack up against Italian food in any moderately sized American city. And if you're in the mood for a break from spicy food, this minimalist chic restaurant is perfect, especially for lunch. Try the Caprese salad to start, then move on to grilled, spiced chicken, or the antipasti bar, with its wide selection of olives, cheeses, Italian meats, and salads. Those who say the food is bland are likely just more used to spicy Indian food. $ *Average main: Rs. 1400* ⊠ *Oberoi, Nariman Point* ☎ *22/6632–4343* ⊕ *www. oberoihotels.com* ✦ *A4.*

$ INDIAN 🍴 **Zaffran.** Oily, spicy biryani and tikkas draw crowds to this once dingy, now oddly nightclub/spaceship-looking joint near CST. This is a spot for the late-night foodie whose taste buds are a bit more discerning than those of the people eating on the street in front of Bade Miya—and, now that it's been redesigned, the cleanliness at this restaurant might actually be Department of Health approved. The chow is unbelievably tasty, if completely traditional, and it comes fast and cheap. Try the chicken biryani, the chicken tikka, or the famous, creamy butter chicken. [$] *Average main: Rs. 500* ✉ *B Block, Sitaram Building, Dr. D.N. Rd., Fort* ☎ *22/2344–2690, 22/2340–1976* 🌐 *www.zaffranrestaurant.com* 🕓 *No lunch* ✥ *D2.*

$$$$ INDIAN 🍴 **Ziya.** Opened in 2010, Ziya quickly shot to the very forefront of Indian cuisine and although other modern, more traditionally minded restaurants (like Neel) have taken its place at the top of the heap, it remains one of the most exciting restaurants to hit India in ages. Here, traditional Indian flavors receive nouvelle cuisine treatment from Chef Vineet Bhatia, the first Indian chef to win Michelin stars. Try his "gourmand" tasting menu—seven to ten courses that vary from mushroom *kichidi* (rice, yogurt, and spices—like risotto, but mushier) with *makhani* (creamy red tomato curry) ice cream to a smoked tandoori lamb chop with lemon-grass foam. [$] *Average main: Rs. 2500* ✉ *Oberoi, Nariman Point* ☎ *22/6632–5757* 🌐 *www.oberoihotels.com* ✥ *A4.*

6

JUHU, BANDRA, AND THE WESTERN SUBURBS

$$$$ EUROPEAN 🍴 **Aurus.** Juhu's most trendy nightspot is also one of its best fine-dining restaurants. Definitively loungey, it feels less forced and more elegant than most lounge bars in Mumbai, and the outdoor area, overhanging a nice stretch of Juhu Beach, has low white couches and sparkling candlelight. Inside, it's a bit too dim, but later on the dance floor fills up with some of Bollywood's most beautiful people, so stick around after your meal. The continental food has local influences, and runs the gamut from traditional pastas to molecular gastronomy. The signature dish—duck prepared by the *sous vide* method—is succulent, but the grilled New Zealand lamb shank is better. [$] *Average main: Rs. 1500* ✉ *Nichani Kutir, Juhu Tara Rd., near Reid & Taylor, Juhu* ☎ *22/6710–6666* 🌐 *www.dishhospitality.com* ✥ *F2.*

$$$$ INDIAN 🍴 **Azok.** Shortly before Ziya stormed Mumbai's culinary world, renowned chef Vineet Bhatia, hailed for his experimental fine-dining Indian food, quietly opened this lower-key version of his revolutionary Indian restaurant. Perched on the rooftop of an apartment building, Azok may look like a lot of the other outdoor lounges in the city, but rooftop dining is a rare treat in Mumbai, and the food heralds the future of Indian cuisine. Try the mustard tempered stir-fried prawns with wasabi, the lamb biryani, and the chicken tikka with creamy red *makhani* sauce (a mild, creamy tomato curry) over penne pasta. [$] *Average main: Rs. 1600* ✉ *29/1 JR Mhatre Rd., opposite Iris Park, Juhu* ☎ *22/6623–8888* 🕓 *No lunch* ✥ *F1.*

$ CAFÉ 🍴 **The Bagel Shop.** Bandra's beautiful people—from Bollywood stars to expats to creative types—flock to this hip, casual café on tony Pali Hill. The laid-back style, plentiful outdoor seating, and excellent quality food more than make up for the fact that the bagels are actually just round

Sliced fruit for sale

bread, not the boiled-then-baked New York variety. Order a whole-wheat bagel with Goan-style chicken sausage and cream cheese, and one of the wonderful seasonal fruit smoothies, as you lounge on one of the rattan couches. [$] *Average main: Rs. 400* ⊠ *Anand Villa, 13 Pali Mala Rd., up the street from Bandra Commissioner's Station, Bandra* ☎ *22/2605–0178* ✛ *F2.*

$ ✕ **Elco Restaurant.** For decades the food stalls in front of Elco Market
INDIAN have been serving some of the best—and cleanest—vegetarian street food Mumbai has to offer, and they were doing so well that the owners were able to open this two-floor restaurant inside the market, offering essentially the same food. Try the cheese *pav bhaji* for a heartier take on a Mumbai classic, the *ragda pattice,* and pretty much any of the other classics listed in the "Street Food Favorites." Finish off with a serving of sweet, doughy *gulab jamuns,* basically doughnut holes in a sweet syrup. [$] *Average main: Rs. 150* ⊠ *C-84 Elco Market, 46 Hill Rd., Bandra* ☎ *22/2643–7206* ▭ *No credit cards* ✛ *F2.*

$ ✕ **Gajalee.** Suburbanites love this quaint seafood joint near Juhu Beach,
SEAFOOD which compares favorably with the best coastal restaurants Fort has to offer. They've opened a branch in High Street Phoenix Mall, so those staying down south don't have to travel too far to enjoy the fried *surmai* fish (a type of mackerel), the savory crab stir fry, the big, fresh grilled tiger prawns, or the baby shark masala (actually *mori* fish). The Phoenix Mall branch is sleek and modern, while the original Vile Parle location is a bit tacky and dated but generally better regarded (as most originals are). [$] *Average main: Rs. 400* ⊠ *Amrapali Shopping Centre, VL Mehta Marg, Vile Parle, Juhu* ☎ *22/2610–7040, 6696–0902* ⊕ *www.gajalee. com* [$] *Average main: Rs. 400* ⊠ *Phoenix Mills, Block 3 ABC, Senapati*

Bapat Marg, Lower Parel, near Big Bazaar (department store), Central Mumbai ☎ *22/2495–0667, 22/2495–0668* ✛ *F2.*

$$$$ ✕ **Hakkasan.** The Mumbai outpost of the Michelin-starred London orig-
CHINESE inal, this Bandra haunt is worth a visit for those who absolutely must have a fancy Chinese dinner, and can't wait until they're in London, New York, or Miami (where prices, because of tax and local markups here, will be a sight lower). Even then, it's likely only worth dining here if you're in Bandra already. Try the Peking duck with Ossetra caviar (we said it was expensive; might as well go all out), the stir-fry tenderloin with black pepper sauce, or the dim sum basket, in which the scallop shumai is likely the star, but all of the dumplings are outstanding. Ⓢ *Average main: Rs. 3500* ✉ *Krystal Bldg., 206 Waterfield Rd., Bandra, Mumbai* ☎ *22/2644–4444* ⊕ *www.hakkasan.com* ✛ *F2.*

$ ✕ **Kareem's.** Popular with college kids, and tucked neatly off Carter
INDIAN Road, Kareem's serves some of the best kebabs in the 'burbs—and it's a good option for those wary of eating street-side kebabs (which, honestly, take kebabs to a whole other level), or not up for a visit to Muhammad Ali Road in the Muslim ghetto. Open-air, but decorated in unpretentious, but modern, dark wood, Kareem's has a casual atmosphere, enhanced by the bench-style seating. Try the chicken tikka, the mutton *seekh* kebabs (minced meat wrapped around a skewer and cooked in the tandoor oven), and, for vegetarians, the *paneer tikka* (grilled cottage cheese with peppers and onions). There's another on Colaba Causeway. Ⓢ *Average main: Rs. 250* ✉ *7A Gagangiri, Off Carter Rd., Bandra* ☎ *22/2643–7206* Ⓢ *Average main: Rs. 250* ✉ *Shop 3 & 4, Radha Estate, 148 A, Shahid Bhagat Singh Rd., Colaba Causeway, near Sassoon Dock, Bandra* ☎ *22/2215–2206* ✛ *F3.*

$$$ ✕ **Pali Village Café.** Quality European bistro food—and the opportunity
EUROPEAN to see a Bollywood star or two—draws suburbanites, and even a few Townies (people from South Bombay), to this converted two-story furniture store in Bandra. While the rest of Mumbai runs headlong into the future, this place harks back to Bombay's bungalow roots with simple wooden tables, wrought iron railings, and exposed brick. The pastas and sandwiches are well executed, but it's the thin-crust pizza, served by the slice—rare in Mumbai—that's the real draw, though the grilled Australian lamb chops might be the best dish on the menu. Ⓢ *Average main: Rs. 1400* ✉ *Pali Naka, next to Janata Lunch Home, Bandra* ☎ *22/2605–0401* ✛ *F3.*

$$ ✕ **Salt Water Café.** This unpretentious restaurant in Bandra Reclamation—
EUROPEAN a section of Bandra—has a classic nouvelle cuisine menu and a simple rooftop terrace. The crab cakes are especially good, the steak is decent (but remember that unless it's crazy expensive, steak in India usually means buffalo), and the drinks are relatively cheap. It gets crowded on weekends so be sure to make a reservation, preferably for the terrace, where the cover of giant palm trees somehow blocks out the cacophony from noisy Chapel Road below. Ⓢ *Average main: Rs. 700* ✉ *Rose Minar Annexe, 87 Chapel Rd., near Mount Carmel Church, Bandra* ☎ *22/2643–4441* ✛ *F3.*

WHERE TO STAY

ABOUT THE HOTELS

In Mumbai, unlike elsewhere in India, even mid-range hotels can be shockingly overpriced, and a hotel shortage means that good deals are few. Many hotels in that middle range aren't quite up to Western standards of cleanliness, despite their high prices, but location means everything in Mumbai, and tourists may have to sacrifice a bit on substance to get proximity to the city's best attractions. Even hotels with the highest of prices can be full because of year-round demand, so you're well advised to make reservations a few months in advance.

Chains like the Taj, Oberoi, Hyatt, Marriott, InterContinental, Hilton, and Sheraton have huge hotels, most of them deluxe; these cater to leisure and business travelers, and movie stars with money to burn. Whether you reserve with a hotel directly or through a travel agent, always ask for a discount. Note that tariffs quoted in this book and at hotels do not include 12% tax. Room rates at the luxury hotels fluctuate depending on occupancy, and they offer the rate of the day; the earlier you book, the better the rate you'll get. If you're paying cash, convert your currency beforehand—most hotels give poor exchange rates.

Most of Mumbai's hotels are collected around three locations: in South Mumbai, primarily in Colaba; near Juhu Beach in the suburbs (note that the beach has been cleaned up, but it's not clean enough for swimming—even though you might see some local boys going in); and in North Mumbai, near the airport. If you're going to be sightseeing, and you have the money, stay in South Mumbai rather than the suburbs. If you're here on business, the airport may be your ideal location, and there are several luxury hotels in the vicinity.

Mumbai's cheaper hotels, usually in South Mumbai, can be decent but are still probably overpriced for what you get. During the monsoon season (mid-May through late September), these hotels are overrun by large groups of vacationers from various Arab nations who come to Mumbai to enjoy the cooler weather and rain, during which time noise levels can be very high—solo women travelers should probably stay elsewhere during this time unless they really aren't going to be bothered by the stares.

Unless otherwise indicated, hotels have air-conditioning, room service, doctors on call, and currency exchange, and rooms have private bathrooms and cable television.

Prices in the reviews are the lowest cost of a standard double room in high season. For expanded hotel reviews, facilities, and current deals, visit Fodors.com.

CENTRAL MUMBAI

$$$　**Four Seasons.** Extremely popular with businesspeople because of
HOTEL　its central location between South Bombay and the western suburbs, India's tallest hotel—33 stories—also boasts a luxury rooftop bar that is one of the city's hottest (and most expensive) night spots. **Pros:** central location; business-friendly. **Cons:** central location—unless you are

BEST BETS FOR MUMBAI LODGING

Fodor'sChoice ★	**$$$$**	**BEST POOL**
Bentley's, p. 359	InterContinental, p. 361	JW Marriott, p. 362
The Oberoi, p. 361	JW Marriott, p. 362	Taj Mahal Palace, p. 361
Taj Mahal Palace, p. 361	The Oberoi, p. 361	
	Taj Mahal Palace, p. 361	**BEST SPA**
By Price		JW Marriott, p. 362
	By Experience	
$		**BEST LOCATION**
Bentley's, p. 359	**BEST VIEWS**	Bentley's, p. 359
Sea Green, p. 361	InterContinental, p. 361	Fariyas, p. 359
Sea Palace, p. 361	The Oberoi, p. 361	The Oberoi, p. 361
	Taj Mahal Palace, p. 361	Taj Mahal Palace, p. 361
$$$		
Four Seasons, p. 358	**BEST HOTEL BAR**	**BEST INTERIOR DESIGN**
The Trident, p. 361	Four Seasons, p. 358	Novotel, p. 362
	Intercontinental, p. 361	
		BEST FOR BUSINESS
	BEST FOR KIDS	Four Seasons, p. 358
	JW Marriott, p. 362	InterContinental, p. 361

on business nearby, you're in no-man's-land, with slum hutments facing your fancy hotel. $ *Rooms from: Rs. 12000* ⊠ *114 Dr. E. Moses Rd., Parel, Central Mumbai* ☎ *22/2481–8000* ⊕ *www.fourseasons.com* ⟳ *176 rooms, 26 suites* ⦿ *No meals* ✣ *F4.*

COLABA

$ ⛭ **Bentley's.** The best deal in Colaba—a clean, quaint, simple tourist
HOTEL   joint in a prime South Bombay location—is the kind of place young
Fodor'sChoice   expats send visiting friends to stay if they don't have room. **Pros:** cheap
★   and clean; friendly, helpful owner. **Cons:** basic, and can be a little musty.
$ *Rooms from: Rs. 2000* ⊠ *17 Oliver St., Colaba, Mumbai* ☎ *22/2284– 1474* ⊕ *www.bentleyshotel.com* ⟳ *55* ✣ *C5.*

$$$ ⛭ **Fariyas.** Just a few minutes on foot from the Gateway of India, the
HOTEL   Fariyas is a solid mid-range hotel, well located in Colaba. **Pros:** well
located; good views. **Cons:** smallish rooms; surprisingly expensive.
$ *Rooms from: Rs. 9000* ⊠ *25 Devshankar V, Vyas Marg, off Arthur Bunder Rd., Colaba* ☎ *22/6141—6141* ⊕ *www.fariyas.com* ⟳ *87 rooms, 6 suites* ⦿ *Breakfast* ✣ *C5.*

$ ⛭ **Godwin.** A great location at a decent price is the main selling point of
HOTEL   this nine-story, low-frills hotel, but room standards (and views) vary so
opt for one of the 10 renovated deluxe rooms with central air and in-room amenities like coffeemakers. **Pros:** cheap, but not that cheap; well located. **Cons:** shabby rooms. $ *Rooms from: Rs. 5900* ⊠ *41 Garden*

DID YOU KNOW?

The Mumbai Marathon, which was first held in 2004, is so popular that registration usually sells out within two to three weeks: 2,800 people run the full marathon; about 11,000 run the half marathon.

Rd., off Colaba Causeway, near Electric House, Colaba ☎ *22/2287–2050, 22/2284–1226* 📠 *22/2287–1592* 🌐 *hotelgodwin.co.in* 🛏 *52 rooms, 18 suites* 🍴 *Breakfast* ✥ *C5.*

$ HOTEL **Sea Palace Hotel.** The location of this mid-range hotel (with bargain prices for Mumbai) is enough to make it a good choice—it's right on the waterfront near the Gateway of India. **Pros:** the staff is attentive; cheap; great location; airy, pleasant rooms. **Cons:** could be classier. [$] *Rooms from: Rs. 5000* ✉ *26 P.J. Ramachandani Marg, Colaba* ☎ *22/2284–1828, 22/2285–4404* 🛏 *50 rooms, 3 suites* 🍴 *Breakfast* ✥ *C5.*

$$$$ HOTEL Fodor's Choice ★ **Taj Mahal Palace.** Foreigners and wealthy Indians choose the Taj over other fancy hotels in town because it's a beautiful and regal landmark—worth visiting even if you don't stay here—with views past the Gateway of India to the Arabian Sea. **Pros:** it's an icon; location, location, location; city's best views. **Cons:** expensive; service can be disorganized. [$] *Rooms from: Rs. 16000* ✉ *Colaba* ☎ *22/6665–3366* 🌐 *www.tajhotels.com* 🛏 *565 rooms, 45 suites* 🍴 *Breakfast* ✥ *C4.*

$$$ HOTEL **Vivanta by Taj–President.** Favored by business travelers, this luxury hotel also offers some great views, a choice of restaurants, and a hip bar. **Pros:** great in-house restaurants and popular bar; well located. **Cons:** small rooms. [$] *Rooms from: Rs. 12200* ✉ *90 Cuffe Parade, Colaba* ☎ *22/6665–0808* 🌐 *www.tajhotels.com* 🛏 *292 rooms, 20 suites* 🍴 *Breakfast* ✥ *A6.*

6

FORT AND MARINE DRIVE

$$$$ HOTEL **InterContinental.** Aside from the ideal Marine Drive location and some of the city's biggest standard rooms, service is a big plus point here, with personal concierges at your beck and call and a complimentary in-room massage to every guest. **Pros:** 500-square-foot rooms as standard; Dome and Kebab Korner restaurants are among the city's best. **Cons:** the Oberoi, its chief competitor, just seems so much more grand. [$] *Rooms from: Rs. 16000* ✉ *135 Marine Dr., Churchgate* ☎ *22/3987–9999* 🌐 *www.intercontinental.com* 🛏 *58 rooms, 5 suites* 🍴 *Breakfast* ✥ *B2.*

$$$$ HOTEL Fodor's Choice ★ **The Oberoi.** Luxury and stellar service are the hallmarks here—every floor has a butler who will make reservations, collect your laundry, shine your shoes, supervise the room cleaning, and bring you chocolates. **Pros:** best new restaurant in town; elegant rooms with views of the Arabian Sea. **Cons:** expensive. [$] *Rooms from: Rs. 14000* ✉ *Nariman Point* ☎ *22/6632–5757* 🌐 *www.oberoihotels.com* 🛏 *214 rooms, 73 suites* 🍴 *Breakfast* ✥ *A4.*

$ HOTEL **Sea Green.** Aside from its friendly service, this hotel's main virtue is that it's a remarkable bargain for the price and location, if you don't mind the somewhat institutional appearance. **Pros:** good location; nice views; large, clean rooms. **Cons:** antiquated and rather worn. [$] *Rooms from: Rs. 3950* ✉ *145 Marine Dr., Churchgate* ☎ *22/2282–2294, 22/6633–6525* 🌐 *www.seagreenhotel.com* 🛏 *34 rooms, 4 suites* 🍴 *No meals* ✥ *B3.*

$$$ HOTEL **The Trident.** The Oberoi's posh—slightly less luxurious—cousin continues the same tradition of excellent service, and because room rates vary according to occupancy, it can be a great value in the off-season. **Pros:** cheaper than the Oberoi, though not significantly

lower in quality; a true high-rise with proper views. **Cons:** you're not staying at the Oberoi. $ *Rooms from: Rs. 10000* ✉ *Nariman Point* ☎ *22/6632–4343* ⊕ *www.tridenthotels.com* ⤴ *550 rooms, 40 suites* ⦿ *No meals* ✛ *B4.*

JUHU, BANDRA, AND THE WESTERN SUBURBS

$ ⊞ **Citizen.** One of the cheapest decent hotels on the Juhu strip, and right
HOTEL on the beach, the Citizen is a deal in a city where you seemingly pay for every square inch. **Pros:** good value for money; on the beach. **Cons:** far from South Bombay. $ *Rooms from: Rs. 5500* ✉ *960 Juhu Tara Rd., Juhu* ☎ *22/6693–2525, 22/2660–7273* ⊕ *www.citizenhotelMumbai. com* ⤴ *45 rooms, 3 suites* ⦿ *Breakfast* ✛ *F1.*

$$$ ⊞ **Novotel.** Built in the 1970s, this Western-style high rise (formerly
HOTEL the Holiday Inn) was completely renovated when Novotel took over in 2009, and the spacious lobby and large rooms now have a modern, sleek feel. **Pros:** beachside location; airport pick-up included in price; close to suburban malls. **Cons:** far from downtown. $ *Rooms from: Rs. 11000* ✉ *Balraj Sahani Marg, Juhu* ☎ *22/6693–4444* ⊕ *www. novotel. com* ⤴ *203 rooms, 12 suites* ⦿ *No meals* ✛ *F1.*

$$$$ ⊞ **JW Marriott.** A grand, luxurious hotel where you can retreat from
HOTEL the chaos of Mumbai but still be able to step out and experience it, though the main sights are distant. **Pros:** airport transfers included in rates; well-appointed rooms; excellent meals. **Cons:** expensive; far from city sights. $ *Rooms from: Rs. 17900* ✉ *Juhu Tara Rd., Juhu* ☎ *22/6693–3000* ⊕ *www.marriott.com* ⤴ *326 rooms, 29 suites* ⦿ *Breakfast* ✛ *F1.*

$$ ⊞ **Ramada Plaza Palm Grove.** Close to the buzz of Juhu Beach, this
HOTEL hotel is handy for people with business in the suburbs and popular with wedding parties. **Pros:** right on Juhu Beach; spacious rooms; airport pick-up included. **Cons:** expensive; far from South Mumbai. $ *Rooms from: Rs. 7500* ✉ *Juhu Tara Rd., Juhu* ☎ *22/2611–2323, 22/6697–2323* ⊕ *www.krahejahospitality.com* ⤴ *115 rooms, 3 suites* ⦿ *Breakfast* ✛ *F1.*

$$$$ ⊞ **Taj Land's End.** Choose this opulent, ocean-facing hotel if you don't
HOTEL mind paying a decent buck for a luxurious stay far from the city's main sights, but close to some of its best bars and clubs. **Pros:** amazing views; close to restaurants and nightlife. **Cons:** expensive; far from city's historic sites. $ *Rooms from: Rs. 13500* ✉ *Land's End, Bandstand area, Bandra* ☎ *22/6668–1234* ⊕ *www.tajhotels.com* ⤴ *493 rooms, 33 suites* ⦿ *Breakfast* ✛ *F3.*

NIGHTLIFE AND THE ARTS

THE ARTS

Nowadays, Mumbai's arts scene has gone as online as any other major city's, so your first stop should probably be the Internet. *You'll find the websites for all of the major playhouses below; check schedules accordingly.* For movies, go to ⊕ *www.bookmyshow.com*, India's answer to Fandango, to book tickets at most Mumbai theaters. For some of the

Taj Mahal Palace

The Oberoi

best cultural goings-on-about-town, check out the websites ⊕ *www. MumbaiBoss.com* and ⊕ *www.BPBweekend.com*, which are hipper versions of *Time Out*. If you're old school, you can check out the fortnightly culture calendar "Programme of Dance, Music and Drama," available free at the Government of India Tourist Office. The daily *Times of India* usually lists each day's films, concerts, and other events; on Friday they publish a guide to city events called *What's Hot* that can be purchased at any newsstand. The afternoon paper *Midday* publishes highlights of the coming week's events in its pullout *What To Do? Where To Go?*, also available online (⊕ *www.mid-day.com*). Program information and details usually appear on the Maharashtra Tourism Development Corporation's (MTDC) city-guide programs, shown regularly on hotel in-house TV stations.

National Centre for the Performing Arts (*NCPA*). This huge complex has dance performances, and occasionally hosts movie revivals. The performance schedule is posted on the website. It also includes a spacious Mediterranean restaurant, Amadeus. Note that some NCPA performances are open to members only; a year's membership is Rs. 2,500. ✉ *Sir Dorab Tata Rd., Nariman Point* ☎ 22/6622–3724, 22/2237–3737 ⊕ *www.ncpamumbai.com*.

Rhythm House Private Ltd. Performance tickets in Mumbai are usually quite inexpensive (from free to Rs. 500) and can be purchased from box offices or from the ticket counter at Rhythm House (across the street from the Jehangir Art Gallery), one of Mumbai's main music stores— selling CDs, DVDs and electronics—and another source of information on what's happening. ✉ *40 K. Dubash Marg, Rampart Row, Kala Ghoda, Fort* ☎ 22/4322–2727 ⊕ *www.rhythmhouse.in*.

FILM Mumbai, aka "Bollywood," is the center of the Indian film industry— the largest film producer in the world. A typical epic Indian musical in the movie theater is three or so hours of song, tears, gun battles, and around-the-trees love dances; in other words, quite a spectacle. Most of these movies are in Hindi, but the plots are pretty basic, so you'll probably get the gist. Seeing a Bollywood movie in an Indian theater is an experience unlike what most Americans are used to: it's a very social scene, often with whole families or groups of friends talking and laughing and eating; indeed, the movie itself is often not the primary entertainment. It's definitely a unique experience, but not for everyone. And even if you go, don't feel obliged to stay to the end. The Inox is a convenient place to go, but there are other Bollywood theaters farther afield; check local entertainment listings.

Inox. A good place to catch a Bollywood film, or the latest English one, is the upscale Inox. ✉ *CR2 shopping mall, opposite Bajaj Bhavan, Nariman Point* ☎ 22/6659–5959.

For English-language movies, there are several options around Mumbai:

IMAX Adlabs. Mumbai's only IMAX theater shows a mixture of popular and documentary films in its main dome theater, but it's in a rather out-of-the-way part of Mumbai, and it's advisable, especially for the dome, to purchase tickets in advance from bookmyshow.com. ✉ *Anik Wadala Link Rd., Wadala* ☎ 22/3989–4040.

A theater performance at Mumbai's National Centre for the Performing Arts

Nehru Centre Auditorium. Interesting art films, some in English, are shown here. ✉ *Dr. Annie Besant Rd., Worli, Central Mumbai* ☎ *22/2496–4676* ⊕ *www.nehru-centre.org.*

Regal Cinema. This Art Deco-style theater usually shows current Hindi-language movies, but often screens Hollywood blockbusters. ✉ *Shaheed Bhagat Singh Rd., opposite Prince of Wales Museum, Colaba* ☎ *22/2202–1017.*

Sterling Cinema. Current English-language (and Bollywood) films are shown here. ✉ *Tata Palace, Murzban Rd., off D.Naoroji Rd., near Victoria Terminus, Fort* ☎ *22/2207–5187, 22/6631–6677, 22/6622–0017.*

MUSIC AND THEATER

Nehru Centre Auditorium. Mumbai's second major venue regularly hosts theater, music, and dance performances. ✉ *Dr. Annie Besant Rd., Worli, Central Mumbai* ☎ *22/2496–4676* ⊕ *www.nehru-centre.org.*

☺ **Prithvi Theatre.** Run by the famous Kapoor acting family (current Bollywood stars Kareena and Ranbir Kapoor are two of them), the theater stages a variety of plays each week, some in English, with reasonably priced tickets. They often host special programs for children, too. It's a 45-minute drive north from downtown Mumbai, or 20 minutes from the airport in nontraffic hours. An evening at Prithvi, which has an arty café and bookstore, can be memorable. ✉ *Janaki Kutir, Church Rd., Juhu* ☎ *22/2614–9546* ⊕ *www.prithvitheatre.org.*

NIGHTLIFE

Simply put, no city in India knows how to have a good time quite like Mumbai. Here you'll find everything from dingy "permit rooms" (basically cafeteria-style rooms with a liquor license) so dirty they make an American dive bar look like the Rainbow Room, and clubs so fancy they make the Rainbow Room look like a permit room. Whatever destination you choose, they all hold their own special charms. If you're in the mood for a cheap tipple, and you appreciate the character of a down and dirty dive bar, head to Gokul, behind the Taj Mahal Palace, it's the most tourist-friendly of Mumbai's permit rooms.

If you're more inclined to clubbing, Mumbai has lots to choose from—though club owners seem to have decided that the only option that works in this city are lounges with blaring music and tiny dance floors: be forewarned, though, that prices are steep, and you'll often pay New York prices, or more, for your drinks. Note, too, that many clubs and bars have "couples" policies, wherein a "stag" (lone man) is not permitted to enter without a woman. This might be a circuitous attempt to prevent brawls, pick-up scenes, and prostitution—or just a club owner figuring that in a country where many more guys are allowed to stay out late than girls, a club full of dudes isn't going to attract much business. To avoid an unpleasant encounter at the door, check with your hotel staff to find out whether your destination club or bar will allow you to enter if you're a man traveling alone or in a group of men. Dress nicely and you'll probably get in; an advance call from your hotel concierge might also make your entry smoother.

One area where the suburbs have it over the city is nightlife, and the after-dark scene in the wealthy enclaves of Juhu and Bandra thrive on suburbia's young nouveau riche as well as city folk willing to travel for a good night out.

Revelry peaks from Thursday to Sunday nights, with an early-twenties-to-mid-thirties crowd. Pubs open daily at around 6 or 7 (except a few, which open in the afternoon) and close by 1:15 am or a little later, depending, quite honestly, on how much they've paid the local cops. Some places collect a cover charge at the door. As in any metropolis, the reign of a nightspot can be ephemeral. ■TIP➔ **Ask a young hotel employee to tell you where the best clubs or bars are, as trends change quickly in Mumbai.**

CENTRAL MUMBAI
BARS AND LOUNGES

Aer. The rooftop club at the Four Seasons is one of the most popular—and most expensive—bars in town, but it offers stunning views of the city in all directions, and is probably worth a drink. ⊠ *Four Seasons Hotel, 114 E. Moses Rd., Worli, Central Mumbai* ☎ *22/2481–8000, 22/2481–8444.*

Busaba. In addition to its excellent Asian restaurant (think a combination of Burmese, Chinese, Vietanmese, and Thai), Busaba has a relaxed but small and attractive bar-lounge. There's another branch near Blue Frog and Café Zoe in Central Mumbai, if you're in the neighborhood.

✉ *4 Mandlik Rd., near Cotton World, Colaba* ☎ *22/2204–3779*
✉ *Mathuradas Mill Compound, N.M. Joshi Marg, near Blue Frog,*
Lower Parel, Central Mumbai ☎ *22/6747–8974.*

CLUBS AND DISCOS

Blue Frog. International bands and local acts play every night except
Monday at this spacious, trendy nightclub, with top-notch acoustics.
International cuisine is served—with munchies like onion rings, burgers,
and cheese platters, as well as full meals like pasta and fried fish. Entry
per head varies from free to Rs. 2,000, depending on whether there
is an international or domestic act playing. Check website for schedule. ✉ *Mathuradas Mills Compound, Tulsi Pipe Rd. entrance, opposite
Kamala Mills entrance, Lower Parel, Central Mumbai* ☎ *022/6158–
6158* ⊕ *www.bluefrog.co.in.*

COLABA

BARS AND LOUNGES

Gokul. The most tourist-friendly of Mumbai's permit rooms, offering a
no-frills, dingy atmosphere—this is the kind of place you want to hit
up for super-cheap drinks (we're talking nearly retail prices per bottle,
which you can order to your table) before you head to the club, or for a
late-night drink post-clubbing, if the owners have paid the cops enough
to stay open past bar time that night. ✉ *10 Tulloch Rd., behind Taj
Mahal Palace hotel and next to Bade Miya, Colaba* ☎ *22/2284–8248,
22/2284–8206.*

Indigo. More famous as a restaurant, Indigo also has a comfortable and
happy bar/lounge area and excellent wine selection, making it a special
place to have drinks, too. ✉ *4 Mandlik Rd., near Cotton World, Colaba*
☎ *22/6636–8980, 22/6636–8981.*

Koyla. Koyla is a rooftop hangout with hookahs, Arabian music, a good
breeze, and tasty barbecue bites. No alcohol is served. ✉ *Gulf Hotel,
Arthur Bunder Rd., near Radio Club, Colaba* ☎ *22/6636–9999.*

Sports Bar Express. Loud music, a giant television screen, and pool tables
in the next room are the attractions here. ✉ *Shaheed Bhagat Singh Rd.,
next to Regal Cinema, Colaba* ☎ *22/6639–6682.*

Wink. One of the more popular bars in south Mumbai, Wink is on the
spendy side because it's located in the 5-Star Vivanta by Taj–President
Mumbai hotel. The main draw is its chill house music. ✉ *Vivanta by
Taj–President Mumbai, 90 Cuffe Parade, Colaba* ☎ *22/6665–0808.*

CLUBS AND DISCOS

Prive and Tetsuma. Patterned on a London nightclub, Prive and Tetsuma
are among the hottest clubs in town with a decent Japanese restaurant
that becomes a bar at night. Both are open until at least 4 am on most
weekend nights, serve expensive drinks, attract a youngish (but not
teenage) crowd, and allow smoking indoors once it's late enough. ✉ *The
Courtyard, 41/44 Monrepos, ground fl., Minoo Desai Road, near Radio
Club, Colaba* ☎ *22/2202–8700.*

6

Song and Dance, Bollywood Style

Nicknamed after its Hollywood exemplar, Bollywood, the famously spirited and wildly popular Indian film industry headquartered in Mumbai, is the largest movie production center in the world. Its devoted Hindi-speaking patrons number in the tens of millions.

For almost 40 years, the blueprint of Bollywood movies hasn't changed much: boy meets girl, boy and girl dance provocatively, but never kiss; something keeps them apart, usually some sort of injustice, or something having to do with religion or family; a poorly staged fight ensues in which one man takes on an entire village, and, finally, love conquers all and the pair live happily ever after. Often a dream sequence is used as an excuse for what basically amounts to a music video, often shot in the Swiss Alps, wherein famous actors otherwise unaffiliated with the movie's plot will appear, and lip synch. You may also notice pieces of your favorite American films popping up, uncredited (one popular Bollywood movie includes pieces of all the following films: *The Godfather, Pulp Fiction, Reservoir Dogs,* and *Goodfellas*; another took the plot of *I Am Sam* and turned it into a post-9/11 film, and managed to fit in a subplot featuring a Katrina-like situation in the American South). Although on the whole, the films, not to mention the acting and writing, aren't quite up to Western standards, production values are improving dramatically.

Hindi films play a special role in the lives of the Indian people. Sure, it's a lot of musical gobbledygook, but for the poor and the illiterate, paying a few rupees for three solid hours of fantasy is a terrific bargain—and middle- and upper-class Indians are no less attached to their movies and the gods of Bollywood. An on-location film shoot, or the arrival of a Hindi star at a restaurant, will attract mobs; these actors and actresses are the demigods of India. (You'll also find them on TV and billboards, hawking everything from cell phones to cement.) The lion of the industry, Amitabh Bachchan, one of India's favorite superstars—think of him as a cross between Burt Reynolds and Ben Kingsley—has a temple dedicated to him in West Bengal.

Moviegoing tips: Remember to stand up for the national anthem before the movie. You could try to brush up on your Hindi before you go, or have a local accompany you to provide a translation (you'll find that patrons talking in the movies is not uncommon, indeed, it's also not unusual for theatergoers to hold full-volume cell-phone conversations in the middle of the movie), but even though the movies are in a foreign language, it's pretty easy to follow along.

FORT AND MARINE DRIVE
BARS AND LOUNGES

★ **Dome.** With some of the best views of the city, the open-air Dome attracts a young, good-looking crowd who sit, amid candlelight, on plush white sofas and chairs. It's one of the best sunset-drink spots in the city, and the fact that the menu includes a selection from the excellent Kebab Korner only sweetens the deal. Drinks are fairly expensive, but if you're on a budget, grab a Kingfisher for Rs. 300—hardly a steal, but you're paying for the view. ⊠ *InterContinental Hotel, 135 Marine Dr., Churchgate* ☎ *22/6639–9999.*

Eau Bar. Facing the Arabian Sea, this bar is elegant and more reserved than many of its peers, and attracts a rather high-class clientele for the live jazz band that plays each night. ⊠ *The Oberoi hotel, Nariman Point* ☎ *22/6632–4142.*

Geoffrey's. A relatively staid yuppie crowd likes to hang out in the clubby (in the British sense) setting here, but it's also one of the few bars with enough TVs to accommodate a big televised sporting event like Wimbledon or the World Cup. ⊠ *Marine Plaza Hotel, 29 Marine Dr., Churchgate* ☎ *22/2285–1212.*

JUHU, BANDRA, AND THE WESTERN SUBURBS
BARS AND LOUNGES

Hawaiian Shack. Small but popular, Hawaiian Shack resembles a Goa beach spot and plays retro music. ⊠ *339 16th Rd., opposite Pal's Fish Corner, off Linking Rd., Bandra* ☎ *22/2605–8753.*

Olive Bar and Restaurant. This candlelit nightspot draws Mumbai's who's who for bites of top-notch antipasto, risotto, seafood salad, and sips of caipiroskas (Caipirinias made with vodka instead of cachaça liqueur). ⊠ *14 Union Park, off Carter Rd., Bandra* ☎ *022/26058228* ⊕ *www. olivebarandkitchen.com.*

Vie. Great food as well as great beats—opt for the lounge on the beach. ⊠ *102 Juhu Tara Rd., opposite Little Italy, Juhu* ☎ *22/2660–2003.*

CLUBS AND DISCOS

Enigma. In the swanky Marriott, Enigma is one of the hottest discos in the burbs. Expect loud music. ⊠ *JW Marriott, Juhu Tara Rd., Juhu* ☎ *22/2693–3000.*

MALABAR HILL AND ENVIRONS
BARS AND LOUNGES

The Ghetto. This is a great late-night spot, and the closest Mumbai has to a true dive bar, complete with a pair of beat up pool tables. ⊠ *30 Bhulabhai Desai Rd., Breach Candy, Malabar Hill* ☎ *22/2353–8418.*

SHOPPING

Mumbai is a shopper's town: in the same day, you can sift through alleys full of antiques in Chor Bazaar, haggle for trinkets on the Colaba Causeway, and stop in at the Brioni showroom at the Taj Mahal Palace Hotel for marked-up luxury goods (though we'd recommend you get your Louis Vuitton and Armani back home to avoid the huge import taxes).

The Causeway, Kemps Corner, and Breach Candy are all trendy shopping areas in South Mumbai; the latter two are chic and pricey. A walk down Colaba Causeway will probably take you past most of the things you want to buy in India—shoes, clothes, cheap knickknacks, cheap cotton clothing, jewelry, and wraps—displayed at stalls lining the road; more expensive items are found in the air-conditioned shops and boutiques behind the stalls on this same road.

The arcades in top hotels offer a little bit of everything for a lot more money than anywhere else, but the merchandise is beautiful and the pace unhurried (and it's climate-controlled). If you're looking for the kind of stuff you can't get anywhere else in the world, and a more vibrant experience, throw yourself into the middle of one of Mumbai's famous bazaars. After all, odds are you didn't come to India to visit the Louis Vuitton boutique.

The city's department stores are good for one-stop shopping, and Fabindia and The Bombay Store both have a large number of branches in the city.

Throughout Mumbai many smaller shops are closed on Sunday (some of the suburbs are closed a different day: in Worli, up to Bandra, they're closed Monday; and in Bandra, up to the suburbs, they're closed Thursday, although many areas are also in the process of switching to Sunday). Malls, however, are open every day. They are especially crowded on the weekend (mall-gazing—that is, large-scale window shopping—has become a new Mumbai leisure activity).

Once you've exhausted Mumbai proper, you can venture out to the suburbs, where prices tend to be lower and the malls more numerous. Linking Road in Bandra is a trendy place to shop, and Juhu's main strip, Juhu Tara Road, is lined with cutting-edge new boutiques, shops, art galleries, and restaurants.

Some good and cheap Mumbai buys: silver jewelry, handicrafts, handloom cotton and silk clothing and household items, eyeglasses, DVDs, CDs, and books.

CENTRAL MUMBAI

CLOTHING

Ensemble. This pricey store has exclusive men's and women's Indian and Western fashions, and lovely costume jewelry, all by high-profile Indian designers. Ask to see the rare Banarasi silk saris, in rich colors woven with real gold and silver thread. ⊠ *Paragon Centre, ground fl., opposite Century Mills, B-1, Worli, Central Mumbai* ☎ *22/2284–3227, 22/2287–2882* ⊕ *www.ensembleindia.com.*

DEPARTMENT STORES AND MALLS

Phoenix Mills. This is an ever-expanding shopping, entertainment, and dining area in an old mill—an island of prosperity and chic modernity amid slums and industry. The complex is divided into different segments. Phoenix Mills itself has department stores like **Big Bazaar,** outlet clothing shop **Pantaloons,** and Hamley's. Palladium is the luxury mall featuring Burberry, Zara, Gucci, Diesel and the like; here too are a number of clubs (frequented by the teenage and college student set) and a Comedy Store, showcasing various comics of varying quality on a nightly basis. High Street Phoenix features high street brands. If you get hungry, outlets of Indigo Deli, Moshe's and McDonald's, among many others, await. ⊠ *Phoenix Mills Compound, Senapati Bapat Marg, Lower Parel, Central Mumbai.*

DID YOU KNOW?

About 1,000 Bollywood movies are released each year, about twice the number from Hollywood.

Getaway to Matheran Hill Station

Perhaps the most pleasant hill station to visit near Mumbai, Matheran, founded by British collector Hugh Malet, is cooler than Mumbai all year long due to the elevation, and it's particularly nice in the months leading up to and during the monsoon, when the hillsides burst into verdant bloom. One big attraction is the fact that Matheran is car-free, and the main forms of transportation are horses, hand-pulled rickshaws, and carts. The late Jimmy Lord, a crusty Parsi gentleman who established a Raj-style hotel (Lords Central) here, was responsible for the push to hang on to Matheran's heritage: he was at the forefront of campaigns to keep the hill station free of vehicles. Over the years this hill station has grown from a tiny hamlet to a budget tourist resort. Horseback riding on the country paths beyond town is a pleasant and popular pastime. Matheran is famed for its handmade shoes, and stalls and stalls of footwear dot the town. Equally famous is the historic "toy" train by which you get here—it's not a toy but, rather, runs on a narrower gauge track.

COLABA

CLOTHING AND CUSTOM TAILORING

Amrapali Creations. Very prompt and efficient, Amrapali Creations largely do Indian clothes, *salwar-kameez*, and sari blouses but if you give them a sample to copy they can make you a Western-style outfit. ⊠ *Shop 38, Ruki Mahal, near H.P. Petrol Pump, Colaba* ☎ 22/2288–5060.

Arjan Matching Centre. This store has brocade and plain silk, and is the best place to find fabric for linings. A reliable tailor (Amrapali) is next door at Shop 38. ⊠ *Ruki Mahal, near H.P. Petrol Pump, opposite Hanuman Mandir, Colaba* ☎ 22/2284–1516, 22/2288–5767.

Colaba Causeway. Colaba Causeway is lined with pavement stalls selling various children's trinkets—leather animals, small drums, purses, beads, and peacock-feather fans—as well as Indian clothing. ⊠ *Colaba Causeway, Colaba.*

Narisons Khubsons. Fine cotton and silk can be made into excellent shirts, trousers, or women's outfits in one day if need be. They also sell readymade women's clothing. There are two shops named Khubsons, back to back; make sure you have the right one (the one closer to Regal Cinema). ⊠ *49 Colaba Causeway, opposite Colaba police station, Colaba* ☎ 22/2202–0614.

Indian Textiles Company. In the Taj Mahal hotel, this store sells quality silks, as does the Burlington store here. ⊠ *Taj Mahal Palace & Tower, Apollo Bunder, Colaba* ☎ 22/2202–8783.

EYEGLASSES

Lunettes. A conveniently located, reasonable, and efficient eyeglass outlet is Lunettes. ⊠ *Ruki Mahal, Colaba Causeway, ground fl., near Kailash Parbat, Colaba* ☎ 22/2283–3338.

HANDICRAFTS AND HOUSEHOLD FURNISHINGS

Atmosphere. Exotic home furnishings and fabrics for the home are sold by the meter here. There's lots of expensive silk, and they'll organize tailoring for you. ⊠ *Vaswani House, 7 Best Marg, Colaba* ☎ *22/2283–1877, 22/2283–1936* ⊕ *www.atmospheredirect.com.*

Good Earth. All sorts of housewares, including linens, pottery, and brass are on offer here. There's one in Juhu, opposite the Marriott Hotel, and one in Lower Parel. ⊠ *2 Reay House, adjacent to Taj Mahal Hotel, Colaba* ☎ *22/2495–1954* ⊕ *www.goodearth.in.*

Mysore Sales International. Regal silks from Mysore are available here. ⊠ *World Trade Center, Cuffe Parade, Colaba* ☎ *22/2218–1658, 22/2218–4952.*

Trimourti. Browse Maharashtra crafts and an outstanding collection of statues, sculptures, and idols at Trimourti. ⊠ *World Trade Center, Cuffe Parade, Colaba* ☎ *22/2218–6283.*

INCENSE AND PERFUME

Ajmal. You'll find a wonderful selection of rare Indian and French perfumes stored in huge decanters here. They also stock *agar* wood, a rare incense base, 1,000 grams of which costs as much as a night at the Taj Mahal hotel. Sandalwood oil is also another fragrance stocked here. ⊠ *4/13 Kamal Mansion, Arthur Bunder Rd., Colaba* ☎ *22/2285–6976.*

JEWELRY

Mangal Palace. You'll find wonderful silver jewelry from all over India here, and there are some good bargains. ⊠ *Colaba Market, Colaba* ☎ *22/2283–4333, 22/2204–8928.*

CST AND ENVIRONS

BAZAARS AND MARKETS

Chor Bazaar. In this bustling but tiny flea market you can find exactly what you don't need but have to have—old phonographs, broken nautical instruments, strange toys, dusty chandeliers, furniture, and brass objects ranging from junky knickknacks to valuable antiques and curios. Keep an eye on your purse or wallet and come relaxed—it can be chaotic. ⊠ *Mutton St., near Kutbi Masjid, off Mohammed Ali Rd., Mandvi, CTS and Environs.*

Zaveri Bazaar. A few blocks northwest of Crawford Market, this is the place to go for diamond, gold, and silver jewelry. The tumultuous streets are lined with tiny, decades-old family jewelry businesses. Duck into one and sip a customary cup of tea or coffee while a salesperson shows you the merchandise. Most shops are authentic, but beware of false silver and gold; it's difficult to spot the fakes, so it might be best to buy primarily for appearance and make intrinsic value a secondary consideration. ⊠ *Sheikh Memon St., Kalbadevi* ⊗ *Mon.–Sat. 11–7.*

JEWELRY

Sheikh Memon Street. The most cost-effective place to buy jewelry is from a smaller outfit, such as **Narandas and Sons, Zaveri Naran Das,** or **Ram Kewalram Popley**—all on Sheikh Memon Street, which begins at Crawford Market and runs northwest through Zaveri Bazaar. Insist on knowing how many karats you're buying and whether or not the store will stand by the piece's purity. ⊠ *Kalbadevi.*

Tribhovandas Bhimji Zaveri. In business since 1865, this is said to be the largest jewelry showroom in India, with five floors of gorgeous 18-, 22-, and 24-karat gold, diamonds, and silver jewelry. ⊠ *241–43 Zaveri Bazaar, Kalbadevi, CST & Environs* ☎ *22/2343–5656* ⊕ *www. tbztheoriginal.com.*

LEATHER AND SHOES
Daboo Street. Brave bargain-hunters should take a trip to chaotic Daboo Street for all sorts of leather goods. ⊠ *Off Mohammed Ali Rd., a 5-minute walk south from Chor Bazaar, CST and Environs.*

FORT AND MARINE DRIVE
ART AND ANTIQUES
Jehangir Art Gallery. At least three art shows are staged here every week, either on the main floor or on the pavement racks outside in fair weather. Prices vary vastly. The whole area adjoining Jehangir Art Gallery has become an art district, and exhibitions can be happening at adjoining buildings, too. Inquire at the gallery. ⊠ *M.G. Rd., Kala Ghoda, Fort* ☎ *22/2284–3989.*

Gallery Chemould. An elegant gallery in the Fort district for those looking for a break, full of works by modern masters like Atul Dodiya and rolling exhibitions. ⊠ *Queens Mansion, G. Talwatkar Rd., 3rd fl., Fort* ☎ *22/2200–0211* ⊕ *www.gallerychemould.com.*

Natesan's Antiqarts Ltd. With branches in many Indian cities, this emporium sells magnificent but expensive curios, subcontinental antiquities, wood carvings, sculptures, and paintings, as well as a few smaller items at better prices. ⊠ *Jehangir Art Gallery, basement, Fort* ☎ *22/2285–2700.*

Phillips Antiques. Established in 1860, Phillips has the best choice of old prints, engravings, and maps in Mumbai. It also sells many possessions left behind by the British—Staffordshire and East India Company china, old jewelry, crystal, lacquerware, and sterling silver. The store is closed for an hour at lunchtime. ⊠ *Regal Circle, Madam Cama Rd., opposite Regal Cinema, Fort* ☎ *22/2202–0564.*

BAZAARS AND MARKETS
Fashion Street. This is a trove of cotton bargains in a long row of open-air stalls, with mounds of colorful, cheap, mainly Western clothing for all ages. The name is completely incongruous—there is nothing fashionable about this street, but the knock-offs are cheap. Come around 11 am, when the crowds are thinner and the sun has not yet peaked—and bargain. ⊠ *M.G. Rd., opposite Bombay Gymkhana, Fort.*

CLOTHING AND CUSTOM TAILORING
Anokhi. Colorful clothes with block-print designs from Rajasthan. ⊠ *Rasik Niwas, Metro Motors La., Dr. A.R. Rangnekar Marg, off Hughes Rd., Marine Drive* ☎ *22/2368–5761, 22/2368–5308* ⊕ *www. anokhi.com.*

Custom Tailors and Fine Fabrics

Mumbai's bazaars boom with some of the richest and widest varieties of cloth, and the Mangaldas Cloth Market has enough bales of material to carpet all of South Mumbai.

Buying clothes tailored to fit in Mumbai is not a difficult proposition: There are a number of tailors who can turn splendid fabric into custom-made clothing—Indian or Western—in a matter of hours, for ladies or men. The tailors are often armed with the latest catalogs and will faithfully copy a design from a picture. They're fast and competent, but be specific about what you want; their improvisations are not likely to go over well.

If you have a shirt or trousers to give as a sample, they can generally make an exact copy. Make sure you preshrink cotton material and any lining before you give it in for stitching (rinse for a few minutes and drip dry; colored cottons need to be rinsed by themselves for just a few seconds to prevent too much bleeding). Fix a rate beforehand, and give an earlier deadline than necessary to allow for refittings if needed. If the material needs a lining, buy it yourself. *See Clothing and Custom Tailoring listings under Colaba, Fort and Marine Drive, and Malabar Hill and Environs.*

6

Bombay Store. Bombay Store has cottons for children, and loads of upscale India trinkets, artifacts and antique reproductions. ⊠ *Sir Pherozeshah Mehta Rd., Fort* ☎ 22/2288–5048.

Christina. This is a tiny, classy boutique with exquisite silk blouses and shirts, scarves, ties, *dupattas* (long, thin scarves for draping), and silk-edge purses and wallets. ⊠ *The Oberoi hotel section of Oberoi Shopping Centre, Nariman Point* ☎ 22/2282–5069.

Roop Milan. Primarily a sari shop, Roop Milan also sells a huge variety of fine silks upstairs. ⊠ *Maharshi Karve Rd., near Marine Lines Station, Churchgate* ☎ 22/2200–1257, 22/2200–5951.

Sheetal. This is probably the best suit shop in Mumbai, with an extensive collection of fabrics and impeccable tailoring. You can get a full suit made here in about five days if you ask them to expedite it, with a trial fitting, for about Rs. 12,000. ⊠ *Sheetal Estate, Grant Rd., near Grant Rd. Station, Marine Drive* ☎ 22/2385–6565, 22/2387–6114.

DEPARTMENT STORES AND MALLS

Bombay Store. The large, attractive, and friendly Bombay Store sells clothing and accessories for men, women, and children, silk by the meter, homewares, organic wellness products, and gifts. There are a number of branches in the city. ⊠ *Sir Pherozeshah Mehta Rd., Fort* ☎ 22/2288–5048, 22/2288–5049.

Fabindia. This store showcases the best of Indian fabrics—*khadis* (home-spun cotton), muslin, vegetable-dyed silks, and embroidered materials. You can find women's clothing (saris, *kurtas*, skirts, trousers, blouses, and *kurtis*) as well as men's shirts and *kurtas,* children's clothes, table-cloths, curtains, cushion covers—and napkins fashioned from these beautiful materials, some of which is also available by the meter. The

Home furnishing for sale inside the Good Earth shop

Fort Fabindia is the address to head to—it's in a high-ceilinged, period building, with a wide selection—but there are a number of branches all over the city. ✉ *Jeroo Bldg., 137 M.G. Rd., Kala Ghoda, Fort* ☎ *22/2262–6539* ⊙ *Daily 10–7:45.* ✉ *Navroze Apartments, Pali Hill, near HDFC Bank, Bandra* ☎ *22/2646–5286.*

Westside. The clothing is unlikely to excite travellers, but the Western style supermarket may entice those wishing for a piece of home, whether in the form of imported cheese or chocolates. ✉ *158 M.G. Rd., Kala Ghoda, Fort* ☎ *22/5636–0495.*

EYEGLASSES
Ganko Optics. An old and trustworthy family-run optician with good frame choices. ✉ *19 Tulsiani Chambers, ground fl., Nariman Point* ☎ *22/2283–2335, 22/2282–4692.*

HANDICRAFTS AND HOUSEHOLD FURNISHINGS
Contemporary Arts and Crafts. There's a small but representative selection of Indian handicrafts at reasonable prices here. ✉ *210 D.N. Rd., opposite Fort House, Fort* ☎ *22/6561–8431.*

JEWELRY
Bombay Store. This is a good bet for silver jewelry. ✉ *Sir Pherozeshah Mehta Rd., Fort* ☎ *22/4066–9999.*

Tanishq. Owned by the Tata Group, a venerable and enormous Indian conglomerate whose founder built the Taj Mahal hotel, Tanishq is a reliable place to buy gold jewelry. The prices, however, are a little higher than elsewhere. ✉ *Veer Nariman Rd., near the Cricket Club of India*

(CCI), Churchgate ☎ *22/2282–1621, 22/2282–6043, 22/2283–8801*
⊕ *www.tanishq.co.in.*

MUSIC AND MUSICAL INSTRUMENTS

Bhargava Musical Enterprise. For Indian musical instruments, try this tiny, hard-to-find shop selling tablas (hand drums), harmoniums (a Western instrument with 42 black-and-white keys that has been adapted for Indian music), sitars (long-necked Indian lutes), and *tanpuras* (similar to sitars, but fretless). ⊠ *156 Khetwadi, Vallabhai Patel Rd., near Opera House, Prarthana Samaj* ☎ *22/2385–1519.*

Rhythm House. If you want to take home some Indian recordings, especially classical music, head for Rhythm House; along with pop, jazz, and everything else, the store has an excellent selection of *pacca gana* (classical vocal music), Indo-Western fusion music, Hindi film music, and Indian instrumental music, as well as English and Hindi DVDs and VCDs. ⊠ *40 K. Dubash Marg, Rampart Row, Kala Ghoda, Fort* ☎ *22/2285–3963.*

JUHU, BANDRA, AND THE WESTERN SUBURBS

CLOTHING

OMO. The women's clothing and silver jewelry sold here are very attractive. ⊠ *204 Sagar Fortune, Waterfield Rd., Bandra* ☎ *22/6698–1804.*

HANDICRAFTS AND HOUSEHOLD FURNISHINGS

Dhoop. Here you'll find a superb, unusual collection of handicrafts that includes upside-down incense holders and palm-leaf lampshades. If you're staying in Bandra, you're only 15 or so minutes away. ⊠ *101 Khar Sheetal Apartments, Dr. Ambedkar Rd. & Union Park, Khar* ☎ *22/2649–8646, 22/2649–8647.*

MALABAR HILL AND ENVIRONS

CLOTHING AND CUSTOM TAILORING

Nalli. The Mumbai branch of the famous Chennai store has a fair selection of classic silk saris. Have a look at the authentic gold-embroidered saris from Kanchipuram, in Tamil Nadu, as well as the Bangalore saris and the uncut silk sold by the meter. ⊠ *Trimurti Apartments, Bhulabhai Desai Rd., Breach Candy, Malabar Hill and Environs* ☎ *22/2353–5577.*

Raymond. This is an outlet for Raymond Mills, which makes some of India's finest men's suits. They can tailor a first-rate suit for about Rs. 8,000 in about a week. During the wedding season (winter) they can get very busy. ⊠ *Bhulabhai Desai Rd., Breach Candy, opposite Breach Candy Hospital, Malabar Hill and Environs* ☎ *22/2368–2644.*

EYEGLASSES

Gangar Opticians. Try upmarket Gangar Opticians, which offers a wide selection of designer brand frames. ⊠ *62 Chinoy Mansions, Warden Rd., Kemps Corner, Malabar Hill* ☎ *22/2789–0614.*

AURANGABAD, AND THE AJANTA AND ELLORA CAVES

Mumbai may not have much in the way of ancient history—and the Elephanta Caves might just be a bit too crowded (with both humans and monkeys)—but just an hour-long flight from the cosmopolitan city are some of the finest examples of centuries-old, rock-cut temples and cave paintings in all of India. Ajanta has famous frescoes full of intricate detail, with once bold but now faded natural colors, and Ellora has some of the most elaborate and awe-inspiring cave architecture in the country. Both have been listed as UNESCO World Heritage Sites.

Dating back more than 2,000 years, the cave temples of Ajanta and Ellora rank among the wonders of the ancient world. Here, between the 2nd century BC and the 5th century AD, great numbers (i.e., thousands) of monks and artisan/laborers carved cathedrals, monasteries, and entire cities of frescoed, sculptured halls into the solid rock. Working with simple chisels and hammers, and an ingenious system of reflecting mirrors to provide light into the dark interiors, they cut away hundreds of thousands of tons of rock to create the cave temples and other carvings. The work of these craftsmen inspires perpetual awe for the evident precision of their planning and knowledge of rock formations, their dedication to creating all this so far from the rest of India, and the delicacy and sheer quantity of the artwork. The cave temples span three great religions—Buddhism, Hinduism, and Jainism.

For optimum appreciation of the caves, allow one full day for each site, and remember Ajanta is closed Monday, and Ellora is closed Tuesday.

Suggested Itinerary: A trip to Ajanta and Ellora, while making your base in Aurangabad, makes a perfect long weekend trip from Mumbai. If you leave Mumbai on Friday morning, you can have dinner in Aurangabad—it's best to estimate more time, rather than less, when it comes to travel in India—and then head out early the next morning for the Ajanta caves, about a two- to three-hour drive away, for the day. Sunday morning you can head to the much closer (about 30 minutes), and more crowded, Ellora Caves, then head back to Mumbai that evening.

GETTING HERE AND AROUND

To get to Ajanta and Ellora, you can take a train, bus, or plane to Aurangabad.

BY AIR Aurangabad is about 45 minutes from Mumbai by air (about US$75, one-way), or 3½ hours from New Delhi (about US$100, one-way); there are also sometimes links between Aurangabad and Jaipur and Udaipur in the winter. Air India and Jet Airways fly to Aurangabad from Mumbai and Delhi. Schedules change every six months for these kinds of hop-and-a-skip flights, so check with the airlines for the most up-to-date information.

BY TRAIN There are only a few trains between Aurangabad and Mumbai, and the timing makes it difficult to see the caves in a timely manner. Indian Rail's *Tapovan Express* is the best option; it departs from Mumbai at 6:10 am and the journey takes just over seven hours.

CLOSE UP

The Deccan Odyssey

Following the success of Rajasthan's luxury Palace on Wheels train, India introduced a Maharashtra counterpart, the *Deccan Odyssey*. Traveling first-class on Indian trains in the heyday of the British Raj was a comfortable, lavish experience, with chefs and attendants taking care of the passengers' every need, in royal surroundings, as the train chugged through breathtaking countryside. The feeling is replicated aboard this train. Over seven nights and eight days you travel down the Maharashtra coast to Goa, then swing upward to Pune, and to Ajanta, Ellora, and the vineyards of Nashik before returning to Mumbai. In high season (October to March) such excursions will set you back US$425 per night in triple-sharing accommodation, US$500 in double-sharing accommodation, or US$650 for a single occupancy rail cabin. The train has several restaurants, lounges, and even a gym. For more information, visit ⊕ www.deccanodyssey.com.

VISITOR
INFORMATION

The Government of India Tourist Office, across from the train station, provides a warm and informative welcome to Aurangabad and is open weekdays 8:30–6 and Saturday and holidays 8:30–2. Ask for Mrs. I.R.V. Rao. The MTDC office in town (open Monday to Saturday 10–5:30; closed the second and fourth Saturday of the month) offers a variety of information about other destinations in Maharashtra, and they have a counter at the airport that's open when flights arrive.

Travel Agency Contacts Blossom Travel Services ✉ *205 Mehar Chambers, Town Centre, Sector C-1, Aurangabad* ☎ *240/248–1955.* **Saibaba Travels Aurangabad** ✉ *Shop No 88, Sindhi Colony, Jalna Rd., Aurangabad* ☎ *240/235–1612* ⊕ *www.saibabatravels.com.*

ESSENTIALS
Airline Contacts Air India ⊕ *www.airindia.com.*
Jet Airways ⊕ *www.jetairways.com.*

Visitor Information Contacts Government of India Tourist Office
✉ *MTDC Holiday Resort, Station Rd, 1st fl., Aurangabad* ☎ *240/236–4999*
⊕ *www.incredibleindia.org.* **Maharashtra Tourism Development Corporation (MTDC)** ✉ *MTDC Holiday Resort, Station Rd., Aurangabad*
☎ *240/233–1513* ⊕ *www.maharashtratourism.gov.in.*

AURANGABAD

388 km (241 miles) east of Mumbai; 30 km (18 miles) southeast of Ellora; 100 km (62 miles) southwest of Ajanta.

With several excellent hotels and a growing number of good restaurants, Aurangabad is a good base from which to explore the cave temples at Ajanta and Ellora.

Although probably not worth a separate trip in itself, Aurangabad does have a few sites that are worth seeing if you have extra time before or after visiting the caves.

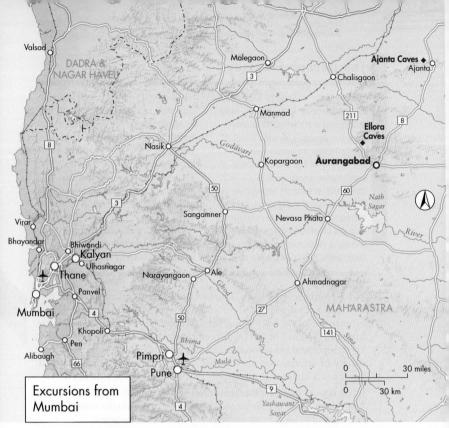

Excursions from Mumbai

The city is known for its *himru* (cotton and silk brocade) shawls and saris, and its gorgeously and painstakingly decorated Paithani *zari*, which are fine gold-embroidered saris—*zari* is the name for the gold metallic thread; and Paithani is a village very close to Aurangabad. If you're interested, pop into the Aurangabad Standard Silk Showroom or Aurangabad Silk, both near the train station; Ajanta Handicrafts in Harsul, on the highway to Ajanta; or Himroo Saris, on the highway to Ellora. An even better option to view Himru saris being woven is to venture over to the Himru Cooperative Society at Jaffer (also spelled Zaffar) Gate, an area in the western part of Aurangabad: There you can see the entire process in action in a traditional environment. The saris (which can be cut up and tailored into other items) are more reasonably priced here.

EXPLORING

Bibi-ka-Maqbara. This 17th-century tomb is also known as the mini Taj Mahal; you can usually see it from the plane when you're flying into Aurangabad. A pale imitation of the original Taj Mahal, it is dedicated to the wife of the last of the six great Mughal emperors, Aurangzeb (founder of Aurangabad and son of the Taj Mahal's creator, Shah Jahan). It was supposed to be a shining, white-marble edifice, but money ran out, so only the bottom 2 feet of the monument were built with marble; the rest is stone with a facade of plaster. Somewhat awkwardly proportioned, the structure can be said to illustrate the decline of Mughal architecture. ✉ *550 yards north of the old town, beyond Mecca Gate* 🎫 *Foreigners US$3* ☉ *Daily sunrise–10 pm.*

Daulatabad Fort. The imposing fort, built in 1187 by a Hindu king, is surrounded by seven giant walls more than 5 km (3 miles) long. Daulatabad was once called Deogiri, or "hill of the gods," but was changed to "city of fortune" when the sultan of Delhi overtook it in 1308. Devote at least half a day to this fascinating fort, considered one of India's most impressive. There's a wonderful view of the plains from the acropolis (fortified city) on the top. As you enter the fort you go through a labyrinth—note the moats, spikes, cannons, and dark maze of tunnels designed to make the fort as impregnable as possible. Equally interesting is the Jami Masjid (large mosque) inside; it was made from horizontal lintels and pillars taken from Jain and Hindu temples. Hindu folks around here put a lot of store in a *puja* (worship) done at the top of the fort and then down below, at the exit. ✉ *13 km [8 miles] west of Old Town, on the highway to the Ellora Caves* 🎫 *Foreigners around US$3* ☉ *Daily sunrise–6.*

Lonar Crater. About 160 km (100 miles) and 3½ to 4 hours east of Aurangabad, beyond Jalna, *not* on the highway to either Ajanta or Ellora, is the Lonar Crater. If you have a day free, or if you have an extra day because the caves are closed, visit this serene 50,000-year-old meteor crater. Off the beaten path and away from postcard sellers, bead hawkers, and soft-drink-stall owners, the 1,800-meter-long crater lake is one of India's more phenomenal sites. It's said to be Asia's largest and youngest crater. Lonar is a peaceful spot, full of wildlife and greenery.

WHERE TO EAT

Aurangabad isn't much of a restaurant destination, though there are some decent options, most of which serve dishes representing multiple cuisine options—Indian (Mughlai and tandoori, or South Indian), Chinese, and the local variant of what passes for continental food. Stick with Indian cuisine outside the luxury hotels, it's generally well prepared and tasty. Most restaurants here don't serve food outside typical meal hours.

$
NORTH INDIAN

✕ **Angeethi.** Named after a traditional Indian cooking vessel, this dark, cozy, slightly tacky restaurant serves Punjabi, continental, and Chinese food, and has a knack for tandoori items. Other specialties include chicken biryani, Afghani kebab *masala* (boneless chicken in a cashew sauce), and two-person *sikandari raan* (marinated leg of mutton). There are plenty of tasty vegetarian choices, too. Service is friendly but not terribly efficient. This is one of Aurangabad's most popular restaurants, and gets busy on weekends. $ *Average main: Rs. 400* ✉ *6 Mehar Chambers, Jalna Rd., Vidya Nagar* ☎ *240/244–1988.*

$
NORTH INDIAN
★

✕ **Balle Balle.** Inside the Hotel Manor, this quaint Indian restaurant is known for having some of the most authentic Punjabi food in town. You can eat vegetarian or nonvegetarian. Liquor is not served, and it's only open in the evening. $ *Average main: Rs. 500* ✉ *Kranti Chowk* ☎ *240/233–3383* ☉ *No lunch.*

Continued on page 393

AJANTA AND ELLORA CAVES

The centuries-old carved cave temples and cave paintings at Ajanta and Ellora are the product of awe-inspiring workmanship and span three great religions—Buddhism, Hinduism, and Jainism.

The caves at Ajanta and Ellora rank among the wonders of the ancient world. Here, between the 2nd century BC and the 5th century AD, great numbers (probably thousands) of monks and artisan laborers carved cathedrals, monasteries, and entire cities into the rock. Working with simple chisels and hammers, and an ingenious system of mirrors to send light into the interiors, the laborers cut away hundreds of thousands of tons of rock to create the cave temples and other carvings. The precision of the planning, the dedication of the laborers in such a remote location, and the delicacy and sheer quantity of the artwork make it obvious why both locations have been designated UNESCO world heritage sites.

CAVE PAINTINGS
Both Ajanta and Ellora have monumental facades and statues but Ajanta also has remarkable cave paintings that have survived the centuries. The paintings cover most of the cave surfaces, except the floor. They were created by spreading a plaster of clay, cow dung, chopped rice husks, and lime onto the rock walls, then painting pictures with local pigments: red ocher, copper oxide, lampblack, and dust from crushed green rocks. The paint brushes were made of twigs and camel hair. The caves are now like chapters of a splendid epic in visual form, recalling the life of the Buddha, and illustrating the life and civilization of the artisans.

(top) The magnificent Kailasa Temple, carved out of solid rock (left) The Ajanta cave painting of Padmapani, also known as "the one with the lotus in his hand"

THE AJANTA CAVES

Set in a wide, steep, horseshoe-shaped gorge above a wild mountain stream, the Ajanta caves reward travelers with a stunning glimpse into ancient India. Tucked in a setting that is lush and green after the monsoon, India's greatest collection of cave paintings dates back two millennia and is housed within massive carved stone caverns.

HISTORY

It's believed that a band of wandering Buddhist monks first came here in the 2nd century BC, searching for a place to meditate during the monsoons. Ajanta was ideal—peaceful and remote, with a spectacular setting. The monks began carving caves into the gray rock face of the gorge, and a new temple form was born.

Over the course of seven centuries, the cave temples of Ajanta evolved into works of incredible art. Structural engineers continue to be amazed by the sheer brilliance of the ancient builders,

who, undaunted by the limitations of their implements, materials, and skills, created a marvel of artistic and architectural splendor. In all, 29 caves were carved, 15 of which were left unfinished; some of the caves were *viharas* (monasteries)—complete with stone pillows carved onto the monks' stone beds; others were *chaityas* (Buddhist cathedrals). All of the caves were profusely decorated with intricate sculptures and murals depicting the many incarnations of Buddha.

As the influence of Buddhism declined, the number of monk-artists became fewer, and the temples were swallowed up by the voracious jungle. It was not

(top) An aerial view of the Ajanta caves (right) A carving of a reclining buddha in an Ajanta cave

until about a thousand years later, in 1819, that an Englishman named John Smith, who was out tiger hunting on the bluff overlooking the Waghora River in the dry season, noticed the soaring arch of what is now known as Cave 10 peeking out from the thinned greenery in the ravine below. It was he who subsequently unveiled the caves to the modern world.

The paintings are dimly lit to protect the artwork, and a number are badly damaged, so deciphering the work takes some effort. The Archaeological Survey of India has, however, put a lot of effort into making the caves more viewable, including installing special ultraviolet lights to brighten certain panels. Shades and nets installed at the mouth of each cave keep out excess sun and bats.

PLANNING YOUR VISIT

A trip to the Ajanta caves needs to be well planned. You can see the caves at a fairly leisurely pace in two hours, but the drive to and from the site takes about two to three hours each way.

There's no longer direct access to the caves. All visitors are required to park their cars or disembark from their buses at a visitor center 3 km (2 mi) from the caves. From here, a Rs. 6 ticket buys you a place on frequently departing green Maharashtra Tourism Development Corporation (MTDC) buses to the caves (it's Rs. 10 for an air-conditioned bus, but they travel less frequently). The visitor complex has stalls with people hawking souvenirs, film, sodas, water, and packaged and fresh hot snacks—plus unknown guides that need to be firmly dismissed.

WHAT TO BRING AND WEAR

Come prepared with water, lunch or snacks, comfortable walking shoes (that can be slipped on and off easily, because shoes are not allowed inside the caves), socks to pad about the cave in so you don't get your feet dirty, a small flashlight, a hat or umbrella for the heat, and patience. Aurangabad can be hot year-round, and touring 29 caves can be tiring.

PRACTICAL INFO

✉ 100 km (62 mi) northeast of Aurangabad; about a 2–3 hour drive.

🎟 Admission Rs. 250, light fee Rs. 5 (includes all caves), video camera fee Rs. 25, parking Rs. 15. Flash photography and video cameras are prohibited inside the caves (shooting outside is fine). There is a cloak room at the visitor center where you can check bags for Rs. 5.

🕐 Tues.–Sun. 9 am–5 pm (Closed Monday); arrive by 3:30

VISITING THE AJANTA CAVES

WHERE TO START

The caves are connected by a fair number of steps. It's best to start at the far end, at Cave 26, and work your way to Cave 1 to avoid a long trek back at the end. The initial ascent, before you reach the cave level, is also quite a climb, at 92 steps. Palanquins carried by helpers are available for the less hardy, for Rs. 400.

MOST IMPORTANT TO SEE

Opinions vary on which of the Ajanta caves is most exquisite: Caves 1, 2, 16, 17, and 19 are generally considered to have the best paintings; caves 1, 6, 10, 17, 19, and 26 the best sculptures. (The caves are numbered from west to east, not in chronological order.) Try to see all eight of these caves, at least.

Cave 1. Ajanta's most popular cave paintings are here; they depict the Bodhisattva Avalokitesvara and Bodhisattva Padmapani. Padmapani, or the "one with the lotus in his hand," is considered to be the alter ego of the Lord Buddha; Padmapani assumed the duties of the Buddha when he disappeared. Padmapani is often depicted with his voluptuous wife. When seen from different angles, the mag-

nificent Buddha statue in this cave seems to wear different facial expressions.

Cave 2. This cave is remarkable for the ceiling decorations and murals relating the birth of the Buddha. For its sheer exuberance, the painting of women on a swing is considered the finest. It's on the right wall as you enter, and when you face the wall it's on the left side.

Cave 6. This two-story cave has lovely detail. Climb the steep steps to the second floor, where there are pillars that emit musical sounds when rapped.

Cave 10. The oldest cave, this shrine dates from 200 BC, and is dominated by a large, squat *stupa* (a dome, or monument,

to Buddha). The exquisite brush-and-line work dates from AD 100: in breathtaking detail, the Shadanta Jataka, a legend about the Buddha, is depicted on the wall in a continuous panel. There are no idols of Buddha in this cave, indicating that idol worship was not in vogue at the time. (Cave 19, which dates from about the 5th century, does contain idols of Buddha, showing the progression of thought and the development of new methods of worship as the centuries wore on.) Guides and caretakers will enthusiastically point out the name of the Englishman, John Smith, who rediscovered the caves. His name, along with 1819 underneath, is carved on the 12th pillar on the right-hand side of this cave—though it's Cave 9, with its domed arch, that Smith first spotted.

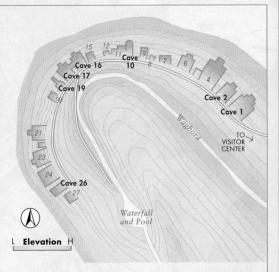

Cave 16. The monk-artists seem to have reached their creative zenith here; the continuous narrative spreads both horizontally and vertically, evolving into a panoramic whole—at once logical and stunning. One painting is especially riveting: known as *The Dying Princess,* it's believed to represent Sundari, the wife of the Buddha's half-brother Nanda, who left her to become a monk. This cave has an excellent view of the river and may have been the entrance to the entire series of caves.

Cave 17. This cave has the greatest number of pictures undamaged by time. Heavenly damsels fly effortlessly overhead, a prince makes love to a princess, and the Buddha tames a raging elephant (resisting temptation is a theme).

Other favorite paintings here include the scene of a woman applying lipstick and one of a princess performing *sringar* (her toilette)—this last is on the right-hand wall as you enter, and as you face the wall on the farthest right pillar.

Cave 19. Dating from about the mid 5th century, when Buddhism was in full swing, the stone sculpture on the exterior of this magnificent chaitya, or cathedral, is incredibly detailed. Inside, too, the faded paintings are overshadowed by the the sculptures. The standing Buddha is especially notable; compared with the stupas from earlier caves, this one is much more detailed and elongated.

Cave 26. This is the most interesting of the caves at the far end. An impressive sculpted panel of a reclining Buddha is on your left as you enter. It's believed to be a portrayal of a dying Buddha on the verge of attaining nirvana. His weeping followers are at his side, while celestial beings are waiting to transport him to the land of no tomorrows (no rebirths).

Unfinished caves. Several unfinished caves were abandoned nearby but are worth a visit if you're up for the steep, 100-step climb (alternatively, you can walk up the bridle path, a gentler ascent alongside the caves). From here you have a magnificent view of the ravine descending into the Waghura River. An even easier way to reach this point is to stop your car as you return to Aurangabad, 20 km (12 mi) from the caves: take a right at Balapur and head 8 km (5 mi) toward Viewpoint, as it's called by the locals.

(top left) A princess and her servant (bottom left) Detail from Cave 2 (middle left) Buddha carving in Cave 6 (left) Inside Cave 26

THE ELLORA CAVES

Unlike the cave temples at Ajanta, those of Ellora are not solely Buddhist. Rather, they follow the development of religious thought in India through the decline of Buddhism in the latter half of the 8th century, to the Hindu renaissance that followed the return of the Gupta dynasty, and to the Jain resurgence between the 9th and 11th centuries. Of the 34 caves here, the 12 to the south are Buddhist, the 17 in the center are Hindu, and the 5 to the north are Jain.

HISTORY

In the 7th century, religious activity shifted from Ajanta to a site 123 km (76 mi) to the southwest—known today as Ellora—although the reason for this move is not known. The focus at Ellora is sculpture, which covers the walls in ornate masses. The carvings in the Buddhist caves are serene, but in the Hindu caves they take on a certain exuberance and vitality—gods and demons do fearful battle, Lord Shiva angrily flails his eight arms, elephants rampage, eagles swoop, and lovers intertwine.

Unlike at Ajanta, where the temples were chopped out of a steep cliff, the caves at Ellora were dug into the slope of a hill along a north–south line, presumably so that they faced west and could receive the light of the setting sun.

WHEN TO GO?

Because Ellora is such a busy tourist destination, try to avoid coming here during school holidays from April to first week of June.

(top) Kailasa Temple (top right) Detail of a religious story carved into Kailasa (bottom right) One of the smaller rock-carved temples

The annual **Ellora Dance Festival,** held on one full moon night in December, draws top classical Indian dancers and musicians from around the country to perform outdoors against the magical backdrop of the Ellora Caves. For more information, ask at the tourist office or the Maharashtra Tourism Development Corporation.

PLANNING YOUR VISIT

Visiting the Ellora caves is in many ways easier than visiting Ajanta, though the rewards are different. Not only is Ellora closer to Aurangabad, when you get there, the line of caves is more accessible, all parallel to the road, and there are not many steps involved. Proximity to Aurangabad and the easy access makes seeing these caves a half-day's

adventure; choose either early morning or late afternoon. The winding drive to Ellora is very pleasant, through low-slung hills past old ruins as well as Daulatabad Fort (try to squeeze at least a half-hour stop there, too).

WHERE TO EAT?

You're best off packing a lunch from Aurangabad, but there are two decent options around caves: The **Ellora Restaurant** (☎ 24/372–4441), by the entrance, is a convenient place to stop for a cold drink and a hot samosa. The outdoor patio has fruit trees (home to many monkeys) and pink bougainvillea flowers. The restaurant closes before the caves do. Outside Kailasa Cave (number 16), past the many souvenir stall, is the Hotel Kailas with its attached restaurant, **Kailas:** it's a simple cafeteria-style restaurant serving basic vegetarian Indian food until 9:30 pm. The food isn't great, but it's a bit nicer than the Ellora Restaurant.

PRACTICAL INFORMATION

✉ 30 km (18 mi) northwest of Aurangabad; about a 1/2 hour drive

🎟 Rs. 250, video camera fee Rs. 25

🕓 Wed.–Mon. (closed Tuesday), 6 am–6 pm

VISTING THE ELLORA CAVES

WHERE TO START

Although the caves are spread out over a large area, they're parallel to the road. Arrange with your driver to pick you up at several points: start at Cave 1 and work your way to 16, where you should have your driver meet you and take you to Cave 21. Then head to Cave 29. Another short drive will take you to the Jain caves.

MOST IMPORTANT TO SEE

Cave 16, the Kailasa temple, is the star attraction here but make sure to see caves from each of the three representative religions so that you can compare and contrast.

The southernmost caves are Buddhist.

Cave 2. The facade of this impressive monastery is deceptively simple, but the interior is lavish: gouged into the block of rock is a central hall with ornate pillars and a gallery of Buddhas and Bodhisattvas seated under trees and parasols.

Cave 5. The largest of the Buddhist caves, this was probably used as a classroom for young monks. The roof appears to be supported by 24 pillars; working their way down, sculptors first "built" the roof before they "erected" the pillars.

Cave 6. A statue of Mahamayuri, the Buddhist goddess of learning—also identified as

Saraswati, the Hindu goddess of learning—is the focus here, surrounded by Buddhist figures. The boundaries between Hinduism and Buddhism are fuzzy and Hindus worship and recognize some Buddhist gods and goddesses as their own, and vice versa: Hindus, for instance, consider Buddha the avatar of Vishnu.

Cave 7. This austere hall with pillars is one of Ellora's two-story caves.

Cave 10. The carvings here are impressive: the stonecutters reproduced the timbered roofs of the period over a richly decorated facade that resembles masonry work. Inside this shrine—the only actual Buddhist chapel at Ellora—the main work of art is

a huge sculpture of Buddha. Check out the high ceiling with stone "rafters" and note the sharp echo. The cave has been dubbed the Sutar Jhopdi or Carpenter's Cave and called a tribute to Visvakarma, the Hindu god of tools and carpentry.

Caves 11 and 12. These two caves rise grandly three floors up and are richly decorated with sculptural panels.

Starting with Cave 13, the Hindu caves are the successors to the Buddhist ones, and a step inside will stop you in your tracks. It's another world—another universe—in which the calm contemplation of the seated Buddhas gives way to the dynamic cosmology of Hinduism. These caves were created around the 7th and 8th centuries.

Cave 16. Ellora is dominated by the mammoth Kailasa Temple (also known as Kailasanatha, or Kailash) complex, or Cave 16. Dedicated to Shiva, the complex is a replica of his legendary abode at Mount Kailasa in the Tibetan Himalayas. The largest monolithic structure in the world, Kailasa reveals the genius, daring, and raw skill of its artisans.

To create the Kailasa complex, an army of stonecutters started at the top of the cliff, where they removed 3 million cubic feet of rock to create a vast pit with a freestanding rock left in the center. Out of this single slab, 276 feet long and 154 feet wide, the workers created Shiva's abode, which includes the main temple, a series of smaller shrines, and galleries built into a wall that encloses the

entire complex. Nearly every surface is exquisitely sculpted with epic themes.

Around the courtyard, numerous friezes illustrate the legends of Shiva and stories from the great Hindu epics, the Mahabharata and the Ramayana. One interesting panel on the eastern wall relates the origin of Shiva's main symbol, the lingam, or phallus. Another frieze, on the outer wall of the main sanctuary on the southern side of the courtyard, shows the demon Ravana shaking Mount Kailasa.

Cave 21. Of the Hindu caves north of Kailash, this cave, also called the Ramesvara, has some interesting sculptures, including the figurines of the river goddesses at the entrance. It's thought to be the oldest Hindu cave.

Cave 29. Past the seasonal waterfall, this cave, also called Dhumar Lena, is similar in layout to the caves at Elephanta, near Mumbai. Pairs of lion sculptures guard the staircases and inside are some interesting friezes.

The Jain caves are at the far end of Ellora, and definitely worth a visit, if just for the contrast. The Jain caves are more modest and subdued

than the Hindu caves, but have some lovely artwork carvings. Climb through the many well-carved chambers and study the towering figures of Gomateshvara (a Jain mythological figure) and Mahavira (an important Jain sage).

Cave 32. The most notable of the Jain caves is a miniature Kailash Temple, on two levels. The bottom floor is rather plain, but elaborate carvings surround the upper story.

(top left) Seven carved buddhas, Cave 12 (middle left) seated buddha, Cave 10 (top right) Detail on Kailasa Temple (bottom right) Cave 29 detail

PLANNING YOUR VISIT

Interior of a cave at Ajanta

GETTING TO THE CAVES

To see the caves from Mumbai takes several days: you'll base yourself in Aurangabad, which is about 400 miles east of Mumbai (an hour-long flight), and make separate day trips to Ajanta and Ellora. Allow one full day for each site, and remember Ajanta is closed Monday, and Ellora is closed Tuesday.

If you can make it only to either Ellora or Ajanta, choose Ajanta: it's farther, but the comparative lack of crowds and the pristine serenity of the forest are worth it.

Suggested itinerary from Mumbai. A trip to Ajanta and Ellora, while making your base in Aurangabad, makes a perfect long weekend trip from Mumbai. If you leave Mumbai on Friday you can be in Aurangabad in the late afternoon, have dinner, and then head out early the next morning for the Ajanta caves, about a 2- to 3-hour drive away, for the day. Sunday morning, you can head to the much closer (about 30 minutes), and more crowded, Ellora Caves, then head back to Mumbai that evening.

Getting to Ajanta and Ellora from Aurangabad. From Aurangabad there are tour buses (check with the Government of India Tourist Office or the MTDC office) but this ends up being rather rushed. You're best off hiring a car and driver. An air-conditioned car for a full day will cost around Rs. 2,400 to Ajanta and Rs. 1,100 to Ellora. You can arrange a car for hire through your hotel a travel agent, or the Government of India Tourist Office; fix a price in advance.

HIRING A GUIDE

It's a good idea to hire a guide, who can explain the iconography and details about how the caves were built. The Government of India Tourist Office (✉ *Krishna Vilas, Station Rd. Aurangabad 431210* ☎ *240/236-4999 or 240/233-1217* ⊕ *www.incredibleindia. org*) oversees about 45 expert, polite, multilingual tour guides. You can hire one through the tourist office; through the MTDC office (✉ *MTDC Holiday Resort, Station Rd. Aurangabad* ☎ *240/233-1513* ⊕ *www.maharashtratourism.gov.in*); or through a travel agent in Aurangabad.

For parties of one to four, the fees are about Rs. 1,000 for a full day to Ajanta, and about Rs. 750 for a full day to Ellora. Hiring a half-day guide (four hours) is about Rs. 450. An extra Rs. 400 or so is charged for trips of more than 100 km (60 mi). It's best to book ahead. There are also some guides availabe to hire at the ticket counters to the caves.

If you opt not to hire a guide, you can ask the guides posted at the caves, for information; tip them ten rupees for their kindness.

QUICK GUIDE TO THE CAVES

Ajanta	Ellora
Farther from Aurangabad (about 3-hour drive)	Closer to Aurangabad (about 1/2-hour drive)
Closed Monday	Closed Tuesday
29 caves were carved (15 are unfinished)	34 caves; Kailasa is the highlight
All Buddhist	Buddhist, Hindu, and Jain
Focus is on cave paintings	Focus is on sculpture
Caves chopped out of steep cliff	Caves dug into slope of a hill

$$ ✕**Madhuban.** Dark furniture, large paintings of Indian scenes, an abun-
INTERNATIONAL dance of green granite, crisp white tablecloths, and a chandelier composed
of multiple *diyas* (traditional Indian lamps) set a regal tone at Madhuban,
one of Aurangabad's top restaurants. A wall of windows opens onto a
garden of lovely tropical trees and flowers. The menu might include butter
chicken and dal *makhani*, a rich black lentil dish; the Chinese food is tasty
too—the chilli chicken, a spicy Chindian concoction is recommended—
though the addition of Mexican and Italian food is hardly necessary. The
buffet lunch is popular. $ *Average main: Rs. 900* ✉ *Welcomgroup Rama
International Hotel, R-3 Chikalthana* ☎ *240/663–4141.*

$$ ✕**The Residency and the Garden Café.** The hotel's two adjoining eateries
INTERNATIONAL share the same menu, which offers a mix of Indian and continental cui-
★ sines. The choice is easy—if it's lunch you're after, the old-world style
Garden Café is easily the loveliest location around for a light lunch,
with white cane garden furniture adorning a marble veranda that looks
out over green lawns and flower beds. For dinner, head to the Residency, where warm colors and lots of wood identify it as a classy place.
It has a good multicuisine buffet, and the local chicken curry is also
recommended, as are the desserts. $ *Average main: Rs. 800* ✉ *8-N-12
CIDCO* ☎ *240/661–3737.*

$ ✕**Surya's Garden Court Restaurant.** About a 15-minute journey from the
INDIAN center of town, the Garden Court Restaurant is on a sprawling estate
often used for weddings and private parties. The restaurant is open
year-round, and serves great Indian food. Try the chicken *seekh* kebabs
(minced chicken grilled in a tandoor), the chicken tikka masala and the
laccha parathas (a flaky bread). Somewhat surprisingly, there's also
some decent Mexican food here—the enchiladas have an Indian twinge
to them, which turns out to be not a bad thing. $ *Average main: Rs.
250* ✉ *Beed Bypass Rd., near Dutta Mandir, Deolai* ☎ *240/696–0500*
⊕ *www.suryalawns.com.*

$ ✕**Tandoor.** The hospitality of manager Syed Liakhat Hussain is one
INDIAN good reason to visit this brightly lit, busy, and cheerful restaurant that
stays open late. The kebabs are another reason, especially the *kasturi*
(chicken) kebab. People come to this local landmark for authentic and
well-made tandoori food. Try the *murg tikka* (chicken kebabs), *paneer
tikka* (cubes of cottage cheese baked in a tandoor), biryani, black *dal*
(lentils), and the fresh, fried local fish. Shoot for lunch instead of dinner
if you're coming by auto-rickshaw—later in the evening it's difficult to
find transportation (it's far from the main hotels). $ *Average main: Rs.
500* ✉ *Shyam Chambers, Station Rd.* ☎ *240/232–8481.*

WHERE TO STAY
For expanded hotel reviews, visit Fodors.com.

Most hotels in Aurangabad discount their rates if you ask. If you book
directly, push for 15% off, or more—and make sure to ask whether
the agreed-on rate includes breakfast and airport or train station pick-
up. Unless otherwise noted, all hotels listed are fully air-conditioned.

$ ⊡ **Lemon Tree Hotel.** Every room at this attractive contemporary hotel,
HOTEL designed around a central garden, has a pool view, and either a patio
★ or a balcony. **Pros:** well-lit, cheerful hotel; comfortable rooms; good

6

value; excellent food. **Cons:** small bathrooms. [$] *Rooms from: Rs. 5300* ✉ *R 7/2 Chikalthana, Airport Rd.* ☎ *240/660–3030* 🌐 *www.lemontreehotels.com* 🛏 *102 rooms, 4 suites* 🍴 *Breakfast.*

$$ HOTEL ★ 🏨 **The Meadows.** Accommodations at this resort-style hotel, which has won architectural awards, are in simple cottages, each with a private patio, and though rooms are a bit spartan, it's wonderfully tranquil—and eco-concious, too: Biotechnology using plant roots purifies the air and wastewater. **Pros:** service above average; good value; airport pick-up; close to Ellora caves. **Cons:** far from the city. [$] *Rooms from: Rs. 6000* ✉ *Aurangabad–Mumbai Hwy., Village Mitmita, Padegaon, 5 km (3 miles from city center)* ☎ *240/267–7412 to 16* 🌐 *www.themeadowsresort.com* 🛏 *48 cottages, 4 suites* 🍴 *Breakfast.*

$$ HOTEL 🏨 **Taj Residency.** Convenient for the World Heritage Sites, this gleaming Mughal palace is all bright white marble and stone, inside and out—its windows and doors arch to regal Mughal points, and the grand dome over the lobby is hand-painted in traditional Jaipuri patterns. **Pros:** city's most elegant hotel; lovely ambience. **Cons:** rather expensive; service disorganized. [$] *Rooms from: Rs. 8000* ✉ *8-N-12 CIDCO* ☎ *240/661–3737* 🌐 *www.tajhotels.com* 🛏 *66 rooms, 2 suites* 🍴 *Breakfast.*

$$ HOTEL 🏨 **WelcomHotel Rama International.** A long driveway through spacious grounds leads to a place where efficient and friendly staffers create the kind of warm, intimate setting you'd normally associate with a smaller hotel. **Pros:** excellent value; attentive personal service; nice views; comfortable rooms. **Cons:** small pool. [$] *Rooms from: Rs. 7000* ✉ *R-3 Chikalthana* ☎ *240/663–4141* 🌐 *www.welcomhotelrama.com* 🛏 *132 rooms, 5 suites* 🍴 *Breakfast.*

THE ARTS

Ellora Dance Festival. This annual festival, held on one full moon night in December, draws top classical Indian dancers and musicians from around the country to perform outdoors against the magical backdrop of the Ellora Caves. Ask at the Tourist office or the MTDC.

Goa

WORD OF MOUTH

"Goa is special because of its mixture of Portuguese and Hindu culture."

—bombayteddy

"Goa has some great food, and the Portuguese influence can be seen in Old Goa and in many parts of the state."

—Lyndie

WELCOME TO GOA

TOP REASONS TO GO

★ **Sand and waves:** Goa's long, sandy, palm-fringed beaches are perfect for more than just sun worship: scores of shacks serving cold beer and fresh seafood make them one long beach party.

★ **Goan cuisine:** If you like spices and caught-that-day seafood, you're in luck.

★ **Backwaters:** Rivers flow across Goa to the Arabian Sea. Escape the crowds at a heritage home or country inn for a couple of days, in a town like Loutolim for scenic nature walks, home-style cooking, and generous hospitality.

★ **Parties:** Goa's party scene is no longer as hedonistic as in years past, but during peak season the famed all-night beach parties still continue to draw young and not-so-young people from around the world.

★ **Portuguese architecture:** Goa was under Portuguese control until 1961, and the colonial past lingers on in its historic buildings, forts, churches, and charming Portuguese homes and mansions.

1 North Goa. For many visitors the heart and soul of Goa is in the bustling beaches and villages north of Panaji. You can find classic Goan beach life in many towns and villages dotting the coast, such as Candolim, Calangute, Baga, and Anjuna. And hotel rooms, restaurants, shops, and water sports are plentiful during the tourist season. Quieter beaches are north of the Chapora River in and around Mandrem; inland villages such as Siolim are lovely alternatives for experiencing Goa's less touristy, rural side.

2 Panaji and Central Goa. Whitewashed Catholic churches, palm-lined plazas, and the narrow streets of Panaji's historic Fontainhas—the Latin Quarter—feel decidedly more European than Indian. The grandiose churches of Old Goa and the temples in Ponda are best accessed from here.

3 South Goa. There are a few historic sights in and around Margao, but most people come to the south for the swanky upscale resorts that offer much quieter beaches. Colva and Palolem have caught up on the party trail, and the area now has a slew of beachside bars and restaurants. Loutolim, one of Goa's prettiest villages, is a charming alternative to go off the beaten path.

Map labels

Fort Tiracol
Arambol
Arambol Beach
Mandrem Beach
Ashvem Beach
Morjim Beach
Vagator Beach
Anjuna Beach
Baga Beach
Calangute Beach
Candolim Beach
Sinquerim Beach
Fort Aguada

Pernem
PERNEM
Chapora
Mapusa
BARDEZ
Dr. Salim Ali Bird Sanctuary
Bitona
Dicholi
Divar Is.
Old Goa
Panaji
TESWAD

Arabian Sea

Gama Vasco Da
Dabolim Airport
MORMUGAO
Bogmalo Beach
Grande Island
Cansaulim Beach
Majorda & Utorda
Colva
Benaulim
Varca

MAHARASHTRA

KARNATAKA

BICHOLIM

SATARI

Valpoi

4A

Ponda

Mandovi

4A

Zuari

PONDA

Loutolim

GOA

SANGUEM

Margao
(Madgaon)

Dudhsagar
Falls

Chandor

17

3

Sanguem

SALCETE

Quepem

Colossim
Beach

QUEPEM

Cabo de
Ramao
(Cape Rama)

17

CANACONA

Chauri

Palolem
Beach

17

Patnem

0   10 mi

0   10 km

GETTING ORIENTED

Goa is best described as short (just 105 km [65 miles] long) and sweet (full of friendly locals). The capital city, Panaji, divides the northern beaches from those in the south, and is the regional transportation and cultural center. Although Goa is India's smallest state (in area), its terrain manages to include sandy beaches, lazy backwaters, acres of emerald-green rice paddies, and thick palm forests, as well as steep, jungle-covered mountains. Its immense popularity means that it has much better tourist infrastructure than elsewhere in India, with plenty of hotel rooms, an increasing number of excellent restaurants, decent roads, and reliable cell-phone connectivity and electricity. Most of the country's development is along its coastline, where visitors will find all the resorts that have made Goa famous, as well as its two major towns—Panaji in the center and Margao in the south.

7

EATING WELL IN GOA

Abundant seafood from the Arabian Sea, coupled with Goa's location on the spice route, ensures a wonderfully diverse cuisine.

(top left) Chicken vindaloo; (top right) The popular Goan sweet called bebinca; (bottom right) A dish of roasted cashews

Goan food is distinguished by the continued presence of Portuguese cooking techniques and ingredients. Chillies from the New World were incorporated into the local arsenal of spices relatively early, possibly with the arrival of Vasco da Gama in the late 15th century. The Portuguese also popularized eating pork, the use of vinegar, and certain dessert techniques. Goan Catholic eating habits are influenced by the Portuguese methods, as well as those of the native Konkani-speaking inhabitants of the area.

The fact that Goa is a major tourist destination has also had an effect on the food you'll find here, and there are serviceable international restaurants (particularly "Italian" cafés and "German" bakeries). The gamut of Indian cuisines is also well represented, with some Punjabi restaurants that are as good as anything in North India.

CASH(EW) CROP

An important cash crop in Goa, cashew trees grow all over the state. The tree, which is native to Brazil, came to Goa with the Portuguese. A local liquor is distilled from the cashew tree's fruit: the cashew apple. The first distillation, called *arrack*, has lower alcohol content than the pungent *feni*, which is the third distillation and can be up to 80 proof. Goan distilleries also make a coconut feni.

BEBINCA

A layered glutinous dessert, **bebinca** is traditionally eaten on special occasions, but due to its popularity with tourists, it's available in Goa all year round. The dish most likely evolved in Goa, possibly with some Portuguese influence, but it has since migrated to Portugal as well. Making bebinca is a slow process: a batter of refined flour, coconut milk, egg yolks, and sugar is poured and baked, in layers, in a low-heat oven. The slight caramelizing between layers makes for an attractive tiger-stripe treat. You can buy bebinca in vacuum-sealed packages to take home.

VINDALOO

A much-replicated Indian dish, vindaloo is the culinary pinnacle of the merging of Konkan and Portuguese cultures. A Portuguese meat dish cooked with red wine and garlic (*vinho* and *alhos*) was baptized in the fire of Goan spices and became vindaloo; the Goan version uses vinegar rather than wine for a slightly acidic-sweet taste. Vindaloo is originally a pork dish, but has since been adapted to chicken and lamb. It may include potatoes, too, and it generally incorporates red chilli for color and green chilli for spice.

SORPOTEL

A dish of Portuguese heritage that was adopted by Goan Christians, **sorpotel** (or *sarapatel*) is often somewhat

toned down for tourists: it's an offal stew that is made using the liver, heart, and tongue of pork or other meats. By some accounts, the stew traditionally also includes the animal's blood, which some cooks still use as a thickener—but probably not in the version tourists encounter. This flavor is enhanced by the use of vinegar.

CHOURIÇO

If you happen to be in town on a market day, you might see strings of bulging Goan sausages gleaming dark red in the sun. Called **chouriço,** these are the local descendents of Portuguese chorizo, and are made with ground pork, vinegar, chilli, and other spices, and stuffed into casings. *Chouriço* can be very spicy or mild and varies in texture from dry to juicy. This type of sausage must be cooked, and is usually eaten with rice or bread.

XACUTI

Chicken **xacuti** is one of Goa's most successful dishes outside of the state—and it can also be made with fish or lamb. It's a milder curry than some of the fiery red Goan curries. Coconut, white poppy, other seeds (peppercorn, cumin, and fennel), and warm spices like cinnamon, star anise, and cloves are roasted and then fried and simmered with the meat for an aromatic addition to rice or a piece of bread (*pao*).

GOA BEACHES

With crescent-shape beaches of white sand and dramatic swathes of cliffs hugging the coastline, Goa continues to attract hordes of domestic and foreign travelers.

(top left) A fishing boat on Palolem beach; (top right) Arambol beach in northern Goa; (bottom right) Sunset at the beach

Goa's northern beaches at Baga and Calangute draw the biggest crowds and have plenty of food and drink shacks, easy access to water sports, trendy restaurants and boutiques, and booming nightlife. There's a Wednesday flea market at the former hippie enclave around Anjuna, while arresting sunset views await visitors to the cliffs at Vagator. The northern-most beaches of Ashvem, Mandrem, and Morjim are quieter and more scenic, but have far fewer places to stay and eat.

Plush all-inclusive resorts dominate the southern coastline of Benaulim, Varca, and Cavelossim, where the beaches are cleaner and the shacks are less in evidence. Colva is popular on the domestic tourist trail, and is often packed with families and tour groups. Palolem beach, with its swaying palms and clean coastline, is becoming more popular but quality accommodations and dining options still lag behind its northern counterparts.

MONSOON SEASON?

Most visitors go to Goa for the beach and the sun, though monsoon season (June to September), with its frequent downpours, is atmospheric and remarkably lush. It's also when the crowds are thinner and the prices lower—though most of the beach shacks and some of the larger properties are closed. And if your dream is to lie out on the beach or by the pool, this definitely isn't the time for you to visit.

WHAT SHOULD I WEAR?

The steady influx of foreign visitors over the years means that bikinis on the beach are commonplace. However, anything more risque, like going topless or nude, is not acceptable. When you leave the beach, drape a sarong or throw on a cover-up to avoid untoward attention. Wandering around town or sitting in a restaurant in only a bathing suit is not advisable. And wear your flip-flops if you're leaving the beach as streets and beach walkways can be dirty.

EATING AND DRINKING

Beach-shack dining is a signature experience in Goa—fresh seafood, a cold beverage, and a golden sunset. What more could you ask for? Stick to simple Goan dishes here, though, and save the bold ordering choices for the better restaurants in town.

RESTROOMS

Public restrooms can be dirty, so tuck some toilet paper in your beach bag, and bring some hand sanitizer unless your hotel is within walking distance. Facilities are cleaner at the nicer restaurants but you'll probably be turned away if you're not a paying customer.

WATER SPORTS

The beaches at Calangute, Baga, and Colva in particular offer plenty of options for water sports, including parasailing, windsurfing, jet-skiing, and banana boating.

BEACH CHAIRS

Beach chairs with umbrellas line the beaches in front of restaurants. If you're a customer these are free to use, otherwise you can ask to rent one for a small, and negotiable, fee.

HAWKERS

You'll find plenty of vendors and stalls selling knickknacks, souvenirs, food, and drinks. Stick to the bottled beverages and be cautious of inflated prices. Vendors can be a nuisance but a firm "No, thanks," is all that's needed.

THE SUN

This is the tropics, and the sun is strong. Wear good sunscreen and reapply often. Local brands with high SPF are available. If you're particular about a specific brand, bring your own as prices here will be higher.

LIFEGUARDS

Major beaches have lifeguards during the day; smaller beaches do not. Undertows can be a danger in some areas, particularly in the monsoon season, so ask the lifeguards or the locals.

NEFARIOUS ELEMENTS

Goa's reputation for wild parties and easy drugs is not undeserved but you can avoid any associated annoyances by sticking to recommended hotels, restaurants, and bars. Again, if approached by anyone undesirable, a firm "No, thank you," should send them on their way.

Updated by
Vandana
Verma

Beguiling white sands, fresh and spicy seafood, and a cold drink under a glowing sun is Goa at its charming best. But there's plenty more: striking Renaissance cathedrals in Old Goa, ancestral homes surrounding the ragtag city of Margao, the ornate Hindu temples of Ponda, and Panaji's Portuguese historic district.

Those who know India well will tell you that Goa, the smallest state in the Indian federation, is an anomaly—a territory that is decidedly its own entity, shaped by a unique set of circumstances and influences.

Goa wasn't much of a tourist spot until the early 1960s, with the arrival of the first hippies from Europe, who were lured by the laid-back culture and picturesque beaches of Anjuna, Calangute, and Vagator. The lax law enforcement made it easy for the beaches to quickly become the site of wild parties, cheap alcohol, and plenty of drugs. The Anjuna flea market was established soon after, in the 1970s, as many of the foreign tourists started selling secondhand goods to fund an extended stay. It was around this time that the beach shacks appeared as well: temporary structures that multitask as restaurant, bar, hotel, bookstall, shop, or just a place to hang out all day.

The era of electronic music in the 1980s changed Goa into a hot spot for raves, and heady full-moon parties were all the rage for the subsequent decade. This golden age of raves has subsided in recent years due to increased government action. However, parties continue to rage on in less publicized venues—you just have to ask around at popular bars to find out what's going on.

As Goa continued to attract more and more visitors, it caught the attention of well-heeled Indian tourists. Five-star hotels and resorts started popping up in the south, while package tours and charter flights from the United Kingdom and elsewhere in Europe became a common feature in the north. It soon became a hip destination for Indians, particularly in the 10 days over Christmas and the New Year, as the affluent flocked to Goa for private parties.

Today, with more and more Indians traveling abroad, this party scene has subsided to a certain degree, but it still remains enough of a party destination to justify sky-high hotel rates during that fortnight around Christmas and New Year's Eve. The next generation of long-term budget foreigners, meanwhile, has retreated to the northern beaches around Morjim. Here you might enter an Internet parlor and find a keyboard in Hebrew or signs in Russian.

All this tourism has had an undeniable influence on Goa's way of life, economy, and identity, and in some areas today you can find a Greek restaurant, a French-food shack, a German bakery, a pizza joint, and an Indian *dhaba* (fast-food joint) all within a 5-mile radius. Much of Goa has evolved to cater to every breed of tourist—top-notch restaurants, boutique hotels, lovely heritage homes, luxury resorts, funky beach shacks, cheap and noisy hotels, and business hotels for the corporate retreats and conferences. You can still get away from it all, or you can just dive in and savor its still-wild reputation. But now, more than ever before, Goa offers so many more options that the hippies might be the only ones complaining.

PLANNING

WHEN TO GO

HIGH SEASON: NOVEMBER TO LATE FEBRUARY

Goa's tourist season begins in November and peaks from the middle of December until after the New Year in January, when the skies are clear and parties are in overdrive. Anyone planning to visit over this time should prepare for sky-high lodging prices, and for beaches, hotels, and restaurants that are packed around the clock.

LOW SEASON: MAY TO OCTOBER

It's wise to avoid Goa in the months of May and October, when it is oppressively hot and humid, and very unpleasant even for the locals. During the monsoon months, from June through September, most of Goa's hotels, beach-shack restaurants, and bars shut down due to the torrential rains and strong winds; violent surf makes water sports impossible, and visitors will struggle to find places to dine that are open. Farther inland the forests are lush, as are the rice plantations, which lie near Goa's many rivers, and most of the larger hotels stay open—it's always worth asking for "monsoon specials" if you are headed to Goa at this time of year.

SHOULDER SEASON: LATE FEBRUARY TO APRIL

Those who visit in the early spring can still enjoy gorgeous weather and Goa's beauty without feeling as if they're just part of a crowd—and there's the added excitement of Carnival.

GETTING HERE AND AROUND

AIR TRAVEL

Most travelers get to Goa by booking an international flight to Mumbai or Delhi, then hopping a domestic flight to Goa's Dabolim Airport, about 29 km (18 miles) south of Panaji, the state capital. Direct flights are available from many of India's major cities, and most can be booked online.

AIRPORT TRANSFERS Buses are infrequent, so it's usually best to take a taxi from here to your destination. You can arrange for a prepaid taxi service at a counter inside the airport, or go straight outside and hire a private cab. Many resorts include airport transfers, or you can prearrange it for a fee. Alternatively, a government taxi desk outside the arrivals hall can organize a prepaid taxi. This is a better option than trying to negotiate fares with persistent drivers yourself. Either way, the fare to Panaji should not exceed Rs. 500.

Airport Information Dabolim Airport ☎ *832/245–0723.*

BIKE OR MOTORBIKE TRAVEL

If you're in reasonable shape and confident riding on potholed, heavily traveled roads, consider renting a bicycle for a jaunt to save on taxi fares, especially if you simply want to get from your hotel to the beach and back. Don't expect more than one gear or anything resembling what you're used to; check the tires and brakes. You can rent motorbikes at bus stops, train stations, markets, and beach resorts and cars at the airport—your hotel will be able to arrange one as well. You'll need an international driver's license to drive anything larger than a 55-cc engine. However, Indian drivers and roads being what they are, think long and hard before renting any motorized vehicle you intend to drive yourself.

BUS TRAVEL

Several private bus companies connect Goa with Mumbai, Pune, Bengaluru, and Mangalore. They are more expensive than public transit but definitely faster and more comfortable. Try Paulo Travels (☎ *832/663–7777* ⊕ *www.paulotravels.com*) for reliable service. Getting around Goa by bus is not advised unless you are traveling very light. Passengers are often packed in tight.

CAR TRAVEL

Goa can be easily explored from one end to the other by car. Everyplace is within a short drive of everyplace else.

TAXI AND AUTO-RICKSHAW TRAVEL

Goa has a unionized taxi system with fixed rates from point A to point B. They are expensive, but this is the best way to get around in Goa if money isn't a constraint. You don't really need to contact a tour operator, as there will usually be a taxi stand outside your hotel. If not, the hotel will call one for you from the nearest stand. Fares are not negotiable (in theory), and drivers charge a fixed rate displayed on a board at every taxi stand. If you are visiting a number of places and covering a lot of ground, it makes more sense to hire a taxi for a four- or eight-hour

FESTIVALS: CARNIVAL

Carnival time—in February, just before Lent—remains the official season for nonstop revelry, directed by King Momo ("King of Misrule"), a Goan appointed by his peers as the life of the party. Festivities include fanciful pageants (with some 50 floats depicting elements of Goa's folk culture, or more contemporary messages like preservation of the environment), hordes of musicians strumming the guitar or playing the banjo, and dancers breaking into the *mando* (a folk fusion of the Portuguese fado and the waltz)—all in streets spangled with confetti.

Brazilian samba dancers on parade at Goa's Carnival celebration

stretch (Rs. 1,500 for four hours), and pay an additional rate (Rs. 12) for every kilometer above 80 km (50 miles). Round-trip distances are calculated even for one-way journeys. Taxis levy a surcharge when they operate at night.

Most hotels can arrange taxis to take you around, either to the beach, restaurants, or shopping, and nothing is too far given the state's small size.

Auto-rickshaws, otherwise known as autos in India and "tuk-tuks" elsewhere in Southeast Asia, are easy to find. They cost less than taxis, but there are no fixed rates, so before climbing in ask a local or a knowledgeable visitor what the fare should be to your destination. Autos are best for short distances in town rather than for jaunts across the state.

TRAIN TRAVEL

You can take a train or bus to Goa from Mumbai, but be warned: such trips can be long—at least 12 hours by train, 17 hours by bus—crowded, and uncomfortable. (Be sure to take a bus or train with reserved seating.) The Konkan Railway (⊕ *www.konkanrailway.com*) runs lines to Mumbai in the north and Mangalore in the South. The Madgaon station in Margao is the main station, and there are smaller ones in Pernem, Thivim, Karmali, and Canacona. Book early online for train reservations: seats fill up quickly during the tourist season. Air-conditioned sleepers are best for overnight journeys.

For complete train schedules and fares, and to book tickets online, go to the Indian Railways website (⊕ *www.indianrail.gov.in*) where you can purchase and upgrade tickets, determine the kind of train you want, and review the rather extensive list of rules.

Train Information Karmali station
☎ *832/228–5798.* **Margao station**
✉ *2 km [1 mile] from the main shopping area, Margao* ☎ *832/271–2790.*

TOURS

There are dozens of private tour operators in Goa. The most reliable are run by the Goa Tourism Development Corporation, which runs bus tours of both North and South Goa—departing from Panaji, Madgaon, and Colva Beach—as well as river cruises from the Santa Monica Pier in Panaji, and the Goa Department of Tourism.

FIND IT ALL GOA

The best resource for up-to-date Goa information is Find All Goa (⊕ *www.findall-goa.com*), which provides detailed calendars for live music, tours, cruises, and cultural and sporting events, as well as useful information regarding plane and train departures. Exceptionally detailed maps of Goa's districts and towns (including walking paths) can be downloaded.

Contacts Department of Tourism
✉ *Tourist Home, Patto Bridge, Panaji* ☎ *832/243–8750* ⊕ *www.goatourism.gov.in.* **Goa Tourism Development Corporation** ✉ *Trionara Apartments, Dr. Alvares Costa Rd., Panaji* ☎ *832/242–4001 to 03* ⊕ *www.goa-tourism.com.*

VISITOR INFORMATION

In Panaji, the Directorate of Tourism fields general inquiries. For assistance with reservations, including bus tours, contact the Goa Tourism Development Corporation (GTDC). There's also a 24-hour "Hello Information" number for Goa (☎ *832/241–2121*), which is extremely useful for finding phone numbers.

Tourist Offices Department of Tourism ✉ *Tourist Home, Patto Bridge, Panaji* ☎ *832/243–8750* ⊕ *www.goatourism.gov.in.* **Goa Tourism Development Corporation** ✉ *Trionara Apartments, Dr. Alvares Costa Rd., Panaji* ☎ *832/242–0779* ⊕ *www.goa-tourism.com.*

ABOUT THE RESTAURANTS

If you like seafood and spicy food in general, you're in luck. You can spend all your time happily eating nothing but searingly hot (spicy) fish day in and day out, both in the best restaurants around (generally found at hotels) and at beachfront open-air shacks. But since Goa has such a huge tourist culture, food can be prepared to your liking—simply grilled or fried or with less spice, if you prefer. Goan food is typically big on flavor, whether it's chilli, tamarind, or coconut that dominates the dish. Make sure you order your meat (pork or beef) cooked through, and only order meat in the better-known larger restaurants, not at the beach shacks. Seafood is usually safe everywhere as long as it's fresh. If you're vegetarian, you'll get by fine, but vegetables are not as plentiful in the Goan diet as are fish, seafood, and meat.

Prices in the reviews are the average cost of a main course at dinner or, if dinner is not served, at lunch.

ABOUT THE HOTELS

Goa has every kind of lodging, from super-exclusive posh resorts to beachside shacks appropriate only for beach bums and seen-it-all globetrotters. Expect to get what you pay for, however, especially during peak season, from December to February, when traveling hordes fill the hotels. Make sure you reserve a room far in advance of this time. During the monsoon season (June–October), prices drop by up to half and the resorts fill up with Indian visitors from the North. Unless noted otherwise, hotels have air-conditioning, TVs, and bathrooms with showers.

Prices in the reviews are the lowest cost of a standard double room in high season. For expanded hotel reviews, facilities, and current deals, visit Fodors.com.

PLANNING YOUR TIME

In Goa, those who love the water can swim, go parasailing or jet-skiing, or hire a banana boat for a couple of hours paddling. Foodies have menus full of fresh seafood, local delicacies and international dishes to choose from. There are lots of markets all over the state for those interested in shopping, and more than enough bars and nightclubs to keep the party crowd going all night. And despite Goa's prominence on the tourist trail, it's still possible to go off the beaten path and experience Goa's quieter and charming side along its rivers and in its villages.

It takes about a week to catch all of Goa's highlights—the beaches, Panaji, Old Goa, and the backwaters. If you're coming mainly for the beaches, a three- or four-day trip will suffice for swimming in the warm waters of the Arabian Sea, shopping at the colorful markets, and enjoying the flavors of Goan food. And there's a beach to suit every desire: those looking for seclusion and clear water can head north to Arambol, currently home to Goa's few remaining hippies, while the resort-lined southern beaches offer swankier shacks and cold bottles of wine on quiet beaches. For nonstop action—all-night parties with DJs and live bands—partygoers should head for Baga in the north or Colva in the south. It's worth putting a day aside to see Panaji and to sample Goa's Portuguese ties firsthand, most apparent in the historic Fontainhas and Sao Tomé districts, as well as in the grand churches of Old Goa, built by the Portuguese in the 16th century.

A wonderful way to properly experience Goan life is to check in for two or three days at one of the state's heritage homes or properties. With antique-filled guest rooms, attentive service, and delicious home cooking, the best of these places amount to a pleasurable window into Goa's past. Ultimately, much of Goa's charm lies in its ability to be so flexible: here you can choose between a tranquil retreat from modern life or party central, a resort spot for a perfect tan, or a destination from which to explore India's heritage.

EXPLORING GOA

Although it is the coastal areas that are the biggest draw for visitors to Goa, if you travel inland you'll find jungles, mountains, and agricultural areas. The north is known for its restaurants, bars and party-hearty beaches. In central Goa you'll find the mammoth ghost town that is Old Goa, as well as Panaji, the state capital. The less-traveled south is home to several high-end hotels and resorts, as well as small villages that allow a glimpse into Goa beyond the beach shacks and all-night parties.

Note that in addresses the terms *wadi, waddo,* and *vado* all mean "street."

NORTH GOA

For plenty of fun in the sun and after-hours parties, head to the busy beaches at Calangute, Baga, and Anjuna, which were important stops on the hippie trails of the 1960s and 1970s. The coastal stretch is increasingly built up, but there are still some quiet areas around Mandrem beach (north of the Chapora River). Nearby, atop the hills, are a few beautiful old forts built of laterite, the local pitted red stone; they offer beautiful vistas of the curvaceous coastline. The villages that sit a few miles inland have charming bed-and-breakfasts and inns with rustic flavor.

You may also want to take an excursion to one of the popular markets. On Wednesday the lively market in Anjuna, not far from the beach, is filled with inexpensive jewelry, cotton sarongs, colorful shoulder bags, and handicrafts marketed by vendors from Goa, Karnataka, and other Indian states. There's also Ingo's Saturday night bazaar, in nearby Arpora. To find late-night beach parties, follow the trance music to any of dozens of beach shacks in Baga, Calangute, and Anjuna.

Goa's restaurant scene continues to refine and reinvent itself, with excellent restaurants serving both Goan and international cuisines. Stop by A Reverie in Calangute for its global fusion menu, Thalassa in Vagator for delicious Greek food, Ciao Bella in Assagao for wonderful Italian cuisine or Lila Café in Baga for a hearty morning-after recovery meal.

ARAMBOL, ASHVEM, MANDREM, AND MORJIM

★ *48 km (30 miles) northwest of Panaji.*

The sands of Arambol are far less congested than those at Baga and Calangute, and as a result the area has become home to a new generation of hippies and free-spirited travelers. You'll catch this bohemian vibe in the European cafés and cheap hotels and shacks that cater to long-haul visitors.

The beach, also known as Harmal, is rugged and lovely. The best stretch is tiny Paliem Beach, at the foot of Waghcolomb Hill. The scenery is spectacular: a freshwater pond stands at the base of the hillside barely 200 yards from the sea. The sea is rougher here than at other beaches—it's still good for swimming, but a bit more fun for those who like a little surf. To avoid the crowds when it's high season, walk past the pond, and you'll find quieter tidal inlets and rock ledges.

A little farther south are the lovely, quiet beaches of Ashvem, Mandrem, and Morjim. Divided by little creeks, the beaches have spectacular windswept stretches of sand, a far cry from the overcrowded beaches south of the Chapora River. Mandrem offers the most accommodation and entertainment options, including a couple of well-tended luxury shacks. Morjim is popular because of the Olive Ridley turtles, which use its dark sands as a nesting ground during the winter. Hatchlings emerge at night after an eight-week incubation period. Conservation efforts have proved difficult, and it's unclear whether turtles will continue to return to nest here. Ashvem is quiet and relaxing in the daytime, but once the sun goes down this is where you'll find the open-air beach parties in high season.

MONSOON MASALA

Chances are you've never experienced anything like the monsoon in Goa. The downpours are heavy and sudden, and the raindrops so huge and close together it's as if someone is throwing buckets of water on you from a second-floor window. The rain may last for days or a mere 30 minutes, disappearing as quickly as it came. Even so, if you're in Goa during a rainy spell, don't let it slow you down. Wear your flip-flops, bring an umbrella, and carry on as the locals do.

GETTING HERE AND AROUND

The best and fastest way of getting here is by taxi. A prepaid non-air-conditioned ride from the airport should set you back about Rs. 1,200 to Arambol. From Panaji, it should take you about 40 minutes for a Rs. 600 taxi ride. Most hotels will arrange taxis, rent motorbikes, or loan bicycles.

WHERE TO EAT AND STAY

For expanded hotel reviews, visit Fodors.com.

$$$ PIZZA 🍴 **Fellini.** Firmly established as the definitive destination for pizza in North Goa, Fellini is tucked away in the busy lanes of Arambol—it takes some finding, but the pepperoni pizzas make it worth the hunt. They don't skimp on the mozzarella, and Fellini's salami pie commands a devoted following that traipses in from all over the North. Vegetarians should try the classic margherita or the spinach and mushroom options. The interior is no-nonsense, with shack-style tables and seating. It's best to skip right over the pasta section of the menu, because it's the giant calzones and pies that are the stars here. [$] *Average main: Rs. 500* ✉ *Socoillo Vaddo, Main Arambol Beach Rd., Arambol Pernem* ☎ *97/6489–3896.*

$$$$ INDIAN ★ 🍴 **La Plage.** Don't let the casual air of the palm trees and simple white tables of this down-to-earth shack fool you. It serves some of the best French food in town (and country, by some estimates). Conceived in 2003 by three old friends, the restaurant has transformed from its humble six-table beginnings into a must-visit destination for any food-lover passing through Goa. Try the warm tiger prawn carpaccio or crispy sardine fillets with parsley, pine nuts, and lime zest; or the sesame-crusted tuna fillet with wasabi mashed potatoes and soy sauce. Dinner reservations are recommended during the Christmas and New Year's season. [$] *Average main: Rs. 1500* ✉ *Ashwem Beach, Morjim* ☎ *98/2212–1712* 💳 *No credit cards* 🕓 *Closed May–Nov.*

$$$$ HOTEL ★ 🏨 **Elsewhere.** On a 500-yard-long spit of outstretched private land, surrounded on three sides by the waters of the Arabian Sea and Otter Creek, is Denzil Sequeira's lovely ancestral property, a reminder of a forgotten Goa. **Pros:** semi-private beach; lovely property. **Cons:**

Goa's Past

Goa's coastal location has made it an influential trading post for many centuries. Hindu merchants flourished for centuries, trading spices, silk, pearls, horses, and ideas with Arab, East African, and Mediterranean cultures. Control of the region shifted between the Bahmani Sultanate of the Deccan Plateau and the Vijayanagar Empire in Hampi, to the east. Goa's fortunes were profoundly altered by the arrival in 1510 of Affonso de Albuquerque, a Portuguese explorer and naval officer who wrestled the tiny realm from the hands of the Sultan of Bijapur. For the next 450 years the Portuguese exerted major pressures as well as a strong influence on Goan culture, language, and religion—they converted many native Hindus and Buddhists to Catholicism by force. The Portuguese ruled with an iron first before, during, and after the rest of the Indian subcontinent was under the thumb of the British.

It was during this period, from the 16th to the 18th centuries, that the grandiose churches of Old Goa were built. The most illustrious structures here include Old Goa's Sé (cathedral) and the Basilica of Bom Jesus, where the remains of St. Francis Xavier lie in a silver casket entombed in a Florentine-style marble mausoleum. A string of cholera epidemics in this city built on swamps eventually saw its decline, and the Portuguese adopted Panaji as its new capital.

Although British-ruled India became a free country in 1947, the Portuguese retained their hold on Goa for 15 more years. They were finally driven out in 1961 through a land assault ordered by India's first Prime Minister, Jawaharlal Nehru. In comparison to some 30,000 Indian troops, the Portuguese force of 3,000 men was nominal.

In the decades since, Goa has retained its own identity, although tourism has changed it a great deal. In day-to-day life, Catholic traditions are evident in its whitewashed village churches, and European influence lives on in the Goans' love for pork, and even in local fashions. Goans, perhaps more than any other Indian state, are quite Western in their outlook, and it is that harmonious blend of East and West that sets it apart from most other parts of the country.

---

a 60-yard bamboo footbridge is the only access route; reservations have to be made via email. $ *Rooms from: Rs. 29000* ✉ *North Goa* ⊕ *www.aseascape.com* ⌑ *4 beach houses, 3 tents* ☉ *Closed June–Sept.* ⦿ *Breakfast.*

$$$ ⬚ **Fort Tiracol.** This small 18th-century Portuguese fort, situated at land's
HOTEL end nearly at Goa's northern border, is now a striking heritage hotel.
Pros: lots of privacy; inspiring views of the Arabian Sea from every room. **Cons:** isolated; no beach access. $ *Rooms from: Rs. 8900* ✉ *Tiracol* ☎ *832/652–9653* ⊕ *www.forttiracol.com* ⌑ *5 rooms, 2 suites* ⦿ *Breakfast.*

$$$ ⬚ **Siolim House.** For the old-world charm of an aristocratic family home,
HOTEL stay at this elegant Portuguese villa on the south bank of the Chapora
★ River, now converted into an all-suites boutique hotel. **Pros:** tranquil rural setting; free Wi-Fi; palatial rooms. **Cons:** no TV; no a/c in some

rooms; the mattresses on some beds are old. *Rooms from: Rs. 6600 ✉ Opposite Vaddy Chapel, Siolim, Bardez ☎ 832/227–2138, 833/227–2941 🌐 www.siolimhouse.com 7 suites 🍴 Breakfast.*

$$$ RESORT **Yab Yum Resorts.** The property's signature thatched and dome-shape roofs are tucked away in a shaded grove of palm trees—a fun and funky location that's minutes from lovely Ashwem Beach. **Pros:** quiet beach. **Cons:** no restaurant on premises. *Rooms from: Rs. 6000 ✉ Ashvem Beach, Mandrem ☎ 832/224–7712, 832/651–0392 🌐 www.yabyumresorts.com 5 cottages, 12 domes ⏲ Closed late Apr.–Oct. 🍴 Breakfast.*

BEACHES

Arambol Beach. Perfect for those keen on sampling a taste of the 1970s hippie trail, and still favorite with Goa's free spirits, this North Goan beach has long, wide swathes of clean sand and shallow water that's great for paddling. Even in season you can find quiet stretches where you can chill out, and with a few fun shacks spread out over the length of the beach, there's always fresh juice and light food to be had. **Amenities:** food and drink. **Best for:** solitude; sunrise; sunset; swimming. ✉ *Arambol Pernem.*

Ashvem Beach. The white sands here are perfect for uninterrupted lazing. Sandwiched between Morjim and Mandrem beaches, Ashvem has a fair few hippie beach shacks, but it still manages to hold onto its air of deserted idyll. Between September and February, this is a nesting spot for the Olive Ridley turtle, and if you're lucky you'll spot a few. No longer off the beaten track, the areas around the beach are now full of thatched beachside accommodations, like Yab Yum Resorts ⇨ *See Where to Stay listings*. And in season it's also home to some of Goa's best seasonal eating, notably at upscale La Plage ⇨ *See Where to Eat listings*. It's not as much of a destination for partyers as some of its neighboring beaches, and just a hop and a skip away from the beach are lush paddies and coconut groves. **Amenities:** food and drink. **Best for:** solitude; sunrise; sunset; swimming; walking. ✉ *Mandrem.*

Mandrem Beach. This quiet hideaway in North Goa has the advantage of not being a popular destination on the tourist trail, which is why it's a top pick for honeymooners and for couples looking for a quiet getaway. There are a few beach shacks and the odd guesthouse in season, but you really have to make your own entertainment on this deserted stretch. **Amenities:** none. **Best for:** solitude; sunset.

Morjim Beach. Best known as a home to Olive Ridley sea turtles, serene Morjim Beach is popular with those keen to see a nesting site of the species. Known to be quiet and peaceful, it is easy to see the attraction for these endangered marine creatures. In recent years, however, the village of Morjim has also become home to most of Goa's Russian expatriates, earning itself the title of "Little Russia," and this influx has brought with it a less peaceful atmosphere. Although the beach is still quiet during the day, it now has a thriving nightlife. **Amenities:** food and drink. **Best for:** swimming; walking; partyers. ✉ *Morjim.*

7

A woman playing an alphorn at Arambol beach

VAGATOR BEACH

★ *25 km (16 miles) northwest of Panaji.*

Jagged cliffs along sandy shores give a rugged wild atmosphere to the beaches at Vagator, which is split by a seaside headland that offers beautiful views on either side. On one side are the dark red walls of the old hill fort of Chapora, built in 1717, which was later taken twice from the Portuguese by the Marathas. (The Marathas ruled a principality that covers much of the modern-day state of Maharashtra, north of Goa.) The view from the ramparts is phenomenal, and farther up the shore are stretches of secluded sand. On the other side is beautiful Ozrant Beach, also called Mini-Vagator, near which you will find an impressive stone face of Shiva that was carved into a boulder by an unknown sculptor.

Little Vagator and Vagator come to life after dark. Beach shacks like Boom Shankar will have information on the ongoing beach parties. Nine Bar, above the beach, is for trance lovers. This part of Goa is not as developed as the beaches farther south, and although there are plenty of shack restaurants, they have a here-today-gone-tomorrow feel; indeed, many disappear from one season to the next, or take on a different name. The best way to figure out where to eat is to ask fellow travelers for the name of the current favorite.

WHERE TO EAT AND STAY
For expanded hotel reviews, visit Fodors.com.

$$$ ✕ **Ciao Bella.** This delightful Italian restaurant is one of Goa's newest,
ITALIAN and is definitely among its best. The Italian couple, Mario and Simona, who are at the helm here are hands-on hosts who tend to customers

CLOSE UP

Water Sports in Goa

Goa offers a variety of water sports, from adrenaline-generating Jet Ski rides and parasailing to more lighthearted banana boat and catamaran rides.

Parasailing. This is the most exciting water-sport experience in Goa: you take off and feel the wind hitting you across the lovely palm-fringed coastline. There are two ways to do it: either you take off and land on a winchboat in the water, or you descend onto the beach. You will find plenty of operators during the tourist season, but some of them have questionable safety standards. Use licensed operators at the luxury resorts if you happen to be staying at one, or use one of those with a history of operating in Goa. Parasailing around Sinquerim-Candolim-Calangute offers a spectacular view of Fort Aguada. Other recommended areas are near the Arrosim-Cansaulim and Utorda stretches, and Mobor Beach, in the south. From Miramar you can catch views of the Mandovi River meeting the sea. Rides last for three to five minutes and cost between Rs. 400 and Rs. 1,000; boat-ride charges are extra. You need to be comfortable with both heights and water.

Jet-skiing and waterskiing. Water sports operators in Colva, Candolim, Calangute, Miramar, Arossim, Utorda, Benaulim, Mobor, and Rajbaga are also set up for jet-skiing. It's an exhilarating, energetic ride, which lasts from 2 to 15 minutes. Usually instructors accompany you on the rides, which cost around Rs. 1,500. If you want to go waterskiing, the cost is between Rs. 400 and Rs. 1,200 depending on the length of the ride and the time of year; operators are at Candolim, Calangute, Arossim, Utorda, Majorda, and Rajbaga.

Scuba diving and snorkeling. Goa is not a great location for these sports, but there are a couple of reputable places to try both. They can both also help you get PADI certified.

as well as cook, and their personal touch is evident in every plate the kitchen sends out. With delicious homemade pasta and bread, a perfect plate of spinach-and-ricotta ravioli, giant portions of black tagliatelle with salmon, and a dessert list that includes a potent coffee granita, everything on the menu is fresh and fantastic. Go early to bag a table at the weekend, but service is so quick that you might not have too long a wait even if you forget. [$] *Average main: Rs. 700* ✉ *569 Assagao Baden Rd., Assagao, Bardez* ☎ *97/6755–7673* 🕒 *No lunch. Closed Mon.*

$$$$ GREEK ★ 🍴 **Thalassa.** Rugged Vagator Beach is the seductive backdrop for Marikketty Grana's popular whitewashed Greek restaurant, which is on top of a low cliff overlooking the rocky shores of Little Vagator. Thalassa's vibrant chef re-creates authentic food from her native Corfu, including much-loved dishes like *sofrito* (veal, slow-cooked in white wine and herbs) and *pastisada* (meat with tomato sauce and spices served with macaroni). The lamb dishes, such as the moussaka, are excellent. There are options for vegetarians, too: try the hot feta cheese, the risotto, or the mushroom saganaki, made with melted cheese. [$] *Average main: Rs. 800* ✉ *Little Vagator, Ozran Beach, Vagator* ☎ *98/5003–3537* 💳 *No credit cards* 🕒 *No lunch; closed late May–Sept.*

7

$$$ HOTEL
[H] **Casa Vagator.** Perched on a hillside high above the Arabian Sea, this smart and stylish contemporary hotel overlooks the wild beauty of Vagator Beach, which guests can reach by following a winding path that descends rather sharply. **Pros:** far from the hustle and bustle of Goa's beach scene; striking sea views. **Cons:** lots of stairs; small pool; the neighboring Nine Bar sometimes has thumping music at night. [$] *Rooms from: Rs. 7000* ✉ *H. No. 594/4 Vozran, Vagator* ☎ *832/727–4931* 🌐 *www.casaboutiquehotelsgoa.com* 🛏 *11 rooms, 1 penthouse suite* 🕒 *Closed roughly June–mid-Sept.* 🍴 *Breakfast.*

$$$ HOTEL
[H] **Sunbeam.** Owned by flamboyant Indian stylist Jivi Sethi, Sunbeam is a gorgeously redecorated Portuguese family home in one of North Goa's most charming villages. **Pros:** excellent food; beautiful family heirlooms and home-style touches; access to some of Goa's best beaches. **Cons:** powercuts; lack of light in the Old House rooms. [$] *Rooms from: Rs. 7000* ✉ *E-13 Saunta Vaddo, Mapusa-Anjuna Rd., Assagao, Vagator Beach* ☎ *832/226–8525* 🛏 *3 rooms* 🍴 *All meals.*

BEACHES

Vagator Beach. The dark sands of Vagator Beach lead on from the red cliffs that line it. Vagator is popular with both local and foreign tourists, and as a result visitors will find lots of vendors and stands selling snacks, sliced local fruit, trinkets, and souvenirs. Plenty of bars and shacks are on hand to cater to this mixed crowd, and in the high season most bars reverberate to the sounds of dance and trance music. Vagator's waters are choppier than some of North Goa's other beaches, which is why this beach isn't a top pick for swimmers. **Amenities:** food and drink; parking; toilets. **Best for:** sunset; partyers; walking. ✉ *Vagator.*

ANJUNA BEACH

★ *20 km (12 miles) northwest of Panaji.*

Discovered by the hippies in the late 1960s, Anjuna and its palm-lined beaches have had many seasons of glory. Although Anjuna can get very crowded and boisterous, its beach is still not as commercial as Calangute and doesn't have the large-scale luxury resorts you'll find at Sinquerim Beach and in the south. With coconut trees framing the sands against jagged laterite cliffs and boulders, the beach is as popular as ever. Drugs are all too easily available here, too, but they are also highly illegal—even if they seem to be part of the atmosphere. Anjuna is known for its **flea market** on Wednesday.

WHERE TO EAT AND STAY

For expanded hotel reviews, visit Fodors.com.

$ BAKERY
🍴 **Baba Au Rhum.** This charming little French pizzeria and bakery, in a sleepy residential lane off the busy Anjuna road, is open all day, but it's best for breakfast. The croissants are buttery and fresh, and the pain au chocolat is far too good to be restricted to the morning. The menu also includes a concise selection of freshly squeezed juices, sandwiches, and salads, as well as fairly good pizzas and burgers, but it's with the sweet stuff that they really excel—try a strawberry and lemon tart or the chocolate passion fruit version, which sounds an unwise blend,

but is actually delightful (with just a little kick). $ *Average main: Rs. 300* ⊠ *Salim House, opposite Uttam Resorts, Arpora* ☎ 98/2207–8759.

$ ✕ **Biryani Palace.** American expats who like the Palace's relaxed service,
INDIAN open-air seating and good food claim this casual eatery is one of the best restaurants in Anjuna. The cook specializes in *biryanis* (Indian rice pilaf made with vegetables, spices, and a choice of seafood, chicken or meat), of course, but also barbecued seafood, mixed seafood grills, and Goan specialties. Soft lighting, mat ceilings, rattan chairs on a sandy floor, and no a/c set the mellow mood that is enhanced by classic sitar music—instead of the driving Goan trance beat played in most area restaurants. $ *Average main: Rs. 200* ⊠ *Anjuna Beach Rd., 500 yds. from beach, Anjuna* ☎ 93/2612–4699 ▭ *No credit cards.*

$$$ ▦ **Casa Anjuna.** History, style, and attitude combine to make spending
★ time in this 200-year-old Portuguese mansion and its lush tropical garden a rare pleasure. **Pros:** beautiful setting; antiques-filled rooms; peace and quiet. **Cons:** 10-minute walk to the beach. $ *Rooms from: Rs. 6000* ⊠ *D'Mello Vaddo 66, Anjuna, Bardez* ☎ 832/227–4123 ⊕ *www. casaboutiquehotels.com* ⤵ *19 rooms, 2 suites, 3 penthouses* ⦿| *Breakfast.*

$ ▦ **Hotel Bougainvillea (Granpa's Inn).** This hotel occupies a 200-year-old
HOTEL restored Portuguese country house on an inland lane. **Pros:** great value; funky; rural setting. **Cons:** too far to walk to the beach; no a/c in some rooms. $ *Rooms from: Rs. 2900* ⊠ *Gaunwadi, Anjuna* ☎ 832/227–3270, 832/227–3271 ⊕ *www.granpasinn.com* ⤵ *7 rooms, 7 suites* ⊙ *Closed July and Aug.* ⦿| *Breakfast.*

$$ ▦ **Laguna Anjuna.** This upscale place to stay is less than a kilometer from
RESORT the beach, in a tree-lined residential area. **Pros:** quiet, relaxed setting. **Cons:** a bit removed from the main attraction. $ *Rooms from: Rs. 4000* ⊠ *Soranto Vado, Anjuna* ☎ 832/227–4131 ⊕ *www.lagunaanjuna.com* ⤵ *19 rooms, 6 suites* ⦿| *Breakfast.*

BEACHES

Anjuna Beach. This is Goa's original hippie haven. Those full-moon parties, now so synonymous with this beach state, first happened on the sands of Anjuna in the 1960s, and even today this northern beach is home to modern-day flower children, international travelers keen on sampling some of that hippie stardust, and everyone looking for a party. It's definitely not one of Goa's most beautiful beaches, but the steady influx of people means that it's got restaurants and bars galore. Anjuna's busiest on Wednesday, when the famed weekly Anjuna Flea Market takes place. The water is safe for swimming and you'll find lots of sunbathers and souvenir vendors year-round. **Amenities:** food and drink; water sports; parking. **Best for:** partyers; sunset; swimming; walking. ⊠ *Anjuna.*

NIGHTLIFE

Curlie's Bar. At the south end of Anjuna, Curlie's is something of an institution, organizing parties in season and *the* place for partyers to congregate year-round. With a great sea view and a basic menu, this is an essential pit stop for anyone who wants to sample the hard-partying side of Goa. ☎ 98/2216–8628.

DID YOU KNOW?

Goa's largest flea market, in hippie-haven Anjuna, is held every Wednesday; it's said that the market started in the 1960s when cash-depleted hippies used to sell their belongings to buy a few more weeks of peace and love.

The Flea Market at Anjuna

Getting to the Wednesday flea market at Anjuna can be half the fun; you can take a bus or a motorcycle taxi, or a fisherman's boat from Baga, which takes 15 minutes or so. (Going by road takes half an hour.) There are still some old-school foreigners around manning the stands, but it really isn't their market anymore. Now the markets are dominated by Lamani, Kashmiris, and Tibetans, who sell all kinds of trinkets while dressed in striking clothing and jewelry, as well as craftspeople from elsewhere in India. The market is a splash of red and orange in a flat area above the rocky beach. Bead and white-metal bangles, necklaces and earrings, silver toe rings, embroidered shoulder bags, silk and cotton sarongs, and ethnic footwear are among the more common products on sale. If you look carefully, there are all sorts of other things here as well, from used motorbikes of uncertain age to do-it-yourself *mehendi* henna-tattoo kits. Buy a crochet bikini, tops and skirts embroidered with tiny mirrors, or a tie-dye bandana to get your wardrobe for those really formal occasions, or just sit back at the market bar and down a ridiculously cheap beer while someone braids your hair deftly or offers to tattoo, pierce, or otherwise mutilate various parts of your anatomy. Be careful not to bargain unfairly, because you run the risk of a sarcastic "take it for free?" from one of the tribal women. When your day's bargains have been struck (and getting things for a third or less of the quoted price is not uncommon), join the rest of Anjuna down at the shore. The market only appears during the tourist season; during the monsoon there's a smaller market in Anjuna just above the main town beach.

Paradiso. This is one of Goa's most popular nightclubs, near Anjuna Beach atop a cliff with a fabulous view. ☎ 832/325–9999.

Primrose Café. Between Anjuna and Vagator, this is another option for starting the night.

Shore Bar. The most popular place to down beer, watch the dramatic sunset over the Arabian Sea, and listen to loud music until the wee hours is the Shore Bar on the beach. The steps of this place are usually packed with people, especially on Wednesday after the flea market. Walk north from the market for about a kilometer to get here. ☎ 98/2238–3795.

BAGA BEACH

15 km (9 miles) northwest of Panaji and 2 km (1 mile) north of Calangute.

One of Goa's top party beaches, Baga is known for its hopping "shack life." The many popular food and drink joints are headlined by St. Anthony's for seafood and the legendary Tito's Bar and Café Mambo for nighttime revelry. The many water sports here include parasailing, windsurfing, and Jet Ski rides.

The beach drops steeply to the shoreline, where fishing canoes make use of the easy boat-launching conditions to provide rides, including trips to the Wednesday market at Anjuna Beach just around the bend (the ride to Anjuna takes 15 minutes by sea, but twice as long by road). A few hundred meters down the beach, to the south of the point where the steep slope meets the sand, you'll find less-crowded areas where you can spread out your towel and sunbathe. The beach gets its name from the Baga River, which meets the sea at the beach's northern end.

WHERE TO EAT AND STAY
For expanded hotel reviews, visit Fodors.com.

$ ✕ **Lila Café.** Cross the river, and you
CAFÉ arrive at picturesquely situated Lila Café, by the banks of the Baga River. The daytime eatery is the perfect antidote to any late-night revelry and is famous for its freshly baked breads and jams, soups, omelets, and continental dishes—don't miss the hot croissants. This German café is among the top breakfast places around; even locals happily make the trip from Panaji. $ *Average main: Rs. 150* ⊠ *House no. 566, near Baga River, Arpora-Baga, Bardez* ☎ *0832/227–9843* ⊕ *www.lilacafegoa.com* ⊟ *No credit cards* ⊘ *Closed Tues. and June–Sept.*

$$ ✕ **St. Anthony's.** This seaside restaurant, a bit above Baga's many beach
SEAFOOD shacks, serves an astonishing variety of fish dishes in a casual setting that draws big crowds due to its location at the mouth of the river. The tuna steaks and pomfret dishes are particularly good. $ *Average main: Rs. 400* ⊠ *near the Baga River* ☎ *832/645–2396* ⊟ *No credit cards.*

$$$ ⬚ **Casa Baga.** This rambling, boutique hotel is far and away the best
HOTEL place to stay in Baga—the lively beach scene is only two minutes away, and the friendly staff treat you like family, making up for any upkeep deficits. **Pros:** not on the noisy main road; exceptional staff. **Cons:** sketchy plumbing. $ *Rooms from: Rs. 7000* ⊠ *40/7 Saunta Vaddo, Baga* ☎ *832/227–6957, 832/228–2930, 832/228–2931* ⊕ *www.casaboutiquehotelsgoa.com* ⇥ *14 rooms* ⦿ *Breakfast.*

$ ⬚ **Cavala.** Quality bargain accommodations are rare in this side of town,
HOTEL which makes this welcoming property, by a tropical garden near Baga beach, a cheery option. **Pros:** minutes to Baga beach. **Cons:** drab, less than thrilling rooms. $ *Rooms from: Rs. 2200* ⊠ *Saunta Vaddo, Baga* ☎ *832/227–6090* ⊕ *www.cavala.com* ⇥ *21 rooms, 9 suites* ⦿ *Breakfast.*

BEACHES
Baga Beach. This long, narrow (at high tide) beach is one of Goa's most popular, and Baga is where you'll find nonstop action, cocktails around the clock, innumerable water-sports vendors, as well as some of North Goa's best-loved party spots like Tito's ⇨ *See Nightlife listings* and Cavala (a short walk away from the beach). In the winter months this beach is filled with package tourists, so although you won't find peace at Baga, you will find everything else. **Amenities:** food and drink; water sports; lifeguards. **Best for:** partyers; sunset; windsurfing. ⊠ *Baga.*

LOOK BOTH WAYS

India is second only to China in traffic fatalities, a high percentage of which involve pedestrians. When walking on Goa's country lanes or potholed city streets, beware of vehicles coming at you from every possible direction. Indian drivers pass on curves, head down the wrong side of the road, and swerve to miss stray dogs, cows, and the occasional wild pig.

7

DID YOU KNOW?

Taking a boat from Baga Beach to Anjuna—to the flea market, for example—is much faster than traveling by road. A boat takes only about 15 minutes, and bypasses any traffic jams.

NIGHTLIFE

Tito's. Always packed, Tito's is the most happening bar and disco in Goa. Café Mambo, on the premises, is open 9:30 am–3:30 am daily, but the party crowd doesn't come in until close to midnight. Expect fashion shows, famous DJ mixers theme nights, popular dance music, and fairly expensive drinks. ☎ *832/227–5028, 832/227–9895.*

CALANGUTE BEACH TO CANDOLIM

12 km (7 miles) northwest of Panaji.

Calangute is by far the biggest draw in Goa—it's an open stretch of white sand with an entrance area crammed with restaurants, stalls, and shops. The mood is especially festive during the high season in winter, when dozens of shacks serving inexpensive beer, mixed drinks, and seafood pop up on the beach.

The beach is accessible by concrete steps. ⚠ Note the sign warning that swimming is dangerous—there's a fairly strong undertow here.

Beyond the beach are some of the area's best restaurants and boutique shopping. You'll also find hundreds of shops, including roadside trinket stalls, branches of the Oxford Bookstore and Café Coffee Day, ATMs, travel agencies, and Malini Ramani's boutique, filled with vibrant clothes. Most of these shops are on the stretch of road running from St. Anthony's Chapel, past a market, to Baga. Candolim Church was first built in 1560 and dedicated to Our Lady of Hope; it was repaired in 1661 and received its current cake-icing look when the village Communidade remodeled it thanks to contributions from Candolim parishioners.

GETTING HERE AND AROUND

Calangute is at the center of the Bardez Coast, bordered by Candolim Beach to the south and Baga to the north. From the airport, a prepaid taxi costs around Rs. 600–Rs. 700.

WHERE TO EAT

$$$$
INTERNATIONAL
★

✕ **A Reverie.** As the name suggests, A Reverie has a dreamlike, elegant ambience: the space is painted in warm earthy tones but there are stylish overtones of bling. Dimmed lounge areas, crystal chandeliers, and wrought-iron decorative furniture accent this popular fine-dining restaurant where dishes are "re-visited, re-interpreted and re-invented." Flavors are truly fused and all the food is beautifully plated. You might start, for instance, with a wasabi-flavored guacamole or a lemongrass-scented seafood dashi consommé with seaweed; intricately prepared seafood, meat, and dessert options hit similarly nuanced notes. The cocktails are intriguing, too—try the Desi Caipirinha made with fresh sugarcane juice or a Goan piña colada with a hint of the local (very potent) feni liquor. There is a live jazz band on weekends. Reservations are recommended. $ *Average main: Rs. 2000* ✉ *Holiday St., next to Goan Heritage, Gauroravaddo* ☎ *91/2350–5550, 98/2317–4927* ☽ *No lunch. Closed May–Oct.*

$$$$
ECLECTIC
★

✕ **I-95.** This open-air dinner lounge and restaurant is chic but casual, with red stone walls and soothing candle-lit ambience. The brainchild of two couples from Mumbai, I-95 is a hit for its well-executed dishes and flair for presentation. The menu is a mixed bag, with some Indian, seafood, and continental fare. The delectable dishes include the blue crab risotto with jalapeño, lime, and cilantro jelly, beef carpaccio with quail egg, and seared tiger prawns dusted with lemon rind. The restaurant has earned a reputation for its lobster creations, and there's also a rich hot-chocolate soufflé to cap a fine meal. [$] *Average main: Rs. 3000* ✉ *Castello Vermelho, behind the Art chamber, 1/115 A Gauravaddo, near Kamat's Holiday Homes* ☎ *832/227–5213, 98/8130–1184.*

$$$$ ASIAN 🍴 **Republic of Noodles.** Its chain restaurant name belies how good the food is here. Slightly more expensive than is the norm in Goa, this Pan-Asian eatery sends out excellent seafood *laksa* (spicy noodle soup) and Asian barbecue to a swanky crowd. The interior is all dark bamboo and sandstone with Indonesian accents, and diners can choose to sit at *teppanyaki* counters (with a built-in hotplate where the chef cooks and serves the food straight onto your plate) or at regular tables to tuck into their bowls of pan-fried noodles or Javanese duck curry. Try the excellent fresh watermelon margaritas to go with a steaming bowl of pan-fried Singapore noodles. [$] *Average main: Rs. 2000* ✉ *Lemon Tree Amarante Beach Resort, Vadi, Calangute* ☎ *832/398-8188* 🌐 *www.republicofnoodles.com* ⏲ *No lunch Mar.–Oct.*

$$$ INDIAN 🍴 **Souza Lobo.** Established in 1932, and now managed by the third generation of the Lobo family, this large, airy no-frills restaurant on hectic Calangute Beach catches the exuberant sea breeze. The seafood is excellent, which means the place is always busy. The Goan masala fried prawns are exactly as they should be—with authentic red masala and fresh, perfectly deveined prawns. Other Goan specialties include the squid *amot tik* (a sour curry), kingfish steak *peri-peri* (in spicy, tangy red sauce), and prawn-stuffed pomfret. The restaurant also serves Western-style seafood with a good garlic butter sauce. There's live music every night. (Be warned: the toilet here is shabby.) [$] *Average main: Rs. 500* ✉ *Calangute Beach, Bardez* ☎ *832/227–6463, 832/228–1234* 🌐 *www.souzalobo.com.*

WHERE TO STAY

For expanded hotel reviews, visit Fodors.com.

$$$ HOTEL ★ 🏨 **Casa Britona.** On a bank of a tributary of the River Mandovi, this boutique hotel 10 km (6 miles) from Sinquerim comes with unique views of inland Goa, mangroves, and freshwater wildlife. **Pros:** lovely location; private, tranquil hideaway. **Cons:** a taxi or scooter is needed to reach the beach. [$] *Rooms from: Rs. 7000* ✉ *H. No. 217 Salvador-do-Mundo, near Charmanos, Britona* ☎ *832/241–0962, 832/241–6737* 🌐 *www.casaboutiquehotelsgoa.com* 🛏 *10 suites* 🍽 *Breakfast.*

$$$$ HOTEL 🏨 **Fortune Select Regina.** In a quiet location off the main road near Candolim, this resort from the Fortune Hotels group is competent and professional in its service and facilities. **Pros:** tranquil location in a busy tourist area. **Cons:** pricey for this type of property; a taxi or scooter is needed to reach the beach. [$] *Rooms from: Rs. 10000* ✉ *376 off Fort Aguada Rd., Candolim* ☎ *832/398–8444* 🌐 *www.fortunehotels.in* 🛏 *96 rooms, 6 suites* 🍽 *Breakfast.*

$$$$ HOTEL 🏨 **Nilaya Hermitage.** Nilaya, which roughly translates to "a hidden dwelling," could not be more aptly named. **Pros:** fabulous tiled pool; dreamy theme rooms; day cruises on the wooden sailing dhow; on-site ayurvedic

spa. **Cons:** remote, requires taxis to go anywhere. [$] *Rooms from: Rs. 21998* ✉ *off Main Calangute Rd., Arpora, Calangute* ☎ *832/226–9794* 🌐 *www.nilaya.com* 🛏 *14 rooms* 🍴 *Some meals.*

$$$$ HOTEL 🏨 **Pousada Tauma.** This beautiful boutique hotel built of laterite (a local red pitted stone) has old Portuguese floor tiles and an abundant, leafy garden, giving it an earthiness and warmth that's especially welcome in this overcrowded part of town. **Pros:** secluded setting; full ayurvedic treatments available. **Cons:** pricey compared to similar hotels in this range. [$] *Rooms from: Rs. 16000* ✉ *Porba-Vaddo, Calangute* ☎ *832/227–9063* 🌐 *www.pousada-tauma.com* 🛏 *13 suites* 🍴 *Breakfast.*

BEACHES

Calangute Beach. Crowded and dirty, particularly in the high season, Calangute Beach is a tourist trap and the main destination for every package tourist to visit Goa. The rampant commercialization means that visitors can take their pick of activities, from water sports to shopping, but space and quiet are harder to find. The beach is accessible by concrete steps. ⚠ **Note the sign warning that swimming is dangerous—there's a fairly strong undertow here. Amenities:** food and drink; water sports; lifeguards. **Best for:** partyers; windsurfing. ✉ *Calangute.*

SPORTS AND THE OUTDOORS

Calangute Beach Watersports. Calangute Beach Watersports is another parasailing outfitter in the area. ☎ *98/2215–1002.*

Sea Waves Water Sports. Offers winchboat parasailing. ✉ *Opposite Tito's, Calangute* ☎ *98/2317–4669.*

Hop aboard a dolphin- or crocodile-spotting tour, which winds past thick mangroves along the Zuari and Mandovi rivers, or take a ride on a banana boat.

Odyssey Tours. Odyssey Tours has a luxury yacht with a license to carry 27 passengers on deck, plus four crew members, including a captain and engineer. (Sorry, you can't rent the yacht and captain it yourself.) They offer half-day dolphin-spotting cruises (9:30 am–1 pm for about Rs. 1,000 per person, including lunch; reservations are necessary). The yacht leaves from Britona, where it has its own jetty. In the afternoon it's available for private charter groups for Rs. 10,000 per hour. ☎ *832/227–6941.*

MAPUSA

15 km (9 miles) north of Panaji.

Friday is the big market day in Mapusa (pronounced *map*-sa)—the main town in the Bardez district. People from adjoining villages and some transplanted hippies convene to sell everything from vegetables to blue jeans to handicrafts. It's an ideal place to buy souvenirs. Mapusa is not a place you'd want to stay for the night, and there's really nothing much to see here, but like Margao in the south, the town is good for brief forays to shop and take care of other necessities. Steer clear of it as much as possible if you want to maintain a cheerful mood—except for the lively Friday market, the town is a bit dreary.

7

Inner Peace

If there's anything that sums up the Goan attitude to life, it's *sussegado,* which means "take it easy." Even with the tourist influx exceeding the local population, the massive star resorts and hotels in the south, and the infamous rave and trance parties in the north, there's a certain peace in Goa that is unlikely to ever be disturbed, because it comes from within. A part of this mood of daylong siesta can be attributed to a widespread love of excellent food and local alcohol—Goa brews its own *feni*, a potent and inexpensive concoction distilled from palm sap or cashew-fruit juice. If you're looking to imbibe the true spirit of Goa, try the coconut-palm feni—it smells less pungent than the cashew variety and goes down a little bit easier. You can buy the alcohol from just about anywhere in Goa (but make sure it's bottled properly) and down it with classic tender coconut water. A morning in the waves, tiger prawns at a seaside shack, and a couple of fenis, and you will come to discover why people come back to Goa year after year to rejuvenate, even as they complain that it's getting crowded and dirty. A week in the company of Goans, with their mellow attitude toward life and their legendary warmth—despite the heavy toll taken on their state by tourism—and you may find yourself, for better or for worse, more than a little intoxicated by the Goan way.

FORT AGUADA

4 km (2½ miles) south of Sinquerim Beach.

★ **Fort Aguada.** Perched high on a hill, with wonderful views west across the Arabian Sea and east across Aquada Bay to Panaji, Fort Aguada was built in 1612 and named for the natural springs that supplied not only the fort but also passing ships. Surrounded by wild grass, the fort is in excellent condition. Inside, you can take a good look at the solid stone architecture and the old lighthouse. The fort's defenses actually enclosed a much larger area than the bastion at the top of the hill; a seaward bastion still juts into the Arabian Sea on Sinquerim Beach, near the Taj cluster of hotels. If you only have time for one of Goa's many forts, hit Aguada—it's the best preserved and most magnificent. Hire a taxi if time is a constraint; it's not an easy walk, as it's 4 km (2½ miles) south of Sinquerim Beach and at least half the way is a fairly steep incline. ⊠ *Sinquerim, Candolim* ⊗ *Weekdays 10–5:30.*

SINQUERIM BEACH

10 km (6 miles) northwest of Panaji.

Along with Bogmalo, also in the Bardez district, Sinquerim is one of the few beaches where you can rent windsurfers, water skis, and other water toys without having to be a guest at a hotel. It's much cheaper to rent equipment from these places, but check the condition of the equipment and make sure lifejackets are provided; also check, if possible, with others on the beach to verify adequate supervision. Stretching in front of the Taj resorts, this small, sandy beach can get crowded with tourists and vendors.

Saris and bathing suits at Calangute Beach

GETTING HERE AND AROUND

Sinquerim is the first beach you'll get to as you head northwest after crossing the Mandovi River from Panaji.

WHERE TO EAT AND STAY

For expanded hotel reviews, visit Fodors.com.

$$ SEAFOOD 🍴 **Morisco.** Goan specialties and the view of the historic fortification are the draws at this seafood restaurant. The catch of the day is marinated in Goan spices and served along with local music. [$] *Average main: Rs. 400* ✉ *Fort Aguada Beach Resort, Sinquerim Beach, Bardez* ☎ *832/664–5858* ⏲ *No lunch.*

$$$$ HOTEL 🏨 **Aashyana Lakhanpal.** This handsome, and sprawling, property provides an excellent base from which to explore North Goa. **Pros:** airy bedrooms and lots of open space; wonderful swimming pool; great food and attentive service. **Cons:** the dense foliage attracts mosquitoes so make sure to carry repellent; the attentive service might be overbearing to some. [$] *Rooms from: Rs. 13800* ✉ *Escrivao Vaddo, Candolim* ☎ *832/248–9225* 🌐 *www.aashyanalakhanpal.com* 🛏 *5 rooms, 3 cottages* 🍽 *No meals.*

$ B&B/INN 🏨 **Marbella Guest House.** This heritage guesthouse is on one of North Goa's narrowest lanes, behind the massive Taj resorts. **Pros:** great value; oozing with charm. **Cons:** no phones in room. [$] *Rooms from: Rs. 2900* ✉ *Between Sinquerim and Candolim beaches, Bardez district* ☎ *832/247–9551* 🌐 *www.marbellagoa.com* 🛏 *3 rooms, 3 suites* 🍽 *Breakfast.*

$$$$ RESORT ★ 🏨 **Taj Holiday Village.** The guest rooms at this resort are housed in charming Goan village–style cottages and villas that face lush gardens or the broad expanse of Sinquerim Beach. **Pros:** spectacular setting;

sophisticated yet friendly service. **Cons:** lots of kids can mean lots of noise. $ *Rooms from: Rs. 11900* ✉ *Sinquerim, Bardez* ☎ *832/664–5858* ⊕ *www.tajhotels.com* ➲ *133 rooms, 9 villa suites* ⦿ *Breakfast.*

$$$$

RESORT

Fodor's Choice

★

⊡ **Vivanta by Taj–Fort Aguada.** Constructed within the boundary and adjoining the ramparts of an old Portuguese fort built in 1612, this hotel has gorgeous views of the fort, sea, and beach. **Pros:** stunning location; beautifully furnished rooms. **Cons:** may be too formal for some guests. $ *Rooms from: Rs. 11400* ✉ *Sinquerim Beach, Bardez* ☎ *832/664–5858* ⊕ *www.tajhotels.com* ➲ *121 rooms, 24 suites, 38 cottages, 15 villas* ⦿ *Breakfast.*

BEACHES

Sinquerim Beach. Close to Panaji, Sinquerim is a quiet, well-kept beach and, with some of Goa's most expensive resorts in the area—including the Vivanta by Taj–Fort Aguada and the Taj Holiday Village ➪ *See Where to Stay listings*—it tends to be a destination for well-heeled local tourists and older international travelers. Having said that, pockets of vendors and tourists can gather around some of the more populist beachfront hotels. Visitors can try their hand at water sports such as windsurfing to snorkeling, and while the water isn't crystal clear, it is clean and makes for a lovely afternoon of paddling about; consistent waves make for good bodysurfing. **Amenities:** lifeguards; water sports. **Good for:** snorkeling; sunrise; swimming. ✉ *Bardez.*

SPORTS AND THE OUTDOORS

John's Boat Tours. Dolphin-watching, snorkeling at Grand Island, crocodile-spotting in the river backwaters and sea fishing are all available from John's. There are also jeep tours to nearby spice plantations, Dudhsagar Falls, and Hampi ruins in the neighboring state of Karnataka. ✉ *Candolim Beach* ☎ *98/2218–2814, 98/2215–6543* ⊕ *www.digitalgoa.com/johnsboattours* ⊘ *Closed June–Sept.*

Thunderwave Water Sports. On Sinquerim Beach, Candolim, this operator has been offering winchboat parasailing for nearly 20 years. ✉ *Near Taj Holiday Village* ☎ *832/249–9779, 98/2217–6985, 98/2217–6986.*

PANAJI

Panaji (also called Panjim), once the capital of the former Portuguese colony and now the state's capital, has a scenic setting along the banks of the Mandovi River, about 29 km (18 miles) north of Goa's Dabolin airport. Apart from its own considerable charms—including the colonial architecture in the city's Fontainhas and Sao Tomé neighborhoods—the small city is a good base to explore Goa's Portuguese past, visible in the grand and ornate churches of Old Goa.

PANAJI

★ *600 km (372 miles) south of Mumbai.*

Panaji has somewhat less of the poverty and hustle and bustle of India's other state capitals, and its palm-lined plazas, elegant Portuguese colonial architecture, and other sights are easy to explore. There are historic homes and churches, restaurants serving flavorful Goan cuisine, and many unique galleries and boutiques. The best way to see the older parts of the city is on foot—in fact, if you leave without having explored the backstreets at leisure, you haven't really seen the best it has to offer. For diehard sun-and-sand lovers, there's the city beach at Dona Paula, but Panaji isn't recommended for its beaches, as they tend to be dirty and crowded.

GETTING HERE AND AROUND

Expect to pay about Rs. 500 for the 40-minute taxi ride to reach Panaji from Dabolim airport. After that, it's an easy stroll to reach the city's main attractions, which are all in a central part of town. Banks and ATMs, Internet cafés, tour operators, and airline offices are all generally found along the city's main arteries, in particular 18th June Road and 31st January Road.

ESSENTIALS

Visitor Information Visitor Information ✉ *Patto, Panaji* ☎ *0832/243–8750, 8751 and 8752* ⊕ *www.goatourism.gov.in.*

EXPLORING

Church of Our Lady of Immaculate Conception. This grand shrine was a mere chapel before 1541. Soon after, in 1600, it became a parish, and its structure was rebuilt entirely. Now the church almost entirely presides over one of Panaji's squares. The building's distinctive zigzag staircases are a 19th-century addition, and the church's large bell was originally in the Church of St. Augustine in Old Goa. An annual December festival here draws huge crowds. At the other times of the year the square is a peaceful place to linger. ✉ *Near Municipal Gardens* 🎟 *Free* ☉ *Mon.– Sat. 9–6, Sun. 10–6.*

Dr. Salim Ali Bird Sanctuary. Just a short distance from Panaji, this delightful bird refuge is on the tip of Chorao, an island in the Mandovi. The ferry jetty for Chorao is on Ribander jetty on the southern bank of the Mandovi River, between Panaji and Old Goa, and boats travel regularly to the island and back. A taxi can bring you to the jetty for the 15-minute ride across the river. The Forest Department in Panaji organizes guided tours to Chorao. The tiny sanctuary, full of mangroves, is named after a dedicated Indian ornithologist. Although October through March is the best time to view migratory birds, the sanctuary is open year-round. ✉ *3km (2 miles) northeast, Panaji* ☎ *832/222–4747.*

Fontainhas. The shady, narrow streets of this largely residential neighborhood do not seem Indian—they are clearly still Portuguese at heart. From tiny *balcaos* (colonnaded porches), inhabitants watch as their quiet, unchanging world goes by, and through the old windows you can hear people practicing the piano and violin. At the heart of Fontainhas is the little whitewashed Chapel of St. Sebastian, which dates only to the late 19th century—new by Goan standards. Its claim to fame is an old crucifix that was once housed in the infamous Palace of the Inquisition in Old Goa. ✉ *Between Ourem Creek and Altinho.*

The Old Secretariat. This heritage building, with sloping tiled roofs, wooden verandas, and carved stone coats of arms, occupies a pleasant spot by the Mandovi River and has several important associations.

DID YOU KNOW?

One of the first churches in Goa, the Church of Mary Immaculate Conception was established in 1541. At night the church is illuminated by thousands of small light-bulbs, making it a prominent sight.

The first building on this site was the palace of the Sultan of Bijapur, who ruled Goa at the time of the Portuguese invasion. The building that the Portuguese erected in its place served as temporary quarters for the viceroys of Goa upon their arrival or departure from the territory until it became their permanent residence in the mid-18th century, when Old Goa was abandoned as the capital. In the early 20th century the Secretariat became a government office. It's slated to become a museum in the future, now that the legislature has moved to Porvorim. ✉ *Mandovi riverfront.*

Sao Tomé. This crumbling old neighborhood contains the General Post Office, a former tobacco trading house, and a maze of extremely narrow streets behind it. The tiny bars of this district are full of old-world character, and indeed you might need that drink to help banish the more grisly images of Goa's past—the area opposite the post office was once the site of Panaji's town executions. ✉ *Between M.G. Rd. and Emidio Gracia Rd.*

WHERE TO EAT

$$$$ ECLECTIC

🍴 **AZ.U.R.** The Goa Marriott's café and lounge, pronounced "As You Are," may be worth a visit for the bay views alone—fortunately, the quality of its limited yet choice menu won't disappoint, either. Western classics like croque monsieur or a BLT are great for either lunchtime or a late afternoon snack. There are also bar-food options such as calamari fritters and potato skins, as well as a selection of teas and coffees. After dark, the coffee shop morphs into a relaxed evening lounge bar. [$] *Average main: Rs. 1200* ✉ *Goa Marriott, Miramar, Panaji* ☎ *832/246–3333.*

$$$$ BARBECUE

🍴 **Ernesto's Bistro.** Brothers Ernesto and Vasquito Alvares are at the helm at this newly renovated Goan barbeque and bistro in the old town, in the protected heritage zone of the Latin Quarter. The menu is dominated by meaty fare, and you'll be in the company of locals and tourists alike, who come for the excellent barbequed ribs and burgers, as well as for Asian-inflected seafood. Wonderful desserts include their specialty, *serradura*—the name means "sawdust," but don't be deterred; the novel creation blends crushed cookies and sweetened cream. In clement weather you can eat outdoors in the courtyard. [$] *Average main: Rs. 1000* ✉ *6/49 Nanu Tarkar Pednekar Rd., below Maruti Temple, Fontainhas, Panaji* ☎ *98/2301–5921.*

$$$ INDIAN Fodor's Choice ★

🍴 **Mum's Kitchen.** Smack-dab in the middle of Panjim, Mum's Kitchen, a Goan institution, is indisputably the best place in town for home-style Goan food. The menu's vast and enticing, so either visit as part of a large group, or when absolutely ravenous. Most of the regulars are locals, so the kitchen doesn't hold back on the spice. Try the *rawa* (semolina)-fried Bombay duck and the spicy prawn *recheado* (a Portuguese-inspired masala). The milder sausage curry, served with fresh *poi* (the Goan bread that's similar to a ciabatta), is a real treat. Go prepared to wait for a table, although service is brisk so the wait shouldn't be too long. [$] *Average main: Rs. 600* ✉ *854 Martins Bldg., D.B. St., Panaji–Miramar Rd.* ☎ *098/2217–5559, 91/90110–95557* 🌐 *www.mumskitchengoa.com.*

$$$ ECLECTIC

🍴 **Panjim Inn.** The veranda, up a flight of stairs at the historic Panjim Inn, is an atmospheric location for those seeking tasty Goan and continental fare, casual dining, and fair prices. The menu includes local favorites such as spicy Goan prawn curry served with rice, but also be sure to check the daily specials, particularly for seasonal seafood items. It's open from 7 am to 10 pm. $ *Average main: Rs. 500* ✉ *E-212 31st January Rd., Fontainhas* ☎ *832/222–1122, 832/222–6523, 832/243–5628.*

$$ ✕ **Rio Rico.** The formal staff of this somewhat somber restaurant at
INDIAN the Hotel Mandovi serve tasty Goan specialties that include *rawa* (semolina)-fried fish and prawns and Portuguese-influenced seafood *caldeirada* (poached fish layered with potatoes and tomatoes and cooked with white wine). $ *Average main: Rs. 300* ✉ *The Mandovi Hotel, D.B. Marg* ☎ *832/222–4405 to 09* ⊕ *www.hotelmandovigoa.com.*

$$$ ✕ **Ritz Classic.** You're likely to be the only foreigner in this family
INDIAN favorite—that is if you can find it. The restaurant may be drab and hidden away on the second floor of an anonymous block on the commercial 18th June Road, but it's certainly worth looking for. Goan specialties, including grilled kingfish, pomfret *recheiado* (marinated in a blend of spices, then grilled), and chicken *xacuti* (coconut and tamarind curry), are prepared wonderfully and without any concession to international tolerance levels for spice. With lines going out the door, especially at lunch, service is quick and sometimes rushed amid the din. $ *Average main: Rs. 500* ✉ *Wagle Vision Building, 18th June Rd., 2nd fl.* ☎ *832/242–6417, 832/664–4796, 832/222–1138.*

$$$ ✕ **Sher-e-Punjab.** Locals and foreigners hungry for North Indian food
NORTH INDIAN seek this diner out for lunch, dinner, or a quick snack while taking a break from the intense shopping of 18th June Road. With an enticing selection of kebabs, tandoori items, and favorites like butter chicken, this is the place for a satisfying meal in a no-frills setting. House specialties include the Peshawari chicken and the mutton dry fry. $ *Average main: Rs. 500* ✉ *18th June Rd., in front of Bombay Bazaar* ☎ *832/222–7204* ⊕ *www.hotelaromagoa.com.*

$$ ✕ **Viva Panjim.** A walk down a narrow alley in the Fontainhas district
INDIAN brings you to one of the city's best-value restaurants. Featuring the award-winning cuisine of chef Linda De Souza, this cheery hideaway is crowded with locals and tourists. The maître d' is happy to make recommendations to anyone unfamiliar with Goan specialties such as kingfish vindaloo, and chicken *cafreal* (marinated and cooked with fresh cilantro, also known as coriander; green chillies, and ginger). Indoor seating can get cramped (there are just a handful of tables there), but tables are also available outside. Reliable Goan classics, conviviality, and bargain prices are the rule, and the prawn curry is possibly the best in the state. $ *Average main: Rs. 300* ✉ *H. No. 178 31st January Rd., behind Mary Immaculate High School, Fontainhas* ☎ *832/242–2405, 98/5047–1363* ☉ *No lunch.* ·

WHERE TO STAY
For expanded hotel reviews, visit Fodors.com.

$$$ ▦ **Goa Marriott Resort.** Walk into the lovely sea-facing lobby, where you
RESORT can watch and listen to the crash of waves along the rocky shores, and
★ you will find it hard to walk away. **Pros:** courteous staff; beautiful location. **Cons:** city beach isn't the best; a bit pricey. $ *Rooms from: Rs. 9350* ✉ *Miramar Beach Rd.* ☎ *832/246–3333* ⊕ *www.marriott.com* ⇗ *175 rooms, 5 suites* ❖| *Breakfast.*

Along the streets of Panaji, Goa's capital

$$ **HOTEL** [☷] **Hotel Fidalgo.** At the corner of a crowded intersection on the bustling 18th June Road, this business hotel has modern rooms that lack personality, but are clean. **Pros:** good value for money. **Cons:** noisy commercial part of town; drab hallway carpets; pool faces a shabby building. [$] *Rooms from: Rs. 4500* ⊠ *18th June Rd.* ☎ *832/222–6291 to 99* ⊕ *www.hotelfidalgo-goa.com* ↷ *101 rooms, 7 suites* [○] *Breakfast.*

$ **B&B/INN** [☷] **Panjim Inn.** Travelers who appreciate a sense of place love the warmth of the Panjim Inn, a unique hotel in the center of historic Fontainhas that was built in the late 1800s and incorporates the former family home of the owner, Ajit Sukhija. **Pros:** great location in the center of the historic district; friendly staff; relaxed atmosphere. **Cons:** traffic noise; no phones in rooms. [$] *Rooms from: Rs. 3693* ⊠ *E-212, 31st January Rd., Fontainhas* ☎ *832/222–6523, 98/2357–2035, 832/222–1122, 832/243–5628* ⊕ *www.panjiminn.com* ↷ *24 rooms* [○] *Breakfast.*

$$$ **HOTEL** **★** [☷] **Panjim People's.** Four-poster beds, carved rosewood dressers, and plenty of windows grace each of the four spacious rooms in this historic annex of the Panjim Inn (it's also home to the Gitanjali art gallery, on the ground floor). **Pros:** spacious rooms; old-world charm. **Cons:** some windows overlook a dumpster below; no elevator; no room phones. [$] *Rooms from: Rs. 9000* ⊠ *E-212, 31 January Rd., Fontainhas* ☎ *832/222–6523, 832/243–5628, 832/222–1122, 98/2357–2035* ⊕ *www.panjiminn.com* ↷ *4 rooms* [○] *Breakfast.*

$ **B&B/INN** [☷] **Pousada Panjim.** On a quiet street across from the Panjim Inn is a stylish property furnished with elegant antique cupboards and teak and rosewood four-poster beds. **Pros:** quiet refuge in a noisy city; memorable, one-of-a-kind setting; exceptional value. **Cons:** no restaurant on premises (there is one across the street though). [$] *Rooms from:*

Rs. 2700 ✉ *E-212, 31 January Rd., Fontainhas* ☎ *832/222–6523, 832/243–5628, 832/222–1122, 98/2357–2035* 🌐 *www.panjiminn.com* 🛏 *9 rooms* 🍴 *Breakfast.*

$$$$ HOTEL 🏨 **Vivanta by Taj–Panaji.** This three-year-old Taj property is more business-oriented than other members of the group, with the added oomph of high-tech features such as surround-sound home theater systems, multimedia panels, and LCD screens in all rooms. **Pros:** top-notch facilities. **Cons:** better suited to business travelers; no nearby beach access. [$] *Rooms from: Rs. 11700* ✉ *D.B. Bandodkar Rd., St. Inez Junction* ☎ *832/663–3687* 🌐 *www.tajhotels.com* 🛏 *158 rooms, 12 suites* 🍴 *Breakfast.*

IT'S A STAKEOUT

Goan taxi drivers stake out tourists by waiting outside hotels and restaurants. As soon as you walk out the door, three or four of them are at your side asking you if you want a cab, and where you are going. They find it hard to believe you'd want to walk when you can afford to pay for a ride.

BOAT CRUISES

Casino Caravela. Gambling, food, and drink can be enjoyed every night from 5 pm until 6 am onboard the Casino Caravela, a floating luxury casino that also has a TV/game room for those under 18, a toddlers' room with babysitters, and an open-air swimming pool. The dress code is smart-casual, which in India means no shorts, bikinis, or swimming trunks are allowed outside the pool area. ☎ *832/223–4044 to 47.*

Department of Tourism. In addition to several private operators, the Department of Tourism organizes river cruises, some with a Goan cultural show, music, and dinner. Most cruises depart from the Panaji jetty on the River Mandovi. ☎ *832/243–8750* 🌐 *www.goatourism.gov.in.*

SHOPPING

Stores are open 10 am to 7 pm, and 18th June Road (named after an anti-colonial protest launched by a socialist leader in 1946) is the city's busiest shopping thoroughfare. It's worth a stroll if you are in the market for dried fruits, curry pastes and powders, or for some examples of Goa's foot-thumping and lively Konkan folk music.

Barefoot. Trendy handcrafted and natural housewares, home furnishings, silk, cotton men's and women's clothing, and jewelry from different parts of the country are sold here. Their ceramic tea sets alone are worth a look. ✉ *H. No. 1/26, 31st January Rd.* ☎ *832/243–6815* 🕒 *Closed Sun.*

Bombay Bazaar. Bombay Bazaar, a department store with a twist, is a gathering of dozens of vendors, each competing for business in the confines of a jam-packed two-story building. Wares include Indian- and Western-style clothing, saris and handicrafts, plus basic needs such as suitcases, shoes, and watches. Everything is well priced. ✉ *18th June Rd.* ☎ *832/222–1985.*

Sinari's. This is the place to buy Indian music of all sorts, including Goan trance, devotional Hindi, Indian pop, and rap. It's in the shopping arcade next to Bombay Bazaar. ✉ *Padmavati Towers, 18th June Rd.* ☎ *832/222–4842.*

CLOSE UP

Take Home the Taste of Goa

If you haven't found your share of slippers and sarongs and bags and bangles at Anjuna or the shack-shops near the main beaches, pay a visit to a local grocery. Look carefully, and you'll find some great stuff to take home as a reminder of your stay in Goa or to give away as unusual "back from India" gifts. There's high-quality *bebinca* (a rich, layered, dense 16-layer cake made of butter, sugar, egg yolk, and coconut) that has a long shelf life, making for easy packing; *feni* (Goan liquor) in fancy bottles (though it smells the same as the stuff in the downmarket bottles),

which you'd be well advised to transport only in your carry-on baggage; *prawn balchao* (in a red chilli sauce) and *mackerel reicheado* (pickled prawns and mackerel soaked in red masala, which have to be fried once you get home); a variety of dried and wet *masalas* (spice mixes) from *cafreal* (green masala) and *vindaloo* (hot red masala) to *xacuti* (a masala with coconut and ground spices), and packets of *tendlim* (a pickled gourd). Chances are the storeowner will wrap it for you with a grin to acknowledge that you know a bit about Goa after all.

Sosa's. Come here for high-end Indian designers, including Goan favorite Savio Jon. Expect bright colors, easy silhouettes, cotton and silk and all manner of resort wear. ⊠ *E-245 Rua de Ourem* ☎ *832/222–8063, 98/2338–1488* ۞ *Closed Sun.*

UK Dry Fruits. This store has an excellent selection of cashew nuts—Goa is famous for its cashew crop. There are exotic varieties such as Pudina Lime, Hot Masala, and Szechuan—sample a couple before buying. You will also find a great selection of Goan curry pastes, powders, and spice mixtures. ⊠ *18th June Rd.* ☎ *832/243–5455.*

Velha Goa Galleria. This is the store for *azulejos*, a traditional Portuguese style of hand-painted tiles and ceramics. In addition to a selection of tiles, frames, and other ceramics, they have the rights to sell the reproduced ceramic artwork of Goa's own celebrated cartoonist Mario Miranda. Fantastic for souvenirs and gifts. ⊠ *4/191 Rua de Ourem* ☎ *832/242–6628* ⊕ *www.velhagoa.com* ۞ *Closed Sun.*

OLD GOA

Fodor'sChoice ★ *10 km (6 miles) east of Panaji.*

Gorgeous Old Goa, with foliage creeping in around the ruins of old churches, served as the capital of the Portuguese colony until repeated outbreaks of cholera forced the government to move to Panaji in 1843. The shift out of Old Goa, however, had begun as early as 1695. It was a slow desertion—first the viceroy, then the nobility, then the customs. By the time the official declaration came, it was already a deserted, ruined city. There are several imposing and beautiful churches, convents, and monasteries that reveal its former glory. Most were begun at a time when European architectural styles were shifting toward the baroque. For anyone with an interest in religious architecture or Catholic history, Old Goa is a must-see destination.

GETTING HERE AND AROUND

Hop into a taxi or auto-rickshaw in Panaji to reach Old Goa. The 20-minute ride will cost Rs. 250 by taxi or Rs. 150 by auto-rickshaw. It's a small area, and you can walk easily from one sight to another. It's worth hiring an English-speaking guide for a one-hour walking tour—they tend to find you around the entrance of the Basilica of Bom Jesus.

TIMING

You'll probably want to spend at least a couple hours exploring Old Goa.

EXPLORING

Archaeological Museum. A part of the Franciscan monastery behind the Church of St. Francis of Assisi, the Archaeological Museum has an intricately gilded and carved interior. The museum's collection is not entirely devoted to Catholic objets d'art; it also has bits and pieces from Goa's early Hindu history. It's worth a quick look around, if only to peruse the portrait gallery of Goa's viceroys. ⊠ *Across the road from Basilica of Bom Jesus* ☎ *832/228–6133* ⬛ *Rs. 5* ☉ *Sat.–Thurs. 10–5.*

Basilica of Bom Jesus. Dedicated to the worship of the infant Jesus, the Basilica of Bom Jesus is also known throughout the Christian world as the tomb of St. Francis Xavier, patron saint of Goa, who was handed the task of spreading Christianity in the Portuguese colony. The saint's body has "survived" almost 500 years now without ever having been embalmed, and lies in a silver casket well out of reach of visitors. Built from local red stone around the turn of the 17th century, the tomb took the Florentine sculptor Giovanni Batista Foggini 10 years to complete. Once every 10 years the missionary's body is exposed to the public at close quarters, drawing thousands of pilgrims. The next such event is scheduled for November 2014. ⬛ *Free* ☉ *Mon.–Sat. 9–6:30, Sun. 10–6:30.*

Museum of Christian Art. Inside the Convent of St. Monica, the Museum of Christian Art has a number of objects of Christian interest, including paintings and religious silverware, some dating back to the 16th century. The convent was the first nunnery of its kind in the East, and functioned as one until the late 19th century. ⊠ *Holy Mount Hill* ⬛ *Rs. 5* ☉ *Tues.–Sun. 10–5:30.*

★ **Sé (St. Catherine's) Cathedral.** The imposing white Sé (St. Catherine's) Cathedral—the largest church in Old Goa—was built between 1562 and 1652 by order of the King of Portugal. Fine carvings depict scenes from the life of Christ and the Blessed Virgin over the main altar, which commemorates St. Catherine of Alexandria. Several splendidly decorated chapels are dedicated to St. Joseph, St. George, St. Anthony, St. Bernard, and the Holy Cross. Only one of the cathedral's two original majestic towers remains; the other collapsed in 1776. ⊠ *Across the road from Basilica of Bom Jesus* ⬛ *Free* ☉ *Mon.–Sat. 9–6:30, Sun. 10–6:30.*

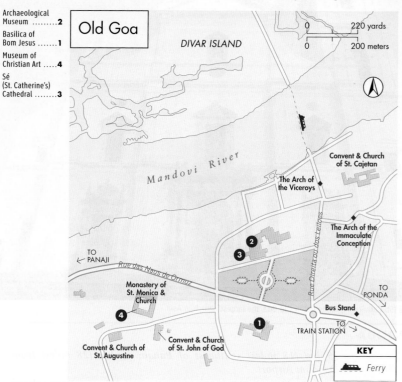

Archaeological
Museum **2**

Basilica of
Bom Jesus **1**

Museum of
Christian Art **4**

Sé
(St. Catherine's)
Cathedral **3**

Old Goa

DIVAR ISLAND

0 — 220 yards
0 — 200 meters

Convent & Church
of St. Cajetan

Mandovi River

The Arch of
the Viceroys

The Arch of the
Immaculate
Conception

TO
← PANAJI

Rue das Naos de Ormuz

Rue Direita ou das Feiras

Monastery of
St. Monica &
Church

TO
PONDA ↘

Bus Stand ◆

TO
TRAIN STATION ↗

4

Convent & Church of
St. Augustine

Convent & Church
of St. John of God

KEY

🚂 *Ferry*

7

DUDHSAGAR FALLS

★ *50 km (31 miles) southeast of Panaji.*

Dudhsagar Waterfalls. With a name that means "sea of milk," these
waterfalls are imposing, with water cascading almost 2,000 feet into
a rock-ribbed valley. They are at their most impressive when the monsoons arrive, but this also makes the approach road inaccessible, so
the ideal time for a trek here is between October and the end of April.
Pack refreshments and beach towels, and plan to spend a morning here;
monkeys, birds, bees, butterflies, and thick foliage complete the wild
experience. The Goa Tourism Development Corporation runs tours
from Panaji and Calangute (9 am–6 pm; around Rs. 700) in a non-
air-conditioned bus, which include the falls and the nearby Tambdi
Surla Hindu temple, built in the 13th century. You could also take a
train to Dudhsagar from Margao and get there in an hour and a half.
✉ *Sanguem District.*

Sé (St. Catherine's) Cathedral in Old Goa, the largest church in Asia

PONDA

29 km (18 miles) southeast of Panaji; 45 km (28 miles) from Dabolim Airport.

Ponda itself is an uninteresting town, but a number of the temples in the hills that surround it shouldn't be missed. The area came under Portuguese control relatively late, in 1764, about 250 years after the Portuguese conquered Goa—which explains why the temples were not destroyed.

Manguesh temple. One of the chief attractions of Ponda is this temple in Priol, 7 km (4 miles) before you reach Ponda. With its domes and other eccentric, un-Hindu architectural features, the temple has evidence of Islamic and Christian influences. Other temples in the vicinity include the always-crowded Shantadurga temple, with its distinctive tower, the Mahalsa temple, with its gargantuan (41-foot-high) oil lamp, and the Lakshmi Narasimha and Naguesh temples, with their lovely temple tanks (large pools with steps leading into them, so that the faithful can bathe).

SOUTH GOA

Margao, about 7 km (4 miles) inland from the coast, is the main town in South Goa. There's a bustling market, and it's worth exploring for its shopping areas, but only if you happen to be passing through; there's no reason to stay here. If you want to check out the sights, make Colva or Benaulim your base, and get the benefit of the beach and the nightlife after your day out. Excursions include the villages of Loutolim and Chandor, which have beautiful ancestral homes, some of which date from the early 1600s. The beaches of the south are more relaxing than those of the north; people here are less prone to partying, although there is more shack life in the south now than there used to be. Some of the state's most luxurious and expensive resorts are in this area.

BOGMALO BEACH

24 km (15 miles) north of Margao; 25 km (16 miles) south of Panaji.

This tiny crescent of fine sand is perfect for swimming and sunning. It's near a low, verdant hill topped by a few modern buildings on one side and the Bogmallo Beach Resort on the other. Two tiny islands sit about 10 km (6 miles) out to sea. For the most privacy, walk down the beach to the far right—there are fewer fishing boats, shacks, and people. Another of Bogmalo's assets is its boating and water-sports facilities for diving and jet-skiing. For a lunch break, try the **Seagull,** a simple, thatched-roof shack on the beach—they serve some of the best prawn-curry rice in Goa. The airport is just a 4-km (2½-mile) ride away.

WHERE TO STAY

For expanded hotel reviews, visit Fodors.com.

$$$ **Bogmallo Beach Resort.** This six-story high-rise hotel seems to have **RESORT** ignored all the rules about being close to the beach. **Pros:** close to the airport. **Cons:** not much character. $ *Rooms from: Rs. 8000* ☎ *832/253–8222 to 235* ⊕ *www.bogmallobeachresort.com* ⇌ *126 rooms, 15 cottages* ⦿ *Breakfast.*

$$ **Coconut Creek.** On a dense coconut plantation, just a two-minute walk **RESORT** (about 500 yds) from Bogmalo Beach and a 3-km (2-mile) drive from Dabolim Airport, this charming little resort with spotless, airy rooms, and a small swimming pool is run by a friendly staff. **Pros:** private jungle setting; one of the nicest mid-range resorts in South Goa. **Cons:** only half the rooms have a/c, the rest have fans and are likely to be uncomfortable in summer. $ *Rooms from: Rs. 5000* ☎ *832/253–8100* ⊕ *www.coconutcreekgoa.com* ⇌ *20 rooms* ⦿ *Breakfast.*

CANSAULIM BEACH

10 km (6 miles) northwest of Margao.

This quiet, clean stretch of beach between Bogmallo and Colva has a fine location—it's conveniently close to both Dabolim Airport and Margao, and yet a good distance from the crowded north and the congested beaches around Colva. The only significant signs of life in these parts are the hotels and resorts in the vicinity, and a couple of sleepy villages.

WHERE TO EAT AND STAY

For expanded hotel reviews, visit Fodors.com.

$$$$ **The Village Plaza.** The Hyatt's food "village" adjacent to the expan- **ECLECTIC** sive lobby has a number of interconnected restaurants: Da Luigi serves wood-fired pizzas and pasta; Casa Sarita has Goan specialties; Masala offers North and South Indian cuisine; and Café is a coffee shop that's open 24 hours. $ *Average main: Rs. 3000* ⊠ *Park Hyatt Goa Resort and Spa, Arossim Beach, Cansaulim* ☎ *832/272–1234.*

$$$$ RESORT   Fodor'sChoice   ★

⌂ **Park Hyatt Goa Resort and Spa.** In the very top bracket of the Goa resorts, the modern and sleek Hyatt has spacious rooms with unusual pebble-floor and glass-wall bathrooms. **Pros:** ultra luxurious; impeccable service; top notch spa and restaurants. **Cons:** very spread out; very expensive. $ *Rooms from: Rs. 12000* ⊠ *Arossim Beach, Cansaulim* ☎ *832/272–1234* ⊕ *www.goa.park.hyatt.com* ⇆ *237 rooms, 12 suites* ⏚ *Breakfast.*

MAJORDA AND UTORDA

★   *10 km (6 miles) from Margao.*

Majorda and nearby Utorda, which both have a number of resorts, are rapidly sacrificing peace and quiet to larger volumes of tourists. Just north of Colva Beach, they are within cycling distance from Colva (5 km [3 miles]) and Betalbatim (3 km [2 miles]), both known for restaurants and shack life. If you stay here, you'll have yourself a good base from which to explore the sights around Margao.

WHERE TO EAT AND STAY
For expanded hotel reviews, visit Fodors.com.

$$$ INDIAN

✕ **Martin's Corner.** This famous family-run restaurant in a village near Majorda grew out of a small shop that was set up with four tables about 20 years ago. With its lamps and cane bar, it still feels like a shack. Its prices, however, are well above the average shack's, and with good reason—Goan seafood dishes like the masala fried king crab are prepared with great care by the acclaimed Mrs. Carafina, who runs the place with her three sons. Pleasant retro music and the aromas of Goan cooking fill the air at lunch and dinnertime. Try the tiger prawns in garlic sauce. $ *Average main: Rs. 500* ⊠ *Bin Waddo, Betalbatim, Salcette* ☎ *832/288–0061* ⊕ *www.martinscornergoa.com.*

$$$ RESORT

⌂ **Alila Diwa Goa.** Overlooking verdant rice plantations and the Arabian Sea, the Alila Goa is a cool open oasis of dark pitched roofs, breezy verandas, and serene courtyards. **Pros:** free Wi-Fi. **Cons:** no direct beach access (it's about five minutes by car or the hotel shuttle). $ *Rooms from: Rs. 9945* ⊠ *48/10 Adao Vado Majorda, Salcette* ☎ *832/274–6800* ⊕ *www.aliladiwagoa.com* ⇆ *153 rooms, 18 suites* ⏚ *Breakfast.*

$$$$ RESORT

⌂ **The Kenilworth Beach Resort.** Lacking the frantic-to-please service typical of some other hotels in Goa—the staff here is experienced and calm—this large resort has a marble lobby with lots of quiet corners for relaxing. **Pros:** all rooms have private balconies. **Cons:** sprawling and crowded at times. $ *Rooms from: Rs. 11000* ⊠ *Utorda, Salcete* ☎ *832/669–8888* ⊕ *www.kenilworthhotels.com* ⇆ *101 rooms, 3 suites* ⏚ *Breakfast.*

$$$ RESORT

⌂ **Majorda Beach Resort.** An old favorite with tourists from Mumbai and Gujarat, this resort has an ayurvedic ashram and spacious rooms. **Pros:** good beach access. **Cons:** dark lobby. $ *Rooms from: Rs. 8000* ⊠ *Sal-*

cete ☎ *832/288–1111 to 13* ⊕ *www.majordabeachresort.com* ⇆ *110 rooms, 10 cottages* ❐ *Breakfast.*

$$$ ❐ **Vivenda Dos Palhacos.** This
B&B/INN 100-year-old restored Portuguese
Fodor's Choice home—with a lovely front porch—
★ has lots of pizzazz thanks to own-
ers Simon and Charlotte Hayward.
Pros: personalized, friendly ser-
vice; rooms with character; free
Wi-Fi. **Cons:** no TV or phones in
rooms. $ *Rooms from: Rs. 6000*
✉ *Costa Vaddo, Majorda, Sal-
cette* ☎ *832/322–1119* ⊕ *www.vivendagoa.com* ⇆ *6 rooms, 1 tent
(seasonal)* ❐ *Breakfast.*

DRESS CODE REVISION

Almost anything goes at Western-style resorts, and in beach towns even Indian women visiting from Mumbai and Delhi might wear shorts and spaghetti strap tops. As a rule, Indians don't wear bathing suits—too immodest—they just wade right in, the men wearing baggy pants and Western-logo T-shirts, the women wearing saris or *salwar-kameez*—long pants with a flowing tunic that hits below the knees.

COLVA

7 km (4 miles) west of Margao.

Colva Beach is the most congested beach in South Goa. Its large park-ing and entrance areas are crowded with shacks selling snacks and souvenirs and young men offering mopeds for rent. The first 1,000 feet of the beach are hectic—stuffed with vendors, cows, and fishing boats—but the sand, backed by palm groves, stretches in both direc-tions, and promises plenty of quieter spots. The water is good for swimming and the restaurants and bar shacks are the nightlife hub of the entire region.

WHERE TO STAY

For expanded hotel reviews, visit Fodors.com.

$ ❐ **Longuinhos Beach Resort.** This old Colva favorite is right on the beach,
HOTEL about a kilometer from the crowded village. **Pros:** great beach access; one of the best mid-range resorts in Colva. **Cons:** a bit run-down. $ *Rooms from: Rs. 3675* ✉ *Salcete* ☎ *832/278–8068 to 69* ⊕ *www.longuinhos.net* ⇆ *51 rooms, 2 suites* ❐ *Breakfast.*

SPORTS AND THE OUTDOORS

Chris Water Sports. Chris Water Sports lets you parasail from the shore of Colva Beach. ☎ *98/2214–2110.*

LOUTOLIM

Fodor's Choice *10 km (6 miles) northeast of Margao.*
★
Loutolim is among Goa's prettiest villages, with lush paddy fields and tranquil village roads that lie under a canopy of forest trees. This is also a lovely area to view some fine examples of Goan-Portuguese architecture. There's not much by way of accommodations except for the charming Casa Susegad. If you are able to get a room, make Loutolim a stopover to experience nontouristy Goa and visit nearby spice plantations, the Brangaza house in Chandor, or the Miranda House—a well-preserved

Goan country house. Lunch at one of Goa's most delightful restaurants, Fernando's Nostalgia, in the courtyard of the chef's house on the Ponda-Margao road, is a must if you venture this side.

WHERE TO EAT AND STAY

For expanded hotel reviews, visit Fodors.com.

$$$ INDIAN Fodor's Choice ★ 🍴 **Fernando's Nostalgia.** In the tranquil, slow-paced old village of Raia you'll find one of the best restaurants in the state. If you sit at certain tables you can catch glimpses of household life in the late chef Fernando's country house. Now run by his wife, the restaurant serves classic Goan and Portugese-Goan dishes, such as salted ox tongue, *fofos* (fish cutlets mixed with mashed potatoes and spices, rolled in breadcrumbs and egg, and shallow-fried), *sopa de bretalha* (spinach soup), and prawn *almondegas* (prawn cutlets), which are rarely found in restaurants; that probably explains why Nostalgia is where many Goans go. The restaurant comes to life in the evening, when the alcohol begins to flow and the band starts to play (Thursday through Sunday). [$] *Average main: Rs. 600* ✉ *608 Uzro, Raia, Salcete* ☎ *832/277–7098, 832/277–7054, 98/2210–3467* 🌐 *fernandosnostalgia.wordpress.com.*

$$$ B&B/INN ★ 🏨 **Casa Susegad.** Loutolim's laid-back charm is captured in Norman and Carol Steele's warm and inviting country inn. **Pros:** very relaxing; lovely food; personalized service; yoga lessons available in season. **Cons:** 30-minute ride to the beach; there might be too many pets here for some. [$] *Rooms from: Rs. 6000* ✉ *Orgao Loutolim, Salcete* ☎ *832/648–3368, 098/2210–6341* 🌐 *www.casasusegad.com* 🛏 *5 rooms* 🍽 *All meals.*

CHANDOR

15 km (9 miles) east of Margao.

This small, sleepy village occupies the site of Chandrapur, ancient capital of the region from AD 375 to 1053.

★ **Braganza House.** The chief reason to visit Chandor is this 400-year-old house—a slice of living history. Two wings are occupied by two branches of the Braganza family, the Menezes Braganzas and the Braganza Pereiras. You can see the style in which the wealthy landed gentry must have lived until the land reformation that followed Independence in 1947; the great rooms are filled with treasures, including beautiful period furniture and Chinese porcelain. Although some parts of the house have been renovated and are in reasonably good shape, it takes a lot of effort to maintain the two wings, and contributions toward upkeep are expected. ☎ *832/278–4201, 832/278–4227* 🎟 *Donations welcome* 🕒 *Usually 9–5, but call ahead for an appointment.*

BENAULIM

9 km (6 miles) southwest of Margao.

Just 2 km (1 mile) south of Colva is the first of the beautiful, secluded beaches of South Goa—a far cry from the action-packed beaches of the north. Head to Benaulim and farther south only if you want to get away from it all. All this isolation comes at a price: the resorts are more expensive here.

Low tide at Palolem Beach

GETTING HERE AND AROUND

Benaulim village has a small supermarket and is centered around a crossroads called Maria Hall. The beach is less than a kilometer from the village. There are some vendors, food shacks, and locals, but none of the crowds you'd find up north.

WHERE TO EAT AND STAY

For expanded hotel reviews, visit Fodors.com.

$$$$
INDIAN
Fodor's Choice
★

✕ **Allegria.** This Goan restaurant in the Taj is reminiscent of an old-fashioned landlord's drawing room, with sepia photographs on the walls and carved wooden furniture. The variety of menu items makes an excellent introduction to local cuisine. Try the *kullanche mass kottnim* (crabmeat with onions, coriander, and garlic), and *sannas* (sweet, delicately flavored, steamed rice cakes) with an assortment of curries, such as classic pork vindaloo, pork *sorpotel* (curry simmered with Goan vinegar), and boneless chicken xacuti. If you want to be adventurous with dessert, try the *adsorachem merend*, a feni-infused coconut mousse with saffron sauce. Live singing accompanied by guitar and mandolin adds to the scene. $ *Average main: Rs. 3000* ✉ *Taj Exotica* ☎ *832/668–3333* ⌨ *Reservations essential.*

$$$
SEAFOOD

✕ **Joecons.** The highlight of this open-air restaurant, a short walk from the Taj Exotica and less than a kilometer from the village, is the well-prepared fresh seafood specialties, including exceptional grilled garlic prawns. The best part may be that you can custom order their fresh seafood with the spice and style of your choice. $ *Average main: Rs. 500* ✉ *Near Taj Exotica* ☎ *832/277–0099.*

$$$$ ⊞ **Taj Exotica.** Beside tranquil Benaulim Beach you'll find one of the most
RESORT attractive places to stay in south Goa. **Pros:** great restaurants; gorgeous
setting. **Cons:** very spread out; very expensive. $ *Rooms from: Rs.
14000* ⊠ *Calwaddo, Salcette* ☎ *832/668–3333* ⊕ *www.tajhotels.com*
↩ *140 rooms, 4 suites* ⏐⊙⏐ *Breakfast.*

VARCA

14 km (8.7 miles) southwest of Margao.

The scenery at Varca is rural: there are deep fields on either side of the
road, and you may get the distinct feeling that you're heading nowhere
in particular. This is an illusion. There are a number of resorts close
to Varca village that take advantage of its perfect, unspoiled stretch of
beach. Stay at Varca for the beach and for the opportunity to take long
walks through the green Goa countryside.

WHERE TO EAT AND STAY
For expanded hotel reviews, visit Fodors.com.

$$ ✕ **Carnaval.** Low-hung black lamps light a woven bamboo ceiling, and
ECLECTIC Mario Miranda cartoons enliven the walls at this restaurant with excel-
★ lent fusion food. Try the jerk potatoes *peri peri* (with hot chilli peppers),
the tandoor-grilled tiger prawns with lemon mustard sauce, and the
naan with pesto. After all this the dessert, such as crepes filled with *gajar
ka halwa* (a sweet made from carrots), seems almost ordinary. $ *Aver-
age main: Rs. 400* ⊠ *Ramada Caravela, Varca Beach* ☎ *832/669–5000*
⊙ *No lunch.*

$$$ ⊞ **Ramada Caravela.** A casino, a fusion Indian-Mediterranean restau-
RESORT rant, and a Polynesian eatery on the beach add to the mix of this
cheery beachfront resort, which is spread-out over 23 acres. **Pros:**
refurbished rooms are a plus. **Cons:** public spaces could use a spruc-
ing up. $ *Rooms from: Rs. 9000* ⊠ *Varca Beach, Salcete* ☎ *832/669–
5000* ⊕ *www.caravelabeachresort.com* ↩ *190 rooms, 4 suites, 5 villas*
⏐⊙⏐ *Breakfast.*

$$$ ⊞ **The Zuri White Sands.** This family-friendly hotel has a massive free-
RESORT form pool, more than 600 feet long, with a swim-up bar. **Pros:** the
★ pool is a fun centerpiece for the resort; free Wi-Fi. **Cons:** no elevators.
$ *Rooms from: Rs. 8000* ⊠ *Pedda, Varca, Salcete* ☎ *832/272–7282
to 84* ⊕ *www.thezurihotels.com* ↩ *154 rooms, 4 suites* ⏐⊙⏐ *Breakfast.*

CAVELOSSIM

20 km (12 miles) southwest of Margao.

The last of the villages before the mouth of the Sal River, Cavelossim is
also the end of the coastal road southward from Bogmalo. If you want
to continue down the coast, you have to head back inland and take
the national highway south, or take a country road up the river and
use a ferry. Given that this is a rural area, Cavelossim is a surprisingly
developed little place, with a shopping arcade; this is chiefly because of
the presence of the Leela, arguably the most luxurious of the southern
Goa resorts. The beach is clean and striking because it's at the mouth
of the Sal River—serene and flanked by fields and coconut plantations.

This part of South Goa is an end in itself, and it's not a good base from which to explore the rest of the state (if you're keen on beach hopping and other touristy activities, stay up north). It's the place to come when you want to relax, take up residence on the beach, and forget about everything, including trips to town.

GETTING HERE AND AROUND

From Dabolim Airport, it will take you about 45 minutes to reach Cavelossim.

WHERE TO STAY

For expanded hotel reviews, visit Fodors.com.

$$$
RESORT
 Holiday Inn. The chief advantage of this international chain is its uniform service and friendly vibe, and the private access to Mobor Beach is a blessing after the crowded beaches of North Goa. **Pros:** well priced for its lovely beach location. **Cons:** could use an update. $ *Rooms from: Rs. 7000 ⊠ Mobor Beach ☎ 832/287–1303 to 312 ⊕ www.holidayinngoa. com ⤳ 200 rooms, 3 suites ⊠ Breakfast.*

$$$$
RESORT
Fodor's Choice
★
 The Leela Goa. For flat-out, over-the-top luxury and sophistication, nothing in Goa can top this well-planned 75-acre resort that includes a secluded beach and a magnificent view of cliffs and coves. **Pros:** the best accommodations rupees can buy. **Cons:** extremely pricey. $ *Rooms from: Rs. 20000 ⊠ Cavelossim, Mobor, Salcete ☎ 832/662–1234 ⊕ www.theleela.com ⤳ 120 rooms, 66 suites ⊠ All meals.*

BEACHES

Cavelossim Beach. One of Goa's lesser-known stretches, Cavelossim Beach is starting to come into its own. With a few swanky hotels in the area, including the Leela Goa ⇨ *See Where to Stay listings*, Cavelossim is primarily popular with older Indian visitors, and as a result is fairly clean, with soft white sand. If you're looking for swinging nightlife, this is not the beach for you, but it is worth a visit for those seeking relaxation, or perhaps some dolphin spotting—contact the area's boat operators who can organize sunset trips to spot the pods of dolphins that inhabit these waters. **Amenities:** food and drink; lifeguard; water sports. **Best for:** solitude; sunset; swimming. ⊠ *Cavelossim Beach.*

PALOLEM BEACH

★   *37 km (23 miles) southwest of Margao.*

Until recently, Goa's southernmost sandy stretch—nicknamed Paradise Beach—really was like a dream. The tourists who reached Palolem, in the Canacona district, were only nature lovers and privacy seekers. Even so, despite the influx of shacks, hotels, restaurants, and discos, this mile-long, crescent-shape stretch of white sand remains one of the most beautiful beaches in India.

Accommodation options are threadbare; there are temporary thatched huts lining the shoreline during the tourist season. Your best bet might be at the Lalit Goa, a few kilometers south, at Raj Baga.

GETTING HERE AND AROUND

From Dabolim Airport, a prepaid taxi will cost you about Rs. 1,200 to make the 67-km (42-mile) trip, which will take roughly 90 minutes.

WHERE TO STAY

For expanded hotel reviews, visit Fodors.com.

$$$
RESORT

🏨 **The Lalit Goa.** They don't get bigger than this sprawling 85-acre all-suites resort. **Pros:** secluded; great for golf enthusiasts. **Cons:** it's quite a walk between all the amenities; not close to the beach. $ *Rooms from: Rs. 7200* ✉ *Raj Baga, Cancona, 3 km (2 miles) from Palolem Beach* ☎ *832/266771* ⊕ *www.thelalit.com* ↪ *255 suites, 8 villas* ⊠*Breakfast.*

BEACHES

Palolem Beach. This once-deserted white-sand beach, backed by palm groves and low, green mountains, is still quieter than its northern counterparts, but Palolem is now a definite destination for sunseekers. It has a solid selection of cheap eateries and shacks, which have sprung up to cater to its bunch of hippie visitors. The farthest south of this coastline's developed beaches, it's no longer quite the idyll that first drew visitors this far south, but it is still very beautiful. **Amenities:** food and drink. **Best for:** solitude; swimming; walking.

Kerala

WORD OF MOUTH

"While the trip itself had its ups and downs like any genuine vacation, the state itself is truly stunning. I have never seen such natural beauty with so much diversity in India, from beaches to backwaters to mountains, Kerala has it all."

—Galactus

WELCOME TO KERALA

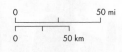

TOP REASONS TO GO

★ **Ease Your stress:** There's no place better than Kerala to get an ayurvedic oil massage and a yoga session. Let your tension melt away and your body kick back into equilibrium.

★ **Sail along the scenic backwaters:** Luxury houseboats come with hotel comforts, but the real attraction is the traditional village life you see drifting by.

★ **Lounge by the sea:** Relax along an isolated stretch of sand in North Kerala, access backwaters minutes from the beach at Marari, or party on Kovalam's Lighthouse Beach.

★ **Indulge your taste buds:** Whether its spicy, coconut based curries, Portugese and Dutch influenced dishes, or North Kerala biryani cooked in bamboo trunks, Kerala's extensive menu is sure to win over your taste buds.

★ **Tap into the past:** Reflect on Kerala's colonial past in Kochi, as you watch the sun set over Fort Cochin harbor, or visit the ancient port of Muziris, India's gateway for world religions.

1 Kochi. This colonial port city is packed with historical homes, churches, mosques, and a centuries-old synagogue where the city's small remaining population of Jews still worship.

2 Central Kerala. Central Kerala is blessed with natural beauty: beaches, the backwaters, stunning tea and spice plantations, and cool mountain wildlife preserves. It's also a busy tourist destination with crowds in season.

3 Southern Kerala. The main attractions here are the beaches in and around Kovalam and the laid-back atmosphere. It also holds the capital city of Trivandrum.

4 Northern Kerala. In this quiet area, you'll find long stretches of pristine sand and Bekal Fort, a 300-year-old beachfront fort that shouldn't be missed.

GETTING ORIENTED

The small state of Kerala is separated from the rest of the country by natural boundaries—the Arabian Sea to the west and the high Western Ghats to the east. The thickly forested and mountainous eastern edge can only be reached by road. Its hilly and fertile midlands are spotted with coconut farms and paddy (rice) fields; its coastal lowlands are famous for the beaches and backwaters. Although most people never venture beyond the central backwater resorts and the well-developed beach towns in the south, the north's long pristine beaches are also getting popular.

8

Kasaragod
Bekal Fort
Bekal
Nileshwar
4
Payyannur
Paygangati
Alikkod
Kannur
Thalassery
Mahé
Badagara
Quilandi
Calicut (Kozhikode)
Ferokh
Shoranur
Ponnani
Cheruthuruthi
Palakkad
Kunnamkulam
Guruvayur
2
Trichur (Thrissur)
Kodungallur
Kaladi
Parur
Aluva
Kochi (Cochin)
Ernakulam
1
Munnar
Vaikam
Shertallai
Kanjikuzhi
Kumarakom
Thekkady
Kochi Backwater
Kottayam
Alleppey (Alappuzha)
Lake Periyar Wildlife Sanctuary
Sabarimala
Haripad
Kayankulam
Pathanamthitta
Punalur
Quilon (Kollam)
Pon Mudi
Varkala
3
Trivandrum (Thiruvananthapuram)
Kovalam

EATING WELL IN KERALA

The Kerala table is eclectic, savory, and adventuresome. Rice is the staple, coconut the essence, seafood the star, and spices the local zing.

(top left) Spicy fried chicken with curry leaves; (top right) Fish curry; (bottom right) Idiyappam

Kerala means "land of coconuts" in Malayalam, and its cuisine certainly bears that out. Keralites use every part of the coconut, and its milk and oil are prominent in all Keralan food, both sweet and savory.

Expect distinctive meat and fish dishes—rich beef or mutton stewed in coconut milk, bread stuffed with fried mussels, *biriyanis* cooked in an assortment of spices, and savory fish curries. Vegetarian dishes are plentiful—gourds, yam, mango, and bananas may be cooked or raw, in appetizers, entrées and desserts. Grated coconut and *jaggery*—semi-refined palm sugar—are commonly used in sweets.

Kerala is known for *iddiappa*, or "string hoppers"—thin strands of dough formed into little nests that are steamed and served with coconut milk and sugar for breakfast or as an accompaniment to soups, stews, or curries. *Appam*, a slight variation on the theme, is a rice-flour pancake, thin and crispy on the edges with a spongy, raised center.

CHRISTIAN CUISINE

Kerala's Syrian Christian cuisine bears the stamp of all those who traversed its coasts. A typical day begins with *Pallappam,* a rice pancake with Portuguese origins. Red meat, not often found in Indian cuisine, is a major ingredient, with lamb *ishtew* (a stew with coconut milk) and *thoran* (dry beef with spices) being favorites.

MEEN POLLICHATHU

A central Kerala delicacy, **meen pollicha-thu** is a fragrant preparation of stuffed fish wrapped in a banana leaf. Any fish in season can be used, but the karimeen pearl spot fish is a Kerala local. The fish is marinated with various spices and a paste of diced tomatoes, onions, ginger, garlic, and coconut milk, then wrapped in a banana leaf sealed with a clove and cooked. This dish is available in almost every restaurant in Kerala.

MEEN PATHIRI

Malabar's stuffed fish pancakes, or **meen pathiri,** are found at almost every highway eatery in the northern part of the state. A pathriri—or parota, as it's often called—is a flatbread based on rice flour and coconut milk. This is filled with fish (usually king fish, sardines, or pearl spot) that is shredded and cooked with spices, including chilli powder and turmeric. While some meen pathiri are so generously stuffed they look like a pie, in some parts of Malabar the pancake is flattened with a rolling pin after being stuffed. Chicken and mutton stuffings are also used.

IDIYAPPAM

String hoppers, or idiyappam, are made with rice flour and can be eaten with a curry, a stew, or at breakfast with *mutta* (egg) roast or simply with coconut milk. This Kerala staple can be sweet or savory and is a standard accompaniment to all

meals, often garnished with grated coconut. Most often you will find it served with potato stew.

PAZHAM PORI

An evening snack available from street vendors, cafeterias, and train stations across the state, **pazham pori** are plantain fritters—deep-fried delights that are best when served hot. A ripe Kerala-grown banana, which is very similar to a plantain, is chopped and coated in a flour-based batter before it's fried. A similar fritter is made using yams.

MEEN MULAKITTATHU

Using the fresh catch of the day, **meen mulakittathu,** or fish curry, is a staple at the dinner table. Traditionally cooked in a brass pot, the gravy is a combination of coconut milk and spices that are all grown in Kerala—and freshly crushed when the dish is cooked in traditional homes. Different kinds of fish can be used, although the most popular are pearl spot and king fish. The emphasis is on freshness. This dish is served with steamed red rice or with idiyappam (see above).

PUTTU

Another specialty of the region, *puttu* is a puddinglike dish made from fresh-grated coconut and rice flour, molded into a cylindrical shape and then steamed.

8

Updated
by Sehrish
Shaban

A charming myth explains the creation of Kerala, the narrow state running 560 km (350 miles) along India's western coast. Parashurama, an avatar of Vishnu, performed a series of penances to atone for a grievous sin, and the god of the sea rewarded his devotion by reclaiming Kerala from the deep.

The reality is no less charming. From pristine beaches and backwaters to extensive stretches of tea and spice plantations and rolling hills, Kerala is a land of diverse natural beauty, added to which is the opportunity to spot unique species of birds and wildlife. The landscape changes across the breadth of the state, and is dotted with waterfalls, fresh springs, and forests. It is also rich in history, with Hindu temples dating back thousands of years and a culture that include dance, martial arts, and age-old ayurvedic treatments. From the more recent past, coastal cities like Kochi preserve colonial mansions and 19th-century godowns (warehouses) used to store spices and teas from the plantations.

In 1956 the Malayalam-speaking states of Kochi and Travancore joined with the district of Malabar to form Kerala. The new Indian state became the first place in the world to adopt a communist government in a free election, an event that caused global speculation. Today this tropical enclave between the western mountains and the Arabian Sea is one of India's most progressive states, with a literacy rate of well over 90% and a life expectancy far higher than the Indian average. Even in the shabbiest backwater "toddy shop," where locals knock back glasses of potent coconut liquor, you'll find a copy of the day's newspaper. However, despite Kerala's very real accomplishments, unemployment remains endemic. Its citizens depend to a large degree on remittances (money sent from abroad). To be able to provide for their families back home, many Keralan men must leave to work in the Persian Gulf.

The Malayalis make up India's most highly educated population; many are conversant in English, Hindi, and Tamil, as well as Malayalam. In the nearly three millennia before the 1795 establishment of British rule, Phoenicians, Arabs, Jews, Chinese, and Europeans came in droves, attracted by the region's valuable cash crops: tea, rubber, cashews, teak, and spices—notably black pepper (Kerala's black gold) and cardamom.

Kerala's diversity is a testament to all those who passed by during the last few centuries. This state is unique in that its population is almost equally divided into Christians, Hindus, and Muslims (India's three largest religious communities).

Since Independence, people have begun using the place names that were used prior to British colonization. The strong British presence here makes name changes particularly germane; hence, Alleppey/Alappuzha, Calicut/Kozhikode, Cochin/Kochi, Quilon/Kollam, Trichur/Thrissur, and Trivandrum/Thiruvananthapuram. Official maps and tourist brochures reflect these changes but both versions are still commonly used.

PLANNING

WHEN TO GO

HIGH SEASON: OCTOBER TO MARCH

Although Kerala used to have a second dip in visitor numbers during October's monsoon, this month now marks the beginning of the high season for all hotels and tour operators, with mostly foreign tourists flocking in to take advantage of "monsoon tourism" deals on offer. December and January are the peak tourist months, so be prepared to pay top rates around Christmas and New Year's Eve. If you plan on visiting during that time be sure to book ahead as many hotels run on full occupancy. Because of Kerala's large Christian community, this time of the year is quite festive and very enjoyable. The climate is ideal for the beach and backwaters, while the hills offer a cooler alternative.

LOW SEASON: MARCH TO JULY

By March the tourists season starts to wind down as temperatures soar to almost 40 degrees Celcius and the air becomes humid. June brings in the monsoon season that lasts up to mid-August (in the last few years). This rainy season deters tourists bound for the beaches and the backwaters, but it's supposed to be the best time for ayurvedic treatments. The hills like Munnar and Kannur are still pleasant during this time and often cater to domestic tourists escaping the heat in the plains.

SHOULDER SEASON: AUGUST AND SEPTEMBER

By mid-August the monsoons are over and the temperature is cooler. The Onam Festival is celebrated across Kerala around this time. Tourists can find some of the best deals during this period and domestic vacationers are already taking advantage of this. The cooler temperature and good prices make this an ideal time to visit, although, because August is the tail end of the monsoon and the sea is on high tide, swimming in the ocean is restricted on several beaches. This is also bug season, so insect repellents and a suitcase full of long pants is advisable to ward off the mosquitoes that can cramp evenings outside.

GETTING HERE AND AROUND

Driving to Kerala is a good option. If you're coming from Tamil Nadu, the drive from Madurai along the Madurai–Kottayam Road is stunning. NH–17 runs along the coast from Mangalore south to Kochi, though it

8

gets a little rough north of Calicut. Roads to the interior *ghats* (mountains) are often breathtaking: the landscape changes from the brilliant lime green of the rice fields to the rich, dark green of the tea plantations and jungle, with breathtaking waterfalls scattered along the way.

The most convenient way to get around Kerala is with a hired car and driver. The journey from Trivandrum to Kochi takes about five hours. Figure about Rs. 12 per km (½ mile) for a non-air-conditioned car and a halt charge of Rs. 150 per night. Shop around, and hire a car from a government-approved travel agency.

In central Kerala boat cruises offer a fascinating look at the backwaters where people still live. Most houseboats are based in the Alleppey district. When booking an overnight stay on one, make sure it comes equipped with solar panels and air-conditioning or a fan, or you're in for a hot night. The going rate for a posh two-bedroom vessel with air-conditioning and meals included is roughly Rs. 14,000; a one-bedroom will run about Rs. 9,000.

AIR TRAVEL

Most international flights land in Trivandrum or Kochi. But the small Calicut airport also has flights coming from the Middle East and Sri Lanka. Air India, Jet Airways, IndiGo, and Go Air cover domestic routes and most local carriers fly between Trivandrum, Kochi, and Calicut.

AIRPORT
TRANSFERS

Calicut's Karipur Airport is 23 km (14 miles) south of town; a cab will cost roughly Rs. 550.

Kochi's international airport is about 40 km (25 miles) east of the city; abominable traffic can make it a two-hour trip. A taxi will cost about Rs. 500. The small airport in Trivandrum is 6 km (4 miles) west of the city center; taxis charge about Rs. 200 to get to the city and about Rs. 700 to reach Kovalam.

BOAT AND FERRY TRAVEL

Private companies, the Kerala Tourism Development Cooperative (KTDC), and the Tourist Desk operate half-day backwater tours from Alleppey for around Rs. 100 to Rs. 400. The Alleppey Tourism Development Cooperative (ATDC) runs daily trips between Alleppey and Quilon (Rs. 300 for eight hours). After Quilon, boats continue south to Trivandrum and Kovalam. Boats leave both Alleppey and Quilon at 10:30 am.

Boat and Ferry Information ATDC ⊠ *Municipal Library, Thathampally, 2nd Fl., Alleppey* ☎ *91/477–2264462* ⊕ *www.atdcalleppey.com.*

TAXIS AND AUTO-RICKSHAWS

Auto-rickshaws are a convenient and quick way to travel around town. In Trivandrum, figure Rs. 10 for the first 1½ km (1 mile) and Rs. 4.50 per additional kilometer—other cities will be slightly less. Don't be alarmed if your driver doesn't use the meter—it usually doesn't work (whether because it was intentionally broken or not is difficult to say). Make sure to agree on a fare before you get in, and don't trust a driver for unbiased shopping recommendations.

Cabs are also a good option for destinations around Kochi. Fares will run about Rs. 100 an hour for a non-air-conditioned car. Most cabs have a Rs. 70 minimum. Ask at any tourist office about the latest legal rates. Taxis hired at your hotel will have a slightly higher rate but drivers are more likely to speak some English. Or you can grab a taxi at cab stands near the Sea Lord Jetty or at the intersection of M.G. Road and Club Road.

TRAIN TRAVEL

Rail journeys in Kerala can be scenic and more comfortable than traveling by car. The KK Express—which travels from Kanya Kumari, at India's southern tip, all the way up to New Delhi—is a good train to take through Kerala, as is the Kerala Express. December is a major pilgrimage season, so you'll need to book tickets in advance if you're traveling during this period. Check with KTDC for the latest schedules and fares, or try ⊕ *www.indianrail.gov.in*, and use a travel agent or your hotel's travel desk to make bookings, unless you don't mind standing in the unruly queue at the train station.

Train Information Ernakulam Junction ☎ *131*. **Ernakulam Town Station** ☎ *484/235–3920*. **Trivandrum Central Station** ☎ *132*.

EMERGENCIES

If you need a doctor or 24-hour pharmacy, ask at your hotel. They'll know the closest place and can send someone to get medicine, or find a doctor.

MONEY MATTERS

ATMS   ATMs are now available in Kerala's major cities: Kochi, Trivandrum, and Calicut. Check for the Cirrus or Plus sign, as many local banks do not accept foreign cards. Look for international banks like ANZ Grindlays, HSBC, and Standard Chartered, as well as the Indian bank ICICI. Make sure your PIN is four digits.

CURRENCY   Most of the major hotels have currency exchange services, but its wise
EXCHANGE   to shop around for the best deal. Thomas Cook offers good rates. ANZ Grindlays and any branch of the Bank of India will cash traveler's checks and change hard currency. Traveler's checks sometimes get marginally higher rates than cash.

TRAVEL AGENTS AND TOURS

The Kerala Tourism Development Council (KTDC) has several inexpensive tours, including wildlife-spotting excursions to the Lake Periyar Wildlife Sanctuary and one- to two-week trips that follow a pilgrim trail through Kerala's sacred shrines. Sita Travels can help with bookings and arrange a car and driver. The Great India Tour Company, one of Kerala's best travel agencies, has offices throughout South India. SATM Tours and Travel designs affordable packages around your particular interests. Trivandrum-based Tourindia created the houseboat phenomenon and offers unusual Kerala backwaters experiences. One intriguing two- to three-day trip—created by Tourindia and the forestry department—sends you deep into the jungle with a local guide, an armed escort, and a naturalist. Destination Holidays specializes in Kerala tours, and has a good reputation among budget operators for good service and local knowledge.

Contacts **Destination Holidays** ✉ *Pallath Bldgs., Kurisupally Rd., Ravipuram, Ernakulam, Kochi* ☎ *484/235–6497, 484/235–7316* ⊕ *www.destinationholidays. net.* **Great India Tour Company** ✉ *Mullassery Towers, Vanross Junction, Trivandrum* ☎ *471/301–1500.* **Tourindia** ✉ *136 M. G. Rd., Trivandrum* ☎ *471/233–0437, 471/233–1507.*

VISITOR INFORMATION

Excellent brochures, maps, pamphlets, and transportation information on all of Kerala's districts are available at any KTDC office. In Kochi, the office is open daily 8–7. Trivandrum's two KTDC offices—one in town and one at the airport—are open weekdays 10–5.

In Kochi, an alternative source of information is the Tourist Desk, a private, nonprofit organization that conducts moderately priced tours and provides clear, straightforward information about the state. In Kannur, the District Tourism Promotion Council is quite active. Central Kerala is well served by the ATDC. The Government of India Tourist Office—open weekdays 9–5:30 and Saturday 9–1—has its own vehicles, boats, lodgings, and tours.

Tourist Offices **ATDC** ✉ *Komala Rd., Alleppey* ☎ *477/226–1693* ⊕ *www.atdcalleppey.com.* **Kannur District Tourism Promotion Council** ✉ *Taluk Office Campus, Kannur* ☎ *497/270–6336* ⊕ *www.dtpckannur.com.*

ABOUT THE RESTAURANTS

Eating out is a relatively new concept in Kerala; the older generation views restaurants with a great deal of suspicion and the act of dining outside the home as some sort of tragedy. Most restaurants, as a result, cater to visitors and are often attached to hotels. (The word hotel, in fact, is often synonymous with restaurant.) This doesn't mean that visitors are denied the opportunity to eat an outstanding, authentic meal in Kerala. On the contrary, you'll often find the best authentic food in the better hotels and resorts. The top independent restaurants are in the major cities of Kochi, Calicut, and Trivandrum, or the tourist hub of Kovalam.

Prices in the reviews are the average cost of a main course at dinner or, if dinner is not served, at lunch.

ABOUT THE HOTELS

Many Kerala resorts make use of traditional regional architecture, from tribal-style huts to elaborate wooden manors. Heritage properties transplant or reassemble traditional teak wood homes, while other hotels are newly built in the old style, helping to support traditional carpentry.

In cities, most hotels have air-conditioning, but many resorts in less populated and cooler areas do not. Beach properties often rely on fan and sea breezes, and in the hilly interior, air-conditioning is usually unnecessary. Some buildings have no window screens, so if a cool and/or bug-free sleep is part of your plan, ask about both. Many resorts, even upscale establishments, don't have TVs in guest rooms. Outside of cities, power supply is tenuous. Most hotels have their own generators, but they take a few seconds to kick in. Don't be surprised if you're left in the darkness for a moment—it's unavoidable.

Some lodgings charge a 10% service fee, and the state government tacks on another 6%–16%, depending on the facilities. In luxury places, count on paying up to 25% in taxes. You may be able to offset such fees with off-season discounts—around 50% during the monsoon season, from June to August. On the other hand, many hotels charge higher-than-usual rates in peak season, from mid-December to mid-January.

Prices in the reviews are the lowest cost of a standard double room in high season. For expanded hotel reviews, facilities, and current deals, visit Fodors.com.

PLANNING YOUR TIME

The most convenient way to tackle Kerala is with a car and driver, allowing for the maximum amount of flexibility. Spend at least a day in Kochi, soaking in the beauty and the cultural offerings. A four-day itinerary can also include two days of ayurvedic massages and great local food in the resort town of Kumarakom and an overnight houseboat cruise through inland waterways. Drive inland to Thekkady or Munnar and spend two days viewing the wildlife in Thekkady's Lake Periyar Wildlife Sanctuary (take the 4 pm boat cruise or a more adventurous jungle trek) and scenic Munnar, Kerala's Switzerland, with the added attractions of wild elephants and the Rajamala sanctuary. Some travelers arrive in Kerala by car from Madurai, in Tamil Nadu; if that's your plan, visit Idukki on your way west toward the coast. Another option is to travel south from Thekkady to Trivandrum, Kerala's capital. Explore its sights and quiet lanes before heading for the mellow beaches, palm-fringed lagoons, and rocky coves near Kovalam and Varkala beach. If you want to get away from the crowds, head for the rarely visited north to see the extraordinary Theyyam festivals of Kannur, the sweeping vistas of the fort at Bekal, near Kasargode, and the pristine beaches along the northern coast.

EXPLORING KERALA

Outside of the historic, spice-trading city of Kochi, attractions are rustic: quiet beaches spiked with palm trees line the west coast; the hilly eastern interior is heavily forested. Kochi is the anchor of low-lying central Kerala, a region dominated by lazy inland waterways, rice fields, and fishing boats; the backwater lifestyle is best experienced from the deck of a slow-moving boat. Farther inland, you'll find tranquil tea and spice plantations as well as two national parks. At Lake Periyar Wildlife Sanctuary, near Thekkady, you can observe creatures in their native habitat from the comfort of a boat. Rajamala Wildlife Sanctuary, in the Evarikulam National Park near Munnar, is where you'll find the endangered *nilgiri tahr,* a shy but sweet-tempered mountain goat. The hills surrounding Thekkady and Munnar are lovely for trekking, rich in waterfalls and birdsong. Southern Kerala is best known for the beaches near Kovalam, which lie south of the stately capital city, Trivandrum (Thiruvanandapuram). Undeveloped, conservative northern Kerala is the state's cultural heartland; you can witness some of the region's most spectacular festivals here. Kerala's Muslim community is concentrated in the north, and Christians in the central and southern regions. Many of Kerala's low-slung, modest temples restrict entry to Hindus only.

KOCHI

1,380 km (860 miles) south of Mumbai.

Kochi, formerly and still commonly known as Cochin, is one of the west coast's largest and oldest ports. The streets behind the docks of the historic Fort Cochin and Mattancherry districts are lined with old merchant houses, godowns (warehouses), and open courtyards heaped with betel nuts, ginger, peppercorns, and tea. Throughout the second millennium this ancient city exported spices, coffee, and coir (the fiber made from coconut husks), and imported culture and religion from Europe, China, and the Middle East. Today Kochi has a synagogue, several mosques, Portuguese Catholic churches, Hindu temples, and the United Church of South India (an amalgamation of several Protestant denominations).

EXPLORING KOCHI

The city is spread out over mainland, peninsula, and islands. Ernakulam, on the mainland 2 km (3 miles) from the harbor, is the commercial center and the one-time capital of the former state of Cochin. Willingdon Island, which was created by dredging the harbor, holds several luxury hotels as well as a navy base. The beautiful Bolghatty Island, north of Ernakulam, is a favorite picnic spot for locals. On it there's a government-run hotel in a colonial structure that was once used by the Dutch governor and later by the British Resident. Another local favorite is Cherai beach on Vypin Island, which is a 10-minute ferry ride from Fort Cochin. The Fort Cochin district, Kochi's historic center, is at the northern tip of the Mattancherry peninsula. Houses here often recall Tudor manors; some have been converted to hotels, others remain in the hands of the venerable tea and trading companies. South of Fort Cochin, in the Mattancherry district, is where you'll find the city's dwindling Jewish community. Their small neighborhood, called Jew Town, which is now dotted with cafés and shops selling curios and antiques, is centered on the synagogue.

GETTING HERE AND AROUND

Cabs are a good option for getting around the city; public ferries and private boats go between Fort Cochin, Willingdon Island, and Ernakulam throughout the day. Ernakulam's main boat jetty is south of the Taj Residency hotel. Boats leave for Fort Cochin roughly every half hour from 6 am to 9 pm. There are frequent ferries to Mattancherry, and limited service to Embarkation Jetty, on Willingdon Island's eastern tip. Ferry rides cost only a few rupees.

TIMING

Spend at least two days here to soak up the history and culture of the city, see all the sights, and enjoy some downtime relaxing by the harbor and dining on local delicacies.

ESSENTIALS

Tourist Offices Government of India Tourist Office ⊠ *Malabar Rd., Willingdon Island, Kochi* ☎ *484/266–8352.* **KTDC** ⊠ *Shanmugham Rd., Ernakulam, Kochi* ☎ *484/235–3234* ⊕ *www.ktdc.com* ⊠ *Museum Complex, LMS Vellayambalam Road, Trivandrum* ☎ *471/232–2279* ⊕ *www.ktdc.com.* **Tourist Desk.**

Traditional Chinese fishing nets

Tourist Desk is a private company providing tours around Kerala. ⊠ *Main Boat Jetty, Ernakulam, Kochi* ☎ *484/237–1761* ⊕ *www.touristdesk.in.*

Travel Agents and Tours Great India Tour Company ⊠ *Ravipuram, Pithuru Smarana, Srikandath Rd., 1st fl., Ernakulam, Kochi* ☎ *484/231–7004.* **Sita Travels** ⊠ *Tharakan Building, M. G. Rd., Ernakulam, Kochi* ☎ *124/470–3400* ⊕ *www.sita.in.* **Travelogics** ⊠ *Warriam Rd., Ernakulam, Kochi* ☎ *484/236–5765* ⊕ *www.travelogics.in.*

A GOOD TOUR

The sleepy, tree-lined streets of Fort Cochin are perfect for a leisurely stroll. Start at the **St. Francis Church,** one of the earliest Indian churches to be built by Europeans. Portuguese explorer Vasco da Gama was once buried here. Continue northeast along Church Street, passing colonial bungalows, to Vasco da Gama Square and the famed **Chinese Fishing Nets.** Follow River Road along the sea front past more colonial buildings. When you come to the end of the small Children's Park, take a right so that the edge of the park is on your right. At the park's far edge you'll hit tiny Princess Street—one of the first streets built in Fort Cochin, it's now crammed with shops, tour agencies, and modest European-style houses. The next major intersection is at Bastion Street. Take a left here and you'll soon see **Santa Cruz Cathedral** on your right. From here, hop in an auto-rickshaw to Mattancherry (a Rs. 30 trip) and visit the **Dutch Palace.** When you exit, take a right and follow the road as it turns a corner. The **Pepper Exchange** is on your right. Visitors aren't admitted and trading now occurs mainly online. Turn right again and you'll reach the **Synagogue.** In the afternoon browse in the antiques and spice shops that line Jew Town Road, or head back north to the jetty and catch a ferry to Ernakulam for shopping on Mahatma Gandhi (M.G.) Road.

TIMING You can see Fort Cochin and Mattancherry in a day. Remember that all houses of worship close for a few hours around lunchtime. The Dutch Palace is closed on Friday, the synagogue is closed to visitors on Friday and Saturday, and many shops are closed on Sunday.

> **HEAD FOR WATER**
>
> Traffic on land and the city's many bridges can be abominable. Private launches and small ferries zip through the waterways, making the journey as enjoyable as the destination.

EXPLORING

Chinese Fishing Nets. The precarious-looking bamboo and wood structures hovering like cranes over the waterfront are Kochi's famous Chinese fishing nets. Although they've become identified with the city, they're used throughout central Kerala. Thought to have been introduced by Chinese traders in the 14th century, the nets and their catch are easily accessible from Fort Cochin's Vasco da Gama Square. You can watch the fishermen haul up the nets around 6 am, 11 am, and 4 pm. They're particularly striking at sunset or at any time when viewed from the deck of a boat. ⊠ *Kochi.*

Dutch Palace. Built by the Portuguese in the mid-16th century as a gift for the Rajas of Cochin, this structure was extended by the Dutch when they took control of the area. The rajas, in turn, added some of India's best mythological murals—the entire story of the *Ramayana* is told on the walls in a series of bedchambers, which also have inviting window seats. In the ladies' ground-floor chamber, you can see a colorful, mildly erotic depiction of Lord Krishna with his female devotees. The coronation hall near the entrance holds portraits and some of the rajas' artifacts, including a fantastic palanquin covered in red wool. The palace has rare, traditional Kerala flooring, which looks like polished black marble but is actually a mix of burned coconut shells, charcoal, lime, plant juices, and egg whites. ⊠ *Palace Rd., Mattancherry, Kochi* 🕮 *Rs. 2* ⊙ *Sat.–Thurs. 10–5.*

NEED A
BREAK?

Kashi Art Café. A favorite hangout for artists and young tourists, Fort Cochin's Kashi Art Café is about as funky as Kerala gets. The front room hosts rotating exhibitions, primarily of South Indian contemporary art, and light continental fare and Western-style coffee is served in the garden café at the rear. The real treat is to experience this tiny little pocket of Kerala subculture. ⊠ *Burgher St., Kochi* 🕾 *484/221–6769* ⊕ *www.kashiartgallery. com* ⊙ *Daily 8:30–7:30.*

St. Francis Church. The Portuguese flag first appeared in Fort Cochin in 1500, and Vasco da Gama arrived in 1502. The following year, Afonso de Albuquerque came with half a dozen ships full of settlers—he built the fort, and five friars in the crowd built India's first European church, St. Francis, in 1510. Da Gama returned in 1524 as Portuguese viceroy of the Indies, died that same year, and was buried in this church. You can still visit his gravestone, but his remains were shipped back to Lisbon in 1538.

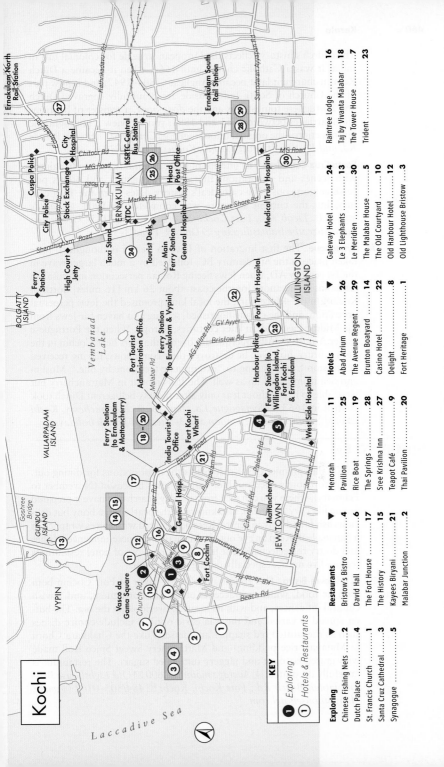

Kochi

KEY

- ▶ Exploring
- ① Hotels & Restaurants

Exploring ▶

Chinese Fishing Nets	2
Dutch Palace	4
St. Francis Church	1
Santa Cruz Cathedral	3
Synagogue	5

Restaurants ▶

Bristow's Bistro	4
David Hall	6
The Fort House	17
The History	15
Kayees Biryani	21
Malabar Junction	2
Menorah	11
Pavilion	25
Rice Boat	19
The Springs	28
Sree Krishna Inn	27
Teapot Café	9
Thai Pavilion	20

Hotels ▶

Abad Atrium	26
The Avenue Regent	29
Brunton Boatyard	14
Casino Hotel	22
Delight	8
Fort Heritage	1
Gateway Hotel	24
Le 3 Elephants	13
Le Meridien	30
The Malabar House	5
The Old Courtyard	10
Old Harbour Hotel	12
Old Lighthouse Bristow	3
Raintree Lodge	16
Taj by Vivanta Malabar	18
The Tower House	7
Trident	23

The church's history reflects the European struggle for colonial turf in India. It was a Catholic church until 1664, when it became a Dutch Reform church; it later became Anglican (1804–1947) and is now part of the Church of South India. Inside are beautifully engraved Dutch and Portuguese tombstones and the *doep boek,* a register of baptisms and marriages between 1751 and 1894; you can view a photographic reproduction—the original is too fragile. ✉ *Church St., between Parade Rd. and Bastion St., Fort Cochin, Kochi* 🕑 *Daily 9:30–5.*

Santa Cruz Cathedral. The interior of this cathedral is colorfully painted with scenes and decorations that some find gaudy and others perceive as gorgeous. The cathedral's history dates from the 16th century, but the current structure was completed in 1904. ✉ *Parade and K.B. Jacob rds., Fort Cochin, Kochi* ☎ *484/221–5799* 🌐 *www.santacruzcathedralbasilica.org* 🕑 *Daily 9–1 and 3–5.*

★ **Synagogue.** The first migration of Jews to Kerala is thought to have taken place in the 6th century BC, followed by a much larger wave in the 1st century AD, when Jews fleeing Roman persecution in Jerusalem settled at Cranganore (on the coast about 26 km [16 miles] north of Kochi). In the 4th century, the local king promised the Jews perpetual protection, and the colony flourished, serving as a haven for Jews from the Middle East and, in later centuries, Europe. When the Portuguese leader Afonso de Albuquerque discovered the Jews near Cochin in the 16th century, however, he destroyed their community, having received permission from his king to "exterminate them one by one." Muslim anti-Semitism flared up as well. The Jews rebuilt in Mattancherry but were able to live without fear only after the less-belligerent Dutch took control in 1663. ✉ *Synagogue La., Jew Town, Mattancherry, Kochi* 🎫 *Free* 🕑 *Sun.–Thurs. 10–noon and 3–5 (except Jewish holidays).*

WHERE TO EAT

As Kerala's premier city, Kochi offers the most options for dining out. Many top hotels open outdoor seafood grills in season (November to February), where you can pick from the day's catch and have it prepared as you like. Try *karimeen,* also known as the pearl spot, a bony but delicious fish found only in central Kerala, prepared with spices wrapped in a banana leaf. Keep an eye out for unusual Portuguese-influenced dishes and do try the eclectic Kochi Jewish cuisine. Lots of hotel restaurants feature live music, especially during peak season.

$$$ ECLECTIC 🍴 **Bristow's Bistro.** This restaurant offers a flavor of Fort Cochin both with its food, which has accents of Dutch, Portuguese, and Jewish cultural influences, and with its location overlooking the sea. The buffet spread is varied and the à la carte options include choice dishes such as the stuffed red snapper and desserts like the Chakkara Choru (a Malabari rice pudding) and Mattanchery Sweet Spice Roll made with grated coconut and jaggery (unrefined sugar). The restaurant is tastefully decorated. [$] *Average main: Rs. 600* ✉ *Old Lighthouse Bristow Hotel, Beach Rd., Fort Kochi, Kochi* ☎ *484/305–0102* 🌐 *www.oldlighthousehotel.com.*

$$
CONTEMPORARY

✕ **David Hall.** This former Dutch home is now an art gallery and café run by the Casino Group. The front room displays the work of contemporary Indian artists and works from art camps held in villages across Kerala. Beyond this is the café, open nonstop from noon to 9 pm, which extends out to the back lawn. Best known for its Italian pizza and panini, the menu changes regularly, depending on what ingredients are in season, making for interesting choices and dependable freshness. $ *Average main: Rs. 300* ✉ *1/264 Princess St., opposite Parade Ground, Fort Kochi, Kochi* ☎ *484/221–8298* ⊟ *No credit cards* ☉ *Closed Mon.*

> ### KOCHI BOAT TOURS
>
> From Ernakulam's High Court or Sealord Jetty you can hire private boats, usually for about Rs. 500 an hour. The Kerala Tourism Development Corporation (KTDC) conducts two inexpensive boat tours of Kochi each day; the 3½-hour trips depart at 9 am and 2 pm from the Sealord Jetty, opposite the Sealord Hotel, between the Main and High Court jetties.

$
SEAFOOD
★

✕ **The Fort House.** Inside a budget hotel in a great location on the pier, this simple, open-air restaurant doesn't skimp on quality or authenticity. The menu is almost entirely seafood—chicken and specialty items (like lobster) must be ordered in advance. Every dish is cooked to order and presented in a clay vessel. The Prawns Kerala—fried—and the braised seerfish are terrific. If you agonize over oil, tell the chef in advance. $ *Average main: Rs. 150* ✉ *Fort House Hotel, 2/6 A Calvathi Rd., Fort Cochin, Kochi* ☎ *484/221–7103, 484/221–5221.*

$$$
ECLECTIC
Fodor's Choice
★

✕ **The History.** The intriguing, extensively researched menu draws on the myriad international influences on Kochi's history. Alongside traditional fare you'll find unusual dishes bearing the stamp of the Middle East, Portugal, the local Jewish community, or the days of the British Raj. Some age-old recipes have been passed on to the restaurant by local communities. The lofty, elegant dining room is windowed on all sides, and capped with a gabled wooden ceiling (resembling an upturned ship) supported by massive wood beams. Live sitar and tabla music is performed every evening. Don't miss out on the Railway Mutton Curry from the British Raj era or the Chuttulli Meen, a grilled fish cooked in spices, which is a favorite in Cochin Jewish cuisine. $ *Average main: Rs. 650* ✉ *Brunton Boatyard Hotel, River Rd., Fort Cochin, Kochi* ☎ *484/221–5461* ☉ *No lunch.*

$
INDIAN

✕ **Kayees Biryani.** Known for its *biryani*, a rice dish cooked with meat and spices, the Kayees in Mattancherry is the original one and people say it's the best (there's another outlet in Ernakulam). Be prepared to wait in line during lunch hours on weekdays, and expect a more limited choice, or no food at all, if you arrive late—they run out. A variety of *biryanis* is on offer, both local to Kerala and other regional specialties such as Malabar style, with shrimp. Other notable dishes include the fish curry with Kerala Porotta (flatbread). Be sure to wash down your meal with Kayees' special *jeera* water (boiled with cumin seeds), an ayurvedic drink known to aid digestion. $ *Average main: Rs. 100* ✉ *Durbar Hall Rd., Mattancherry, Kochi* ☎ *484/222–6080.*

8

$$$ ECLECTIC Fodor's Choice ★ 🍴 **Malabar Junction.** The mix of regional specialties and Mediterranean cuisine at this small, quirky restaurant with an open side facing a garden and swimming pool, isn't as crazy as it sounds—most dishes veer closer to one side or the other. A tasty mahimahi fillet for instance, is flavored with local spices. If you're craving Western food, the pastas are excellent. Seafood is always fresh and perfectly cooked. Don't miss the chocolate-filled samosas in mango sauce, the restaurant's signature dessert. The restaurant has a large selection of Indian and foreign wines. [$] *Average main: Rs. 700* ✉ *The Malabar House, 1/268–1/269 Parade Rd., Fort Cochin, Kochi* ☎ *484/221–6666.*

$$$ ECLECTIC 🍴 **Menorah.** Menorah, a fine tribute to Cochin's rich Jewish history, is in the former mansion of the city's best-known Jewish family, and the waitstaff will elaborate on the history and the family if you ask. Traditional Cochin-Jewish cuisine is served—try the *plav*, a rice and chicken dish, and the mutta roast (egg cooked with a variety of spices)—and the fine table linens and stately surroundings recall the royalty, prime ministers and dignitaries that once dined here. Sip a glass of wine while looking out onto the courtyard with a pool to complete the picture of a bygone era. [$] *Average main: Rs. 700* ✉ *Koder House, Tower Rd., Fort Cochin, Kochi* ☎ *484/221–8485* 🌐 *www.koderhouse.com.*

$ ECLECTIC 🍴 **Pavilion.** In an out-of-the-way hotel south of Mattancherry, this plain-looking restaurant is a well-kept secret. Ignore the multicultural cuisine and go straight for a fish dish like the prawn curry or the *meen pollichathu* (spiced fish steamed in a banana leaf), which is so hot even Malayalees break a sweat. If you'd like it toned down, send a message to the chef when you order. [$] *Average main: Rs. 200* ✉ *Hotel Abad, near intersection of Moulana Azad Rd. and Kochangadi Rd., Chullickal, Kochi* ☎ *484/222–8211.*

$$$$ SEAFOOD ★ 🍴 **Rice Boat.** This perennial favorite of Kochi's well-to-do is shaped like a traditional wooden boat. Most tables overlook the waterfront. The menu focuses on seafood and Kerala specialties made with saltwater- and local freshwater fish grilled and cooked in traditional curries. The showpiece is an interactive kitchen where you can chat with the chef as he prepares your meal. [$] *Average main: Rs. 1200* ✉ *Vivanta by Taj Malabar Hotel, Malabar Rd., Willingdon Island, Kochi* ☎ *484/664–3000.*

$$ ECLECTIC 🍴 **The Springs.** The lunch buffet at the Avenue Regent's multicuisine restaurant is so popular that even visiting chefs pop in for a bite when they're in town. There's a variety of South Indian, North Indian, Mexican, Thai, Burmese, and Chinese specialties, but most people come for the hot, fresh, perfectly prepared *appam* (a traditional rice pancake), served with a mildly spicy coconut stew. [$] *Average main: Rs. 300* ✉ *Avenue Regent Hotel, 39/206 M. G. Rd., Ernakulam, Kochi* ☎ *484/237–7088, 484/237–7688, 484/237–7977.*

$ INDIAN 🍴 **Sree Krishna Inn.** Vegetarian meals and a pleasant, air-conditioned dining room draw in the business crowd to this handsome tile-roof building just off M. G. Road. The restaurant serves North and South Indian and Chinese dishes and snacks, as well as a large selection of ice creams. [$] *Average main: Rs. 100* ✉ *Warriam Rd., Ernakulam, Kochi* ☎ *484/236–6664.*

An antique shop in Kochi

$ ✕**Teapot Café.** This charming café, tucked away off Princess Street across
ECLECTIC the Chinese Fishing Nets at the harbor, has teapots and kettles dangling
from the ceiling and tables made from tea crates. It's almost like being in
a tea museum. There's an extensive menu of both Indian and continental
food, but the café is best known for its sandwiches and freshly baked
cakes—in particular the one they call Death by Chocolate. The relaxed
atmosphere and extensive range of teas makes this place popular with
tourists and locals alike. $ *Average main: Rs. 60 ✉ Peter Celli St., Fort
Kochi, Kochi* ☎ *484/221–8035* ⊘ *No dinner.*

$$$ ✕**Thai Pavilion.** Don't be surprised if your waiter explains each dish to
THAI you upon presentation—this is, after all, Kerala's first Thai restaurant.
The menu features plentiful seafood offerings and is reasonably authen-
tic, though some dishes are on the sweet side. The *pla rad prik* includes
a very soft fish, nicely flavored with basil, and the spicy classic *tom yam
goong* soup, made with prawns, doesn't disappoint. The dining room is
done up in warm woods, with silver accents on the ceiling and chairs.
Beveled glass windows give you a glimpse of the sea. $ *Average main:
Rs. 700 ✉ Vivanta Taj Malabar Hotel, Malabar Rd., Willingdon Island,
Kochi* ☎ *484/266–6811.*

WHERE TO STAY

For expanded hotel reviews, visit Fodors.com.

$ ▥ **Abad Atrium.** This impressively modern Western-style hotel is set back
HOTEL from M. G. Road, shielded from traffic noise by its sister establishment
Abad Plaza. **Pros:** good value; rooftop swimming pool. **Cons:** smallish
bathrooms; many rooms have views of a construction site. $ *Rooms*

from: Rs. 3500 ✉ *M. G. Rd., Ernakulam, Kochi* ☎ *484/238–1122, 484/238–4380* 🌐 *www.abadhotels.com/atrium* 🛏 *48 rooms, 4 suites* 🍴 *Breakfast.*

$$ HOTEL 🏨 **The Avenue Regent.** The spiffy marble lobby of this high-rise business hotel has art deco red bands around the ceiling molding and in the floor pattern. **Pros:** good spot for shopping; clean, spacious rooms; in-room Internet access. **Cons:** noisy location; basic lobby lacks character; no room safes. [$] *Rooms from: Rs. 5500* ✉ *39/2026 M. G. Rd., Ernakulam, Kochi* ☎ *484/237–7977, 484/237–7688* 📠 *484/237–5329* 🌐 *www.avenuehotels.in* 🛏 *49 rooms, 4 suites* 🍴 *Breakfast.*

$$$$ HOTEL Fodor's Choice ★ 🏨 **Brunton Boatyard.** Built in a combination of Dutch and Portuguese colonial styles, this elegant hotel is on the site of a former boatyard, facing the harbor's Chinese Fishing Nets. **Pros:** all rooms and bathrooms are sea-facing; swanky hotel bar is one of the few in Kochi stocked with foreign liquor; great restaurants; Wi-Fi in all rooms. **Cons:** pricey; doesn't offer no-smoking rooms. [$] *Rooms from: Rs. 16000* ✉ *Calvetty Rd., Fort Cochin, Kochi* ☎ *484/221–5461* 🌐 *www.cghearth.com* 🛏 *26 rooms, 4 suites* 🍴 *Breakfast.*

$$$ HOTEL 🏨 **Casino Hotel.** This modern hotel has rustic touches like coir carpeting in the hallways and tiny earthenware pots for bathroom amenities. **Pros:** a relative bargain for a full amenties hotel, especially since taxes are included in the tariff; quiet location; great restaurant. **Cons:** a bit far from the sites in Fort Cochin; location is a bit drab; no spa. [$] *Rooms from: Rs. 7400* ✉ *K. P. K. Menon Rd., Willingdon Island, Kochi* ☎ *484/266–8221, 484/266–8421* 🌐 *www.cghearth.com* 🛏 *66 rooms, 1 suite* 🍴 *Breakfast.*

$ B&B/INN ★ 🏨 **Delight.** This spotless homestay is wildly popular with budget travelers, in no small part because of the warm, knowledgeable, and extraordinarily helpful hosts who can arrange for great English-speaking taxi- and auto drivers. **Pros:** quiet location across from cricket field and a short walk from the Chinese Fishing Nets; great value. **Cons:** showers aren't separate so bathroom gets wet; extra 500 rupees charged for a/c. [$] *Rooms from: Rs. 2000* ✉ *Parade Ground, Post Office Rd., Fort Cochin, Kochi* ☎📠 *484/221–7658* 🌐 *www.delightfulhomestay.com* 🛏 *6 rooms* 🍴 *Breakfast.*

$ B&B/INN 🏨 **Fort Heritage.** Each room in this restored 17th-century Dutch mansion is slightly different from the next, though all are enormous and have towering wooden ceilings and period reproduction furniture. **Pros:** great location; good price; friendly atmosphere. **Cons:** ground-floor rooms open directly into the restaurant; no Internet access; no swimming pool. [$] *Rooms from: Rs. 3000* ✉ *1/283 Napier Street, Elphinstone Road, Fort Cochin, Kochi* ☎📠 *484/221–5333, 484/221–5455* 🌐 *www.fortheritage.com* 🛏 *9 rooms, 3 suites* 🍴 *Breakfast.*

$$$$ HOTEL 🏨 **Gateway Hotel.** The large sea-facing rooms have spectacular views, in this beautifully maintained downtown hotel, although standard rooms are on the small side, and their bathrooms have showers rather than tubs. **Pros:** nice pool; rooms upgraded with new furniture and flooring a few years ago. **Cons:** basic; lacks Kerala charm. [$] *Rooms from: Rs. 13600* ✉ *Marine Dr., Ernakulam, Kochi* ☎ *484/667–3300* 🌐 *www.thegatewayhotels.com* 🛏 *96 rooms, 12 suites* 🍴 *Breakfast.*

$$ **Le 3 Elephants.** Tucked between a quieter part of Cherai beach and its

B&B/INN   backwaters, Le 3 Elephants has eco-friendly cottages all facing the back-

Fodor'sChoice   waters. **Pros:** spa; environmental credentials; good value for money.

★   **Cons:** Cherai beach isn't very clean. *$ Rooms from: Rs. 5000 ⊠ 1078 Convent Beach, Pipeline Rd., North Cherai Beach, Kochi* ☎ *93/4917– 4341* ⊕ *www.3elephants.in* ⤴ *11 rooms* ⦿| *Breakfast.*

$$$ **Le Meridien.** On 25 landscaped acres on the outskirts of Ernakulam,

HOTEL   this imposing, green-tile-roofed complex houses a massive hotel and

★   South India's largest convention center. **Pros:** world class amenities; plenty of entertainment options, including one of Kerala's few night-clubs. **Cons:** several kilometers from anything worth seeing; tasteful, but lacks local flavor. *$ Rooms from: Rs. 6000 ⊠ Kundannur Junction, NH–47 Bypass, Maradu, Ernakulam, Kochi* ☎ *484/270–5777* ⊕ *www. lemeridien.com/cochin* ⤴ *223 rooms* ⦿| *Breakfast.*

$$$ **The Malabar House.** Luxurious but homey, this early-18th-century

HOTEL   Dutch villa once housed European traders and bankers. **Pros:** restau-rant might be Kochi's best; deluxe rooms open into private garden; hotel staff is friendly and helpful. **Cons:** pricey; some standard rooms lack amenities like closets. *$ Rooms from: Rs. 7000 ⊠ 1/268–1/269 Parade Rd., Fort Cochin, Kochi* ☎ *484/221–6666* ⊕ *www.malabarhouse.com* ⤴ *17 rooms* ⦿| *Breakfast.*

$$ **The Old Courtyard.** Slightly decrepit but still charming, this late-18th-

B&B/INN   century refurbished mansion in the heart of Fort Cochin has eight rooms overlooking a central courtyard. **Pros:** restaurant menu has both con-tinental and Kerala options; great location; friendly staff. **Cons:** a lit-tle worn around the edges; basic accommodations without phones or Internet. *$ Rooms from: Rs. 4000 ⊠ 1/371 Princess St., Fort Cochin, Kochi* ☎ *484/221–5035, 484/221–6302* ⊕ *www.oldcourtyard.com* ⤴ *6 rooms, 2 suites* ⦿| *Breakfast.*

$$$ **Old Harbour Hotel.** Just opposite the Chinese Fishing Nets, this

HOTEL   300-year-old Dutch mansion, which reopened in 2006 after a two-

★   year restoration, is a standout in Fort Cochin's ever-expanding field of boutique heritage hotels. **Pros:** restaurant serves very good Kerala delicacies. **Cons:** pricey. *$ Rooms from: Rs. 9250 ⊠ 1/328 Tower Rd., Fort Cochin, Kochi* ☎ *484/221–8006, 484/221–8007* ⊕ *www. oldharbourhotel.com* ⤴ *13 rooms, 3 cottages* ⦿| *Breakfast.*

$$$ **Old Lighthouse Bristow.** This tastefully decorated hotel is the former

HOTEL   home of the late Sir Robert Bristow, the architect of the modern port of Cochin. **Pros:** spa offers a variety of ayurvedic massages; Wi-Fi is available in all rooms. **Cons:** service is somewhat lacking; can be noisy because its on busy Cochin beach. *$ Rooms from: Rs. 9000 ⊠ Beach Rd., Fort Cochin, Kochi* ☎ *484/305–0102* ⊕ *www.oldlighthousehotel. com* ⤴ *11* ⦿| *Breakfast.*

$ **Raintree Lodge.** At the quiet end of busy Petercelle Street, this simply

B&B/INN   furnished hotel inside a 1700s Dutch building has earned raves for its reasonable rates and good-looking rooms, furnished with two-poster beds, other characterful wood furniture and art. **Pros:** great location; atmospheric rooms. **Cons:** expensive for the limited facilities available; no restaurant. *$ Rooms from: Rs. 2400 ⊠ 1/618 Petercelli St., Fort Cochin, Kochi* ☎ *484/325–1489* ⊕ *www.fortcochin.com* ⤴ *5 rooms* ⦿| *No meals.*

8

$$$$
RESORT
Fodor'sChoice
★

Taj by Vivanta Malabar. Isolated at the tip of Willingdon Island, this grand hotel offers a heritage sensibility and style, and absolute luxury. **Pros:** unmatched water views; spacious rooms; fantastic restaurants. **Cons:** isolated on an island where there's little to do; not cheap. $ *Rooms from: Rs. 10000 ⊠ Malabar Rd., Willingdon Island, Kochi ☎ 484/664–3000 ⊕ www.tajhotels.com ✈ 87 rooms, 9 suites ❚❍❙ Breakfast.*

$
HOTEL

The Tower House. Converted from an interesting 17th-century house, this hotel, directly opposite the Chinese Fishing Nets, strikes the right balance between providing modern amenities and retaining the integrity of the historic building. **Pros:** reasonably priced; in the heart of historic Fort Cochin; has a garden pool. **Cons:** service is not their strongest point; no in-room safes. $ *Rooms from: Rs. 3500 ⊠ 1/320 Tower Rd., Fort Cochin, Kochi ☎ 484/221–6960 ⊕ neemranahotels.com/tower-house ✈ 13 rooms ❚❍❙ Breakfast.*

$$$$
HOTEL

Trident. This tasteful and stylish hotel, outfitted for both business and leisure travelers, is a low-rise, tile-roof building that wraps around a central courtyard, so hallways are full of natural light. **Pros:** bar, which overlooks the pool, stocks international liquor. **Cons:** Willingdon Island location is not ideal for sightseeing. $ *Rooms from: Rs. 10700 ⊠ Bristow Rd., Willingdon Island, Kochi ☎ 484/308–1000 ⊕ www.tridenthotels.com ✈ 76 rooms, 9 suites ❚❍❙ Breakfast.*

NIGHTLIFE AND THE ARTS

BAR

Seagull. Popular with both locals and tourists, Seagull is Cochin's best option for a chilled beer by the sea—in fact, it's one of the few places that serves liquor. The restaurant offers a large selection of local seafood and other dishes, and though the interior is rather basic, its outdoor seating on the pier makes it the ideal place to enjoy a relaxing meal to the sound of the ocean. Thoughtfully, the Seagull has provided a separate area for locals who just come in for a drink. ⊠ *Calvathy Rd., Fort Cochin, Kochi ☎ 484/221–8128.*

ART GALLERY

Kerala Lalita Kala Akademi Gallery. The former home of the Parishith Thampuran Museum now houses the Kerala Lalita Kala Akademi Gallery. There's not much here by way of explanation, but the traditional tile-roof building is cool and airy, and the interesting collection features contemporary works by Indian artists. ⊠ *D. H. Rd., Ernakulam, Kochi ☎ 484/236–7748 ⊠ Free ⊘ Mon.–Sat. 11–7.*

DANCE

Dating back to the 17th century, Kathakali is an art form in which elaborately made-up and costumed dancers tell epic stories using stylized hand gestures. For centuries, Kathakali performances were the only after-dark entertainment in Kerala; shows began at sundown and lasted all night. Today, for the benefit of tourists, performances are often shortened to one or two hours. Many centers also offer the chance to watch dancers being made up, which can be as entertaining as the show.

Cochin Cultural Centre. Kathakali performances in the air-conditioned room of the Cochin Cultural Centre start daily at 6 pm, though you should arrive an hour before the show to see makeup being applied. ✉ *K.B. Jacob Rd., near police station, Fort Cochin, Kochi* ☎ *484/221–6911* ⊕ *www.cochinculturalcentre.com.*

Kerala Kalamandalam. This revered arts academy is credited with the revival of traditional arts in Kerala, providing training in Kathakali, Mohiniattam, and at least 14 different native art forms. All-night Kathakali performances are staged here a few nights each year, and you're welcome to watch students in practice sessions, weekdays from 8:30 to noon and 3:30 to 5:30. ✉ *Cheruthuruthy, 29 km (18 miles) north of Thrissur) near NH 17, Thrissur* ☎ *488/426–2418* ⊕ *www. kalamandalam.org.*

Kerala Kathakali Centre. This is a pleasant outdoor venue, where makeup starts at 5 pm and Kathakali shows follow at 6 pm daily. There is also a daily *kalaripayattu* (Kerala martial arts) show that starts at 4 pm. Short-term courses in dance and music are offered here. ✉ *River Rd., near the bus stand, opposite Brunton Boatyard, Fort Cochin, Kochi* ☎ *484/221–5827* ⊕ *www.kathakalicentre.com* 📧 *Kathakali: Rs. 250; martial arts: Rs. 200.*

See India Foundation. The director here provides lively explanations of the Kathakali dance before every 6:45 pm show. Makeup starts at 6 pm. ✉ *Kalthil Parambil La., Ernakulam, Kochi* ☎ *484/237–6471* 📧 *Rs. 200.*

MARTIAL ARTS

Kerala's dramatic, high-flying martial art, Kalarippayattu, may be the oldest in Asia. Some think it started in the 12th century, others think it began earlier, and still others say later. Some scholars believe that Buddhist monks from India introduced Kalarippayattu to China along with Buddhism. Participants learn both armed- and unarmed-combat techniques. One of the more unusual skills involves defending yourself against a knife-wielding attacker using only a piece of cloth. In peak season, many hotels stage performances.

★ **E.N.S. Kalari Centre.** If you call in advance, you can watch Kalarippayattu practitioners here. ✉ *Nettoor, Ernakulam, Kochi* ☎ *484/270–0810* ⊕ *www.enskalari.org.in.*

SHOPPING

The streets surrounding the synagogue in Mattancherry are crammed with stores that sell curios, and Fort Cochin's Princess Street has sprouted several small shops worth a browse. For saris, jewelry, handicrafts, and souvenirs, head to M. G. Road in Ernakulam. Be suspicious of the word "antique" in all stores, and bargain hard.

Kathakali dancers

Cinnamon. A branch of the chic Bangalore boutique, Cinnamon stocks stylish ethnic and modern housewares, silk scarves and purses, jewelry, and Indo-Western designer clothing. The store is closed Sunday. ⊠ *1/658 Ridsdale Rd., Parade Ground, Fort Cochin, Kochi* ☎ *484/221–7124, 484/221–8124* ⊕ *www.cinnamonthestore.com.*

Cochin Gallery. Jewelry, carpets, cushion covers, bronze figurines, and wooden boxes are sold at this gallery. ⊠ *6/116 Jew Town Rd., Mattancherry, Kochi* ☎ *484/222–1225, 484/221–0851.*

Crafter's. Local hotels often get their antiques here. The store is crammed with stone and wood carvings, pillars, and doors as well as such portable items as painted tiles, navigational equipment, and wooden boxes. Crafter's also has a café upstairs. ⊠ *6/141 Jew Town Rd., Mattancherry, Kochi* ☎ *484/222–3346.*

Fort Royal. This is an expensive all-in-one shop with goods from all over India. You can find brocade work, marble inlay boxes, and Kashmiri carpets, plus local handicrafts and precious and semiprecious jewelry. ⊠ *1/258 Napier St., Fort Cochin, Kochi* ☎ *484/221–7832.*

Glada. Cochin's upscale ladies buy the latest designer fineries at this pricey boutique. ⊠ *Convent Junction, Ernakulam, Kochi* ☎ *484/236–4952.*

Idiom Books. Whether you're looking for a little information on Kerala or a little something to while away the hours, stop by Idiom Books, a small bookshop opposite the synagogue, or its branch in Fort Cochin. You can find an intriguing collection of recent Western and Indian fiction, as well as books on history, culture, cooking, and religion. ⊠ *Jew Town Rd.,*

Mattancherry, Kochi ☎ *484/222–5604* ✉ *1/348 Bastion St., near Princess St., Fort Cochin, Kochi.*

Indian Arts and Curios. This is one of Kerala's oldest and most-reliable curio shops. ✉ *6/189 Jew Town Rd., Mattancherry, Kochi* ☎ *484/222–8049.*

Jayalakshmi. A mind-blowing selection of saris (including Kerala saris), *lehangas* (long skirts with fitted blouses), and the like are on offer here, as well as Indian and Western clothes for men and children. There are also branches in Trivandrum and Calicut. ✉ *M. G. Rd., near Rajaji Rd., Ernakulam, Kochi* ☎ *484/408–9899.*

Kairali. A fixed-price government shop, Kairali has a good selection of local handicrafts and curios. It's closed on Sunday. ✉ *M. G. Rd., near Jose Junction, Ernakulam, Kochi* ☎ *484/235–4507.*

Surabhi. Run by the state's Handicrafts Cooperative Society, Surabhi has an impressive selection of local products. ✉ *M. G. Rd., Ernakulam, Kochi* ☎ *484/237–7978.*

KERALA CRAFTS

Look for cups, vases, spoons, and teapots carved from coconut shells and baskets, floor and table mats, and carpets hand-woven from coir (coconut fiber), and sleeping mats and handbags made of resilient, pliable kova grass. Other goods include brass lamps, rosewood elephants, lacquered wooden boxes with brass fittings—traditionally used to store the family jewels—and metal mirrors from Aranmula, northeast of Trivandrum. Cinnamon, cloves, cardamom, and other spices are also sold throughout Kerala.

8

CENTRAL KERALA

Between Kochi and Quilon (Kollam), to the south, is the immense labyrinth of waterways called *kayals,* through which much of the life of the Malayalee has historically flowed. From the vastness of Vembanad Lake to quiet streams just large enough for a canoe, the backwaters have carried Kerala's largely coconut-based products from village to market for centuries, and continue to do so today. You can relax at some of Kerala's finest resorts, or briefly join the floating lifestyle by taking a boat cruise.

The terrain rises and the temperature drops as you move inland, up into the teak-forested hills of Thekkady and Munnar. Kerala's interior is elephant country—you'll find them roaming in Lake Periyar Wildlife Sanctuary and even appearing in the mists of Munnar's tea plantations.

KUMARAKOM

80 km (50 miles) south of Kochi.

Some of Kerala's finest resorts are hidden in this tiny, rapidly developing paradise on the shores of Vembanad Lake. Novelist Arundhati Roy's birthplace, Ayemenem (featured in her 1997 novel *The God of Small Things)* is close by. Birds abound in the backwaters, as well as in the sanctuary on the lake's eastern shore.

WHERE TO EAT AND STAY

For expanded hotel reviews, visit Fodors.com.

$ ECLECTIC 🍴 **Lakshmi Hotel.** If you want a change of pace from your resort's dining room, the restaurant of this locally owned hotel offers reliable local fare along with North Indian specialties, though the menu is not lengthy. Service is leisurely, but the food is freshly prepared and the air-conditioned dining room is clean and comfortable. The restaurant is known for its Karimeen fish wrapped in a banana leaf and its traditional vegetable *thali*, which includes 10 items for Rs. 60. [$] *Average main: Rs. 70* ✉ *Kottayam–Kumarakom Rd., Kumarakom North* ☎ *481/252–3313.*

$$ HOTEL 🏨 **Abad Whispering Palms.** In a natural backwater on the banks of Vembanadu Lake, this hotel combines natural beauty and tranquillity with modern conveniences. **Pros:** friendly and helpful staff; nice views; well priced **Cons:** rooms need an upgrade. [$] *Rooms from: Rs. 5000* ✉ *New Nazarath Rd., Kumarakom* ☎ *481/252–3820* 🌐 *abadhotels.com/lakeresort* 🛏 *53 rooms* 🍽 *Breakfast.*

$$$$ RESORT ★ 🏨 **Coconut Lagoon.** This ground-breaking and much-imitated Vembanad Lake resort put Kerala's backwaters on the map. **Pros:** good restaurants; kid-friendly; staff naturalists can take guests on a tour of the local bird sanctuary and the hotel's small butterfly garden. **Cons:** the pricey two-story mansions have bathroom and bedrooms on different floors (opt for the one-level bungalow); can only be accessed by boat. [$] *Rooms from: Rs. 13500* ✉ *Vembanad Lake* ☎ *481/252–4491* 🌐 *www.cghearth.com* 🛏 *42 rooms, 8 suites* 🍽 *Some meals.*

$$$ RESORT Fodor's Choice ★ 🏨 **Kumarakom Lake Resort.** In the heritage section of this beautiful 25-acre lakefront property, palatial traditional villas, reassembled from old houses, are set around a network of canals. **Pros:** amazing 820-foot meandering pool; gorgeous setting; large and varied buffet. **Cons:** pricey. [$] *Rooms from: Rs. 9500* ✉ *Kumarakom North P.O.* ☎ *481/252–4900, 1800/425–5030* 🌐 *www.kumarakomlakeresort.in* 🛏 *66 rooms* 🍽 *Breakfast.*

$$$$ RESORT 🏨 **Taj by Vivanta Kumarakom.** The main building of this tranquil, verdant resort is an 1891 plantation house, built by the son of an English missionary. **Pros:** trees are populated by winged residents of the nearby bird sanctuary; nice pool-facing gym; plenty of activities for children. **Cons:** not as carefully maintained as other Taj properties—the central lake, for example, has a stagnant green tinge; pricey. [$] *Rooms from: Rs. 18000* ☎ *481/252–5711* 🌐 *www.vivantabytaj.com* 🛏 *28 rooms* 🍽 *Breakfast.*

$$$$ RESORT ★ 🏨 **Zuri Kumarakom Resort and Spa.** The four-headed statue of a Kathakali dancer in the gleaming lobby, the boat-shape check-in desk, and the backwater setting all locate the property soundly in Kerala; but guests checked into this luxurious resort can easily forget where they are as they indulge in the decidedly untraditional couples massage or relax with a Havana stogie in the cigar bar. **Pros:** enormous modern spa has both ayurvedic and Western treatments. **Cons:** room and massage rates among the highest in South India; look elsewhere if you want a Kerala experience. [$] *Rooms from: Rs. 13857* ✉ *Karottukayal, Kumarokom* ☎ *481/252–7272* 🌐 *www.thezurihotels.com/kumarakom* 🛏 *72 rooms* 🍽 *Breakfast.*

ON THE BACKWATERS

houseboat cruise. A houseboat cruise provides a window into traditional local life. Shaded by a woven bamboo canopy and fanned by cool breezes, you can drift past simple, tile-roof houses with canoes moored outside; tiny waterfront churches; and people washing themselves, their clothes, their dishes, and their children in the river. Women in bright pink-and-blue dresses stroll past green paddy fields, their waist-length hair unbound and smelling of coconut oil. Graceful palms are every-where, as are village walls painted with political slogans and ads for computer-training courses. Backwa-ter trips can be designed to suit any time constraint or budget. Motorized or punted canoes squeeze into nar-row canals, taking you to dreamy roadless villages, and big ferries ply the eight-hour Quilon–Alleppey route as if it were a major highway. Romantic houseboats give you the opportunity to stay overnight on the water; there's even an Oberoi luxury cruise ship offering every imaginable comfort. Any travel agent, hotel, or the Kerala Tourism Development Corporation (KTDC) (☎ *484/235–3234,* ⊕ *www.ktdc. com*), can help you hire a private boat or plan a trip. Most cruises depart from Quilon, Alleppey, or Kumarakom. In addition, the Trident Hilton in Kochi can book you a stateroom on the MV *Vrinda*, an eight-bedroom luxury cruise ship.

ALLEPPEY

35 km (22 miles) southwest of Kumarakom.

This coir-manufacturing city was once known as the Venice of India, though most residents have abandoned their canoes for cars. Alleppey (Alappuzha) is an important gateway to the backwaters—tour opera-tors abound, and several resorts here offer a good alternative to the pricier properties in Kumarakom.

On the second Saturday in August throngs of supporters line the shore to watch the annual Nehru Cup Snake Boat Race, which starts with a water procession and concludes dramatically as the boats (propelled by as many as 100 rowers) vie for the trophy. Several snake-boat races take place in the area from mid-July to mid-September. Check with the Alleppey Tour-ism Development Cooperative (ATDC) for exact times and locations.

WHERE TO STAY

For expanded hotel reviews, visit Fodors.com.

$$$$
HOTEL
A Beach Symphony. Each of these private cottages, in a beach garden with coconut palms, has a spacious veranda where all meals are served, and some have their own private swimming pool (the others share a pool). **Pros:** high levels of privacy; cottages have Wi-Fi. **Cons:** gets booked up fast; spa needs soundproofing; Marari Beach is not pristine. **$** *Rooms from: Rs. 11500* ⊠ *Marari Beach Rd., Alleppey* ☎ *97/4429–7123* ⊕ *www.abeachsymphony.com* ⨾ *4 cottages* ⊚| *Some meals.*

$$$
RESORT
Kayaloram Heritage Lake Resort. Just steps from the waterfront, this is a pleasant, small-scale heritage resort consisting of four buildings surrounded by a common veranda. **Pros:** quiet, intimate environment.

8

Cons: no TV; a/c is only on at night. $ *Rooms from: Rs. 6100* ⊠ *Punnamada* ☏ *477/223–2040* ⊕ *www.mirresorts.in/kayaloram-lake-resort-alleppey.html* ↝ *12 rooms* ¶○¶ *Breakfast.*

$ ⛨ **Keraleeyam.** This quaint waterfront property specializes in ayurvedic
B&B/INN   treatments. **Pros:** inexpensive; pretty location; great deals on all-inclusive ayurvedic packages. **Cons:** very basic; spotty service; no television or Internet. $ *Rooms from: Rs. 1512* ⊠ *Thathampally* ☏ *477/223–1468, 477/223–6950* ⊕ *www.keraleeyam.com* ↝ *13 rooms* ¶○¶ *Breakfast.*

$$$$ ⛨ **Marari Beach.** With a private and unspoilt palm-fringed beach, an excel-
RESORT   lent ayurvedic center, and easy access to both Kochi and the backwa-
★   ters, Marari packs a lot of Kerala into one bundle. **Pros:** spacious rooms; friendly and professional staff; tennis courts. **Cons:** no TVs; beach is closed during monsoons. $ *Rooms from: Rs. 13000* ⊠ *Mararikulam* ☏ *478/286–3801* ⊕ *www.cghearth.com* ↝ *59 rooms, 3 suites* ¶○¶ *Breakfast.*

$$$$ ⛨ **Marari Villas.** On the secluded Marari beach—thought to be one of
RESORT   Kerala's finest—this select group of villas is run by a European couple who found a gap in the private hospitality market: each villa has its own butler and chef. **Pros:** private setting on the beach; super-attentive service. **Cons:** lacks the functionality of a hotel. $ *Rooms from: Rs. 10000* ⊠ *Marari Beach, Pollathai* ☏ *994/794–8707* ⊕ *www.mararivillas.com* ↝ *4 villas* ¶○¶ *Breakfast.*

$ ⛨ **Palm Grove Lake Resort.** Simplicity rules the day at this coconut planta-
RESORT   tion hideaway near the starting point of the Nehru Cup Snake Boat Race. **Pros:** large, clean rooms. **Cons:** no a/c in most rooms. $ *Rooms from: Rs. 1650* ⊠ *Punnamada* ☏ *477/223–5004, 477/224–3474* 🖷 *477/225–1138* ⊕ *www.palmgrovelakeresort.com* ↝ *6 cottages* ¶○¶ *Some meals.*

$$$ ⛨ **Punnamada Backwater Resort.** Small design details and a recent reno-
RESORT   vation make this typical backwater resort sparkle, and four lake-view rooms with private patios are just steps from the water. **Pros:** beautiful lake views; relatively good value. **Cons:** secluded location may be too quiet for some; no Internet in rooms. $ *Rooms from: Rs. 9300* ⊠ *Punnamada Jetty Rd.* ☏ *477/223–3690, 477/223–3692* ⊕ *www.punnamada.com* ↝ *26 rooms* ¶○¶ *Breakfast.*

QUILON

71 km (44 miles) north of Trivandrum; 87 km (54 miles) south of Alleppey.

If you're coming up from Trivandrum, central Kerala starts here, with the peaceful waters of eight-armed Ashtamudi Lake. You can catch a ferry from Quilon (Kollam) in the morning and reach Alleppey eight hours later. The waterfront here is not nearly as developed as Vembanad Lake, and the few resorts are utterly peaceful and reasonably priced.

WHERE TO STAY

For expanded hotel reviews, visit Fodors.com.

$$ ⛨ **Aquaserene.** The gorgeous lakeside setting, the private beach, and
RESORT   the total backwater experience will quickly help you forget the bumpy
☾   ride that got you here, on a barely paved road through a fishing vil-
lage. **Pros:** room rates typically include an early-morning fishing trip, guided village cycling tours, and a half-hour boat ride; many amenities

A houseboat on the backwaters

for youngsters, including volleyball, table tennis and a children's park. **Cons:** a bit too remote for some. $ *Rooms from: Rs. 5750* ✉ *South Paravoor* ☏ *474/251–2410 to 17* ⊕ *www.aquasereneindia.com* ⟳ *27 rooms, 1 suite* ⎮⦿⎮ *Breakfast.*

$$$
HOTEL 🏨 **Club Mahindra Backwater Retreat.** Ayurveda is the focus of this soothing resort on the shores of Ashtamudi Lake, but even without undergoing treatment, you can expect to find peace here, where Chinese fishing nets flicker like a mirage in the morning mists that rise off the silvery lake. **Pros:** plenty of activities for children, including clay modeling and video games. **Cons:** no gym; no bar. $ *Rooms from: Rs. 7500* ✉ *Chavara South* ☏ *476/288–2310, 476/288–2357, 476/288–2655* ⊕ *www. clubmahindra.com* ⟳ *22 rooms, 3 suites* ⎮⦿⎮ *Breakfast.*

THEKKADY

130 km (81 miles) east of Kumarakom.

Due east of Kumarakom and Kottayam, this cool mountain town sits at 3,000 feet above sea level in the Cardamom Hills, midway between Kochi and the temple city of Madurai in Tamil Nadu. ■**TIP**➔ **You don't need a room with air-conditioning here.**

★ **Lake Periyar Wildlife Sanctuary.** In the vicinity of Thekkady, the Lake Periyar Wildlife Sanctuary is one of India's best animal parks for spotting elephants, bison, wild boar, oxen, deer, and many species of birds. The best viewing period is October through May.

Lake Periyar, its many fingers winding around low-lying hills, is the heart of the 300-square-mile sanctuary. Forget exhausting treks or long safaris: here, you lounge in a motor launch as it drifts around bends and comes upon animals drinking at the shores. In dry season, when forest watering holes are empty, leopards and tigers also pad up to the water. ■ **TIP→ Be prepared: Indian children (and adults) love to scream and shout at wildlife sightings.** On a quiet trip, elephants hardly notice the intrusion, although younger pachyderms will peer at you out of curiosity and then run squealing back to their elders when your boat comes too close. If you're brave-hearted, you can spend a night in a jungle lodge (if you go on a forest trek, look out for leeches on the ground, especially during the monsoon); if you're less adventurous you can commune with nature from the safety of a moated watchtower. Half-hour elephant rides are also available. For information about treks and the park, contact the Kerala Tourism Development Corporation (KTDC; ✉ *Shanmugham Rd., Ernakulam, Kochi;* ☎ *484/235–3234*). 🌐 *www.ktdc.com* 🎫 *Boat safaris: Rs. 150; video camera charge: Rs. 100* 🕒 *Boat safaris: daily at 7, 9:30, 11:30, 2, and 3:30; book one day in advance with KTDC or at the boat landing point in Thekkady.*

WHERE TO STAY

For expanded hotel reviews, visit Fodors.com.

$$ HOTEL 👶 🏨 **Aranya Nivas.** One of only two hotels that are actually inside the Periyar Tiger Reserve (the other is the luxurious Lake Palace), Aranya Nivas is a former hunting lodge with a location that enables guests to closely interact with wildlife. **Pros:** superb location for viewing wildlife; good standard of service. **Cons:** entry into the resort is possible only between 6 am and 6 pm; rooms need an upgrade. [$] *Rooms from: Rs. 4100* ✉ *Thekkady* ☎ *486/922–2023* 🌐 *www.aranyanivasthekkady.com* 🛏 *30 rooms* 🍴 *Some meals.*

$$$ HOTEL 👶 🏨 **Club Mahindra Tusker Trails.** On a former coffee plantation, this woodsy Club Mahindra property offers concrete cottages raised on stilts; balconies are nice touches, as is the thatch piled on the roofs. **Pros:** good location and restaurant; cottages have private terraces; has plenty of activities geared toward children. **Cons:** room interiors need renovation. [$] *Rooms from: Rs. 8900* ✉ *Ambalambika Rd.* ☎ *486/922–2273, 486/922–2401 to 07* 🌐 *www.clubmahindra.com* 🛏 *49 rooms* 🍴 *Some meals.*

$$$$ HOTEL 🏨 **Hotel Lake Palace.** A ferry transports you to this former maharaja's hunting lodge on an island inside the Lake Periyar Wildlife Sanctuary, where you can spot wildlife from your balcony. **Pros:** the best lodge in Thekkady for watching wildlife; all meals included in tariff. **Cons:** very basic accommodations; no safe in rooms. [$] *Rooms from: Rs. 23000* ✉ *Lake Periyar Wildlife Sanctuary* ☎ *486/232–2023* 🌐 *www.lakepalacethekkady.com* 🛏 *6 rooms* 🍴 *All meals.*

$$$ RESORT 👶 🏨 **Muthoot Cardamom County.** Views from this steeply pitched resort are gorgeous and on the grounds there's a fishpond where you can catch your own dinner. **Pros:** great ayurvedic massage center with a well-trained doctor; large swimming pool. **Cons:** fills up with package tourists; can be noisy. [$] *Rooms from: Rs. 10000* ✉ *Thekkady Rd.* ☎ *486/922–4501 to 03* 🛏 *42 rooms, 2 suites* 🍴 *Breakfast.*

$$$ RESORT ★ 🏨 **Shalimar Spice Garden.** This rustic retreat is 20 bone-jarring minutes off the main road to Thekkady, but once there the emphasis is on serenity and relaxation; most guests come for ayurvedic treatment and

yoga. **Pros:** gorgeous setting; rooms include complimentary slippers and heaters. **Cons:** remote; rooms are somewhat small. [$] *Rooms from: Rs. 10000* ✉ *Murikkady* ☎ *486/922–2132, 486/922–3232* 🌐 *www.shalimarkerala.net* ⇆ *20 rooms* 🍴 *Breakfast.*

$$$ RESORT Fodor's Choice ★ 🏨 **Spice Village.** Just outside the Lake Periyar Wildlife Sanctuary, this is not only Thekkady's finest resort, with top-notch service, it is also eco-friendly, running on solar energy and recycling all its waste within the premises. **Pros:** plenty of activities; good location; oxidized, chlorine-free pool. **Cons:** easy to get lost in this large resort. [$] *Rooms from: Rs. 8500* ✉ *Kummily Rd.* ☎ *486/922–2314, 486/922–2315* 🌐 *www.cghearth.com* ⇆ *52 rooms* 🍴 *Breakfast.*

MUNNAR

100 km (62 miles) north of Thekkady; 130 km (80 miles) east of Kochi.

On the drive from Thekkady to Munnar, a good road winds through lofty forests as well as spice and tea plantations. The town of Munnar itself is small and unattractive. However, most of the land around it is owned by the Tata tea company and a few smaller concerns, resulting in a kind of unspoiled hill station, with hundreds of acres of tea, coffee, and cardamom plantations amid hills, lakes, streams, and waterfalls. During your visit you can tour these plantations; arrange trekking, rock-climbing, paragliding, and river trips; or just sit on your hotel balcony with a cup of tea, taking in the scenery.

Most lodgings can arrange a tea plantation tour, where you can walk through the steeply pitched, dense green hedges, and see how the leaf is processed. (Historically, the dregs of the batch get shipped to America, although this has been changing in recent years.) Cardamom plantations are just this side of heaven. The shade-loving spice needs plenty of forest cover, so a walk through a plantation feels like a stroll in the woods, complete with dappled sunlight, mountain streams, and birdsong. It's quite cool here, so you don't need to find a hotel with air-conditioning.

Rajamala Wildlife Sanctuary. This park, 15 km (9 miles) northwest of Munnar, is home to the endangered nilgiri tahr. You can get close to this endearingly tame mountain goat, pushed to the brink of extinction by its utter lack of suspicion toward human beings. Half the world's remaining population lives here. ■ **TIP→ The sanctuary is closed for 45 days during the calving season, roughly from January to February (check ahead of time).** ✉ *Evarikulam National Park, Idukki District* ☎ *486/523–0460* 🌐 *www.ktdc.com* 🎟 *Rs. 200* 🕒 *Daily 8–5.*

WHERE TO STAY

For expanded hotel reviews, visit Fodors.com.

$$ HOTEL ALL-INCLUSIVE 👶 🏨 **Camp Noel.** Known for its stunning views, tranquil surrounding, and warm hospitality, Camp Noel is tucked away on 15 acres of grassland. **Pros:** friendly and helpful staff. **Cons:** difficult to get to; amenities are basic. [$] *Rooms from: Rs. 5500* ✉ *Pazhathottam, Koviloor, 30 km (18 miles) west of central Munnar, Munnar* ☎ *85/9050–7050* ⇆ *20 rooms* 🍴 *All-inclusive.*

8

Picking tea leaves

$$$ 🏨 **Club Mahindra Lakeview.** Set between a mountain peak and a tea
HOTEL plantation, this large, family-oriented resort has guest quarters in the
main building or in hillside cottages. **Pros:** clean; modern facilities;
good value. **Cons:** no Internet in rooms; a bit noisy when tour groups
roll in; breakfast not included. $ *Rooms from: Rs. 9000* ✉ *22 km (14
miles) east of Munnar, Chinnakanal Village* ☎ *486/824–9290* ⊕ *www.
clubmahindra.com* ➽ *120 rooms* ⊙ *No meals.*

$$ 🏨 **Kaivalyam Retreat.** This is essentially a yoga retreat run by a couple
B&B/INN who are both instructors and, with 11 scenic acres of vegetation and
tea plantations, it certainly sets the scene for a holistic, organic lifestyle.
Pros: nice views; eco-friendly. **Cons:** service is slow; can get noisy with
families around. $ *Rooms from: Rs. 4000* ✉ *Pallivasal Estate, opposite
Workers Recreation Center, Moolakada,, Munnar* ☎ *94/9582–1617*
⊕ *kaivalyamretreat.com* ➽ *8 rooms* ⊙ *All meals.*

$$ 🏨 **Siena Village.** Some of the rooms at this hotel capture the country-
HOTEL lodge feeling perfectly—ignore the single-story standard rooms and
opt for a split-level deluxe one. **Pros:** outdoor buffet with musical
performances and campfire during high season; play area and play
room for children. **Cons:** rooms are basic. $ *Rooms from: Rs. 4750*
✉ *22 km (14 miles) east of Munnar, Chinnakanal* ☎ *486/824–9461,
486/824–9261* ⊕ *www.thesienavillage.com* ➽ *26 rooms, 2 suites*
⊙ *Some meals.*

$$$ 🏨 **The Tall Trees.** You can hardly spot the wood-and-stone structures of
HOTEL this hushed, breezy resort on a 66-acre cardamom plantation where
the views are of trees, trees, and more trees. **Pros:** large rooms; hotel
arranges lots of activities. **Cons:** tiring walk uphill to the restaurant;
a lot to pay for relatively basic accommodations. $ *Rooms from: Rs.*

6400 ✉ *Bison Valley Rd.* ☎ *986/523–0641, 986/523–0593, 986/523–2716* 🌐 *www.ttr.in* 🛏 *16 rooms, 3 suites* 🍴 *Some meals.*

$$$ HOTEL 🏨 **Windermere Estate.** Plantation life can be pretty darn good, especially when you're not working in the fields and are instead made to feel like the guest of a planter, either in one of the five bedrooms of the main guesthouse, which has a communal balcony, or in an individual cottage. **Pros:** service is warm and personalized; great views. **Cons:** basic amenities, with no bar and no safe in rooms; pricey. [$] *Rooms from: Rs. 10000* ✉ *Pothamedu* ☎ *484/242–5237 reservations, 486/523–0512* 🌐 *www.windermeremunnar.com* 🛏 *18 rooms* 🍴 *Some meals.*

LAKSHADWEEP

250 km (160 miles) off the coast of Kerala.

Of the 36 or so coral atolls that make up the isolated paradise of Lakshadweep, only about 10 are inhabited, and their population is devoutly Sunni Muslim. Tourism here is severely restricted to protect the fragile ecosystems and the traditional peoples. If you don't have an Indian passport, your visit will be limited to Agatti, Kadmat, or Bangaram Island, each of which has one resort property. (You need to obtain a government entry permit with passport details.)

Crystal waters and soft sands are Lakshadweep's main attraction; all resorts offer water sports, and there's even a scuba diving school on Kadmat Island.

Society for the Promotion of Recreational Tourism and Sports (*SPORTS*). Trips to Lakshadweep can only be arranged through the Society for the Promotion of Recreational Tourism and Sports, which runs tours from October to May. Foreign tourists are not allowed in Kavaratti and SPORTS arranges the Special Permit for tourists to visit the other two main islands. The accommodations at the beach hotels there are basic at best. ✉ *Harbour Rd., Willingdon Island, Kochi* ☎ *484/266–8387, 484/266–8647* 🌐 *www.lakshadweeptourism.com.*

SOUTHERN KERALA

The beaches near Kovalam are southern Kerala's main attraction—in fact, they're what brought Western tourists to the state in the first place, as the hippie scene from Goa moved down the coast. Parts of Kovalam are overdeveloped and full of touts selling cheap tie-dye clothes. There are, however, still some pleasant spots to relax within a few miles of the main beach. Just a half hour from Kovalam is Kerala's capital city of Trivandrum (Thiruvanandapuram), former home of the rajas of Travancore and now home to Kerala's primary international airport.

TRIVANDRUM

222 km (138 miles) south of Kochi; 253 km (157 miles) southwest of Thekkady.

Built on seven low hills and cleansed by ocean breezes, Kerala's capital is surprisingly calm and pleasant. Trivandrum's few sights and quiet lanes outside the town center make it an enjoyable place to spend the day.

EXPLORING

Kuthiramalika (Puthenmalika) Palace Museum. The 18th-century Kuthiramalika (Puthenmalika) Palace Museum, or Horse Palace, has carved rosewood ceilings and treasures of the royal family, including an ivory throne, weapons, paintings, and gifts from foreign dignitaries. Lifesize Kathakali figures stand in the dance room. Carved horses, for which the palace is named, line the eaves of an inner courtyard. Only one-third of the enormous compound is open to visitors; the entrance fee includes a knowledgeable guide. Also note that you must remove your shoes upon entering. ⊠ *next to Padmanabhaswamy Temple, East Fort* ☎ *471/247–3952* ⊠ *Palace: Rs. 20; shoe-storage charge Rs. 1* ☉ *Tues.–Sun. 8:30–12:45 and 3–4:45.*

Museum and Art Gallery Complex. In an 80-acre park at the north end of M. G. Road are the many attractions of the Museum and Art Gallery Complex. Buy your ticket at the Natural History Museum, a musty collection of animal skeletons, dioramas, and stuffed birds, then head straight to the second floor to see an interesting model of a traditional *nalakettu* home (the traditional home of the Nairs, a warrior clan), complete with costumed figurines and a full explanation. The art museum's collection of local arts and crafts—including bronze and stone sculptures and musical instruments—is as noteworthy as the building itself, with its Cubist pattern of gables and its decorative interior. Memorabilia donated by the royal family, including a golden chariot used by the Maharaja of Travancore, is displayed in the tiny Sree Chitra Enclave. On the opposite side of the park, the Sree Chitra Art Gallery has an eclectic collection of paintings, including works of the Rajput, Mogul, and Tanjore schools; copies of the Ajanta and Sigirya frescoes; and works from China, Japan, Tibet, and Bali, along with canvases by modern Indian painters. ⊠ *Museum Rd.* ☎ *471/231–8294* ⊠ *Rs. 10* ☉ *Tues. and Thurs.–Sun. 10–4:30, Wed. 1–4:30.*

Padmanabhaswamy Temple. The handsome Padmanabhaswamy Temple, dedicated to Vishnu, has a seven-story *gopuram* (entrance tower). The date of its original construction has been placed at 3000 BC; legend has it that it was built by 4,000 masons, 6,000 laborers, and 100 elephants over the course of six months. In the main courtyard there's intricate granite sculpture, supplemented by more stonework on the nearly 400 pillars supporting the temple corridors. The complex is technically open only to Hindus and keeps erratic hours, so call ahead to be assured of at least a glimpse. ⊠ *M. G. Rd., at Chali Bazaar* ☎ *471/245–0233* ☉ *Daily 8–10, 10:30–11:15 and 5:15–6:15.*

OFF THE BEATEN PATH

Vijnana Kala Vedi Cultural Center. About 120 km (75 miles) north of Trivandrum, this institute, established by a French woman in 1977, is dedicated to preserving the arts and heritage of Kerala. People from all over the world come to study everything from singing to cooking to language with experienced masters in a simple village atmosphere. You can choose to give back by participating in a volunteer program to teach English in a local school. Short stays are available for Rs. 1600 per night. A one-week stay is Rs. 12,000, all-inclusive; there are discounts for longer stays. ⊠ *Tarayil Mukku Junction, Aranmula* ☎ *468/221– 4483, 468/231–0451* ⊕ *www.vijnanakalavedi.org.*

WHERE TO EAT AND STAY

For expanded hotel reviews, visit Fodors.com.

$
INDIAN

✕ **Azad.** The food won't disappoint here, even if the interior isn't much to look at. Specialties include *biryani,* a flavorful rice cooked with chicken or mutton, and *kuthu paratha,* a Kerala Muslim delicacy of flat bread stuffed with minced fish. Azad has become a chain, but this, the original restaurant in East Fort, is probably the best. $ *Average main: Rs. 150* ⊠ *M. G. Rd., East Fort* ☎ *471/247–2895.*

$
INDIAN

✕ **Hotel Aryaas.** There's nothing fancy here—just simple, tasty, vegetarian food like *amma* (mom) would make. The air-conditioned restaurant is comfortable and clean, and menu options range from soups and salads to french fries. Opt for the traditional *thali,* a meal of rice and vegetable accompaniments—one extra-special thali comes with a whopping 18 dishes. $ *Average main: Rs. 100* ⊠ *Subramaniam Rd.* ☎ *471/233–8999* ▭ *No credit cards.*

$
ECLECTIC

✕ **Orion.** Although it offers a variety of cuisines, this restaurant has acquired a reputation with locals for its traditional Indian dishes. The lunchtime South Indian buffet features such Kerala specialties as *elisseri* (pumpkin with red beans), *avial* (mixed vegetables in a mild coconut gravy), and fish curry. $ *Average main: Rs. 250* ⊠ *The Residency Tower, Press Rd.* ☎ *471/233–1661.*

$
HOTEL

▨ **South Park.** One of Trivandrum's premier hotels, the South Park has recently been renovated, including the replacement of carpets with wood floors, among other improvements. **Pros:** good location; affordable; in-room Wi-Fi. **Cons:** large and impersonal; on a noisy street. $ *Rooms from: Rs. 2900* ⊠ *Spencer Junction, M. G. Rd.* ☎ *471/233– 3333* ⊕ *www.fortunehotels.in* ⤴ *76* ⅋ *Breakfast.*

SHOPPING

Most shops are closed Sunday, and smaller shops occasionally shut down for a few hours at lunchtime on weekdays.

The Craft Shop. For crafts from all over India, head to The Craft Shop. ⊠ *G. A. K Rd., off M. G. Rd.* ☎ *471/232–3335.*

Karalkada. Weavers for Travancore's royal family sell traditional Kerala saris (made of plain white cotton) at Karalkada. ⊠ *Kaithamukku Junction* ☎ *471/247–2932.*

Natesan's. This is a respected art and antiques dealer. ⊠ *M. G. Rd.* ☎ *471/233–1594* ⊗ *Closed Sun.*

SMSM. For Kerala handicrafts and souvenirs, hit this government emporium. ⊠ *Statue Junction, off M. G. Rd.* ☎ *471/233–1668.*

KOVALAM

16 km (10 miles) south of Trivandrum.

Kovalam's sandy beaches are lined with palm-fringed lagoons and rocky coves. Fishermen in *lungis* (colorful cloth wraps) drag in nets filled with the day's catch, then push their slender wooden boats out again with a Malayalam "Heave ho." Here you can spend the day loafing on warm sand or rocky outcroppings, watch the sun set, then sit back as the dim lights of distant fishing boats come on. In peak season, outdoor eateries spring up right on the beach—just point to the fish of your choice and specify how you'd like it prepared. **■ TIP→ Be sure to find out how much it's going to cost—a little discreet bargaining might be in order.**

Overdevelopment had nearly ruined Kovalam, but it's experiencing something of a revival, with luxury hotel groups like the Leela coming to the area. The main beach, Lighthouse, has been cleaned up; the concrete promenade is lined with shops, restaurants, and budget hotels. It's well lighted at night, allowing for a pleasant evening stroll as well as some semblance of nightlife. For peace and solitude, however, stick to the secluded beaches in villages to the north and south of Kovalam town.

OFF THE BEATEN PATH

Padmanabhapuram Fort and Palace. Believed to be the largest wooden palace in Asia, this magnificiant, 18th-century, carved-teak palace is actually across the border in neighboring Tamil Nadu, about a 1½-hour (63 km [39 miles]) drive south of Kovalam on National Highway 47. Once the home of the Travancore rajas (Travancore was the southernmost state, which was combined with Cochin and Malabar to form Kerala), it's one of the best-preserved examples of old wooden architecture in India. ✉ *Thuckalay, Kanyakumari, Tamil Nadu* 🌐 *www.ktdc.com* ⏲ *Tues.–Sun. 9–4:30.*

WHERE TO EAT AND STAY

For expanded hotel reviews, visit Fodors.com.

$$ INDIAN — 🍴 **Hotel Rockholm Restaurant.** What might be Kovalam's best chef prepares excellent international and local dishes. Try the seasonal seafood dishes, such as fried mussels or prawns Kerala-style, which are cooked in coconut oil with a variety of spices. You can eat indoors or on a terrace overlooking the ocean. [$] *Average main: Rs. 400* ✉ *Lighthouse Rd.* ☎ *471/248–0406, 471/248–0407.*

$ RESORT — 🏨 **Beach & Lake.** Sandwiched between the roar of the Arabian Sea and the ripple of a backwater lagoon, this basic resort north of Kovalam—accessible only by boat—has ayurvedic treatments and plenty of quiet as its main draws. **Pros:** cheap; gorgeous views; friendly staff. **Cons:** can only be reached by boat; basic accommodations; few eating options near the hotel. [$] *Rooms from: Rs. 2145* ✉ *Pozhikkara Beach, Pachalloor Village* ☎ *471/238–2086* 🌐 *www.beachandlakeresort.com* 🛏 *19 rooms* 🍽 *Breakfast.*

$$ HOTEL — 🏨 **Coconut Bay.** In an undeveloped area about 2 km (1 mile) south of Kovalam, this 3-acre property has a secluded beach and ayurvedic center. **Pros:** large, comfortable beds. **Cons:** no bathtubs. [$] *Rooms from: Rs. 5700* ✉ *Mulloor* ☎ *471/248–0566, 471/248–0668, 471/248–4566* 🌐 *www.coconutbay.com* 🛏 *27 rooms* 🍽 *Breakfast.*

A temple in Trivandrum

$ RESORT 🏨 **Ideal Ayurvedic Resort.** This small, homey resort south of Kovalam has specialized in ayurvedic treatment since 1997. **Pros:** friendly staff; little to distract guests from their treatment. **Cons:** few amenities; not on the beach. [$] *Rooms from: Rs. 1700* ✉ *Just before Somatheeram, Chowara* ☎📠 *471/226–8632* 🌐 *www.idealayurvedicresort.com* 🛏 *30* 🍴 *Some meals.*

$$$$ RESORT 🏨 **The Leela Kempinski Kovalam Beach Resort.** Once run by the government, the best-sited property in Kovalam recently completed a major renovation under the Kempinski Hotels group. **Pros:** spectacular views; private beach area; good ayurvedic center. **Cons:** pricey; getting to the bars and restaurants on Lighthouse Beach requires a bit of a walk. [$] *Rooms from: Rs. 11000* ☎ *471/248–0101* 🌐 *www.theleela.com* 🛏 *178 rooms, 2 suites* 🍴 *All meals.*

$$ HOTEL 🏨 **Manaltheeram.** Quieter and even closer to the water than its neighboring sister property, Somatheeram Beach Resort, Manaltheeram has rooms in simple, circular brick cottages that are neatly arrayed on ascending terraces. **Pros:** quiet, exclusive beachfront; some restaurant tables set up on the beach. **Cons:** ayurveda being offered is below average; a little short on amenities. [$] *Rooms from: Rs. 4000* ✉ *Chowara* ☎ *471/226–6222* 🌐 *www.manaltheeram.com* 🛏 *61 rooms* 🍴 *Some meals.*

$ HOTEL 🏨 **Neelakanta.** This beachfront budget hotel, a low-rise building right on Kovalam's main drag, is popular with foreigners. **Pros:** beach views. **Cons:** building looks a bit shabby. [$] *Rooms from: Rs. 3300* ✉ *Lighthouse Beach* ☎ *471/248–0321, 471/248–6004* 🌐 *www.hotelneelakantakovalam.com* 🛏 *28 rooms, 6 suites* 🍴 *No meals.*

$$ HOTEL **Nikki's Nest.** Among bougainvillea, coconut palms, banana trees, orchids, and acacia are thatch-roof, circular cottages and traditional wooden houses, most with commanding sea views. **Pros:** great hilltop beach views **Cons:** uphill walk to the hotel from the beach. [$] *Rooms from: Rs. 5000* ✉ *Azhimala Shiva Temple Rd., Chowara* ☎ *471/226–8822, 471/226–8821* 🌐 *www.nikkisnest.com* 🛏 *47 rooms* 🍴 *Breakfast.*

$$ RESORT **Somatheeram Ayurvedic Health Resort.** Stress-free Westerners in green robes roam the winding pathways of this popular ayurvedic beach resort. **Pros:** plenty of activities, including yoga and meditation. **Cons:** smallish, basic rooms. [$] *Rooms from: Rs. 4860* ✉ *Chowara* ☎ *471/226–6501* 🌐 *www.somatheeram.org* 🛏 *66 rooms* 🍴 *Some meals.*

$$$$ RESORT Fodor's Choice ★ **Surya Samudra Private Retreats.** Overlooking the sea, this rambling resort has an exquisite beach, lovely views, and a great deal of peace (loud noise isn't permitted). **Pros:** great beach; some massive rooms; a don't-miss swimming pool cut out of rock with underwater sculptures. **Cons:** no television; no activities for children. [$] *Rooms from: Rs. 15000* ✉ *10 km (6 miles) south of Kovalam, Pulinkudi* ☎ *471/248–0413* 🌐 *www.suryasamudra.com* 🛏 *21 rooms, 4 suites* 🍴 *Breakfast.*

NORTHERN KERALA

If Kerala is unspoiled India, then Malabar—as the northern part of the state was once known—is unspoiled Kerala. Arab traders landed here long before Vasco da Gama, and many trading families converted to Islam. Various conquerors built forts along spectacular stretches of coastline, and some of Kerala's most unique and colorful religious festivals take place in this region. With the exception of the hill station of Wyanad, tourism has yet to make in-roads into the northern part of Kerala. Resorts, cruises, and sunbathing are almost unheard of. Nothing you see here has been prepackaged for your convenience, so making a visit to northern Kerala is a bit more work—but highly rewarding.

CALICUT

146 km (91 miles) northwest of Kochi.

This city doesn't hold much excitement in itself, but Calicut (Kozhikode) has an airport and is a good base for exploring several interesting sights nearby, including the lushly forested Wyanad district to the northeast. The city's historical ties with the Middle East are clearly apparent due to the strong Arab presence.

EXPLORING

Tasara Center for Creative Weaving. You can see weavers working on giant hand looms here, and Tasara also hosts programs for artists-in-residence. Call ahead to arrange a visit. ✉ *Beypore North, 10 km (6 miles) south of Calicut* ☎ *495/241–4832* 🌐 *www.tasaraindia.com* 🕒 *Mon.–Sat. 8:30–5 by appointment.*

Theeram Nature Conservation Society. A group of local fishermen started the Theeram Nature Conservation Society when they discovered that the Olive Ridley turtles they'd been eating were an endangered species. The center and its small turtle hatchery are on the beach at Kolavippalam, near Payyoli, about 30 km (19 miles) north of Calicut and off National Highway 17. If you're lucky, you can catch female turtles arriving on the beach in November and December to lay their eggs, which hatch in January and February.

WHERE TO EAT AND STAY

For expanded hotel reviews, visit Fodors.com.

$ ECLECTIC 🍴 **Kingsbay.** The friendly owner's passion for food is much in evidence in this bungalow restaurant specializing in seafood. A rubber planter by profession, he offers a varied menu that encompasses other regional and national cuisines, including South Indian, North Indian, Thai, and continental. Most popular is the Squid and Prawn Masala Fry, while South Indian cuisine is represented by Kudla Dreams, a mixed platter of six seafood specialties from nearby Mangalore. You won't find many vegetarian dishes on the menu. This is predominantly a family restaurant for well-heeled locals and often hosts a lively crowd. Alcohol is not served. [$] *Average main: Rs. 250* ✉ *1414 Customs Rd., Vellayil, Calicut* ☎ *495/4054422.*

$ ECLECTIC 🍴 **Mezban.** In the heart of the city, in a business hotel, this modern and comfortable restaurant serves a range of local, Chinese and continental dishes, including squid *tawa peralan* (a dry curry prepared with numerous spices) and prawn biryani. Another favorite is the barbecued chicken, which is marinated with a spicy sauce. The restaurant does not serve alcohol, which is common in this largely Muslim part of Kerala. The place gets busy at dinner, especially on weekends, and as a result waiting time can vary. Mezban does not have the best service. [$] *Average main: Rs. 250* ✉ *Hotel Asma Tower, Mavoor Rd., Calicut* ☎ *495/408–8000* 🌐 *www.asmatower.com/restaurant.htm.*

$ INDIAN 🍴 **Paragon.** It's not much to look at, and it can get noisy when crowded, but this Calicut stalwart serves up tasty food. The chicken *biryani* is excellent, as is the unusual fried shrimp dish that goes very well with *parathas* (local type of bread). Other favorites include the prawn pepper fry and tamarind fish curry. [$] *Average main: Rs. 200* ✉ *Kannur Rd.* ☎ *495/276–1020, 495/276–7020* 🌐 *www.paragonrestaurant.net* 💳 *No credit cards.*

$ SOUTH INDIAN 🍴 **Zain's Hotel Restaurant.** Zain's hotel, close to the beach, is the place to go to for authentic Malabari cuisine—a brightly painted former home that has become one of Calicut's most popular restaurants. It's owned by a Kerala Moplah woman who not only prepares dishes to family recipes passed down through generations, but also creates innovative fusion dishes. With plastic chairs and tables laid out both indoors and outdoors, this is a no-fuss dining experience. The owner-chef Zainabi and her daughter Sherin, the dessert chef, are always there and are very hospitable. Go here for the biryani, *unnakkaya* (a sweet, banana- and coconut-based snack), mussel pie, and the different types of *pathiri* (North Kerala stuffed flatbreads). [$] *Average main: Rs. 100* ✉ *Convent crossroads, behind Tagore Centenary Hall, Calicut* ☎ *495/236–6331.*

Bekal Fort in North Kerala

$ HOTEL [H] **Fortune Hotel.** Slim wooden pillars encircle the pleasant lobby of this modern business hotel, and there's a beautiful terra-cotta-tile atrium with a traditional brass lamp. **Pros:** rooftop pool affords nice city views; mid-size rooms are comfortably furnished; Wi-Fi; great value. **Cons:** a little noisy; no safe in the rooms. [$] *Rooms from: Rs. 3000* ✉ *Kannur Rd.* ☎ *495/276–8888* 🌐 *www.fortunehotels.in* 🛏 *60 rooms, 3 suites* 🍴 *Breakfast.*

$$ HOTEL [H] **Gateway Hotel, Calicut.** Formerly the Taj Residency, Calicut's premier hotel is frequented by airline crews and wealthy Omanis, who come for lengthy treatments at the well-regarded ayurvedic center. **Pros:** great pool. **Cons:** smallish rooms; unremarkable by Taj standards. [$] *Rooms from: Rs. 4500* ✉ *P. T. Usha Rd.* ☎ *495/276–5354* 🌐 *www.thegatewayhotels.com* 🛏 *70 rooms, 4 suites* 🍴 *Breakfast.*

$$$ RESORT [H] **Kadavu.** One of the first swank, world-class riverside resorts in the Calicut area, Kadavu signaled Malabar's foray into tourism. **Pros:** stunning river views; good value. **Cons:** front-desk staff is less than proficient in English; 30-minute auto ride to Calicut. [$] *Rooms from: Rs. 6000* ✉ *Off N. H. Bypass, Azhinjilam, 18 km (11 miles) south of Calicut, Feroke* ☎ *483/283–0023, 483/283–0027* 🌐 *www.kadavuresorts.com* 🛏 *117 rooms* 🍴 *Breakfast.*

KANNUR

92 km (57 miles) northwest of Calicut.

The Kannur district is the heartland of the Moppilahs (Kerala's Muslim community). It's also a center for the hand-loom industry as well as the manufacture of *beedis,* potent hand-rolled cigarettes made from tobacco sweepings. The town itself was for many years at the center of the maritime spice trade. The ruling Kolathiri rajas profited from the spice trade as did the European colonists. Today Kannur is a good hub for visiting several coastal sights—to the north and the south—including forts and undeveloped beaches. Come quick, though; massive development in the works at Bekal could change everything in five years.

EXPLORING

Bekal Fort. The drive north from Kannur to Bekal, in the Kasargode district, is a dreamy trip through sleepy towns with nothing but coconut and rice fields in between. The largest fort in Kerala, Bekal Fort, covers more than over 40 seafront acres. The 300-year-old structure rises from a green lawn, and looks out over the Arabian Sea in one direction and distant coconut groves in the other. You can easily spend a peaceful hour or two clambering around the ruins. The loudest noise you'll hear is the crashing of the waves against the ramparts. A massive resort development project is planned in the area, however, with grandiose plans to one day turn Bekal into a top Asian tourist destination. The closest airport is Mangalore which is 60 km (37 miles) away. ⊠ *NH–17, 72 km (45 miles) north of Kannur, Bekal* ☎ *467/223–6580* 🖃 *Rs. 100 (non-Indians); Rs. 5 (Indians)* ⊙ *Daily 8:30–5:30.*

Fort St. Angelo. In 1505 the Portuguese built Fort St. Angelo, with the consent of the ruling Kolathiri Raja, in order to protect their interests in the area. After passing into Dutch and then British hands, it's now maintained by the Archaeological Survey of India. There are still a few British cannons intact, and lovely views of the fishing activity in Moppillah Bay. ⊠ *Off NH–17, 3 km (2 miles) north of Kannur* 🖃 *Free* ⊙ *Daily 8–6.*

Kanhirode Weaving Cooperative. The Kanhirode Weaving Cooperative is strewn with yarns of all colors, set out to dry after dyeing. You can watch the weavers at their giant, clackety-clacking looms, making bed sheets and upholstery for export as well as brightly colored saris. Cloth is available for purchase. ⊠ *Off Kannur–Mysore Rd., 13 km (8 miles) east of Kannur, Kanhirode* ☎ *497/285–7865* ⊕ *www.weaveco. com* 🖃 *Free* ⊙ *Mon.–Sat. 9–5:30.*

Sri Muthappan Temple. The unusual Sri Muthappan Temple sits on the bank of the Valapattanam River at Parassini Kaduvu. It's devoted to Lord Shiva in the form of a tribal hunter, and it hosts Theyyam performances almost every day of the year. Though it's not as colorful as traditional outdoor festivals, you can at least get a taste of Theyyam. As Sri Muthappan is usually pictured with a hunting dog, friendly mutts roam the sanctuary, and offerings at the shrine take the form of bronze dog figurines. ⊠ *Off NH–17, 18 km (11 miles) north of Kannur, Parassini* 🖃 *Free* ⊙ *Theyyams usually daily 5:30–8 am and 6:30–8 pm.*

★ **Theyyam.** A unique regional draw is the spectacular dance called Theyyam. More than an art form, it's a type of worship that is tribal in origin and thought to predate Hinduism in Kerala. Theyyams aren't held in traditional temples, but rather in small shrines or family compounds. Dancers don elaborate costumes and terrifying makeup for the ritual dance, during which its believed they become possessed by the spirit of the deity they represent, allowing them to perform such feats as dancing with a 30-foot headdress, a flaming costume, or falling into a pile of burning embers. The ritual is accompanied by intense drumming, howling, and chanting. Theyyam season is from November to May.

WHERE TO EAT AND STAY

For expanded hotel reviews, visit Fodors.com.

$ ✕ **Coachman's Inn.** Local well-to-do
INDIAN families often dine here at tables made more private by small dividers, and though the interior is somewhat dark and drab, the food is top notch. The *naan* (bread) here, garnished with black sesame seeds, is particularly good. Try also the fish *malabari* (cooked in a mild curry) or the justly popular butter chicken. $ *Average main: Rs. 200* ✉ *Kamala International, S. M. Rd.* ☎ *497/276–6910.*

$$$$ 🏠 **Ayisha Manzil.** A stay in this 1862 clifftop home may be the best
B&B/INN way to experience what north Kerala is all about—people come for
ALL-INCLUSIVE the gorgeous sea views and the local cuisine, cooked by host and TV chef Faiza Moosa. **Pros:** taxes, great meals, and non-alcoholic drinks included in the room price; great views. **Cons:** basic accommodations. $ *Rooms from: Rs. 15500* ✉ *Court Rd., Thalassery* ☎ *490/234–1590* ⤴ *7 rooms* ⊘ *Closed April 30–July 31* ⦿ *All-inclusive.*

$ 🏠 **Mascot.** A terrific hillcrest location provides a great sea view, and a
HOTEL cliffside walkway leads to the large swimming pool and ayurvedic center. **Pros:** fantastic sea views from most rooms. **Cons:** the closest beach has been taken over by the navy. $ *Rooms from: Rs. 1600* ✉ *Near Baby Beach, Burnassery* ☎ *497/270–8445* ⦿ *www.mascotresort.com* ⤴ *25 rooms* ⦿ *No meals.*

UNDERSTANDING INDIA

BOOKS AND MOVIES

BOOKS AND MOVIES

Books
Nonfiction

The best general surveys of Indian history are John Keay's *India: A History* and Stanley Wolpert's *New History of India* (6th ed.), with Keay focusing more on antiquity. Three sparkling introductions to the modern nation are *India: From Midnight to the Millennium,* by Shashi Tharoor; *India Unbound: From Independence to the Global Information Age,* by Gurcharan Das; and *The Idea of India,* by Sunil Khilnani.

Mark Tully's books, including *No Full Stops in India* and *India in Slow Motion* (with Gillian Wright), combine travel with social analysis. William Dalrymple's *The Age of Kali* is a collection of incisive essays on aspects of the modern subcontinent, as are Gita Mehta's *Snakes and Ladders* and Octavio Paz's *In Light of India,* by the Nobel Laureate and former Mexican ambassador. Elisabeth Bumiller's *May You Be the Mother of a Hundred Sons* is an American reporter's take on the varied lives of Indian women. *Freedom at Midnight,* by Larry Collins and Dominique Lapierre, is a spellbinding account of India's break from Britain; *City of Joy,* by the same authors, is a powerful portrait of Calcutta. Nirad Chaudhuri's classic *Autobiography of an Unknown Indian* recounts the Bengali author's youth in colonial India, with insightful descriptions of Indian customs, castes, and relations with the British. James Cameron's *An Indian Summer* is a glib but loving memoir by a British journalist who lived in India during and after the Raj. Sudha Koul's *The Tiger Ladies* recalls life in beautiful Kashmir before it became a war zone in the late 1980s. While not his best writing, *India: A Million Mutinies Now* is the most optimistic of Nobel Laureate V.S. Naipaul's three books on India.

The classic works on early India are A.L. Basham's *The Wonder That Was India* and Romila Thapar's *History of India,* Volume I. India's first prime minister, Jawaharlal Nehru, was a peerless writer and left some inspiring works including his autobiography and *The Discovery of India,* a unique rendition of the country's history. William Dalrymple's *White Mughals* illuminates the bicultural lives of British traders in Hyderabad during the 18th century. Among the great Sanskrit texts, the best translations of the *Bhagavad-Gita* are Barbara Stoler Miller's and Eknath Easwaran's; Easwaran has also translated the sacred *Upanishads.* The epics known as the *Mahabharata* and *Ramayana* are available in countless translations, the most popular of which are Krishna Dharma's and Eknath Easwaran's. Classical Hindu myths are retold in prose form in *Gods, Demons, and Others,* by the master writer R. K. Narayan, and more recently in *Ka,* by Roberto Calasso. Diana Eck's *Banaras: City of Light* is an engaging profile of the holy city.

Stuart Cary Welch's *India: Art and Culture, 1300–1900* is a lavishly illustrated catalog by a great connoisseur, while Vidya Dehejia's *Indian Art* is a good textual survey. *Myths and Symbols in Indian Art and Civilization,* by Heinrich Zimmer (edited by Joseph Campbell) is helpful to the art or mythology buff. The famously erotic *Kama Sutra* has been freshly translated by Wendy Doniger and Sudhir Kakar. The colorful minibook *India and the Mughal Dynasty,* by Valérie Berinstain, makes a great pocket companion in much of North India, and William Dalrymple's *City of Djinns* brings Mughal Delhi to life. Royina Grewal's *In Rajasthan* is an excellent travelogue by an Indian. For ravishing photographs, see *A Day in the Life of India,* people going about their business; *Living Faith,* Dinesh Khanna's renditions of sacred spaces and scenes; *India Modern,* a contemporary treatment of traditional buildings and crafts; and any of several collections by Raghubir Singh, Raghu Rai, and Henri Cartier-Bresson.

Fiction

Indian novelists took the literary world by storm in the 1980s and '90s, and the flood has not abated. Vikram Seth's mesmerizing *A Suitable Boy* portrays middle-class life in the 1950s through a timeless story of young love. Rohinton Mistry's novels center on the Parsi community of Bombay; his masterpiece, *A Fine Balance,* is an extraordinary study of the human condition as experienced by a motley group in the 1970s, and *Family Matters* and *Such a Long Journey* weave poignant tales of family ties and personal misfortune. Another fine Bombay novel, Manil Suri's *The Death of Vishnu,* features an old homeless man whose neighbors squabble over the best way to deal with him. *Love and Longing in Bombay,* by Vikram Chandra, is a collection of short stories with a single narrator.

Midnight's Children, by Salman Rushdie, is the epic tale of a boy who was born the moment India gained independence. Rushdie's *The Moor's Last Sigh,* narrated by a young man of mixed heritage, paints incomparably sensual portraits of Bombay and Cochin. Arundhati Roy's *The God of Small Things,* set in 1960s Kerala, tells a disturbing story of brother-and-sister twins raised by a divorced mother. Roy has since become a political activist in New Delhi. David Davidar's *The House of Blue Mangoes* is a South Indian family saga.

Amit Chaudhuri's short novel *A Strange and Sublime Address* (published in the United States with Chaudhuri's *Freedom Song*) is a gorgeous story of a 10-year-old boy's stay with relatives in Calcutta. Anita Desai's *Fasting, Feasting* concerns an Indian family whose son goes off to college in the United States. Khushwant Singh's *Delhi* is a bawdy but ultimately moving romp through Delhi's tumultuous history. *The Impressionist,* a picaresque novel by Hari Kunzru, shows the adventures of a half-English, half-Indian boy in both countries in the early 20th century. Upamanyu Chatterjee's *English,*

August is a funny account of a rookie in the Indian Civil Service.

Bengali poet and Nobel Laureate Rabindranath Tagore wrote some enduring novels including *Gora* and *Home and the World*; to read his poetry in translation, look for *Gitanjali*. Rudyard Kipling's *Kim* is still one of the most intimate works of Western fiction on India; in E. M. Forster's *A Passage to India* the conflict between Indians and their British rulers is played out in the story of a man accused of rape. Ahmed Ali's 1940 novel *Twilight in Delhi* gives a poignant account of 19th-century urban Muslim society.

Not all good Indian writing has been published in the West. In India you'll find plenty of English-language fiction and nonfiction on the issues of the day. Reading fiction from other languages is another way to penetrate India's regional cultures; top writers available in translation include Sunil Gangopadhyay (Bengali), Nirmal Verma (Hindi), Intizar Husain and Ismat Chugtai (Urdu), U. R. Ananthamurty (Kannada), Vaasanthi and Ambai (Tamil), and Paul Zacharia (Malayalam).

Films

Indian films can be roughly divided into Bollywood fare—musical romances from Bombay's prolific industry—and independent art films. A prime example of classic costume melodrama is *Aan* (1952), directed by Mehboob, a story of royalty tamed by peasants. The late Satyajit Ray adapted and directed the internationally known *Pather Panchali* (1955), *Aparajito* (1956), and *The World of Apu* (1959), a breathtaking trilogy depicting poverty and tragedy in the life of a Bengali boy. *Salaam Bombay* (1988), directed by Mira Nair, is a heartbreaking fictionalized exposé of Bombay's homeless and slum children. Roland Joffe's *City of Joy* (1992), starring Patrick Swayze, is based on Dominique Lapierre's book about Calcutta. Deepa Mehta's best-known films are *Fire* (1996), in which two beautiful but neglected sisters-in-law turn to each other for love, and *Earth* (1999), an adaptation of Bapsi Sidhwa's novel on the partition of India and Pakistan, *Cracking India*. Another Mira Nair film, *Monsoon Wedding* (2001), takes on several contemporary issues in the context of a high-class Punjabi wedding. Although not set in India, Gurinder Chadha's *Bend It Like Beckham* (2002) is worth watching for its funny, life-affirming portrait of a soccer-loving Punjabi girl in London. Aparna Sen's *Mr. and Mrs. Iyer* (2002) won accolades for its sensitive treatment of interfaith relations.

Bollywood's exuberant musicals are now widely available on DVD. Blockbusters include *Kal Ho Naa Ho* (2003), which places a fetching Bollywood cast in photogenic New York; *Dil Chahta Hai* (2001), a romantic comedy set in Bombay; and *Lagaan* (2001), featuring a 19th-century cricket match with the British.

Films set in India by Western directors are numerous. The excellent *Shakespeare Wallah* (1965), written by Ruth Prawer Jhabvala and James Ivory and directed by Ivory, fictionalizes the experience of the Kendal family's traveling theater troupe. Ivory's *Heat and Dust* (1982), an adaptation of Jhabvala's novel, re-creates the past through a young woman's discovery of a series of her grandmother's letters. *Phantom India* (1969), directed by Louis Malle, is an epic documentary of Indian life. Richard Attenborough's *Gandhi* (1982) traces the adult life of the leader of India's independence movement. *A Passage to India* (1984), based on E. M. Forster's novel, was directed by David Lean. *The Jewel in the Crown* (1984), an epic TV series based on part of Paul Scott's *Raj Quartet*, features a romance between a British woman and an Indian man in the waning years of British rule. Most recently, the multiple Oscar-winning *Slumdog Millionaire* (2008), directed by Danny Boyle, is an adaptation of Vikas Swarup's novel, *Q & A*, which explores the life of a Mumbai youth and his success on a TV quiz show.

Travel Smart
India

WORD OF MOUTH

"From my experience of hiring a private driver, what I can say is that its total freedom, you can stop where ever you want whenever you want, you get to see great sights on your way."

—pgill26

"Taking the train is a great way to meet Indians who don't work in the tourist biz, at least in 2AC."

—thursdaysd

"The Delhi Metro is fast, clean, and very easy to use. . . . Women traveling alone can use the women-only car, which is the first car of each train."

—Hank54

GETTING HERE AND AROUND

The major international tourist hubs are Delhi, in the north, and Mumbai, 1,407 km (874 miles) to the south. All the major cities are connected by a national highway system, air service, and trains.

Road travel is definitely an easy way to take in local color in a leisurely way. Unfortunately, most roads still have just two lanes and are in poor condition, and progress can be painstaking. However, that's changing as India continues to work on its modernization project, which has already produced the "Golden Quadrilateral," a massive four-lane highway network, similar to those in America, that connects Delhi, Kolkata, Chennai, and Mumbai.

An onslaught of domestic airlines competing for business has made air travel throughout the subcontinent relatively hassle-free and convenient. It's the best option for those who are on a tight schedule, although flight delays—due to congestion and weather (usually fog or monsoon rains)—are common. Always be prepared for flights to be delayed or even canceled.

The Indian train system is an intricate network shuttling millions of people across the country every day. It's very reliable, if run-down, and practically every point of interest in the nonmountainous areas of India has a train station nearby. Train travel is also likely to be the cheapest option for going long distances, making it perfect for travelers on a budget and those who want to travel the way many Indians do.

Common terms for the word "road" in local languages (India has many) include *marg, galli, rasta, salai, peth,* and *sarani.* Many streets and roads have an older British name and a newer, post-Independence name. Residents often refer to roads by their old names or use abbreviated versions of cumbersome names. Mumbai and its pre-Independence name,

FINDING YOUR WAY

Indian addresses are often haphazard. Building numbers may appear in postal addresses, but they don't always appear prominently on the buildings themselves. Some neighborhoods use lettered block systems—each block has a corresponding letter and each house a number (i.e., B-139 is house number 139 in B block). In some towns and some residential areas, houses are not numbered sequentially—number 45/234 could be next to 32/342. This makes neighborhood names and landmarks, often included in urban addresses, very important. Addresses in small villages may include the name of the district or nearest large town or city. Postal codes play a big part in ensuring that letters reach their destinations.

Bombay, are used interchangeably. The city's Netaji Subhash Chandra Marg is still called by its old, easy-to-remember name of Marine Drive, and Jay Prakash Road is referred to as J.P. Road. And many cities have a main drag that's now called M.G. (for Mahatma Gandhi) Road. In Delhi, however, M.G. Road stands for Mehrauli-Gurgaon Road.

▌ **AIR TRAVEL**

Flying to and within India has become easier in recent years with new international routes and the emergence of several new low-cost Indian domestic airlines. Flying from Delhi to Mumbai, for example, is just about as easy as flying between two major cities in America. Domestic tickets can generally be purchased through traditional travel agents, airline websites, travel websites, and even at Indian airports if you've decided to make a last-minute trip.

Security in Indian airports, however, often requires considerable time. You'll need to attach blank luggage tags (provided at the check-in counter) to all of your hand luggage (including purses). When you clear screening, these tags will be rubber stamped and reverified by a police officer or airline staff member at the time of boarding. Passengers are routinely patted down at security, irrespective of whether the metal detector goes off. Women are frisked in a separate dressing-room-like box by female security guards, whereas men are checked out in the open. Because of these time-consuming procedures, it's a good idea to check in at least two hours before a flight within India.

Flying time to either Delhi or Mumbai is 16 hours from New York and 18 hours from Chicago.

Airline Security Issues Transportation Security Administration. Answers for almost every question that might come up are available here. ⊕ www.tsa.gov.

AIRPORTS

India's two major international gateways are Indira Gandhi International Airport (DEL) in New Delhi and Chhatrapati Shivaji International Airport (BOM) in Mumbai. Delhi is best for all the major tourist spots in the north, including Rajasthan. Mumbai is more convenient for Goa and Kerala. Both airports are reasonably close to the city centers and to the train stations if that's your next mode of travel.

The airports in Delhi and Mumbai, which also accommodate domestic flights, are as comfortable as those in the United States or Europe, but with fewer shopping and dining options. In 2010 a new, ultramodern international terminal, T3, opened at the Delhi airport, which has vastly improved the experience for everyone passing through.

Airport Information Chhatrapati Shivaji International Airport (Mumbai) ☎ 22/6685–1010 ⊕ www.csia.in. Indira Gandhi International Airport (Delhi) ☎ 124/337–6000 ⊕ www.newdelhiairport.in.

GROUND TRANSPORTATION

The best way to get to and from India's major international airports is by taxi or auto-rickshaw (the latter if you're feeling adventurous and don't have that much luggage). Your hotel can also arrange for a private pickup at the airport, in which case the driver will be holding a sign with your name at the exit point. Hotel pickups are considerably more expensive than any other option and vary greatly in price (expect a charge of at least Rs. 800 in big cities).

If you are on a budget, you can also arrange a basic, usually non-air-conditioned taxi at the prepaid, government-approved stands beyond immigration and customs. In most cities, you'll state your destination, pay in advance, and be given a voucher to give to your driver when he drops you off. He may need to take it from you when leaving the airport parking lot, to show to the parking attendant who will record the voucher number and your name in a log. If you want an air-conditioned car, you can book through one of the private taxi companies whose desks resemble those of car-rental companies. These are all reputable companies and they will either charge you a preset or a metered fair, depending on your destination. Luggage room is ample in taxis in Delhi, but the cars used in Mumbai are older and smaller, with less room. Taxi drivers might try to charge you an extra fee (around Rs. 10) per bag, but again, this varies from city to city.

TRANSFERS BETWEEN TERMINALS

If you need to transfer between terminals (for example, between domestic and international) you can use the airport-run terminal transfer bus for free, provided you have a ticket for a departing flight from the destination terminal.

FLIGHTS

TO INDIA

International companies are constantly reevaluating their service to southern Asia. Call the air carriers listed here to confirm their flights and schedules, or work with a travel agent who's knowledgeable about the region. That said, you can get to India, usually with a stop in Europe, on many international carriers. Those offering daily direct flights include United Airlines (Newark to Delhi or to Mumbai), American Airlines (Chicago to Delhi), and Air India (New York JFK to Mumbai and Delhi, and Chicago to Mumbai). Jet Airways flies daily from New York JFK or Newark to Delhi and Mumbai. All flights are via Brussels.

WITHIN INDIA

India's domestic airline scene has boomed since the millennium, although the world economic downturn in 2008 has taken some of the wind out of future expansion plans. In addition to the so-called legacy carriers, Jet Airways and Air India, which both also fly internationally, there is a newer crop of carriers—including ones you've probably never heard of—each with its own quirks.

Jet Airways is often the most expensive carrier, but provides very good service. Air India, the government carrier, can be a little stodgy and prices a bit high. Popular low-cost, no frills carriers include SpiceJet, IndiGo, and GoAir.

Airline Contacts Air India ☎ 800/223–7776 (US), 022/2758–0777 (India) ⊕ www.airindia. com. **American Airlines** ☎ 800/433–7300 (in US), 124/309–0700 (in India) ⊕ www.aa.com. **British Airways** ☎ 800/247–9297 in US, 800/1023–5922 in India ⊕ www.britishairways. com. **Delta Airlines** ☎ 800/241–4141 (in US), 800/180–0099 (in India) ⊕ www.delta.com. **Luftansa** ☎ 800/399–5838 (in US), 124/488–8888 (in India) ⊕ www.lufthansa.com. **United Airlines** ☎ 800/864–8331 in US, 124/431–5500 in India ⊕ www.united.com.

Within India Air India ☎ 22/2758–0777 in India, 800/223–7776 in US ⊕ www.airindia. com. **IndiGo** ☎ 99/1038–3838, 800/180–3838 ⊕ www.goindigo.in. **Jet Airways** ☎ 11/3989–3333 in India, 877/835–9538 in US ⊕ www.jetairways.com. **SpiceJet** ☎ 800/180–3333 ⊕ www.spicejet.com.

❚ BUS TRAVEL

Bus travel isn't the safest or most comfortable way to travel in India, especially at night. Service within cities, especially in Delhi, is crowded and dangerous for women, with men literally hanging outside the bus (if they can manage to grab hold while the bus is still moving). The situation is a bit better in Mumbai, but a lack of published bus schedules and routes makes the city bus experience best left to locals or those who have time to figure it out. If you decide on bus travel between cities, try to take the most luxurious privately run air-conditioned coaches, such as Volvo buses, and have a local travel agent make the arrangements. Buses rarely if ever have restrooms on board, but they usually stop every 2–4 hours at restaurants or roadside cafés so that passengers can use the restrooms and drink a cup of tea. Whatever bus you take, it's a good idea to bring earplugs or earphones, as many play Bollywood movies or music at high volumes.

❚ CAR TRAVEL

Travel by car in India isn't for the faint of heart, but if you can get over India's extremely different road philosophy, it can be an enjoyable, never boring way to see the country and get from one city to the next.

ROAD CONDITIONS

Roads in India may be wide and smooth in big cities, but they're usually narrow and terribly maintained in the countryside. Traffic in major cities is so erratic and abundant that it is hard to pin down local rush hours. Roads are filled with countless cars at all times of the day and even late at night, especially around the airports (international flights tend to arrive in the wee morning hours). Always be ready for some kind of traffic jam or other road drama if traveling by car.

Traffic is multifarious: you'll see slow-moving cyclists, bullock carts, cows, goat flocks, and even camels or elephants sharing the road with speeding, honking, quick-to-pass, ready-to-brake-for-animals and vehicles of all shapes and sizes. Barring a few principal routes and highways built under the continuing modernization project, Indian roads are often dilapidated and become worse during monsoon season. Speed limits, set according to road conditions, are frequently ignored. Road signs, when they exist, are often just in Hindi or the local language.

FROM DELHI TO	DISTANCE	
City	Distance in kilometers	Distance in miles
Agra	203	126
Jaipur	258	160
Mumbai	1,407	874
Goa	1,912	1,188

Because of India's European influence, newer sections of cities are filled with traffic circles. Older parts of the cities, however, are generally made up of extremely narrow, winding streets. Old Delhi's streets tend to be one-way, although you won't be able to tell which way that is unless you simply look at the traffic. Locals drive fast when they can and show little regard for pedestrians.

In rural areas two-way roads are often only one-lane wide, so vehicles frequently dodge oncoming traffic for hours on end. Some roads also serve as innovative extensions to farms, with grain laid out to dry on the pavement or sisal rope strung over the route so that vehicles tramp the grain or rope down. British-style left-side driving creates one more challenge to many motorists.

RULES OF THE ROAD

Hard copies of road regulations are difficult to come by in India. It's no wonder, because it seems as if Indians either ignore or genuinely aren't aware of road rules across the subcontinent. Take, for instance, speed limits. They aren't always posted, and different states have different speed limits for cars traveling on the national highways. Any speed less than 100 km (about 60 miles) per hour is probably legal. Locals drive faster than that if not stifled by gridlock, and punishment for speeding is spotty at best. On the off chance that you're driving and you get stopped for speeding, you might have to pay a fine or a bribe depending on the officer's mood.

There are also laws requiring the use of seatbelts and laws against using your cell phone while driving. However, you'll be hard-pressed to find any local who wears a belt religiously or gets punished if he doesn't. People do seem to be more aware of restrictions on cell-phone use, and talkers in cities like Delhi and Mumbai, especially foreigners, do get singled out by the cops—it's best not to use your cell phone behind the wheel. The most serious offense—drunk driving—is taken very seriously and is punishable by jail time.

The website ⊕ *www.indiandrivingschools. com* has a fairly comprehensive outline of basic Indian traffic regulations. Nevertheless, it's not too much of a stretch to call Indian roads a free-for-all where traffic rules are theoretical at best.

HIRING A CAR AND DRIVER

Don't rent a self-drive car. The rules and road conditions are probably like nothing you've ever experienced, so taking taxis or hiring a car and driver are the best choices. The good news: hiring a car and driver is affordable by Western standards, and even Indians use this option for weekend getaways. However, the price can add up for long trips, so be sure to establish terms, rates, and surcharges in advance. Drivers are usually paid by the company they work for, and every company has unique policies. It's not uncommon for you to pay for the whole trip in advance, or to pay for half at the front end while settling the balance at the end of the trip. Rates generally include gasoline.

Shorter trips are usually priced by kilometer. Figure Rs. 11 to Rs. 13 per kilometer for a non-air-conditioned Ambassador—a hefty, roomy car designed by the British in the 1950s. Ambassadors, which sometimes come with air-conditioning, are not as universal as they used to be, and now the most economic rates often get you a Tata Indica, a small but also practical choice. Indicas are not quite as comfortable as the Ambassador, as these are lighter cars that get bounced about on pot-holed roads. In some locations a higher rate gets you a diesel Sumo jeep or an air-conditioned Cielo or Contessa; still more cash gets you a Toyota, a minivan, or, at some agencies, even a Mercedes-Benz or a BMW.

On longer trips one price usually covers a certain number of hours and kilometers; beyond that you pay extra. Expect to pay at least Rs. 1,000 a day to have a driver at your disposal—more if you're using an expensive hotel car. Add to this a "night halt charge" of Rs. 150 to Rs. 200 per night for overnight trips. Some companies also charge a driver's fee for an eight-hour day.

Arrange a car and driver only through a reputable travel agency or licensed, government-approved operator or, for quite a bit more money, through your hotel. Be sure to discuss your itinerary up front—what seems like a reasonable day's drive on a map can often take much longer in reality. Roads in some areas—wildlife sanctuaries, for example—require a jeep; better to iron out all the details than to miss sights because you don't have the right sort of vehicle. On long journeys, decide in advance where and when you'll stop for tea or meal breaks. The daredevil road maneuvers that are the norm in India can be unsettling. Ask the driver to travel slowly, or have the operator inform the driver of your request.

▌TAXI AND AUTO-RICKSHAW TRAVEL

Probably the best way to get around an Indian city is by taxi or motorized auto-rickshaw. Auto-rickshaws, especially, are fast and cheap, although not as comfortable as an air-conditioned taxi.

Auto-rickshaws are practically everywhere and are easy to flag down. Taxis are also easy to hail on the street in Mumbai, but much harder to find in Delhi. One drawback is that most drivers don't speak English. If your driver can't understand your pronunciation of a landmark or hotel, pen and paper may do the trick. Bystanders are also often helpful in getting from point A to B.

Most important, find out in advance the approximate fare for the distance you will be going—someone at your hotel can give you a ballpark figure. This is crucial, because even if your taxi or rickshaw has a meter, the driver might not use it. That is the standard practice in Delhi, where it's common for rickshaw drivers to quote outrageous fares and claim that the meter is "broken." Don't fight the system—just have an idea of a fair price before you get in, and expect that negotiation will usually be part of the game. A good rule of thumb is that no rickshaw ride should cost more than Rs. 150 (most are much less), and no taxi ride should cost more than Rs. 600, unless you are going really, really far away. In Mumbai, drivers are good about using the meter and rate conversion cards that are used to convert the rates on outdated meters to current, government-approved norms. Once you're at your destination, the card shows how much you should pay based on the figure displayed on the meter. If you think you're going to a place that may not have vehicles for the return journey (you will probably know for sure only when you reach your destination, unfortunately), then when you arrive, negotiate a waiting fare and a return fare with the driver.

Remember that there are prepaid taxi and auto-rickshaw counters at airports and train stations in major cities, as well as at some top tourist spots. You tell the clerk your destination and pay for it in advance. He may ask you how much luggage you have—paying an extra Rs. 10 is the norm for each large bag or suitcase. The clerk will give you a receipt, at which point you might have to stand in line for the taxi or rickshaw. The driver might also be standing next to you and escort you to his vehicle. Do not get waylaid by aggressive drivers who try to persuade you to come to them instead of going to the counter. They'll certainly charge you more than the published rate at the counter. At your destination, do not pay the driver anything extra, even if he claims you gave the wrong destination to the counter clerk (unlikely) or gives other excuses.

Drivers supplement their incomes by offering to find you a hotel or to take you shopping at the "best" stores, which means they'll get a commission if you get a room or buy anything. The stores are usually very expensive, so if you don't want this kind of detour, you must be very firm. Finally, taxis close to luxury hotels are notorious for swindling customers who hire them outside the hotel. Establish beforehand, with the help of the doorman, that the taxi driver will follow his meter or rate card, or negotiate the fare in the presence of the doorman. Or, better yet, walk a block or two away from the hotel's entrance.

▌ TRAIN TRAVEL

Traveling by train in India can be a fine experience if you plan it well. Trains connect the tiniest places across the subcontinent, and train journeys are a terrific way to see off-the-beaten-track India. Traveling on second-class non-air-conditioned trains can be tough, but you'll get better views of the countryside, because the windows are wide open, not sealed, and don't have a smoky film on them, as they do in air-conditioned cars. On the other hand, air-conditioned trips are much more comfortable. Trains, especially on smaller routes, can often be late, so be prepared to cope with delays.

Like its international airports, India's train stations are rather chaotic—though highly entertaining to observe. Hawkers sell everything a typical traveler would want: hot *puris* (deep-fried whole wheat bread), boiled eggs, squeaky toys, and hot tea and coffee made on a crude portable stove. Porters, also known as coolies, weave in and out, balancing unimaginable configurations of trunks and bags on their heads. Invariably, when one person sets out on a journey, five come to see him off. The platforms swirl with crowds and luggage. You need to be careful to hang on to your possessions and your bearings so you don't get bumped or swept away. Plan to be early, and keep your tickets safe. If the train is delayed or has not yet arrived, try to find a waiting room. Though usually drab and not very comfortable, these places are safe and might have attached bathrooms. Many large train stations have restaurants or at least snack counters where you can take a break, too.

Train ticket prices vary greatly depending on where and how you're traveling. The *Shatabdi* and *Rajdhani* expresses are fast and have air-conditioned cars and either reclining seats (in *Shatabdis*) or berths (in *Rajdhanis*), but only offer services between major cities. The next-fastest trains are called "mail" trains. "Passenger" trains, which usually offer only second-class accommodations, make numerous stops, and are crowded. Even on the best trains in this group, seats can be well worn and lavatories less than pleasant. But traveling by air-conditioned first class makes for a leisurely and fun journey.

The *Bhopal Shatabdi Express* (train 2002 or 2002A) and *Taj Express* (train 2280) travel between Delhi's Hazrat Nizamuddin station (NZM) and Agra's Cantonment station (AGC). (Many other trains also travel between the two cities daily.) Both expresses leave early in the morning from Delhi; the *Shatabdi* takes about two hours, the *Taj* 2½. Either option allows for a full day of sightseeing before returning to Delhi on a similar express. There are also express trains connecting Delhi with Mumbai and other major cities. The website of the Indian Railway system has comprehensive schedules of every train running across India.

For long train rides, buy a yard-long chain with loops and a padlock to secure your luggage. (You might find a vendor on the platform at a large train station.) After you've locked your bag and stowed it in its place, loop the chain through its handle and attach it to a bar or hinge below the seat. Be sure to chain your luggage as soon as possible; a lot of small bag thefts take place during journey embarkation and disembarkation. Your journey will be more pleasant if you bring along packaged snacks, sandwiches, juice, and bottled water. Bigger trains provide meals as part of the ticket/tariff, and you can expect a number of the items on a food tray to be packaged.

Trains have numerous classes. The air-conditioned cars consist of first-class air-conditioned (also known as 1AC; lockable compartments with two or four sleeping berths), second-class air-conditioned (also known as 2AC; two or four berths that convert to sleepers, but no lockable compartments), and third-class air-conditioned (also known as 3AC; just like 2AC but with six berths in each seating bay). Ordinary first class are the non-air-conditioned lockable compartments with two or four sleeping berths. The a/c chair car (AC chair class) is a comfortable way to go on day trips, with rows of two or three seats on each side. Seats are covered in either vinyl or cloth. Any of the previous classes are adequate, although 3AC can make for slightly cramped quarters. Sleeper class is laid out just like the 3AC car without the air-conditioning. Finally there's second seating, the cheapest because no reservations are required. But it's not recommended for long distances—the car has an open-air plan with rows of padded or plain wood benches.

Berths are in configurations of four or six in an open coupe arrangement on one side of a train car. On the other (corridor) side, berths are against the wall, in pairs of two; corridors run parallel past these "side" berths and bring in noise and traffic, but have more room to sit up in than the other berths. You'll find two kinds of lavatories, the Western-style commode lavatory and the Indian-style toilet (essentially a hole over which you squat). Although it can be hard to get used to Indian-style facilities, they're actually more sanitary in the sense that there's no contact. Definitely bring enough toilet paper (and some hand sanitizer)—you won't find it on most trains.

In large cities you may be able to buy tickets with major credit cards. Elsewhere, expect to pay cash. Most local travel agents can get train tickets for you.

You must reserve seats and sleeping berths in advance, even with a rail pass. If your plans are flexible, you can make reservations once you arrive in India. To save time, use a local travel agent (who may need to photocopy your passport); otherwise, head to the train station and prepare for long lines and waits. Large urban stations have a special office for foreigners, where you can buy "tourist quota" tickets. (Every train reserves a few seats for tourists who haven't made reservations.) If you arrive early in the morning— around 8—getting a ticket shouldn't take you more than half an hour; however, in peak season tourist quotas fill quickly, and you may have to change your dates altogether. When it's time to travel, arrive at the station at least half an hour before departure so you have enough time to find your seat. Sleeper and seat numbers are displayed on the platform and on each car, along with a list of passengers' names and seat assignments.

If you are not buying from the tourist quota and are booking during nonpeak season, booking online is a convenient option. You can buy e-tickets, which must be printed out and can often be bought on the day of travel, at ⊕ *www.irctc.co.in*. A good resource for train schedules is ⊕ *www.indianrail.gov.in*.

LUXURY TRAINS

In recent years India has expanded its range of luxury trains. They all offer elaborate meals from a variety of cuisines and luxury quarters as well as fine (albeit extremely busy) itineraries. Packages, which are very expensive, include food, bus tours from stations (after you disembark you're loaded onto a luxury bus for sightseeing), rail travel, and more. High-season rates for seven- or eight-day tours on some of the trains start at around $3,000, based on double occupancy, but the *Maharajas' Express*, introduced in 2010, is much more: around $6,400. All tickets are cheaper in the off-season (March–October).

Rajasthan's *Palace on Wheels*, the original luxury train, and the *Royal Rajasthan on Wheels* both depart from Delhi and in their most popular routes have nearly identical destinations, passing through such tourist hot spots as Jaipur, Jaisalmer, Jodhpur, Udaipur, and Agra. The *Maharajas' Express* operates several different thematic routes and departs from either Delhi or Mumbai.

The *Deccan Odyssey*, leaving from Mumbai, includes stops at the Ellora and Ajanta caves, Goa, and Sevagram, one of Gandhi's bases of operations.

Luxury Trains *Deccan Odyssey* ☏ 97/1717–9408 in India ⊕ *www. thedeccanodysseyindia.com*. *Maharajas' Express* ☏ 022/6690–4747 ⊕ *www.irctc.com*. *Palace on Wheels* ☏ 800/103–3500 in India, 800/463–4299 toll free in US ⊕ *www.palaceonwheels.net*. *Royal Rajasthan on Wheels* ☏ 11/2338–3837 ⊕ *www.royalrajasthanonwheels.com*.

Train Information *Indian Railways* ⊕ *www.indianrail.gov.in*. To make online reservations, go to www.irctc.co.in. **Indian Railways International Tourist Bureau** ⊠ *New Delhi Railway Station, Paharganj side, 2nd fl.* ☏ 11/2340–5156, 11/2334–6804 ⊗ *Mon.–Sat. 8–8, Sun. 8–2.*

ESSENTIALS

▌ ACCOMMODATIONS

Staying in India can be a pleasure, regardless of whether you've paid top price at a world-class luxury hotel or gone the no-frills route at a local hostel. For average accommodations somewhere in the middle, you often can expect to pay significantly less than what you'd pay at a comparable hotel in America, which makes getting the bill a pleasant surprise. Whether a room has plush carpets and chairs or a simple bed and table, most tend to be clean and neat.

The lodgings we list are the cream of the crop in each price category. We always list the facilities that are available, but we don't specify whether they cost extra. When pricing accommodations, always ask what's included and what costs extra. Properties are assigned price categories based on the rate for a standard double room in the high season, which in most of India is approximately October through March, peaking at Christmas and New Year's, when even higher rates apply. When you book a room at a hotel, however (especially an expensive hotel), ask for their best rate and push them to include breakfast and a station or airport pickup. Be a hard bargainer; consider asking them to knock the rate down further, even after they have given you a discount. You can always shop around and come back.

Try to secure all room reservations before arrival, especially during peak season and in the major cities and popular tourist destinations such as Mumbai, Delhi, Agra, and Goa. But give yourself a little leeway to make plans on arrival, especially if you have more than two weeks. In the off-season and in smaller cities it's often fairly easy to change plans at the last minute. This is especially true during monsoon season (late June through August) when many hotels have vacancies and deep discounts. Indians vacation during school holidays in April, May, and early June; for a few days in October or November (for Diwali, or, in eastern India, Durga Puja); and for 10 days between Christmas and the New Year. Reservations are extra-difficult to secure during these times.

Room rates can be extremely expensive in business-oriented cities like Mumbai and Delhi. Urban hotels rarely have off-season discounts, though some international chains have incentive programs for frequent guests. In other areas, hotels may be seeking guests, so you may be able to negotiate your price. When you reserve, ask about additional taxes and service charges, which increase the quoted room price. Do not agree to an airport pickup or breakfast without asking whether these services involve extra costs. Airport pickups organized by luxury hotels are generally overpriced.

As in restaurants, practically every hotel in India will gladly put up with children running around. Most allow children under a certain age to stay in their parents' room at no extra charge or for a nominal charge, but others charge for them as extra adults. Confirm the cutoff age for children's discounts. Only in the more upscale hotels will you find extra special accommodations like a cot or a crib. The same goes for structured children's programs: Oberoi and Taj hotels offer pretty reliable plans for kids with staff supervision, but programs vary from hotel to hotel, so you'll need to ask when making reservations. Most Oberoi hotels also have a library of kid-friendly DVDs. Beyond the luxury realm, however, there's nothing that kids will find particularly spectacular about the average Indian hotel—that is, no over-the-top playgrounds. You're better off trying to impress them with the sights.

CATEGORY	COST
$$$$	over Rs. 10,000
$$$	Rs. 6,000–Rs. 10,000
$$	Rs. 4,000–Rs. 5,999
$	under Rs. 4,000

All prices are in rupees for a standard double room in high season, with no meals, excluding tax and service charges, which vary by region.

Most hotels and other lodgings require you to give your credit-card details before they will confirm your reservation. If you don't feel comfortable using the Internet for this information, give it over the phone or ask if you can fax it (some places even prefer faxes). However you book, get confirmation in writing and have a copy of it handy when you check in.

Be sure you understand the hotel's cancellation policy. Some places allow you to cancel without any kind of penalty—even if you prepaid to secure a discounted rate—if you cancel at least 24 hours in advance. Others require you to cancel a week in advance or penalize you the cost of one night.

GOVERNMENT LODGING
The state-government-run tourism departments and the forestry department manage inexpensive accommodations throughout India. Most of these facilities are poorly maintained, and government employees and officials receive priority booking. Some states, including Rajasthan and Maharashtra run fairly competent hotels—and some are in former palaces or other heritage buildings. For more information, contact the tourist office in the capital of the state you plan to visit.

HERITAGE HOTELS
The Indian government has an excellent incentive program that encourages owners of traditional *havelis* (mansions), forts, and palaces to convert their properties into hotels or bring existing historic hotels up to government standards. (But do be careful where you stay, because "government standards" aren't always ideal for Westerners.) Many of these official heritage hotels—noted in reviews throughout this guide—are well outside large cities. Their architecture and style are authentically Indian, not Western. If this type of lodging appeals to you, contact one of the Indian tourist offices for more information. There are more than 60 such establishments in Rajasthan and a smattering elsewhere in India.

HOSTELS
Hostels offer bare-bones lodging at low, low prices—often in shared dorm rooms with shared baths—to people of all ages, though the primary market is young travelers, especially students. Most hostels serve breakfast; dinner and/or shared cooking facilities may also be available. In some hostels you aren't allowed to be in your room during the day, and there may be a curfew at night. Nevertheless, hostels provide a sense of community, with public rooms where travelers often gather to share stories.

Hostels in India are found mainly in the big cities and are a good option if you're on a very tight budget. However, because India is an inexpensive country they aren't nearly as common as they are in Europe. People of all ages and genders are usually welcomed, and many can accommodate you on a walk-up basis. You'll often find several types of sleeping options, including single rooms (which usually cost more) as well as shared ones. Some hostel rooms can be as good as those at inexpensive hotels, with air-conditioning and TVs.

Information New Delhi YMCA Tourist Hostel ☎ 11/4364–4000 ⊕ www.newdelhiymca.org. **Youth Hostels Association of India** ☎ 11/2611–0250 ⊕ www.yhaindia.org. **YWCA Hostels of Bombay International Center** ☎ 22/2202–5053 ⊕ www.ywcaic.info.

LOCAL DO'S AND TABOOS

CUSTOMS OF THE COUNTRY

In India, food and food-related hospitality is very important. Indians believe in showing their warmth by feeding a guest endless cups of tea, snacks, and meals. If you refuse entirely to eat a meal or have a cup of tea you may offend your host. Indians also believe in offering food over and over again, to make sure the guest has had enough, in case he or she is too shy to ask for more. So if you don't want more of something, be firm but polite in your refusals.

Higher-income households in the big cities are increasingly more westernized, so you might not feel too out of place if you're invited to such a home. However, if you're invited to an extremely traditional Indian home, you should observe certain customs. Men often sit separate from women. Sometimes, when the men entertain a foreign visitor (even a woman), the women of the house keep their distance or don't emerge; they may not speak English, or may be shy. Don't be surprised if the woman of the house serves you but doesn't join the gathering. Don't protest, and don't follow her into the kitchen—in some "upper-caste" Hindu homes the kitchen is frequently off-limits—just accept her behavior as the tradition of this particular home. Often, shoes are taken off before entering, so be sure to inquire, or watch what the family does.

Numerous customs govern food and the partaking of meals. In many households you arrive, sit and talk, and then have your meal; after you eat, the evening is over. Consequently, the meal might not start until 10 pm or later. When you eat in remote areas, you may not be given utensils; eat only with your right hand, as the left is considered unclean. (Left-handers can use utensils if available.) If you want a second helping or are buying openly displayed food, don't help yourself with your hands, which is considered by some as "polluting" the food. Let your host or vendor serve you.

GIFTS

If you visit someone's home for dinner or you're staying with an Indian family, it's a kind gesture to bring a gift from abroad. If there are youngsters in the home, bring something for them. Toys, cosmetics, perfume, and aftershaves are all good options, as is liquor if you're sure that your guests are drinkers—many Indians are not.

GREETINGS

People in India are not overly ceremonious on a day-to-day basis. The common greeting is a simple hello or *namaste* in Hindi. Beyond that, people tend to keep to themselves, especially in big cities, and there's no body contact—no friendly hugs. However, you may see young men walking down the street holding hands or with arms intertwined—this is an expression of friendship, not romance. For safety's sake, foreign women are better off not making eye contact with or smiling at strange men on the street—it could be perceived as an invitation for more communication. When you're leaving, a simple good-bye or expression of thanks will do. A firm handshake has become common, especially in professional contexts in Delhi, Mumbai, and Bangalore.

SIGHTSEEING

Religious monuments demand respect. Remove your shoes before entering a temple or shrine, even if it appears to be in ruins (this is also the case in many Christian churches in India). All religions forbid smoking, alcohol consumption, and loud talking on the premises. Some temples and mosques are off-limits to foreigners who don't practice the faith (or, in the case of Hindu temples, of non-Indian descent), or to unaccompanied women; don't try to bribe your way inside. Women should dress modestly—no shorts or tank tops—and should cover their heads before entering a mosque. Both men and women must cover their heads before entering a Sikh temple. Cameras and video cameras are not always permitted.

LOCAL DO'S AND TABOOS

On rare occasions a Hindu or Muslim festival involves animal sacrifice; do a little research on the festival rituals ahead of time if you are worried this may upset you or your child. Some Hindu and Jain temples don't allow any leather products inside their premises—and the prohibition includes wallets, purses, shoes, belts, and camera cases. Some temples also expect you to purify yourself by washing your hands and feet in a nearby tap or tank before you enter. In Sikh temples, don't point your feet toward the Holy Book or step over anyone sitting in prayer or meditation. Play it safe in both Hindu and Sikh temples: if you sit on the floor, sit cross-legged or with your feet tucked beneath you. In some shrines the sexes are separated; look around (or follow instructions) and let the situation govern what you do. Step into the courtyards of mosques with your right foot first.

Many well-meaning travelers commit an unforgivable sacrilege when they visit a Buddhist monastery. You're welcome to spin any prayer wheel, but just as you must circumambulate the interior and exterior of a monastery, *stupa*, or *mani* wall in a clockwise direction, you must spin prayer wheels clockwise only. Inside the monastery, cushions and chairs are reserved for *lamas* (monks), so sit on the steps outside or on the floor. If you meet a *rimpoche* (head lama) or a respected monk, it's polite not to turn your back on him when you leave. Also remove your hat and lower your umbrella in the confines of a monastery and in the presence of a lama.

LANGUAGE

Try to learn a little Hindi or the local language. You need not strive for fluency; even just mastering a few basic words and terms is bound to make chatting with the locals more rewarding.

Contrary to popular belief, English is not spoken by the majority of Indians. The country does function in English alongside Hindi and other local languages, however, so barring rural areas, you aren't likely to experience too much of a language barrier, especially in cities and tourist hubs where command of English is widespread. Hindi is the national language, but India isn't truly unified linguistically, and many Indians don't speak Hindi at all. Most states and countless smaller areas have their own unique tongues that bear no resemblance to the national language. For example, the languages of South India have completely different scripts and origins from those of the north—one reason why a command of both Hindi and English comes in handy.

HOTELS AND GUESTHOUSES

Hotels and guesthouses are easy to find in most cities. Hotels include chains, company-run, and privately owned properties—anything from a bare-bones budget hotel at a train station to a lavish palatial property in the choicest part of town or a luxurious beach resort. Overall, they tend to be larger, more formal, and more expensive than guesthouses. The term guesthouse refers to small, independent budget digs that usually lack some of the standard hotel amenities (TVs and in-room telephones, for example). Especially popular with foreign backpackers, they often have fewer rooms than hotels and the owners tend to live on-site. Room service is available in most guesthouses, although meals are not generally included in the rates.

India's tourism department approves and classifies hotels based on a rating system of five stars (the fanciest) to no stars (no frills). The ratings are based on the number of facilities and on hotel and bedroom size. Hotels without pools or those that serve only vegetarian food or that don't have a 24-hour restaurant—including some historic, charming, comfortable properties—don't qualify for five-star status but are often just as luxurious as those that do. The rating system also fails to take service and other important intangibles into account. Although these ratings can be misleading, tour operators often use them, so ask what a star rating means when booking.

If a room you're taking looks a little dingy, chances are the staff will clean it again for you. Make sure the door locks and that the bathroom's plumbing works.

If you opt for room service outside a luxury hotel, here are a few things to keep in mind: Tea or coffee usually comes pre-mixed—ask to have a pot of tea or coffee with the milk, sugar, and tea bags or instant coffee brought separately. You can probably get food cooked according to your preferences, but you have to make the request. Ask for fruit juice without ice (you may or may not be successful in getting it without added sugar). Make sure the mineral water is sealed, and do not use water from pitchers in the room unless you are certain it's safe.

▌COMMUNICATIONS

INTERNET

High-speed Internet access is available almost everywhere in India at Internet cafés and hotels, and connection speeds often approach what you're used to at home. Upscale private cafés in major cities sometimes offer Wi-Fi free to customers. Hotel service is generally more reliable, but it's also usually more expensive—business-class hotels may charge as much as Rs. 1,000 or more a day. Rates at Internet cafés are very cheap (around Rs. 30–Rs. 50 for an hour), so it's probably best to leave your computer at home unless you absolutely need it.

If you plan to bring a laptop to India, remember to never plug your computer into a socket before asking about surge protection—some hotels don't have built-in current stabilizers, and extreme electrical fluctuations can damage your adapter.

Contacts Cybercafes. More than 4,000 Internet cafés worldwide are listed here.
⊕ *www.cybercafes.com.*

PHONES

The good news is that you can now make a direct-dial telephone call from virtually any point on earth. The bad news? You can't always do so cheaply. Calling from a hotel is almost always the most expensive option; hotels usually add huge surcharges to all calls, particularly international ones. You can phone from call centers, roadside shops, or even the post office. Calling cards usually keep costs to a minimum, but only if you purchase them locally. And then there are cell phones *(⇨ below)*, which are more prevalent than landlines in some areas; as expensive as cell-phone calls can be, they are still usually a much cheaper option than calling from your hotel.

Using landlines as well as cell phones in India can be frustrating—sometimes the connections are great, sometimes they're lousy, and you'll almost always have to repeat yourself at least once because connections just don't seem to be that crisp.

A few peculiarities to keep in mind: Indian businesses usually have a series of phone numbers instead of just one, because networks can get congested. If a number reads "562/331701 through 331708," for example, you can reach the establishment using any number between 331701 and 331708. Some of the numbers may be telefax numbers, so if you're trying to send a fax and someone answers, ask them to put the fax machine on. Homes may also have two (or more) phone lines, although this is becoming less common with the near-universality of cell phones, especially among young urbanites.

There is no standard number of digits in landline phone numbers across the country. The norm, however, is 10 digits, which includes a city code of two or three digits. Cell-phone numbers are always 10 digits and start with the number 8 or 9. If the cell number is from another state, you'll need to dial 0 first.

The country code for India is 91, after which you dial the city code, and then the phone number. Delhi's city code is 11, and Mumbai's is 22. Some city codes are three digits, such as the code for Amritsar, which is 183.

CALLING WITHIN INDIA

If you're calling long distance within India to any of the landline numbers listed in this book, dial a zero, then the city code, then the phone number. You only have to dial a zero before a 10-digit cell-phone number—there is no city code. When calling from a cell phone to another one in a different city, the call is considered long distance.

Aside from the quality of connections at times, the local telephone system is adequate for getting in touch when you need to. All phone numbers can be dialed directly from pretty much every public access phone, eliminating the need for an operator.

If you don't have a cell phone, the easiest option is to make a call from one of the ubiquitous public call offices (PCOs), easily identifiable by their bright yellow signs. They're not really offices so much as open-air booths, and they're pretty much on every street corner in Indian cities and in small villages, too, as well as in airports and train stations. PCOs are equipped with ISD/STD capabilities, meaning you can make both international and long-distance domestic calls in addition to local ones. (ISD stands for "international subscriber dialing," STD for "subscriber trunk [direct distance] dialing.") You'll make a call from a regular telephone connected to a meter that keeps track of the time. Once you hang up, an attendant will give you a receipt with the meter reading and tell you how much you owe. Rates are on a per-minute basis, and there is no surcharge. At less than Rs. 10 per minute, domestic calls won't break the bank. It's much more expensive to call internationally, though, so inquire about current rates to different countries. Still, if you just want to call home quickly, a PCO is extremely convenient and hassle-free. Try to avoid making calls from hotels. They often come with huge surcharges, and it's just as convenient to use the PCO down the street.

Directory assistance is spotty in India. The private company JustDial (⊕ *www.justdial.com*) is reliable and has numbers all over the country. Two national numbers—6999 and 9999—can be called for assistance from anywhere in India.

CALLING OUTSIDE INDIA

International calls can be subject to long delays, but most hotels, airports, train stations, post offices, and PCOs are connected to the International Subscriber Dialing (ISD) system. You just dial 00, followed by the country code, the area code, and the number. If calling from a public phone stall, you'll be handed a receipt with the number of minutes and an attendant will calculate how much you owe. Remember that hotels add an enormous surcharge to international calls and faxes; in addition, they sometimes charge a fee per call made on your calling card. Find out what the charges are before you dial. To avoid the surcharge, make your calls at a PCO. There are no reduced-rate calling hours for international calls. Some Internet cafés are set up to let you use an Internet-based calling service such as Skype. This allows very inexpensive international rates.

The country code for the United States is 1.

Using an AT&T access code to reach an operator can be helpful if you absolutely must use your own calling card from home or want to have charges billed to your personal account. However, it's usually more trouble than it's worth, and calling cards bought locally are guaranteed to be cheaper. Some hotels might not let you use the access number, and surcharges are always involved.

Access Codes AT&T USADirect ☎ *000117* ⊕ *www.att.com.*

CALLING CARDS
Calling cards for use within India are fairly common. The Indian cell phone service providers Airtel, Reliance, and Vodafone sell international prepaid calling cards that you can use to call domestically, too. International rates are less than Rs. 10 per minute. The cards work on cell phones and landlines, including at PCOs, and can be bought at practically any stall or shop selling cell phone services. Remember that there might be a surcharge for connecting with these cards on hotel phones.

CELL PHONES
If you have an unlocked multiband phone (some countries use different frequencies from those used in the United States) and your service provider uses the world-standard GSM network (as do T-Mobile, Cingular, and Verizon), you can probably use your phone abroad. Roaming fees can be steep, however: 99¢ a minute is considered reasonable. And overseas you normally pay the toll charges for incoming calls. It's almost always cheaper to send a text message than to make a call, since text messages have a very low set fee (often less than 5¢).

If you just want to make local calls, consider buying a new SIM card (note that your provider may have to unlock your phone for you to use a different SIM card) and a prepaid service plan in the destination. You'll then have a local number and can make local calls at local rates.

Cell phone technology is excellent in India, and whether you have your own phone or rent one, you'll likely be connected wherever you go because of extensive network coverage all over the country—even in small towns.

If you're based in Europe or another Asian country, your cell phone will probably work in India. American cell phones increasingly have international roaming capabilities, so inquire with your provider. But also confirm how much the provider charges per minute for international roaming, which is expensive unless you have a special plan.

If you are planning on staying several weeks, it may be worth your while (and the least hassle) to simply buy a prepaid local SIM card. In most cities there are cell phone shops on just about every corner, and they often sell good-quality used phones as well as inexpensive new ones.

As an anti-terrorism measure, Indian cell-phone shops are required to have a proof of address for anyone buying a new SIM card or cell phone. Although not all shops are stringent about this, the law does mean that buying a card or phone for a short trip may be more trouble than it's worth. If you do find a shop that's willing to work with you, you'll have to provide a copy of your passport, two passport-size photos, and your local address (normally that of your hotel) to register for a

SIM card. You'll usually be up and running with a phone number in less than 15 minutes. Some upscale hotels also offer phone rentals to their guests.

You will have to pay a certain number of rupees in advance to get talk time. Non-residents do not have the option of "post-pay" plans. Rates are generally around Rs. 1 per minute, depending on who you are calling. When you've run out of minutes, you can easily recharge your phone at a cell phone service shop. Airtel and Vodafone are two of the country's largest cell phone service providers.

Contacts **Cellular Abroad.** You can rent and buy GMS phones and buy SIM cards that work in many countries from Cellular Abroad. ☎ 800/287–5072 ⊕ www.cellularabroad.com. **Mobal.** This company rents mobiles and sells GSM phones (starting at $29) that will operate in 190 or more countries. Per-call rates vary throughout the world. ☎ 888/888–9162 ⊕ www.mobalrental.com. **Planet Fone.** You can rent cell phones here, but the per-minute rates are expensive. ☎ 888/988–4777 ⊕ www.planetfone.com.

▌CUSTOMS AND DUTIES

You're allowed to bring goods of a certain value back home without having to pay any duty or import tax. There's a limit on the amount of tobacco and liquor you can bring back duty-free, and some countries have separate limits for perfumes; for exact figures, check with your customs department. The values of so-called "duty-free" goods are included in these amounts. When you shop abroad, save all your receipts, as customs inspectors may ask to see them as well as the items you purchased. If the total value of your goods is more than the duty-free limit, you'll have to pay a tax (most often a flat percentage) on the value of everything beyond that limit.

The customs process at the international gateways isn't difficult, although the line you have to wait in is likely to be long. If you're entering India with dutiable or valuable articles, you must mention this when you stop at customs. Officials may ask you to fill out a Tourist Baggage Re-Export Form (TBRE), as such articles must be taken with you when you leave India. You'll have to pay a duty on anything listed on the TBRE that you plan to leave in India. Depending on the attitude of the customs official, you may have to list your laptop computer, camera or video equipment, and cell phone on a TBRE form. It's a good idea, though, not to go searching for forms or a customs official unless someone questions you.

Among other things, you may bring the following into India duty-free: personal effects (clothing and jewelry); a camera, a video camera, a laptop computer, a cell phone, 200 cigarettes or 50 cigars or 250 grams of tobacco, up to two liters of alcohol, and gifts not exceeding a value of Rs. 8,000 (about US$175). You may *not* bring in illegal drugs, firearms, Indian currency (although a small amount is unlikely to cause any trouble, especially if you don't declare it), pornographic material, gold or silver that's not jewelry, counterfeit or pirated goods, or antiquities. Consult India's Central Board of Excise and Customs website for complete details.

LEAVING INDIA

Rupees aren't technically allowed out of India; you must exchange them before you depart, although you are unlikely to be questioned or searched for a few small bills you may have kept for a coffee in the airport. Foreign-exchange facilities are usually in the same airport halls as the check-in counters, but there's no access to these facilities once you pass through immigration. Tourists cannot take out more foreign currency than they brought in. There is no limit on gold jewelry.

All animal products, souvenirs, and trophies are subject to the Wildlife Protection Act of 1972. The export of ivory (unless you can prove it's antique) and the skins of protected species aren't allowed. Export of exotic birds, wildlife, orchids, and other flora and fauna is forbidden as well.

In general, items more than 100 years old cannot be exported without a permit from the Archaeological Survey of India (ASI), which has offices in many cities, including Delhi and Mumbai. Reputable shops will provide you with the necessary permit or help you get it.

Information in India Central Board of Excise and Customs ⊕ *www.customs.gov.in.*

US Information US Customs and Border Protection ☏ *877/227–5511* ⊕ *www.cbp.gov.*

▌ EATING OUT

Indian culture definitely revolves around food, and there's no shortage of local restaurants and international chains serving foreign cuisines and fast food in big cities as well as regional Indian cuisine everywhere. There are also lots of little no-frills cafés and food stalls lining the streets where locals can pick up all kinds of snacks in between meals (although you may want to take a cautious stance with its famous street food). India is also a haven for vegetarians, with tons of "veg" restaurants, as they're called. Even "non-veg" places usually have delicious meat-less options.

⇨ *For information on food-related health issues, see Health below.*

Almost all restaurants in India are kid-friendly, even many of the fancier ones in top hotels. If your child doesn't like Indian food, it's almost always possible to order things like sandwiches and pizzas.

American fast food is easily accessible in the larger cities, which often have branches of McDonald's, Pizza Hut, and Domino's Pizza. Nirula's is a well-known fast-food chain in Delhi and other points in the north, and they serve Indian fast food, burgers, and ice cream. In villages and smaller towns across the subcontinent such eateries are nonexistent. In that case, an order of plain bread such as *naan* and lentils may be just the ticket.

MEALS AND MEALTIMES

A regular Indian meal consists of some rice or bread, served with spiced vegetables, meat, and lentils. Accompaniments to the meal can include *chaas* (spiced buttermilk), *lassi* (a sweet or salty yogurt drink), pickle, *papad* (a deep-fried or dry roasted waferlike savory made from lentil or rice), chutney, and *raita* (spiced yogurt). A sweet, usually very sugary and milk-based, is the last course. At the end of the meal, *paan* (a stimulating concoction of sugar and various spices wrapped in the leaves of the betel pepper plant), *supari* (plain betel nut), rock sugar, or anise seed may be served as a breath-freshener/digestive.

Although lots of Indians eat cornflakes or toast to start the day, traditional Indian breakfasts are often much heavier. They can consist of any of the following South Indian foods: *idlis* (steamed rice and lentil cakes) with chutney; *rasam wada* (deep-fried lentil fritters served with a hot, spicy watery lentil curry); *dosas* (a crisp pancake, made with a fermented ground-rice-and-lentil batter); *upma* (light semolina, also known as farina, with vegetables); or *aloo poha* (spicy potatoes mixed with rice flakes).

A good portion of the Indian population is vegetarian for religious reasons, and many people who are not vegetarian don't eat meat every day (and certainly not at every meal). Most Hindus consider the cow sacred and do not eat beef. Muslims (and many Hindus) do not touch pork. And many Hindus choose to eat only chicken and seafood and stay away from red meat. Many Jains are not only vegetarian but also don't eat any vegetable grown under the ground—one reason may be that plucking up the root destroys life. As you travel through India, expect to encounter folks who don't eat meat on Tuesday (in honor of Hanuman, the monkey-god servant of Rama); much of India's religious and ethical life, indeed, revolves around food.

Although South Indian restaurants often start serving lunch early, in North India people tend to eat lunch later in the afternoon than in the United States, sometimes around 2 or 3 pm. Restaurants in cities normally stay open until 11 pm or midnight, as Indians are known for starting dinner quite late (past 10 pm). In other areas, expect an earlier dinner in restaurants (finished by 9 pm) unless you're staying in a luxury hotel. Coffee shops in urban luxury hotels are often open 24 hours.

Snacking is also popular, and common treats include samosas, white-bread sandwiches, *jalebis* (deep-fried bright yellow flour fritters soaked in sugar syrup), and the fudgelike milk sweets. *Masala chai* (spiced milk tea) and ginger tea are extremely popular and are often consumed four to five times a day. But as you go south, coffee becomes equally important and is served boiling hot, creamy, and foamy (sort of like a triple espresso with cream and sugar).

Unless otherwise noted, the restaurants listed in this guide are open daily for lunch and dinner.

RESERVATIONS AND DRESS

Regardless of where you are, it's a good idea to make a reservation if you can, but they also aren't required, except in the fanciest restaurants of upscale, big-city hotels. We only mention them specifically when reservations are essential or when they are not accepted. For popular restaurants, book as far ahead as you can (often 30 days), and reconfirm as soon as you arrive in India. (Large parties should always call ahead to check the reservations policy.)

Very few restaurants require formal attire. By and large India is very casual about dress codes. However, certain clubs do not allow anyone—even in daylight hours—to wear shorts or men to wear sandals.

WINES, BEER, AND SPIRITS

India produces many kinds of liquor, and exorbitant duties make imported spirits unaffordable to all but the wealthiest of its citizens. Its locally produced versions of international brands of rum, vodka, and gin are adequate but generally unmemorable. The sweet local red rum, Old Monk, is worth a try. Kingfisher beer is ubiquitous, refreshing, and bland. With every year more and more Indian wine is produced, and much of it is good, although not overly complex. Scotch whisky is by far the most popular kind of hard liquor in India: Director's Special is a mild and reliable brand.

Alcohol at luxury hotels is vastly marked up. Consider buying your own liquor and having it in your room—you can always call for a glass, bottled water, and soda. If you're a woman traveling alone, drinking in your room is probably a better option in any case.

Indian customs may appear prudish toward drinking—but open a bottle and you may find you're quite popular. According to proper Indian etiquette, alcohol is excluded from many occasions. When you visit someone's house you may not be offered a drink even in the evening, and the strongest beverage you may get is tea. At some Hindu and virtually all Muslim weddings and at festival time, alcohol may not be served. Women are infrequent drinkers, at least in public. Don't be surprised if you encounter quite a few male teetotalers.

Dry days—when alcohol isn't available anywhere in the country—are observed on January 26, August 15, October 2, and on certain festival dates. Some states observe additional dry days, which are usually on or around election days; others prohibit everything but beer.

ELECTRICITY

Blackouts lasting anywhere from 30 minutes to 12 hours are a part of everyday Indian life, particularly in summer when the load is high. But if you're staying at a mid- to high-end hotel, there will, no doubt, be a generator that can restore electricity within seconds. Storms can play havoc with electricity, and low-voltage electricity and surges are problems. It's always a good idea to have a flashlight or a small hand-held fan if you plan on being in rural, rugged areas for any length of time.

The electrical current in India is 220 volts, 50 cycles alternating current (AC). There are two types of wall outlets in India: large, three-pronged ones used for large appliances such as refrigerators and air-conditioners, and smaller ones that take plugs with two round prongs, like those used in continental Europe.

Consider making a small investment in a universal adapter, which has several types of plugs in one lightweight, compact unit. Most laptops and mobile phone chargers are dual voltage (i.e., they operate equally well on 110 and 220 volts), so they require only an adapter. These days the same is true of small appliances such as hair dryers. Always check labels and manufacturer instructions to be sure. Don't use 110-volt outlets marked "for shavers only" for high-wattage appliances such as hair-dryers.

Contacts Help for World Travelers Global & Electric Phone Directory. This directory has information on electrical plugs and telephones around the world. ⊕ www.kropla.com.

EMERGENCIES

Delhi's 24-hour East West Medical Center has a referral list of doctors, dentists, pharmacists, and lawyers throughout India. Its staff can arrange treatment wherever you are in the country. It also provides air ambulances that can evacuate you from remote areas in the case of a medical emergency. Note: You must pay the center when you receive assistance—credit cards are accepted—and then apply for reimbursement by your insurance company later. It's necessary to get in touch with East West first so that they can verify your policy details. This can take anywhere from a few hours to a day, depending on the day of the week and whether the details are in order; at that point East West will organize payment.

Contact Meera Rescue, based in Delhi with branches in Mumbai and Goa, if international evacuation is necessary. (Whatever happens, don't go to a government hospital. In a grave emergency, contact your embassy.) Meera Rescue is a professional evacuation service recognized by international insurance companies; the company evacuates from anywhere in the country to hospitals in major cities and overseas if necessary; it's open 24 hours. Like East West, you must pay Meera and be reimbursed by your insurance company.

General Emergency Contacts East West Medical Centre ⊠ 28 Greater Kailash 1, New Delhi ☎ 11/2464–1494. **Meera Rescue** ⊠ 112 Jor Bagh, New Delhi ☎ 11/2465–3170, 11/2465–3175 ⊕ www.meera-rescue.com.

Consulates and Embassies Indian Consulate General ⊕ www.indiacgny.org. **Indian Embasssy** ☎ 202/939–7000 ⊕ www.indianembassy.org. **US Consulate (Mumbai)** ⊠ Bandra Kurla Complex, C-49, G-Block, Bandra East, Mumbai, Maharashtra ☎ 22/2672–4000 ⊕ mumbai.usconsulate.gov. **US Embassy** ⊠ Shantipath, Chanakyapuri, New Delhi ☎ 11/2419–8000 ⊕ newdelhi. usembassy.gov.

HEALTH

No vaccination certificate or inoculations are required to enter India from the United States, Canada, or the United Kingdom unless you're coming via certain parts of sub-Saharan Africa, in which case you'll need proof of inoculation against yellow fever. If you're coming from Africa, it's crucial to have proof of inoculation against yellow fever or you could be quarantined on arrival in dismal government facilities.

Ultimately you must decide what vaccinations are right for you before you travel to India. Talk to your doctor about this three months before departure. The Centers for Disease Control and Prevention (CDC) post a list of recommended vaccinations for the Indian subcontinent on their website; these include hepatitis A and typhoid fever.

In areas where malaria and dengue fever—both carried by mosquitoes—are prevalent, use mosquito nets, wear clothing that covers the body, apply repellent containing DEET, and use spray for flying insects in living and sleeping areas. On arrival in India, consider purchasing repellents that plug into the wall and release a mosquito-repelling scent. These are effective in keeping a room mosquito-free and can be found in any market. Also you may want to consider taking malaria prophylactics, as the disease exists in many regions of India. There's no vaccine to combat malaria and dengue, and mosquitoes can pass on other infections, such as the Chikungunya virus, so preventing bites should always be your first line of defense.

While traveling in remote areas or in small towns, it's a good idea to have a medical kit containing a pain reliever, diarrhea medication, moist towelettes, antibacterial skin ointment and skin cleanser, antacids, adhesive bandages, and any prescription medications.

The precautions you take for yourself in India are the same ones you should take for your child. Make sure they have all their vaccinations, and consult a pediatrician about anti-malaria medication. Bring a mosquito repellent spray from home that you know to be safe for children. And only give them bottled water to help guard against stomach problems that could spoil a short trip.

The most common types of illnesses are caused by contaminated food and water.

If you have problems, mild cases of traveler's diarrhea may respond to Imodium (known generically as loperamide) or Pepto-Bismol. Be sure to drink plenty of fluids; if you can't keep fluids down, seek medical help. Infectious diseases can be airborne or passed via mosquitoes and ticks and through direct or indirect physical contact with animals or people. Some, including Norwalk-like viruses that affect your digestive tract, can be passed along through contaminated food. Speak with your physician and/or check the CDC or World Health Organization websites for health alerts, particularly if you're pregnant, traveling with children, or have a chronic illness.

SPECIFIC ISSUES IN INDIA

The major health risk in India is traveler's diarrhea, caused by eating contaminated fruit or vegetables or drinking contaminated water, so it's important to watch what you eat. Avoid ice, uncooked food, and unpasteurized milk and milk products, and **drink only bottled water or water that has been boiled for at least one minute.** Avoid tap water, ice, and drinks to which tap water has been added. **You may want to turn down offers of "filtered" water;** it may have been filtered to take out particles but not purified to kill parasites. Water purified through an Aquaguard filter system, however, is generally safe (as long as the filter has been maintained correctly). You'll be fine at most places catering to foreign tourists. **When buying bottled water, make sure that the cap hasn't been tampered with.** Bottles are sometimes refilled with tap water. However, moves to encourage people to refill bottles with Aquagard water to help reduce the country's mountain of plastic waste is blurring this issue. Many mid-range tourist hotels offer free or very cheap boiled or filtered water. Soft drinks, in bottles or cans, and packaged fruit juices are safe, readily available options. And always **keep at least one bottle of water in your hotel room** for brushing your teeth as well as for drinking.

If your stomach does get upset, try to drink plenty of purified water or tea—ginger tea (*adrak chai*) is a good folk remedy. In severe cases, rehydrate yourself with a salt-sugar solution—½ teaspoon salt (*namak*) and 4 tablespoons sugar (*shakar or cheeni*) per quart of water.

Avoid raw vegetables and fruit outside of fancy restaurants, even those that have been peeled, unless it was you who did the cutting and peeling. Make sure that all meats are thoroughly cooked. It's not necessary to go vegetarian, and to do so would mean missing out on some delicious dishes. Just choose restaurants with care, and eat hot foods while they're hot. A little bit of personal hygiene can also go a long way in preventing stomach upsets. Wash your hands before you eat anything, and carry moist towelettes or hand sanitizer. **Locally popular, worn-looking restaurants often serve the safest food.** Such restaurants often can't afford refrigeration, so the cooks prepare food acquired that day—not always the case with the upscale places. Some hotel chefs buy in bulk and, thanks to temperamental electricity, a refrigerator may preserve more than just foodstuffs. That said, stomach upsets often are due more to the richness and spice of Indian cuisine than to the lack of hygiene. Many hotel restaurants cook Indian dishes with quite a bit of oil. If you have a sensitive stomach, order carefully and don't overdo things, especially in your first few days when your stomach is getting used to the new flavors. Fried foods from street vendors often look delicious, but inspect the oil: if it looks as old as the pot, it could be rancid.

Stomach issues are what tend to scare first-time visitors the most, and if you're only going to be in India for a short time, it makes sense to take as many precautions as possible so sickness won't cut into your vacation. However, if you're going to be in India for a longer period, try to acclimate yourself to things like street food, filtered water, ice, and the wonderful abundance of fresh-squeezed

juices, because avoiding every single thing that could possibly make you sick in India is not only impractical, but also limiting. Chances are that your body will simply adjust and become resistant to most stomach problems.

All Indian cities are heavily polluted, though serious efforts have been going on for years to reduce vehicle pollution. Mumbai and Delhi require their taxis to run on compressed natural gas (CNG), which has considerably reduced the smog. People with breathing problems, especially asthma, should **carry the appropriate respiratory remedies.** India's heat can dehydrate you, and dust can irritate your throat, so **drink plenty of liquids.** Dehydration will make you weak and more susceptible to other health problems. Seek air-conditioned areas when possible, and plan your day so you're visiting tourist sites in the early morning or late afternoon, when the sun is less strong.

If you travel into jungle areas during or right after the monsoon, you may fall victim to the disgusting but generally non-dangerous plague of leeches, which lie in wait on damp land. Help protect yourself by covering your legs and carrying salt. Applying DEET and strong-smelling chemicals such as deodorant to your skin and pants will also help make your flesh less appealing. Don't wear sandals. If a leech clings to your clothing or skin, dab it with a pinch of salt and it will fall off.

For bedbug bites, buy a bar of Dettol soap (available throughout India) and use it when you bathe to relieve itching and discomfort. If you're staying in a dubious hotel, **check under the mattress** for bedbugs, cockroaches, and other unwanted critters. Use Flit, Finit, or one of the other readily available spray repellents on suspicious-looking furniture and in mosquito-infested rooms. Mosquito coils (*kachua*), which you must light, and Good Knight pellets, which are plugged into an outlet, are fairly effective at "smoking" mosquitoes away. On the road, **treat scratches, cuts, or blisters at once.** If you're trekking, save the bottle and cap from your first bottled water so you can refill it with water that you purify yourself.

Beware of overexposure even on overcast days. To avoid sunburn, **use a sunscreen** with a sun-protection factor of at least 30. To play it safe, **wear a wide-brimmed hat.**

OVER-THE-COUNTER REMEDIES

You don't necessarily need to lug a medicine cabinet with you to India—**practically every over-the-counter medication and medical supply under the sun is available** in the big cities should you need them. The pharmacies, or "chemists"—which are also abundant—will carry a wide variety of both recognizable name brands and Indian versions. If you're not sure what you need to make yourself feel better, shopkeepers can usually make good recommendations.

CHILDREN IN INDIA

Bringing your kids to India may seem daunting, but most children love it. India is like a giant circus, with color, chaos, and a sideshow every minute. Kids are warmly welcomed everywhere except, perhaps, in the stuffiest of restaurants, and most Indians will bend over backward to help you with a child-related need. In fact, so much affection is lavished on children here—everyone wants to pick them up, pinch their cheeks, talk to them—that your little ones may even get overwhelmed.

There are a couple of thing to remember: Many diseases are prevalent in India that no longer exist elsewhere, so **check with your pediatrician first** and make sure your child's immunizations are current. It's easiest to bring an infant (who cannot yet crawl, and who is still dependent on breast-feeding or formula) or children who are a bit older and can walk on their own.

Something you might find strange is the fact that no one really uses car seats in India; even educated women think nothing of holding infants in their arms while sitting in the front seat of a moving vehicle (or on the back of a motorbike). So if you plan on getting a car and driver, **don't expect to get a car seat**—bring your own (don't expect, either, that seat belts will always work).

Health Warnings National Centers for Disease Control & Prevention (*CDC*). ☎ *800/232–4636* ⊕ *www.cdc.gov/travel.* **World Health Organization** (*WHO*). ⊕ *www.who.int.*

▌ HOURS OF OPERATION

Most banks are open weekdays 10–2 and Saturday 10–noon, and most ATMs are open around the clock. International airports and some top hotels have 24-hour currency-exchange facilities, and the major American Express branches have extended hours for check cashing. Post offices are generally open Monday–Saturday 10–5.

Gas stations are usually open daily 6 am–10 pm. In larger cities, some stay open 24 hours.

Most museums are closed on Monday. Site museums (adjoining archaeological monuments) are normally closed on Friday.

Pharmacies are usually open daily 9:30–8, though in cities there are some 24-hour establishments. In some places you can also buy medications from the 24-hour pharmacies at large hospitals. (Note that in India pharmacies are called "chemists.")

Outside the major metropolitan areas, many shopkeepers close their establishments for lunch and an afternoon siesta. Many stores are closed Sunday.

Bars and nightclubs in the big cities are usually done by 2 am, although some local laws mandate much earlier closing times, such as 11.

HOLIDAYS

India's fixed date national holidays are January 26 (Republic Day), August 15 (Independence Day), October 2 (Gandhi's birthday), and December 25 (Christmas). Endless festivals enliven—and shut down—different parts of the country throughout the year. Festivals often affect availability of travel connections or the time needed to reach the airport, so look into the holidays that are coming up as you plan your itinerary.

▌ MAIL

The Indian postal system is fairly reliable, and stamps can be bought in post offices and various other shops. Airmail letters and postcards take a week to 10 days to reach most destinations from India. Postal delays are caused by holiday rushes (during Diwali and the Christmas season) and strikes.

Airmail letters (weighing 20 grams, or 0.7 ounce) to Australia, New Zealand, United States, Canada, South Africa, or Europe cost Rs. 15; postcards cost Rs. 12. Aerograms to anywhere in the world are Rs. 15. Although your postcards are likely to arrive, they may take a very long time to do so.

SHIPPING PACKAGES

There are many options for shipping gifts and other purchases home. Many stores—especially those that cater to tourists—ship items using courier services or other private methods. It's usually reliable and fast, but reconsider shipping anything special that you would absolutely hate to lose. You can send parcels home "surface air lifted" (SAL), a special service provided by the Indian postal department that's cheaper than airmail. A letter or parcel of 250 grams or less costs Rs. 310 to North America. Each additional 250 grams cost Rs. 65. Different rates apply for other countries.

▌ MONEY

A trip to India can be as luxurious and expensive—or as bare-bones and cheap—as you want it to be. The economy has really spiked since 2000, along with domestic travel and international foot traffic, and as a result, room rates at fancy urban hotels are comparable to those in New York, London, or Paris. You'll pay substantially more for everything in popular tourist spots and big cities compared with the rest of the country, although certain goods (including soda, cigarettes, chips, etc.) have a maximum retail price (MRP) printed on their packaging. It's illegal to sell such products for more than the printed amount, although sometimes vendors try to charge foreigners more, assuming they are unaware of this price regulation.

If you're willing to stay at modest hotels and eat where the locals do, you might find that the most expensive part of your trip turns out to be the international airfare ($1,000–$2,000, depending on when you go). It's possible to find good hotels for less than US$70 a night, and the cheapest run less than US$30 (sometimes a lot less). You could also conceivably eat every meal for less than US$2.

Many merchants, even in big cities, still only accept payment in cash. Always carry sufficient rupees as well as a credit card in your wallet. (Although it's possible to cash traveler's checks in big cities, it's rarely convenient to do so.) Shopkeepers appreciate it when people pay with the exact amount, or as close to it as possible. In fact, they balk at giving change in general. The 1,000 rupee note should definitely not be used to pay for, say, something that costs Rs. 100, because merchants might not even have that much change on hand. It's advisable to stick to denominations of Rs. 100 or less, and don't flaunt Rs. 500 and Rs. 1,000 notes.

A cup of tea from a stall costs about Rs. 5 (US9¢), but in top hotels it can cost more than Rs. 80 (US$1.45). A 650-ml bottle of beer costs about Rs. 75 (US$1.40) in a shop, Rs. 250 (US$4.50) without taxes in a top hotel. A 6-km (4-mile) taxi ride in Delhi is supposed to cost about Rs. 60 (US$1.10), though it rarely does because taxi drivers often do not want to use their meters and try to charge higher prices for tourists.

ITEM	AVERAGE COST
Cup of Coffee	Rs. 10–Rs. 50, fancy Rs. 80
Glass of Wine	Rs. 250–Rs. 500
Glass of Beer	Rs. 250 in a bar or hotel
Sandwich	Rs. 30–Rs. 70
Museum Admission	Rs. 200–Rs. 250 (foreigner rates)

Prices throughout this guide are given for adults. Substantially reduced fees are almost always available for children, students, and senior citizens.

ATMS AND BANKS

Your home bank will probably charge a fee for using ATMs abroad; the foreign bank you use may also charge a fee. Nevertheless, you'll usually get a better rate of exchange at an ATM than you will at a currency-exchange office or even when changing money in a bank. And extracting funds as you need them is a safer option than carrying around a large amount of cash.

■TIP➜ PINs with more than four digits are not recognized at ATMs in many countries. If yours has five or more, remember to change it before you leave.

There are only a few cash machines in smaller towns in India, but larger cities are dotted with ATMs. Look for ICICI, HDFC, or HSBC ATMs, which generally accept foreign cards. Other ATMs might only accept Indian cards, especially in smaller towns. If you know you'll be traveling to a rural area, it's crucial to have enough cash on hand.

If you think you'll need cash from your bank account or cash advances through your credit card, make sure that your bank and credit cards are programmed for ATM use in India before you leave home, and inform your bank that you'll be using your cards in India. All ATMs function in English, and most have security guards.

CREDIT CARDS

It's a good idea to inform your credit-card company before you travel, especially if you're going abroad and don't travel internationally very often. Otherwise, the credit-card company might put a hold on your card owing to unusual activity. Record all your credit-card numbers—as well as the phone numbers to call if your cards are lost or stolen—in a safe place, so you're prepared should something go wrong. Both MasterCard and Visa have general numbers you can call (collect if you're abroad) if your card is lost, but you're better off calling the number of your issuing bank, since MasterCard and Visa usually just transfer you to your bank.

If you plan to use your credit card for cash advances, you'll need to apply for a PIN at least two weeks before your trip. Although it's usually cheaper (and safer) to use a credit card abroad for large purchases (so you can cancel payments or be reimbursed if there's a problem), note that some credit-card companies *and* the banks that issue them add substantial percentages to all foreign transactions, whether they're in a foreign currency or not. Check on these fees before leaving home, so there won't be any surprises when you get the bill.

■TIP➜ Before you charge something, ask the merchant whether or not he or she plans to do a dynamic currency conversion (DCC). In such a transaction the credit-card processor (shop, restaurant, or hotel, not Visa or MasterCard) converts the currency and charges you in dollars. In most cases you'll pay the merchant a 3% fee for this service in addition to any credit-card company and issuing-bank foreign-transaction surcharges.

Dynamic currency conversion programs are becoming increasingly widespread. Merchants who participate in them are supposed to ask whether you want to be charged in dollars or the local currency, but they don't always do so. And even if they do offer you a choice, they may well avoid mentioning the additional surcharges. The good news is that you *do* have a choice.

Credit cards are widely accepted in large Indian cities, especially at the retail chain stores and the upscale restaurants. Smaller merchants and street stalls, however, are likely to take only cash. It's a good idea to keep at least Rs. 1,000 (in small denominations) in your wallet at all times in the cities, along with your credit card, so you'll always have both options. In rural India, don't ever count on being able to pay with a credit card, and always have enough cash to see you through.

American Express is rarely accepted in India, Diners Club is not widely accepted, and Discover isn't accepted at all.

Reporting Lost Cards American Express ☎ 800/528–4800 in the US, 336/393–1111 collect from abroad ⊕ www.americanexpress. com. **Diners Club** ☎ 800/234–6377 in the US, 303/799–1504 collect from abroad ⊕ www. dinersclub.com. **MasterCard** ☎ 800/627–8372 in the US, 636/722–7111 collect from abroad ⊕ www.mastercard.com. **Visa** ☎ 800/847–2911 in the US, 410/581–9994 collect from abroad ⊕ www.visa.com.

CURRENCY AND EXCHANGE

The units of Indian currency are the *rupee* and the (rare) *paisa*—100 paise equal one rupee. Paper money comes in denominations of 2 (also rare), 5, 10, 20, 50, 100, 500, and 1,000 rupees. Coins are worth 5, 10, 20, 25, and 50 paise (all rare), 1 rupee, 2 rupees, 5 rupees, and 10 rupees, but it's unlikely that you'll see anything less than 1 rupee. At this writing, the rate of exchange is approximately US$1 to Rs. 55, so that a 500-rupee note is worth just over $9. The price of big-ticket items, such as real estate or cars, is usually given in units of *lakh* or *crore*. A lakh is equal to 100,000, and a crore is equal to 100 lakh. Therefore, 1 lakh rupees is equal to roughly $1,800, and 1 crore is $180,000.

India has strict rules against importing or exporting its currency. The currency-exchange booths at the international airports are always open for arriving and departing overseas flights. When you change money, remember to get a certain amount in small denominations (in 10s is best) to pay taxi drivers and such. Reject torn, frayed, taped, or soiled bills, as many merchants, hotels, and restaurants won't accept them, and it's a hassle to find a bank to get them exchanged.

Always change money from an authorized money changer and insist on receiving an encashment slip. Some banks now charge a nominal fee for this slip, which you might need if you want to reconvert rupees into your own currency on departure from India. Don't be lured by illegal street hawkers who offer you a higher exchange rate.

For the most favorable rates, change money at banks. Although ATM transaction fees may be higher abroad than at home, ATM rates are excellent because they're based on wholesale rates offered only by major banks. India's state-run banks can take forever to cash traveler's checks. If you must use them, save time and use an American Express office or the foreign-exchange service at your hotel. Rates will be slightly lower, but you'll save irritation and time. Rates are also unfavorable in airports, at train and bus stations, and at restaurants, hotels, and stores.

TRAVELER'S CHECKS AND CARDS

Fewer establishments accept traveler's checks these days than ever before. Nevertheless, they're a cheap and secure way to carry extra money, particularly on trips to urban areas. Both Citibank (under the Visa brand) and American Express issue traveler's checks in the United States, but Amex is better known and more widely accepted; you can also avoid hefty surcharges by cashing Amex checks at Amex offices. Whatever you do, keep track of all the serial numbers in case the checks are lost or stolen.

You can use traveler's checks in India, but in most cases it's just not that convenient to cash them. Cash (both brought in and withdrawn from an ATM) and credit cards are better options. You can cash traveler's checks only in big cities, and most merchants, whether urban or rural, don't accept them. Lost or stolen checks can usually be replaced within 24 hours. To ensure a speedy refund, buy your own traveler's checks—don't let someone else pay for them, as the purchaser is the only one able to request a refund. Don't leave traveler's checks in your hotel room, and keep the counterfoil with the check numbers separate from the checks.

Contacts American Express ☎ 888/412–6945 *in the US, 801/945–9450 collect outside of the US to add value or for assistance* ⊕ *www.americanexpress.com.*

▌ PACKING

India is full of beautiful, colorful, over-the-top fashions, but your visit here probably shouldn't include lots of fancy things from your own closet. Make it a point to buy Indian statement pieces during your travels if that's your thing, keeping the original contents of your suitcase simple: shirts made of plain cotton or cotton-synthetic blends and a couple of pairs of comfortable pants—all of which can be washed easily and worn again throughout your trip. Avoiding completely synthetic fabrics that don't breathe is key, since much of India is hot year-round, with temperatures topping 110 degrees or more in the summer months. Delicate fabrics just don't respond well to vigorous Indian washing and powerful detergents, let alone profuse amounts of sweat. Dry cleaning is available across every city and in all major hotels, but even if you think it's a safe bet, quality can vary significantly among dry cleaners, and they tend to use harsh chemicals.

Don't worry about looking too casual—India is not a dressy society. If an upscale function or fancy dinner at a big-city restaurant is on the itinerary, men can often get away with just a formal shirt and pants. Women can wear a simple dress or a dressier blouse with pants and heels.

Bring sunglasses, a bottle of nonsticky, high-SPF sunblock (the amount of protection in sunblocks sold in India is questionable) and two good pairs of footwear—sandals with rubber soles and lightweight walking shoes are smart options. Skip anything that's difficult to maneuver in, such as hiking boots—unless you'll be trekking in the north—since you'll often be required to remove your shoes to enter religious sites.

Most important is to dress modestly, especially at sacred sites. In such places, long pants are appropriate for men; for women, stick to below-the-knee skirts, dresses, or neat pants. T-shirts are fine, but the male topless look should be left to wandering *sadhus* (Hindu ascetics). Women should always avoid wearing tight tank tops or tops that are sheer or have plunging necklines. It's not that Indian women never wear revealing clothing, but foreigners wearing such items often attract unwanted attention. If you must wear shorts, keep them on the long side, because only children can get away with short shorts. Avoid doing odd things like wearing a long Indian tunic as a dress or a tight sari blouse as a top. Bathing suits worn in public pools frequented by Indians should be on the conservative side, but women should feel free to wear bikinis at beach resorts and large hotels that cater to a foreign clientele.

Things to keep handy at all times are toilet paper and moist towelettes or hand sanitizer, especially on long train trips. Few public restrooms provide toilet paper or a way to wash your hands thoroughly. In any case, there probably won't be any hand towels, so a handkerchief for drying your hands is also useful. Consider also carrying a money pouch or belt, a basic first-aid kit, and a small flashlight. Good sanitary napkins are sold in India, but women should pack their own tampons unless they don't mind using ones without applicators, which are generally the only kind readily available in India.

If you visit in monsoon season, bring a collapsible umbrella. Instead of bringing your own rain boots, buy a cheap pair once you arrive, or just don some sandals. Locals call rain boots gum shoes. In winter, bring a sweater or a light jacket for cool evenings.

WITH CHILDREN

If you have a young child, it's probably not worth the bother of packing a stroller: sidewalks in Indian cities often have cracks or even holes, and in any case they don't usually have enough space for them. Be extra careful in Delhi and Mumbai, as streets are crowded and cars unforgiving. **Pack all necessary medications as well as rash creams, zinc oxide, sunscreen, diapers, and diaper wipes.**

Although major brands of disposable diapers, as well as Nestlé instant baby cereals, are available in most cities, they can be hard to find. Powdered milk produced by such companies as Amul and Nestlé is readily available, as is sterilized (UHT) milk sold in sealed boxes. Use those products instead of looking for fresh milk, which needs to be boiled properly—in fact, it's a wise precaution to boil UHT milk as well. If you run out of formula, Lactogen is a reliable Indian brand. Bottled mineral water and packaged snacks—potato chips, cookies, chocolate bars, fruit juices, and soft drinks—are sold throughout India. Though not nutritious, such snacks are often preferable to food that may be spicy or not entirely hygienic. If you're heading out for a day of sightseeing, ask your hotel staff if they can pack a lunch for your child. A small hot pot or kettle can be useful for making instant soup or noodles, which are also available throughout India.

If you'll be taking any air-conditioned trains, bring a few pieces of warm clothing, as the cars get very cold. Leggings help protect against mosquitoes in the evening, hats shade faces from the sun, and rubber slippers or sandals are always practical. A few pairs of socks can come in handy. If you plan to travel by car **bring a portable car seat.** *See the transportation section (above) for further information.* Choose accommodations that are air-conditioned or have rooms equipped with mosquito netting to protect your child from mosquito bites. **Pack plenty of insect repellent as well as a 3-square-foot piece of soft cloth netting** (available in fabric stores), which you can drape over a carriage or car seat to shield your child from insects. Pellet repellents that plug into the wall and release a mosquito-repelling scent are available in stores across India, and are effective in keeping a room mosquito-free. It's a good idea to purchase such a gizmo on arrival (try Good Knight or ALLOUT).

▌ PASSPORTS AND VISAS

Unless you hold an Indian passport or are a citizen of Nepal or Bhutan, you need a visa to enter India. This applies to children and infants as well.

Info Travisa
⊕ *indiavisa.travisaoutsourcing.com.*

PASSPORTS

US passports are valid for 10 years. You must apply in person if you're getting a passport for the first time; if your previous passport was lost, stolen, or damaged; or if your previous passport has expired and was issued more than 15 years ago or when you were under 16. All children under 18 must appear in person to apply for or renew a passport. Both parents must accompany any child under 14 (or send a notarized statement with their permission) and provide proof of their relationship to the child.

▌**TIP→** Before your trip, make two copies of your passport's data page (one for someone at home and another for you to carry separately). You can also scan the page and email it to someone at home and/or yourself.

There are 13 regional passport offices, as well as 7,000 passport acceptance facilities in post offices, public libraries, and other governmental offices. If you're renewing a passport, you can do so by mail. Forms are available at passport acceptance facilities and online.

The cost to apply for a new passport is $165 for adults, $120 for children under 16; adult renewals are $140. Allow up to six weeks for processing, both for first-time passports and renewals. For an expediting fee of $60 you can reduce this time to about two to three weeks. If your trip is less than two weeks away, you can get a passport even more rapidly by going to a passport office with the necessary documentation. Private expediters can get things done in as little as 48 hours, but charge hefty fees for their services.

VISAS

A visa is essentially formal permission to enter a country. India no longer handles visa applications directly, except on an emergency basis. Instead, you must go to the website of Travisa Outsourcing to submit an application and pay electronically. A standard, multiple-entry six-month tourist visa costs US$73 for American citizens. Non-US citizens pay different fees. If you're traveling on business or as a student or journalist, you require a different (and more expensive) visa.

Travisa has offices in Washington, New York, Chicago, San Francisco, and Houston, and you can submit your passport in person at those locations. Refer to the Travisa website for detailed instructions. Your Indian visa should be processed within five days from the time Travisa receives your passport, but start the process at least two weeks before your departure to allow for glitches.

As far as the visa's validity goes, the clock starts ticking the day the government issues you one, not the day you arrive in India, so note the expiration date. You must enter and leave during the specified time period, and your passport must have a remaining validity of at least six months. If you need to extend your visa, go to the Foreigners' Regional Registration Office (FRRO) in one of the major cities. But beware—the Indian government makes it extremely difficult to extend a visa for any reason, and if you overstay your visa, you may be required to get clearance from

India's Ministry of Home Affairs to leave the country. Punishment can range from heavy fines to actually being jailed. Bottom line: Follow the visa rules and don't expect exceptions to be made, even if you think you have a good excuse.

US Passport Information
US Department of State ☎ 877/487-2778 ⊕ travel.state.gov/passport.

US Passport and Visa Expediters
A. Briggs Passport & Visa Expeditors ☎ 800/806-0581, 202/338-0111 ⊕ www.abriggs.com. **American Passport Express** ☎ 800/455-5166 ⊕ www.americanpassport.com. **Passport Express** ☎ 800/362-8196 ⊕ www.passportexpress.com. **Travel Document Systems** ☎ 800/874-5100 Washington D.C., 877/874-5104 New York, 888/874-5100 San Francisco, 866/797-2600 Houston ⊕ www.traveldocs.com. **Travel the World Visas** ☎ 202/223-8822 ⊕ www.world-visa.com.

❙ RESTROOMS

When you need a restroom, ask for the "loo," the washroom, or the toilet. Two types of toilets are available wherever you go in India. Traditional Indian toilets are holes in the ground—a squat variety with two steps to put your feet. There are also Western-style toilets, but the toilet seat, except in luxury hotels and better restaurants, may be messy. In many bathrooms you'll see a faucet, a small hand-held showerhead, and/or a bucket with a beaker or other small vessel; Indians use these to rinse, bidet-style, after using the toilet. Hands are always washed elsewhere, usually in an area right outside the bathroom. Outside of hotels, malls, and some restaurants, public restrooms are rarely clean, and ideally avoided. On long road journeys, finding any public restroom—let alone a clean one—is difficult. Always use the restroom before you set out and ration your fluid intake during a long journey. Be on the lookout for a decent hotel or opt for the outdoors. Luxury hotels and fancier restaurants usually have clean bathrooms.

Nicer hotels and restaurants provide toilet paper, but you can't depend on this, as most Indians don't use the stuff (they use their left hand and running water to clean themselves, which is why this hand is considered unclean). And often soap and paper towels are not available for washing up afterward. Keep toilet paper and towelettes with you at all times, which are readily available in pharmacies and grocery stores in large cities. Never throw anything other than a small amount of toilet paper in a toilet; India's septic systems clog easily.

Find a Loo **The Bathroom Diaries.** This site has a searchable map of restrooms the world over—each one located, reviewed, and rated. ⊕ *www.thebathroomdiaries.com.*

▌ SAFETY

There are no generalizations that can be made regarding potential dangers for all tourists in India, but urban areas do have their particular crime patterns, and everyone is vulnerable in bad parts of town. For example, Delhi is known to be dangerous for women at night and has more crime in general than other big cities in India. In Mumbai, however, women are relatively safe at all hours, with fewer crimes taking place, which is the main reason a reported rape there is almost always a big deal, but not so newsworthy in Delhi.

Scams for targeting foreigners abound. One of the better-known, yet not that common routines comes from the shoe shiners at Delhi's Connaught Place, who furtively sling mud at your feet and then point out how badly your shoes need to be cleaned. Just be cautious everywhere you go, and know that in a country in which most tourists stand out—and that is filled with locals vying for their business—you're always a potential target.

Theft in hotels is not common, but you should never leave money, traveler's checks, passports, or jewelry in plain sight. If your hotel has a safe, definitely use it, but if there's nothing to lock up valuables, you may wish to take them with you. Follow the lead of locals: avoid wandering around late at night, especially in smaller towns where shutters close early, and avoid road journeys after dark. As anywhere, never leave suitcases unattended in airports or train stations.

India has no tourist police, except in Mumbai, and they patrol infrequently in orange jeeps. The most visible police officers are traffic cops, clad in white and khaki; they can usually help out, even with a nontraffic problem (though taxis are in their jurisdiction). Otherwise, look for a regular police officer, in a khaki uniform.

Avoid strangers who offer their services as guides or money changers, and do not agree to be taken anywhere with anyone. In crowds, be alert for pickpockets—wear a money belt, and/or keep your purse close to your body and securely closed. If you travel by train, don't accept food or beverages from fellow passengers. Those who accept such generosity—and Indians are most commonly the victims—sometimes ingest drug-laced refreshment and are robbed once the drug takes effect. It's likely that you will be offered food on a train; Indians feel uncomfortable eating meals in front of another without sharing, but it's safest to offer an excuse and refuse. In train stations, ignore touts who tell you that your hotel of choice is full or has closed; they hope to settle you into a place where they get a kickback for bringing in business. Do not agree to carry a parcel for anyone.

Women need to take extra precautions. If you're alone, don't travel late at night, especially in Delhi. Avoid seedy areas, touts volunteering their services, or over-friendly strangers and jostling crowds of men. Also, never get into a taxi or auto-rickshaw if a second man accompanies the driver. If you find yourself in a tricky situation—a taxi driver demanding a king's ransom, a hawker plaguing you, a stranger following you—head straight for a police officer or at least threaten to do so, which often works just as well. Don't hesitate to protest loudly if you're harassed.

Overnight trains are safe for women traveling alone provided they take sleeper class or better, where you'll be in an open compartment packed with other people. Just remember to chain your luggage to the loops provided below your sleeping berth (luggage chains and locks are available at every major train station). You may want to avoid first-class air-conditioned trains, because on those you're locked in a room with three others—who may all be male. However, this is also the most comfortable compartment and chances are that your fellow travelers—irrespective of their gender—will be educated and respectful.

It's easy to get upset by the number of beggars who beseech you for spare rupees, motioning from hand to mouth to indicate they have nothing to eat. Most disturbing are the children, as young as three years old, roaming in between cars on busy streets with no adult figure in sight. Sometimes, especially in big cities, such beggars are part of a ring and may not be as destitute as they look. If you give a beggar money, a dozen more may immediately spring up, and you may feel pressured to provide for all; it can also be difficult to get the first beggar, or the entire group, off your tail. Be firm and do not allow a beggar to follow you—a raised voice or mild threats usually work. If you're not firm, expect to be followed by a pack for a while—they do not give up easily.

If you want to contribute, seek out an established charity that's in a position to substantially help those in need. It also doesn't hurt to pass out small trinkets or candy to child beggars if you really can't stand the thought of ignoring them—but do it discreetly.

Hawkers and touts can also be a tremendous nuisance. If you're not interested in what a hawker is offering, give him a firm, polite no and ignore him after that. If he persists, tell him to clear off and employ some mock anger or else he will follow you for blocks. Do not encourage touts at all.

GOVERNMENT ADVISORIES

As different countries have different worldviews, look at travel advisories from a range of governments to get more of a sense of what's going on out there. And be sure to parse the language carefully. For example, a warning to "avoid all travel" carries more weight than one urging you to "avoid nonessential travel," and both are much stronger than a plea to "exercise caution." A US government travel warning is more permanent (though not necessarily more serious) than a so-called public announcement, which carries an expiration date.

The US Department of State's website has more than just travel warnings and advisories. The consular information sheets issued for every country have general safety tips, entry requirements (though be sure to verify these with the country's embassy), and other useful details. By registering on the site, you can have the DOS email you travel warnings as they are posted.

The US Department of State generally does not list broad travel warnings for India because the majority of the country is safe for tourists. Still, there are a few unstable areas, and riots and other disturbances can arise quickly in otherwise-safe areas. It's always a good idea to know where the closest consulate or embassy is.

General Information and Warnings US Department of State ⊕ *www.travel.state.gov.*

▌ TAXES

Airport departure tax is Rs. 500 for non-Indians, and it's included in the price of your ticket. The tax is the same no matter which country you fly to.

V.A.T., or Value-Added Tax, can be 1%, 4%, 12.5%, or nothing depending on the item purchased and the state where it was purchased. The V.A.T. is included in the listed price of items, except at restaurants and some hotels. For your hotel room, you will probably pay a service tax (around

12%), V.A.T. (12.5% and included in rates) and possibly even a luxury tax (10%). Rates differ from state to state.

▌ TIME

There are no time changes from region to region in India. The entire country operates on Indian Standard Time, which (in summer) is 5½ hours ahead of Greenwich Mean Time, 10½ hours ahead of Eastern Standard Time, 13½ hours ahead of Pacific Standard Time, 4½ hours behind Sydney time, and 7½ hours behind Auckland time. India does not observe daylight saving time, so add an hour to the above times when DST is not in effect elsewhere.

▌ TIPPING

It's true that much of India runs on tips, but you can get a skewed understanding of the system if you stay only in top hotels, where wealthy tourists and businesspeople are a majority of the clientele. In those situations, hotel employees have come to appreciate modest tips. In smaller towns, however, tipping is less institutionalized and not expected in many instances. Always trust your instincts and reward good service accordingly wherever you are. Some guidelines:

Always tip in cash. You should leave up to 10% on any restaurant bill, 15% for exceptional service. At some large luxury hotel chains, such as Oberoi, tips to individuals are not encouraged, but they ask you to leave one tip at the end of your stay, which management then divides among staff. At other hotels, you won't go wrong if you tip your room valet Rs. 20 per night. Bellboys and bell captains should be paid Rs. 10 per bag. For room service, tip 10% of the bill. Tip the concierge about Rs. 10 if he gets you a taxi, or consider a Rs. 100 tip at the end of your stay if he has helped you in several situations. Train-station porters should be paid Rs. 40 or more per bag, depending on the weight, plus Rs. 40 per 30

minutes waiting fees, if applicable. Set the rate before you let him take your bags (a sign may be posted with official rates). Taxi drivers don't expect tips unless they go through a great deal of trouble to reach your destination; in such a case Rs. 10–Rs. 20 is fair. Some taxi and auto-rickshaw drivers may ask for Rs. 10 per piece of luggage over and above the meter charge. If you hire a car and driver, tip the driver about Rs. 50–Rs. 100 per day, depending on the distance traveled and about Rs. 50 for each lunch or dinner; also give him a larger amount at the end of the journey if you have been using him for many days. Tip local guides 10% of the price of the tour.

TIPPING GUIDELINES FOR INDIA	
Bartender	10% percent of bill
Bellhop	Rs. 10 per bag
Hotel Concierge	Depends on level of service. At least Rs. 10–Rs. 20 for getting a car or taxi.
Hotel Doorman	Rs. 5 if he opens car door
Room Valet	Rs. 20 per day
Hotel Room-Service Waiter	10% of bill
Porter at Train Station	Negotiate price before accepting service. Official rates start at Rs. 40 per bag.
Skycap at Airport	Same as porter
Taxi Driver	None, or up to Rs. 40
Tour Guide	Depends on extent of tour. 10% of total price is acceptable
Valet Parking Attendant	Rs. 10–Rs. 20
Waiter	10% at a regular restaurant. 15% at high-end and five-star hotel restaurants. Make sure service has not been added to the bill.
Hired Driver	Rs. 50–Rs. 100 per day

▌TOURS

A package tour to India can help tremendously when you have a short amount of time and want to pack in as much as possible. You'll save time by not having to arrange everything yourself or learn too much about the great Indian art of haggling, and you'll also know in advance what you're getting. The downside is that you'll often end up paying much more. Because tour companies assume, in general, that foreigners traveling to India expect Western standards of accommodations and dining, they'll often book you in business-class or luxury hotels and have you eating pricey meals. This approach often neglects a more authentic understanding of India, where independent travel and exploration can be very fulfilling—not to mention much cheaper—if you're willing to do a little research and branch out from the typical tourist spots.

Organizations American Society of Travel Agents (*ASTA*). ☏ *703/739-2782* ⊕ *www.astanet.com.* **United States Tour Operators Association** (*USTOA*). ☏ *212/599-6599* ⊕ *www.ustoa.com.*

▉ **TIP→** Local tourism boards can provide information about lesser-known and small-niche operators that sell packages to only a few destinations.

GUIDED TOURS

Guided tours are a good option when you don't want to do it all yourself. You travel along with a group (sometimes large, sometimes small, sometimes just your party and the guide), stay in prebooked hotels, eat with your fellow travelers (the cost of meals sometimes included in the price of your tour, sometimes not), and follow a schedule.

A knowledgeable guide can take you places that you might never discover on your own, and you may be pushed to see more than you would have otherwise. Tours aren't for everyone, but they can be just the thing for trips to places where

making travel arrangements is difficult or time-consuming (particularly when you don't speak the language).

Whenever you book a guided tour, find out what's included and what isn't. A "land-only" tour includes all your travel (by bus, in most cases) in the destination, but not necessarily your flights to and from or even within it. Also, in most cases prices in tour brochures don't include fees and taxes. And remember that you'll be expected to tip your guide (in cash) at the end of the tour.

The number of tours to India is overwhelming. Quality and price vary greatly, but the ones listed here have proven track records. Overseas Adventure Travel offers a good, "classic" tour of India in which you'll visit points in Rajasthan as well as Agra, Khajuraho, and Varanasi. OAT tends to attract older Americans who can afford a high standard of travel—standards reflected in the tours' cost. Tours usually cost somewhere around $200 a day (including international airfare).

Four Wheel Drive India is a Jaipur-based tour company that provides several tour options, including honeymoon and wildlife packages. The major advantage here is that if you don't see the exact tour you want, they can customize one for you and help coordinate every aspect. Siddharth Travels Interserve, based in Delhi, is a responsive company that has many suggested tours that can also be personalized. Compass Tours and Travel offers a dizzying array of options all over the subcontinent, from four-day jaunts in Goa to luxury tours of Rajasthan at all price points. Djoser offers the opportunity of traveling with small groups of Europeans (mostly Dutch) and caters to a more independent-minded traveler. Their tours lack the cookie-cutter features of more mainstream tour companies.

Recommended Companies Compass India ☏ *877/772-6672* ⊕ *www.compasstours.com.* **Djoser** ☏ *877/356-7376, 484/595-0480*

⊕ www.djoserusa.com. **Four Wheel Drive India** ☎ 141/272-2025 ⊕ www.fourwheeldriveindia.com. **Overseas Adventure Travel** ☎ 800/955-1925 ⊕ www.oattravel.com. **Siddharth Travels Interserve** ☎ 11/4656-5500 to 5530 ⊕ www.siddharthtravels.com.

CULTURE TOURS

Both Smithsonian Journeys and National Geographic Expeditions have tours that come with highly educated guides, lodging in high-end hotels, and hefty price tags. Their tours will involve you in local culture, as in having dinner in an Indian family's house or a visit to an ashram. Alumni associations are another source for interesting (albeit also often expensive), culturally oriented trips to India.

Contacts National Geographic Expeditions ☎ 888/966-8687 ⊕ www.nationalgeographicexpeditions.com. **Smithsonian Journeys** ☎ 855/330-1542 ⊕ www.smithsonianjourneys.org.

PHOTO TOURS

Photo Safari India, run by photographer Vandit Kalia, can put together custom tours whose destinations maximize the chances of getting great shots of wildlife. (Group tours to national parks—Ladakh, Goa, and Arunachal Pradesh—are also run on occasion.) National Geographic takes advantage of its publication's traditional strength by offering a 10-day tour tailored to photographers.

Contacts Photo Safari India ⊕ www.photosafariindia.com.

VOLUNTOURISM

Transitions Abroad, a clearinghouse for creative ways to travel at low cost, lists many organizations that accept volunteers for their programs in India.

Contact Transitions Abroad ⊕ www.transitionsabroad.com.

▌VISITOR INFORMATION

The America-based Indian tourism offices can send brochures and help with plans, but it's better to call or visit the website for information—trying to get a response by email usually doesn't work.

Contacts Ministry of Tourism ☎ 11/2371-0518 in India, 212/586-4901 in US ⊕ www.incredibleindia.org.

For travelers spending more than a few days in Delhi, Mumbai, or another vast, rapidly changing Indian city, the Eicher series of maps is useful. National English-language newspapers include *Indian Express* (⊕ www.indianexpress.com) and *Hindustan Times* (⊕ www.hindustantimes.com). The Indian answer to 411, JustDial (☎ 22/6999-9999) helps callers find out about local businesses and answers lots of other questions. Listings can be text messaged to a cell phone. (The prefix in the phone number dials Mumbai, but substituting other local area codes will work equally well.) They also run a search engine (⊕ www.justdial.com) of their listings, which is useful for locals and visitors in urban areas alike. Google works pretty well, too. Rediff (⊕ www.rediff.com) dissects current events and pop culture across India.

INDEX

A

A Reverie ✕ , *421*
Addresses for buildings, *492*
Adinath Temple, *188*
Agra, *159–165, 173–176*
  children, attractions for, *174,
    175*
  dining, *165, 173–174*
  exploring, *161–165*
  festivals and seasonal events,
    160
  lodging, *174–175*
  shopping, *175–176*
  tour options, *161*
  transportation, *160–161*
  visitor information, *161*
  when to go, *161*
Agra Fort, *161–164*
Agra Gate, *177*
Ahuja Residency 🖫 , *128*
Air travel, *14, 32, 492–494*
  Delhi, *87–88*
  Delhi side trips, *155*
  Goa, *403–404*
  Kerala, *452*
  Mumbai, *311–313*
  Rajasthan, *225–226*
  travel times, *41*
Airports, *11, 32, 492–493*
Ajanta Caves, *13, 378–379,
    383–387*
Ajit Bhawan 🖫 , *287*
Akbar's Tomb, *161, 164–165*
Akshardham Temple Complex,
    85, 101–102
Albert Hall Museum, *241*
Alcoholic drinks, *509*
Allegria ✕ , *441*
Alleppey, *471–472*
Alsisar Haveli 🖫 , *246*
Amarya Haveli 🖫 , *128*
Amber (Amer) Fort and Palace,
    236–237
Anandamayi Ghat, *200*
Anguri Bagh, *163*
Anjuna Beach, *414–415, 418*
Annapurna Temple, *204–205*
Anokhi (shop), *253*
Antique shops, *374*
Apno Gaon, *241*
Apoorva ✕ , *351*
Arambol, *408–411*
Archaeological Museum (Goa),
    434
Archaeological Museum
  (Khajuraho), *184*

Architecture, *50*
Armories, *238*
Art galleries and museums
  Delhi, *100, 102, 106, 109,
    131–132*
  Goa, *434*
  Jaipur, *241, 242, 252*
  Jodhpur, *283, 285–286*
  Kerala, *466, 478*
  Khajuraho, *187*
  Mumbai, *326, 327, 330, 374*
  Shekhawati, *252*
  Udaipur, *266, 274, 280*
  Varanasi, *197, 204, 210*
Arts in India, *9, 11, 74–75*
Ashvem, *408–411*
Assi Ghat, *200*
Astrology, *46*
ATMs, *515*
Aurangabad, *13, 378–381,
    393–394*
Aurangzeb's Mosque, *201*
Auto-rickshaws. ⇨ *See* Taxi
  and auto–rickshaw travel

B

Babulnath Temple, *332*
Bada Bagh, *292*
Badal Mahal, *277*
Badal Vilas, *296–297*
Bade Miya ✕ , *343*
Baga Beach, *418–421*
Bagore ki Haveli, *266*
Bahá'í faith, *57*
Bahá'í House of Worship, *85,
    110*
Balle Balle ✕ , *381*
Banaras Art Center, *210*
Banganga Water Tank, *309,
    332*
Bangla Sahib Gurdwara, *107*
Banks, *515*
Bargaining, *70, 306*
Bars, pubs, and lounges
  Delhi, *134–136*
  hours, *513*
  Kerala, *466*
  Mumbai, *366–367, 368–369*
Basil & Thyme ✕ , *119*
Basilica of Bom Jesus, *434*
Bathing ghats, *258*
Bazaars and markets
  Delhi, *138–139, 144*
  Goa, *414, 418*
  Mumbai, *306–307, 335, 337,
    338–339, 373*

Beaches
  Goa, *400–401, 408–409, 411,
    412–423, 424–426, 437–439,
    443-444*
  Mumbai, *325–326*
Bedbugs, *512–513*
Beggars, *521*
Bekal Fort, *485*
Bellevue ✕ , *165*
Benaulim, *440–442*
Bentley's 🖫 , *359*
Bharat Kala Bhavan Museum,
    197, 204
Bharat Milap festival, *160*
Bharatiya Lok Kala Mandal,
    266
Bharatpur, *256–257*
Bhendi Bazaar, *338–339*
Bibi-ka-Maqbara, *380–381*
Bijamandala Temple, *189*
Bikaner House, *102*
Bike travel, *404*
Birbal's Palace, *179*
Bird-watching, *256–257, 427*
Blue Ginger ✕ , *119*
Boat and ferry travel, *452*
Boat cruises, *432, 461, 471*
Bogmalo Beach, *437*
Bollywood, *368*
Books on India, *488–490*
Bookstores, *139, 144–145*
Braganza House, *440*
Brahma Kumaris Spiritual Uni-
  versity, *278*
Brahma Temple (Khajuraho),
    188
Brahma Temple (Pushkar),
    258–259
Britannia & Co. ✕ , *352*
Brunton Boatyard 🖫 , *464*
Buddhism, *57*
Bukhara ✕ , *119*
Bundi, *280–281*
Bundi Palace, *281*
Bus travel, *40–41, 494*
  Delhi, *88*
  Delhi side trips, *156*
  Goa, *404*
  Mumbai, *313*
  Rajasthan, *226*
Busaba ✕ , *343*
Business hours, *513–514*

C

Calangute Beach, *421–423*
Calicut, *482–484*

Camel Fair, *259*
Camel safaris, *30*, *218–219*, *299*
Candolim, *421–423*
Cansaulim Beach, *437–438*
Caowki Ghat, *200–201*
Car and driver travel, *14*, *38–39, 41, 494–496*
Delhi, 88
Delhi side trips, 156
Goa, 404
Mumbai, 313, 315
Rajasthan, 226–227
tipping, 522
Carnaval ✕, *442*
Carnival, *404*
Carpet shops, *145–146*
Casa Anjuna ⬚, *415*
Casa Britona ⬚, *422*
Casa Susegad ⬚, *440*
Cashew trees, *398*
Casinos, *432*
Caste system, *48–49*
Catholicism, *309*
Cavelossim, *442–443*
Caves
Ajanta and Ellora, 13, 378–379, 383–392
Elephanta, 321, 324
Cenotaphs, *292*
Chandela ⬚, *193*
Chandor, *440*
Chandra Mahal, *238*
Char Bagh, *236*
Chattarpur Temples, *115*
Chaturbhuj Temple, *189*
Chaukhandi Stupa, *211*
Chausath Yogini Temple (Khajuraho), *183*
Chausath Yogini Temple (Varanasi), *201*
Chet Singh Ghat, *200*
Chhattarpur Temples, *115*
Children and travel, *24, 513, 518*
Children, attractions for
Delhi, 117
Delhi side trips, 174, 175, 193
Kerala, 472–473, 474, 475
Mumbai, 333–334, 365
Rajasthan, 236, 259, 266–267, 289
Children's science center, *267*
Chinese Fishing Nets, *457, 458*
Chitragupta Temple, *186*
Chittaurgarh, *278, 280*
Chokhi Dhani, *241–242*
Chor Bazaar, *335*
Chor Bizarre ✕, *118*

Chowpatty Beach, *325–326*
Christianity, *56, 448*
Christmas, *59*
Churches
Goa, 427, 434
Kochi, 457, 458, 460
Church of Our Lady of Immaculate Conception, *427*
City Palace (Jaipur), *238*
City Palace (Udaipur), *263*
Class structure in India, *47*
Clothing in Indian society, *49, 142, 439*
Clothing shops
Delhi, 138, 139–140, 146
Mumbai, 370, 372, 374–375, 377
Clubs and discos
hours, 513
Jaipur, 249
Mumbai, 367, 369
Coconut Lagoon ⬚, *470*
Colva, *439*
Commonwealth Games, *10*
Consulates, *510*
Cooking schools, *216, 478–479'*
Costs, *514–515*
Cottons (shop), *253*
Crawford Market, *338*
Credit cards, *5, 515–516*
Cremation rituals, *205*
Crocodile-spotting tours, *423, 426*
Cruises, *432, 461, 471*
CST (Chhatrapati Shivaji Terminus), *335, 338*
Cuisine of India, *64–69*
Culture tours, *524*
Currency, *15, 453, 516*
Customs and duties, *507–508*
Customs of India, *502*
Cycle-rickshaw travel, *14, 157*

D

Dabbawallas, *304*
Dance, *75*
Delhi, 133
Ellora Dance Festival, 389, 394
Kerala, 466–467, 486
Khajuraho Festival of Dance, 160
Mumbai, 364
Darabhanga Ghat, *201*
Dargah Sharif, *221, 259*
Dasaprakash ✕, *165*
Dashashvamedh Ghat, *200, 204*
Daulatabad Fort, *381*

Deeg, *256*
Delhi, *12, 78–147*
Central Delhi, 101–109, 119, 122–123, 127–128, 134–135, 138–142, 143
Chandni Chowk, 94
children, attractions for, 117
dining, 80–81, 118–126, 139, 146
emergencies, 89–90
exploring, 90–117
Gali Paranthe Wali, 96
getting oriented, 79
history of, 92
holy sites, 84–85
Internet, mail, and shipping, 90
lodging, 127–130
nightlife and the arts, 131–136
Old Delhi (Shahjahanabad), 93–101, 118, 127, 137–138
planning your time, 86–87
shopping, 82–83, 136–147
South Delhi, 110–117, 123–126, 128, 130, 135–136, 144–147
top reasons to go, 78
transportation, 87–89
visitor information, 90
walking tour, 95
when to go, 87
Delhi side trips, *12, 150–212*
⇨ *See also Agra; Khajuraho; Taj Mahal; Varanasi*
children, attractions for, 174, 175, 193
dining, 152–153, 158, 165, 173–174, 181, 187, 189, 192, 204, 206–208
Fatehpur Sikri, 176–181
festivals and seasonal events, 160, 183
getting oriented, 151
lodging, 158, 174–175, 193–194, 208–209
nightlife and the arts, 183, 210
planning your time, 158
Sarnath, 210–212
shopping, 175–176, 194, 210
top reasons to go, 150–151
tours, 157, 159
transportation, 155–157
visitor information, 157–158
when to go, 155
Delight ⬚, *464*
Department stores and malls, *370, 375–376*
Desert Culture Centre, *294*
Devi Art Foundation, *131*
Devi Jagadamba Temple, *186*

Dhabas, *39*
Dhamekh Stupa, *211*
Dharavi, *318–320*
Dhobi Ghats, *332*
Dilli Haat, *144*
Dilwara Temples, *221, 278*
Dining, *5, 15, 508–509.* ⇨ See
    also specific destinations
cuisine of India, 64–69
tipping, 522
Diwali festival, *59*
Diwan-i-Khas, *98*
Dr. Salim Ali Bird Sanctuary,
    427
Dolphin-spotting cruises, *423,
    426*
Dome (bar), *368–369*
Dudhsagar Falls, *435*
Duladeo Temple, *189*
Dum Pukht ✕ , *119*
Durga Puja festival, *160*
Durga Temple, *200, 204*
Dussehra festival, *160*
Dutch Palace, *457, 458*
Duties, *507–508*

E

E.N.S. Kalari Centre, *467*
Economy of India, *8*
Eid-ul-Adha festival, *59*
Eid-ul-Fitr festival, *59*
Eklingji, *275*
Eklingji Temple Complex, *221*
Electricity, *510*
Elephanta Caves, *321, 324*
Elephants, *30*
Ellora Caves, *13, 378–379,
    383, 388–392*
Ellora Dance Festival, *389, 394*
Elsewhere 🏠 , *409–410*
Embassies, *510*
Emergencies, *510*
Delhi, 89–90
Kerala, 453
Mumbai, 316–317
Rajasthan, 228
Esphahan ✕ , *173*
Etiquette and behavior, *308,
    502–503*
Etmad-ud-Daulah's Tomb, *161,
    165*
Exchanging money, *15, 516*
Eyeglasses shops, *372, 376,
    377*

F

FAQs, *22–23*
Fatehpur Sikri, *176–181*
Fernando's Nostalgia ✕ , *440*

Festivals and seasonal events,
    58–59, 74
Delhi side trips, 160, 183
Goa, 404
Kerala, 486
Mumbai, 315, 389, 394
Rajasthan, 229, 259, 266
Film, *75*
Delhi, 132
Jaipur, 249
Mumbai, 364–365
Film industry, *368*
Films about India, *488–490*
Fire ✕ , *119, 122*
Flea markets, *414, 418*
Flying Fox (tours), *285, 289*
Fontainhas, *427*
Foreigner ticket tax, *14*
Fort Aguada, *424*
Fort House, The ✕ , *461*
Fort St. Angelo, *485*
Forts
Delhi, 97–99, 114–115
*Delhi side trips, 161–164,
    205–206*
Goa, 424
Kerala, 480, 485
Mumbai, 381
*Rajasthan, 236–237, 241, 242,
    255, 257, 266, 277, 278,
    280, 281, 283, 285, 292, 294*

G

Gadsisar Lake, *292, 297*
Galwar Bagh, *243*
Gandhi, Indira, *108–109*
Gandhi, Mohandas
    Karamchand, *100, 108,
    332–333*
Gandhi Smriti, *108*
Ganesh Chathurthi festival,
    59, 315
Ganga Dussehra festival, *160*
Ganges, *198–203*
Gardens
Delhi, 114
Jaipur, 236, 242
Jodhpur, 283
Mumbai, 334
Taj Mahal, 168
Udaipur, 267
Gateway of India, *324*
"Gem dealer" scams, *222*
Gem Palace (shop), *251*
Gender roles in Indian society,
    48
Ghantai Temple, *188*
Gharial Sanctuary, *194–195*
Ghats

Delhi, 100
Mumbai, 332
Pushkar, 258
Varanasi, 200–201, 204
Gift-giving, *502*
Globalization, *11*
Goa, *13, 396–444*
*beaches, 400–401, 408–409,
    411, 412–423, 424–426,
    443–444*
*dining, 398–399, 406, 409,
    412–413, 414–415, 419,
    421–422, 425*
*festivals and seasonal events,
    404*
getting oriented, 397
history of, 410
*lodging, 406–407, 409–411,
    414, 419, 422–423, 425–426,
    430–432*
monsoon season, 400, 409
*nightlife and the arts, 415, 418,
    421, 429–430*
North Goa, 408–426
Panaji, 426–436
planning your time, 407
shopping, 414, 418, 432–433
South Goa, 436–444
*sports and the outdoors, 413,
    423, 439*
top reasons to go, 396
tour options, 406
transportation, 403–406, 432
visitor information, 406
when to go, 403
Goa Marriott Resort 🏠 , *430*
Golden Fort (Sonar Qila), *292,
    294*
Government advisories, *521*
Government buildings, *102–
    103, 427, 429*
Government lodging, *501*
Greetings, *502*
Guda Vishnoi, *290*
Guesthouses, *504*
Gulta Ji Mandir, *243*
Guru Nanak Jayanti holiday,
    59
Guru Shikhar, *278*
Gyan Bhandar, *294*
Gyanvapi Mosque, *204–205*

H

Haji Ali Shrine, *309, 332, 333*
Handicrafts shops
Delhi, 138, 140–141, 146
Jaipur, 249–251
Kerala, 467–469
Mumbai, 373, 376, 377

Udaipur, 274–275
Hanging Gardens, *334*
Hanuman Ghat, *200*
Hanuman Mandir, *84*
Harish Chandra Ghat, *200*
Hauz Khas Village, *110, 112*
Hawa Mahal (Fatehpur Sikri),
179
Hawa Mahal (Jaipur), 238–239
Hazrat Nizamuddin Darga,
85, 112
Health concerns, *510–513*
Heritage hotels, *501*
Hinduism, *55*
gods and goddesses, 60–63
Hiran Minar, *180*
History, The ✕ , *461*
History of India, *50–53*
Holi festival, *59*
Holidays, *58–59, 513–514*
Home furnishings shops
Delhi, 141, 143, 147
Mumbai, 376, 377
Hostels, *501*
Hotel Ganges View 🖼 , *208*
Hotels, *501, 504.* ⇨ *See also*
Lodging
House of Mariam, *179*
Houseboat cruises, *471*
Houses of historic interest
Delhi, 102–103, 108
Goa, 440
Jaisalmer, 292, 294, 296
Mumbai, 332–333
Humayun's Tomb, *112, 114*

I

Imperial, The 🖼 , *127*
Incense shops, *373*
Independence Day, *59*
India Gate, *108*
Indira Gandhi Memorial
Museum, *108–109*
I-95 ✕ , *421–422*
Internet access, *504*
Delhi, 90
Rajasthan, 228
Irani cafés, *352*
ISKCON Temple, *115, 117*
Islam, *55*
ITC Mughal 🖼 , *174*
Itineraries, *26–29*

J

Jagat Niwas Palace Terrace
Restaurant ✕ , *269*
Jagat Shiromani Temple, *237*
Jagdish Temple, *263, 265*

Jag Mandir Island Palace, *265*
Jahangiri Mahal, *163*
Jaigarh Fort, *237, 242*
Jain (Bachraj) **Ghat,** *200*
Jain Temple (Mumbai), *309,*
333
Jain Temple (Ranakpur),
276–277
Jain Temples (Jaisalmer), *294*
Jainism, *57*
Jaipur, *232–261*
children, attractions for, 236
dining, 240, 241–242, 243,
245–246, 251
exploring, 236–243
lodging, 246–249, 255, 257
nightlife and the arts, 249
shopping, 249–254
side trips, 254–261
tour options, 236, 237
transportation, 233, 236, 245
village complexes, 240
visitor information, 236
when to go, 236
Jaipur House, *102*
Jaisalmer, *291–300*
camel safaris, 299
dining, 297–298
exploring, 292–297
lodging, 298–299
shopping, 300
tour options, 292
transportation, 292
Jaisalmer Fort Palace Museum
and Heritage Centre, *294*
Jama Masjid (Delhi), *85, 96–97*
Jama Masjid (Fatehpur Sikri),
177, 180
Jantar Mantar (Delhi), *102*
Jantar Mantar (Jaipur), *240*
Jaswant Thada, *283*
Javari Temple, *188*
Jawahar Kala Kendra, *242*
Jayanti festival, *160*
Jehangir Art Gallery, *326*
Jet-skiiing, *413*
Jewelry shops
Delhi, 138, 143, 147J
aipur, 251
Mumbai, 373–374, 376–377
Udaipur, 275
Jhankar ✕ , *286*
Jodh Bai Palace, *179*
Jodhpur, *281–290*
children, attractions for, 289
dining, 283, 286–287
exploring, 283–286
lodging, 287–288
nightlife and the arts, 288

shopping, 289–290
side trips, 290
sports and the outdoors,
288–289
tour options, 283, 285, 289
transportation, 282
visitor information, 282
Judaism, *54, 330*
Juna Mahal, *294*

K

Kainoosh ✕ , *124*
Kamala Nehru Park, *332,*
333–334
Kanak Vrindavan Gardens,
242
Kandariya Mahadev, *185–186*
Kanhirode Weaving Coopera-
tive, *485*
Kannur, *484–486*
Karni Mata, *221*
Kartik festival, *160*
Kashi Vishvanath Temple,
204–205
Kebab Korner ✕ , *353*
Keoladeo National Park,
256–257
Kerala, *13, 446–486*
Central Kerala, 469–477
children, attractions for,
472–473, 474, 475
dining, 448–449, 454, 458,
460–463, 470, 479, 480,
483, 486
emergencies, 453
festivals and seasonal events,
486
getting oriented, 447
Kochi, 456–469
lodging, 454–455, 462, 463–
466, 471–473, 474–477, 479,
480–482, 484, 486
money matters, 453
nightlife and the arts, 466–467
Northern Kerala, 482–486
planning your time, 455
shopping, 467–469, 479
Southern Kerala, 477–482
top reasons to go, 446
tour options and travel agents,
453–454, 461, 471
transportation, 451–453
visitor information, 454
when to go, 451
Khajuraho, *159, 181–195*
children, attractions for, 193
dining, 187, 189, 192
exploring, 183–189

festivals and seasonal events, 160, 183
lodging, 193–194
nightlife and the arts, 183
shopping, 194
side trips, 194–195
transportation, 182–183
visitor information, 183
when to go, 183
Khajuraho Festival of Dance, 160
Khajuraho Village, 195
Khan Chacha ✕, 122
Khas Mahal (Agra), 163
Khas Mahal (Delhi), 98
Knesseth Eliyahoo Synagogue, 309, 327
Konkan Café ✕, 346–347
Kovalam, 480–482
Kumarakom, 469–470
Kumarakom Lake Resort ⌐, 470
Kumbhalgarh, 277
Kumbhalgarh Sanctuary, 277
Kuthiramalika (Puthenmalika) Palace Museum, 478

L

Lake Palace, 265
Lake Periyar Wildlife Sanctuary, 473–474
Lake Pichola, 263, 265
Lakshadweep, 477
Lakshmana Temple, 185
Lala Dulli Chand Naresh Gupta ✕, 118
Lalguan Mahadeva, 184
Lali (Dhobi) Ghat, 200
Lal Qila (Red Fort), 97–99
Language, 503
La Plage ✕, 409
Laxmi Vilas Palace Hotel ⌐, 257
Le Meridien ⌐, 465
Le Pain Quotidien ✕, 347
Le 3 Elephants ⌐, 465
Leather shops, 374
Leela Goa, The ⌐, 443
Lemon Tree Hotel ⌐, 393–394
Leopold Café ✕, 347, 350
Lodarva Temples, 297
Lodging, 5, 25, 500–501, 504. ⇨ *See also* specific destinations
meal plans, 500, 504
tipping, 522
Lodhi Gardens, 114
Lohagarh Fort, 257
Lohar Chawl, 338

Lonar Crater, 381
Lotus Temple, 85, 110
Loutolim, 439–440
Lutyens' Delhi, 102

M

Machhi Bhavan, 163
Magen Hassidim Synagogue, 335
Magique ✕, 124
Mahadeva Temple, 186
Mahamandir, 283
Maha Navrati festival, 58
Mail and shipping, 90, 514
Majorda, 438–439
Makar Sankranti festival, 59, 160
Malabar Junction ✕, 462
Man Mandira Ghat, 201
Mandore Gardens, 283
Mandrem, 408–411
Mangaldas Market, 338
Manguesh Temple, 436
Mani Bhavan, 332–333
Manikarnika Ghat, 201
Mapusa, 423
Marari Beach ⌐, 472
Marriage in Indian society, 48
Martial arts, 467
Matangesvara Temple, 184
Matheran Hill Station, 372
Meadows, The ⌐, 394
Meal plans, 500, 504
Meals and mealtimes, 508–509
Medical assistance. ⇨ *See* Emergencies
Mehrangarh Fort, 283, 285
Meteor craters, 381
Metro travel, 88
Mittal Tea House, 143
Monasteries, 283
Money matters, 5, 10, 15, 514–517
Kerala, 453
Rajasthan, 228
Monkey Temple, 200, 204
Morjim, 408–411
Mosques
Agra, 164
Delhi, 85, 96–97, 98–99, 114–115
Fatehpur Sikri, 177, 179, 180
Mumbai, 309
Taj Mahal, 169, 172
Varanasi, 201, 204–205
Moti Masjid (Agra), 164
Moti Masjid (Delhi), 98–99
Motorbike travel, 404
Mount Abu, 277–278

Mughal Room ✕, 173
Mulagandha Kuti Vihari Temple, 211–212
Mumbadevi Temple, 339
Mumbai, 13, 302–394
Bandra, 309, 339–340, 355–357, 362, 369, 377
Central Mumbai, 334–335, 341, 343, 358–359, 366–367, 370
children, attractions for, 333–334, 365
Colaba, 320–325, 343, 346–347, 350–351, 359, 361, 367, 372–373
CST and environs, 335, 338–339, 373–374
dining, 304–305, 325, 326, 327, 338, 340–357, 381, 393
emergencies, 316–317
exploring, 320–340
festivals and seasonal events, 315, 389, 394
Fort and Marine Drive, 325–330, 351–355, 361–362, 368–369, 374
getting oriented, 303
history of, 313
holy sites, 308–309
Juhu, 339–340, 355–357, 362, 369, 377
lodging, 358–362, 393–394
Malabar Hill and environs, 330, 332–334, 369, 377
name change from Bombay, 319
nightlife and the arts, 362–369, 394
planning your time, 318–320
shopping, 306–307, 337, 369–377
slum tours, 318–320
top reasons to go, 302–303
transportation, 311–316, 379
visitor information, 317–318
western suburbs, 339–340, 355–357, 362, 369, 377
when to go, 311
Mum's Kitchen ✕, 429
Munnar, 475–477
Museum and Art Gallery Complex, 478
Museum of Christian Art, 434
Museums. ⇨ *See also* Art galleries and museums
archaeology, 184, 212, 434
crafts, 102, 106
in Delhi, 100, 102, 106, 107, 108–109, 117

folk art and culture, 187, 241,
  266, 285–286, 294, 327, 330
Gandhi, Indira, 108–109
Gandhi,
Mohandas Karamchand, 100
  in Goa, 434
  Hindu culture, 106
  in Kerala, 478
  in Khajuraho, 184
  in Jaipur, 241, 242
  in Jaisalmer, 294
  in Jodhpur, 283, 285–286
  in Mumbai, 327, 330
  Nehru, 107
  railroads, 117
  in Sarnath, 212
  Taj Mahal, 169
  in Udaipur, 266, 267, 280
  in Varanasi, 197, 204
Music, 75
  Delhi, 133, 147
  Mumbai, 365
Music shops, 143, 377
Mussaman Burj, 163

N

Nagar Sagar Kund, 281
Nagda, 275
Nagina Masjid, 164
Nahargarh Fort, 241
Najina Masjid, 179
Nakki Lake, 278
Nandi Temple, 186
Nasiyan Temple, 259
Nathmal-ki Haveli, 292, 297
**National Gallery of Modern
  Art** (Delhi), 109
**National Gallery of Modern
  Art** (Mumbai), 327
National Gandhi Museum, 100
**National Handicrafts and Han-
  dlooms Museum**, 102, 106
National Museum, 106
National Rail Museum, 117
National Zoological Park, 117
Naubat Khana, 177
Neel ✕ , 341
Neemach Mata, 263, 266
Neemrana Fort Palace , 247
Nehru Memorial Museum, 107
Nepali Ghat, 201
North and South Secretariats,
  102

O

Oberoi, The (Delhi) , 130
Oberoi, The (Mumbai) , 361
Oberoi Amarvilas , 174–175

Oberoi Rajvilas , 248
Oberoi Udaivilas , 271
Oberoi Vanyavilas , 255
Observatories, 102, 240
Oh! Calcutta ✕ , 341
Old Goa, 433–434
Old Harbour Hotel , 465
Old Secretariat, 427, 429
Over-the-counter remedies,
  513

P

Packing tips, 15, 517–518
**Padmanabhapuram Fort and
  Palace**, 480
Padmanabhaswamy Temple,
  478
Palaces
  Delhi, 98
  Delhi side trips, 163, 179,
    205–206
  Kerala, 457, 458, 478, 480
  Rajasthan, 236–238, 240, 242,
    263, 265, 266, 277, 280,
    281, 285, 294, 296–297
Palolem Beach, 443–444
Panaji, 426–436
Panch Mahal, 179
Panchganga Ghat, 201
Panjim People's , 431
Panna National Park, 195
Pantry, The ✕ , 353–354
Parasailing, 413, 423, 426, 439
Park Hyatt Goa Resort and Spa
   , 438
Parks
  Delhi side trips, 195
  Mumbai, 332, 333–334
  Rajasthan, 254–257, 278
Parsvanath Temple, 188
Parvati Temple, 187
Passports, 518–519
Patwon-ki Haveli, 292, 294,
  296
Peace Park, 278
Pepper Exchange, 457
Perfume shops, 373
Peshawri ✕ , 173
Photo tours, 524
Police, 520
Politics in India, 8, 49
Ponda, 436
Pottery shops, 251
Pradeep , 208–209
Prayaga Ghat, 201
Price categories, 5
Prince of Wales Museum, 327,
  330
Purana Qila, 114–115

Pushkar, 257–261
Pushkar Bramha Temple, 221

Q

Qila-i-Kuhna Masjid, 114–115
Quilon, 472–473
Qutub Minar, 115
Quwwat-ul-Islam Masjid, 115

R

Raj Ghat, 100
Rajasthan, 12–13, 214–300.
  ⇨ *See also* Jaipur; Jaisalmer;
    Jodhpur; Udaipur
  camel safaris, 218–219, 299
  children, attractions for, 236,
    259, 266–267, 289
  dining, 216–217, 229–230,
    240, 254–246, 251, 259–260,
    265–266, 267, 269–270, 275,
    283, 286–287, 297–298
  emergencies, 228
  festivals and seasonal events,
    229, 259, 266
  getting oriented, 21
  5holy sites, 220–221
  Internet access, 228
  lodging, 230, 246–249, 255,
    257, 261, 270–271, 278,
    281, 287–288, 298–299
  money matters, 228
  nightlife and the arts, 249, 288
  planning your time, 230
  shopping, 222–223, 249–254,
    274–275, 289–290, 300
  sports and the outdoors,
    288–289
  top reasons to go, 214–215
  tour options, 228–229
  transportation, 218–219,
    225–228
  visitor information, 229
  when to go, 225
Rajputs, 231
Ramada Khajuraho , 194
Rambagh Palace , 248
Ramlila performances, 74
Ramnagar Fort and Palace,
  205–206
Ranakpur, 276–277
Ranakpur Temple, 221
Rang Mahal, 98
Raniji ki Baori, 281
Ranthambhore National Park,
  254–255
Ranthambhore Fort, 255
Rashtrapati Bhavan, 102–103
Recycling, 11

Religions of India, *9, 49, 54–57*
Republic Day, *59*
Residency and the Garden Café ✕, *393*
Restrooms, *519–520*
Rice Boat ✕, *462*
Rick's (bar), *134–135*

S

Safdarjang's Tomb, *115*
Safety, *419, 520–521*
Sahelion Ki Bari, *267*
St. Francis Church, *457, 458, 460*
Sajjan Garh, *263, 266*
Salim Chisti's Tomb, *180, 181*
Salim Singh-ki Haveli, *292, 297*
Samode Haveli ☒, *248*
Sam Sand Dunes, *296*
Sanganer, *253–254*
Sankat Mochan Temple, *206*
Sansad Bhavan, *102*
Santa Cruz Cathedral, *457, 460*
Sao Tomé, *429*
Sarnath, *210–212*
Sarnath Archaeological Museum, *212*
Satiyon ka Pagthiya, *294*
Savitri Temple, *259*
Scams targeting foreigners, *222, 520*
Scindia Ghat, *201*
Scuba diving, *413*
Sé (St. Catherine's) Cathedral, *434*
Shaare Rahamim Synagogue, *338*
Shalimar Spice Garden ☒, *474–475*
Shantinath Temple, *188*
Sheesh Mahal (Agra), *163*
Sheesh Mahal (Jaipur), *237*
Shekhawati, *252*
Sher Mandal, *114–115*
Shiladevi Temple, *237*
Shilpgram, *266*
Shilpgram Utsav, *266*
Shitala Temple, *206*
Shiva Temple Complex, *275*
Shivala Ghat, *200*
Shoe shops, *374*
Shopping, *70–73.* ⇨ *See also* specific destinations
    hours, 513
Siddhivinayak Temple, *309*
Sightseeing etiquette, *308, 502–503*

Sikhism, *56*
Sinquerim Beach, *424–426*
Siolim House ☒, *410–411*
Sis Ganj Sahib Gurdwara, *85, 101*
Sisodia Rani ka Bagh, *242*
Slum tours, *318–320*
Slumdog Millionaire, *10*
Smoke House Grill ✕, *126*
Snorkeling, *413, 426*
Soam ✕, *354*
Social conditions of India, *46–49*
Society for the Promotion of Recreational Tourism and Sports, *477*
Spice Village ☒, *475*
Sri Muthappan Temple, *485*
State emporiums, *141*
State Museum of Tribal and Folk Arts, *187*
Step wells, *281*
Street food, *64, 145, 348–349*
Sunset Point, *278*
Surya Samudra Private Retreats ☒, *482*
Sussegado, *424*
Suvarna Mahal ✕, *246*
Suzette ✕, *354*
Svetamber Jain Temple, *99*
Swastikas, *220*
Symbols, *5*
Synagogues
    Kerala, 457–458, 460
    Mumbai, 309, 327, 335, 338

T

Table, The ✕, *350*
Taj by Vivanta Malabar ☒, *466*
Taj Gateway Hotel Ganges ☒, *209*
Taj Holiday Village ☒, *425–426*
Taj Lake Palace ☒, *271*
Taj Mahal, *166–172*
    inside the Mausoleum, 171
    Outer Taj, 168–169
    visiting tips, 172
Taj Mahal Palace ☒, *361*
Taj Mahotsav festival, *160*
Taj Nadesar Palace Hotel ☒, *209*
Taragarh, *281*
Tasara Center for Creative Weaving, *482*
Taxes, *14, 521–522*
Taxi and auto-rickshaw travel, *14, 40–41, 496–497*

Delhi, *88–89*
Delhi side trips, *155–156*
Goa, *404–405, 432*
Kerala, *452–453*
Mumbai, *315–316*
Rajasthan, *227*
tipping, 522
Tazia Tower, *296–297*
Tea and coffee shops, *143, 352*
Technology and science in India, *9*
Telephones, *504–507*
Temples
    Ajanta cave temples, 13, 384
    Delhi, 84, 85, 99, 101–102, 107, 110, 115, 117
    Ellora cave temples, 13, 391
    Goa, 436
    Jaipur, 221, 243
    Jaisalmer, 294, 297
    Kerala, 478, 485
    Khajuraho, 183–189
    Mumbai, 309, 332, 333, 339
    Pushkar, 258–259
    Rajasthan, 221, 243, 258–259, 275, 276–277, 278, 280
    Sarnath, 211–212
    Udaipur, 263, 265, 276–277, 278, 280
    Varanasi, 200, 201, 204–205, 206
Textile shops, *253–254*
Textiles, *70–71, 72*
Thalassa ✕, *413*
Theater, *74, 75*
    Delhi, 133–134
    Jaipur, 249
    Mumbai, 364, 365
Theeram Nature Conservation Society, *483*
Thekkady, *473–475*
Theyyam, *485–486*
Tigers, *254–255*
Time, *522*
Timing the trip, *14*
Tipping, *522*
Tombs
    Agra, 161, 164–165
    Aurangabad, 380–381
    Delhi, 110, 112, 114, 115
    Fatehpur Sikri, 180, 181
    Taj Mahal, 168
Top attractions, *16–17*
Top experiences, *18–19*
Tours and tour guides, *15, 392, 523–524*
Towers
    Agra, 163
    Chittaurgarh, 280

Delhi, *114–115*
Fatehpur Sikri, *180*
Jaisalmer, *296–297*
Mumbai, *334*
Taj Mahal, *169*
Towers of Silence, *334*
Train travel, *14, 33–37,
497–499*
classes of train, 35
Deccan Odyssey, *379*
Delhi, *89*
Delhi side trips, *157*
Goa, *405–406*
Kerala, *453*
luxury trains, *37, 499*
Mumbai, *316, 379*
Palace on Wheels, *245*
Rajasthan, *227–228, 245*
toy trains, *36*
travel times, *41*
Transportation, *14, 30–41,
492–499*
Traveler's checks and cards,
516–517
Trident Agra , *175*
Trishna ✕, *354*
Trivandrum, *478–479*
Tulsi Ghat, *200*
Turtles, *483*

U

Udaipur, *261–281*
children, attractions for,
266–267
dining, *265–266, 267–270, 275*
exploring, *263–267*
lodging, *270–271, 278, 281*
shopping, *274–275*
side trips, *275–281*

tour options, *263*
transportation, *262*
Umaid Bhawan Palace 🖼, *288*
**Umaid Bhawan Palace
Museum,** *283, 285–286*
Utorda, *438–439*

V

Vagator Beach, *412–414*
Vamana Temple, *187–188*
Varaha Temple, *185*
Varanasi, *159, 195–212*
dining, *204, 206–208*
exploring, *197–206*
festivals, *160*
getting oriented, *197*
lodging, *208–209*
nightlife and the arts, *210*
shopping, *210*
transportation, *197*
visitor information, *197, 202*
Varca, *442*
Victoria Terminus, *335, 338*
**Vijnana Kala Vedi Cultural
Center,** *478–479*
Visas, *518–519*
Vishnoi community, *290*
Vishvanath Temple (Khaju-
raho), *186*
Vishvanath (Golden) **Temple**
(Varanasi), *201*
Visitor information, *524*
Agra, *161*
Delhi, *90*
Delhi side trips, *157–158*
Goa, *406*
Jaipur, *236*
Jodhpur, *282*
Kerala, *454*

Khajuraho, *183*
Mumbai, *317–318*
Rajasthan, *229*
Varanasi, *197, 202*
Vivanta by Taj-Fort Aguada
🖼, *426*
Vivenda Dos Palhacos 🖼, *439*
Voluntourism, *524*

W

Wasabi by Morimoto ✕,
350–351
Water for drinking, *511–512*
Waterfalls, *435*
Waterskiing, *413*
Weaving centers, *482, 485*
When to go, *14*
Wildlife preserves
Delhi side trips, *194–195*
Goa, *427*
Kerala, *473–474, 483*
Rajasthan, *254–257, 277*
Women traveling alone,
520–521

Y

Yum Yum Tree, The ✕, *126*

Z

Zaveri Bazaar, *338–339*
Zip-line tours, *285, 289*
Zoos, *117*
Zoroastrianism, *57*
**Zuri Kumarakom Resort and
Spa** 🖼, *470*
Zuri White Sands, The 🖼, *442*

PHOTO CREDITS

1, cmittman, Fodors.com member. 3, Dinodia/ age fotostock. Chapter 1: Experience India 6-7, Luca Tettoni / age fotostock. 8, AbhijeetRane/Flickr. 9 (left), thefi nalmiracle/Shutterstock. 9 (right), NCPA Photo/ Narendra Dangia. 10, h0usep1ant/Jeff Karpala/Flickr. 11 (left), Oberoi Hotels & Resorts. 11 (right), R-photos/Shutterstock. 13 (left), Sreeganesha, Fodors.com member. 13 (right), Joan Saba, Fodors.com member. 16 (left), paul prescott/Shutterstock. 16 (top middle), Rafal Cichawa/Shutterstock. 16 (bottom), Terraxplorer/iStockphoto. 16 (top right), anneblock, Fodors.com member. 17 (top), Taj Hotels Resorts and Palaces. 17 (bottom), Polly Ryan, Fodors.com member. 17 (right), Steven Miric/ iStockphoto. 18, Pangfolio.com/Shutterstock. 19 (left), emin kuliyev/Shutterstock. 19 (right), highviews/Shutterstock. 20, Günter Gollnick/ age fotostock. 21, RABOUAN Jean-Baptiste / age fotostock. 22, Anne Clark/iStockphoto. 23 (left), paul prescott/Shutterstock. 23 (right), Caroline Gaines, Fodors. com member. 24, Dana Ward/Shutterstock. 25, Taj Hotels Resorts and Palaces. 26, mcgregorjn, Fodors. com member. 28, Jeremy Richards/iStockphoto. 29 (left), Mikhail Nekrasov/Shutterstock. 29 (right), Aleksandar Todorovic/Shutterstock. 30-31, Ian Cumming / age fotostock. 32, Navin Mistry / Alamy. 33, Neil Barclay / age fotostock. 34 (top), Dinodia / age fotostock. 34 (middle), Lukas Hlavac/Shutterstock. 34 (bottom), Ben Sutherland/Flickr. 35, Boaz Rottem / age fotostock. 36 (both), Dinodia / age fotostock. 37 (top), 2010 SuperStock. 37 (bottom), ARCO / Therin-Weise / age fotostock. 38, Dana Ward/Shutterstock. 39, Kharidehal Abhirama Ashwin/Shutterstock. 40 (left), Christian Haugen/Flickr. 40 (right), Terraxplorer/iStockphoto. 41, Honza Soukup/Flickr. 42, Taka / age fotostock. Chapter 2: Portrait of India 43, Photosindia.com / age fotostock. 44, Kulpreet_Photography/iStockphoto. 45, James Burger / age fotostock. 46, Marco Cristofori / age fotostock. 47 (bottom left), Teresa Zau, Fodors.com member. 47 (top right), Nikhil Gangavane/iStockphoto. 48, Nick Hanna / Alamy. 49, Vikram Raghuvanshi/iStockphoto. 50, Ivan Vdovin / age fotostock. 51 (bottom left), Alan Lagadu/ iStockphoto. 51 (top right), Rafal Cichawa/Shutterstock. 52, Jan S./Shutterstock. 53, Walter Bibikow / age fotostock. 54, Wikimedia Commons. 55 (bottom left), paul prescott/Shutterstock. 55 (top right), AJP/Shutterstock. 56, Lebedinski Vladislav/Shutterstock. 57, paul prescott/Shutterstock. 58, Christophe Boisvieux / age fotostock. 59 (bottom), JeremyRichards/Shutterstock. 59 (top), AJP/Shutterstock. 60, Matthias Rosenkranz/Flickr. 61 (bottom), Vassil/Wikimedia Commons. 61 (top), jaimaa/Shutterstock. 62, Dinodia / age fotostock. 63, saiko3p/Shutterstock. 64, Joe Gough/iStockphoto. 65 (bottom), Jehangir Hanafi /iStockphoto. 65 (top), Monkey Business Images/Shutterstock. 66, Joe Gough/iStockphoto. 67, Colin & Linda McKie/iStockphoto. 68, WITTY234/Shutterstock. 69, Bartosz Hadyniak/ iStockphoto. 70, JTB Photo / age fotostock. 71 (bottom), Sid B. Viswakumar/Shutterstock. 71 (top), RABOUAN Jean-Baptiste / age fotostock. 72, Ian Cumming / age fotostock. 73, Wikimedia Commons. 74, M Balan / age fotostock. 75 (bottom), testing/Shutterstock. 75 (top), NCPA Photo/ Harkiran Singh Bhasin. 76, Eitan Simanor / age fotostock. Chapter 3: Delhi 77, Arco Images/age fotostock. 78, Rajibnandi/Wikimedia Commons. 79 (top left), Terra plorer/iStockphoto. 79 (top right), Dana Ward/Shutterstock. 79 (bottom), indigreen.co.in. 80 and 81 (bottom), highviews/Shutterstock. 81 (top), sanskarshan/Wikimedia Commons. 82, Chumbak. 83 (bottom), Mahima Mehra/Haathi Chaap. 83 (top), www.artbyaarohi.com. 84, Varun Shiv Kapur/Flickr. 85 (bottom), Kylelovesyou/Wikimedia Commons. 85 (top), Russ Bowling/Flickr. 86, Sreeganesha, Fodors.com member. 91, Helene Rogers / age fotostock. 94, Massimo Pacifi co / age fotostock. 99, Dinodia /age fotostock. 100, Mel Longhurst / age fotostock. 103, The Print Collector / age fotostock. 106, ARCO / Therin-Weise / age fotostock. 109, McPHOTOs / age fotostock. 113, Tibor Bognar / age fotostock. 116, Oriental Touch / age fotostock. 122, A+B Company. 129 (top), The Imperial Hotel. 129 (bottom left), Ahuja Residency. 129 (bottom right), Oberoi Hotels & Resorts. 133, Edmund Sumner/VIEW / age fotostock. 136, Smoke House Grill. 141, Varun Shiv Kapur/Flickr. Chapter 4: Side Trips from Delhi 149, Alexander Pöschel/ age fotostock. 150, Polly Ryan, Fodors.com member. 151 (top left), NGail, Fodors.com member. 151 (top right), Rudolf Tepfenhart/Shutterstock. 151 (bottom), jennyt/Shutterstock. 152, paul prescott/Shutterstock. 153 (both), Bon Appetit / Alamy. 154, Guillermo Garcia/Shutterstock. 164, Mel Longhurst / age fotostock. 166-67, Redtigerxyz/Wikimedia Commons. 166, J Hauke / age fotostock. 168 (bottom left), Mark Henley / age fotostock. 168 (top left), Hashim/Wikimedia Commons. 168 (top center), Gavin Hellier / age fotostock. 168 (bottom right), Wikimedia Commons. 168 (top right), Samir Luther/Wikimedia Commons. 169, Dinodia / age fotostock. 170, John Henry Claude Wil / age fotostock. 171 (top), Rafal Cichawa/Shutterstock. 171 (second), William Donelson/Wikimedia Commons. 171 (third), Alexey Fateev/Shutterstock. 171 (fourth), Galyna Andrushko/Shutterstock. 171 (bottom), JeremyRichards/Shutterstock. 172, Oriental Touch / age fotostock. 180, Tibor Bognar / age fotostock. 187, Richard Ashworth / age fotostock. 190-91, Jose Fuste Raga / age fotostock. 198-99, Aleksandar Todorovic/ Shutterstock. 200 (left), Christopher Soghoian/Flickr. 200 (right), Rumi Arpita-devi/Flickr. 201 (top left), Lebedinski Vladislav/Shutterstock. 201 (bottom), Aleksandar Todorovic/Shutterstock. 201 (top

NOTES

ABOUT OUR WRITERS

Chaya Babu, a freelance journalist from New York, has worked in Chicago and Mumbai, writing on arts, culture and social issues. Her work has appeared in the *Huffington Post, Salon,* the *Wall Street Journal,* and Indian publications including *OPEN Magazine* and the *Sunday Guardian.* Her time in India informed her work on this edition of *Fodor's Essential India,* for which she updated the "Experience India" and "Portrait of India" chapters.

Margot Bigg has lived and worked in India for many years and has written for a number of Indian publications, including local editions of *Rolling Stone, Condé Nast Traveller,* and *Time Out.* She's also the author of *Moon Living Abroad in India* and *Moon Taj Mahal, Delhi & Jaipur.* Margot contributed to the first edition of *Fodor's Essential India* and for this edition she updated the "Travel Smart" chapter. Find out more about her at www.margotbigg.com.

Abhishek Madhukar, born and raised in Bihar, followed his wanderlust into the travel industry, leading specialized cultural, historical, and photography tours in India, primarily in Rajasthan. He is also a freelance writer and photographer, including reporting for Thomson Reuters on Tibetan issues and the Dalai Lama. For *Fodor's Essential India,* Abhishek updated the "Rajasthan" chapter.

Neil Munshi is an inveterate traveler and compulsive mover who has lived in eight cities in the last seven years, but has spent the past three in Mumbai. His work has appeared in *Esquire, GQ India,* the *Boston Globe,* the *Chicago Tribune,* and what he believes is the greatest college paper in history, the *Minnesota Daily.* For *Fodor's Essential India,* Neil updated the "Mumbai" chapter.

Malia Politzer is a staff writer at *Mint,* India's second-largest business and economics newspaper, and her articles include social and political issues, food, and travel. Her work has appeared in the *Wall Street Journal Asia, Far Eastern Economic Review, Foreign Policy Magazine,* and *Migration Policy Institute.* For this edition of *Fodor's Essential India,* Malia updated the "Side Trips from Delhi" chapter.

Sehrish Shaban has reported for Reuters, PBS, NewsHour, washingtonpost.com and other media outlets, is a consultant at the *Times of India,* and teaches postgraduate journalism courses. Her writing interests range from food and travel to business and social issues. Sehrish established "No Man's Land," a Delhi-based trust that promotes design and ideas in southern Asia. For *Fodor's Essential India,* Sehrish wrote the "Kerala" chapter.

Sonal Shah is the editor of *Time Out Delhi,* and writing interests include food, travel, art, and anthropology; her work has appeared in *Time Out Delhi, Food & Wine, Departures, Art India,* and other publications. For the first edition of *Fodor's Essential India,* Sonal wrote the "Eating Well" Spotlights that appear in each chapter and most of the "Portrait of India" chapter; for this edition she updated the "Delhi" chapter.

Vandana Verma is the editor of The India Tube, a Delhi-based travel website. Formerly the Food & Drink and Lifestyle editor at *Time Out Delhi,* Vandana has a degree in journalism from the University of London and writes about food, travel, music, and popular culture. For this edition of *Fodor's Essential India,* Vandana updated and added to the "Goa" chapter.